DATABASE DESIGN AND PROGRAMMING FOR
DB2/400

PAUL CONTE

DUKE PRESS

A Division of
DUKE COMMUNICATIONS INTERNATIONAL
Loveland, Colorado

Library of Congress Cataloging-in-Publication Data

Conte, Paul, 1948-
    Database design and programming for DB2/400 / by Paul Conte.
      p. cm.
    Includes bibliographical references (p.   ) and index.
    ISBN 1-882419-06-5 (pbk.)
    1. Database design. 2. IBM Database 2. I. Title.
QA76.9.D26C65 1996
005.75'65—dc20   96-35673
                              CIP

Copyright © 1997 by DUKE PRESS
DUKE COMMUNICATIONS INTERNATIONAL
Loveland, Colorado

This book was printed and bound in the United States of America.

ISBN 1-882419-06-5

123456 PO 9876

To my wife, Janice, who has filled my life
with joy, inspiration, and peace.

About the Author

Paul Conte is president of Picante Software, Inc., a software development company in Eugene, Oregon. He's also a senior technical editor for *NEWS/400* magazine. Paul is a widely published expert on database systems, database design, software engineering, and programming languages. He's considered a leading authority on DB2/400, and his articles have appeared in *NEWS/400, Database Programming & Design, Computer Language,* and numerous other publications. Paul also consults and speaks frequently on database issues. His past clients have included IBM, Apple Computer, the Relational Database Institute, Fidelity International, the Ford Foundation, and many other prominent organizations. Paul has presented more than 100 seminars and courses throughout North and South America, as well as in Europe.

Paul has developed applications on a variety of platforms and relational DBMS, including the AS/400, S/38, S/370, DEC, and PCs with DB2, Oracle, Ingres, and Access. He is the principle architect and developer of several commercial software products, including Flex/EDIT, a widely used Windows-based AS/400 programmer's workbench. His language expertise covers a wide range: C/C++, COBOL, RPG IV and RPG/400, Delphi, and Visual Basic, to name a few. Paul has written several high-level language preprocessors used by AS/400 development groups.

Paul has a B.A. in psychology from Georgia State University and an M.S. in computer science from the University of Oregon. He served on the University of Oregon faculty for eight years and ran his own consulting firm before starting Picante Software. Paul has received several awards for his writing, including the prestigious "Award of Excellence" from the Society for Technical Communication's international competition. His other publications include *Common Sense C,* a highly acclaimed book on C and C++ programming. Paul is a member of the Association for Computing Machinery and the IEEE Computer Society.

Paul's personal interests include fly fishing, wine tasting, and cooking — and combining the results of all three interests in the kitchen.

Acknowledgments

A book as extensive as *Database Design and Programming for DB2/400* can't be created alone, or by just a few months of intensive writing. During the past decade, many people have helped me develop the understanding of DB2/400 that is the foundation of this book. Just as importantly, I've been mentored in the art of technical writing by many excellent wordsmiths at *NEWS/400* magazine.

Three good friends have been there from the beginning of my association with Duke Communications International (the company that encompasses Duke Press and *NEWS/400* magazine). Dave Duke, president of Duke Communications, has provided me and many other authors the support and encouragement to research and write about topics that are important to AS/400 developers. Dave is obsessed with quality (a commendable obsession in my opinion) and has invested heavily in the authors and staff who produce Duke Communications publications. Dave's commitment over the years has enabled me to tackle complex topics, examine them in depth, and try to explain them thoroughly. From this effort came much of the knowledge that was required to tackle a comprehensive textbook about DB2/400.

Dave Bernard, publisher of Duke Press, edited my first article for what was then called *NEWS 34-38* magazine, as well as my previous book for Duke Press. He's been a steady source of encouragement, and after repeated efforts he finally convinced me I could successfully tackle writing a DB2/400 book I would be satisfied with. Dave also took on the burden of final editing and organizing the production to meet both tight deadlines and my sometimes maddening attention to every detail — from the cover layout to the way code samples are presented. Dave's combination of skill, enthusiasm for the project, and good humor kept us on track and made the demanding writing schedule an exciting challenge for me rather than a burden.

Trish Faubion, former editor of *NEWS/400*, edited many of my magazine articles and more than anyone else has shaped my approach to technical writing. Much to my delight, Trish took on the primary editing job of this book, even though now, as production editor for Interweave Press (including *PieceWork* magazine), she's more involved with articles about designing quilts than articles about designing databases. Trish wielded a firm and precise scalpel in her editing, and readers will benefit from her many refinements.

Many others, some old friends, some new acquaintances, provided help that was essential to producing the book. My original manuscript was much improved by the comments of a number of reviewers. Four instructors — Janice Weinberg at Madison Area Technical College, Penny Ellis and Bernie Cinkoske at IVY Tech State College in Indianapolis, and Ted Tucker at Metropolitan Community College in Omaha — read almost the entire book and gave me invaluable suggestions to increase its usefulness as a college-level text. Bryan Meyers provided thoughtful comments on various DDS coding styles I used. Bryan and Julian Monypenny checked the RPG IV advice and sample programs in Chapters 7 and 15, and Dan Riehl did likewise for the COBOL/400 advice and programs in those chapters. Carol Ramler and Sue Romano of IBM provided exceptionally detailed technical reviews of Chapters 13 through 16, covering SQL/400 and DB2/400 constraints. The SQL material would not have had the same depth without their expertise. Carol Woodbury provided a similar review for Chapter 18 on database security. I very much appreciate the time reviewers took to read the manuscript and write their comments. Of course, I take responsibility for any errors that may remain in the final version.

I drew on several previously published sources for some of the material. Julian Monypenny provided the idea and original version of the "soft coded" trigger program presented in Chapter 17. Dan Riehl and Bryan Meyers wrote the original versions of Appendix C (PDM) and Appendix D (SEU). I appreciate all three of them granting me permission to use their work.

Over the years, numerous IBMers have helped explain many of the topics covered in this book. Among them, I wish to thank Jon Paris for help with RPG IV; John Broich for help with stored procedures; and Kent Milligan, Mark Anderson, and John Fulton for help with a wide variety of DB2/400 questions. I'd also like to thank Frank Soltis for his explanations of the AS/400 architecture, as well as for graciously agreeing to write the Foreword.

I have also benefited from numerous discussions on programming and database design with Roger Pence, Mike Otey, Richard Rubin, Nick Knowles, Carson Soule, Wayne Madden, and many others. Thanks to you all for keeping the work interesting.

Several other people provided substantial help in producing the book. My wife Janice Gotchall and friend Linda Russial typed and edited much of Appendix A (DDS keywords) and Appendix B (database commands). Janice also helped with much of the copying, faxing, and other logistics. Most importantly, Janice bore the impact of this book on our personal lives with enormous good humor and extra effort to maintain a pleasant and functioning household. At Duke Press, John Morris-Riehl designed a sharp-looking cover, Sharon Hamm coordinated the scheduling and free-lance editing to keep things moving, and Jan Caufman managed the production of the book. I'm grateful to you all for your help and patience.

There are also many editors, technical editors, and other staff of Duke Communications who have helped with earlier articles on topics covered in this book. Thanks to all of you for your help getting it right.

Finally, I would like to thank the many AS/400 programmers I've spoken or corresponded with over the years for their observations, tips and techniques, stimulating questions, and encouragement. I hope all of you take pleasure in being a part of this book.

Table of Contents

Foreword

You hold in your hands a new standard for database textbooks, and the timing couldn't be better. Many companies are just beginning to make their business applications more competitive, to implement client/server and network computing applications, and to recognize the advantages of data warehousing and data mining applications. Playing a major role in the transformation of business applications all over the world is the AS/400, and top-notch AS/400 development programmers are in great demand.

The AS/400 is, and always has been, a database machine. DB2/400 is the most widely used multiuser relational database in the world. More business data is contained in DB2/400 databases than in any other kind of database. As a result, the AS/400 is in a perfect position to capitalize on the trend toward data warehousing and client/server or network database serving. That is, of course, assuming we have enough application programmers with knowledge about DB2/400. Education on DB2/400 has been sorely lacking; and until now, a good textbook on the subject has not existed.

In general, database textbooks seem to be theoretical works written more for a computer science student than for a professional application programmer. There is nothing wrong with teaching database concepts and theory, but unless they are anchored to something that is tangible for developing applications, there is little for a real-world application programmer to take away. If this is also your view of database textbooks, you are in for a pleasant surprise with this book.

Paul Conte has written a practical database design textbook specifically for AS/400 application developers. The integrated nature of the AS/400 helps tie all the pieces of an application together, but Paul's experience and understanding of the whole application development process provides the real value in this book. He is able to present DB2/400 and database design techniques in a way that AS/400 application programmers at all levels, from beginners to seasoned professionals, can easily understand and immediately begin to use.

I particularly like Paul's inclusion of numerous examples throughout the text, as well as exercises at the end of each chapter. As a teacher myself, I know that the only way to truly learn new concepts is through practice. Paul also is not shy about offering his personal opinions on various topics. His tips alone are worth the price of the book.

I first met Paul in 1985. He had come to Rochester to find out more about the System/38 — its history and its future — for an article he was writing for *NEWS 34/38* magazine (now *NEWS/400*). Unknown to Paul at the time, the future of the System/38 was bleak. The Fort Knox project, an attempt to combine five dissimilar IBM systems — including Rochester's System/36 and System/38 — into a single new system was a dismal failure. The System/38 had earlier been declared non-strategic by IBM, and there were no plans for a follow-on product. In fact, the AS/400 project was not officially approved until December 1985.

But as one of those who firmly believed the System/38 had a strong future and that we would soon convince IBM management to let us create its successor, the AS/400, I was anxious to meet with Paul. I soon found a kindred spirit, and we spent several hours that day talking about our favorite computer system.

The System/38, a marvelous system, was way ahead of its time. It was the first commercial system to have an integrated database with relational characteristics. Paul was particularly intrigued by this database and wanted to know more about its internal design and how it came to be. I was impressed with the way Paul approached these topics. He always put them in the context of practical application development. *Database Design and Programming for DB2/400* clearly shows that Paul has never lost this focus.

To develop high quality AS/400 applications, every AS/400 application programmer needs to fully understand DB2/400 and database design. The best way to provide that understanding is not to treat database design as an isolated entity totally devoid of any real-world practicality, but to continually focus on how the database design relates to the application. At last, Paul Conte has given us a database textbook that does just that. It is long overdue.

Frank Soltis
Chief architect of the AS/400 (IBM) and
Professor of Computer Engineering,
University of Minnesota

Preface

By many measures, including number of units sold and customer satisfaction ratings, the AS/400 is the most successful business computer ever developed. One reason for that success is its integrated database management system, known as DB2/400. DB2/400 provides a highly functional, efficient, and reliable system for storing and manipulating large volumes of data and is the foundation for most of the business applications that run on the AS/400. For that reason, it's no overstatement to say that a well-designed database is a prerequisite for top quality AS/400 application software. The obvious corollary is that a successful AS/400 application developer must have a solid understanding of DB2/400 and database design.

This book provides that understanding to students and practicing programmers. Once you master the topics covered in *Database Design and Programming for DB2/400*, you'll be able to design and create *professional-level* databases for real applications. A professional application developer requires skills in several areas, among them:

- Modeling the system[1]
- Designing the system implementation
- Implementing the system's database and software

In other words, you need to understand a system from the user's point of view, design a suitable system conceptually, and then implement it with the tools at hand. You can't neglect any of these areas and expect much success.[2] That's why this book covers database *design*, as well as *programming* — the programming world doesn't need more "hacks" who charge into development projects with a little knowledge of syntax and not much more.

Of course, pure theory alone isn't enough either. Ultimately, somebody has to create the files and programs that comprise a system. You'll find that if you get a good education in basic design and programming principles, along with some practical coding knowledge, the implementation part gets much easier as you gain more experience. Modeling and design, on the other hand, remain challenging throughout a developer's career because the world is both complex and rapidly changing. In the long run, modeling and design skills are the most difficult to master; but you have to start somewhere, and my experience teaching and "mentoring" new programmers suggests that most people find it easier to learn something tangible — like how to create a file — before they get too deeply into conceptual areas.

---

[1] Another common term for this part of the process is "systems analysis." I prefer "modeling" because it captures both the *analysis* and the *synthesis* aspects of the process.

[2] Of course, there are many other associated skills required: Project planning, quality assurance, and a certain amount of "political savvy" are all important for a developer.

So in this book, by the end of Chapter 2, you'll know how to create a DB2/400 file to hold data, and by the end of Chapter 7 you'll know almost all the ways you can set up and use various kinds of DB2/400 files. At that point, you'll be "armed and dangerous" and ready for the second part of the book, which covers data modeling and database design. The third and fourth parts of the book cover additional design and programming topics that are also crucial to working with DB2/400. I'll preview the content of each section of the book in a moment, but first let's go over where this book fits into your education.

The broad subject of application development can be sliced several ways. I've already suggested that there's theory and practice — this book is practical, but includes one chapter on the relational database model, which is the conceptual foundation of both DB2/400 and widely used data modeling and design techniques. The discussion of the relational model minimizes formal mathematics and emphasizes the model's "intuitive" nature, which is one of its great strengths. Another split is high-level language programming (e.g., RPG IV, COBOL, or C++) versus database programming. Both types of programming are essential to application development, of course. This book concentrates on database programming, but includes two full chapters and many discussions about accessing DB2/400 files from HLL programs. I urge the reader to pursue comparable courses (or books) on HLL design and programming in conjunction with the use of this book. The annotated bibliography in the appendices includes a number of highly recommended books about HLL programming.

As with any topic, database material can range from introductory level to advanced. I've tried to write this book so that anyone with at least some familiarity with computers and programming finds it accessible. On the other hand, I haven't shied away from challenging material if I thought it was important to help the reader become a professional-level developer. This shouldn't be your first book about computers or programming, although it may be the first book you've read that concentrates on database issues. For college-level Information Systems or Applied Software Development programs, this book should work well for a course (or sequence) that requires at least one HLL programming course as a prerequisite. Naturally, the pace of instruction can be significantly faster if the book is used in an upper division course, as opposed to early in the student's exposure to software development. (Instructors should note that this book isn't intended to provide comprehensive enough treatment of relational database theory or DB2/400 system internals to be used as the only text for in-depth courses on those topics. See the annotated bibliography for books that cover these topics in more detail.)

For programmers — or readers who wish to become programmers — who aren't enrolled as students, I recommend that you have a fairly good knowledge of at least one programming language and at least a superficial exposure to the AS/400. Naturally, having an AS/400 available to try out solutions to exercises will be a big advantage. This is an ideal book for programmers coming from other database platforms, such as Oracle, MS SQL Server, or other versions of DB2 (e.g., on IBM mainframes). If that's your situation, you should be able to blast through most of the chapters and get a very rapid start with DB2/400.

This is a textbook, not a technical reference manual. However, I've tried to provide numerous examples, tables, appendices, and detailed technical explanations so that no AS/400 manuals are necessary to create, manage, and use DB2/400 files. Fortunately, the AS/400 provides extensive fill-in-the-blank prompting and online help for DDS, SQL, and CL commands. With this text and online resources, you should be able to perform almost any DB2/400-related task without too much trouble. For many AS/400 development groups, copies of this book can serve in place of additional copies of IBM's database-related manuals.

Finally there's the mix of personal opinion and technical fact that goes into any book. While this book is packed with facts, it also offers some opinions and recommendations on various design and programming techniques. In my experience, the most capable developers *think* about why they do things the way they do. Over time, this attitude leads to improvement; and after 10 years' of experience, the developer who's been paying attention will have far surpassed the developer who kept doing the same thing over and over — whether from ignorance, superstition, or habit. I've tried to pass along the results of some of my own observations — for instance, about the importance of a consistent and meaningful approach to file and field names. Every one of these opinions is debatable, but I've spared you lengthy arguments for my point of view. Wherever I make a recommendation, consider it, and if you think of a better solution, use it instead. Hopefully, some of my "tips" will save you time and headaches as you accumulate experience.

On a technical note, this edition is based on Version 3 of DB2/400 and AS/400 HLLs. If you're using an earlier release, you may find that your system doesn't support some of the functions used. This is especially true with SQL/400, which changed significantly in both V2R3 and V3R1. Because of the rapid development of DB2/400 and the unavoidable span of releases that any edition of a text covers, I've targeted the most recent release available at the time of publication.[3] For that same reason, the file and field names in the examples all conform to Version 3 RPG IV (as well as ILE COBOL/400) syntax, but not to RPG/400 syntax. Almost all DB2/400 features and techniques are still applicable to RPG/400 — and this text can be used quite successfully when only the RPG/400 compiler is available; but shorter names are necessary to use the sample files directly in RPG/400 programs. Part I provides more discussion on HLL naming restrictions and suggests coding practices for various languages, including both versions of RPG.

---

[3]At the time of publication, the current release was V3R2 for CISC systems and V3R6 for RISC systems. The most widely used version was still V3R1, however. Where an item is new in V3R6 or V3R2, I've noted that fact either in the body of the text or in a footnote.

A Closer Look at the Contents of This Book

The book is divided into four major parts, as well as a collection of appendices.

Part I introduces DB2/400 and the so-called "native" interfaces available to create and access database files. These interfaces include Data Description Specifications (DDS), the Create Physical File (CRTPF) and Create Logical File (CRTLF) commands, and the built-in I/O operations of AS/400 high-level languages.

At this stage in DB2/400 development, it's still essential to understand DDS and AS/400 HLL I/O operations, so Part I should be included in any course on DB2/400. With the exception of Chapter 5, the chapters in this section build on each other and should be read (and fully understood) in sequence, unless the reader already has a good foundation in a chapter's topics. Exercises at the end of each chapter provide a way to check that the information is fully comprehended. Chapter 5 covers some less-frequently-used advanced features and can be skipped if necessary to fit other material into a course. Chapter 7 provides an introduction to using RPG IV and COBOL/400 database file declarations and I/O operations to access DB2/400 data. This chapter assumes that the reader is already familiar with RPG IV, RPG/400, or COBOL/400. The material focuses on database issues and is not by itself an adequate introduction to HLL programming.

Part II covers database modeling and design. This material is based on the relational database model and provides both an introduction to that model, as well as a description of how this model can be used as the foundation of a design process.

Part II provides the reader with important foundation concepts for understanding why the designers of DB2/400 (and other relational database management systems) set things up the way they did; consequently, this section also gives the reader a better grasp of how to use DB2/400 effectively. This section also teaches how to model and design application databases. Students shouldn't get too far in their study without understanding the topics covered in this part of the book. To fit chapters into different curriculum plans, Chapter 9 on the relational database model may be presented as an independent topic. Chapters 10, 11, and 12, which go into specific modeling and design techniques more extensively, require a firm grasp of the relational model and should be taught only after Chapter 9 (or the student gets an equivalent foundation from another course). If chapters need to be pruned to fit course constraints, Chapter 11 on entity-relationship diagramming or Chapter 12 on physical database design could be left to a later course or self-study.

Part III covers SQL/400 (Structured Query Language/400), the other important interface to DB2/400. SQL is a newer facility than DDS and HLL built-in I/O operations, and SQL will arguably be the more important of the two DB2/400 interfaces in the future.

IBM — and the rest of the computer industry — is putting most of its database development efforts into SQL. A professional application developer will require SQL skills to further his or her career on the AS/400, as well as on other platforms. SQL is an extensive topic, so this part of the book may be appropriate for a second course in a DB2/400 (or a more general database-oriented) sequence. Although the SQL material doesn't require the student to have worked through Part I, it does assume a solid understanding of the structure of DB2/400 (e.g., libraries, files, members). SQL also is directly based on the relational model, and the material covered in Chapter 9 is essential. The three chapters in this part should be studied in sequence, and they're all necessary for a student to write SQL-based applications.

Part IV is a collection of material that is important in "real-world" database programming, including database constraints, security, and backup and recovery. Before you tackle any of this material, Part I should be covered thoroughly. Chapter 16 on database constraints should be preceded by Chapter 9, as well. Other than these prerequisites, the topics may be covered in any order. An instructor may prefer to use Chapter 18 on database security as part of the syllabus for an entire course on AS/400 security (which covers other types of security, as well). Similarly, an instructor may want to cover backup and recovery (Chapter 19) in a course on AS/400 operations.

The **Appendices** provide reference material to enable the reader to use DB2/400, and related OS/400 development tools, in a classroom or production environment.

The appendices include concise, but detailed, references for all DDS keywords that apply to logical and physical files, as well as descriptions of the CRTPF and CRTLF commands. A condensed guide to more than 20 additional database-related commands is also provided. Three short appendices instruct the reader in the use of the AS/400 Programming Development Manager (PDM), the Source Entry Utility (SEU), and Interactive SQL (ISQL) — tools that are used to work with DDS source code and interactive SQL statements. I've included an extensive annotated bibliography, which readers can use to expand their knowledge of DB2/400, database design, and other software development areas. Instructors may want to explore some of the recommended books for additional material for their course syllabus. A glossary recaps the important terms used in this book, for easy lookup.

The four parts are designed to fit comfortably (for the student and instructor) into a two-course sequence. Parts I and II as the first course provide the student a mix of design and programming. From my own experience, most students will find this easier to digest than cramming both "native" DB2/400 and SQL programming into a single course. It also provides an effective mix of tangible and conceptual so the student is better prepared to tackle SQL and advanced topics. The second course can provide a thorough treatment of SQL, and — to the degree that time allows — the course can cover selected topics from Part IV. Students who complete this sequence will be well-prepared for handling database design and programming.

An Instructor's Guide is available to those instructors who adopt this text for classroom use. The guide includes answers to the exercises, as well as some additional notes on the topics covered in each chapter of the text. The guide includes a diskette with source and data files for the examples and exercises.

As a final introductory comment, let me say that in my own career, database design and programming have frequently been the pivotal areas that determined the success of major application development projects. Unfortunately, these skills are often neglected in the training of business programmers. Fortunately for the reader, people who have these skills are in high demand and are usually well compensated. If you learn the material in this book, you can expect to be ahead of the pack in finding interesting and well-paying jobs. On a personal note, I've also found that the early stages of data modeling are especially challenging and fun. I hope a little of both comes through in this book.

Eugene, Oregon   *Paul Conte*

P A R T   I

THE DB2/400 DATABASE

Chapter 1

Basic Concepts

Chapter Overview

This chapter introduces the concept of a database and describes DB2/400, which is the database management system that's part of the AS/400. You'll get a general idea of how the AS/400 and its operating system, OS/400, are architected. You'll also get an overview of DB2/400 physical and logical files.

Databases and Database Management Systems

A **database** is a set of computer files for storing information that's used by a business or other organization. A typical business might keep information about customers and their orders, suppliers of raw materials, and employees who work for the company. Storing this type of information in computer files provides for easy retrieval and updating, as well as flexible analysis of the raw data to produce management reports, such as sales trends or average employee benefit costs. Of course, how "easy" and "flexible" it is to work with the data is largely determined by how well the database has been set up and the capabilities of the **database management system** (**DBMS**), which provides the software to create files and retrieve and update file contents. In this chapter, we'll look at the building blocks of the **DB2/400** DBMS that runs on IBM **AS/400** computer systems.

DB2/400 is an integrated part of **OS/400,** the AS/400's operating system, which means that you don't have to buy it as a separate software product and that any AS/400 application you write can take advantage of DB2/400 features. Figure 1.1 shows a simplified view of how DB2/400 fits into the AS/400 architecture.

As you can see, DB2/400 provides a layer that all **high-level language** (**HLL**) programs (i.e., RPG IV, COBOL, C, and C++) use to access application data. You can also see that all utilities and remote applications (e.g., from PCs using Client Access/400) must go through DB2/400 to access data on the AS/400.[1] This integrated, uniform interface provides a high degree of consistency and control for AS/400 application developers.

---

[1] In V3R1 of OS/400, IBM introduced the **Integrated File System** (**IFS**), which is a Unix-like directory structure and set of interfaces. Under IFS, what used to be the QSYS system

Figure 1.1
DB2/400 and the
AS/400 Architecture

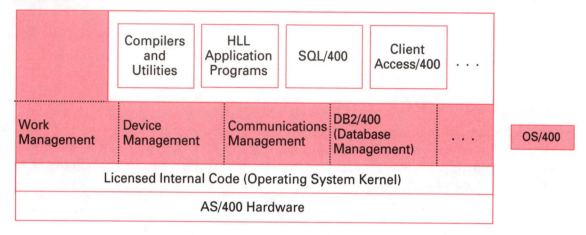

If you're familiar with other operating systems and DBMS products, you'll find that DB2/400 has features of both conventional operating systems' file management facilities and relational DBMS products. For example, like a conventional file management facility, DB2/400 lets you use built-in HLL I/O operations, such as COBOL's Read and Write verbs, to access data. Like other relational DBMS products, DB2/400 lets you access the same data using **Structured Query Language** (**SQL**). The "dual" nature of DB2/400 is even expressed in the nomenclature: files and fields are referred to as tables and columns when you work with SQL/400, the DB2/400 version of SQL.

OS/400 Objects, Libraries, and User Profiles

Because DB2/400 is an integral part of OS/400, it helps to have a general understanding of how OS/400 is organized and where DB2/400 fits in. Everything in the OS/400 operating system, including the database, is organized as **objects**. Examples of OS/400 objects are programs, **database files**, **user profiles**, message queues, and about 80 other types of objects.[2] Like other operating systems (e.g., Unix), OS/400 stores program instructions,

library that contained all other OS/400 objects is now the /QSYS.LIB subdirectory under the root directory of IFS. Other IFS subdirectories, such as /QOpenSys, contain Unix-like and other new types of files. This book treats only the "traditional" OS/400 architecture; that is, only the /QSYS.LIB part of IFS. Most AS/400 installations still use only these traditional facilities, and anyone who wants to work with the other parts of IFS will find Unix-oriented books more appropriate.

[2] You may have heard of "object-oriented" (OO) languages and databases, and wonder how these apply to OS/400. Like OO languages, OS/400 organizes everything into objects of different types, which have restricted interfaces. The implementation of how an object, such as a file, carries out its operations is *encapsulated* in the object implementation, hidden from

application data, and other system components on disk, loading them into main memory as needed. But, unlike most other operating systems, OS/400 doesn't let you get at the bytes on disk or in memory directly. Instead you must always use specific **commands** or other system interfaces that are valid for each type of object. For example, you can't *execute* a database file or perform a file *update* operation on a program object.[3] As we progress through DB2/400's capabilities, you'll learn about various types of OS/400 objects and the way to use them.

OS/400 controls how you use an object by storing some descriptive information with the actual content of the object. Figure 1.2 depicts the storage layout (disk or memory) for an OS/400 object.

Figure 1.2
OS/400 Object
Storage Layout

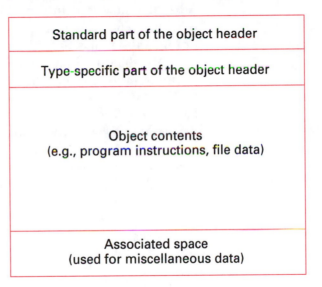

As you can see, all objects have a header, the object-specific contents (e.g., program instructions or file data), and an area known as the associated space where system or user programs store miscellaneous data related to the object.

the application programmer. However, application programmers can't create new OS/400 object types as they can in most OO languages; essentially, only IBM can do that.

DB2/400, which is part of OS/400, is generally considered a *relational* DBMS, not an object-oriented DBMS. Object-oriented databases are designed to store irregular, complexly structured data, such as the engineering plans for an airplane. Relational databases are a good fit for table-oriented data, but need some additional features to handle the types of data for which object-oriented databases are typically used.

[3] Most other operating systems treat everything on disk as a "file" and let you attempt nonsensical operations, such as executing a file that contains data instead of instructions. These operating systems may offer some protection by setting file attributes (e.g., "executable"). But you can still create a file with the "executable" attribute that contains data instead of instructions. With OS/400, it's impossible to change an object's type (e.g., from *FILE to *PGM), so you can't have the wrong type of contents in an object.

The object header has two parts. All objects have at least the following information in the *standard* part of their header:

- The library that contains the object
- The object's name
- The object's type
- The object's subtype
- The user profile that owns the object

An AS/400 **library** is an object that contains other objects. Think of an AS/400 library as a Unix or MS-DOS directory or a Windows 95 folder. The only difference is that you can't nest AS/400 libraries as you can directories or folders — that is, a library can't contain another library object.[4]

AS/400 object names are generally up to 10 alphanumeric characters, beginning with a letter or national character (e.g., $, #, @ in the U.S.). Thus, CUSTOMER might be the name of the customer master file. Libraries also have names; for example, you might use APPDTA as the name of the library that contains your production application data files. An object's **qualified name** is the combination of the name of the library that contains it and the object's unqualified name, separated with a forward slash. For example, APPDTA/CUSTOMER would be the qualified name of the customer master file if it were stored in library APPDTA.

We've already touched on the notion of object type, and on the AS/400 each object type is designated by a special value, such as *PGM for program and *FILE for file. Some object types are further broken down into subtypes. The *FILE object type, for instance, includes **physical files**, **logical files**, printer files, display files, and communications files — all of which are kinds of record-oriented sources or targets for external program data. In this book, we'll use the term "file" to mean either a physical or logical file. When it's necessary to refer to another kind of file, we'll use an unambiguous term, such as "printer file."

An OS/400 object is uniquely defined by the combination of its qualified name and its object type, which means OS/400 allows only one object on an AS/400 that has a given combination of library, name, and object type. As a result, you can have a CUSTOMER *FILE object in the APPDTA library and another CUSTOMER *FILE object in the TSTDTA library, but you can't have two files with the same name in the same library. You *can* have two objects with the same name in the same library, as long as they aren't the same type, but it's not good practice because of the potential for

---

[4] Actually, one OS/400 library, QSYS, can contain other library objects. QSYS is essentially the "system" and contains all other libraries. See also the earlier footnote about the Integrated File System.

confusion. Generally you should give unique names to all the objects in the same library, regardless of their types.

Each OS/400 object is owned by a user profile — another type of OS/400 object. Each user profile stores information about a system user, including the user's name, password, and authority to access data or use system functions. Whenever you sign on, you supply a user profile name and password, and this lets OS/400 control your use of the system, including access to the database. Chapter 18 covers database security in more detail; the main thing to know as you learn about creating and accessing files is that each file object has a user profile designated as its owner and all access to the database is controlled based on the authority granted to one or more user profiles.

Files, Record Formats, and Members

While studying DB2/400, we'll spend a lot of time talking about database files. In simple terms, a database file is a named collection of **records**. In a typical example (Figure 1.3), the CUSTOMER file would contain a record for each of the company's customers. A record is a collection of **fields**, which are named items of data, such as CUSTID (customer ID) and NAME (customer name), that represent attributes of some item (e.g., a customer) of interest to the organization.

An OS/400 file object contains the object header information discussed previously. For files, this header is often referred to as the **file description** and includes a description of the file's **record format** — the byte-by-byte

Figure 1.3
Sample CUSTOMER
File Contents

FIELDS

CUSTID	NAME	SHPLINE1	SHPCITY	SHPSTATE	STATUS
10001	Ajax Plumbing	12 Main St.	Seattle	WA	A
10002	Sherod Sign Co.	576 Pearl St.	Eugene	OR	X
10003	Picante Software	132 E. Broadway	Portland	OR	A
10004	Cobblestones	340 Willamette St.	Seattle	WA	B
10005	Kinetic Bagel	501 6th Ave.	Seattle	WA	C
10006	Full City Coffee	11 Monument Ave.	Richmond	VA	X
10007	Zenon's Cafe	6 Ventura Blvd.	Loveland	CO	C
10008	Bubba's Grill	491 High St.	Denver	CO	A
10009	The West Bros.	2601 Stratford Rd.	Portland	OR	A

RECORDS

Figure 1.4
Record Format for the
CUSTOMER file

layout of all the fields in the file's records.[5] (Some kinds of logical files, which we discuss in the next section, have multiple record formats.) Figure 1.4 depicts a simple record format for the CUSTOMER file and a sample record.

Field Name	Data Type	Length	Decimal Positions	Start Position	Size	Usage	Column Heading
CUSTID	Packed Decimal	7	0	1	4	In/Out	Cust. ID
NAME	Character	30	n/a	5	30	In/Out	Customer Name
SHPLINE1	Character	100	n/a	35	100	In/Out	Customer Shipping Line 1
SHPCITY	Character	30	n/a	135	30	In/Out	Customer Shipping City
SHPSTATE	Character	2	n/a	165	2	In/Out	Cust. Ship. State
STATUS	Character	1	n/a	167	1	In/Out	Cust. Sts.

Sample record with starting positions of each field

10001	Ajax Plumbing	12 Main St.	Seattle	WA	A
1	5	35	135	165	167

You can organize the data in a particular file into one or more file **members**, each with its own member name. Single-member files are the most common organization you'll encounter in AS/400 applications, and typically the one member has the same name as the file (and, of course, holds all the file's data). In some cases, however, a file might have multiple

---

[5] You can create a DB2/400 file that contains simple fixed-length records without any field definitions. This type of file is referred to as a **program-described** file because you must code the file's layout in any HLL program that uses the file. Program-described files are not very common any more in AS/400 business applications. The types of files that we discuss in this book (those that do have field descriptions) are known as **externally described** files because they have definitions that are external to the HLL programs that use the files.

members. For example, a SALE96 file, which holds sales records for 1996, could have 12 members: JAN, FEB, . . ., DEC, with each member containing the sales records for a single month.[6] Members can be added to or removed from a file at any time; you don't have to specify a fixed number of members when you create a file. If a file has multiple members, they all have the same record format.

Physical and Logical Files

There are two types of DB2/400 files:

- Physical files
- Logical files

You store application data in physical files. DB2/400 takes care of low-level details such as reading and writing disk sectors. Application programs and database utility programs see the data in a physical file member as a sequence of records, as in Figure 1.5.

Figure 1.5

Record Placement in a DB2/400 Physical File

Relative Record Number (RRN)	"Deleted Record" Flag	Contents
1		Record for customer number 10004
2	On	(no record)
3		Record for customer number 10007
4		Record for customer number 10001
. . .	. . .	. . .
(highest RRN)		Record for customer number 10009

Each record occupies a unique location in a member, and the records are not necessarily in any order based on their content. A record's location is identified by its relative record number (RRN), which starts at 1 for the first record in the member and increases by 1 for each location. When you

---

[6] Members are not a type of AS/400 object; they are a component of a file object, just like record formats and access paths. The statement "Everything in the OS/400 operating system, including the database, is organized as objects" may seem a little confusing in this light. The statement is true, but there are further degrees of organization within various types of objects.

delete a record, DB2/400 sets on an internal "deleted record" flag in the record's location. When you insert a new record, DB2/400 puts it in either the first available location with a "deleted record" flag set or after the last record in the file.

A physical file always has just one record format, and all records in the same physical file (regardless of how many members the file has) have the same record layout. For most business applications, the record layout is a fixed length, although DB2/400 does support variable-length records, as well.

Logical files provide an alternative way to access data in one or more physical files. You can use a logical file to

- Select a subset of the records in a physical file (e.g., only customers in Seattle)
- Merge the records from multiple physical file members (e,g., combine twelve members that contain monthly sales records)
- Select a subset of the fields in a physical file's record format (e.g., only the name and status of customers)
- Combine ("join") related records in two or more physical files (e.g., combine detailed customer data with the sales records for the customer)
- Provide an index so records can be retrieved in particular order (e.g., by customer name)

Figure 1.6 provides a conceptual view of the relationship between a logical file and a physical file.

It's important to understand that logical files have no data in them; data is always stored in physical file members. Logical files do have members, however. You specify for each logical file member which physical file member(s) it spans. Logical files also have record formats. Although most logical files have a single record format, logical files can have multiple formats. Chapters 4 through 6 cover the details of logical files and explain the relationship between logical file and physical file record formats and members.

File and Field Descriptions

One thing that distinguishes DB2/400 from a traditional operating system file management facility is that every DB2/400 file contains a description of itself.[7] The file description includes the following items:

- File name
- File subtype (physical or logical)

---

[7] Recall that this book focuses only on externally described files. As mentioned in an earlier footnote, DB2/400 also supports program-described files that do not contain descriptions.

Figure 1.6
Relationship Between
Logical and Physical Files

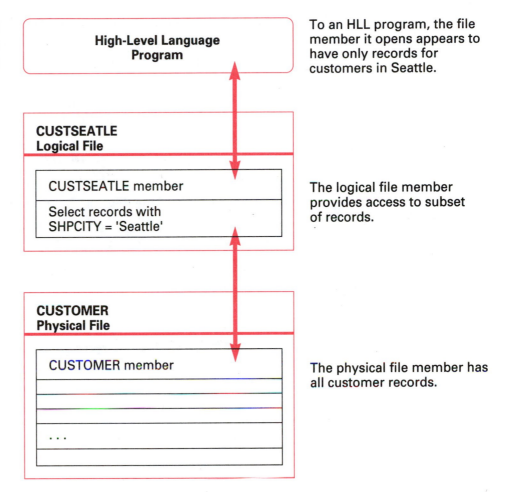

High-Level Language Program

To an HLL program, the file member it opens appears to have only records for customers in Seattle.

CUSTSEATLE
Logical File

CUSTSEATLE member

Select records with
SHPCITY = 'Seattle'

The logical file member provides access to subset of records.

CUSTOMER
Physical File

CUSTOMER member

. . .

The physical file member has all customer records.

- Record format
- Access path description (discussed in the next section)
- List of members

AS/400 HLL compilers (which are all written by IBM) read the file descriptions for any files you declare in your programs. AS/400 HLLs have extended I/O-related statements that take advantage of the fact that the compiler has this file information. For example, you don't have to declare a record layout in your RPG input specs or your COBOL Data Division: With the appropriate file declaration in your program, the compiler does that automatically. As another example, the compiler can automatically use the correct fields for keyed record access (e.g., by customer number) based on the key field(s) you define for a file. In addition, utility programs, such as report generators, can use file descriptions to determine a file's layout and keyed sequence (if any) without requiring the end-user to enter anything other than the file's name.

One of the most useful parts of the file description is the record format, which stores the following information for each field in the record:

- Name
- Data type (e.g., character, packed-decimal number)
- Length (for character fields) or precision and scale (i.e., number of digits and decimal positions, for numeric fields)
- Starting position in the record (the first field starts at position 1)
- Size (number of bytes occupied in the record)
- Usage (whether the field can be used for input, output, or both types of access)
- An optional column heading
- An optional descriptive text of up to 50 characters

In later chapters, you'll learn how to specify this field-level information when you create a database file.

Access Paths and Indexes

So far, we've seen that DB2/400 stores data as a sequence of records in a physical file. DB2/400 also provides a variety of ways to access records. There are two types of DB2/400 **access paths,** which describe the order in which records can be retrieved: **arrival sequence** access path and **keyed sequence** access path.

An arrival sequence access path is the order of records as they're stored in the database (i.e., by relative record number). "Arrival sequence" is a bit of a misnomer because a new record can be inserted in a "deleted record" location that has a lower RRN than a record that "arrived" earlier. The term originated before the AS/400 supported re-using deleted record locations and has hung on. The COBOL language uses a more descriptive term — "relative" file organization — for this type of access.

A keyed sequence arrival path is the order of records based on ascending or descending values in one or more **key fields** that you specify when you create the file. DB2/400 also supports access paths that select a subset of the records in a physical file. For example, an access path might include just those customer records with a SHPCITY value of "Seattle." Internally, DB2/400 maintains one **index** per file member for any physical or logical file that has key fields, as well as for most logical files that specify record selection. Indexes are stored as part of an OS/400 file object. The file description includes the index description, if the file has an index.

As you might expect, your programs can always use an arrival sequence access path to access records in a physical file; no special coding is required when you create the file. You can also define one keyed access path as part of a physical file, and DB2/400 will create an index for each member of the physical file. (Note that the *definition* of the keyed access path is the same for all of a physical file's members, but each member has its own index.)

Using logical files, you can have multiple access paths for the same data in a physical file, and thus, can access it in various ways. Each logical file can have one keyed access path definition. So, for example, if you want to retrieve customers in order by name or by address, you need two logical files (assuming you didn't use either of these fields for the physical file's keyed access path). Like physical files, each logical file member has its own index.

You can read and write DB2/400 data with either **sequential access** or **direct access**.[8] With sequential access, your program essentially performs a series of "read next record" operations to retrieve records. If you use an arrival sequence access path, your program receives records in their physical order (DB2/400 will automatically skip "deleted record" locations). If you use a keyed access path, your program receives records in the order defined by the key fields. With direct access, you specify either a RRN or a specific key value and DB2/400 returns the specific record you've identified (if one exists, of course).

As you insert, delete, or update records in a physical file member, DB2/400 maintains the necessary entries in any indexes that exist for keyed access paths (this includes logical file members over the physical file member). Although you can tune database performance by choosing from several alternative methods of index maintenance, generally, your applications can count on all keyed access paths reflecting the current contents of the database.

Accessing Files from HLL Programs

When you want to access DB2/400 data, your program performs three steps:

- Open a physical or logical file member
- Process (read, insert, update, or delete) records in the file member
- Close the file member

In some cases, you use explicit HLL statements, such as Open and Close in RPG or COBOL, to open and close a file member. In other cases, such as with RPG's built-in cycle, the HLL runtime does this for you automatically. Note that in HLL terminology you "open a file," which in DB2/400 means you open a file member. In this book, the two expressions are equivalent unless otherwise noted.

Whether you open a file explicitly or implicitly, DB2/400 creates a temporary internal control structure known as an **open data path** (**ODP**), which your program uses to access the records in a file member. DB2/400 uses information from the file description (e.g., the record layout and access

---

[8] Direct access is often referred to as random access — but there's usually nothing random about it.

path description) to set up an ODP. Then during your program's execution, HLL runtime routines and DB2/400 use the ODP for such purposes as keeping track of your position in the file and locking records to avoid conflicting updates by multiple users. To understand some of DB2/400's more advanced features, you need to understand the role of ODPs; however, for most of the topics covered in this book, the ODP is taken for granted, and we can treat DB2/400 files as if HLL operations operated on them directly, rather than through the ODP.

Creating Files with Data Description Specifications and SQL

You create DB2/400 files in two ways: [9]

- Enter **Data Description Specifications** (**DDS**) in a source file member and execute a command to compile the source into a file object
- Execute an SQL/400 Create statement

DDS is a language that, as its name suggests, describes file data. You use a source code editor, such as **Source Entry Utility** (**SEU**, covered in Appendix D), to enter DDS statements into a **source file** member.[10] Figure 1.7 shows some of the DDS source code for the CUSTOMER physical file.

The syntax of DDS is fairly simple; each line is split into a number of fixed-width columns. The last column (positions 45 to 80) provides a free-format area where you can place keyworded entries. In subsequent chapters, we'll explore the details of various DDS facilities to define physical and logical files.

After you've entered the DDS to define a file, you execute one of the following OS/400 CL commands to create the file object:

- CRTPF (Create Physical File)
- CRTLF (Create Logical File)

Figure 1.8 illustrates the process of creating a new file object from DDS.

---

[9] Actually, there's a third OS/400 method you can use to create database files. The Interactive Data Definition Utility (IDDU) is a carryover from the S/36 and is on the AS/400 to aid migration of S/36 applications. IDDU isn't intended for new AS/400 applications.

[10] DB2/400 further categorizes physical files into data files and source files. Data files are the ones you create for your applications (in other words, any type of file except a source file). Source files are files with three specific fields: source sequence (SRCSEQ), source date (SRCDAT), and source data (SRCDTA). You store HLL, DDS, and other source code in source files. The SEU editor, the HLL compilers, and several other AS/400 utilities are designed to work with source files. You create a source file with the CRTSRCPF (Create Source Physical File) command, which creates the file with the required fields — no DDS is necessary to create a source file.

Figure 1.7
DDS for the CUSTOMER
Physical File

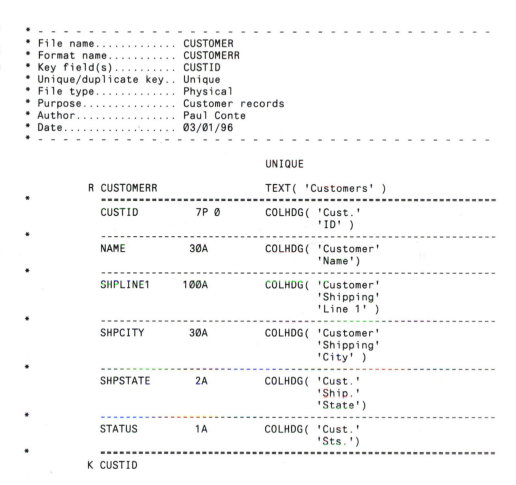

```
* - - - - - - - - - - - - - - - - - - - - - - - - - - - - - - - - -
* File name.............. CUSTOMER
* Format name........... CUSTOMERR
* Key field(s).......... CUSTID
* Unique/duplicate key.. Unique
* File type............. Physical
* Purpose............... Customer records
* Author............... Paul Conte
* Date..................'...... 03/01/96
* - - - - - - - - - - - - - - - - - - - - - - - - - - - - - - - - -

                                        UNIQUE

        R CUSTOMERR                     TEXT( 'Customers' )
*       ==================================================================
          CUSTID          7P 0          COLHDG( 'Cust.'
                                                 'ID' )
*       -------------------------------------------------------------------
          NAME            30A           COLHDG( 'Customer'
                                                 'Name')
*       -------------------------------------------------------------------
          SHPLINE1        100A          COLHDG( 'Customer'
                                                 'Shipping'
                                                 'Line 1' )
*       -------------------------------------------------------------------
          SHPCITY         30A           COLHDG( 'Customer'
                                                 'Shipping'
                                                 'City' )
*       -------------------------------------------------------------------
          SHPSTATE        2A            COLHDG( 'Cust.'
                                                 'Ship.'
                                                 'State')
*       -------------------------------------------------------------------
          STATUS          1A            COLHDG( 'Cust.'
                                                 'Sts.')
*       ==================================================================
        K CUSTID
```

Most AS/400 development installations also have the IBM Application Development ToolSet product installed, which provides a utility known as **Programming Development Manager (PDM)**. PDM provides a list-based, interactive interface for working with AS/400 libraries, objects, and source file members. PDM options are available to simplify execution of the CRTPF and CRTLF commands. Appendix C provides an introduction to PDM.

To revise a file's definition, you edit its DDS source, then delete the file (and its contents) and execute the CRTPF or CRTLF command to re-create the file. In a production environment, you typically copy the file before deleting it and then copy back the records from the old file to the new file, using the CPYF (Copy File) command. With V3R2 or V3R6 of DB2/400, you can use the CHGPF (Change Physical File) command or the SQL Alter statement to make most file changes and re-create the file, all in one step.

Figure 1.8
Creating a DB2/400
Physical File from DDS

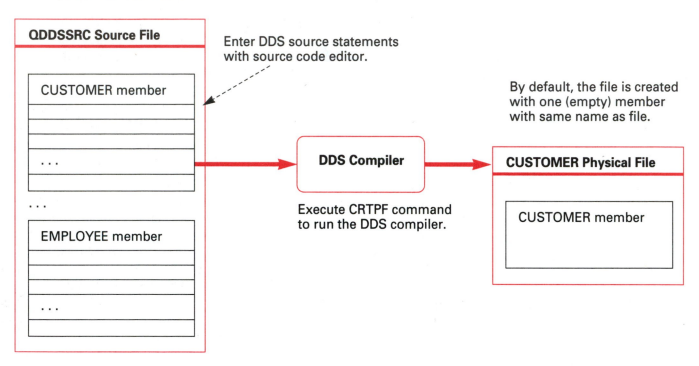

DDS was available with the first version of OS/400, and most AS/400 installations still use it to create database files. If IBM's **DB2 Query Manager and SQL Development Kit for OS/400** product is installed on an AS/400, you can use the following SQL statements to create and revise DB2/400 files:

- Create Table
- Create View
- Create Index
- Alter Table
- Comment on
- Label on

In standard SQL terminology, a **table** is a physical file and **views** and **indexes** are logical files (Chapter 13 explains the differences). SQL refers to records as **rows** and to fields as **columns.** In the chapters that cover SQL, this book uses the table-oriented terminology; elsewhere it uses conventional file terminology.

You can execute these SQL statements either interactively (using the interface the SQL Development Kit provides) or as **embedded statements** compiled into an HLL program (again using a feature of the SQL Development Kit). The latter approach raises an interesting aspect of DB2/400's support for SQL. Although you must buy the SQL Development Kit to get the interactive SQL interface and the facility that lets you embed SQL statements in HLL programs, *all* AS/400's include in DB2/400 the ability to *run* compiled HLL programs that were created using embedded SQL.

Whether you create a database file with DDS or SQL, you get the *same* type of object — a physical or logical file.[11] What's more, you can create a file with DDS and then read and update the contents with SQL, or create a file with SQL and read and update the contents with HLL I/O operations. Because DB2/400 includes as part of the "native" file support features that SQL requires, there was no need to add a separate DBMS layer just to support applications written with SQL.

Chapter Summary

A database is a set of computer files to store business information. A database management system (DBMS) is the system software for creating database files and updating their contents. DB2/400 is the AS/400's integrated DBMS, and is part of OS/400, the AS/400's operating system.

Everything in OS/400 is an object. There are more than 80 OS/400 object types, including programs and database files. An object contains a header and the actual content (e.g., program instructions or file data) of the object. OS/400 lets you use objects only through commands or other system interfaces that are valid for the specific type of object. Library objects contain other types of OS/400 objects (except other library objects). User profile objects own objects. An object is uniquely identified by its library, name, and object type.

There are two types of DB2/400 database file objects: physical files, which contain data, and logical files, which provide alternative ways to access data in physical files. File objects contain a file description, which includes the record format of the records in the file. The record format describes the type, length, and other attributes of the fields in a record. The data in a physical file is organized into one or more members, all of which have the same record format. Logical files also have members; each logical file member provides access to the data in one or more underlying physical file members.

DB2/400 has two types of access path: arrival sequence, which orders records by their relative location in a physical file member, and keyed, which orders records by values in the records' key fields. You can read and write records sequentially (in order of the access path) or directly (by specific relative record number or key value).

---

[11] There are actually some file attributes that are set differently depending on whether you use DDS or SQL to create a file. However, the OS/400 object types are the same, and you can generally use DDS-based and SQL-created files interchangeably.

To access DB2/400 data from a high-level language (HLL) program, you open a file member, process the records, then close the file member. When you open a file member, DB2/400 creates an open data path (ODP) that your program and DB2/400 use to keep track of the file position and other runtime information.

You can create database files with Data Description Specifications (DDS) or SQL. Files created either way can generally be used interchangeably.

Key Terms

access path
arrival sequence
AS/400
column
command
Data Description
    Specifications (DDS)
database
database file
database management
    system (DBMS)
DB2/400
DB2 Query Manager and
    SQL Development Kit
    for OS/400
direct access

embedded statement
externally described file
field
file description
high-level language (HLL)
index
Integrated File System (IFS)
key field
keyed sequence
library
logical file
member
object
open data path (ODP)
OS/400
physical file

program-described file
Programming Development
    Manager (PDM)
qualified name
record
record format
relative record number (RRN)
row
sequential access
Source Entry Utility (SEU)
source file
Structured Query Language
    (SQL)
table
user profile
view

Exercises

1. List several advantages of using a database. Are there any disadvantages?

2. Why do you think the designers of OS/400 made everything an "object"? Do you think OS/400 objects make programming easier or harder? Do you think OS/400 objects will affect performance?

3. What are the disadvantages to the OS/400 restriction that you can't nest libraries? Are there any advantages to this approach. *[Hint: Consider how Unix and DOS implement searches for executable and non-executable files.]*

4. Why do you think OS/400 considers as "files" all of the following: database files, display files, printer files, communications files? Do you think OS/400 allows the same set of file operations for all types of files?

5. What are the two types of database files, and what are their respective purposes?

6. What part of a file describes the arrangement of the fields in the file's records? What advantage does this offer to application programmers? To non-programmers?

7. Draw a "box" diagram that shows the relationship of the following: library, file, member, record, field.

8. What is an RRN? How does DB2/400 use it?

9. What are key fields? Give at least two important uses of key fields.

10. Give several possible ways you might want to access the data in a customer master file (e.g., accessing only customers in Seattle).

Exercises Continued

Exercises continued

11. When would you use sequential access? When would you use direct access? Would you ever use both in the same program?

12. List several things you think DB2/400 might use the ODP for?

13. Describe two ways to create a database file. Do you think a physical file must exist before you can create a logical file over it? Why or why not? *[Note: You'll find the answer in Chapter 4.]*

Chapter 2

Physical Files

Chapter Overview

In this chapter you learn how to use Data Description Specifications (DDS) and the CRTPF (Create Physical File) command to create a DB2/400 physical file. You learn about file-level, record-level, field-level, and key field-level DDS entries. You also learn how DB2/400 uses key fields to guarantee unique record identifiers and how to let your applications access records by key value.

DDS for Physical Files

As you learned in Chapter 1, a DB2/400 physical file is the OS/400 object that contains data. Each physical file has a single record format, which describes the layout of fields in the file's records; all records in a physical file have the same layout. Data records are stored in physical file members. A physical file must have at least one member to contain any data. Although most files you encounter in AS/400 business applications have a single member, a physical file may have multiple members, each containing a portion of the file's records.

To define a physical file, you code DDS statements in a **source file member** using a **source code editor**, such as SEU.[1] (You may also use SQL to create physical files, but Chapter 13 covers that approach.) If you're not already familiar with SEU and OS/400 source files, Appendix D provides an introduction. IBM supplies the QDDSSRC source file in library QGPL as a default file where you can keep your DDS source members. Many AS/400 installations

---

[1] SEU is a full-screen (5250 display) style editor that's part of IBM's Application Development ToolSet/400 (ADTS/400) product, which also includes the Programming Development Manager (PDM), Screen Design Aid (SDA), Report Layout Utility (RLU), and Interactive Source Debugger (ISDB). Most AS/400s used for application development will have ADTS/400 installed. At this writing, two — more modern — editors are available for entering DDS (and other AS/400 source code) — IBM's CODE/400 product, which runs under OS/2, and Aldon Computer Group's Flex/EDIT product, which runs under Windows. Both products provide a graphical user interface (GUI), multiple editing windows, mouse selection and navigation, and other features typically found in workstation-based source-code editors.

use source files other than QGPL/QDDSRC for their production source code,[2] but the process of entering DDS and creating files is the same.

You use one source member for the DDS for each physical file. Normally, you should make the source member name the same as its physical file name (e.g., use CUSTOMER as the name of the source member that has the DDS for the CUSTOMER physical file). Source file members have a **source type attribute**, which is PF for physical file DDS and LF for logical file DDS.[3] SEU provides fill-in-the-blank prompting for DDS based on the source type of the member you're editing. Figure 2.1 shows an SEU editing window with a prompt for a DDS source statement. SEU also provides online help, as shown in Figure 2.2.

Figure 2.1
SEU Display with a
Prompt for DDS

```
Columns . . . :    1  71              Edit              DB2BOOK/CHP2PF
SEU==> █                                                        CUSTOMER
FMT A* .....A*. 1 ...+... 2 ...+... 3 ...+... 4 ...+... 5 ...+... 6 ...+... 7
0012.00      *.........T.Name++++++RLen++XDcU......Keyword++++++++++++++++++
0014.00                                     UNIQUE
0015.00
0016.00           R CUSTOMERR              TEXT( 'Customers' )
0017.00      *    ============================================================
0018.00           CUSTID          7P 0     TEXT( 'Customer ID' )
0019.00
0020.00                                     COLHDG( 'Cust.'
0021.00                                             'ID' )
0022.00      *    ------------------------------------------------------------
 Prompt type . . .   PF       Sequence number . . .  0018.00

 Name                                 Data     Decimal
 Type         Name       Ref   Length Type     Positions    Use
 _            CUSTID      _       7    P           0         _
 Functions
 TEXT( 'Customer ID' )

 F3=Exit    F4=Prompt   F5=Refresh          F11=Previous record
 F12=Cancel             F23=Select prompt   F24=More keys
```

[2] Because the IBM-supplied defaults for the CRTPF (Create Physical File) and CRTLF (Create Logical File) commands specify QDDSRC as the source file containing the DDS to be compiled, some installations use a source file named QDDSRC in a locally created library (e.g., APPSRC/QDDSRC) for their DDS source. Note, however, that a Q as the first letter of an object name usually indicates that the object is supplied by IBM. Normally, you should not start your application object names with a Q.

An alternative way to organize DDS source code is to use a separate source file for each source type; for example, PFSRC for physical file source and LFSRC for logical file source. Note that you can change the CRTPF and CRTLF commands' default source file names from QDDSRC to your own file names, using the CHGCMDDFT (Change Command Default) command.

[3] When AS/400 programmers refer to a physical or logical file, they often use the shorthand PF or LF, pronounced "pee-ef" and "el-ef."

Figure 2.2

Online Help Display
for DDS

```
Columns . . . :   1  71              Edit                   DB2BOOK/CHP2PF
..............................................................................
:                          DDS for Physical Files - Help                      :
:                                                                             :
: █Name                                                                       :
:                                                                             :
:      Type a Record Format, Field, or Key Field Name in this position. The   :
:      maximum length allowed is 10 characters, beginning in column 19.       :
:                                                                             :
:   Reference                                                                 :
:                                                                             :
:      Type R in this field to use the reference function to copy             :
:      attributes of a previously defined named field to the field you are    :
:      now defining.                                                          :
:                                                                             :
:   Length                                                                    :
:                                                                             :
:      Type a value to indicate the number of bytes in a Character field or   :
:      the number of digits in a Numeric field. The following are valid       :
:                                                                  More...    :
:   F3=Exit help    F10=Move to top    F11=Search Index    F12=Cancel         :
:   F13=Information Assistant          F14=Print help                         :
:                                                                             :
:..............................................................................:
```

When you add a new source member or edit an existing member, you can specify a 50-character description for it.[4] You should always provide a description for each member that clearly states what's in the physical file, as in the following examples:

```
Customers

Customer status codes and descriptions
```

By default, the source member description is copied to the physical file object's description when you create the latter, so don't use descriptions such as "Customer physical file DDS" (you already know that the member contains physical file DDS from its PF source type).

DDS is primarily a fixed-format language where you place entries in designated columns on each line of source. Figure 2.3 shows the source columns for physical file DDS.

All columns except the last are fixed format and are called **positional entries**. The last column is a free-format area in which you code **keyword entries** for a variety of DDS functions. Each DDS keyword entry begins with a **keyword**. (Figure 2.4 summarizes the keywords for physical files, grouped by section. Appendix A provides detailed descriptions for all the keywords available for physical and logical files.)

---

[4] You can subsequently change the source member text using SEU, PDM, or the CHGPFM (Change Physical File Member) command.

Figure 2.3

Source Columns for
Physical File DDS

Column	Positions	Content
Sequence number	1–5	Optional sequence number or comment
Form type	6	A or blank to indicate DDS
Comment flag	7	Place a * in this column to identify the entire line as a comment
Unused	8–16	Leave blank unless the line is a comment
Type of Name	17	One of the following: Blank — field name K — key field name R — record format name
Unused	18	Leave blank unless the line is a comment
Name	19–28	An identifier for one of the following: Record format name Field name Key field name
Reference	29	Code R in this position to refer to the attributes of a previously defined field
Length	30–34	For character fields, the maximum number of characters; For numeric fields, specify the maximum number of digits (including any decimal positions)
Data Type	35	One of the following: A — character H — hexadecimal P — packed decimal S — zoned decimal B — binary F — floating point L — date T — time Z — timestamp If you leave this column blank, the default is: A — if decimal positions (36-37) is blank P — if decimal positions (36-37) contain a number in the range 0 to 31
Decimal positions	36–37	For character fields, leave blank For numeric field, enter an integer in the range 0 to 31 (and not greater than the Length you enter in 30-34) for the number of positions to the right of the decimal point
Usage	38	Blank or B — both input and output operations are always valid for physical file fields
Unused	39–44	Leave blank unless the line is a comment
Function	45–80	Keyword entries (see Appendix A)

Figure 2.4
Physical File DDS
Keyword Summary

File level	Record level	Field level	Key field level	Field-level entries for reference by display and printer files
ALTSEQ	FORMAT	ALIAS	ABSVAL	CHECK
CCSID	TEXT	ALWNULL	DESCEND	CHKMSGID
FCFO		CCSID	DIGIT	COMP, CMP
FIFO		COLHDG	NOALTSEQ	EDTCDE
LIFO		DATFMT	SIGNED	EDTWRD
REF		DATSEP	UNSIGNED	RANGE
UNIQUE		DFT	ZONE	REFSHIFT
		FLTPCN		VALUES
		REFFLD		
		TEXT		
		TIMFMT		
		TIMSEP		
		VARLEN		

Note: See Appendix A for a description of each keyword.

Some keyword entries (e.g., DESCEND) have no parameters, and the keyword is all you code to specify the DDS function. For example, to specify that a key field should be in descending order, you code

```
...2....+....3....+....4....+....5.
K TOTAMT                DESCEND
```

Other keyword entries require one or more parameters to complete the entry. You code keyword entries with parameters as the keyword followed immediately (no intervening spaces) by a left parenthesis, then the parameter value(s), followed by a right parenthesis. For example, to specify the date format for a date field, you code the keyword entry as

```
DATFMT(*YMD)
```

You may optionally put one or more spaces after the left parenthesis and before the right parenthesis:

```
DATFMT( *YMD )
```

This style improves the readability of your DDS and is used in the source code examples in this book.

Character-string parameter values must be enclosed in single quotation marks. For example, to specify descriptive text for a field, you code the keyword entry as

```
TEXT( 'Customer name' )
```

If you want an apostrophe within a character string, code two adjacent single quotation marks, for example

```
TEXT( 'Customer''s name' )
```

For this example, DB2/400 uses

```
Customer's name
```

as the description it displays or prints for the entry.

If a keyword entry takes more than one parameter value, you separate the values with one or more blanks or place them on separate lines. The following entries show two ways you could specify a two-line column heading:

```
COLHDG( 'Customer' 'Name' )
```

or

```
COLHDG( 'Customer'
        'Name' )
```

You may also continue a series of keyword entries across successive source lines. (Although you can put more than one keyword on a line, separating the keywords by at least one space, it's more readable to begin each keyword entry on a new line.) If a character-string parameter won't fit on a single line, you can continue the parameter on the next line by coding a **continuation symbol** — a plus (+) or a minus (–) — as the last character on the line to be continued.

- A plus (+) means the continuation begins with the first nonblank character in the functions column (positions 45–80) of the next line.
- A minus (–) means the continuation begins in position 45 of the next line.

A simple and readable technique for long character strings is to break the string between words and continue with a plus (+), aligning the first word of the continued line(s) under the first word of the line where the parameter starts, as in the following example:

```
TEXT( 'This is a long +
       string continued +
       across 3 lines' )
```

For this example, DB2/400 uses the string

```
This is a long string continued across 3 lines
```

as the parameter value.

Note that all names, keywords, and other unquoted entries used in DDS must be uppercase. Most DB2/400 names, including library, file, member, record format, and field names can be up to 10 characters long and must begin with an alphabetic or national character: A through Z, @, $, or # (in the U.S.). All subsequent characters can be alphanumeric: A through Z, 0 through 9, @, $, #, or _ (underscore)[5]. Although many AS/400 programmers use the national characters to identify fields with special meaning (e.g., unique key fields, such as #CUSTNBR), this practice can cause problems if your applications are used in countries that have different characters for the national character set. For example, AS/400 systems in Italy allow $, £, and § in DB2/400 names. Also note that RPG/400 and COBOL do not allow the underscore (_) character in identifiers. The best approach for DB2/400 names is to use only letters and digits.

The DDS you code for physical files is grouped into four sections:

- File-level statements (optional)
- A record-level statement (exactly one required)
- Field-level statements (normally, one or more)
- Key field-level statements (optional)

These sections must appear in the order listed above. Figure 2.5 shows sample DDS for the CUSTOMER physical file and identifies the four sections. The remainder of the chapter examines these sections of DDS code.

Figure 2.5
DDS for CUSTOMER
Physical File

```
* - - - - - - - - - - - - - - - - - - - - - - - - - - - - - - - - - - -
* File name............. CUSTOMER
* Format name.......... CUSTOMERR
* Key field(s)......... CUSTID
* Unique/duplicate key.. Unique
* File type............. Physical
* Purpose.............. Customer records
* Author............... Paul Conte
* Date.................. 03/01/96
* - - - - - - - - - - - - - - - - - - - - - - - - - - - - - - - - - - -
*
*.........T.Name++++++RLen++XDcU......Keyword++++++++++++++++++++++++++++
```

File-level entries
```
                                        UNIQUE
```

```
*
```

Record-level entry
```
         R CUSTOMERR              TEXT( 'Customers' )
```

Field-level entries
```
         CUSTID         7P 0      TEXT( 'Customer ID' )

                                  COLHDG( 'Cust.'
                                          'ID' )
```
Figure 2.5 continued

[5] OS/400 has a quoted-name feature that allows names with lowercase and special characters, but this isn't used in most AS/400 sites.

Figure 2.5
Continued

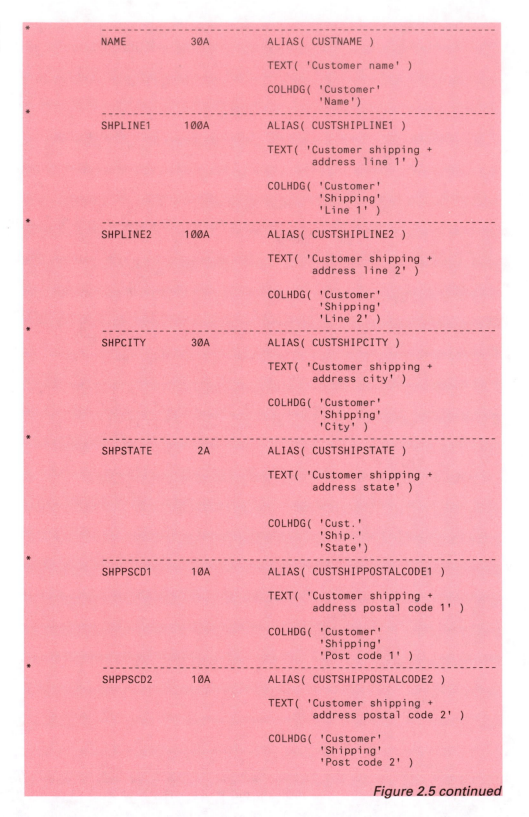

```
*   ------------------------------------------------------------
    NAME        30A             ALIAS( CUSTNAME )

                                TEXT( 'Customer name' )

                                COLHDG( 'Customer'
                                        'Name')
*   ------------------------------------------------------------
    SHPLINE1    100A            ALIAS( CUSTSHIPLINE1 )

                                TEXT( 'Customer shipping +
                                       address line 1' )

                                COLHDG( 'Customer'
                                        'Shipping'
                                        'Line 1' )
*   ------------------------------------------------------------
    SHPLINE2    100A            ALIAS( CUSTSHIPLINE2 )

                                TEXT( 'Customer shipping +
                                       address line 2' )

                                COLHDG( 'Customer'
                                        'Shipping'
                                        'Line 2' )
*   ------------------------------------------------------------
    SHPCITY     30A             ALIAS( CUSTSHIPCITY )

                                TEXT( 'Customer shipping +
                                       address city' )

                                COLHDG( 'Customer'
                                        'Shipping'
                                        'City' )
*   ------------------------------------------------------------
    SHPSTATE    2A              ALIAS( CUSTSHIPSTATE )

                                TEXT( 'Customer shipping +
                                       address state' )


                                COLHDG( 'Cust.'
                                        'Ship.'
                                        'State')
*   ------------------------------------------------------------
    SHPPSCD1    10A             ALIAS( CUSTSHIPPOSTALCODE1 )

                                TEXT( 'Customer shipping +
                                       address postal code 1' )

                                COLHDG( 'Customer'
                                        'Shipping'
                                        'Post code 1' )
*   ------------------------------------------------------------
    SHPPSCD2    10A             ALIAS( CUSTSHIPPOSTALCODE2 )

                                TEXT( 'Customer shipping +
                                       address postal code 2' )

                                COLHDG( 'Customer'
                                        'Shipping'
                                        'Post code 2' )
```

Figure 2.5 continued

Figure 2.5
Continued

```
*     -------------------------------------------------------------
      SHPCNTRY      30A        ALIAS( CUSTSHIPCOUNTRY )

                               TEXT( 'Customer shipping +
                                     address country' )

                               COLHDG( 'Customer'
                                       'Shipping'
                                       'Country' )
*     -------------------------------------------------------------
      PHNVOICE      15A        ALIAS( CUSTPHONEVOICE )

                               TEXT( 'Customer voice phone +
                                     number' )

                               COLHDG( 'Customer'
                                       'Phone' )
*     -------------------------------------------------------------
      PHNFAX        15A        ALIAS( CUSTPHONEFAX )

                               TEXT( 'Customer Fax phone number' )

                               COLHDG( 'Customer'
                                       'Fax' )
*     -------------------------------------------------------------
      STATUS        1A         ALIAS( CUSTSTATUS )

                               DFT( ' ' )

                               TEXT( 'Customer status' )

                               COLHDG( 'Cust.'
                                       'Status')
*     -------------------------------------------------------------
      CRDLIMIT      7P 0       ALIAS( CUSTCREDITLIMIT )

                               ALWNULL

                               DFT( *NULL )

                               TEXT( 'Customer credit limit' )

                               COLHDG( 'Cust.'
                                       'Credit'
                                       'Limit' )
*     -------------------------------------------------------------
      ENTDATE       L          ALIAS( CUSTENTRYDATE )

                               DATFMT( *ISO )

                               TEXT( 'Customer info data entry +
                                     date' )

                               COLHDG( 'Cust.'
                                       'Entry'
                                       'Date' )
```

Key field-level entries   K CUSTID

Defining File Attributes

You can specify several physical file attributes by using DDS file-level statements. Only the function column (i.e., keyword entries in positions 45–80) is used on file-level statements. The DDS for CUSTOMER in Figure 2.5 has only one file-level statement, which uses the UNIQUE keyword to specify that DB2/400 should prevent duplicate values for the key field defined for the file. This file attribute prevents two customer records in the same physical file member from having the same CUSTID value (CUSTID, the CUSTOMER file's key field, is discussed later). UNIQUE is a commonly used entry for physical files whose record format includes a field, such as CUSTID, that provides a unique identifier for each record in the file.

The less-commonly used ALTSEQ, FCFO, FIFO, and LIFO file-level keywords also affect the way DB2/400 handles files with key fields. "Defining a Key," later in this chapter, discusses these keywords.

The REF keyword lets you specify another file that contains field definitions referenced in the current file's field-level statements. Chapter 3 covers this technique in detail.

Defining a Record Format

The DDS for a physical file has one record-level statement. This statement must have an R in the Type of Name column (17) to indicate that it defines a record format. The record-format name goes in the Name column (19–28). The record-format name can be any valid DB2/400 name but typically is either the same as the file name or has an R as the last character to signify that it's the file's record-format name.[6] The examples in this book use the R suffix for all record-format names.

---

[6] The practice of appending an R to a file name to form its record format name is especially common in installations that use RPG/400 or RPG IV because both versions of RPG require unique file- and record-format names. Other AS/400 HLLs don't have this restriction, and with these languages it's simpler to have identical file- and record-format names, especially because this convention lets you use full 10-character file names without worrying about how you form the record-format name.

If you have two or more related physical files and plan to create a single-format, nonjoin logical file that encompasses them, all the physical files should have the same record-format name. Chapter 4 covers nonjoin logical files.

Also, if you open two files in an RPG/400 or RPG IV program, the files can't have a field with the same name. Many RPG/400 and RPG IV installations adopt a convention of a unique two-letter prefix for each file's field names. In RPG IV, you can use the Prefix keyword on a file specification (discussed in Chapter 7) to add the prefix characters to the beginning of each field name in a file. Many RPG/400 installations actually code the prefix as part of the field name on the DDS field definition (e.g., all fields in the CUSTOMER file might begin with CS.)

Also note that RPG/400 (but not RPG IV) places some more severe restrictions on DB2/400 name lengths. In most cases, RPG/400 permits a maximum of eight characters in file- and record-format names and six characters in field names. If RPG/400 programs will use your database files, be sure to consider these language restrictions.

The TEXT keyword lets you specify a 50-character description for the record format. Although it's not required, including this description with all your record- and field-level definitions is a valuable documentation practice. DB2/400, some HLL compilers, and many utilities display or print this text, making it easier when you work with a file to understand the purpose of its components. DB2/400 also lets you specify descriptive text when you create a file object, and because physical files always have just one record format, a good practice is to use the same (or at least consistent) descriptions for both the physical file and its record format.

In most cases, TEXT is the only keyword specified on a physical file's record-format definition. Usually the field-level statements that define the record format's fields immediately follow the record-level statement. Occasionally, however, you may want two physical files to have the same record format; in this case, you can specify the FORMAT keyword in one physical file's record format and *not* include any field-level statements in the DDS for that physical file. For example, if you were to put each year's sales records in a separate file, you might use the following statement to simplify the file definitions for the second and later years' files:

```
...2....+....3....+....4....+....5....+....6.
R SALER                        FORMAT( SALE95 )
```

In this example, SALER is the record format being defined, and SALE95 is the name of an existing file whose format you want to copy. The file you specify as the FORMAT parameter must contain a format with the same name you're defining (e.g., SALER). When you use a FORMAT keyword, the two files, their members, and their record formats are completely separate; the DDS compiler copies the previously defined fields. The DDS compiler also copies the reference format's TEXT description (if any), and you can't specify both FORMAT and TEXT keywords on the same record-level statement.

Using FORMAT isn't a common practice because you might add new fields as you track more sales data each year, and you can't put additional field definitions after a record-level statement with the FORMAT keyword. Field referencing, which Chapter 3 covers, provides an alternative approach to reusing previous definitions that's almost as convenient, and a lot more flexible, than the FORMAT function.

Defining Fields

Unless you use the FORMAT keyword described above, you follow the record-level statement with one or more field definitions. A field definition is indicated by leaving the Type of Name column (17) blank. Each field definition requires a name (10–28). You can define the field's attributes explicitly by entering values in the other columns, or you can code an R in the reference column (29) to define the field as having the same attributes as a previously defined field.

To explicitly define a field, you must supply at least the following information in addition to a field name:

- Length
- Data type
- Decimal positions (for numeric fields only)

Optionally, you can specify one or more of the keywords listed in the field-level column of Figure 2.4. You can optionally specify a Usage attribute (position 38), but because all physical file fields can be used for both input and output operations, you should just leave this column blank.

After its name, the first thing to decide about a field is what **data type** to use: character (or hexadecimal), numeric, or date/time. A field's data type determines both the encoding DB2/400 uses to store field values and the allowable uses of the field (e.g., whether a field can be used in arithmetic operations).

When a field value is stored on disk or in memory, the AS/400 uses one or more 8-bit bytes to represent the value. For example, to represent characters, the AS/400 normally uses the **EBCDIC (Extended Binary Coded Decimal Interchange Code)** representation.[7] Each character takes one byte of storage; thus, there are 256 possible characters, including the uppercase and lowercase letters, digits, punctuation, and an assortment of graphical symbols and control characters.[8] The uppercase letter A, for example, is represented in EBCDIC by the eight bits 11000001. The AS/400 has several encoding schemes for numeric values, each offering advantages and disadvantages. Although it's useful to know how data is encoded on the AS/400, the more important aspect to understand about DB2/400 field data types is the purpose and relative advantages and disadvantages of each data type.

Character and Hexadecimal Data Types
Character fields are typically used for textual data in applications: names of things, addresses, descriptions, etc. Many applications also use short character codes in place of longer descriptions; for example, a customer status value of A might mean "active, in good standing." In some cases, codes can

---

[7] Many other systems, such as Unix and DOS on PCs, use the ASCII (American National Standard Code for Information Interchange) set of character codes. The AS/400 also provides ASCII support both within DB2/400 and the Integrated File System. When data is moved between an EBCDIC and an ASCII file, the character codes must be translated. IBM and other vendors provide support in a variety of translation and communications software products to handle this conversion.

[8] DB2/400 also supports international applications with features for non-English character sets (specified by the CCSID file- or field-level keyword), and double-byte character sets (DBCS), which use two bytes for each character. DBCS support is an operating-system option that's beyond the scope of this book.

save significant disk storage and simplify data entry. Most AS/400 applications use only fixed-length character fields, whether for text or codes, although DB2/400 supports variable-length character fields if you specify the VARLEN keyword. Fixed-length fields are significantly simpler to work with in HLL programs and are what you'll see in the examples in this book.

To define a character field, specify A in the Data Type column (35). Although the DDS compiler treats a blank data type as A when the Decimal Positions column (36–37) is also blank, it's better to code the data type explicitly. In the Length column (30–34), specify the *maximum* length (number of characters, including blanks) for any potential value you might store in this field. Believe it or not, picking the right length for character fields is a challenge for the following reasons:

- The greater a field's length, the more disk storage the file requires for each record. For files with lots of records, this may be a significant amount of storage.
- If you code too small a length, you may have to truncate values or re-create the file at some point to increase the field's length.

Except for very large files (more than a million records), you should normally err on the side of making a field (character or numeric) longer than you ultimately need. Disk storage has become fairly inexpensive (per byte), and it can be cumbersome to change field definitions once a file is in production use.

Another good practice is to use only a limited number of values for field lengths. For example, make all fields that hold some type of textual description 50 characters (the same as DB2/400 uses for descriptions of files, fields, etc.), use only 1- or 3-character codes, make all address fields the same length, and so on. Don't try to fine-tune each field's length (e.g., by using 23 characters for one kind of name and 37 characters for some other kind of name). This practice becomes confusing, is hard to maintain, and is error-prone in HLL programs. The field referencing techniques covered in Chapter 3 provide an easy way to implement a set of standard field data types and lengths for all your files.

The **hexadecimal** (or **hex**) data type is rarely used in business applications, which deal primarily with text, numbers, and codes. A hex field can be used for storing binary data that doesn't represent characters or numbers (e.g., bitmaps of graphical images). DB2/400 treats hex fields as it treats character fields, except functions that perform character display or translation don't treat hex values as actual characters.

Numeric Data Types

For **numeric fields**, you have a choice of several data types: packed decimal, zoned decimal, binary, and floating point. Each data type uses a different scheme to store numbers as a series of bytes in the file, and each has its advantages and disadvantages.

For any numeric field, you must specify the maximum length number it can hold and the number of decimal places, in addition to the data type. A numeric field's length is specified as the maximum number of digits, *not* bytes. Figure 2.6 lists the valid field lengths and amount of disk storage occupied for various data types.

Figure 2.6

Valid Field Lengths for Data Types

Data type	Valid lengths	Bytes occupied in storage
Character (A)	1 to 32,766 characters	Number of characters
Hexadecimal (H)	1 to 32,766 bytes	Number of bytes
Zoned decimal (S)	1 to 31 digits	Number of digits
Packed decimal (P)	1 to 31 digits	For even lengths: (number of digits / 2) + 1 For odd lengths: (number of digits + 1) /2
Binary (B)	1 to 9 digits	1 through 4 digits: 2 bytes 5 through 9 digits: 4 bytes
Floating point (F) single-precision	1 to 9 digits	4 bytes
Floating point (F) double-precision	1 to 17 digits	8 bytes
Date (L)	6, 8, or 10 characters (implicit)	4 bytes
Time (T)	8 characters (implicit)	3 bytes
Timestamp (Z)	26 characters (implicit)	10 bytes

For numeric fields that will contain integer (nonfractional) values, enter 0 for the decimal positions (positions 36–37). For fractional values, enter a number from 1 to 31 for the number of places to the right of the decimal point. The number of decimal positions (obviously) can't be greater than the field's length in digits. DB2/400 *doesn't* store an actual decimal point for fractional fields, regardless of the data type. Instead DB2/400 functions, as well as HLL applications and utilities that access the field, make the appropriate adjustment when they perform an arithmetic operation. For example, if 123 is stored in the bytes of a packed-decimal field with two decimal positions, when you use this field, DB2/400 automatically treats it as 1.23 — you *don't* have to adjust the number in your programs.

If you specify a value for the Decimal Positions column (36–37) and do not specify a Data Type (position 35), the field is treated as a packed-decimal field. Don't rely on this default, however, because coding an explicit data type provides clearer documentation.

Packed decimal (P in position 35) represents a number by using a *half-byte* (four bits) for each digit and the low-order half-byte (rightmost four bits) of the low-order byte for the sign.[9] The half-byte 1111 is used for positive values, and the half-byte 1101 is used for negative values. Thus, a 4-byte packed-decimal field can hold a number up to seven digits long. The number +1234567 would be represented as

1	2	3	4	5	6	7	+
0001	0010	0011	0100	0101	0110	0111	1111

A 6-digit number would also require a 4-byte packed-decimal field because a field must be an integral number of bytes; in a 6-digit packed-decimal field one half-byte would be unused[10]. Thus, the number –123456 would be represented as

0	1	2	3	4	5	6	–
0000	0001	0010	0011	0100	0101	0110	1101

In general, you should declare packed-decimal fields with an odd number for the length.

Packed decimal has been around for a long time on IBM systems and is both compact and fast to process (on the AS/400). Its main disadvantage is that it's not found on many other systems or in the standards for some widely used languages, such as C and C++. (IBM's C and C++ compilers for the AS/400 do provide support for packed-decimal fields.) If portability or cross-system data access is a concern, be sure to check on the language and data translation capabilities that will be used.

Zoned decimal (S in position 35) represents a number as one byte (eight bits) per digit. Thus, to hold a 7-digit number, you need a zoned-decimal field that occupies seven bytes. Each byte is simply the EBCDIC character representation of the digit, except the last byte has the high-order half-byte (leftmost four bits) set to indicate the number's sign (1111 for positive, 1101 for negative, or 1110 for unsigned). The number +123 would be represented in a 4-byte field as

0		1		2		+	3
1111	0000	1111	0001	1111	0010	1111	0011

The number –123 would be represented in a 4-byte field as

0		1		2		–	3
1111	0000	1111	0001	1111	0010	1101	0011

---

[9] You can represent numbers in the range 0 to 15 with four bits, but packed decimal uses only the range 0 to 9 for each half-byte.

[10] In some cases, DB2/400 actually performs *extra* steps to handle packed-decimal fields with an even length.

Zoned decimal is a legacy of computer punch card days and is not as compact or efficient to process as packed decimal or binary.[11]

The **binary** data type (B in position 35) represents a number as a base-2 value, with one bit used for the number's sign.[12] The value +1234 would be represented as

```
0000 0010 1101 0010
```

The value –1234 would be represented as

```
1111 1011 0010 1110
```

Binary fields are compact, and most computer systems and languages support binary values (although some languages support only integers, not decimal fractions). In DB2/400, binary fields can hold values only up to 9 digits, whereas packed-decimal and zoned-decimal fields can hold numbers up to 31 digits long. In the past, binary fields were also somewhat slower to process on the AS/400, but this has improved with recent models.

For many business applications, the packed-decimal data type is a good choice for most numeric fields. The binary data type may be a preferable alternative if data is shared with a non-AS/400 system and translation from packed decimal isn't convenient.

Floating point (F in position 35) is generally used for scientific or mathematical applications (and by C or C++ programs) and is not very common in AS/400 business applications. Both RPG IV and COBOL/400 are limited in their support for floating point (see Chapter 7), so be sure you're familiar with the capabilities of the HLLs that may be used to access the file before setting up floating-point fields. The default maximum length for a floating-point field is 9 digits, and you can use the FLTPCN(*DOUBLE) keyword entry to specify a double precision floating-point field that can have a maximum length of 17 digits.

Date, Time, and Timestamp Data Types

DB2/400 supports special data types for **date**, **time**, and **timestamp** values. For these three data types, you specify the data type (L, T, or Z, respectively) but *not* a length or decimal positions. The system determines the length of

[11] Because zoned-decimal numbers are stored like character strings, there are some programming "tricks" you can use with them. For example, you can map date data type fields (which contain a separator character) to zoned-decimal fields in logical files, and then treat the zoned-decimal field like an ordinary number. Generally you should avoid these kinds of tricks, unless there's no cleaner solution.

[12] Our normal numbering system is base-10 — from right to left, the positions in a number represent the number of 1s, 10s, 100s, and so on. In base-2, the positions correspond to powers of 2 — 1, 2, 4, 8, and so on. Both systems, of course, can represent the full range of integers — 1, 2, 3, etc. The AS/400 uses "two's complement" encoding for binary numbers. This approach actually flips bits for negative numbers, so that -1 is represented by the bit pattern 11111111. This encoding allows the processor to perform faster arithmetic.

these types of fields. SQL, RPG IV, and some utilities support date arithmetic on date fields. With date arithmetic, you can add a number of days (or months or years) to a date field, and the result will take into account month and year boundaries. For example 1996-12-31 + 1 (day) would equal 1997-01-01. Date fields and date arithmetic can simplify how many common business applications handle dates.

DB2/400 stores all date fields in the same four-byte *internal* format on disk. When your application program or a utility uses the date, DB2/400 decodes it into an *external* format, as determined by the DATFMT and DATSEP keyword entries. The DATFMT keyword can have any of the values shown in Figure 2.7.

Figure 2.7
DATFMT Values
for Date Fields

Format name	DATFMT parameter	Date separator	Field length	Example
Job default	*JOB			
Month/Day/Year	*MDY	DATSEP	8	12/31/97
Day/Month/Year	*DMY	DATSEP	8	31-12-97
Year/Month/Day	*YMD	DATSEP	8	97.12.31
Julian	*JUL	DATSEP	6	97/364
International Standards Organization	*ISO	– (dash)	10	1997-12-31
IBM USA standard	*USA	/ (slash)	10	12/31/1997
IBM European standard	*EUR	. (period)	10	31.12.1997
Japanese Industrial Standard Christian Era	*JIS	– (dash)	10	1997-12-31

If you don't specify a DATFMT keyword, the date format is *ISO. If you specify DATFMT(*JOB), the field has the date format associated with the interactive or batch job that runs the CRTPF command that creates the file. The external length of a date field is determined by the DATFMT value, as listed in Figure 2.7. Your HLL program works with the external length, as well as the date's external format. For several of the date formats, you can also code a DATSEP keyword entry to specify a separator. The allowable DATSEP parameter values are slash ('/'), dash ('–'), period ('.'), comma (','), or blank (' '). For example, to use a yy/mm/dd format for the date a customer's information was entered in the database, you code

```
...2....+....3....+....4....+....5....+....6.
ENTDATE         L          DATFMT( *YMD )
                           DATSEP( '/'  )
```

You can also specify DATSEP(*JOB) to use the date separator associated with the interactive or batch job in which the file is created.

Although applications in the past often used 2-digit years, the fact that many files now contain dates that span two centuries makes 4-digit years necessary. Thus, you should normally chose either *ISO, *USA, *EUR, or *JIS for DATFMT and omit the DATSEP keyword.

Time fields work similarly to date fields. You code the field name and T for the data type. Then (optionally) you code TIMFMT and TIMSEP keyword entries. Figure 2.8 lists the alternative time formats.

Figure 2.8
TIMFMT Values
for Time Fields

Format name	TIMFMT parameter	Time separator	Field length	Example
Hours:Minutes:Seconds	*HMS	TIMSEP	8	13:01.01
International Standards Organization	*ISO	. (period)	8	13.01.01
IBM USA standard	*USA	: (colon)	8	1:01 pm
IBM European standard	*EUR	. (period)	8	13.01.01
Japanese Industrial Standard Christian Era	*JIS	: (colon)	8	13:01.01

The TIMSEP parameter can be a colon (' : '), period (' . '), or blank (' '). The *USA time format does *not* include seconds (even though the internal storage of the field does). You can also specify TIMSEP(*JOB) to use the time separator associated with the interactive or batch job in which the file is created.

The timestamp (Z) data type has a system-defined format, so you don't code length, decimal positions, or formatting keywords. Timestamps appear externally as

```
yyyy-mm-dd-hh.mm.ss.uuuuuu
```

where *uuuuuu* is millionths of a second. Use timestamps when you need to maintain a precise record of the sequence in which events occur.

Additional Field-Level Keywords

Several other field-level keywords are available for physical files. TEXT and COLHDG let you specify descriptive information that can be used in interactive displays or in reports. TEXT takes a single parameter, which is a character string up to 50 characters long. For documentation purposes, as well as report labels, it's good practice to code a TEXT entry for each field.

COLHDG takes one, two, or three parameter values for a 1- to 3-line column heading. For example,

```
COLHDG( 'Cust.'
        'Credit'
        'Limit' )
```

will result in the heading

```
Cust.
Credit
Limit
```

The string for each line can be up to 20 characters long; however, you may want to take into consideration the length of the field when you pick a column heading. For example, you might want a narrow column heading for a field that holds a 1-character code.

COBOL/400 and SQL/400 both support identifiers longer than the DB2/400 limit of 10 characters. You can take advantage of this capability by specifying an **alias**, or longer name, for a field. The following statement defines a more descriptive alias for the SHPPSCD1 field:

```
...2....+....3....+....4....+....5....+....6....+....7..
  SHPPSCD1        10A           ALIAS( CUSTSHIPPOSTALCODE1 )
```

The ALIAS value can be up to 30 characters long. It must be uppercase and begin with a letter (A through Z); subsequent characters must be letters, digits, or an underscore (A through Z, 0 through 9, or _). COBOL/400 and RPG/400 don't allow underscores in identifiers,[13] so it's better not to use them. Unfortunately, DDS doesn't allow mixed-case names (e.g., CustPostalCode1) so longer names can be a bit cumbersome. SQL/400 and COBOL/400, however, treat lowercase and uppercase the same in identifiers, so you *can* use mixed case to refer to database fields, even though field name and alias names are uppercase. You can't use (and wouldn't want to, of course) the same alias name for multiple fields in the same record format, and an alias name can't be the same as any field name in the file.

When an HLL program reads and writes records to a physical file, it has all the fields available. The program must put "sensible" values in every field before it inserts a record into a file or updates an existing record. But, as you'll see in Chapter 4, a program can insert a *logical* file record that does *not* have all the fields of the underlying physical file (a logical file record format can contain a subset of a physical file's fields). What DB2/400 puts in those physical file fields that the program doesn't fill depends on how you define the physical file field.[14]

---

[13] The COBOL/400 compiler provides an option to convert underscores into dashes, which are an allowable character in identifiers. If you're in a COBOL installation, you may want to use this feature so you can define more readable aliases.

[14] As Chapter 6 explains, DB2/400 also uses a physical file field's default value to fill fields in a join logical file record when there's no matching secondary record and the JDFTVAL keyword is specified in the join logical file's DDS.

You can specify a **default field value** with the DFT keyword as in the following example:

```
...2....+....3....+....4....+....5....+....6
   STATUS          1A          DFT( 'U' )
```

DB2/400 will store a U in the physical file's STATUS field when a new record is inserted through a logical file that doesn't include the STATUS field. The DFT parameter value must be a valid value for the data type and length of the field you're defining.

You can also specify the ALWNULL (allow null) keyword for the field, and you can use a special **null** flag or placeholder[15] as the default:

```
...2....+....3....+....4....+....5....+....6
   STATUS          1A          ALWNULL
                               DFT( *NULL )
```

You can also specify ALWNULL with or without a default value to let languages such as SQL/400 explicitly set the field to null. In database terminology, null means "no value" or "not known." DB2/400 actually stores a hidden bit for each **null-capable** field. When the field is null, DB2/400 sets this hidden bit to 1; when the field has a normal value, DB2/400 sets this bit to 0. SQL/400 and some HLLs have built-in tests to check whether a field is null.

If you don't specify either a default value or ALWNULL, DB2/400 uses a default of blanks for character and hex fields, zero for numeric fields, and the current date and time for date, time, and timestamp fields. If you don't specify a default, but you do specify ALWNULL, DB2/400 uses null as the default.

If the DB2/400 defaults are satisfactory, you don't need to code a DFT entry. Here's a simple decision process to decide whether to code ALWNULL:

1. If the field must *always* have a valid value, do *not* code ALWNULL (e.g., the CUSTOMER file's CUSTID field shouldn't have ALWNULL because every customer should have an identifying number).

2. If it's valid for the field to not have any value, use ALWNULL if *either* of the following conditions is true:

   a. You want to use the system-defined null placeholder to identify missing or unknown values

   b. All the valid values for the field's data type and length might occur as actual data, and thus you *can't* use one of them to indicate "missing" or "unknown"

Note that null is different than, say, 0 for numeric fields. For example, the EMPLOYEE file's CHILDCNT (child count) field might contain 0 if you *know* that the employee has no children, but the field might be null if you

---

[15] Null isn't actually a field value; rather it serves as a placeholder to represent "value unknown."

don't know how many children (if any) the employee has. Also, keep in mind that using your own special values for missing or unknown data requires special handling when you run queries over the file. For example, if you use –1 as the CHILDCNT value for "unknown," you (and any end-user) must be careful to exclude these records when you calculate an average number of children per employee. Chapter 12 provides more information about different ways to represent unknown or inapplicable data.

The rightmost column of Figure 2.4 shows a final group of field-level keywords that can be coded for a physical file but that have no effect on the file itself. These keywords, such as EDTCDE, can be referenced when you code DDS for AS/400 display or printer files or when a utility program accesses the file. This book doesn't cover the topic of display and printer files, but you'll see how you might use these keywords when we discuss field reference files in Chapter 3. One thing to be sure you understand: *DB2/400 does not enforce constraints such as those specified in the RANGE and VALUES keyword entries.* Even with a RANGE(0 1000) keyword on a physical file field, your programs can store an out-of-range value of 9999 in the field. The RANGE constraint may be enforced as the end-user enters data into an AS/400 workstation display, but that's the extent of the protection that these DDS keywords provide. Chapter 12 discusses techniques you can use to enforce constraints when a record is added to or updated in a physical file.

Defining a Key

The final section of physical file DDS is for defining **key fields**. This section is optional, and you can always use logical files to define **keyed access paths** for a physical file, regardless of whether the physical file itself has any key fields. A file key serves either or both of the following purposes:

- Provides a unique identifier so you can directly access a record by its key field value
- Allows sequential processing of records in the order determined by their key field values

A customer master file provides a good example of a file that needs a **unique key**.[16] It would be difficult to manage a database where two distinct customers might be indistinguishable, so it's common practice (even in non-computerized systems) to assign a unique identifier to each customer. In our CUSTOMER file, the CUSTID field serves this purpose. The key-level entry to specify that CUSTID is a key field requires a K in position 17 and the field name in positions 19–28. Any key field you specify must be a field that you've

---

[16] When we discuss the relational database model in Chapter 9, we examine the concept of a unique **primary key** more formally. For now, the informal idea of a unique identifier will suffice.

already defined in the field-level entries for the same file (or that is part of a record format referenced by the FORMAT record-level entry).

When you create a file with one or more key fields, DB2/400 creates, as part of the file object, an internal **index** for each member. In the index, DB2/400 stores the key values for all records in a member and the relative record number (RRN) of the record that goes with each key value.[17] This means that when your program requests DB2/400 to retrieve a record by key, DB2/400 can do a very fast lookup in the index to find which RRN holds the requested record. The index also allows DB2/400 to return records sequentially to your program, starting with the record that has the first key value and moving in order — by key value — through the file member. As you insert, delete, and update records, DB2/400 keeps this index up to date.

When a file's definition contains the UNIQUE file-level keyword, DB2/400 blocks any attempt to insert into a member a new record that has the same key value as an existing record. If your HLL program attempts this, it will receive a "duplicate key" I/O error (a condition that your application programs must be prepared to handle).

As a general rule, most physical files should have a unique key, which is used as the primary means of identifying records. In many cases, this key is a single field, such as CUSTID or ORDERID. In other cases, however, it may take the combined values of two or more fields to guarantee uniqueness. For example, a particular classroom on a college campus might require both the building name and the room number. For such **composite keys**, you code multiple key-field entries:

```
...2....+....3....+....4....+....5....+....6.
K BLDNAME
K ROOMNBR
```

The first key field is the **major key**; the succeeding ones are the **minor keys**. In this example, the order of key values is illustrated by the following list:

```
BLDNAME          ROOMNBR
...              ...
'SCIENCE I'      101
'SCIENCE I'      201
...              ...
'SMITH HALL'     101
'SMITH HALL'     103
...              ...
```

The order in this example is ascending, which is the default unless you specify the DESCEND keyword for a key field. The key definition

```
...2....+....3....+....4....+....5....+....6.
K BLDNAME
K ROOMNBR                      DESCEND
```

---

[17] DB2/400's internal index is a sophisticated data structure known as a **B-tree**. B-trees provide a very compressed format to store the keys and one in which any key can be located quickly (without a sequential search of all the key values).

results in the key values shown below. Note that the order of key values doesn't affect their uniqueness.

```
BLDNAME         ROOMNBR
...             ...
'SCIENCE I'     201
'SCIENCE I'     101
...             ...
'SMITH HALL'    103
'SMITH HALL'    101
...             ...
```

The remaining key field-level keywords let you specify special treatment of field values when they're used as keys. For example, ABSVAL treats the field value as an absolute value (i.e., non-negative), so a field value of –5 would be considered a key value of 5. These keywords are used infrequently but are valuable in special applications.

Before leaving the topic of key fields, we need to revisit briefly several file-level keywords. We've looked at the UNIQUE keyword. If you use UNIQUE and one or more key fields have the ALWNULL keyword specified on their field definitions, you can specify whether DB2/400 should consider nulls when determining uniqueness. The default method is to treat the nulls just like any other value. For a file with a single key field, this would mean that at most one record could have null for the key field. If you code UNIQUE(*EXCNULL), for purposes of the key field, DB2/400 treats every null as if it were different from every other null (i.e., two nulls won't be considered duplicates). Be careful before you use either this option or ALWNULL for the field-level entry of a unique key field; generally unique key fields should not allow nulls.

If you don't specify the UNIQUE keyword, DB2/400 lets you store records with duplicate key values. By default, DB2/400 doesn't sequence records with duplicate keys in any particular order. You can specify the following file-level keywords to determine the order in which duplicates are retrieved during sequential processing:

- FIFO — lowest RRN first
- LIFO — highest RRN first [18]
- FCFO — least recently changed key value first

---

[18] FIFO stands for "first-in first-out," and LIFO stands for "last-in first-out," which at one time corresponded to "lowest RRN first" and "highest RRN first." When DB2/400 added the ability to reuse "deleted" record locations, FIFO and LIFO became misnomers. Be sure you don't depend on true FIFO and LIFO handling of duplicates.

The Create Physical File Command

Once you've entered your physical file DDS, you execute a CRTPF (Create Physical File) command to create the file object from the DDS.[19] You can enter the CRTPF command from any display screen that lets you enter CL commands. Or, if you're using PDM (discussed in Appendix C), you enter option 14 (Compile) beside the source member name to execute the CRTPF command. In either case, you can press the F4 key to prompt for the command's parameter values. Appendix B provides a full description of the CRTPF command parameters; this section discusses the most important parameters you need to be familiar with.

We'll start by looking at one of the simplest commands[20] you might enter to create the CUSTOMER file:

```
CRTPF FILE( appdta/customer )
      SRCFILE( appsrc/qddssrc )
```

The CRTPF command's FILE parameter specifies the physical file you're creating (which can't already exist). Normally you should provide a qualified name (library and file name) to ensure that the new file object is placed in the correct library. The SRCFILE parameter identifies the source file where the file's DDS is stored. By default, the CRTPF command uses the same source member name as the file name you specify in the FILE parameter (e.g., CUSTOMER).

Also by default, the CRTPF command creates the physical file with one member and gives this physical file member the same name as the physical file. You can specify the optional MBR parameter if you want to create a member with a different name — e.g., MBR(FEB). Figure 2.9 lists other CRTPF command parameters and their defaults, which you may want to change.

The following command specifies explicit values for the maximum number of members and the initial and incremental file size limits. The command also specifies that DB2/400 should reuse record locations that are marked as deleted when it inserts new records and that the file's **public authority** should allow read-only access.

---

[19] The CRTPF command runs a DDS compiler that reads your source code and produces an OS/400 object. It may sound odd to talk about "compiling" a file because few other operating systems have files that are as complex or that contain the type of descriptive information as OS/400 files. Nevertheless, the process is much like that of compiling an HLL program — it's just that the resulting object is a file, not an executable program. The DDS compiler produces a compile listing (spooled file) that has the same name as the CRTPF's FILE parameter. This listing shows any syntax errors.

[20] In this book's examples, CL commands are generally shown with one parameter per line (without the CL + continuation character), and the keyword is shown for each parameter. CL is a free-format language and allows positional parameter values (without keywords) for some parameters. The easiest way to enter commands when you first learn the AS/400 is to use the prompting facility (by entering the command name and pressing F4). OS/400 also provides extensive online help for all commands and their parameters.

Figure 2.9
Commonly Used CRTPF
Command Parameters
and Defaults

Parameter	Purpose	Default
FILE	Physical file to be created	
SRCFILE	Source file that contains DDS source member	*LIBL/QDDSSRC
SRCMBR	Source member containing DDS that defines file	*FILE
MBR	Name of added file member	*FILE
MAXMBRS	Maximum number of members allowed	1
MAINT	For files with key field(s) — how DB2/400 maintains the keyed access path (if any) when the file is not open	*IMMED
SIZE	Three values: Initial number of records to allow The additional number of records to allow for each increment The maximum number of increments	10000 1000 3
REUSEDLT	Whether DB2/400 should reuse "deleted" record locations for new records	*NO
ALWUPD	Allow record updates	*YES
ALWDLT	Allow record deletions	*YES
AUT	Allow public authority	*LIBCRTAUT
TEXT	Description of the file	*SRCMBRTXT

```
CRTPF FILE( appdta/customer )
      SRCFILE( appsrc/qddssrc )
      MAXMBRS( 12 )
      SIZE( 1000000  10000  5 )
      REUSEDLT( *yes )
      AUT( *use )
```

After you create a physical file, you can change many of its attributes using the CHGPF (Change Physical File) command. For example, to increase file size limits, you enter a command such as the following:

```
CHGPF FILE( appdta/customer )
      SIZE( 2000000  20000  10 )
```

If you want to change the DDS field definitions for a file, you must delete or rename the file,[21] edit the DDS, and re-create it. Figure 2.10 shows a simple sequence of commands you could use to re-create a physical file and copy its previous records to the new file object.

---

[21] Before you can delete a physical file, you also have to delete any logical files defined over the physical file. After re-creating the physical file, you have to re-create the logical files, too.

Figure 2.10

Sample Steps to Re-Create a Physical File

```
/* Revise DDS source, then execute the following */
/* commands...                                    */

/* Rename the old version of the file:            */

RNMOBJ OBJ( appdta/customer ) +
       OBJTYPE( *FILE )       +
       NEWOBJ( customerx )

/* Create the new file without any members:       */

CRTPF FILE( appdta/customer )   +
      SRCFILE( appsrc/qddssrc ) +
      MBR( *none )

/* Copy the data from the old version to the new */
/* file:                                          */

CPYF  FROMFILE( appdta/customerx ) +
      TOFILE( appdta/customer )    +
      FROMMBR( *all )              +
      TOMBR( *frommbr )            +
      MBROPT( *add )               +
      FMTOPT( *map *drop )

/* After verifying that the new file has the     */
/* complete and correct data, you can delete the */
/* old version of the file:                       */

DLTF FILE( appdta/customerx )
```

The CPYF (Copy File) command's FMTOPT parameter lets you specify that data from the from-file should be copied to the to-file on a field-by-field basis (*MAP) and that data in any fields in the old version that don't exist in the new version should be dropped (*DROP).

In V3R2 and V3R6, the CHGPF (Change Physical File) command was enhanced to let you re-create a physical file by revising the file's DDS and then specifying the DDS source member on the CHGPF command. In effect, this new version of the CHGPF command does all the steps illustrated in Figure 2.10 (and more), providing a much simpler approach to re-creating physical files.

Figure 2.11 lists other commands that deal with physical files. Appendix B provides a more comprehensive list, as well as the commands' parameters.

Coding Suggestions

- Use PF for the source type for source members that have physical file DDS.
- Use the name of the physical file you're creating as the name of its DDS source member.
- Enter a source member description that's the description of the physical file.
- Use only letters (A through Z) and digits (0 through 9) in names of files, members, record formats, fields, and aliases.

Figure 2.11
Commonly Used Physical
File Commands

Command	Full command name	Notes
ADDPFM	Add Physical File Member	
CHGPF	Change Physical File	
CHGPFM	Change Physical File Member	
CLRPFM	Clear Physical File Member	
CPYF	Copy File	
CRTPF	Create Physical File	
DLTF	Delete File	
DSDBR	Display Database Relations	Displays the names of physical and logical files that are dependent on a specified file
DSPFD	Display File Description	
DSPFFD	Display File Field Description	
DSPPFM	Display Physical File Member	
INZPFM	Initialize Physical File Member	
MOVOBJ	Move Object	Move physical file from one library to another
OVRDBF	Override Database File	
RGZPFM	Reorganize Physical File Member	Reclaim "deleted" record locations, sort records by key value
RMVM	Remove Member	
RNMM	Rename Member	
RNMOBJ	Rename Object	Rename physical file
WRKF	Work with Files	

- Use a maximum of nine characters in file names, and create a physical file's record format name by appending R to the file name.
    - If RPG/400 or RPG IV programs will *never* access the file, you can use the full 10-character file name and use the same name for the record format name.
    - If primarily RPG/400 programs will access the file, use a maximum of seven characters for file names and append an R to form the format name.
    - Where possible, use unabbreviated singular names of application entities for file names (e.g., CUSTOMER, not CUSTMAST or CUSTOMERS).
- Use a maximum of eight characters for field names.
    - If RPG/400 or RPG IV programs will *never* access the file, you can use the full 10-character field names.

- If primarily RPG/400 programs will access the file, use a maximum of six characters for field names, and use a unique one- or two-letter prefix for all fields within a file (e.g., use CS to begin all names in the CUSTOMER file, and don't use CS to begin field names in any other physical file).

- For most physical files, define one or more fields as a unique key.
  - Generally, use the physical file key as the primary means to identify records (use logical file keys to provide alternative record sequencing).

- Leave the Form type (position 6) and Usage (position 38) columns blank.

- Always explicitly code the Data Type column (position 35).

- Generally, use packed decimal for numeric fields.

- Use standard lengths (and decimal positions) for field definitions.
  - Use an odd length for all packed-decimal fields.
  - Use a length of 4 or 9 for all binary fields.

- Use a consistent order for field-level keyword entries (e.g., ALIAS, ALWNULL, DFT, . . ., TEXT, COLHDG).

- Code the ALIAS keyword for any field whose short name isn't clear.

- Code the ALWNULL keyword for any field that should accept the system null value.

- Generally, don't code ALWNULL for key fields.

- Code the DFT keyword for fields for which the DB2/400 defaults aren't acceptable.

- Code the TEXT and COLHDG keywords for all fields.

- Place comments at the beginning of your DDS to describe the file (see Figure 2.5).

- Use spaces, blank lines, and separator line comments to improve the readability of your source code (see Figure 2.5).

- Align multiline TEXT and COLHDG parameters for readability.

- For date fields, use one of the formats that has 4-digit years (e.g., *ISO)

- Generally, a physical file should have a single member with the same name as the file.

Chapter Summary

Physical files contain actual data. A physical file has a single record format. Generally, a physical file has a single member but may have multiple members, each containing some of the file's records.

You create physical files by coding DDS source code in a source file member and executing a CRTPF command. There are four sections to the DDS for a physical file: file level, record level, field level, and key field level. Each DDS statement has positional and keyworded entries. Figure 2.3 shows the contents of these entries.

The most common file-level entry is the UNIQUE keyword, which specifies that DB2/400 should not allow records in a member to have duplicate key values. A physical file has one record-level statement, which specifies the record format name. Following the record-format name are usually one or more field definitions. Each field definition has a name, data type, length, and (for numeric fields) number of decimal positions. You can optionally specify one or more keyword entries for each field.

There are three categories of data types: character (or hex), numeric, and date/time. Character fields are used for storing names, descriptions, and codes. Character fields are generally fixed-length in DB2/400 files, although you can specify variable-length fields. There are four numeric data types: packed decimal, zoned decimal, binary, and floating point. Packed decimal is the most commonly used numeric data type in DB2/400 files. The date, time, and timestamp data types have system-defined lengths. For date and time fields, you specify a date format or time format, and optionally a separator character. Figure 2.12 shows a "sampler" of field-level entries for the allowable data types.

Figure 2.12
Sample Physical File
Field Definitions

```
* - - - - - - - - - - - - - - - - - - - - - - - - - - - - - - - - - - -
* File name............. SAMPLEFLD
* Format name........... SAMPLEFLDR
* Key field(s).......... IDFLD
* Unique/duplicate key.. Unique
* File type............. Physical
* Purpose............... Sample field definitions
* Author................ Paul Conte
* Date.................. 03/01/96
* - - - - - - - - - - - - - - - - - - - - - - - - - - - - - - - - - - -
*
*.........T.Name++++++RLen++XDcU......Keyword+++++++++++++++++++++++++++++

                                      UNIQUE

          R SAMPLEFLDR                TEXT( 'Sample field definitions' )
*           ===============================================================
            IDFLD         7P Ø        TEXT( 'Numeric ID field' )

            CHARFLD      10A          TEXT( 'Character field' )

            HEXFLD       10H          TEXT( 'Hexadecimal field' )
```

Figure 2.12 continued

Figure 2.12
Continued

```
         SNGFLTPNT      9F 0      TEXT( 'Single precision floating +
                                        point field' )

         DBLFLTPNT      17F11     FLTPCN( *DOUBLE )
                                  TEXT( 'Double precision floating +
                                        point field' )

         ZONEDECFLD     7S 0      TEXT( 'Zoned decimal field' )

         TINYPCKDEC     1P 0      TEXT( 'Tiny packed decimal field' )

         LRGPCKDEC      31P30     TEXT( 'Large packed decimal field' )

         BINARYFLD      9B 5      TEXT( 'Binary field' )

         DATEFLD        L         DATFMT( *USA )
                                  TEXT( 'Date field' )

         TIMEFLD        T         TIMFMT( *ISO )
                                  TEXT( 'Time field' )

         TIMESTAMP      Z         TEXT( 'Timestamp field' )
*        ================================================================
    K IDFLD
```

You can specify for a field whether it's null capable and an explicit default value. You can also code some field-level keywords that apply to display and printer files (e.g., EDTCDE), which have no effect on the physical file, but which can be referenced when you define an OS/400 display or printer file or by utility programs.

You can define a key for a physical file. The key can comprise one or more fields. Each key field can be in ascending or descending order. As mentioned above, you can specify either a unique or nonunique (allows duplicate values) key.

The CRTPF command runs the DDS compiler, which reads a source member and (if there are no errors) creates the physical file. This command has optional parameters to specify file attributes, such as maximum size and public authority to the file.

Key Terms

alias
binary
character field
composite key
continuation symbol
data type
date
default field value
Extended Binary Coded
   Decimal Interchange
   Code (EBCDIC)
floating point
hexadecimal (hex) field

index
key field
keyed access path
keyword
keyword entry
major key
minor key
null
null capable
numeric field
packed decimal
positional entry
primary key

public authority
source code editor
source file member
source type attribute
time
timestamp
unique key
zoned decimal

Exercises

1. Explain the relationship between a source file member and a physical file.

2. List the four sections of DDS for physical files.

3. Explain why the UNIQUE keyword is a file-level entry rather than a key field-level entry.

4. Show how to code the DDS TEXT entry for the following description:

```
1....+....2....+....3....+....4....+....5
This is a sample file's full description.
```

5. In Figure 2.5, why do you think the CUSTOMER file's two postal code fields are defined as 10-character fields? What problems might occur if you used numeric fields for ZIP code and ZIP+4 fields?

6. Describe a file for which it might make sense to allow duplicate key values. When would it matter whether you specified FIFO, LIFO, or FCFO for duplicates?

7. Code the physical file DDS for a file to hold the following employee information:

    Identification number

    Name (last, first, middle initial)

    Birth date

    Address (street, city, state, postal code)

    Identification number of employee's manager

    Annual salary

    Health insurance plan (coded)

Be sure to consider the following:

    Appropriate file, record format, and field names

    Field data types and lengths

    Default values

    The file's key (if any)

    Good documentation

Exercises Continued

Exercises continued

8. Code the CRTPF command for the file in Exercise 7, specifying the following file attributes (either by default, or explicitly, if necessary):

Maximum of two members

The first member should be named HDQRTRS

Allow DB2/400 to reuse "deleted" record locations

Allow the public to use, but not update the file (the special value for this authority is *USE)

Chapter 3

Field Reference Files

Chapter Overview

This chapter describes field reference files, an important tool for improving your productivity and increasing the quality of your DB2/400 file definitions. You'll learn how to define a physical file field as having the attributes of a previously defined field. Then you'll see how you can create a field dictionary that provides the basis for all your file definitions. We'll also take a deeper look at the concept of a field's data type, and you'll learn about a basic set of user-defined data types that apply to many business applications. You'll also learn the principles of an effective naming standard for your fields.

The Importance of Code Reuse

Experienced programmers know that one "silver bullet" for fast, high-quality application development is **code reuse**.[1] There are several benefits to code reuse:

- You don't have to re-enter the reused code. This is more than just a matter of saving keystrokes; you also don't have to relearn the detailed coding techniques that are embodied in the existing code.

- The reused code is (hopefully) already working correctly so you're likely to have fewer syntax and logic errors than if you started from scratch.

- Applications are more consistent — both in the way they operate and how they're implemented — when they share common code.

[1] You may have already discovered the value of using previously created code to get a fast start on a programming assignment. A typical approach to creating a new program is to copy the contents of an existing source member to a new member and then delete the parts that won't be used in the new program. This technique is sometimes called "cloning" or "cannibalizing." For student-level and "quick-and-dirty" programs, this approach works pretty well. However, for major applications, there's a serious shortcoming — it takes a lot of effort to keep all the "clones" up-to-date when some of the common code changes. A more effective way to reuse code is with language features, such as RPG's /COPY and COBOL's COPY compiler directives or DDS's field referencing. These features let you reuse code without making an additional copy. That way, if the shared code changes, you have to edit only the *one* copy and recompile the objects (e.g., programs and files) that use it.

The same principles that apply to good code reuse in HLL programs apply to database implementation — in particular, reusing field definitions is a productive way to increase consistency and reduce errors.

Referring to Previously Defined Fields

In physical file DDS, the REFFLD field-level keyword lets you define one field based on a previously defined field. In the simplest case, you can define a field based on another field defined earlier in the same file. For example, suppose you have a SALE file in which you store products' list prices (PRDPRICE) and actual sales prices (SALPRICE). You could code these two fields with the following statements:

```
...2....+....3....+....4....+....5....+....6....+....7..
  PRDPRICE        7P 0        TEXT( 'Product list price' )
  SALPRICE   R                REFFLD( PRDPRICE )
                              TEXT( 'Actual sale price' )
```

The R in position 29 of the SALPRICE definition indicates that the field is defined by referencing another field. The REFFLD keyword entry specifies that the referenced field is PRDPRICE. Figure 3.1 lists the attributes that a referencing field takes on from the field it references.

In this example the SALPRICE definition is equivalent to the following explicit definition:

```
...2....+....3....+....4....+....5....+....6....+....7.
  SALPRICE        7P 0        TEXT( 'Actual sale price' )
```

When you reference a field, you can also code some of the new field's attributes explicitly. In the example above, the SALPRICE definition overrides the TEXT attribute of the PRDPRICE field. You must be very careful when overriding attributes of referenced fields because coding one attribute may cause others to be dropped. For example, if you change the length of a field, in addition to the length being overridden, *all* validity-checking keyword entries (CHECK, etc.), as well as EDTCDE and EDTWRD, are dropped. The third column of Figure 3.1 shows which attributes of the referenced field are ignored when you explicitly specify a related attribute for the field you're defining.

In general, you should avoid "tricky" combinations of field referencing and overriding attributes. For example, you should *not* change the data type, length, and decimal positions of referenced fields.[2] After all, the point is to have one field defined like another, not just to save a few keystrokes. There are some attributes that do make sense to override in many cases. These

---

[2] DDS even lets you specify a field's length and/or decimal positions as *relative to* the referenced field's length and/or decimal positions, respectively. For example, you can code +1 in the length column of the field you're defining to specify that its length is one greater than the referenced field's length. *Don't do this!* The technique makes file definitions harder to understand and defeats the purpose of standardizing field definitions. (Exercise 4 at the end of this chapter considers a possible exception to this rule.)

Figure 3.1
Field Attributes Defined
by Referencing
Another Field

Category: attribute or KEYWORD	Positions or description	Ignored if referencing field specifies:
Field definition:		
length	30-34	length
data type	35	data type
decimal positions	36-37	decimal positions
ALIAS	Alias name	ALIAS
COLHDG	Column heading	COLHDG
DATFMT	Date format	DATFMT
DATSEP	Date separator	DATSEP or a DATFMT that doesn't allow a DATSEP entry
FLTPCN	Floating-point precision	FLTPCN
REFSHIFT	Keyboard shift	REFSHIFT
TEXT	Descriptive text	TEXT, COLHDG
TIMFMT	Time format	TIMFMT
TIMSEP	Time separator	TIMSEP or TIMFMT that doesn't allow a TIMSEP entry
VARLEN	Variable-length attribute	VARLEN
Display file validity-checking attributes:		
CHECK	Input editing validity check	Data type, length, decimal positions, any of the validity-checking keywords or DLTCHK (display files only)
CHKMSGID	Validity-checking message ID	
COMP, CMP	Comparison validity check	
RANGE	Range validity check	
VALUES	Values validity check	
Display file editing attributes:		
EDTCDE	Edit code	Data type, length, decimal positions, any of the editing keywords, or DLTEDT (display files only)
EDTWRD	Edit word	

include ALIAS, COLHDG, and TEXT. Remember that all ALIAS names must be unique within a file, and an ALIAS name can't be the same as a field name in the same file. Also, note that when you override the COLHDG attribute, the referenced field's TEXT attribute is dropped. If you don't specify an explicit TEXT attribute for the field you're defining, its TEXT is formed by concatenating the new COLHDG value(s).

To verify the effect of field referencing (and overriding attributes), you can look at the listing that the CRTPF command produces. This listing shows the resulting DDS definitions after overrides are applied to referenced fields. You can also use the DSPFFD (Display File Field Description) command to see the detailed layout of a file's record format. The following command displays the type of information shown in Figure 3.2:

```
DPSFFD FILE( appdta/customer )
```

Figure 3.2
Partial DSPFFD
Command Output

```
                                Display Spooled File
 File . . . . . :    QPDSPFFD                      Page/Line   1/26
 Control . . . . .   ▮_____                       Columns     1 - 78
 Find . . . . . .    _____
*...+....1....+....2....+....3....+....4....+....5....+....6....+....7....+...
  Field Level Information
                    Data      Field  Buffer   Buffer      Field    Column
     Field          Type      Length Length  Position     Usage    Heading
     CUSTID         PACKED      5  0    3         1         Both     Cust.
                                                                     ID
        Field text . . . . . . . . . . . . . . . :  Customer ID
     NAME           CHAR         30    30         4         Both     Customer
                                                                     Name
        Field text . . . . . . . . . . . . . . . :  Customer name
        Alternative name . . . . . . . . . . . . :  CUSTNAME
        Coded Character Set Identifier . . . . . :    37
     SHPLINE1       CHAR        100   100        34         Both     Customer
                                                                     Shipping
                                                                     Line 1
        Field text . . . . . . . . . . . . . . . :  Customer shipping address li
        Alternative name . . . . . . . . . . . . :  CUSTSHIPLINE1
                                                                       More...
 F3=Exit    F12=Cancel    F19=Left    F20=Right    F24=More keys
```

While field referencing is convenient within one file, it becomes much more valuable when you use a central **field reference file** to store definitions that are shared among all your database files. Before we look at how you set up a field reference file, we need to cover how to reference a field in another file. There are two approaches you can take. The first technique is to specify a file name as the second REFFLD parameter value:

```
...2....+....3....+....4....+....5....+....6....+.....
 SALPRICE  R               REFFLD( PRDPRICE
                                   APPDTA/PRODUCT )
```

The file name can be qualified with a library name, as in this example, or it can be specified without a library. If you use an unqualified name, the referenced file must be in a library that's part of the library list[3] for the job in which you execute the CRTPF command. The referenced file must exist at the time you compile the source member that contains the REFFLD entry, and the referenced field must exist in the referenced file. The referenced field can have the same name as the field you're defining or a different name. Note that the reference is to a physical file object, *not* to a DDS source member.[4] The DDS compiler copies any referenced attributes at the time you create a file. Once you've created the new file, deleting the old file or changing its field definitions has no effect on the referencing file until you re-create the referencing file.[5]

The second way you can reference fields in another file is to specify the REF file-level keyword, as in the following example:

```
...2....+....3....+....4....+....5....+,...6....+..
                              REF( APPDTA/PRODUCT )

R SALER                       TEXT( 'Product sales' )
  ...
  SALPRICE   R                REFFLD( PRDPRICE )
```

When you use REF to specify a referenced file, any field in a REFFLD entry that doesn't specify an explicit file must be in the REF file. If you reference a field in a file (specified with the REF keyword) that has the same name as the field you're defining, you don't have to specify the REFFLD entry. Assume there's an existing SALE95 file with a SALPRICE field and you want to create a new SALE96 file with an identical SALPRICE field. Here's the DDS to do that:

```
...2....+....3....+....4....+....5....+....6....+....7..
                              REF( APPDTA/SALE95 )

R SALE96R                     TEXT( 'Product sales 1996' )
  ...
  SALPRICE   R
```

---

[3] A library list is the ordered list of library names associated with an OS/400 job. Many OS/400 object references allow an *unqualified* object name (that is, without the name of the containing library), in which case OS/400 searches the job's library list for the first library that contains an object of the specified type with the specified name. In many cases, the *LIBL special value can also be used to explicitly specify the library list.

[4] Remember that an OS/400 file object contains the full description of the file's fields as part of the object. The DDS compiler extracts the definitions for referenced fields from this description. Even if the referenced file's original DDS were deleted, you could still reference fields defined in the file.

[5] This approach makes sense, of course. It would hardly be desirable to have a file definition change on-the-fly just because a file it referenced was changed, or worse yet, deleted.

As you can see, field referencing provides a tool for simplifying your physical file definitions. The next section explains how field referencing can help *standardize* your field definitions, as well.

Creating a Field Reference File

A field reference file is simply a physical file that you create to hold field definitions rather than store application data. When you define fields in physical files that are intended to store application data, you do so by referencing fields in the field reference file. There are several strategies you can choose when you use a field reference file — you can store in the field reference file just a base set of reference fields so you have a definition to reference for all your physical file field definitions, or you can define in the field reference file *all* fields that are used in physical files, or you may use something in-between. Let's start with the base set of reference fields.

In Chapter 2, one of the coding suggestions was to use standard lengths to define fields. Let's say you decide to use a 50-character field as the standard field for any kind of description (e.g., product description, account description). You can do this very effectively by creating a physical file called FIELDDFN to hold field definitions and then defining a DESC field in FIELDDFN as follows:

```
...2....+....3....+....4....+....5....+....6....+..
  DESC          50A            ALIAS( DESCRIPTION )
                               TEXT( 'Description' )
                               COLHDG( 'Description' )
```

Once you create the FIELDDFN file, you specify REF(FIELDDFN) in the DDS for all your other physical files. To define a description field, you reference the standard DESC field in one of two ways — by using the same name and definition or by specifying a new name and (optionally) new alias, text, and/or column heading:

```
...2....+....3....+....4....+....5....+....6....+..
                               REF( APPDTA/FIELDDFN )

R PRODUCTR                     TEXT( 'Products' )
  ...
  DESC        R
or
  PRODDESC  R                  REFFLD( DESC )
                               ALIAS( PRODUCTDESCRIPTION )
                               TEXT( 'Product description' )
                               COLHDG( 'Product'
                                       'Description' )
```

You don't need to do anything special to create a field reference file. You don't need to define any key fields (and consequently shouldn't specify the UNIQUE file-level keyword) in the DDS for the field reference file. And you may want to create it without any members (because you won't be storing any actual data in it). The following example is a typical command to create a field reference file:

```
CRTPF FILE( appdta/fielddfn )
      SRCFILE( appsrc/qddssrc )
      MBR( *none )
```

When you need to add new field definitions to the field reference file, you just edit the DDS for it, delete the current physical file, and create the field reference file again. Because the file has no data, you don't need to worry about copying any data from the previous version. If you change a field's definition in the field reference file (e.g., increase the length of a field), you must re-create any physical file whose definition references the field for the change to take effect in that physical file. In typical AS/400 installations, a field reference file may initially have lots of additions made, but then it becomes fairly stable. The initial effort required to set up a field reference file is repaid many times over by simplifying physical file field definitions and by the high degree of standardization it encourages.

It's important to define a good base set of reference fields in the field reference file. Although there are no hard and fast rules for what constitutes a good reference field, there are several rules of thumb that can help. A reference field represents the way you want to store a particular *kind* of thing.[6] For example, in your applications you might want to track people (customers, employees, and contractors), products (both ones you buy and ones you sell), and dates (employee hire dates, dates customers place orders, etc.). Both people and products have names, but they're quite different kinds of things and, as a result, have names with different structures. In your business, you might decide to track people's names as first, last, and middle initial, whereas, you might decide to use a single (perhaps long) name for products. Based on that decision, you could define the reference fields for names, along with a reference field for descriptions, as shown in Figure 3.3.

Let's look at some of the decisions we made in defining the five reference fields in Figure 3.3. We defined the fields for people's first and last names as different sizes. This design decision is based on the idea that many first names fit in 20 characters, and we can afford to truncate the few longer ones; but we need room to hold all (or almost all, anyway) last names in their entirety. In some circumstances, we might decide to make both fields the same length (either long enough to hold almost all names without truncation, or shorter, accepting that we can truncate last names, too). In that case, we'd need only a single reference field: PPLNAME. There's no "right" way to define these reference fields — the choice depends on how the organization needs to treat the information stored in the database (e.g., the acceptable level of truncated first or last names).

---

[6] What I've informally called a "*kind* of thing" is known more formally as a **data type**. To avoid confusion with the DDS Data Type field attribute (e.g., character or packed decimal), we'll use **user-defined data type** as the formal term in this text.

Figure 3.3

Sample Base Fields for a
Description and Different
Kinds of Names

```
*.........T.Name++++++RLen++XDcU......Keyword+++++++++++++++++

          DESC        50A          ALIAS( DESCRIPTION )
                                   TEXT( 'Description' )
*                                  COLHDG( 'Description' )
          ----------------------------------------------------
          FSTNAM      20A          ALIAS( FIRSTNAME )
                                   TEXT( 'First name' )
                                   COLHDG( 'First'
*                                          'Name' )
          ----------------------------------------------------
          LSTNAM      30A          ALIAS( LASTNAME )
                                   TEXT( 'Last name' )
                                   COLHDG( 'Last'
*                                          'Name' )
          ----------------------------------------------------
          MDLINL      1A           ALIAS( MIDDLEINITIAL )
                                   TEXT( 'Middle initial' )
                                   COLHDG( 'M'
*                                          'I' )
          ----------------------------------------------------
          PRDNAM      50A          ALIAS( PRODUCTNAME )
                                   TEXT( 'Product name' )
                                   COLHDG( 'Product'
                                           'Name' )
```

We also decided to allow 50 characters for product names. Because we already have a 50-character reference field for descriptions, why not just use it for product names, too? Well, what if we decide at some point to increase the maximum length of product names, but don't want to change the length of all the description fields in our physical files — we want to have *separate* reference fields to allow for that possibility. In general, you want one reference field for each kind of thing you plan to store in your database. This will let you more easily handle future changes in how you store different kinds of things. Keep in mind, however, that this type of design decision is something that requires experience, good judgment, and a little bit of luck.

You can see how a field reference file lets you reuse many field definitions when you define physical files. You can increase your code reuse and add another level of organization to your definitions by *layering* the field definitions in your field reference file. This technique, shown in Figure 3.4, starts with some very fundamental reference fields (e.g., TDIGIT, TSMLINT, TINT, TLRGINT, and THUGINT for different size integers, as well as a similar set for non-negative integers) and uses them to define more application-oriented reference fields (e.g., YEARSAL).[7]

---

[7] Comment lines with ". . ." mark places in Figure 3.4 where some field definitions have been omitted to reduce the size for publication. For example, TDIGITGE0 would be followed by TSMLINTGE0, and TINTGE0 would be followed by TLRGINTGE0. The omitted numeric field definitions follow the same pattern as for the TDIGIT through THUGINT field definitions.

Figure 3.4
Partial FIELDDFN
"Layered" Field
Reference File

```
*  -  -  -  -  -  -  -  -  -  -  -  -  -  -  -  -  -  -  -  -  -  -  -  -  -  -  -  -  -
* File name.............. FIELDDFN
* Format name........... FIELDDFNR
* Key field(s).......... None
* Unique/duplicate key.. None
* File type............. Physical
* Purpose.............. Field Reference File
* Author............... Paul Conte
* Date................. Ø3/Ø1/96
*  -  -  -  -  -  -  -  -  -  -  -  -  -  -  -  -  -  -  -  -  -  -  -  -  -  -  -  -  -

*.........T.Name++++++RLen++XDcU......Keyword++++++++++++++++++++++++++++++++

          R FIELDDFNR               TEXT( 'Field reference file' )

*         ************************************
*         *   Fundamental reference fields   *
*         ************************************

*         ============================================================
*         Integers (smallest to largest)

          TDIGIT         1P Ø       TEXT( ' Type: Integer, 1 digit ' )
*         ------------------------------------------------------------
          TSMLINT        3P Ø       TEXT( ' Type: Integer, 2 small' )
*         ------------------------------------------------------------
          TINT           7P Ø       TEXT( ' Type: Integer, 3 standard' )
*         ------------------------------------------------------------
          TLRGINT       15P Ø       TEXT( ' Type: Integer, 4 large' )
*         ------------------------------------------------------------
          THUGINT       31P Ø       TEXT( ' Type: Integer, 5 huge' )

*         ============================================================
*         Non-negative integers: GE Ø (smallest to largest)
*         -- Note that COMP( GE Ø ) only applies to display
*            file validity checking of keyboard input.

          TDIGITGEØ R               REFFLD( TDIGIT )

                                    TEXT( ' Type: Integer, GE Ø, +
                                           1 digit')

                                    COMP( GE Ø )
*    ...
*         ----------------------------------------------------------
          TINTGEØ   R               REFFLD( TINT )

                                    TEXT( ' Type: Integer, GE Ø, +
                                           3 standard' )

                                    COMP( GE Ø )
*    ...
*         ----------------------------------------------------------
          THUGINTGEØR               REFFLD( THUGINT )

                                    TEXT( ' Type: Integer, GE Ø, +
                                           5 huge' )

                                    COMP( GE Ø )
```

Figure 3.4 continued

Figure 3.4

Continued

```
*    ========================================================
*    Decimal fractions (DEC): Grouped as 1/10ths (DEC1),
*                              1/100ths (DEC2), etc.
*                              (smallest to largest within group)

     TSMLDEC1        5P 1        TEXT( ' Type: Decimal fraction, +
                                 (  1/10ths), 1 small' )
*    ...
*    --------------------------------------------------------
     TDEC2     R         2       REFFLD( TDEC1 )
                                 TEXT( ' Type: Decimal fraction, +
                                 ( 1/100ths), 2 standard' )
*    ...
*    --------------------------------------------------------
     THUGDEC3  R         3       REFFLD( THUGDEC1 )
                                 TEXT( ' Type: Decimal fraction, +
                                 (1/1000ths), 4 huge' )


*    ========================================================
*    US dollars (USD): Grouped as 1/10ths (USD1), 1/100ths (USD2),
*                       etc.    (smallest to largest within group)
*
*    ...
*    --------------------------------------------------------
     TUSD2     R                 REFFLD( TDEC2 )

                                 TEXT( ' Type: US dollar +
                                 ( 1/100ths), 2 standard' )
*    ...
*    ========================================================
*    Standard identifier: non-negative integer

     TID       R                 REFFLD( TINT )

                                 TEXT( ' Type: ID, standard ' )

                                 COMP( GT 0 )
*    ========================================================
*    Alpha codes, uppercase letters

     TALPHACDE1      1A          TEXT( ' Type: Code, alpha, +
                                 1-character' )

                                 VALUES( 'A' 'B' 'C' 'D' 'E' 'F'
                                 'G' 'H' 'I' 'J' 'K' 'L'
                                 'M' 'N' 'O' 'P' 'Q' 'R'
                                 'S' 'T' 'U' 'V' 'W' 'X'
                                 'Y' 'Z' ' ' )
*    --------------------------------------------------------
     TALPHACDE2      2A          TEXT( ' Type: Code, alpha, +
                                 2-character' )

*                                Note: There's no way in DDS to
*                                      specify only letters and
*                                      blanks for validity.
*    ...
```

Figure 3.4 continued

Figure 3.4
Continued

```
*       ================================================================
*       Standard date, time, and timestamp

        TDATE           L       TEXT( ' Type: Date' )

                                DATFMT( *ISO )
*       ----------------------------------------------------------------
        TTIME           T       TEXT( ' Type: Time' )

                                TIMFMT( *ISO )
*       ----------------------------------------------------------------
        TTIMESTAMP      Z       TEXT( ' Type: Timestamp' )

*       ================================================================
*       Address-related information, shipping and other
*       Ordered by US conventions

        TSMLADRLIN     25A      TEXT( ' Type: Address line, +
                                      1 small' )
*       ----------------------------------------------------------------
        TADRLIN        50A      TEXT( ' Type: Address line, +
                                      2 standard' )
*       ----------------------------------------------------------------
        TLRGADRLIN    100A      TEXT( ' Type: Address line, +
                                      3 large' )
*       ----------------------------------------------------------------
        TCITY          30A      TEXT( ' Type: City' )
*       ----------------------------------------------------------------
        TSTATEABV R             REFFLD( TALPHACDE2 )

                                TEXT( ' Type: State abbreviation, +
                                      2-character' )
*       ----------------------------------------------------------------
        TPOSTALCDE     10A      TEXT( ' Type: Postal code' )
*       ----------------------------------------------------------------
        TCOUNTRY       30A      TEXT( ' Type: Country' )

*       ================================================================
*       Telephone number

        TPHONE         15A      TEXT( ' Type: Phone number' )


*       ****************************************
*       * Application fields (alphabetically) *
*       ****************************************

*       ----------------------------------------------------------------
        CRDLIMIT  R             REFFLD( TUSD2 )

                                ALIAS( CREDITLIMIT )

                                ALWNULL

                                DFT( *NULL )

                                TEXT( 'Credit limit' )

                                COLHDG( 'Credit'
                                        'Limit' )
```

Figure 3.4 continued

Figure 3.4
Continued

```
*           -------------------------------------------------------------
            CUSTID    R                    REFFLD( TID )
*                                          No explicit ALIAS
                                           TEXT( 'Customer ID' )
                                           COLHDG( 'Cust.'
*                                                  'ID' )
            -------------------------------------------------------------
            ENTDATE   R                    REFFLD( TDATE )
                                           ALIAS( ENTRYDATE )
                                           TEXT( 'Entry date' )
                                           COLHDG( 'Entry'
*                                                  'Date' )
            -------------------------------------------------------------
            STATUS    R                    REFFLD( TALPHACDE1 )
                                           TEXT( 'Status' )
*                                          COLHDG( 'Sts.' )
            -------------------------------------------------------------
            YEARSAL   R                    REFFLD( TUSD2 )
                                           ALIAS( YEARLYSALARY )
                                           TEXT( 'Yearly salary' )
                                           COLHDG( 'Yearly'
                                                   'Salary' )
                                           COMP( GE Ø )
*           -------------------------------------------------------------
```

The fundamental reference fields serve as user-defined data types. They are given names that begin with T because they are *type-defining* fields. (This is strictly a naming convention and isn't required by DDS.) Type-defining fields should never be referenced without renaming them in an application file. The application-oriented reference fields (e.g., YEARSAL) don't have the T prefix because they may appear, without renaming, in an application file.

For field reference files in which there are more than about a hundred reference fields, using a layered approach to the field reference file can save work, reduce errors, and provide clearer documentation of the intent of a particular field *definition*. For example, if you have lots of fields that need to store a standard-sized count, you can use REFFLD(TINTGE0) rather than repeatedly coding 7P 0 and COMP(GE 0) on all the individual field definitions.[8]

There are several coding practices that are helpful with field reference files. Earlier in this chapter, I said you shouldn't generally override the data type, length, decimal positions, or most keyword entries of a referenced field.

[8] Exercise 6 at the end of this chapter considers an even clearer way to define application count fields.

There are a few exceptions to this rule that can improve the way you define new fundamental reference fields. Look in Figure 3.4 at how the non-negative integers are defined. They reference the corresponding signed integer (e.g., TINTGE0 uses REFFLD(TINT)) and add a COMP(GE 0) validity check. This approach means that if you change the length of a signed integer field, the non-negative field definition automatically changes as well. A similar approach is used for the set of decimal fraction field definitions. For example, TDEC2 uses REFFLD(TDEC1) but overrides the number of decimal positions from 1 to 2. In this way, the lengths of the corresponding type definitions stay synchronized.[9] Overriding attributes in the definition of fundamental reference fields should be done only when there's a clear, fixed relationship between the fields, as in the case where a non-negative integer should always be the same length as its signed counterpart. Don't use a REFFLD with overrides just because there's some coincidental similarity between two fields' attributes.

Another thing to note about the base reference field definitions is the absence of COLHDG and ALIAS entries. Because these fields won't be used directly in any database files, these two entries aren't useful. In addition, coding ALIAS on these fields would force you to define an ALIAS for any fields that reference them (to avoid duplicate ALIAS names). Some fields, such as STATUS, don't need an ALIAS, and you can't use the field's own name as the value of the ALIAS entry.

DDS requires that a referenced field be defined before any references to it, so that dictates in part the order in which you specify fields in a field reference file. The major order is that type-defining reference fields are defined first, then application-oriented fields. Application-oriented fields can be ordered alphabetically because their definitions should reference only the type-defining fields. The type-defining fields can be grouped, as in Figure 3.4, and ordered by some relevant attributes (e.g., length or number of decimal positions).

Once a field reference file is fairly complete, it may become difficult for a programmer to find an appropriate field to reference just by reading a source listing. But using a standard approach to the TEXT specified for fields and a few DB2/400 tools, you can produce a *field dictionary* such as the one in Figure 3.5.

[9] Defining a set of decimal fraction reference fields requires tradeoffs among several goals. First, packed-decimal numbers should generally have an odd length for both storage and execution efficiency. However, ideally the non-fractional part of a "standard" decimal fraction with one decimal place should have the same number of digits as the non-fractional part of a "standard" decimal fraction with two decimal places. The challenge of designing an alternative approach to the one shown in Figure 3.4 is found in Exercise 7 at the end of this chapter.

Figure 3.5
Field Dictionary Listing

Field Text Description	External Field Name	Field Length In Bytes	Field Type	Number Of Digits	Decimal Positions
Type: Address line, 1 small	TSMLADRLIN	25	A	0	0
Type: Address line, 2 standard	TADRLIN	50	A	0	0
Type: Address line, 3 large	TLRGADRLIN	100	A	0	0
Type: City	TCITY	30	A	0	0
Type: Code, alpha, 1-character	TALPHACDE1	1	A	0	0
Type: Code, alpha, 2-character	TALPHACDE2	2	A	0	0
Type: Code, alpha, 3-character	TALPHACDE3	3	A	0	0
Type: Country	TCOUNTRY	30	A	0	0
Type: Date	TDATE	10	L	0	0
Type: Decimal fraction, (1/10ths), 1 small	TSMLDEC1	3	P	5	1
Type: Decimal fraction, (1/10ths), 2 standard	TDEC1	5	P	9	1
Type: Decimal fraction, (1/10ths), 3 large	TLRGDEC1	9	P	17	1
Type: Decimal fraction, (1/10ths), 4 huge	THUGDEC1	16	P	31	1
Type: Decimal fraction, (1/100ths), 1 small	TSMLDEC2	3	P	5	2
Type: Decimal fraction, (1/100ths), 2 standard	TDEC2	5	P	9	2
Type: Decimal fraction, (1/100ths), 3 large	TLRGDEC2	3	P	5	2
Type: Decimal fraction, (1/100ths), 4 huge	THUGDEC2	3	P	5	2
Type: Decimal fraction, (1/1000ths), 2 standard	TDEC3	5	P	9	3
Type: Decimal fraction, (1/1000ths), 3 large	TSMLDEC3	3	P	5	3
Type: Decimal fraction, (1/1000ths), 3 large	TLRGDEC3	9	P	17	3
Type: Decimal fraction, (1/1000ths), 4 huge	THUGDEC3	16	P	31	3
Type: Integer, GE 0, 1 digit	TDIGITGE0	1	P	1	0
Type: Integer, GE 0, 2 small	TSMLINTGE0	2	P	3	0
Type: Integer, GE 0, 3 standard	TINTGE0	4	P	7	0
Type: Integer, GE 0, 4 large	TLRGINTGE0	8	P	15	0
Type: Integer, GE 0, 5 huge	THUGINTGE0	16	P	31	0
Type: Integer, 1 digit	TDIGIT	1	P	1	0
Type: Integer, 2 small	TSMLINT	2	P	3	0
Type: Integer, 3 standard	TINT	4	P	7	0
Type: Integer, 4 large	TLRGINT	8	P	15	0
Type: Integer, 5 huge	THUGINT	16	P	31	0
Type: ID, standard	TID	4	P	7	0
Type: Phone number	TPHONE	15	A	0	0
Type: Postal code	TPOSTALCDE	10	A	0	0
Type: State abbreviation, 2-character	TSTATEABV	2	A	0	0
Type: Time	TTIME	8	T	0	0
Type: Timestamp	TTIMESTAMP	26	Z	0	0
Type: US dollar (1/100ths), 1 small	TSMLUSD2	3	P	5	2
Type: US dollar (1/100ths), 2 standard	TUSD2	5	P	9	2
Type: US dollar (1/100ths), 3 large	TLRGUSD2	3	P	5	2
Type: US dollar (1/100ths), 4 huge	THUGUSD2	3	P	5	2
Credit limit	CRDLIMIT	5	P	9	2
Customer ID	CUSTID	4	P	7	0
Entry date	ENTDATE	10	L	0	0
Fax phone number	PHNFAX	15	A	0	0
Order date	ORDDATE	10	L	0	0
Shipping address city	SHPCITY	30	A	0	0
Shipping address country	SHPCNTRY	30	A	0	0
Shipping address line 1	SHPLINE1	50	A	0	0
Shipping address line 2	SHPLINE2	50	A	0	0
Shipping address postal code 1	SHPPSCD1	10	A	0	0
Shipping address postal code 2	SHPPSCD2	10	A	0	0
Shipping address state	SHPSTATE	2	A	0	0
Status	STATUS	1	A	0	0
Voice phone number	PHNVOICE	15	A	0	0
Yearly salary	YEARSAL	5	P	9	2

This listing provides a concise ordered list of the available fundamental and application field definitions. For each field, the dictionary provides its name, data type, length, and decimal positions. (The Field Length in Bytes column is the length of character fields; the Number of Digits column is the length of numeric fields.) It's easy to produce similar lists that are ordered by data type and length or field name.

To produce the dictionary list from a field reference file, you use the DSPFFD command to produce an output file with one record for each field defined in FIELDDFN:

```
DSPFFD FILE( appdta/fielddfn )
       OUTPUT( *outfile )
       OUTFILE( appdta/fieldlst )
```

After you produce this file, you can use SQL/400 or another report generator to order and list the contents. The SQL/400 statement used to produce Figure 3.5 is

```
Select     whftxt, whflde, whfldb, whfldt, whfldd, whfldp
  From     appdta/fieldlst
  Order by whftxt
```

The file produced by the DSPFFD command is an externally described file with fields named WHFxxx, which are referenced in the SQL/400 Select statement. SQL/400's interactive environment displays field lists, including the descriptive text for each field, so constructing this statement is quite easy, even if the names are a bit cryptic.

Using SQL/400's selection capabilities interactively, you can also search the FIELDLST file for all entries that might be useful in a particular application. For example, to display a list of all fields that relate to customer information, you could enter

```
Select     whftxt, whflde, whfldb, whfldt, whfldd, whfldp
  From     appdta/fieldlst
  Where    whftxt Like '%cust%'
  Order by whftxt
```

The SQL/400 Like predicate compares a value against a string pattern. In this case, the output includes any field that has "cust" anywhere in its text.

For this simple approach to creating a field dictionary to work, you must enter TEXT strings that properly group and order field definitions. Several techniques were used in Figure 3.4 to achieve the field dictionary in Figure 3.5:

- All type-defining reference field definitions' text start with ' Type: '. Notice the single blank at the beginning; when you order a list by field text (e.g., WHFTXT), this sequences these fields before all application reference fields.

- We used consistent descriptive terms, abbreviations, capitalization, and punctuation (e.g., only Integer, not Integer, integer, and Int).

- We used a sequence of descriptive terms, separated by commas, starting with the most encompassing (e.g., Integer, GE 0, 1 digit).

- In some cases, we used leading blanks to get the desired sequence within a set of terms (e.g., (1/10ths), (1/100ths), (1/1000ths)).

- Where we needed to explicitly sequence a set of terms, we prefixed each term with a number (e.g., 1 small, 2 standard, 3 large, 4 huge)

This example is a fairly simple, but workable, approach to creating a field reference file and associated dictionary. DDS's referencing capability makes more sophisticated approaches possible; for example, you can layer field definitions by using multiple field reference files rather than just sections in a single file. By using separate files, you can group reference field definitions for each major application (e.g., order processing, accounting, personnel) in a separate file. For large organizations, this may help distribute the task of maintaining a complete set of field definitions among several teams of developers. Of course, partitioning the definitions also requires coordination to avoid conflicts or inconsistencies.

Naming Conventions

A field reference file goes a long way toward standardizing your file definitions; a good naming convention helps as well. Field names (and names of other elements of your application) should meet three criteria:

- They must be syntactically correct
- They should be consistently formed
- They should communicate as clearly as possible

For field names, the syntactic restrictions are pretty straightforward: [10]

- Field names must begin with a letter (A through Z) and should use only letters and digits (0 through 9) in the rest of the name (avoid national characters (#, $, @ in the U.S.) and the underscore (_) because of international character set conflicts and HLL syntax restrictions).

- Field names can't be longer than 10 characters, and 8 characters is the recommended maximum if files will be accessed by RPG IV programs (6 characters, if accessed by RPG/400 programs).

---

[10] Although it's not a DB2/400 syntactic restriction, you should avoid COBOL/400 and SQL/400 reserved words (such as FILE, ORDER, and SEQUENCE) to avoid conflicts when you use these languages. The COBOL/400 and SQL/400 reference manuals list the reserved words for each language.

It's much easier to work with a database if its fields follow a regular pattern and use consistent and clear abbreviations. The value of these two principles is easy to see if you consider the problems that arise when names *aren't* formed this way. If you came across the field name CAL1, would you have any idea that it meant "customer address, line 1"? Even if you could guess what the C, A, and L stood for, would you know whether it was a shipping or billing address? While a more meaningful name like SHPLINE1 isn't completely unambiguous, you have a reasonable chance of comprehending it when you first encounter it. In addition, you'll find it very easy to follow code that uses this field once you've had a brief period to familiarize yourself with the file definition.

Consistency helps comprehension, as well — especially when names must be formed with abbreviations. Consider the frequently occurring need to have a field that stores a count of something (e.g., how many of an item are ordered). If some fields use different abbreviations for "count" — CNT, COU, CN — and others use a variety of abbreviations for "number (of)" — NBR, NO, NUM — it becomes difficult to quickly recognize the meaning of a field name, especially when you're working with HLL code that uses the fields. You can avoid this problem by following a simple naming convention, such as

> *The term "count" and its abbreviation CNT are used for fields that store an integral count of some item.*

This convention specifies both the term that will be used and its abbreviation.

The people who designed the OS/400 interface studied abbreviations extensively and came up with a simple and effective scheme for creating abbreviations. The two main principles that they followed are

- Whenever possible, use three-letter abbreviations, except for items, such as ID, that have a well-established shorter abbreviation.
- Form a three-letter abbreviation with the first letter of the term and the two consonants that are most prominent in pronouncing the word (e.g., for "number", use NBR, not NUM).

Because database field names are limited to 10 characters (and for use with RPG IV programs, 8 is recommended [11]), you'll inevitably have to squeeze one or more of the abbreviations in a name. Thus, it's a good idea to develop a list of terms that appear in your applications and 2- and 3-character abbreviations for each of them. Figure 3.6 is a partial list of terms that occur in many applications.

---

[11] Chapter 7 explores how to specify a prefix for a file's field names to keep them unique within an RPG IV program.

Figure 3.6
Sample List of Terms
and Abbreviations

Term	Three-character	Two-character	Other	Notes
Address	ADR	AD		
Amount	AMT	AM		
Application	APP	AP	APLC	For libraries, such as APPDTA and APPSRC
Building	BLD	BL	BLDG	
City	CTY	CT	CITY	
Code	CDE	CD	CODE	
Count	CNT	CN		
Country	CRY	CR	CNTRY	
Credit	CRD	CR		
Customer	CUS	CS	CUST	
Date	DAT	DT	DATE	
Description	DSC	DC		
Employee	EMP	EM	EMPL	
Entry	ENT	EN		
First	FST	FS	FIRST	
Initial	INL	IN		As in middle initial of a name; use INZ for initialize
Initialize	INZ	IZ		
Identifier, Identification		ID		Use for unique identifier (e.g., CUSTID)
Last	LST	LS	LAST	
Limit	LMT	LM	LIMIT	
Line	LIN	LN	LINE	
Middle	MDL	MD		
Name	NAM	NM	NAME	
Number	NBR	NB		
Phone	PHN	PH		
Product	PRD	PD	PROD	
Production	PDC	PR	PRDC	Don't use PRD, which is for Product
				Figure 3.6 continued

Figure 3.6
Continued

Term	Three-character	Two-character	Other	Notes
Room	ROM	RM	ROOM	RM is preferred over ROM
Shipping	SHP	SH		
State	STA	ST	STATE	ST is preferred over STA; avoid ambiguity with ST for Status
Status	STS	ST	STATUS	Avoid ambiguity with ST for State
Text	TXT	TX	TEXT	
Total	TOT	TT		

Note: The IBM *Programming Reference Summary* has lists of the abbreviations IBM uses for CL commands and DDS keywords.

Create and maintain your own list of terms using a word processor document or a database file. Here are some further naming guidelines:

- In forming a three-part name that's only eight characters (for RPG IV), use a two-character abbreviation for the first or third part (not the middle): TOTSHPWT, not TOTSHWGT.

- If you must use two or more two-character abbreviations in a name, keep the two-character abbreviations adjacent: BILPSCD1, not BLPOSCD1, for the billing address's first postal code.

- If you have only one or two terms in a name and the field name can be formed using the full spelling of one or both terms, you can use one or both full terms: NAME, STATUS, SHPSTATE, FILENAME.

- Within a single file's definition, don't use the full spelling of a term in some fields' names and its abbreviation in other field names: not PHONEFAX and PHNVOICE, but PHNFAX and PHNVOICE.

- Try to avoid a mix of two- and three-character abbreviations for the same term in the same file: BILLINE1 (BIL+LINE+1) and BILPSCD1 (BIL+PS+CD+1), not BILLINE1 and BLPSCOD1 (BL+PS+COD+1), in the same file.

- If you have a file in which a number of fields can use a three-character abbreviation (e.g., CNT) but one field can't, and the two-character abbreviation is cryptic (e.g., CN), it's better to handle the one exception with the shorter abbreviation. Often, you can avoid this situation by adjusting the other parts of the name.

- Sometimes it's better to reduce the number of terms, rather than use a bunch of one- and two-letter abbreviations. For example, for a field that contains the first line of a shipping address, use SHPLINE1, instead of SHPADLN1, for the shipping address's first line.

- When you create a new file, consider the consistency among the names as a group. Although you may have to vary from your general conventions slightly, it's more important that the names within a file be as descriptive as possible and consistent among themselves.

Notice also in Figure 3.4 that most application-oriented names don't have any indication of the file that contains them. For example, YEARSAL is used instead of EMPYERSL. When YEARSAL is defined in the EMPLOYEE file, it's obvious that YEARSAL means "employee's yearly salary." If there were a separate CONSULTNT file that also had a YEARSAL field, it would be clear that YEARSAL in that file meant "consultant's yearly salary." There's also no programming problem if a field with the same name is used in two files because the record format name can serve as a qualifier to make the names unique within any program that uses both files. In COBOL/400, this qualifier support is built in to compiler support, and a field can be referenced as

```
YearSal of EmployeeR
```

or

```
YearSal of ConsultntR
```

In RPG IV, you can use the File Specification (F-spec) Prefix keyword to add a unique file abbreviation to the beginning of all fields in a file. For example, specifying Prefix(Em) on the F-spec for the employee file would allow the YEARSAL field to be referenced as EmYearSal within the RPG IV program.[12] (Chapter 7 covers this technique in detail.)

There's one case in which the field name *should* incorporate some indication of the containing file — a key field used as the unique identifier for records in the file. For example, CUSTID explicitly indicates that the field is the unique ID for the CUSTOMER file. The reason for including CUST in the field name is not that ID alone would be an inadequate name within the CUSTOMER file itself. Rather, the reason for this explicit indication of the containing file is that a CUSTID field may also be defined in other files that have some relationship to the CUSTOMER file. For example, a SALE file's record format would normally have a CUSTID field to contain the customer ID of the customer placing the order. Obviously, it wouldn't be a good idea to use just ID as the name of the customer ID field in the SALE file. (What name would you give the field that contained the order ID?). Because CUSTID (or a similar name) is the best choice for a field in a file

---

[12] As mentioned in Chapter 2, explicit field name prefixes may be necessary for database files that will be accessed primarily by RPG/400, which doesn't support qualifiers or the Prefix keyword.

that's related to the CUSTOMER file, it's good practice to use the same name in the CUSTOMER file itself.

As you can see from this set of guidelines, an effective approach to naming requires a balance between consistency and meaningfulness. With the 10- (or 8-) character limit on field names, if you pay attention only to consistency, you end up with coded, hard-to-read names like CAL1. On the other hand, if you follow no guidelines when you create field names, you're likely to end up with a confusing hodge-podge of field names.

Coding Suggestions

- Set up a physical file with no members to serve as a field reference file.
- Use the DSPFFD command to produce an output file with information about all fields in the field reference file. Use SQL/400 or a report utility to print this information as a data dictionary.
- Define *all* fields in application physical files by reference to the central field reference file.
- Establish and follow a good naming convention for files, fields, and other OS/400 elements.
- Maintain and use a list of all terms and abbreviations that are used in file, field, and other names.

Chapter Summary

Reuse of existing code can increase productivity and quality. The DDS REF and REFFLD keywords let you define a physical file field based on a previously defined field. The new field can use an existing field's data type, length, and decimal positions, as well as other attributes, such as column heading. You can override referenced attributes, but generally the data type, length, decimal positions, and editing and validity attributes should be left the same when you reference a field.

You can reference a previously defined field in the same file or in a different file. The ability to reference fields in a different file lets you set up a field reference file to hold field definitions on which you base some or all of your application physical files' field definitions. The field reference file should have at least a base set of reference fields so you can reference one of them for any field definition. These fundamental reference fields provide a set of user-defined data types for other field definitions. You can also choose to define *all* your application fields in the field reference file, in which case it serves as a comprehensive data dictionary for the database.

A consistent and meaningful naming standard is important for your database's file and field names. You should create standards and lists for how you abbreviate terms and how you create names from the abbreviations.

Key Terms

code reuse   field dictionary   user-defined data type
data type   field reference file

Exercises

1. List the information you'd ideally like to have about terms and abbreviations that you use in your database file and field names. Consider how you'd deal with the following concerns:

   • synonymous terms (e.g., "start" and "begin")

   • special terms that end users have for data they work with

   • existing files and programs that were created before you developed naming standards

   • Two- and three-letter combinations that are the natural abbreviation for more than one term (e.g., PRD for product and production)

2. Design and code the DDS for one or more physical files to store the information you've listed for Exercise 1.

3. Why do you think IBM decided to use mostly consonants in its three-letter abbreviations? Consider the results of combining abbreviations.

4. Show an alternative to Figure 3.4 for coding a set of type-defining reference fields for decimal fractions. Use an approach that will minimize the chances of truncating the integer part of a decimal fraction when you assign one decimal field's value to another (e.g., when you assign the value

of a field based on TDEC3 to a field based on TDEC2). Would this be a good place to use the DDS relative length override (e.g., putting +1 in positions 30–34) as discussed in Footnote 2? Why or why not?

5. What advantages and/or disadvantages are there to referencing TDATE and TTIME to define an application field (e.g., ENTDATE), rather than just using L or T in position 35 (data type)?

6. How could you improve on the suggestion to use REF(TINTGE0) for application "count" fields?

7. Suggest a better way to organize the field definitions in the field reference file. Consider the types of tasks people do when they work with the field reference file. Do you see any potential for accidental coding errors with the suggested approach to the field reference file? Suggest ways to reduce the chance of errors.

8. Exercise 7 in Chapter 2 had you code the DDS for an employee file. Create a field reference file that has field definitions so you can define all the employee file fields by referencing fields in the field reference file. Modify the DDS for the employee file to use field referencing and re-create the file.

Chapter 4

Introduction to Logical Files: Keyed Access Paths, Record Selection, and Field Selection

Chapter Overview

This chapter introduces logical files, one of the most flexible DB2/400 facilities for working with the contents of your database. After looking at the general way a logical file works, we cover three of the most common ways they're used. You'll learn how to define a logical file to provide an access path based on a key that's different from the underlying physical file's key. Then you'll see how you can create a logical file that appears to application programs as a file with a subset of the records in the physical file on which the logical file is based. The third use of logical files that this chapter examines is defining a new record format that has only a subset of the fields in the underlying physical file's record format. This chapter also covers the CRTLF (Create Logical File) command, which compiles DDS into a logical file object. Finally, we look at some additional coding techniques, including naming guidelines, for logical files and their record formats and fields.

How Logical Files Work

In Chapter 1, we said that logical files don't actually contain data but provide a means for HLL programs and utilities to access physical file data in an alternative way. One example given was enabling records to be retrieved in a different order from either their arrival sequence (i.e., physical locations in the file) or the keyed sequence defined by the physical file's key field(s). Before we take up the details of logical file access paths, it may help to see why this feature of DB2/400 is so useful.

Suppose you have a CUSTOMER physical file (like the example in Chapter 2) with CUSTID as its key. How would you print a list of customers sequenced by the NAME field? One option would be to **sort** the records using the OS/400 sort utility [1] so the records are physically sequenced in the physical file member by the contents of the NAME field. Then, by accessing

---

[1] The OS/400 sort utility is documented in the *Utilities: Sort User's Guide and Reference* manual (IBM publication SC09-1826). To use the sort utility, you code sort specifications in a source member, then execute the FMTDTA (Format Data) command.

the records in arrival sequence[2], you would get them in order by name. Of course, there are several problems with this technique. For starters, after adding any new customer or changing a customer's name, you'd have to resort the records. And if you wanted to access the records by shipping address, you'd have to use a different sort (and sort them back into name order again when you needed the name sequence). With a customer file, which interactive applications are likely to use heavily, you probably couldn't have exclusive use of the file to sort it except after normal business hours so accessing the data in a variety of sequences would be limited to off hours. As you can see, sorting isn't very convenient.

In most cases, logical files with keyed access paths provide a better solution than sorting. The DDS for one of the simplest logical files you can create is shown in Figure 4.1.

Figure 4.1
Logical File with Keyed
Access Path Based on
NAME Field

```
...1....+....2....+....3....+....4....+....5....+....6....+....7....
        R CUSTOMERR                    PFILE( CUSTOMER )
                                       TEXT( 'Customers by name' )

        K NAME
```

The record level statement (R in position 17) uses a PFILE keyword entry to specify that the logical file is over the CUSTOMER physical file. Every non-join logical file must have a PFILE entry that identifies the scope of the logical file. This file definition specifies that the logical file has the same record format (i.e., the same format name and the same field definitions) as the CUSTOMER file and a single key field: NAME. To create the logical file object from the DDS, you enter the following CRTLF command:[3]

```
CRTLF FILE( appdta/custname )
      SRCFILE( appsrc/qddssrc )
```

This command, like the CRTPF command discussed in Chapter 2, has defaults for most parameters. This example creates the CUSTNAME file in the APPDTA library using the DDS source in the CUSTNAME member in source file APPSRC/QDDSSRC. The new logical file has one member, named CUSTNAME, and this member is based on all members in the CUSTOMER physical file. "The Create Logical File Command" section below discusses this command in more detail.

---

[2] Remember that "arrival sequence" is a bit of a misnomer. A sorted file is one example, because after sorting, the records won't be in the same order that they originally arrived in the database. Because all IBM DB2/400 technical documentation uses "arrival sequence" to mean relative record number sequence, we use that terminology in this text, too.

[3] You can enter CRTLF commands directly through an OS/400 command prompt or use PDM option 14 to execute the command.

When you create a logical file, DB2/400 creates an OS/400 *FILE object, with the logical file (LF) subtype. A logical file object has a record format and members, but instead of containing actual data, the members generally consist of a keyed access path that has key values paired with the relative record numbers (RRNs) of the corresponding physical file records. To your HLL programs, the record layout of the CUSTNAME logical file looks identical to the record layout of the CUSTOMER file. And if your program reads the CUSTNAME file sequentially by key (e.g., to produce a listing), you can use the *same* program with either the physical or logical file. When an HLL program performs a sequential read operation, the compiled code calls a DB2/400 routine to ask for the next record. To find the location of the next record, DB2/400 steps through the open file member's access path — either arrival or keyed. This record is then retrieved and returned to your program. Thus, the order in which records are presented to an HLL program that does sequential processing depends on the access path of the physical or logical file that's opened.

We'll cover HLL program's access of database files more throroughly in Chapter 7, but the code in Figure 4.2 and the diagrams in Figures 4.3 and 4.4 show the steps necessary to access different files (with the same record format) from a single program.

Figure 4.2

Code to Access Two Different Files with the Same Program

```
/* The following Override with Database File command */
/* tells DB2/400 to open the APPDTA/CUSTOMER file    */
/* member CUSTOMER, when the LISTCUST program opens  */
/* the internal file named CUSTOMER.                 */
/* See Figure 4.3                                    */

OVRDBF FILE( customer )
       TOFILE( appdta/customer )
       MBR( customer )

CALL listcust

/* The following Override with Database File command */
/* tells DB2/400 to open the APPDTA/CUSTNAME file    */
/* member CUSTNAME, when the LISTCUST program opens  */
/* the internal file named CUSTOMER.                 */
/* See Figure 4.4                                    */

OVRDBF FILE( customer )
       TOFILE( appdta/custname )
       MBR( custname )

CALL listcust
```

In a normal production environment, the first OVRDBF command probably wouldn't be required because when a program opens a file with the internal name CUSTOMER, by default DB2/400 opens the first member of the first CUSTOMER file that's found in the job's library list. (However, it's not a bad idea to use explicit OVRDBF commands in production systems to avoid problems if the library list or file's member composition changes.)

Figure 4.3

The OVRDBF (Override
with Database File)
Command and Opening a
File in an HLL program

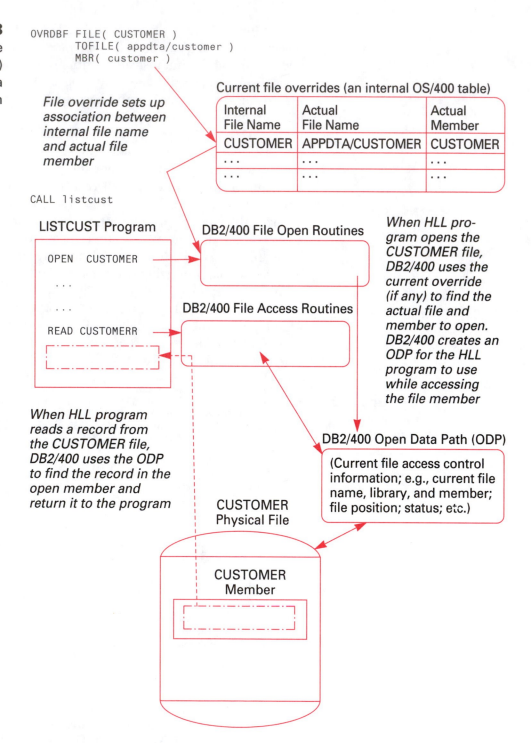

```
OVRDBF FILE( CUSTOMER )
    TOFILE( appdta/customer )
    MBR( customer )
```

*File override sets up
association between
internal file name
and actual file
member*

Current file overrides (an internal OS/400 table)

Internal File Name	Actual File Name	Actual Member
CUSTOMER	APPDTA/CUSTOMER	CUSTOMER
. . .	. . .	. . .
. . .	. . .	. . .

```
CALL listcust
```

LISTCUST Program

```
OPEN  CUSTOMER

...

...

READ  CUSTOMERR
```

DB2/400 File Open Routines

DB2/400 File Access Routines

*When HLL pro-
gram opens the
CUSTOMER file,
DB2/400 uses the
current override
(if any) to find the
actual file and
member to open.
DB2/400 creates an
ODP for the HLL
program to use
while accessing
the file member*

*When HLL program
reads a record from
the CUSTOMER file,
DB2/400 uses the ODP
to find the record in the
open member and
return it to the program*

DB2/400 Open Data Path (ODP)

(Current file access control
information; e.g., current file
name, library, and member;
file position; status; etc.)

CUSTOMER
Physical File

CUSTOMER
Member

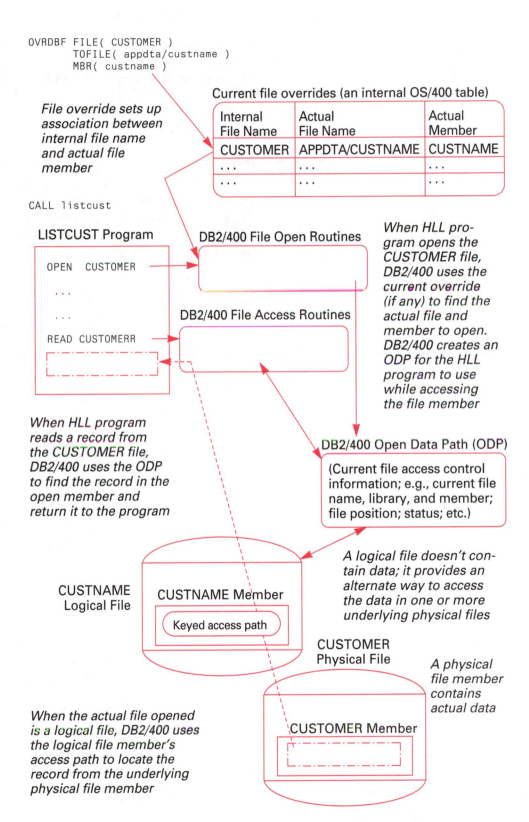

Figure 4.4
Using OVRDBF to Open
a Logical File

```
OVRDBF FILE( CUSTOMER )
       TOFILE( appdta/custname )
       MBR( custname )
```

File override sets up association between internal file name and actual file member

Current file overrides (an internal OS/400 table)

Internal File Name	Actual File Name	Actual Member
CUSTOMER	APPDTA/CUSTNAME	CUSTNAME
. . .	. . .	. . .
. . .	. . .	. . .

```
CALL listcust
```

LISTCUST Program

```
OPEN  CUSTOMER
   . . .
   . . .
READ CUSTOMERR
```

DB2/400 File Open Routines

DB2/400 File Access Routines

When HLL program opens the CUSTOMER file, DB2/400 uses the current override (if any) to find the actual file and member to open. DB2/400 creates an ODP for the HLL program to use while accessing the file member

When HLL program reads a record from the CUSTOMER file, DB2/400 uses the ODP to find the record in the open member and return it to the program

DB2/400 Open Data Path (ODP)

(Current file access control information; e.g., current file name, library, and member; file position; status; etc.)

A logical file doesn't contain data; it provides an alternate way to access the data in one or more underlying physical files

CUSTNAME
Logical File

CUSTNAME Member

Keyed access path

CUSTOMER
Physical File

A physical file member contains actual data

CUSTOMER Member

When the actual file opened is a logical file, DB2/400 uses the logical file member's access path to locate the record from the underlying physical file member

As you can see, there's no magic to logical files. DB2/400 just maintains the necessary indexes (and other mechanisms) so it can handle I/O requests from HLL programs whether the file an HLL program opens turns out to be a logical file or a physical file. Logical files let HLL programs process records in a sequence that's different from their physical order and eliminate the need for record sorts.

Creating a New Keyed Access Path

With this introduction to how DB2/400 supports logical files, let's look at the features you can use when you want to create a new keyed access path or take advantage of other logical file capabilities. The DDS source layout for non-join logical files is identical to that for physical files, although the values allowed in each column are different in some cases, as shown in Figure 4.5.

Figure 4.5
Source Columns for
Logical File DDS

Column	Positions	Content
Sequence number	1–5	Optional sequence number or comment
Form type	6	A or blank to indicate DDS
Comment flag	7	Place a * in this column to identify the entire line as a comment
Unused	8–16	Leave blank unless the line is a comment
Type of name	17	One of the following: Blank — field name or (select/omit field name in multi-line select/omit condition) J — join specification (join logical files only) K — key field name R — record format name O — omit field name S — select field name
Unused	18	Leave blank unless the line is a comment
Name	19–28	An identifier for one of the following: Record format name Field name Key field name Select/omit field name
Reference	29	Leave blank unless the line is a comment

Figure 4.5 continued

Figure 4.5
Continued

Column	Positions	Content
Length	30–34	Specify this field only to override the length of the corresponding field in the physical file For character fields, the maximum number of characters; For numeric fields, specify the maximum number of digits (including any decimal positions)
Data type	35	Specify this field only to override the data type of the corresponding field in the physical file. One of the following: A — character H — hexadecimal P — packed decimal S — zoned decimal B — binary F — floating point L — date T — time Z — timestamp
Decimal positions	36–37	Specify this field only to override the decimal positions of the corresponding field in the physical file. For numeric fields, enter an integer in the range 0 to 31 (and not greater than the Length as defined in the physical file, or entered in 30-34) for the number of positions to the right of the decimal point
Usage	38	Blank — for non-join logical files, defaults to B; for join logical files, defaults to I. B — both input and output operations are valid for this field I — only input operations are valid for this field (i.e., the field is "read-only") N — (valid only for join logical files) neither input nor output operations are valid for the field; it can be used only as a join field
Unused	39–44	Leave blank unless the line is a comment
Function	45–80	Keyword entries (see Appendix A)

Like physical files, logical files can have file-level, record-level, field-level, and key field-level entries. In addition, logical files can also have select/omit-level entries (discussed later in this chapter) and join-level entries (discussed in Chapter 6). The keywords allowed for non-join logical files[4] are shown in Figure 4.6 (appendix A provides a complete description of each keyword).

Figure 4.6

Keywords for Non-Join Logical Files

File level	Record level	Field level	Key field level	Select/Omit level
ALTSEQ	FORMAT	ALIAS	ABSVAL	ALL
DYNSLT	PFILE	COLHDG	DESCEND	CMP/COMP
FCFO	TEXT	CONCAT	DIGIT	RANGE
FIFO		DATFMT	NOALTSEQ	VALUES
LIFO		DATSEP	SIGNED	
REFACCPTH		FLTPCN	UNSIGNED	
UNIQUE		RENAME	ZONE	
		SST		
		TEXT		
		TIMFMT		
		TIMSEP		
		TRNTBL		
		VARLEN		

Note: Logical files also support all the display file related, field-level keywords: CHECK, CHKMSGID, COMP, CMP, EDTCDE, EDTWRD, RANGE, REFSHIFT, VALUES. See Chapters 2 and 3 for a discussion of these keywords.

The DDS for a logical file can have any of the file-level keywords that apply to keyed access paths (e.g., ABSVAL), which were explained in Chapter 2. The most important of these keywords is UNIQUE, and it's not unusual to have one or more logical files with unique keyed access paths, in addition to the physical file's unique keyed access path. When a physical file record is inserted or updated, DB2/400 enforces the unique key requirement for *all* access paths created over a physical file. For this reason, you want to be sure there will *never* be duplicate key values for a logical file's key before you specify UNIQUE for the logical file.

The most common way to define a logical file's access path is to list the key fields, just as you do for a physical file with a keyed access path, as described in Chapter 2. The key fields are listed after the record format is defined, starting

[4]Join logical files are covered in Chapter 6; the information in the rest of this chapter applies to non-join logical files.

with the major key field and ending with the minor key field (if there are multiple key fields). Each key field-level entry can have the same keywords (listed in Figure 4.6) allowed for physical file key fields. Figure 4.7 shows the DDS for a logical file with two key fields; the major key is the customer's city and the minor key is the customer's credit limit in descending order.

Figure 4.7

Logical File with Keyed
Access Path Based
on SHPCITY and
CRDLIMIT Fields

```
...1....+....2....+....3....+....4....+....5....+....6....+....7....
          R CUSTOMERR                    PFILE( CUSTOMER )
                                         TEXT( 'Customers by city and +
                                               descending credit' )

          K SHPCITY
          K CRDLIMIT                     DESCEND
```

When an HLL program reads records sequentially using this logical file, it would see them as follows:

CUSTID	SHPCITY	CRDLIMIT
. . .		
10568	Richmond	9500
12989	Richmond	7500
11006	Richmond	5000
. . .		
10024	Seattle	10000
17651	Seattle	5000

Non-join logical files allow an additional file-level keyword, REFACCPTH, which lets you specify that the logical file has the same access path definition as the referenced file. The items that are referenced include key field definitions, select/omit specifications, and alternative collating information (e.g., ABSVAL). This is a fairly restricted feature and is useful mainly when you have logical files with different field selections but the same key fields. The following example shows how to specify the DDS for a logical file that uses the same access path specification for an existing file:

```
...2....+....3....+....4....+....5....+....6....+....7..
                            REFACCPTH( APPDTA/CUSTNAME )

R CUSTOMERR                 PFILE( APPDTA/CUSTOMER )
  CUSTID
  NAME
  SHPCITY
```

In this example, the record format has the CUSTID, NAME, and SHPCITY fields (we'll discuss field selection later in this chapter), and the access path definition is the same as the CUSTNAME (presumably, logical) file. The new logical file's record format must contain the field(s) used in the referenced file's access path. For example, if NAME is the key field for the CUSTNAME file, any logical file referencing it with REFACCPTH must contain the NAME field, too. Other than the key fields, the file being defined isn't restricted as to fields it includes in the record format.

Selecting a Subset of Records

The logical file examples we've looked at so far present the records of the underlying physical file member in a different sequence, but *all* records are included in the logical file's access path. You can use **select/omit** DDS entries to include only a subset of a physical file's records in a logical file's access path. Select/omit entries follow the key field entries (if any) and are the last entries in a DDS source member.

Figure 4.8 shows a logical file that selects only customer records with a credit limit greater than or equal to 5000.

Figure 4.8

Logical File Selecting Records with Credit Limit of at Least 5000

```
...1....+....2....+....3....+....4....+....5....+....6....+....7....
          R CUSTOMERR                      PFILE( CUSTOMER )
                                           TEXT( 'Customers with credit +
                                                  limit at least 5000' )

          K CUSTID

          S CRDLIMIT                        COMP( GE 5000 )
```

This logical file also has a keyed access path, which orders the selected records by CUSTID. When an HLL program reads this file sequentially, it will get only those records that meet the selection criteria and will get them in CUSTID sequence. For this type of logical file, the internal index that DB2/400 maintains as part of the file's access path contains key values and corresponding RRNs for only those records whose values satisfy the select/omit specifications. If a new record is added to the underlying physical file member, DB2/400 examines the CRDLIMIT field to determine whether to include an access path entry for the record. When an existing record's CRDLIMIT field is changed, DB2/400 adds or removes an entry in the access path, if necessary. (Keep in mind that DB2/400 maintains changes to *all* related access paths when a change is made to a record in a physical file member — the change can be made through any physical or logical file that provides access to the member's data.) To any HLL program that uses a logical file with record selection, the logical file member appears the same as a physical file member that contains only the selected records.[5]

Although record selection is conceptually a matter of stating the logical condition that records must satisfy to be in the subset of selected records,

---

[5] There's one interesting anomaly with record selection, however. An HLL program can add a record to a logical file member and subsequently not be able to retrieve it. In the example where only records with CRDLIMIT ≥ 5000 are selected, if an HLL program uses this logical file to add a customer record with a CRDLIMIT of 1000, DB2/400 will (properly) *not* add an

the syntax for DDS select/omit entries is a bit more complicated.[6] The select/omit section of DDS can have one or more specifications, each beginning with an S (select) or O (omit) in position 17 (Name Type column). To determine whether a particular record is selected, the DB2/400 selection process steps sequentially down the list (i.e., the first S or O condition is tested, then the next condition, etc.). When a condition is satisfied, the record is selected if S is specified on the condition, or omitted (i.e., not selected) if O is specified on the condition. Once some condition is satisfied, no subsequent conditions are evaluated for that particular record — the record's fate is sealed. If no S or O condition is satisfied, a final ALL condition (either explicit or implicit) determines the record's disposition. This final condition can be coded explicitly as follows:

```
...2....+....3....+....4....+....5....+....6
O                          ALL
```

An explicit ALL condition can have either an S (to select) or an O (to omit) all records that don't satisfy a previous select/omit condition. If no explicit ALL condition is coded, an implicit ALL condition is assumed to have the *opposite* S/O specification to that of the last condition. In other words, if the last condition has an S, then records that don't satisfy any condition will be omitted, and vice versa. Figure 4.9 shows a logical file with several select/omit entries.

Figure 4.9
Logical File with Multiple
Select/Omit Conditions

```
...1....+....2....+....3....+....4....+....5....+....6....+....7....
          R CUSTOMERR                  PFILE( CUSTOMER )
                                       TEXT( 'Cust not in Richmond +
                                             w crdt 1000-9999 or +
                                             sts A,B,C' )

          K CUSTID

          O SHPCITY                    COMP( EQ 'Richmond' )
          S CRDLIMIT                   RANGE( 1000 9999 )
          S STATUS                     VALUES( 'A' 'B' 'C' )
```

access path entry. Subsequent attempts to retrieve this record (through the same logical file), even using direct access by CUSTID, will fail with a "record not found" error. A similar problem can occur if an existing record with CRDLIMIT $\geq$ 5000 is retrieved, and its CRDLIMIT is changed to 1000. The result is a so-called "phantom" update because the record seems to "disappear." In practice, this isn't a big problem because it's not common to update the select/omit fields when you access data through a logical file that has record selection.

[6] And the DDS approach doesn't always allow you to express the complete selection criteria you might want, either. We'll see in Chapter 13 how SQL provides more powerful means of record selection. DDS limitations arise both from its simple fixed-columnar syntax, as well as from early limitations of the S/38 database (where DDS originated).

Here's the process DB2/400 follows to determine whether a record is included in the logical file:

1. Is SHPCITY = "Richmond"?
   If Yes, omit the record and don't check further select/omit entries for this record.
2. Is the CRDLIMIT between 1000 and 9999, inclusive?
   If Yes, select the record and stop checking.
3. Is the STATUS = "A" or "B" or "C"?
   If Yes, select the record and stop checking.
4. Omit the record

Each condition (except a final ALL condition) is specified with a field name and a keyword entry. The field name must appear in *both* the underlying physical file's record format and the logical file record format.[7] The allowable keyword entries (in addition to ALL) are COMP,[8] RANGE, and VALUES.

The COMP keyword takes two parameters: a relational operator and a field name or value. The following list summarizes allowable relational operators:

Operator	Meaning
LT	Less than
LE	Less than or equal to
NG	Not greater than (equivalent to LE, which is preferred)
EQ	Equal to
NE	Not equal to
GE	Greater than or equal to
NL	Not less than (equivalent to GE, which is preferred)
GT	Greater than

The second parameter provides the field or value to be compared with the field specified in positions 19–28. The following example compares the CRDLIMIT field's relation to 10000, and omits records whose credit limit is greater than 10000.

```
...2....+....3....+....4....+....5....+....6
O CRDLIMIT                COMP( GT 10000 )
```

The field specified in positions 19–28 is always considered to be on the left side of the relational test; the above example can be read as CRDLIMIT > 10000.

---

[7] In the logical file, the field can appear either in positions 19–28, or as the argument of a CONCAT or RENAME keyword entry. (Chapter 5 discusses CONCAT and RENAME.)

[8] CMP is an allowable synonym for COMP, but COMP is the preferred keyword.

You specify character values in single quotation marks. Date, time, and timestamp values must also be enclosed in single quotation marks and in the same format as the field's definition. For example, to specify an *ISO date, you use `'1995-11-30'`. You can also specify COMP(EQ *NULL) or COMP(NE *NULL) for fields with the field-level ALWNULL keyword specified in the physical file definition.

The RANGE keyword takes two values: low-value and high-value. The following statement selects records with CRDLIMIT greater than or equal to 1000 and less than or equal to 9999.

```
...2....+....3....+....4....+....5....+....6..
S CRDLIMIT                 RANGE( 1000 9999 )
```

The VALUES keyword takes one to a hundred values. The condition is true if the value of the field specified in positions 19–28 matches any of the values specified. The following statement selects records with a STATUS of A, B, or C.

```
...2....+....3....+....4....+....5....+....6....+
S STATUS                   VALUES( 'A' 'B' 'C' )
```

So far, we've looked at simple conditions. You can create compound conditions by coding multiple COMP, RANGE, or VALUES entries on successive lines and using S or O in position 17 on *only* the first line. The following 2-line compound condition selects records only if they have a credit limit from 1000 to 9999 *and* have a status of A, B, or C.

```
...2....+....3....+....4....+....5....+....6....+
S CRDLIMIT                 RANGE( 1000 9999 )
  STATUS                   VALUES( 'A' 'B' 'C' )
```

Notice that the second line does *not* have an S in position 17. Contrast this test with the following two lines, which select records if they have a credit limit from 1000 to 9999 *or* have a status of A, B, or C.

```
...2....+....3....+....4....+....5....+....6....+
S CRDLIMIT                 RANGE( 1000 9999 )
S STATUS                   VALUES( 'A' 'B' 'C' )
```

RANGE and VALUES conditions are simply convenient alternatives to equivalent COMP specifications. The RANGE specification

```
...2....+....3....+....4....+....5....+....6....+
S CRDLIMIT                 RANGE( 1000 9999 )
```

is equivalent to the COMP specifications

```
...2....+....3....+....4....+....5....+....6....+
S CRDLIMIT                 COMP( GE 1000 )
  CRDLIMIT                 COMP( LE 9999 )
```

And the VALUES specification

```
...2....+....3....+....4....+....5....+....6....+
S STATUS                   VALUES( 'A' 'B' 'C' )
```

is equivalent to the three COMP specifications

```
...2....+....3....+....4....+....5....+....6....+
S STATUS                    COMP( 'A'  )
S STATUS                    COMP( 'B' )
S STATUS                    COMP( 'C' )
```

Knowing these equivalencies can be useful when you want to specify a range or set of values using fields rather than literals. A field is allowed as an argument for the COMP keyword, but not as an argument for the RANGE or VALUES keywords.

Because DB2/400 steps through the select/omit specifications in order and quits as soon as a condition is satisfied, you can improve the runtime efficiency of select/omit specifications by putting the conditions that are most likely to be matched toward the beginning of a series of multiple conditions, *as long as the order results in the desired record selection*. For example, suppose that customers have the following average distribution:

- 80 percent are in Richmond
- 50 percent have a maximum credit amount between 1000 and 9999
- 20 percent have a status of A, B, or C

The following order of select/omit specifications results in the best runtime performance:

```
...2....+....3....+....4....+....5....+....6....+
O SHPCITY                   COMP( EQ 'Richmond' )
S CRDLIMIT                  RANGE( 1000 9999 )
S STATUS                    VALUES( 'A' 'B' 'C' )
```

Be careful that you don't arbitrarily reorder the statements if you have a mixture of S and O specifications. For example, suppose that customers were distributed as follows:

- 80 percent have a status of A, B, or C
- 50 percent have a maximum credit amount between 1000 and 9999
- 20 percent are in Richmond

You should *not* use the following order of select/omit specifications because it wouldn't be equivalent to the previous ordering:

```
...2....+....3....+....4....+....5....+....6....+
S STATUS                    VALUES( 'A' 'B' 'C' )
S CRDLIMIT                  RANGE( 1000 9999 )
O SHPCITY                   COMP( EQ 'Richmond' )
```

This ordering would omit *all* customers in Richmond (as intended), because those who had a status or credit limit that satisfied one of the first two conditions would be included in the selected records. Furthermore, *all* customers not in Richmond would be selected — because the last test is an omit specification, all records that satisfy no test are selected. The order that performs best and still selects the right records is

```
...2....+....3....+....4....+....5....+....6....+
O SHPCITY                      COMP( EQ 'Richmond' )
S STATUS                       VALUES( 'A' 'B' 'C' )
S CRDLIMIT                     RANGE( 1000 9999 )
```

DB2/400 maintains all access paths over a physical file member so a logical file with select/omit specifications adds overhead to any application that updates the underlying physical file member, even if the application isn't using the logical file with the select/omit entries. To shift the overhead for select/omit tests so the tests impact only applications using the logical file that contains the select/omit entries, you code a DYNSLT file-level keyword in the DDS for a logical file with select/omit entries. DYNSLT specifies **dynamic record selection**, which means that DB2/400 performs the selection (and omission) tests at the time an HLL program reads a record from the logical file. With dynamic selection, select/omit conditions are not tested when records are inserted, deleted, or changed; and the logical file's access path (if any) has entries for all records. Figure 4.10 shows a logical file with dynamic record selection.

Figure 4.10
Logical File with Dynamic
Record Selection

```
...1....+....2....+....3....+....4....+....5....+....6....+....7....
                                 DYNSLT

         R CUSTOMERR            PFILE( CUSTOMER )
                                TEXT( 'Cust not in Richmond +
                                      w crdt 1000-9999 or +
                                      sts A,B,C' )


         K CUSTID

         O SHPCITY              COMP( EQ 'Richmond' )
         S CRDLIMIT             RANGE( 1000 9999 )
         S STATUS               VALUES( 'A' 'B' 'C' )
```

This file still has a keyed access path, based on CUSTID, but because the file specifies dynamic record selection, the access path contains entries for all records in the underlying physical file member.[9]

---

[9] The logical file in Figure 4.10 would probably also benefit from a **shared access path**. Recent releases of DB2/400 do an excellent job of *automatically* sharing an access path, if two (or more) files have identical or closely related key fields. In this case, the underlying physical file is likely to also have a keyed access path based on CUSTID so DB2/400 must maintain only one access path. Without dynamic record selection (as in Figure 4.9), the logical file requires a separate access path. Access paths don't have to be identical to be shared. For example, if one file has two key fields, SHPCITY and CRDLIMIT, and another file has the single key field, SHPCITY, the second file can share the first file's access path. You don't have to code anything to share access paths, DB2/400 handles it "under the covers."

Dynamic record selection is required if the logical file doesn't specify any key fields.[10] Dynamic record selection is also a good choice for logical files with select/omit entries when the following conditions exist:

- The underlying physical file member is *updated* frequently
- The logical file is *read* infrequently

Also, if a logical file with select/omit entries is used only in batch jobs (e.g., producing reports), the overhead of dynamic record selection may not be a serious issue, so DYNSLT may be appropriate.

Defining a New Record Format

So far we've looked at how a logical file can provide access to records in a particular sequence based on a keyed access path and how a logical file can select a subset of records from the underlying physical file. In most of these examples, the logical files have had the same record format as the underlying physical file; that is, the logical file has the same field definitions as the physical file. Another common use of logical files, however, is to provide access to a subset of the physical file's fields by defining a new record format.

To define a new logical file record format that has a subset of the underlying physical file's fields, you simply list the fields you want after the record-level entry. Figure 4.11 shows the DDS for the CUSTSHIP logical file based on the CUSTOMER physical file, but having only the customer ID and address fields in the record format.

Notice how nothing is required except the field names — all field attributes are the same as in the physical file. When an HLL program reads a record from this logical file, DB2/400 copies, or **maps**, the data from the corresponding field in the physical file record into its location in the logical file record format. When an HLL program inserts or updates a record in the logical file, the data is mapped back to the proper locations in the physical file. On record insert operations, any field in the physical file record format that's not in the logical file record format is given a default value. The default value is the value specified on a DFT field-level entry in the DDS for the physical file or a DB2/400-determined default based on the field's data type: spaces for character fields, zero for numeric fields, or the current date and time for date, time, and timestamp fields. Figure 4.12 pictures the relationship between the logical file defined in Figure 4.11 and the underlying CUSTOMER physical file.

---

[10] DB2/400 doesn't create an internal index unless at least one key field is specified. Without an internal index, a logical file has no place to store entries for selected records, so dynamic record selection is necessary.

Figure 4.11
CUSTSHIP Logical File
with Subset of Fields from
CUSTOMER Physical File

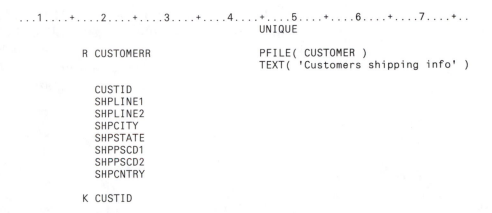

```
...1....+....2....+....3....+....4....+....5....+....6....+....7....+..
                                       UNIQUE

         R CUSTOMERR                   PFILE( CUSTOMER )
                                       TEXT( 'Customers shipping info' )

           CUSTID
           SHPLINE1
           SHPLINE2
           SHPCITY
           SHPSTATE
           SHPPSCD1
           SHPPSCD2
           SHPCNTRY

         K CUSTID
```

Figure 4.12
Mapping Between
CUSTSHIP Logical File
and CUSTOMER
Physical File

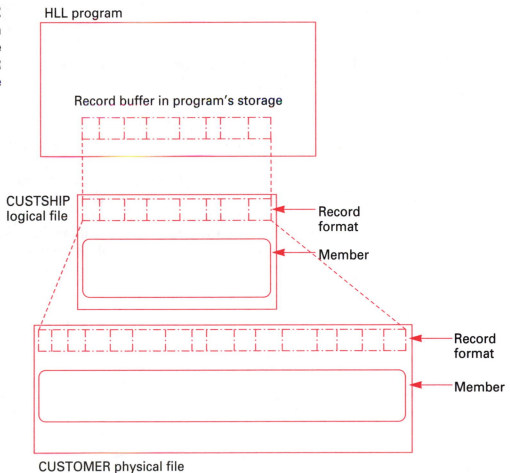

To a program reading the CUSTSHIP logical file, the logical file's record format appears just as if the file were a physical file with the same fields as the logical file — there aren't any "gaps" between fields or any other anomalies in the logical file's record layout. You can reorder fields in a logical file record format, or rename them, as shown in Figure 4.13.

Figure 4.13
Reordering and Renaming Fields in a Logical File Record Format

```
...1....+....2....+....3....+....4....+....5....+....6....+....7....
                                  UNIQUE

       R CUSTR                    PFILE( CUSTOMER )
                                  TEXT( 'Customer shipping info +
                                        for RPG/400' )

         CSSTRT                   RENAME( SHPLINE2 )
         CSCITY                   RENAME( SHPCITY )
         CSST                     RENAME( SHPSTATE )
         CSZIP                    RENAME( SHPPSCD1 )
         CSCRRT                   RENAME( SHPPSCD2 )
         CSATTN                   RENAME( SHPLINE1 )
         CSCNRY                   RENAME( SHPCNTRY )
         CUSTID

       K CUSTID
```

In this example, the fields are renamed to meet the six-character length restriction of RPG/400 and have been given a common prefix (CS) to help ensure unique field names within any RPG/400 program that uses the logical file.[11]

You can also change the attributes of a logical file field, including data type, length, decimal positions, and those field-level keywords listed in Figure 4.6. The rules for overriding attributes are the same as described for field referencing in Chapter 3. Generally it's not a good idea to change attributes, except perhaps in read-only logical files used to map logical file data to a format that's more convenient for display or printing. Among the problems you can encounter is unexpected truncation (e.g., when a logical file shortens or lengthens a field). In some cases, you may have to change a field's data type — either to meet the requirements of an existing HLL program; so you can

---

[11] This renaming technique is an excellent way to bridge between RPG/400 — which requires six-character names, two of which should be a unique prefix — and RPG IV, for which eight characters is the recommended maximum, and no prefix is needed as part of the field name. If you have an existing physical file that has short names because it was used by RPG/400 applications and you are now using RPG IV, you can replace it with a new physical file that has long names and create a new logical file that corresponds to the old physical file, using RENAME to associate the old field names with the new field names. RPG/400 programs that accessed the old physical file can access the new logical file, while new RPG IV programs can access the new physical file. When all the RPG/400 programs have been migrated to RPG IV, the logical file can be deleted. Note that the RPG IV requirements let you effectively double the length of the meaningful part of a field name (from four characters to eight), so creating new physical files with longer field names can be a significant improvement in the comprehensibility of database file definitions.

use the SST (substring) or CONCAT (concatenation) keywords; or to use as a join field. (The SST and CONCAT keywords are covered in Chapter 5, and join logical files are covered in Chapter 6.) If so, Figure 4.14 shows the allowable combinations, and Figure 4.15 shows an example of a logical file that combines several field mapping features and how the contents of this logical file's record format relates to the underlying physical file record format.

Figure 4.14
Allowable Data Type Overrides

Physical file field data types	Logical file data types
C (character)	C, H, S[1]
H (hex)	C, H, S[1]
S (zoned decimal)	C[1], H[1], S, P, B[2], F
P (packed decimal)	S, P, B[2], F
B (binary)	S[2], P[2], B[4], F[2]
F (floating point)	S, P, B[2], F
L (date)	S[3], L
T (time)	S[3], T
Z (timestamp)	L[5], T[5], Z

Notes:
[1] Number of characters (or hex bytes) must be equal to the number of digits.
[2] Binary field must have zero decimal positions.
[3] Do not specify a field length, the system calculates it.
[4] Both fields must have the same number of decimal positions.
[5] Field must have I (input-only) in position 38 (Usage column).

Field usage — whether a field can be used for input and output, input only, or neither input nor output — is another attribute that you can specify for a logical file field. All fields in a physical file can be used for both input and output. In non-join logical files, if you don't specify anything in the Usage column (position 38), fields are also input/output. By default, fields in join logical files are input only, since join logical files are always read-only.

If you specify an I in position 38, a logical file field is input only. A program can read data from this field, but even if the program changes the field's value, DB2/400 ignores the new value when the record is updated in the physical file. When a new record is inserted in a logical file, any physical file fields that correspond to input-only fields in the logical file are given the default value (as specified in the physical file definition, either explicitly or DB2/400-assigned). The primary purpose of input-only fields is to restrict updates to certain fields in logical files that are made available to end users through general-purpose file update utility programs.

Figure 4.15

A Logical File Record Format that Selects, Renames, Reorders, and Changes the Attributes of the Underlying Physical File's Fields

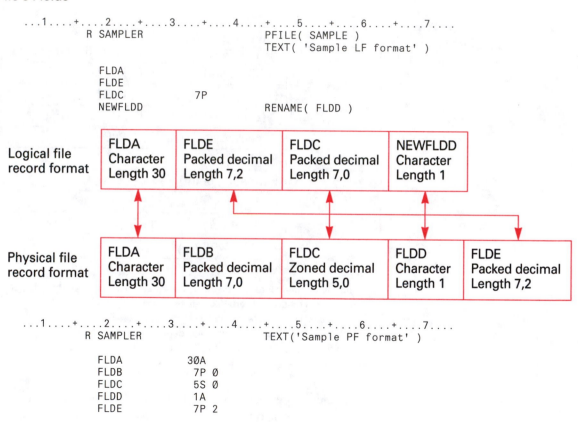

```
...1....+....2....+....3....+....4....+....5....+....6....+....7....
          R SAMPLER                         PFILE( SAMPLE )
                                            TEXT( 'Sample LF format' )

          FLDA
          FLDE
          FLDC           7P
          NEWFLDD                           RENAME( FLDD )
```

Logical file record format

| FLDA
Character
Length 30 | FLDE
Packed decimal
Length 7,2 | FLDC
Packed decimal
Length 7,0 | NEWFLDD
Character
Length 1 | |

Physical file record format

| FLDA
Character
Length 30 | FLDB
Packed decimal
Length 7,0 | FLDC
Zoned decimal
Length 5,0 | FLDD
Character
Length 1 | FLDE
Packed decimal
Length 7,2 |

```
...1....+....2....+....3....+....4....+....5....+....6....+....7....
          R SAMPLER                         TEXT('Sample PF format' )

          FLDA           30A
          FLDB           7P 0
          FLDC           5S 0
          FLDD           1A
          FLDE           7P 2
```

In general, creating new logical file formats can be very useful for read-only files that limit access to sensitive data or that simplify record layouts for use by end users with ad hoc reporting or analysis tools. In Chapters 5 and 6 we'll look at even more ways to take advantage of logical files to simplify data retrieval. To a lesser degree, specialized logical file formats can also provide access control for applications that update a file. However, in most real business applications, the rules that govern updates are complex enough to require program logic, in which case, the program itself limits the fields a user can update, even if internally the program reads the entire physical file record format.

The Create Logical File Command

Before you can create a logical file, all the physical files it encompasses must exist. In the simplest case, a logical file is created over a single physical file, and both the physical and logical files have just one member. In this situation, the access path for the logical file member encompasses the records in the one physical file member. In the first part of the chapter, we looked at an example of a simple CRTLF command that creates this type of logical file. Like physical files, however, logical files can have multiple members. Each logical file member can span one or multiple physical file members. A logical file member can even span several members in *different* physical files. The possibilities can get complex, so we'll work through several examples that demonstrate the alternatives. All examples are based on two physical files: SALE95 and SALE96, each of which has 12 members: JAN, FEB, . . ., DEC. As the members' names suggest, each member has the sales records for one month.

Example 1. One logical file member for each physical file member

Let's say we want a way to access the sales records by date, so we code logical file DDS with the appropriate key field. The first step after coding the DDS is to create the logical files, including the first member for each logical file:

```
CRTLF FILE( appdta/sale95date )
      SRCFILE( appsrc/qddssrc )
      MBR ( jan )
      DTAMBRS( ( sale95 jan ) )
      MAXMBRS( *nomax )

CRTLF FILE( appdta/sale96date )
      SRCFILE( appsrc/qddssrc )
      MBR ( jan )
      DTAMBRS( ( sale96 jan ) )
      MAXMBRS( *nomax )
```

The first command creates the SALE95DATE file and adds the JAN member to it. The DTAMBRS parameter specifies one or more physical file members. In this case, just one member is specified: the JAN member in the SALE95 physical file. A program that opens the JAN member of SALE95DATE will see the same records it would see if it opened the JAN member of SALE95 (assuming there are no select/omit specifications in the DDS for SALE95DATE). The second command creates the SALE96DATE logical file with a JAN member that includes records from the JAN member of the SALE96 physical file.

To add the remaining 22 members (one for each remaining month in 1995 and 1996), you enter an ADDLFM (Add Logical File Member) command for each member:

```
ADDLFM FILE( appdta/sale95date )
       MBR ( feb )
       DTAMBRS( ( sale95 feb ) )
. . .
ADDLFM FILE( appdta/sale96date )
       MBR ( dec )
       DTAMBRS( ( sale96 dec ) )
```

Figure 4.16 depicts the relationships among the members of the SALE95DATE and SALE95 files.

Figure 4.16

Each Logical File Member
Spans One Physical
File Member

SALE95DATE logical file

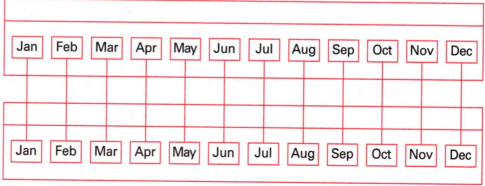

SALE95 physical file

Example 2. A logical file member that spans multiple physical file members
Now let's say we want four logical file members that contain all sales records for a quarter, in order by date. We can again use ADDLFM to add the desired members:

```
ADDLFM FILE( appdta/sale95date )
       MBR ( qtr1 )
       DTAMBRS( ( sale95 ( jan feb mar ) ) )
...
ADDLFM FILE( appdta/sale96date )
       MBR ( qtr4 )
       DTAMBRS( ( sale96 ( oct nov dec ) ) )
```

Notice how each DTAMBRS parameter now has a set of member names (enclosed in parentheses) instead of a single member name. A program that opens the QTR1 member of SALE95DATE sees all the records in the JAN, FEB, and MAR members of SALE95 — as if they were in a single physical file member. Figure 4.17 depicts the relationships among these members of the SALE95DATE and SALE95 files.

Figure 4.17

Each Logical File Member
Spans Three Physical
File Members

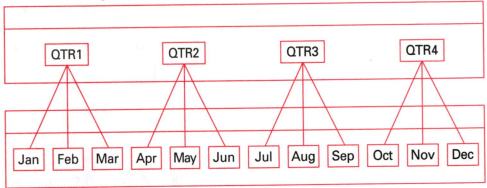

SALE95DATE logical file

SALE95 physical file

Example 3. A logical file member that spans all the members in a physical file
We can even create logical file members that contain *all* sales records for a
particular year:

```
ADDLFM FILE( appdta/sale95date )
       MBR ( year )
       DTAMBRS( *all )

ADDLFM FILE( appdta/sale96date )
       MBR ( year )
       DTAMBRS( *all )
```

Specifying *ALL on the DTAMBRS parameter means you want the log-
ical file member to encompass all members in all underlying physical file(s).
Figure 4.18 depicts the relationships between the YEAR member in
SALE95DATE and the SALE95 members.

Figure 4.18

A Logical File Member
that Spans All Physical
File Members

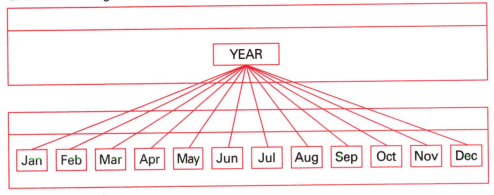

SALE95DATE logical file

SALE95 physical file

Example 4. A logical file member that spans members in *two* physical files
So far, we've looked at logical files that are based on a single physical file. You can list additional files on the record-level PFILE entry to span multiple files.[12] For example, the following DDS defines a logical file that's based on both SALE95 and SALE96 physical files, has the same record format as the underlying physical files, and has a keyed access path based on the SALDATE field:

```
...1....+....2....+....3....+....4....+....5....+....6....+..
          R SALER                          PFILE( SALE95 SALE96 )
                                           TEXT( 'Sales by date' )


          K SALDATE
```

All files specified in the PFILE entry must contain all fields included in the record format. (In this example, SALE95 and SALE96 must have identical formats because the logical file's SALER record format includes all fields of the underlying physical files.)

The CRTLF command has a default value of *ALL for the DTAMBRS parameter, so we might want to first create this logical file without any members:

```
CRTLF FILE( appdta/sale9596dt )
      SRCFILE( appsrc/qddssrc )
      MBR ( *none )
      MAXMBRS( *nomax )
```

To add a member that has the *combined* records for the first quarter, we use

```
ADDLFM FILE( appdta/sale9596dt )
       MBR ( qtr1 )
       DTAMBRS( ( sale95 ( jan feb mar ) )
                ( sale96 ( jan feb mar ) ) )
```

Figure 4.19 shows the relationship between the members in SALE9596DT and the physical file members they span in SALE95 and SALE96.

Look over the syntax of this example's DTAMBRS parameter carefully. In CL, parentheses are used to group lists of values. The DTAMBRS parameter accepts a list of one or more two-element sublists. Each sublist's first element is a file name, and the second element is a list of one or more member names. So in this example, there are two sublists (one on each line), and each sublist is enclosed in a matching pair of parentheses. The first element of the first sublist is sale95 and the second element is (jan feb mar), another list enclosed in parentheses. When a list has only one element, you

---

[12] Although you can access a logical file that spans multiple physical files in RPG/400, RPG IV, and COBOL/400, you can't name this type of file on an RPG F-spec or a COBOL/400 SELECT statement. This restriction exists because DB2/400 actually creates one record format for each file named on the PFILE entry. All of these record formats have the same name, which isn't allowed in RPG or COBOL/400. The workaround is simple: on the RPG F-spec or COBOL/400 SELECT, specify a physical file (or logical file that spans one physical file) with the same format as the logical file you want to access and use an OVRDBF command at runtime to associate the program's internal file name with the logical file that spans multiple physical files.

Figure 4.19

Logical File Members that Span Members in Two Physical Files

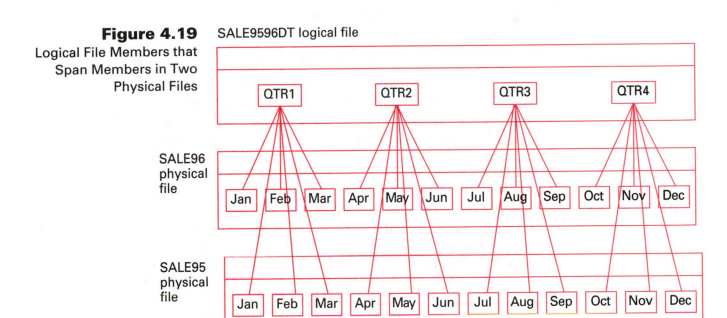

don't usually need the enclosing parentheses, which is why some of the earlier examples had a simpler form. Don't worry too much about getting the number of parentheses right — the interactive prompting available for CL makes entering complex DTAMBRS values quite simple. The key thing is to understand the way you use the combination of the PFILE keyword in the DDS and the DTAMBRS parameter of the CRTLF command to define the scope of a logical file member. Note that any physical file you specify in the DTAMBRS parameter must also be in the PFILE keyword entry.[13]

Because many logical files include key fields, it's important to consider the performance impact of DB2/400's keeping current the internal indexes that are part of keyed access paths as records are inserted, deleted, or changed in physical files. DB2/400 is fairly efficient at maintaining access paths, so you don't generally need to worry if you have five or fewer keyed access paths over an active physical file or 10 to 20 over a less frequently modified file.[14] And, for physical files that are primarily read-only, with little

---

[13] A common mistake is to try to add a new logical file member that includes records from a physical file with an identical record format as the (different) physical file specified on the logical file's PFILE entry. Although this might seem reasonable, DDS doesn't allow it. You can, however specify multiple physical files on a PFILE entry and then add a logical file member that refers to only *one* of these files in the DTAMBRS parameter.

[14] Keep in mind that these are very approximate rules-of-thumb. Tuning a database implementation requires an in-depth knowledge of the operating characteristics of the particular release of DB2/400 you're using (performance characteristics can change with each new release), and careful measurement. See also footnote 9, earlier in this chapter.

update activity, there's not likely to be any significant overhead from having numerous keyed access paths. However, for actively updated physical files, you want to avoid an excessive amount of system access path maintenance, or you may slow down your application's database updates.

If the number of keyed access paths over a physical file starts to become a concern, you can — in some cases — use the CRTPF and CRTLF commands' MAINT parameter to adjust how DB2/400 manages keyed access paths. The MAINT parameter determines when DB2/400 actually makes changes to a non-unique keyed access path. For unique keyed access paths (i.e., the file's DDS contains the UNIQUE file-level keyword), you must use MAINT(*IMMED), the CRTPF and CRTLF command default. **Immediate maintenance** of keyed access paths means DB2/400 updates the access path simultaneously with the record insert, delete, or update. Immediate maintenance is necessary for unique keys because DB2/400 must check the access path for a duplicate key before an insert or update can be permitted. Also, no matter which MAINT value you specify, a keyed access path is always maintained immediately when one or more programs open the associated file member. Obviously, the access path must be current while it's in use.

For physical and logical files with non-unique keyed access paths, you can specify *REBLD (rebuild) or *DLY (delayed) instead of *IMMED for the MAINT parameter. With **rebuild maintenance**, DB2/400 does no access path updating while the file is unopened. At the time a program opens the file, DB2/400 creates the entire access path. Rebuilding an access path can take noticeable time even for moderate-sized files, so it's not a good idea for most interactive programs. But for logical files that are used infrequently and in batch jobs, *REBLD can be a good choice.

With **delayed maintenance**, DB2/400 logs key field changes (including additions and deletions) while the file is unopened, but doesn't actually update the access path. When the file is opened, DB2/400 applies the changes in the log to the access path to bring it up to date. If more than about 10 percent of the key fields are changed before an open, DB2/400 temporarily quits logging changes and does a complete rebuild on the next open. Generally, *DLY is appropriate when the number of key field changes between successive file opens is relatively small. If you know that more than 10 percent of the records' key values will typically be changed between file opens, it's better to use *REBLD instead of *DLY.

The CRTLF command has a number of other parameters, which are described fully in Appendix A. Figure 4.20 lists some of the most commonly used parameters and their default values.

You can also work with logical files using other commands, many of which are listed in Figure 4.21. When you want to change the definition of a logical file, you can just delete it with the DLTF (Delete File) command, modify the DDS, and recompile it. Because deleting a logical file doesn't affect the actual data, you don't need to go through any backup and copy steps as you do when you re-create a physical file. However, if you want to

Figure 4.20
Commonly Used CRTLF
Command Parameters
and Defaults

Parameter	Purpose	Default
FILE	Logical file to be created	
SRCFILE	Source file containing DDS	*LIBL/QDDSSRC
SRCMBR	Source member	*FILE
MBR	Name of added file member	*FILE
DTAMBRS	Physical file members included in member specified in MBR	*ALL
MAXMBRS	Maximum members allowed	1
MAINT	For files with key field(s) — how DB2/400 maintains the access path when the file's not open	*IMMED
AUT	Allow public authority	*LIBCRTAUT
TEXT	Description of file	*SRCMBRTXT

Figure 4.21
Commonly Used Logical
File Commands

Command	Full command name	Notes
ADDLFM	Add Logical File Member	
CHGLF	Change Logical File	
CHGLFM	Change Logical File Member	
CPYF	Copy File	
CRTLF	Create Logical File	
DLTF	Delete File	
DSDBR	Display Database Relations	Displays the names of physical and logical files that are dependent on a specified file
DSPFD	Display File Description	
DSPFFD	Display File Field Description	
MOVOBJ	Move Object	Move logical file from one library to another
OVRDBF	Override with Database File	
RMVM	Remove Member	
RNMM	Rename Member	
RNMOBJ	Rename Object	Renames logical file
WRKF	Work with Files	

re-create a physical file that has logical files defined over it, you must first delete *all* the dependent logical files.[15] After the physical file is re-created, you then must re-create all the logical files. This may sound like unnecessary work, but when you delete a physical file, there's nothing left for DB2/400 to base the dependent logical files on, and after the physical file is re-created, DB2/400 must reprocess all the new data (even if it's just copied from a back-up of the previous version of the physical file) to create the access paths.[16] Also, as explained in Chapter 2, IBM enhanced the CHGPF (Change Physical File) command in releases V3R2 and V3R6 of OS/400 to do these steps automatically. With the enhanced CHGPF command, changing a physical file is much easier.

Coding Suggestions

• Use a clear, consistent approach to naming logical files. Begin all logical file names with consistent two-, three-, or four-character abbreviations for the underlying physical file(s).

    Naming logical files is a bit more challenging than naming physical files because there may be numerous logical files for a single physical file, making it harder to form a unique, descriptive, 10-character name for every logical file. For example, with a CUSTOMER physical file, you may have (among others) a CUSTNAME logical file that has a keyed access path over the customer name and a CUSTCTYNAM logical file the has a keyed access path over the city and the customer name. For logical files whose only purpose is to provide an alternative keyed access path, two- or three-part names are fairly easy to form using the guidelines presented in Chapter 3.

    Note that with RPG IV, COBOL/400, and other AS/400 HLLs (but not RPG/400), it's fine to use the full 10 characters for logical file names — rather than the recommended 9-character limit for physical files — because the record format name should generally be the same as the underlying physical file. For logical files, you don't need to limit the file name to 9 characters to allow an R to be appended to form the record format name.

    Naming gets more difficult for logical files that have complex select/omit specifications, field-mapping, and key fields. Consider a logical file that selects only customers in Richmond who have a high credit rating and that uses customer name as the key field. While CUSTOMER-IN-RICHMOND-WITH-HIGH-CREDIT-BY-NAME would be a fully descriptive file name, it's too long for a DB2/400 file. Obviously, you have to abbreviate, and you may also have to omit some important terms from the name. A reasonable name for this logical file might be CSRCHCRDNM

---

[15] The DSPDBR (Display Database Relations) command displays all the logical files that are dependent on a physical file. For example, DSPDBR FILE(APPDTA/SALE95) shows all the logical files that reference SALE95.

[16] Several AS/400 software vendors market tools to automate the rebuilding of logical files when a physical file is changed.

(CS+RCH+CRD+NM). Another choice might be: CUSTRICH01 (CUST+RICH+01). While this second alternative doesn't convey all the important aspects of the file's contents, it is quickly recognizable as a file that has customers from Richmond. The 01 suffix is a meaningless way to guarantee a unique name; but using 01 through 99 leaves you two four-letter terms to convey the underlying physical file (<u>CUST</u>OMER) and the major category in which to place this particular file (customers in <u>RICH</u>mond). You can see the importance of having standard abbreviations and deciding in advance what approach you take to naming logical files.

- Logical file record format names must be identical to the underlying physical file format name[17] when you don't specify explicit fields. Using the same format name as the physical file also works well when you specify explicit fields.

  For physical files that have the same format and are used to group records (e.g., the SALE95 and SALE96 examples), use the base part of the file name plus R (e.g., SALER) for all the physical files' record format names. This practice lets you reference any of the files from the same HLL program (using an OVRDBF command) and simplifies the definition of logical files that span multiple physical files.

- Don't use the RENAME field-level entry, unless there's a DDS or HLL requirement to rename a physical file field. (*Do* consider using RENAME to meet RPG/400 name restrictions, as discussed in footnote 11.)

- Generally, don't change field attributes. Be especially careful about changing length or decimal positions in logical files that may be used for file updating.

- Create logical files in the same library as the underlying physical file(s) they reference. This greatly simplifies file management, including save/restore operations.

- Use the UNIQUE file-level keyword if, and only if, you need to prevent duplicate key values for the logical file's key.

- Code select/omit specifications in the most efficient order that still provides the proper record selection.

- Assess how a logical file with select/omit specifications will be used to determine whether to code DYNSLT.

- Assess how a logical file with a non-unique keyed access path will be used to determine which type of access path maintenance to use (*IMMED, *DLY, or *REBLD).

---

[17] In the case of a PFILE that specifies multiple physical files, the logical file record format name must be the same as the first physical file's record format name.

Chapter Summary

Logical files let you access physical file data in alternative ways. You direct an HLL program to a specific file member (either physical or logical) by using the OVRDBF command before you open the file in the program. DB2/400 provides the necessary control structures and access routines to enable the same program to work with different files.

You can use key field entries in logical file DDS to create new keyed access paths so records can be accessed in a different order. Alternatively, you can use the REFACCPTH file-level keyword to define a logical file's access path based on an existing physical or logical file's access path.

You can specify select/omit entries so a logical file includes a subset of the records in a physical file. Record selection can be based on simple or compound AND/OR conditions that compare a field's value against a literal or another field. You can specify whether DB2/400 should maintain access path entries only for selected records or should perform dynamic record selection when a program reads a file with select/omit entries.

A logical file can have either the same record format as the physical file upon which it's based or an explicitly defined record format. With an explicitly defined record format, you can select a subset of the physical file's fields, rename fields, reorder them in the record layout, or change field attributes, such as data type and length.

A logical file member can include the records from a single physical file member, from multiple members in the same physical file, or from members in multiple physical files. The PFILE keyword on the logical file record format specification and the CRTLF command's DTAMBRS parameter determine the physical file members that are included in a logical file member.

DB2/400 maintains all unique keyed access paths and the access paths of open files immediately — that is, the access path is updated at the time records are inserted, deleted, or changed. You can use the CRTLF command's MAINT parameter to specify delayed or rebuild access path maintenance for non-unique keyed access paths.

Key Terms

delayed access path
    maintenance
dynamic record selection
field mapping
field usage

immediate access path
    maintenance
rebuild access path
    maintenance
select/omit

shared access path
sort

Exercises

1. Code the DDS for a logical file that can be used to process the CUSTOMER file (Figure 2.5) in order by state (major key) and city (minor key). The logical file record format should be the same as the physical file's.

2. Code the CRTLF command to create the logical file you defined in Exercise 1. Use appropriate command parameters to also add a member with the same name as the logical file and span the CUSTOMER member in the CUSTOMER physical file.

3. Code the DDS for a logical file that contains a subset of the records in the CUSTOMER file. Selected records should satisfy the following conditions:

    Status must not be X. Also, either Postal Code 1 must be 23225, 23227, or 23229, or the credit limit must be between 500 and 1000 (inclusive). The logical file record format and key specifications should be the same as the physical file's. Use the most efficient selection specifications, given the following average distributions:

    • 45 percent of customers have a status X

    • 70 percent of customers have 23227 as their Postal Code 1
    12 percent of customers have 23225 as their Postal Code 1
    3 percent of customers have 23229 as their Postal Code 1

    • 60 percent of customers have a credit limit less than 500

    10 percent of customers have a credit limit over 1000

4. Describe two advantages that the COMP keyword has over RANGE and VALUES. What advantages, if any, do RANGE and VALUES have over COMP?

5. Modify the DDS you created for Exercise 3 to use dynamic record selection.

6. Describe a record selection criteria for the CUSTOMER file that could not be specified using DDS. How could DDS syntax be changed to allow more flexible selection criteria?

7. Use field selection and mapping to code the DDS for a logical file that simplifies the printing of customer address labels using labels that are 5 lines by 60 columns. Draw the layout of where the logical file fields will be put on each label.

8. Use the field usage attribute to code the DDS for a logical file that contains all the fields in the CUSTOMER physical file but allows output only to the address-related fields. The file should have the same access path as the file created in Exercises 1 and 2.

9. Code the DDS for a logical file that has the same record layout and access path as the CUSTOMER physical file but that has file, record format, and field names that are appropriate for use with RPG/400 programs.

Exercises Continued

Exercises continued

10. Using the SALE95 and SALE96 physical files and the SALE95DATE and SALE9596DT logical files described in "The Create Logical File Command" section, show the commands to add the following logical file members:

   - To SALE95DATE, a member that spans the summer months: June, July, and August of 1995

   - To SALE9596DT, a member that spans the summer months: June, July, and August of 1995 and 1996

11. Revise the CRTLF command used in Exercise 2 to create the logical file with delayed access path maintenance.

12. Explain why DB2/400 requires immediate access path maintenance for unique keyed access paths.

13. Why do you think DB2/400 quits logging access path changes for delayed maintenance when the number of changes reaches approximately 10 percent of the number of records in the file?

14. Describe two alternative naming strategies for logical files, in addition to those suggested in this chapter. List the advantages and disadvantages of each method.

Chapter 5

Logical Files: Advanced Features

Chapter Overview

This chapter continues the discussion of non-join logical files begun in Chapter 4. First, we look at ways to define new, derived fields in a logical file's record format. Then we examine logical files that have multiple record formats.

Deriving New Fields

Chapter 4 described how DB2/400 lets you map the underlying data in a physical file to a logical file's record format. In the simplest case, a logical file's record format is identical to the record format of the underlying physical file. But, we also saw how a logical file format could specify the following transformations:

- Drop some fields, so they don't appear in the logical file format
- Change the order of fields within the format
- Rename fields
- Change a field's data type, length, and/or decimal positions
- Change a field's usage from input/output to input only
- Change keyword-specified attributes, such as COLHDG

There are several additional ways to map physical file fields to logical file fields: translating character data, extracting a substring from a field, and concatenating fields.

Translating Character Field Data

Occasionally a program may require character input data in a different form from that stored in the physical file — for example, a program may work properly only on uppercase values (e.g. "RICHMOND") even though the physical file stores the values in mixed case (e.g., "Richmond"). The TRNTBL field-level keyword specifies a **translate table** (an OS/400 *TBL object type) that DB2/400 uses on file read operations when it maps the field data from a physical file to the corresponding logical file field. Each character in the physical file's field value is looked up in the translate table, and the corresponding character specified in the table is put in the logical file's field value. The following field definition uses the IBM-supplied QSYSTRNTBL translate table, which maps all lowercase letters to uppercase:

```
...2....+....3....+....4....+....5....+....6....+....7..
  SHPCITY              I      TRNTBL( QSYS/QSYSTRNTBL )
```

The TRNTBL keyword is valid only for input usage — it provides a *one-way* translation feature. Also, if you want to use translated data (e.g., all upper-case) only to sequence records in a keyed access path and want to read the data in its untranslated form, the proper approach is to use the ALTSEQ file-level keyword to specify a translate table for the file's access path. Appendix A provides information about the ALTSEQ keyword.

IBM supplies many translate tables in the QSYS and QUSRSYS libraries. Entering the following command displays a list of these tables:

```
DSPOBJD OBJ( *ALL ) OBJTYPE( *TBL )
```

To create your own translation table, use the CRTTBL (Create Table) command and a source file member that defines the table, as described in the online help for the CRTTBL command.

Substring Fields

The SST (substring) keyword provides another way to derive an input-only field. A **substring** is a part of a string (string is another term for the contents of a character field). When you define a new field as a substring of an existing field, DB2/400 copies only the specified part of the underlying field's contents into the derived field on an input operation. Suppose the CUSTOMER physical file has a PHNVOICE field that stores U.S. telephone numbers as a left-justified character value with the format 541-345-7271 (i.e., area code, dash, prefix (exchange), dash, individual number). The following specification defines a logical file field with only the prefix part of the phone number:

```
...2....+....3....+....4....+....5....+....6....+....7..
  PFXVOICE             I      SST( PHNVOICE 5 3 )
```

The syntax of the SST keyword is

SST(*field-name starting-position length*)

The first argument for the SST keyword is the name of a field from which the substring is extracted. The field must exist in the underlying physical file or be defined earlier in the same logical file record format. This field must be a character, hexadecimal, or zoned decimal data type. The SST keyword also requires a starting position for the substring (5, in this example) and takes an optional third argument that specifies the length (3, in this example). The starting position is relative to the beginning of the field; that is, the first character of the field has starting position 1. Alternatively, you can specify the derived field's length in the Length column (positions 30–34):

```
...2....+....3....+....4....+....5....+....6....+....7..
  PFXVOICE        3    I      SST( PHNVOICE 5 )
```

The data type of a field derived using the SST keyword is character, unless the field specified in the SST entry is hexadecimal, in which case the derived field is hexadecimal also. The derived field's length is the specified length of the substring.

You can use a two-step approach to derive a character field from a substring of the digits in a packed decimal field. If the PHNVOICE field in the physical file were, for example, an 11-digit packed decimal field that stores phone numbers as 05413457271, the following specifications would create a derived field with only the prefix part of the phone number:

```
...2....+....3....+....4....+....5....+....6....+....7..
  PHNVOICE        S
  PFXVOICE        I       SST( PHNVOICE 5 3 )
```

The first statement maps the packed-decimal physical-file field to a zoned-decimal logical-file field, which is then used as the basis for the substring specified in the second statement. When the DDS compiler searches for the field specified in the SST entry, it first checks in the same logical file record format definition for a prior field-level entry with that field name; then the compiler checks the physical file(s) specified in the PFILE[1] keyword on the record-level entry.

You can use substring fields as key fields and on select/omit specifications. These two capabilities can be helpful when you're faced with an existing field that has some part that needs to be used for sequencing or record selection. But don't go overboard in using substring fields in keys or for record selection when you design new files. Generally, you should define a separate field for any application element that'll be used in keys or record selection.

Concatenated Fields

Whereas the SST keyword lets you decompose an existing field to derive a new field, the CONCAT keyword lets you **concatenate**, or put together, two or more fields to form a new field. The primary purpose of this feature is to derive composite fields that can be used by end-user query and reporting utilities. Here's an example of concatenating three separate employee name fields to form one longer field with the entire name in it:

```
...2....+....3....+....4....+....5....+....6....+....7..
  FULLNAME                CONCAT( FSTNAM MDLINL LSTNAM )
```

If the lengths of the underlying fields are

FSTNAM	20
MDLINL	1
LSTNAM	30

the resulting length of FULLNAME would be 51. The DDS CONCAT function is a fairly primitive capability — when you concatenate fields, DB2/400

---

[1] Or the JFILE entry for join logical files, which are discussed in Chapter 6.

doesn't remove excess blank characters or insert blanks between the component fields.

The data type of the derived field is determined by the concatenated fields' data type(s), according to these rules:

1. If any underlying field is hexadecimal, the derived field is hexadecimal.
2. Otherwise, if any underlying field is character, the derived field is character.
3. Otherwise, the derived field is zoned decimal.

You can't use numeric fields with decimal positions other than zero, floating point, date, time, or timestamp fields in a CONCAT entry. Also, the calculated length of the derived field must be less than or equal to 32,766 for character and hexadecimal fields and 31 for zoned-decimal fields.

A derived numeric field gets its sign (positive or negative) from the rightmost field specified in the CONCAT entry. There's a potential danger in concatenating numeric fields when any field except the rightmost may be negative. DB2/400 embeds the sign of these fields in the concatenated value, which results in invalid zoned decimal data if a negative sign occurs in any field except the rightmost. Although you can use HLL code to get around this problem, it really doesn't make sense to use DDS to concatenate fields for signed numeric values. Most uses of the CONCAT keyword are for character fields (e.g., that hold parts of a name) or for positive numeric fields that store elements of a date (e.g., year, month, day).

Like substring fields, concatenated fields can be used as key fields or in select/omit specifications. In most cases, however, you don't need to concatenate fields to use them for sequencing records (just specify a key that includes all the fields as key fields) or record selection (just use multiple select/omit specifications).

Unlike substring fields, concatenated fields can generally be used for output as well as input. However, if one of the underlying fields is null capable (i.e., has the ALWNULL entry), the derived field is input only.[2] When DB2/400 reads a record with a concatenated field and any underlying field for the derived field has the null value, the derived field is also null.

Because a program can use a concatenated field for output, the situation can arise where an underlying physical file field might be updated both directly and indirectly — via a concatenated field — through the same logical file record format. The following field definitions show how this could happen:

---

[2] The derived field is also input only if any of the underlying fields are variable-length character fields.

```
...2....+....3....+....4....+....5....+....6....+....7..
  FSTNAM
  MDLINL
  LSTNAM
  FULLNAME                        CONCAT( FSTNAM MDLINL LSTNAM )
```

When multiple logical file fields map to the same underlying physical file field, DB2/400 updates the physical file field from *all* the output-capable logical file fields in the order the fields are defined in the logical file record format. In this example, DB2/400 first uses the logical file's FSTNAM field to update the physical file's FSTNAM field, then DB2/400 uses part of the data from the FULLNAME field — even though this may be "old" data — to update the physical file's FSTNAM field. Thus, if a program puts a new value in the FSTNAM field and the first name part of the FULLNAME field isn't also changed, the *old* first name value from the FULLNAME field overwrites the change made to the FSTNAM field.

You can ensure that changes to the individual fields are the ones that change the corresponding physical file fields by specifying the logical file field definitions in the following order:

```
...2....+....3....+....4....+....5....+....6....+....7..
  FULLNAME                        CONCAT( FSTNAM MDLINL LSTNAM )
  FSTNAM
  MDLINL
  LSTNAM
```

In most cases, however, the better solution is to explicitly define the concatenated field as input only, regardless of the order in which you define the fields:

```
...2....+....3....+....4....+....5....+....6....+....7..
  FULLNAME              I        CONCAT( FSTNAM MDLINL LSTNAM )
  FSTNAM
  MDLINL
  LSTNAM
```

When you define the derived field as input only, DB2/400 does not copy back the field's contents to the underlying physical file fields.

Multiformat Logical Files

So far, all the files we've looked at have a *single* record format. Physical files always have just one record format. But logical files can have up to 32 different record formats within the same file. **Multiformat logical files** are not as common as single-format logical files and have become less useful since the introduction of join logical files, which are discussed in Chapter 6. Nevertheless, you may encounter this type of logical file in existing applications, so it's good to be familiar with them.

In multiformat files, there are two or more record-level entries (R in position 17), and each record-level entry begins the definition of a separate record format within the file. Each record format must have a unique name, and each record-level entry is followed by the same types of entries — field-level, key-level, and select/omit-level entries — that follow the record-format name in a single-format logical file. Figures 5.1 and 5.2 show the DDS for two physical files, AUTOLOAN and MORTGAGE, each of which holds information about a type of loan.

Figure 5.1
AUTOLOAN Physical File

```
...1....+....2....+....3....+....4....+....5....+....6....+....7....
                                  REF( FIELDDFN )

                                  UNIQUE

          R AUTOLOANR              TEXT( 'Auto loans' )
            LOANID    R
            CUSTID    R
            PRNAMT    R
            INTRATE   R
            TRMMONTH  R
            EFCDATE   R

          K LOANID
```

Figure 5.2
MORTGAGE Physical File

```
...1....+....2....+....3....+....4....+....5....+....6....+....7....
                                  REF( FIELDDFN )

                                  UNIQUE

          R MORTGAGER              TEXT( 'Mortgage loans' )
            LOANID    R
            CUSTID    R
            PRNAMT    R
            INTRATE   R
            TRMYEAR   R
            EFCDATE   R

          K LOANID
```

Figure 5.3 shows sample records from each physical file. Figure 5.4 shows the DDS for LOANCUST01, a multiformat logical file that contains records from both physical files.

Multiformat logical files must be keyed, and the key-level specifications determine the sequence of the records as they are drawn from different underlying files. In the LOANCUST01 file, the records are ordered by EFCDATE within CUSTID. In cases where records in different formats can have duplicate key values (as in LOANCUST01), the order of the record format definitions (in the DDS source) determines the sequence of records with duplicate keys. Records with the same record format and duplicate key values are sequenced according to the FIFO, LIFO, or FCFO keyword (if any) specified for the logical file.

Figure 5.3
Sample Records for
AUTOLOAN and
MORTGAGE Physical Files

AUTOLOAN

RRN	LOANID	CUSTID	PRNAMT	INTRATE	TRMMONTH	EFCDATE
1	2021	7970221	23000	10.50	60	1995-03-06
2	3022	9933607	16500	9.75	24	1995-07-30
3	2026	5150768	35250	9.25	30	1996-01-25
4	1025	2908761	17000	9.25	24	1996-03-11
5	2027	5150768	8000	11.50	36	1996-03-25
6	3030	7970221	26000	10.00	12	1995-11-21

MORTGAGE

RRN	LOANID	CUSTID	PRNAMT	INTRATE	TRMYEAR	EFCDATE
1	1098	5150768	225000	8.75	25	1996-02-29
2	2022	3200944	78500	9.00	15	1995-10-11
3	2023	2908761	123225	9.25	20	1996-04-01
4	3018	5150768	185000	8.25	30	1996-03-12
5	2024	9933607	94200	7.90	15	1995-04-06
6	3031	3023376	167000	8.50	25	1995-08-22

Figure 5.4
LOANCUST01 Logical File

```
    ...1....+....2....+....3....+....4....+....5....+....6....+....7....+...
         R AUTOLOANR                    PFILE( AUTOLOAN )
                                        TEXT( 'Auto loans by customer ID +
                                              and effective date' )

         K CUSTID
         K EFCDATE

*        -------------------------------------------------

         R MORTGAGER                    PFILE( MORTGAGE )
                                        TEXT( 'Mortgages by customer ID +
                                              and effective date' )

         K CUSTID
         K EFCDATE
```

Figure 5.5

Sequence of Records for
LOANCUST01 Logical File

With the physical file data shown in Figure 5.3, an HLL program reading the LOANCUST01 file sequentially by key would get the records in the sequence shown in Figure 5.5.

Record format	LOANID	CUSTID	PRNAMT	INTRATE	TRMMONTH or TRMYEAR	EFCDATE
AUTOLOANR	1025	2908761	17000	9.25	24	1996-03-11
MORTGAGER	2023	2908761	123225	9.25	20	1996-04-01
MORTGAGER	3031	3023376	167000	8.50	25	1995-08-22
MORTGAGER	2022	3200944	78500	9.00	15	1995-10-11
AUTOLOANR	2026	5150768	35250	9.25	30	1996-01-25
MORTGAGER	1098	5150768	225000	8.75	25	1996-02-29
MORTGAGER	3018	5150768	185000	8.25	30	1996-03-12
AUTOLOANR	2027	5150768	8000	11.50	36	1996-03-25
AUTOLOANR	2021	7970221	23000	10.50	60	1995-03-06
AUTOLOANR	3030	7970221	26000	10.00	12	1995-11-21
MORTGAGER	2024	9933607	94200	7.90	15	1995-04-06
AUTOLOANR	3022	9933607	16500	9.75	24	1995-07-30

At each relative key-field position in the key (i.e., the first-listed key field, the second-listed key field, and so on), the corresponding key fields in all record formats must have the same data type, length, decimal positions,[3] and access path keywords (e.g., DESCEND). This requirement is natural because DB2/400 uses a single internal index for all records in the logical file, and key value entries in an index must have the same structure. You don't have to have the same number of key fields for all record formats; any key fields present for one format but not for others are simply used to sequence records within the same format. Thus, a set of key field definitions such as the following would be valid:

RCDFMT1	**RCDFMT2**	**RCDFMT3**
KEYFLDA	KEYFLDA	KEYFLDA
KEYFLDB		KEYFLDB
KEYFLDC		

---

[3] Floating-point key fields can have different lengths and decimal positions but must have the same data type and precision.

For multiformat logical files, there's a special case for key field specifications that provides flexibility in the way records are sequenced. When you specify *NONE instead of a field name for a key-level entry, DB2/400 uses only key fields specified in key positions *before* the position of the first key field with *NONE to merge records from different formats. Key fields specified in key positions at or after the position of the first key field with *NONE are used to sequence records within the same format. The LOANCUST02 file defined in Figure 5.6 merges records from the AUTOLOAN and MORTGAGE physical files and sequences them by CUSTID. Within a CUSTID, however, all AUTOLOAN records appear before the MORTGAGE records for the same customer. Each customer's auto loans are sequenced by the number of months loan term and loan ID, while each customer's mortgage loans are sequenced by the number of years loan term and loan ID.

Figure 5.6

LOANCUST02 Logical File

```
...1....+....2....+....3....+....4....+....5....+....6....+....7....+...
          R AUTOLOANR                  PFILE( AUTOLOAN )
                                       TEXT( 'Auto loans by customer ID, +
                                              term length, and loan ID' )
          K CUSTID
          K *NONE
          K TRMMONTH                   DESCEND
          K LOANID

*         --------------------------------------------------------

          R MORTGAGER                  PFILE( MORTGAGE )
                                       TEXT( 'Mortgages by customer ID, +
                                              term length, and loan ID' )
          K CUSTID
          K *NONE
          K TRMYEAR                    DESCEND
          K LOANID
```

For this DDS to be valid, the TRMMONTH and TRMYEAR fields must have identical data type, length, and decimal positions. Note that both are specified with the DESCEND keyword.[4]

Figure 5.7 shows how the records from Figures 5.3 would be sequenced.

---

[4] Note that the logical file defined in Figure 5.6 does *not* sequence *all* loans for the same customer by the TRMMONTH and TRMYEAR fields. TRMMONTH is used only for sequencing auto loan records and TRMYEAR is used only for sequencing mortgage loans. The fact that TRMMONTH and TRMYEAR have the same data type, length, decimal positions, and order is a coincidence that lets us code them both in the second key field position. The next example shows a different case.

Figure 5.7
Sequence of Records for
LOANCUST02 Logical File

Record format	LOANID	CUSTID	PRNAMT	INTRATE	TRMMONTH or TRMYEAR	EFCDATE
AUTOLOANR	1025	2908761	17000	9.25	24	1996-03-11
MORTGAGER	2023	2908761	123225	9.25	20	1996-04-01
MORTGAGER	3031	3023376	167000	8.50	25	1995-08-22
MORTGAGER	2022	3200944	78500	9.00	15	1995-10-11
AUTOLOANR	2027	5150768	8000	11.50	36	1996-03-25
AUTOLOANR	2026	5150768	35250	9.25	30	1996-01-25
MORTGAGER	3018	5150768	185000	8.25	30	1996-03-12
MORTGAGER	1098	5150768	225000	8.75	25	1996-02-29
AUTOLOANR	2021	7970221	23000	10.50	60	1995-03-06
AUTOLOANR	3030	7970221	26000	10.00	12	1995-11-21
AUTOLOANR	3022	9933607	16500	9.75	24	1995-07-30
MORTGAGER	2024	9933607	94200	7.90	15	1995-04-06

You can get quite tricky with the *NONE special value. For example, if fields TRMMONTH and TRMYEAR were different lengths, you could use the DDS shown in Figure 5.8 to create a valid logical file.

DB2/400 treats any key specification with *NONE as compatible with any other key field, no matter what the key field's attributes. Thus, the two *NONE key specifications for the MORTGAGER record format essentially shift the "real" key fields beyond the last key field in the AUTOLOANR record format. The record sequence for the file defined in Figure 5.8 is identical to the sequence for the file defined in Figure 5.6.

To create multiformat logical files, you use the same CRTLF command that you use for single-format logical files. If the AUTOLOAN and MORTGAGE physical files each have a single member, the following command creates the LOANCUST01 file with a single member:

```
CRTLF FILE( appdta/loancust01 )
      SRCFILE( appsrc/qddssrc )
```

The command options for spanning multiple members that are available for single-format logical files (discussed in Chapter 4) are also available for multiformat logical files.

The most common use of multiformat logical files is for report programs. Because a multiformat logical file can merge different types of

Figure 5.8

Alternate LOANCUST02
Logical File

```
...1....+....2....+....3....+....4....+....5....+....6....+....7....+...
          R AUTOLOANR                    PFILE( AUTOLOAN )
                                         TEXT( 'Auto loans by customer ID, +
                                               term length, and loan ID' )
          K CUSTID
          K TRMMONTH                     DESCEND
          K LOANID

 *        -------------------------------------------------

          R MORTGAGER                    PFILE( MORTGAGE )
                                         TEXT( 'Mortgages by customer ID, +
                                               term length, and loan ID' )
          K CUSTID
          K *NONE
          K *NONE
          K TRMYEAR                      DESCEND
          K LOANID
```

records from multiple files, an HLL program can use a simple sequential read of one file to get the records in the order needed for a report. AS/400 HLL I/O facilities return the record format name to the program when it reads a multiformat logical file, so the program knows which type of record has been read. In many cases, however, join logical files (which the next chapter covers) provide a simpler alternative to multiformat files for report programs. Also, although you can perform file updates through a multiformat logical file, it's almost always simpler — and in many cases, more efficient — to handle updates by accessing multiple physical files or single-format logical files in an HLL program, rather than using a multiformat logical file. Chapter 7 looks at some of the issues in using multiformat logical files in HLL programs.

Coding Suggestions

- Use the TRNTBL field-level keyword when an existing program needs uppercase or lowercase character data and the physical file field contains mixed-case data.

- Use the SST field-level keyword to extract part of a physical file field's contents. Typical uses are for date values stored as a single character or numeric field.

- Use the CONCAT field-level keyword to create a field that's the concatenation of several character fields.

- Generally specify input-only (I) usage for concatenated fields.

- Consider using a join logical file before creating a multiformat logical file.

- Generally, use separate single-format files (physical or logical) rather than a multiformat logical file for updating data.

- Use a key field specification with the *NONE special value to handle mismatched key fields in multiformat logical files.

Chapter Summary

DDS provides additional ways to derive logical file fields. The TRNTBL keyword specifies translation of character data on input fields. The SST keyword derives an input field from a substring of a character, hexadecimal, or zoned decimal field. The CONCAT keyword derives a field by concatenating two or more fields.

Although most logical files have a single record format, you can create a multiformat logical file with up to 32 distinct formats. Multiformat files must have a keyed access path, and key fields in corresponding positions of the file's key must be compatible. Join logical files may provide a better alternative than multiformat logical files for many input file requirements. Generally, file updates should be done through single-format physical or logical files rather than multiformat logical files.

Key Terms

concatenate
multiformat logical file
substring
translate table

Exercises

1. Code the definition for a logical file field that contains a customer's name (using the NAME field from the CUSTOMER file defined in Figure 2.5) in all uppercase characters, using the IBM-supplied QSYSTRNTBL translation table in library QSYS.

2. Use the SST keyword to code the definition for a logical file field that contains only the three-character area code for a telephone number. Assume the underlying physical file field, PHNVOICE, is a character field that stores phone numbers in the format 541-345-7271.

3. Code a logical file field that contains only the area code *without* using the SST keyword. Explain the advantages and disadvantages of each technique.

4. Code a logical file field that concatenates into a single field the city, state, and postal codes for a customer (using the SHPCITY, SHPSTATE, SHPPSCD1, and SHPPSCD2 fields from the CUSTOMER file defined in Figure 2.5).

Explain two problems you might have using this derived field in an HLL program. Can you think of any advantage to using a concatenated field in an HLL program?

5. Code the DDS for a multiformat logical file that merges records from the AUTOLOAN file in Figure 5.1 and the MORTGAGE file in Figure 5.2. The records should

   - sequence all records by effective date
   - within the same effective date, sequence all mortgage loans first, followed by all auto loans
   - within the same effective date, sequence mortgage loans by (ascending) loan ID, and auto loans by descending principal amount

Chapter 6

Join Logical Files

Chapter Overview

This chapter covers join logical files, a type of DB2/400 file that combines data from related records in different physical files into a single logical file record. Join logical files are a convenient way to let DB2/400 assemble data from various files for use in report programs or with end-user query utilities.

Basic Concepts

In Chapter 5, we saw how a multi-format logical file can be used to merge records from physical files with different record formats. Each record in a multi-format logical file gets its data from a *single* record in an underlying physical file, and — as the name "multi-format" indicates — different records in a multi-format logical file may have different record layouts. **Join logical files** (often referred to simply as **join files**) also let you combine data from physical files with different formats, but each record in a join logical file gets its data from *multiple* records in two or more underlying physical files.[1] And, unlike multi-format logical files, join logical files always have only one record format. One other difference between the two types of logical files is that join logical files are read only, while multi-format logical files are updatable. The primary purpose of join logical files is to combine related information from two or more files to simplify report programs and data retrieval through end-user query tools.

The easiest way to understand the idea of joining files is to look at a simple example that joins two files.[2] Suppose that our database has CUSTOMER and SALE physical files with the definitions shown (in part) in Figures 6.1 and 6.2 and that these files contain the records shown in Figures 6.3 and 6.4.

Note that both files have a CUSTID field. This field is the unique key for the CUSTOMER file; in the SALE file, CUSTID identifies the customer to whom the sale was made. Suppose that we want to produce the report shown in Figure 6.5.

---

[1] That is, the data from two or more physical file records is "joined" together in a single logical file record.

[2] In Chapter 9, we'll look at the concept of a join operation more formally.

Figure 6.1
CUSTOMER Physical File

```
...1....+....2....+....3....+....4....+....5....+....6....+..
                                    UNIQUE

          R CUSTOMERR                 TEXT( 'Customers' )

            CUSTID          7P Ø       TEXT( 'Customer ID' )
            NAME            3ØA        TEXT( 'Customer name' )

          K CUSTID
```

Figure 6.2
SALE Physical File

```
...1....+....2....+....3....+....4....+....5....+....6....+..
                                    UNIQUE

          R SALER                     TEXT( 'Sales' )

            ORDERID         7P Ø       TEXT( 'Order ID' )
            SALEDATE        L          TEXT( 'Sale date' )
            SALETOT         7P 2       TEXT( 'Sale total' )
            CUSTID          7P Ø       TEXT( 'Customer ID' )

          K ORDERID
```

Figure 6.3
Sample Records in
CUSTOMER Physical File

CUSTID	NAME
10001	Ajax Plumbing
10003	Picante Software
10008	Bubba's Grill

Figure 6.4
Sample Records in
SALE Physical File

ORDERID	SALEDATE	SALETOT	CUSTID
3678	1996-02-29	567.25	10003
3679	1996-03-06	1089.00	10001
3680	1996-03-06	376.50	10008
3681	1996-03-22	2012.90	10001
3682	1996-03-23	1233.00	10001
3683	1996-04-02	440.00	10003

We could write an HLL program that reads the CUSTOMER file sequentially by key and, for each CUSTOMER record, reads the SALE file to retrieve all records with the same customer ID as the current CUSTOMER record. But we don't really need to go to all this trouble — join logical files provide a simpler way to bring the necessary information into our program, letting DB2/400 do much of the work to match related records.

Figure 6.5

Report Showing
Combined Customer and
Sale Information

Customer ID	Customer name	Order ID	Sale date	Sale total
10001	Ajax Plumbing	3679	1996-03-06	1089.00
10001	Ajax Plumbing	3681	1996-03-22	2012.90
10001	Ajax Plumbing	3682	1996-03-23	1233.00
10003	Picante Software	3678	1996-02-29	567.25
10003	Picante Software	3683	1996-04-02	440.00
10008	Bubba's Grill	3680	1996-03-06	376.50

Figure 6.6 shows the DDS for the CUSTSALE join logical file, and Figure 6.7 shows how an HLL program would receive records if it read this file sequentially by key.

Each join logical file record has data from one CUSTOMER and one SALE record. In this example, there's exactly one CUSTSALE record for each SALE record, and data from a particular CUSTOMER record is repeated for each SALE record that has the same customer ID. Producing the report in Figure 6.5 is now quite simple because each row in the report is simply the formatted data from a single CUSTSALE record. Using a join logical file, it would be straightforward to produce this report without any HLL programming at all, using a report generator utility, such as IBM's Query/400 product.

Figure 6.6

CUSTSALE Join
Logical File

```
...1....+....2....+....3....+....4....+....5....+....6....+..
          R CUSTSALER                    JFILE( CUSTOMER SALE )
                                         TEXT( 'Sales with +
                                               customer info' )

          J                              JOIN( CUSTOMER SALE )
                                         JFLD( CUSTID CUSTID )
                                         JDUPSEQ( ORDERID )

            CUSTID                       JREF( CUSTOMER )
            NAME
            ORDERID
            SALEDATE
            SALETOT

          K CUSTID
```

Figure 6.7

Record Sequence for
CUSTSALE Join
Logical File

CUSTID	NAME	ORDERID	SALEDATE	SALETOT
10001	Ajax Plumbing	3679	1996-03-06	1089.00
10001	Ajax Plumbing	3681	1996-03-22	2012.90
10001	Ajax Plumbing	3682	1996-03-23	1233.00
10003	Picante Software	3678	1996-02-29	567.25
10003	Picante Software	3683	1996-04-02	440.00
10008	Bubba's Grill	3680	1996-03-06	376.50

The DDS for a join logical file has the following elements:

- One record-level statement (R in position 17) with a JFILE keyword entry that specifies all the physical files that the join logical file references.[3] You must specify at least 2, but no more than 32, files for the JFILE entry. The first physical file you list is known as the **primary file**, and all other files are known as **secondary files**.

- One or more **join specifications**. Each join specification begins with a source statement that has J in position 17 and a JOIN keyword entry that specifies exactly two physical files. A join specification ends when another source statement with J in position 17 or a field name in positions 19 - 28 is encountered.

    Each join specification has one or more JFLD (**join field**) keyword entries. Each JFLD entry lists a pair of fields. The first field is from the first file listed in the preceding JOIN entry, and the second JFLD field is from the second file listed in the preceding JOIN entry. DB2/400 "joins" records from the two physical files based on matching values for the join fields. Thus, for the join file defined in Figure 6.6, DB2/400 joins together all records in the CUSTOMER and SALE files that have identical CUSTID values.

    A join specification can also have a JDUPSEQ entry to specify how multiple matching records (from the second file listed in the JOIN entry) are sequenced. Later in this chapter, we'll take a detailed look at how you join files.

- One or more field-level entries. As with non-join logical files, these entries define the fields in the join logical file's record format. The fields can come from any of the files listed in the JFILE entry. If a field occurs in more than one file listed in the JFILE specification, a JREF field-level entry can be used to specify from which file the field is drawn.

- Optional key-field-level entries. A join file can have an arrival sequenced or keyed access path. Typically, join files have a keyed access path so the records can be processed in a particular sequence (e.g., for a report). All key fields must exist in the primary file (the first file specified on the JFILE entry).

- Optional select/omit specifications. As with non-join logical files, these entries define criteria for which records are included in the join logical file's access path. Select/omit specifications can reference fields in any of the files listed in the JFILE entry.

---

[3] In join logical files, the JFILE entry is used instead of the PFILE entry that's used in non-join logical files. The files listed in the JFILE must be physical files; you cannot join other logical files.

Figure 6.8 lists the DDS keywords that are valid for join logical files. Appendix A provides a more detailed description of each keyword. Note that join logical files also support all the display file related, field-level keywords: CHECK, CHKMSGID, COMP, CMP, EDTCDE, EDTWRD, RANGE, REFSHIFT, VALUES. See Chapters 2 and 3 for a discussion of these keywords.

Figure 6.8

Keywords for Join Logical Files

File level	Record level	Join level	Field level	Key field level	Select/Omit level
ALTSEQ	FORMAT	JDUPSEQ	ALIAS	ABSVAL	ALL
DYNSLT	JFILE	JFLD	COLHDG	DESCEND	CMP/COMP
FCFO	TEXT	JOIN	CONCAT	DIGIT	RANGE
FIFO			DATFMT	NOALTSEQ	VALUES
JDFTVAL			DATSEP	SIGNED	
LIFO			FLTPCN	UNSIGNED	
UNIQUE			JREF	ZONE	
			RENAME		
			SST		
			TEXT		
			TIMFMT		
			TIMSEP		
			TRNTBL		
			VARLEN		

How DB2/400 Creates Join File Records

Conceptually, the way DB2/400 returns records from a join logical file that has a primary file and one secondary file is fairly straightforward, and goes like this (in pseudocode):

While there are more records in the primary file
  Read the next record (either in arrival or keyed sequence) from the primary file
  While there are matching records in the secondary file
    Read the next matching record for the current primary file record
    Return the "joined" current primary and secondary file records
  End while
End while

Several situations can arise as DB2/400 processes records:

Case 1. A primary file record has *no* matching secondary file record.
If you do not specify the JDFTVAL file-level keyword, DB2/400 skips the unmatched primary file record entirely.

If you specify JDFTVAL, DB2/400 returns one record with the primary file record data and default values for all fields from the secondary file. The default value for a field is the value specified on the DFT keyword for its definition in the physical file, or the DB2/400 default of blanks for character and hexadecimal fields, zero for numeric fields, and the current date and time for date/time fields.

Case 2. A primary file record has exactly *one* matching secondary file record.
DB2/400 returns one logical file record that has data from the matching records.

Case 3. A primary file record has *two or more* matching secondary file records.
DB2/400 returns a logical file record for each matching secondary file record. Each of these records will have the same data for fields from the primary file.[4]

If you don't specify the JDUPSEQ keyword for the join specification, the sequence of records within the matching set is undetermined.

If you specify one or more JDUPSEQ entries for the join specification, these entries determine the sequence of records within the matching set. (JDUPSEQ is discussed in more detail below.)

Case 4. A secondary file record has *no* matching *primary file* record.
DB2/400 ignores the unmatched secondary file record.

Defining a Join Logical File

The valid file-level keywords for join logical files are the same as for non-join logical files, except REFACCPTH is not allowed and JDFTVAL is a keyword allowed *only* for join logical files. JDFTVAL takes no arguments and specifies that DB2/400 should return one record for unmatched primary file records, filling in all the fields from secondary file(s) with default values. If the following records exist for CUSTOMER and SALE:

[4] Because DB2/400 returns each successive record based on a match for the primary record's join field(s) value(s), there's one anomaly that can occur when a different job is updating the primary file while it's being read through a join file (DB2/400 allows this unless your job places a "lock" on the primary file to prevent concurrent updates). Suppose a primary file record has two or more matches in the secondary file, and your program has just read the first resulting join file record (i.e., DB2/400 has retrieved the primary file record and its first match in the secondary file). If another job changes the value in the join field of the current primary record, DB2/400 will use this *new* value to find the next match. To your program, it may appear that the primary record has inconsistent matching secondary records. This is a rare situation, but if you want to be sure it doesn't happen, you have to explicitly lock the underlying physical files while your program has the join logical file open.

CUSTOMER	
CUSTID	**NAME**
10001	Ajax Plumbing
10003	Picante Software
10008	Bubba's Grill

SALE			
ORDERID	**SALEDATE**	**SALETOT**	**CUSTID**
3678	1996-02-29	567.25	10003
3680	1996-03-06	376.50	10008
3683	1996-04-02	440.00	10003

the CUSTSALE records returned if you *don't* specify JDFTVAL would be

CUSTSALE				
CUSTID	**NAME**	**ORDERID**	**SALEDATE**	**SALETOT**
10003	Picante Software	3678	1996-02-29	567.25
10003	Picante Software	3683	1996-04-02	440.00
10008	Bubba's Grill	3680	1996-03-06	376.50

Note that there is no join logical file record for customer 10001, which has no matching sale record. The records returned if you *do* specify JDFTVAL in the CUSTSALE file would be

CUSTSALE				
CUSTID	**NAME**	**ORDERID**	**SALEDATE**	**SALETOT**
10001	Ajax Plumbing	0	1996-05-15 [5]	0
10003	Picante Software	3678	1996-02-29	567.25
10003	Picante Software	3683	1996-04-02	440.00
10008	Bubba's Grill	3680	1996-03-06	376.50

In this case, the join logical file contains a single record for customer ID 10001 with default values for the secondary file (SALE) fields.

---

[5] The system default value for a date field is the current date.

As mentioned earlier, a join file's record-level entry provides a record format name and lists the files to be joined in a JFILE entry. The JFILE entry lists 2 to 32 physical files. Recall that the first file is known as the primary file, and all other files are known as secondary files.

Following the record-level entry are one or more **join specifications**. Files are always joined in pairs, thus you need exactly the same number of join specifications as secondary files, which is one less than the number of files listed in the JFILE entry. Later we'll look at different ways to join three or more files. You start a join specification with a source statement that has a J in position 17 and a JOIN keyword. If only two files are being joined, these two files are listed in the JOIN entry in the same order they're listed in the preceding JFILE entry (on the record-level specification). Following the JOIN entry you code one or more JFLD entries to list the corresponding join fields that DB2/400 uses to match records in the two files being joined. If you have two or more JFLD statements for a join specification, their order doesn't matter, since they're used only for matching (not to sequence records).

The first field in a JFLD entry must be from the first file in the preceding JOIN entry and the second JFLD field must be from the second file in the preceding JOIN entry. The join fields can be included in or omitted from the join logical file's record format. In other words, you can join on a field that's not in the resulting logical file's records.

The two join fields can have the same or different names. The two fields must have the same data type, length, and decimal positions, except character fields can have different lengths (the shorter field is treated as if it were the same length as the longer field, and all the shorter field's values are padded with blanks to the length of the longer field). If you need to join on two fields that don't have the same data type, length, and decimal positions, you can derive an appropriate field in the join logical file record format and use it in the JFLD entry. For example, suppose you need to join on two fields: FLDA — a seven-digit packed decimal field with no decimal positions — and FLDB — a five-digit zoned decimal field with no decimal positions. The following JFLD entry and FLDB field definition in the join logical file provide the desired results:

```
...2....+....3....+....4....+....5....+....6....+....7..
                        JFLD( FLDA FLDB )

   ...
   FLDB            7P Ø
```

If you need to redefine a field so it can be used as a join field, yet you don't want it to be accessible to programs that read the join logical file, you can specify N (neither input nor output) for the field's usage (position 38).[6] The following example is similar to the preceding one, except the FLDB

---

[6] Note that because join logical files are read only, fields not defined with usage N are implicitly usage I. You can optionally code the I (although that's unnecessary clutter), but you *cannot* code a B (both input and output) usage.

join field won't appear in the record when read by an HLL program or database utility:

```
...2....+....3....+....4....+....5....+....6....+....7..
                            JFLD( FLDA FLDB )
   ...
  FLDB           7P 0N
```

You can use fields derived with RENAME, SST, or CONCAT as join fields.

If you want to retrieve records in a particular sequence when a record from the first file of the JOIN entry has more than one match in the second file of the JOIN entry, you must specify one or more JDUPSEQ entries for the join specification. Each set of JDUPSEQ entries serves as a sequencing "key" within matching records for that particular join. Be aware that JDUPSEQ entries *don't* specify a key that applies across multiple joins (if three or more files are joined) or across the whole set of join logical file records (for that purpose, an optional key for the entire file can be specified with key field-level entries). The following example shows how you would sequence join file records by the sale date and order ID within a single customer ID's set of records:

```
...2....+....3....+....4....+....5....+....6....+....7..
J                           JOIN( CUSTOMER SALE )
                            JFLD( CUSTID CUSTID )
                            JDUPSEQ( SALEDATE )
                            JDUPSEQ( ORDERID )
```

Naturally, any field you specify for JDUPSEQ must exist in the second file listed in the preceding JOIN entry and must not be one of the field(s) listed in a JFLD entry for this join specification. A JDUPSEQ field can be a field derived with the CONCAT or SST keywords. You can optionally specify *DESCEND as the second parameter for a JDUPSEQ entry, if you want descending sequence, as in

```
...2....+....3....+....4....+....5....+....6....+....7..
                            JDUPSEQ( SALEDATE *DESCEND )
```

The field-level entries in which you define the fields in the logical file's record format, follow the join specifications. The fields can come from any of the files listed in the JFILE entry. The rules for specifying fields are generally the same as for non-join logical files. There are a couple of additional considerations, however. One restriction is that fields specified as parameters for a particular CONCAT keyword must all come from the same physical file. The other issue is how to identify which file a field comes from if more than one file has a field with the same name.

In the case of duplicate names, you add the JREF keyword to the field specification. For example, to include the CUSTID field — which occurs in both the CUSTOMER and SALE files — in the CUSTSALE file shown in Figure 6.6, we had to code a JREF entry, as follows:

```
...2....+....3....+....4....+....5....+....6....+....7..
  CUSTID                    JREF( CUSTOMER )
```

The JREF parameter specifies the physical file name for the field. If the same physical file is specified more than once in the JFILE entry, as is the case when you join a file to itself, you specify the **relative file number** (the primary file is 1, the next file listed in the JFILE entry is 2, etc.).

Join logical files can have key-field entries, which follow the rules for non-join logical files (see Chapter 4 for a discussion of these rules) with the additional constraint that all key fields must come from the primary file. This often determines which of the joined files to list as the primary file. Key fields must also be in the join logical file's record format, and you cannot specify N usage for a key field.

Join logical files can also have select/omit specifications, which follow the rules for non-join logical files (again, see Chapter 4), including that any field used in a select/omit specification must be in the join logical file's record format and must not have N usage. In a number of cases, you must specify DYNSLT (dynamic record selection) for join logical files with select/omit specifications. Dynamic selection is required when JDFTVAL is specified or when select/omit fields come from more than one underlying physical file, and any one of the following is true (assuming FLDA and FLDB are in different physical files):

- The fields from different files are on the same select/omit specification

```
...2....+....3....+....4....+....5....+....6
S FLDA                     COMP( GE FLDB)
```

- Both select (S) and omit (O) specifications are used

```
...2....+....3....+....4....+....5....+....6
S FLDA                     COMP( GT 3 )
O FLDB                     COMP( LT 5 )
```

- Multiple select (S) specifications are OR'd

```
...2....+....3....+....4....+....5....+....6
S FLDA                     COMP( GT 3 )
S FLDB                     COMP( LT 5 )
```

- Multiple omit (O) specifications are AND'd

```
...2....+....3....+....4....+....5....+....6
O FLDA                     COMP( GT 3 )
  FLDB                     COMP( LT 5 )
```

All the cases listed above are ones in which DB2/400 can't determine whether to select or omit an access path entry based on current access path entries and the data in a record from just one physical file.

Joining a Physical File to Itself

You can list the same physical file more than once in the JFILE entry — that is, a physical file can be joined to itself. For example, if you had the EMPLOYEE physical file shown in Figure 6.9, you might join it to itself, as shown in

Figure 6.9
EMPLOYEE Physical File

```
...1....+....2....+....3....+....4....+....5....+....6....+....7....+.
                                      UNIQUE

          R EMPLOYEER                 TEXT( 'Employees' )

            EMPID         7P 0        TEXT( 'Employee ID' )
            LSTNAM        30A         TEXT( 'Employee last name' )
            MGREMPID   R              REFFLD( EMPID )
                                      TEXT( 'Employee''s manager ID' )

          K EMPID
```

Figure 6.10, to have the manager's name in the same join logical file record as the employee's name.

Figure 6.10
EMPMGR Join Logical File

```
...1....+....2....+....3....+....4....+....5....+....6....+....7
                                      JDFTVAL

          R EMPMGRR                   JFILE( EMPLOYEE EMPLOYEE )
                                      TEXT( 'Employee with +
                                            manager info' )

          J                           JOIN( 1 2 )
                                      JFLD( MGREMPID EMPID )

            EMPID                     JREF( 1 )
            LSTNAM                    JREF( 1 )
            MGREMPID                  JREF( 1 )
            MGRLSTNM                  RENAME( LSTNAM )
                                      JREF( 2 )

          K EMPID
```

With the EMPLOYEE file records shown in Figure 6.11, you'd see the EMPMGR file records shown in Figure 6.12.

Figure 6.11
Sample Records in
EMPLOYEE Physical File

EMPID	LSTNAM	MGREMPID
22712	Faubion	76503
65112	Pence	22712
76503	Gotchall	0
82001	Sotherby	22712

Figure 6.12
Sample Records in
EMPMGR Join Logical File

EMPID	LSTNAM	MGREMPID	MGRLSTNM
22712	Faubion	76503	Gotchall
65112	Pence	22712	Faubion
76503	Gotchall	0	*blank*
82001	Sotherby	22712	Faubion

Notice in Figure 6.10 how the JOIN keyword uses relative file numbers, rather than file names, because the file name (EMPLOYEE) could refer to either the file's use as the primary file or its use as the secondary file. All the join logical file's fields require a JREF entry (with a relative file number) because every field occurs in both the primary and secondary files. To include both the employees' and managers' names, we rename the LSTNAM field from the secondary file (which is used to provide the managers' records) as well as use JREF(2) to specify that the field comes from the secondary file.

You might at first think that it wouldn't matter which of the two uses (primary or secondary) of the EMPLOYEE file you use in most of the JREF entries — because the fields exist in both the primary and secondary files. But it *does* matter because the two joined records aren't (usually) the same record. For example, if you specified JREF(2) for the EMPID field, you'd get the employee ID of the *manager*, not the *employee*.

One final technique used in the DDS for the EMPMGR file is specifying JDFTVAL. Doing so ensures that we see all employees in the join logical file, even if the join file record has a default value (e.g., blanks) for the manager's name. There's certainly likely to be at least one employee (the president of the company, for instance) who has no manager, and we probably wouldn't want DB2/400 to leave him or her out of the join logical file.

Joining Three or More Files

You can join up to 32 physical files. When you join more than 2 physical files, you still specify each join between a pair of files. The primary file must be specified as the first file on the first JOIN entry (it can also be specified as the first file on additional JOIN entries), and every secondary file must be specified exactly once as the second file on a JOIN entry (a secondary file can also be specified as the first file on subsequent JOIN entries). The secondary files must first appear on JOIN specifications in the same order they're listed in the JFILE entry. For example, with the following record-level entry

```
...2....+....3....+....4....+....5....+....6....+....7..
R FILEABCR                  JFILE( FILEA FILEB FILEC )
```

you could join FILEA to FILEB and FILEB to FILEC

```
...2....+....3....+....4....+....5....+....6....+....7..
J                           JOIN( FILEA FILEB )
...
J                           JOIN( FILEB FILEC )
```

or you could join FILEA to FILEB and FILEA to FILEC

```
J                           JOIN( FILEA FILEB )
...
J                           JOIN( FILEA FILEC )
```

If you rearranged the JFILE entries as follows

```
...2....+....3....+....4....+....5....+....6....+....7..
R FILEABCR                  JFILE( FILEA FILEC FILEB )
```

you could use either of the following pairs of JOIN entries:

```
...2....+....3....+....4....+....5....+....6....+....7..
J                           JOIN( FILEA FILEC )
...
J                           JOIN( FILEC FILEB )
```

or

```
J                           JOIN( FILEA FILEC )
...
J                           JOIN( FILEA FILEB )
```

These alternatives are *not* necessarily equivalent because the handling of unmatched and multiple-match records may differ.

To clarify how records are joined from three files, let's consider the following four physical files and their contents:

File	DDS	File Contents
CUSTOMER	Figure 6.1	Figure 6.3
SALE	Figure 6.2	Figure 6.4
PART	Figure 6.13	Figure 6.15
SALEITEM	Figure 6.14	Figure 6.16

Figure 6.13
PART Physical File

```
...1....+....2....+....3....+....4....+....5....+....6....+....7
                                    UNIQUE

          R PARTR                   TEXT( 'Parts' )

              PARTID      7P Ø       TEXT( 'Part ID' )
              PARTDESC    5ØA        TEXT( 'Part description' )

          K PARTID
```

Figure 6.14
SALEITEM Physical File

```
...1....+....2....+....3....+....4....+....5....+....6....+....7
                                        UNIQUE

     R SALEITEMR                        TEXT( 'Sale items' )

       ORDERID    R                     REFFLD( ORDERID SALE )
       PARTID     R                     REFFLD( PARTID  PART )
       QTY                7P Ø          TEXT( 'Quantity ordered' )

     K ORDERID
     K PARTID
```

Figure 6.15
Sample Records in
PART Physical File

PARTID	PARTDESC
2654	Fax machine
3620	Stapler
4101	Desk

Figure 6.16
Sample Records in
SALEITEM Physical File

ORDERID	PARTID	QTY
3678	2654	1
3679	3620	10
3679	4101	2
3680	4101	3
3681	2654	2
3682	2654	1
3682	4101	1
3683	3620	5

Together these files contain detailed information about sales of parts to customers. The information can be brought together through the CUSSALPRT join logical file defined in Figure 6.17. The resulting contents of the CUSSALPRT file are shown in Figure 6.18. (Not all the underlying physical file fields are included in CUSSALPRT.)

You can see in this example how DB2/400 creates a join logical file for all the matching combinations of records. In a join logical file such as this, where the primary file is joined to the first secondary file, and the first secondary file is joined to the second secondary file, and so on down the line, the pseudocode algorithm presented earlier can be extended with more inner loops. It may help to think of the process as somewhat like an automobile odometer, with the miles wheel clicking off values for the tens-of-miles, then

Figure 6.17
CUSSALPRT Join
Logical File

```
...1....+....2....+....3....+....4....+....5....+....6....+....7....+....8
                                        JDFTVAL

          R CUSSALPRTR                  JFILE( CUSTOMER SALE SALEITEM PART )
                                        TEXT( 'Customers with sales and +
                                             parts info' )

          J                             JOIN( CUSTOMER SALE )
                                        JFLD( CUSTID   CUSTID )
                                        JDUPSEQ( SALEDATE )

          J                             JOIN( SALE     SALEITEM )
                                        JFLD( ORDERID ORDERID )
                                        JDUPSEQ( PARTID )

          J                             JOIN( SALEITEM PART )
                                        JFLD( PARTID   PARTID )

            CUSTID                      JREF( CUSTOMER )
            NAME
            SALEDATE
            PARTDESC

          K CUSTID
```

Figure 6.18

Sample Records in
CUSSALPRT Join
Logical File

CUSTID	NAME	SALEDATE	PARTDESC
10001	Ajax Plumbing	1996-03-06	Stapler
10001	Ajax Plumbing	1996-03-06	Desk
10001	Ajax Plumbing	1996-03-22	Fax machine
10001	Ajax Plumbing	1996-03-23	Fax machine
10001	Ajax Plumbing	1996-03-23	Desk
10003	Picante Software	1996-02-29	Fax machine
10003	Picante Software	1996-04-02	Stapler
10008	Bubba's Grill	1996-03-06	Desk

the tens-of-miles wheel clicking off values for the hundreds-of-miles, and so on. Conceptually, DB2/400 does something similar to produce the records in this type of join logical file.[7]

As is the case with joining only two physical files, when you don't specify JDFTVAL for a join of three or more files, a primary record is included only if a complete match (a record from each of the joined files) exists. If you do specify JDFTVAL, every primary file record appears at least once in the join logical file. Incomplete matches are filled out with default values, as needed.

---

[7] The actual DB2/400 runtime implementation may use a more efficient approach to retrieving and matching records.

When you specify JDFTVAL, for a join of three or more files, there's one unusual result you should be aware of. Consider the case in which FILEA, FILEB, and FILEC are joined on FLDA, a field that exists in each of the physical files. Assume FILEA is the primary file and is joined to FILEB, the first secondary file. As explained earlier, to complete the join you can join either FILEA or FILEB to FILEC. If you don't specify JDFTVAL, the results are always the same — any incomplete match is omitted from the join logical file. But if you specify JDFTVAL and a FILEA record has a match in FILEC, but not in FILEB, the results are different. With FILEB joined to FILEC, the resulting record will be

FILEA fields	**FILEB fields**	**FILEC fields**
From FILEA	Default	Default

On the other hand, if FILEA is joined to FILEC, the resulting record will be

FILEA fields	**FILEB fields**	**FILEC fields**
From FILEA	Default	From FILEC

When more than one way exists to join three or more logical files, be sure to consider the result of missing matches when you specify how files are joined.

Coding Suggestions

- Code any N (neither) usage fields first in the record format because their purpose is closely related to the join specifications that precede field-level entries.

- When the join logical file record format includes a field from a physical file that's listed more than once in the JFILE entry, be careful that the JREF entry specifies the correct relative file number for the intended use of the file.

- Use RENAME when you need to include two or more fields with the same name from different files.

- If you want to sequence join file records, you should list a physical file with the key field(s) as the first JFILE entry (i.e., make it the primary file).

- If you have a choice of the order in which to specify physical files on the JFILE entry, specify the file(s) with fewest records first. The way files are related or your requirements for a keyed access path may restrict the possible orderings. However, if you have more than one valid alternative, joining files with the fewest records first can significantly improve performance.

- Consider using dynamic selection (i.e., specifying the DYNSLT file-level entry) for files with select/omit entries, even if DYNSLT isn't required. Dynamic selection can reduce the overhead required to maintain the join logical files access path (See the "Selecting a Subset of Records" section in Chapter 4 for more details on dynamic selection.)

Chapter Summary

Join logical files are read-only logical files with a single record format. The fields in a join logical file can come from up to 32 underlying physical files. Join logical files' primary purpose is to simplify report programs and end-user data retrieval with query utilities.

The DDS for a join logical file definition lists 1 primary and 1 to 31 secondary files. One join specification is required for each secondary file, and the join specification lists one or more pairs of fields that are used to match records between the two files listed on the join specification. (In each pair of fields, one field comes from each of the two files being joined.) Optionally, one or more JDUPSEQ entries can be coded for a join specification to determine how multiple matches are sequenced.

DB2/400 returns all combinations of records from the underlying files that have matching values for the pair(s) of fields listed on the join specification(s). If the JDFTVAL file-level keyword is not specified, unmatched records are not part of the logical file. If JDFTVAL is specified, DB2/400 uses default values for secondary file fields with unmatched primary file records. Unmatched records from secondary files are never included in the join logical file.

A join logical file's record format can include fields from any of the underlying physical files. By default, a join logical file's fields are usage I (input-only), but you can specify usage N (neither input nor output) for join fields so they won't appear in the join logical file's records when read by an HLL program or utility. When a field name exists in more than one of the underlying physical files, you must specify a JREF entry for the field to identify which physical file it comes from. A join logical file can optionally have a keyed access path, but key fields must exist in the primary physical file. A join logical file can optionally have select/omit specifications, using fields from any of the underlying physical files.

You can join a file to itself, in which case you must use relative file numbers (based on the order files are listed in the JFILE entry) instead of the file name for any JOIN entry that includes the file. You must also use JREF with a relative file number for any field that's included in the join logical file's record format and that comes from the repeated file.

When you join three or more files, you need one join specification for each secondary file. The first join specification must list the primary file as the first file on the JOIN entry. The other join specifications can join either the primary file or a secondary file to another secondary file. The secondary files must first appear in JOIN entries in the same order they're listed on the JFILE entry. When you specify JDFTVAL, the order of join specifications can affect how unmatched records are handled.

Key Terms

join field
join logical file (join file)

join specification
primary file

relative file number
secondary file

Exercises

1. Modify the definition of the CUSSALPRT join logical file in Figure 6.17 so that

   a. only items that were ordered in quantities of two or more are included in the join logical file's records, and

   b. if an order doesn't include any items ordered in quantities of two or more, the order itself isn't in the join logical file's records, and

   c. if a customer doesn't have any orders that include items ordered in quantities of two or more, the customer isn't in the join logical file's records.

   Hint: The required modifications may be simpler than you first think.

2. Is it possible to modify the definition of the CUSSALPRT join logical file in Figure 6.17 so that it meets criteria a. and b. in Exercise 1 but still lists *all* customers? If so, show the necessary modifications; if not, explain what would be necessary to add to DDS to allow this definition.

3. Using the EMPLOYEE physical file definition in Figure 6.9 and the records in Figure 6.11, show the records that would be contained in the EMPSTF join logical file with the following definition:

```
...1....+....2....+....3....+....4....+....5....+....6....+....7....
       R EMPSTFR                JFILE( EMPLOYEE EMPLOYEE )

       J                        JOIN( 1 2 )
                                JFLD( EMPID MGREMPID )
                                JDUPSEQ( EMPID )

         EMPID                  JREF( 1 )
         LSTNAM                 JREF( 1 )
         STFEMPID               RENAME( EMPID )
                                JREF( 2 )
         STFLSTNM               RENAME( LSTNAM )
                                JREF( 2 )

       K EMPID
```

What does this join logical file provide (i.e., what's its purpose)?

Exercises Continued

Exercises continued

4. Create a join logical file that can be used to produce a "bill-of-materials" report listing parts that are used to build other parts. The two physical files to use are the PART file in Figure 6.13 and the PARTCOMP file defined below:

```
...1....+....2....+....3....+....4....+....5....+....6....+....7....
                               UNIQUE

     R PARTCOMPR                TEXT( 'Parts composition' )

       PARTID        7P Ø       TEXT( 'Part ID' )
       CTPARTID      7P Ø       TEXT( 'Contains part ID' )

     K PARTID
     K CTPARTID
```

The logical file should include the ID and name of both the containing part and the parts it contains. Parts that do not contain any other parts should *not* be included in the join logical file.

Hint: You'll need to use the PART file twice in the join logical file.

5. Modify the join logical file definition created for Exercise 4 so that all parts are included, even those that don't contain other parts.

6. Explain why you think DB2/400 join logical files are read only. Describe (in general terms) a reasonable way to overcome the problems with updatable join logical files.

Chapter **7**

Accessing Database Files from High-Level Languages

Chapter Overview

In Chapters 2 through 6, we learned how to create DB2/400 physical and logical files. This chapter covers how to retrieve, update, insert, and delete records in a database file using AS/400 HLL I/O operations. To access a file from an HLL program, you have to declare the file in the program and then code appropriate I/O statements, so this chapter begins with a discussion of file declarations for different types of access. The next sections cover various types of file operations. The explanations and examples cover RPG IV and COBOL/400, the two most widely used HLLs on the AS/400. The chapter also explains how to use an Override with Database File CL command to identify which actual file member should be opened when the program runs. This chapter isn't a comprehensive treatment of RPG IV and COBOL/400 file I/O; however, with a basic knowledge of either language, you should be able to use DB2/400 files effectively in your programs after studying this chapter.

Declaring a File

An HLL program that accesses a DB2/400 physical or logical file requires several types of statements:

- File declaration(s), and in some cases record format declarations
- File open and close statements
- Record access statements: positioning, read, update, write, and delete

File and record format declarations are *not* executable statements. They identify to the compiler which file objects and record formats to use as the compiler generates code for subsequent I/O statements. A file declaration also specifies the **access method** (e.g., sequential by key) the program uses for the file. Different programs can use different access methods for the same file.[1] Briefly, when the compiler encounters a file declaration in your source code, it retrieves the file's definition — including its record format and access path definition — and merges this information with the items you explicitly specify on the file declaration. During the rest of the compile process, whenever the compiler encounters an I/O statement for this file, it uses the

---

[1] In fact, you can declare the *same* file more than once in a program, and use a different access method for each declaration.

merged information to check the validity of the I/O statement and to generate the appropriate executable code in the program object produced by a successful compilation.

Besides the file name, the most important thing you specify on a file declaration is the access method, which is one of the following:

- **Sequential access** by relative record number (RRN)
  Use this access method to process an entire file when the sequence of records doesn't matter (or the file has been sorted into the proper sequence). Typical uses are for file-wide summarization or to update records en masse.

- **Direct access** by RRN
  Use this access method when you know the RRN of the record you want. This is a fairly uncommon access method because AS/400 applications don't usually store RRNs as "links" to other records but use key values instead.[2]

- Sequential access by key
  Use this method to process an entire file when the sequence of records is important. Typical uses are for detail listings or reports with subtotals where the number of subtotal categories is large. Combined with direct access by key (below), this method also can be used to process a subset of records (e.g., all the order item records for one order ID).

- Direct access by key
  Use this method to access a specific record by a unique key value. Typical uses are for file lookups (e.g., to retrieve data for a particular customer) and individual record updates.

Obviously, sequential and direct access by key can be used only with a file that has a keyed access path. (Recall from Chapter 3 that one main use of a logical file is to provide a keyed access path over a physical file so the data can be accessed in a particular sequence.) Sequential and direct access by RRN can be used with files that have either arrival sequence (i.e., no key) or keyed access paths. Both RPG IV and COBOL/400 let you declare a file so you can use a combination of sequential and direct access for the same file; however, you can't combine access by RRN and access by key for the same file declaration.

The access method determines how you can retrieve records. What about the other operations: insert, update, and delete? Although each HLL has its own particular rules for file declarations, generally the access method isn't important for record inserts. The only requirements are that the file isn't read-only (e.g., a join logical file), the program opens the file for output

---

[2] This method is sometimes used as a fast way to re-retrieve records. If a program saves the RRN of a record the program has previously retrieved by key, direct access by RRN can be used for subsequent retrievals.

(or input and output), and the inserted record doesn't violate a unique key or other file constraint. Most AS/400 HLLs provide "update current" and "delete current" I/O operations, which require you to first read a record (by any access method), thus making it "current." Some HLLs also support direct-by-RRN and/or direct-by-key update and delete operations, which allow a one-step approach to record updates and deletes.

RPG IV File Description Specifications

In RPG IV, you code a **file description specification** (**F-spec**) to declare a database file. Figure 7.1 shows the column layout and values for an F-spec, and Figure 7.2 shows the keywords you can use on an F-spec.[3]

Figure 7.1

Source Columns for RPG IV File Description Specification

Column	Positions	Content
Sequence number	1–5	Optional sequence number or comment
Form type	6	F — to indicate file description specification
Comment flag	7	Place a * in this column to identify the entire line as a comment
File name	7–16	DB2/400 file name
File type	17	One of the following: I — Input file O — output file U — update file
File designation	18	One of the following: Blank — if position 17 is O F — if position 17 is I or U
End of file	19	Always blank for a full procedural file
File addition	20	One of the following: Blank — no records can be added to input or update file A — a Write operation can be used to add records to an input or update file (This column is ignored for output files.)
Sequence	21	Always blank for a full procedural file
File format	22	E — to indicate an externally described file
Record length	23–27	Always blank for an externally described file

Figure 7.1 continued

[3] Figures 7.1 and 7.2 include only columns, values, and keywords relevant to externally described, full procedural, database files. They do not include entries for non-database files (e.g., display files), program-described files (ones that are not created with DDS or SQL), or files that are accessed with the built-in RPG record-processing cycle rather than standard I/O statements. The annotated bibliography lists several sources of information on these other types of files.

Figure 7.1
Continued

Column	Positions	Content
Limits processing	28	Always blank for a full procedural file
Length of key	29–33	Always blank for an externally described file
Record address type	34	One of the following: Blank — Records are accessed by RRN K — Records are accessed by key
File organization	35	Always blank for an externally described file
Device	36–42	Disk — to indicate a database file
Unused	43	Leave blank unless the line is a comment
Function	44–80	Keyword entries (Figure 7.2)

Figure 7.2
Partial List of RPG IV
File Description
Specification Keywords

Keyword	Purpose
Commit(*commit-flag*)	Process file under commitment control. Optional *commit-flag* can be set to "0" (*Off) or "1" (*On) to control commitment control.
Ignore(*rcdfmt₁* : *rcdfmt₂*, : ...)	Ignore one or more record formats in a multiformat logical file.
Include(*rcdfmt₁* : *rcdfmt₂*, : ...)	Include one or more record formats in a multiformat logical file — and ignore all others.
InfDs(*data-structure*)	Specify a data structure to contain feedback information associated with the file.
InfSr(*subroutine-name*)	Specify a subroutine to receive control when an I/O error occurs for the file
Prefix(*pfx*)	Specify a string of characters to add to the beginning of all field names defined in the file's record format(s)
RecNo(*rrn-field*)	Specifies a field that contains a RRN for output files accessed by RRN
Rename(*external-rcdfmt* : *internal-rcdfmt*)	Rename a record format
UsrOpn	File is opened only when Open operation is executed (not during program initialization)

Despite the myriad possible combinations for F-spec columns and key-words, F-specs for the types of files we consider are straightforward. The file name is normally the unqualified name of an existing physical or logical file.[4] RPG IV, unlike DDS (and RPG/400), permits mixed-case names, such as the file name Customer. Mixed-case names are more readable than all uppercase names, and you should use them in your HLL programs where permitted.[5]

If you want to access a file by key, the file must have a keyed access path and you must specify K in position 34 of the F-spec; otherwise, the file is accessed by RRN.

The types of I/O operations that you plan to use for the file determine the entries you should code in positions 17, 18, and 20 (see Figure 7.3), as well as the optional RecNo keyword in positions 44-80.

Figure 7.3

F-Spec Entries for Various Types of I/O Operations

Type of operation	File type (position 17)	File designation (position 18)	File addition (position 20)
Read, ReadP, ReadE, ReadPE, Chain, SetGT, or SetLL	I or U	F	blank or A (A is required to use the Write operation)
Write	O	blank	blank
Write	U	F	A
Update or Delete	U	F	blank or A (A is required to use the Write operation)

---

[4] The file name on the F-spec doesn't have to be the name of an existing file, however. You can use an OVRDBF command before the compile (i.e., before executing the CRTRPGMOD or CRTBNDRPG command) to associate the file name (on the F-spec) with an existing file that has a different name. This technique can be used in RPG IV to declare the same file twice in the same program, using different names on the F-specs. In any case, an F-spec for an externally described file must be associated with an existing DB2/400 file when you compile the program because the compiler has to retrieve the file's definition from the file object.

[5] Because of the amount of discussion surrounding DDS file definitions in Part I, this chapter uses the DDS format (all uppercase) when referring to a DB2/400 file (e.g., CUSTOMER). The RPG IV and COBOL/400 code examples use the more readable mixed case (e.g., Customer). When the text refers to an identifier (e.g., a file or field name) on a specific RPG IV or COBOL/400 statement, the exact form of the identifier is used. Keep in mind that, for the most part, neither RPG IV nor COBOL/400 are case sensitive.

The following examples illustrate the most common cases with keyed access:

- To use sequential and direct access, for input only (e.g., Read, Chain) operations

```
....1....+....2....+....3....+....4....+....5....+....6
FCustomer  IF   E           K Disk
```

- To use only Write operations to add records

```
....1....+....2....+....3....+....4....+....5....+....6
FCustomer  O    E           K Disk
```

- To use sequential and direct access for input (e.g., Read, Chain), Update, and Delete (but not Write) operations

```
....1....+....2....+....3....+....4....+....5....+....6
FCustomer  UF   E           K Disk
```

- To use sequential and direct access for input (e.g., Read, Chain), Update, Delete, and Write operations

```
....1....+....2....+....3....+....4....+....5....+....6
FCustomer  UF A E           K Disk
```

For access by RRN, the following examples illustrate the most common cases:

- To use sequential and direct access, for input only (e.g., Read, Chain) operations

```
....1....+....2....+....3....+....4....+....5....+....6
FCustomer  IF   E             Disk
```

- To use only Write operations to add records

```
....1....+....2....+....3....+....4....+....5....+....6
FCustomer  O    E             Disk
```

- To use sequential and direct access for input (e.g., Read, Chain), Update, and Delete (but not Write) operations

```
....1....+....2....+....3....+....4....+....5....+....6
FCustomer  UF   E             Disk
```

- To use input (e.g., Read, Chain), Update, Delete, and Write (to a specific RRN) operations

```
....1....+....2....+....3....+....4....+....5....+....6
FCustomer  UF A E             Disk    RecNo( CsRRN )
```

In RPG IV, both sequential and direct access are allowed for keyed access with input (file type I) or update (U) files; no special coding is necessary on the F-spec. Normally only sequential access is used for output (O) files (the records are appended to the end of the physical file member), regardless of whether the file is declared for keyed or RRN access.

When you declare an externally described file, RPG IV generates the necessary **input specifications** (**I-specs**) and **output specifications** (**O-specs**) for the file's record format(s). Figure 7.4 shows part of a compiler listing produced for the declaration of an abbreviated version of the CUSTOMER file.

All comment lines and I- and O-specs are compiler-generated. You can see that an I-spec and an O-spec have been generated for each database field. (The field names all begin with Cs, which is a field prefix discussed below.)

Figure 7.4

F-spec and Compiler-Generated I-specs and O-specs for Externally Described CUSTOMER File

```
+....1....+....2....+....3....+....4....+....5....+....6....+....7....+...
 8 FCustomer  UF A E          K DISK     InfDs( CsInfDs )
 9 F                                     UsrOpn
10 F                                     Prefix( Cs )
11
   *-----------------------------------------------------------------
   *                                     RPG name      External name
   * File name. . . . . . . . :          CUSTOMER      APPDTA/CUSTOMER
   * Record format(s) . . . . :          CUSTOMERR     CUSTOMERR
   *-----------------------------------------------------------------
   .
   .
   .
59=ICUSTOMERR
   *-----------------------------------------------------------------
   * RPG record format  . . . . :        CUSTOMERR
   * Prefix . . . . . . . . . . :        CS
   * External format  . . . . . :        CUSTOMERR : APPDTA/CUSTOMER
   * Format text  . . . . . . . :        Customers
   *-----------------------------------------------------------------
60=I                          P     1    4 ØCSCUSTID
61=I                          A     5   34  CSNAME
   .
   .
   .
317=OCUSTOMERR
   *-----------------------------------------------------------------
   * RPG record format  . . . . :        CUSTOMERR
   * Prefix . . . . . . . . . . :        CS
   * External format  . . . . . :        CUSTOMERR : APPDTA/CUSTOMER
   * Format text  . . . . . . . :        Customers
   *-----------------------------------------------------------------
318=O                         CSCUSTID        4P PACK    7,Ø (CUSTID)
319=O                         CSNAME         34A CHAR    3Ø (NAME)
```

You can optionally use the InfDs keyword to specify a data structure, known as the **file information data structure**, that DB2/400 and the RPG IV runtime update after every I/O operation with information associated with the file. The following statement shows how to specify the CsInfDs data structure as the file information data structure for the CUSTOMER file:

```
....1....+....2....+....3....+....4....+....5....+....6
FCustomer  UF A E          K Disk     InfDs( CsInfDs )
```

To declare the data structure, you code **definition specifications** (**D-specs**) such as

```
....1....+....2....+....3....+....4....+....5....+....6
D CsInfDs           DS
D  CsFileName        *File
D  CsFileSts         *Status
D  CsOpcode          *Opcode
```

You must use a different data structure for each file's information data structure. A good programming practice is to use standard names for the data structure and its subfields and to begin the names with the same two letters (e.g., Cs) that you specify on the associated F-spec's Prefix keyword (discussed below).

After each I/O operation, the RPG IV runtime updates the contents of the file information data structure. For example, with the declaration above, after an Open operation is executed for the CUSTOMER file, the CsFileName subfield contains the first eight characters of the F-spec file name, the CsFileSts subfield contains a five-digit file status (0 if OK, 1 to 99 for a warning, and 100 or greater for an error), and the CsOpcode subfield contains the first five characters of the opcode (e.g., OPEN). The RPG IV reference manual lists the complete layout of the file information data structure, as well as all file status values. Although a file information data structure is optional, by always specifying one you get valuable error detection and diagnosis information. Later in this chapter, we look at a complete RPG IV program to see how the file information data structure can be used to provide comprehensive I/O error handling.

By default, RPG IV opens all files when you first call a program. Although this is convenient (you don't have to code an explicit Open operation), you gain better control over file resources by opening and closing files explicitly. One advantage is that you can test the error indicator or file status value after the Open operation to ensure that the open succeeded before attempting other I/O operations. You can also avoid keeping a file open when it's not needed — something that can reduce the system resources your program uses and can also reduce the chance of object-locking conflicts when other jobs need to use the same file. To specify that you want to open and close files explicitly, code the UsrOpn keyword on the F-spec.

When you declare two or more files in an RPG IV program, the compiler treats fields with the same name in different files as if they were one program variable. This means that when you read a record from one file, the field values overwrite any values for fields with the same name(s) in other files.[6] Generally, this is not a good idea so the Prefix keyword can be used to add one or more characters to the beginning of all the field names in a file to make them unique within the program. To add a two-character prefix to the fields in the CUSTOMER file, you'd code

```
....1....+....2....+....3....+....4....+....5....+....6
FCustomer  UF A E             K Disk    Prefix( Cs )
```

---

[6] This error-prone RPG IV "feature" is a legacy of the original version of RPG, which (as the name "Report Program Generator" suggests) was used to read card decks and produce printed reports. At the time, the automatic movement of an input field to an output field was considered a useful coding shortcut. Unfortunately, with the advent of more complex programs, this outdated feature now requires *additional* coding.

With this declaration, a field declared as NAME in the DDS for the CUSTOMER file should be referred to as CsName in the program. A good coding practice is to use field names with a maximum of eight characters in your DDS field definitions and to use a standard two-character prefix for each file's prefix — for example, Cs for the CUSTOMER file and Sl for the SALE file.

Although you don't have to use a prefix when no name conflicts exist, always using a standard prefix increases the consistency of your programs. For example, all references to the NAME field in the CUSTOMER file will be CsName, not CsName in some programs and Name in others.

When you combine the three recommended keywords, a typical F-spec looks like the following:

```
....1....+....2....+....3....+....4....+....5....+....6
FCustomer  UF A E          K Disk    InfDs( CsInfDs )
                                     UsrOpn
                                     Prefix( Cs )
```

If you follow this standard approach to declaring database files, you'll have the basis for excellent control of the I/O parts of your applications.

COBOL/400 File Declarations

COBOL/400 requires two kinds of declarations for a database file:

- A Select clause to declare the file — the Select clause is coded in the File-Control paragraph of the Input-Output Section of the Environment Division.
- A file description (FD) entry to declare the record layout — the FD entry is coded in the File Section of the Data Division.

The following code shows a sample COBOL/400 declaration for a file that's declared for sequential access by key:

```
Environment division.
Input-Output section.
File-Control.

Select        CustomerFile
  Assign      Database-Customer
  Organization Indexed
  Access Mode Sequential
  Record Key  Externally-Described-Key
  File Status CustomerSts.
      .

      .
Data division.
File section.

FD  CustomerFile.
01  CustomerRcd.
    Copy DDS-All-Formats of Customer with Alias.
```

The Select statement identifies an internal file name (e.g., Customer-File) that's used throughout the program. This name must be the same as the name specified on a subsequent FD entry (as shown). The Select statement associates the internal file name with an existing DB2/400 file that's specified in the Assign clause following the Database- device prefix (e.g., Customer).

You specify an access method on a COBOL/400 Select statement by a combination of the Organization and Access Mode clauses. The table below shows the allowable combinations.

Organization	Access Mode		
	Sequential	**Random**	**Dynamic**
Sequential	Sequential by RRN	Not allowed	Not allowed
Relative	Sequential by RRN	Direct by RRN	Sequential or direct by RRN
Indexed	Sequential by key	Direct by key	Sequential or direct by key

Notice that COBOL/400 uses the term "random" for what's called "direct" access in this book.[7] Also, COBOL/400 requires that you specify dynamic access mode if you want to use both sequential and direct access.

For sequential access by RRN, note that the only difference between sequential and relative organization is that with sequential organization, you must always start reading the file at the first record. With relative organization you can use the Start verb.[8]

When you specify sequential organization, neither a Record Key nor a Relative Key clause is specified.

When you specify relative organization, you must specify a Relative Key clause such as

```
Relative Key CustomerRRN
```

where the variable specified is an unsigned integer declared elsewhere in the program. For direct by RRN Read, Rewrite, Write, and Delete operations, you move an RRN to this variable before executing the I/O statement. In COBOL/400, the first record location in a file has an RRN of 1.[9]

---

[7] "Random" is a misnomer because (hopefully) there's nothing random about an application's choice of records to access. "Direct" is a more accurate term when a record is retrieved by key or RRN.

[8] The Start verb lets you position to a specific RRN or key value.

[9] The first active record may not be in record location 1 if this location is marked as "deleted."

With sequential and relative organization, the file can have either a keyed or arrival-sequenced access path. When you specify indexed organization, the DB2/400 file specified on the Assign clause must have a keyed access path; and you must specify the Record Key Externally-Described-Key clause.[10] If the file's keyed access path allows duplicates (i.e., the UNIQUE keyword is not specified in the file's DDS), you should add With Duplicates to the end of this clause, as in

```
Record Key Externally-Described-Key with Duplicates
```

For direct by key Read, Rewrite, Write, and Delete operations, you move values to the key fields of the record declared in the FD entry before executing the I/O statement.[11] The COBOL/400 runtime passes these values to DB2/400 to identify the record.

The File Status clause is optional but recommended. The clause specifies a two-character variable defined in the Working-Storage Section. The system places an I/O status code in this variable after each I/O operation. You can and should check this status code after each I/O operation. The value "00" indicates success; any other value indicates a warning or error. The COBOL/400 reference manual lists all the file status key values and their meanings.

The record layout for a file is declared in an FD entry, such as the one shown in the example above. As mentioned, the FD entry specifies the internal file name that immediately follows the Select keyword on the file's declaration. No other FD entry clauses are necessary for externally described database files.[12]

Immediately following the FD entry, you code an 01-level entry for the file's record format. With externally described files, you generate the contents of the record structure using a COBOL/400 extension of the Copy compiler directive. The result of the Copy DDS-All-Formats in the example above is shown in the portion of the compiler listing in Figure 7.5. All lines beginning with a + are compiler-generated.

For physical files and logical files other than multiformat logical files the Copy DDS-All-Formats form of the directive generates a single record structure. For multiformat logical files, the directive generates one record structure per record format, all redefined to share the same storage area. You can move the appropriate record (group item) from this area to a separate area in Working-Storage after a Read, or you can move data from Working-Storage to the appropriate record before a Write or Rewrite operation. In

[10] The Externally-Described-Key phrase is used for externally described files. For program-described files, you specify actual key fields in this clause.

[11] Of course, if the key fields already contain valid values from a previous Read operation, you don't need to move the same values in again.

[12] With ILE COBOL/400, you can specify Is External to make a file available to other programs in the COBOL/400 run unit.

Figure 7.5

FD Entry and
Compiler-Generated
Record Structure for
Externally Described
CUSTOMER File

```
21      003400 FD  CustomerFile.
22      003500 01  CustomerRcd.
        003600     Copy DDS-All-Formats of Customer with Alias.
23     +000001      05  CUSTOMER-RECORD PIC X(34).                          <-ALL-FMTS
       +000002*    I-O FORMAT:CUSTOMERR  FROM FILE CUSTOMER   OF LIBRARY APPDTA   <-ALL-FMTS
       +000003*                         Customers                             <-ALL-FMTS
       +000004*THE KEY DEFINITIONS FOR RECORD FORMAT  CUSTOMERR               <-ALL-FMTS
       +000005*  NUMBER              NAME                RETRIEVAL    ALTSEQ    <-ALL-FMTS
       +000006*  0001   CUSTID                           ASCENDING       NO     <-ALL-FMTS
24     +000007      05  CUSTOMERR    REDEFINES CUSTOMER-RECORD.              <-ALL-FMTS
25     +000008        06 CUSTID            PIC S9(7)      COMP-3.            <-ALL-FMTS
       +000009*            Customer ID                                       <-ALL-FMTS
26     +000010        06 CUSTOMERNAME      PIC X(30).                        <-ALL-FMTS
       +000011*            Customer name                                     <-ALL-FMTS
```

Working-Storage, you can generate a separate group item for a particular record format by using the Copy DDS-*format-name* variation of the directive.

To use the long names defined with the DDS ALIAS keyword rather than the file's standard field names, add the With Alias phrase to the end of the Copy directive. Even though DDS requires all uppercase field names for an ALIAS entry, COBOL/400 allows mixed case to refer to the same name. For example, in a COBOL/400 program, you can use RecordAction for a field that has ALIAS(RECORDACTION) specified in its DDS.

Opening and Closing a File

Before any I/O operations to a file can be executed, the file must be opened. When you open the file, DB2/400 uses the information from your program's file declaration, along with information from previously executed OVRDBF commands to locate the appropriate file member and allocate an Open Data Path (ODP) that contains buffer areas and control blocks for accessing the file. As long as the file is open, DB2/400 maintains the ODP. Other jobs may access the file member at the same time, but DB2/400 uses a separate ODP for each job so each job's current position in the file and other status information isn't affected by other job's I/O operations.

A file must be in the closed state when you attempt to open it; and a file must be open when you attempt to close it. You can open and close a file multiple times in the same program (although this isn't very common), and in COBOL/400 a file can be opened for different uses (e.g., input and output) at different times.

RPG IV Open and Close Operation Codes

As I noted earlier, by default, RPG IV opens all files when you first call a program. If you specify the UsrOpn keyword on a file's F-spec, an explicit Open operation must be executed before any I/O operations to the file can be performed. Although this is an additional step, it gives you explicit control over when the file is opened, as well as the ability to detect and handle any errors that occur when the file is opened. The Open statement has the following syntax:

```
....1....+....2....+....3....+....4....+....5....+....6....+....7....+
C*      Factor1+++++++Opcode++++Factor2+++++++                        ER
C                     Open     file-name                             xx
```

File-name is the name declared on the F-spec. The error resulting indicator is optional and is set to "0" if the open is successful or to "1" if an error occurs.[13]

After an Open, you should always check the error indicator or file status field in the file information data structure. A file status of 0 indicates a successful open. Other values indicate a warning or error that should be handled.

To close a file, you execute a Close operation, using the following syntax:

```
....1....+....2....+....3....+....4....+....5....+....6....+....7....+
C*      Factor1+++++++Opcode++++Factor2+++++++                        ER
C                     Close    file-name                             xx
```

File-name is the name declared on the F-spec and used on the Open (if an explicit Open was done). The error resulting indicator is optional.

RPG IV also closes all files if the LR (last record) indicator is on when you return from a called program or if the program terminates abnormally.

COBOL/400 Open and Close Statements

Before you can perform any I/O operations to a file, you must explicitly open it using the COBOL/400 Open statement. The Open statement syntax is quite simple:

```
Open file-usage file-name
```

where *file-usage* is Input, Output, I-O, or Extend; and *file-name* is the internal file name that immediately follows the Select keyword on the file's declaration.[14] The file usage determines which I/O operations are subsequently allowed, as shown in the table on page 152.

---

[13] You should always specify an error resulting indicator on an Open statement. If you don't and an error occurs, the system transfers control to the subroutine specified in the InfSr keyword of the file's F-spec (if any). If no InfSr subroutine exists, the default exception handler receives control.

[14] Although you can open multiple files in one Open statement by specifying multiple sets of *file-usage* and *file-name* entries, it's better to use separate statements so the file status can be checked after each open attempt.

	Input	Output	I-O	Extend (see note 1)
Start (see note 2)	Yes		Yes	
Read	Yes		Yes	
Write		Yes	Yes (see note 3)	Yes
Rewrite			Yes	
Delete (see note 2)			Yes	

Notes:

1. Valid only for sequential organization; records are added to end of file

2. Valid only for relative or indexed organization

3. If file is a physical file, the file member is cleared when opened. If file is a logical file, records are appended to end of underlying physical file member.

After an Open, you should always check the file status variable. A status of "00" indicates a successful open. Other values indicate a warning or error that should be handled.

To close a file, you execute a Close operation, using the following syntax:

```
Close file-name
```

where *file-name* is a file name specified on a prior successful Open operation. All open files are also automatically closed when the COBOL/400 run unit ends (e.g., when a program in the run unit executes a Stop Run statement).

Reading a File and Positioning in a File

You can read records sequentially or directly by RRN or by key. Every read operation has an implicit or explicit way to identify which record is to be read. As you're reading a file, DB2/400 maintains a **file pointer** that logically points at or between physical record locations (for access by RRN) or at or between key entries in the keyed access path. Different I/O operations move or set this pointer, which affects which records are accessed in subsequent I/O operations. Understanding the file pointer concept can help you determine which record DB2/400 retrieves on a read operation.

When you open a file for sequential access, DB2/400 sets the file pointer before the first record position or key entry.[15] The first read next operation reads the first record and moves the pointer so it's just before the second record position or key entry. When you do a read previous, DB2/400 reads

[15] In some cases, you can use the POSITION parameter of the OVRDBF command to specify a different position of the file pointer when the file is opened. Also, for sequential access by RRN, DB2/400 automatically skips any record locations marked internally as "deleted."

the record "behind" the current pointer position and moves the pointer backward. When you read a file directly, you supply an RRN or key value for the read operation, and DB2/400 uses that value to set the file pointer and read the specified record. Both RPG IV and COBOL/400 also provide I/O operations to set the file pointer before a subsequent read operation. In RPG, the file positioning operations are SetGT and SetLL; in COBOL/400, the Start statement positions the file pointer.

On a read (or file positioning) operation, several conditions can result in no record being returned to your program:

- A sequential read next when the file pointer is after the last record or key entry; an "end-of-file" (EOF) status is returned.

- A sequential read prior when the file pointer is before the first record or key entry; a "beginning-of-file" (BOF) status is returned.

- A direct read by key when no record exists with that key value; a "no record found" status is returned.

- A direct read by RRN when either no such location exists or the location is marked internally as "deleted" (and thus contains no active record); a "no record found" status is returned.

- Any other type of I/O error; an error status is returned.

Your program should always check for these conditions after a read (or file positioning) operation.

RPG IV Chain, Read, ReadP, ReadE, ReadPE, SetLL, and SetGT Operation Codes

RPG IV provides several ways to read a file.[16] With sequential access, to read the next record, you use a Read opcode with the following syntax:

```
....1....+....2....+....3....+....4....+....5....+....6....+....7....+.
C*      Factor1+++++++Opcode(N)+Factor2+++++++                         EREF
C                     Read      file-name                              xxyy
```

File-name is the name declared on the F-spec. The error resulting indicator (*xx*) is optional and is set to "0" if the read is successful or to "1" if an error occurs. The EOF indicator (*yy*) is required and is set to "0" if the read is successful or to "1" if the end of the file is encountered.

When a record is read successfully, its contents are moved to the fields in the compiler-generated record structure, and the file pointer is advanced to the next record.

To read the previous record, you use the ReadP opcode, which has the same syntax and behavior as the Read opcode, except a ReadP reads

---

[16] In the following discussions of RPG IV opcodes, we treat only single-format files. Handling multiformat files is deferred until a later section.

backward in the file. The indicator in positions 75–76 indicates whether the beginning-of-file condition was encountered on the ReadP.

The Chain opcode provides direct access, either by key or by RRN. The syntax for a Chain is

```
....1....+....2....+....3....+....4....+....5....+....6....+....7....+
C*      Factor1+++++++Opcode(N)+Factor2+++++++                      NRER
C       search-arg    Chain     file-name                          yyxx
```

File-name is the name declared on the F-spec. *Search-arg* is a variable, constant, literal, or (for keyed access only) a key list name that provides the key value for a file accessed by key or the RRN for a file accessed by RRN. The no-record indicator (*yy*) is required and is set to "0" if the read is successful or to "1" if no matching record is found for the key or RRN specified in Factor 1. The error resulting indicator (*xx*) is optional and is set to "0" if the read is successful or to "1" if an error occurs.

If the Chain is successful, you can use a subsequent Read, ReadE, ReadP, or ReadPE operation to read the record after or before the one returned by the Chain. If the Chain fails, you must use another Chain, SetGT, or SetLL to reset the file pointer before a subsequent Read, ReadE, ReadP, or ReadPE.[17]

For access by key, if the file has a composite key (i.e., more than one key field) you must declare a **key list** in your program and use the key list name in Factor 1. A key list declaration includes one KList **calculation specification** (**C-spec**) and one or more KFld C-specs. Although they're C-specs, the KList and KFld entries are declarations, not executable statements. A good programming practice is to put all key list declarations together, at the beginning of the C-specs (along with other C-spec declarations, such as parameter lists). The following code shows an example of using a key list:

```
....1....+....2....+....3....+....4....+....5....+....6....+....7....+
FCustCity  IF   E          K Disk    InfDs( CcInfDs )
                                      UsrOpn
                                      Prefix( Cc )

        .
        .
        .

C*      Factor1+++++++Opcode++++Factor2+++++++                      NRER
C       CcKList      KList
C                    KFld       CcShpCity
C                    KFld       CcCustID

        .
        .

C       CcKList      Chain      CustCity                            9899
```

---

[17] For files that allow records with duplicate key values, a successful Chain returns the first record, based on the explicit or default FIFO, LIFO, or FCFO attribute of the file's key. (See Chapter 2 for a discussion of these DDS file-level keywords.)

Notice how this example uses Cc as the prefix for the CUSTCITY logical file and uses the prefix with both the key list name (CcKList) and the key field names. This approach uses the file's key fields as the key list key fields. Alternatively, you can use work variables (ones declared with a D-spec) as the key list key fields, but they must be declared with the same data type, length, and decimal positions as the file's key fields. Also, the order of the KFld entries must agree with the order of the key fields, as declared in the DDS for the file.[18]

RPG IV has two opcodes that can be used to position the file pointer before a read operation. The SetLL (set lower limit) opcode positions the file at the next record that has a key or RRN greater than or equal to a specified key or RRN. The SetGT (set greater than) opcode is similar but positions to the next record that has a key or RRN greater than a specified key or RRN. The two opcodes have the following syntax:

```
....1....+....2....+....3....+....4....+....5....+....6....+....7....+.
C*      Factor1++++++Opcode++++Factor2+++++++                    NREREQ
C       search-arg   SetLL     file-name                         yyxxzz
C       search-arg   SetGT     file-name                         yyxx
```

File-name is the name declared on the F-spec. *Search-arg* is a variable, constant, literal, or a key list name, as described for the Chain opcode above. The no-record indicator (yy) is also optional and is set to "0" if a record is found that matches the search criteria or to "1" if no record is found that matches the search criteria. The error resulting indicator (xx) is optional and is set to "0" if the positioning operation is successful or to "1" if an error occurs. For the SetLL opcode, the equal-key-match indicator (zz) is set to "1" if a record is found that matches the search key or RRN exactly or to "0" otherwise.

If a SetLL or SetGT is successful, you can use a subsequent Read, ReadE, ReadP, or ReadPE operation to read the record after or before the one pointed to by the SetLL or SetGT.[19] If a SetLL or SetGT results in a no-record condition, the file pointer is positioned to the end of the file.

Instead of an actual key or RRN, you can specify either the *LoVal or *HiVal figurative constants as the search argument in Factor 1 for a Chain, SetLL, or SetGT operation. These represent the lowest and highest valid values for the file's key field(s); for example, for numeric fields, the values are –99999 . . . and +99999 . . ., respectively. If all the key fields for a file have ascending order, using *LoVal positions to or before the first record in the file, and *HiVal positions to or after the last record in the file. With

---

[18] For a file with a composite key, a key list can contain a KFld entry for each of the file's key fields or for a subset of the key fields. The use of partial key lists is discussed later in the chapter.

[19] Generally, you shouldn't use a ReadPE after a SetGT (when both statements have the same set of key fields – either full or partial); the statement will normally fail because the record before the one pointed to by a successful SetGT always has a different key value.

descending keys, the respective positions are reversed; with a mixture, the position may end up in the middle of the file.[20]

For access by key, RPG IV has two variations of the read operation that can be used to sequentially read a set of records that have the same value for all or part of their key fields. Suppose you have a program that displays all the customers in a selected city in order (within the city) by customer ID. This type of access is possible with a logical file that's defined over the CUSTOMER file and that has a composite key consisting of the SHPCITY and CUSTID fields. One way to read a particular city's records is to move the city value to the first key field (e.g., CcShpCity) and a value lower than any customer ID (e.g., –1) to the second key field (e.g., CcCustID), then execute a SetGT to position to the first customer in the city (if any). If there aren't any customers in the specified city, the file pointer will be positioned to the first customer in the city after the specified city, or at the end of the file. A subsequent Read operation retrieves the first customer that satisfies the SetGT search criteria (or the Read sets the end-of-file condition). If the Read succeeds, the returned record must then be checked to see that it's for the specified city. If this record is for the specified city, a read loop can get the rest of the customers in that city until either the end-of-file condition occurs or the record returned has the next city.

This process is fairly straightforward; however, it's even simpler with the ReadE operation and a **partial key**. The ReadE operation has the following syntax:

```
....1....+....2....+....3....+....4....+....5....+....6....+....7....+.
C*      Factor1+++++++Opcode(N)+Factor2+++++++                    EREF
C       search-arg    ReadE      file-name                        xxyy
```

The ReadE operation reads the next sequential record (after the current record or from the beginning of the file if there's no current record) that has a key value equal to the key value specified in Factor 1 (the search argument).[21] The error resulting indicator (*xx*) is optional and is set to "0" if the read is successful or to "1" if an error occurs. The EOF indicator (*yy*) is required and is set to "0" if the read is successful or to "1" if the end of the file is encountered or no more records matching the search argument are found.

The ReadE wouldn't be particularly useful for files with unique keys[22] without another RPG IV feature — partial keys. The search argument for a SetLL and ReadE (as well as the SetGT, ReadPE, Chain, and Delete operations)

---

[20] A common RPG programming mistake is to treat *LoVal as if it means "beginning-of-file" and *HiVal as if it means "end-of-file." These aren't the meanings, and the actual position depends on the ascending/descending order of the file's keys as well as on whether any record in the file has a key value that is equivalent to *LoVal or *HiVal.

[21] You can omit Factor 1, and the key value of the current record will be used as the search argument. However, this isn't a particularly useful (or safe) feature.

[22] Because there'd be only one record that satisfied the ReadE search argument.

can include fewer than the number of key fields defined for the file. In our earlier example of the CUSTCITY file, the search argument can be just the first key field (i.e., SHPCITY in the file and CcShpCity in the program). Thus, to read the customers in Portland, we could use the following code:[23]

```
....1....+....2....+....3....+....4....+....5....+....6....+....7....+.
D UpMoreRcds      S               1A
D IOErrInd        S               1A
  .
  .
  .
C*      Factor1++++++Opcode(N)+Factor2++++++                    NRER
C                   Eval      CcShpCity = 'Portland'
C       CcShpCity   Chain     CustCity                         9799
C                   Eval      IOErrInd =      *In99
C                   Eval      MoreRcds = Not *In97
C                   DoW       ( IOErrInd = *Off ) And ( MoreRcds = *On )
*                      Process the input record here ....
C*                                                             EREF
C       CcShpCity   ReadE     CustCity                         9998
C                   Eval      IOErrInd =      *In99
C                   Eval      MoreRcds = Not *In98
C                   EndDo
```

The Chain operation sets the no-record indicator (97 here) to "0" (*Off) if there's any customer with Portland as its shipping city. This value is negated (i.e., *Off is changed to *On, and vice versa) and assigned to the MoreRcds variable which controls the subsequent loop. The read loop continues as long as more records exist with Portland as the shipping city. When the first customer in the city after Portland is encountered or there are no more customer records, the EOF indicator (98 here) on the ReadE statement will be set to "1" and the loop ends. The first record in the city after Portland is not actually read into the program.

The ReadPE opcode works like ReadE, but reads the previous sequential record (before the current record or from the beginning of the file if there's no current record[24]) that has a key value equal to the key value specified in the search argument.

Normally, DB2/400 places a record lock when you read a record through a file opened for update. While the lock is in effect, no other job[25] can read

---

[23] This example uses the resulting indicators to check for errors and other I/O conditions after I/O operations and to control subsequent program flow. In the complete RPG IV program example discussed later in this chapter, a better approach – using the file status – is shown. For now, note that values of the resulting indicators are moved to meaningfully named, one-character variables immediately after each I/O operation. If you do use resulting indicators, be sure to follow this practice. Do *not* use the indicators themselves (e.g., *In98) to control subsequent program flow because it makes code hard to comprehend and is prone to errors if an indicator gets reused and unintentionally wipes out an existing value.

[24] This will set the beginning-of-file condition.

[25] Actually not even a separate ODP for the same file in the same job can read the record, unless the file is opened under commitment control.

the same record for update, which keeps another job from unintentionally wiping out the first job's record update. A record lock is normally released when you read a different record from the same file (in the same program), when you update the record, or when you close the file. The Chain, Read, ReadP, ReadE, and ReadPE opcodes allow an optional opcode extender when you read a file opened for update. You can code (N) after the opcode to specify that DB2/400 should not place a lock on the record that's read, as in the following example:

```
....1....+....2....+....3....+....4....+....5....+....6....+....7....+
C*      Factor1++++++Opcode(N)+Factor2++++++                        NRER
C       CsCustID      Chain (N) Customer                            9899
```

The (N) extender is appropriate when you have no intention of updating the record, even though you're reading a record from a file opened for update.

You can also use the Unlock opcode to explicitly release the lock on the most recently read record, as in the following statement:

```
....1....+....2....+....3....+....4....+....5....+....6....+....7....+
C*      Factor1++++++Opcode++++Factor2++++++                         ER
C                    Unlock    Customer                              99
```

The Unlock opcode requires the name of an update file in Factor 2 and allows an optional error resulting indicator.

COBOL/400 Read and Start Statements

COBOL/400 provides several variations of the Read statement. For sequential access mode, a Read looks like[26]

```
Read file-name
  At End statement
  Not At End statement
End-Read
```

This type of read is always a read next. The At End phrase specifies the action to take when end-of-file is returned (and no record is read); the Not At End phrase specifies the action to take if a record is read successfully. If an I/O error (other than an end-of-file condition) occurs, *neither* the At End nor the Not At End phrase is executed. Although the At End and Not At End phrases can be used to handle the end-of-file and successful completion conditions, they don't provide a way to handle the important case where an I/O error occurs. Later in this chapter, we look at a simple, comprehensive way (that doesn't use these two phrases) to handle all conditions.

More options are available when you read a file sequentially, but to use them, you must declare the file with dynamic access mode (i.e., for both sequential and direct access). The basic Read statement structure is the same, but you can specify any of the following options after the file name:

---

[26] The next few Read examples omit some optional phrases; we cover some of them later.

- Next
- Prior
- First
- Last

With any of these options, the At End condition is true when there's no record available (i.e., EOF, BOF, or an empty file).

For direct access the Read statement looks like

```
Read file-name
  Invalid Key statement
  Not Invalid Key statement
End-Read
```

If the file was declared (on the Select statement) with relative organization, DB2/400 attempts to read the record location at the RRN contained in the variable specified on the Relative Key clause of the Select. If the file's organization was declared as indexed, DB2/400 attempts to read the record identified by the key values in the key fields of the record declared under the FD entry. If no record is found at the location or with the key specified, the Invalid Key condition is true. If a record is read successfully, the Not Invalid Key condition is true. As with the At End and Not At End phrases, the Invalid Key and Not Invalid Key phrases provide no way to handle error conditions (other than invalid key). However, the error-handling technique we look at later covers these cases, too.

One thing to remember about COBOL/400 Read statements is that they always take a file name, not a record name. The old COBOL rule is "read a file, write a record." After you successfully read a file, the record is placed into the record structure defined (usually with the help of a Copy directive) under the file's FD entry. Optionally, you can specify an Into phrase

```
Read file-name Into variable ...
```

to move the record into a Working-Storage variable. This is simply a shortcut that's equivalent to a Move statement after the Read.

Normally, DB2/400 places a record lock when you read a record through a file opened for update. While the lock is in effect, no other job[27] can read the same record for update, which keeps another job from unintentionally wiping out the first job's record update. A record lock is normally released when you read a different record from the same file (in the same program), when you update the record, or when you close the file. Another optional Read phrase is No Lock, used as follows

```
Read file-name No Lock  ...
```

---

[27] Actually not even a separate ODP for the same file in the same job can read the record, unless the file is opened under commitment control.

to specify that DB2/400 should not place a lock on the record that's read. This option only applies if the file is opened for input-output (I-O). The No Lock phrase is appropriate when, you have no intention of updating the record even though you're reading a record from a file opened for update.

COBOL/400 provides the Start statement as a means to position the file pointer to a record other than one that can be specified using the Read statement. The Start statement has the form

```
Start file-name
  Key relationship Externally-Described-Key
  Invalid Key statement
  Not Invalid Key statement
End-Start
```

where *relationship* is either =, >, or >=. You might use this statement with a composite key; for example, with a logical file with a key of CustID and SaleDate that was defined over a SALE physical file. Because you wouldn't normally know the date of the first sale to a customer, a Read by key would be difficult. But you could move the customer's ID into the CustID field and the lowest possible sale date into the SaleDate field and then execute a Start using >=. If the Start succeeds, the Not Invalid Key condition is true, and a subsequent Read retrieves the record that the Start moved the file pointer to. Of course, you must check the CustID field of this record to ensure it's the same as the one you wanted because the >= condition can be satisfied by a higher CustID value if no record has the specified CustID value. If there are no records that satisfy the key relationship, the Invalid Key condition will be true. If an error (other than invalid key) occurs, neither the Invalid Key nor the Not Invalid Key phrase is executed.[28]

Updating Records

Updating a record replaces the record in the physical file member. You can update records by opening the physical file member or by opening a non-join logical file member over one or more physical file members. (Join logical files can be used only for input.) When you update a record, all the record's fields (in your program) must have valid values before the update operation. The most common approach is to read the existing record first so the fields all have the record's current values. The program then can assign values only to those fields that need to be changed. Some HLLs (e.g., COBOL/400) let you assign values to all a record's fields and then update the record in the file without first retrieving it.

RPG IV Update Operation Code

To update an existing database record, you must first read the record to be updated, using a Read, ReadP, Chain, ReadE, or ReadPE operation on a file opened for update. The read operation must not have specified the N (no

---

[28] See the earlier discussion on error handling.

record lock) opcode extender. There must not be any intervening I/O operations to the same file between the read and update operations. (I/O operations to other files are permitted.) The Update operation for an externally described file specifies a record format name (not a file name), with the following syntax.

```
....1....+....2....+....3....+....4....+....5....+....6....+....7....+
C*      Factor1+++++++Opcode++++Factor2+++++++                        ER
C                     Update    rcd-fmt-name                          xx
```

The error resulting indicator (*xx*) is optional and is set to "0" if the update is successful or to "1" if an error occurs.

RPG IV (unlike COBOL/400) does not provide a way to replace an existing record without first reading it.

COBOL/400 Rewrite Statement

The COBOL/400 Rewrite statement replaces an existing record. If the file is declared with sequential access mode, the record to be updated must first be read successfully, using a Read statement. The retrieved record's data can then be updated or replaced entirely (except you cannot change the value of key fields for files declared as indexed organization). To replace the record in the database, you use a Rewrite statement such as the following for files declared as sequential organization:

```
Rewrite record-name
```

For files declared as indexed or relative organization, you use a Rewrite statement such as the following:

```
Rewrite record-name
  Invalid Key statement
  Not Invalid Key statement
End-Rewrite
```

You specify the record name (not a file name), which is the identifier on the 01-level entry under the FD entry for the file.

A Rewrite for a file declared with indexed or relative organization and with random or dynamic mode does not require you to read the existing record before updating it (although if only some fields are being updated, you may still need to first read the record). For indexed files, you must move the value of an existing record's key to the key fields in the FD entry record, as well as make certain the non-key fields have the intended values (either from a previous Read operation or by explicit assignments). For relative files, you must put the RRN of an existing record in the variable specified in the Select statement's Relative Key clause, as well as place the intended values in all fields of the FD entry record. Note that you can change the key value of a record when you use direct by RRN access. Of course, the new key value must not be an existing key value in another record if the keyed access path doesn't allow duplicates. When a Rewrite is executed for an indexed or relative file, the

Invalid Key condition is true if there's not an existing record for the specified key or RRN value. The Not Invalid Key condition is true if the record is successfully replaced in the file.[29]

One aspect of the Rewrite and Write statements catches many programmers by surprise when they first learn COBOL/400: After a successful Rewrite, the data in the FD entry's 01-level group item is no longer available.[30] You should not try to use the fields in subsequent statements (until they're filled again), and you must fill all the fields (either with a Read or explicit assignments) before you perform another Rewrite or you may get an "invalid data in record" error when DB2/400 attempts the update. This may sound mysterious, but what happens is that, after a Rewrite or Write, the COBOL/400 runtime releases the current memory location of the FD entry (and the 01-level group item) to DB2/400 to update the file. The COBOL/400 runtime then relocates the FD entry to a new memory location, which you must fill before you do anything with it.

The Rewrite (and Write) statement can have an optional From phrase such as

```
Rewrite record-name From variable ...
```

which is equivalent to

```
Move variable to record-name
Rewrite record-name ...
```

After a Rewrite with a From phrase, the data in the "from" variable is still available, even though the data in the record isn't. For this reason, some programmers adopt the practice of always manipulating a Working-Storage copy of a record that's going to be used in a Rewrite or Write operation and using the From phrase.

Writing New Records

When you write a new record, the record is either added to the end of the physical file member or put in a record location that's marked internally as "deleted." You can't write to a record location that's already occupied by an active record — you use an update operation for that purpose. In RPG IV, you can only add records to a file member. If you want to replace all the records in a file member, you must use a CLRPFM (Clear Physical File Member) command to clear the member before opening it for output. In COBOL/400, you have the option (based on the way you declare and open the file) to replace or add records.

---

[29] See the earlier discussion on error handling under the "COBOL/400 Read and Start Statements" section.

[30] This behavior of the Rewrite and Write operations is true of all versions of COBOL, not just COBOL/400.

As you add new records, DB2/400 automatically extends the auxiliary storage (i.e., disk space) for the file, if necessary. The CRTPF command's SIZE parameter lets you specify the initial number of records and number of additional increments allowed for a file (see "The Create Physical File Command" section in Chapter 2).

RPG IV Write Operation Code

The Write opcode adds a new record to a file.[31] The file must be declared either as an output file (O in position 17 of the F-spec) or as an input or update file with A coded in position 20 of the F-spec. The Write operation for an externally described file specifies a record format name (not a file name), with the following syntax:

```
....1....+....2....+....3....+....4....+....5....+....6....+....7....+
C*      Factor1+++++++Opcode++++Factor2+++++++                      ER
C                     Write    rcd-fmt-name                         xx
```

The error resulting indicator (*xx*) is optional and is set to "0" if the write is successful or to "1" if an error occurs.

Before a Write operation is executed, the program should ensure that all fields in the record format contain valid values. If the file is accessed by key, DB2/400 uses the value of the key fields as the record's key value when it adds the record to the file. Ordinarily, new records are appended to the end of the file. However, if the file is accessed by RRN and the RecNo keyword is specified on the file's F-spec, you must first set the value of the variable specified on the RecNo entry to the RRN you wish to write. This RRN should be a location that's marked internally as "deleted" (i.e., a location that doesn't contain an active record).

COBOL/400 Write Statement

The Write statement adds a new record to a file. There are lots of infrequently used variations of the Write, but three cases cover most database needs. The first two cases are to add records to a file with no key (i.e., an arrival sequenced access path) — either by first clearing the file member or by appending records to the end of the file. Both cases use a Write statement such as the following:

Write *record-name*

To clear the file member before adding records, open it for Output.[32] To append records, open it for Extend.

The third case is to add records to a file with a keyed access path that's been declared with indexed organization and random or dynamic access

---

[31] RPG IV also has the Except opcode for writing new records, but for externally described, full-procedural files, you should always use the Write opcode.

[32] The file must be a physical file for the member to be cleared.

mode. This is a typical way to declare a file that the program opens for I-O, so that records can be updated, added, and deleted. This situation requires a Write statement such as

```
Write record-name
   Invalid Key statement
   Not Invalid Key statement
End-Write
```

Before the Write, all the fields (key and non-key) in the FD entry record must be filled. The Invalid Key condition is true if the key value already exists in another record in the file and the file's Select statement doesn't include the With Duplicates phrase (i.e., the file has a unique keyed access path). The Not Invalid Key condition is true if the record is successfully written to the file.[33]

Like the Rewrite statement, the Write statement allows an optional From phrase to move data from a variable before the I/O operation. Also, as with a Rewrite operation, the contents of the FD entry record are not accessible after a successful Write operation.

Deleting Records

When you perform a delete operation, DB2/400 doesn't actually remove the record from the file member; it just marks the record location internally as "deleted." Locations flagged as "deleted" are reclaimed when you reorganize a file using the RGZPFM (Reorganize Physical File Member) command or copy the file member to another member. You can also specify the REUSEDLT(*YES) parameter on the CRTPF command to specify that DB2/400 should use locations flagged as "deleted" when you add new records to the member. Unless you're using direct access by RRN, you normally don't have to worry about how DB2/400 keeps track of deleted records.

RPG IV Delete Operation Code

To delete a record, the file must be declared for update (U in position 17). The Delete opcode can be used to delete the current record that was previously read by a Read, ReadP, Chain, ReadE, or ReadPE operation on a file opened for update. The read operation must not have specified the N (no record lock) opcode extender. There must not be any intervening I/O operations to the same file between the read and delete operations. (I/O operations to other files are permitted.) The syntax for a Delete statement to delete the current record specifies the file name and an optional error indicator:

```
....1....+....2....+....3....+....4....+....5....+....6....+....7....+
C*      Factor1+++++++Opcode++++Factor2+++++++                      ER
C                     Delete    file-name                          xx
```

---

[33] See the earlier discussion on error handling under the "COBOL/400 Read and Start Statements" section.

The error resulting indicator, if specified, is set to "0" if the delete is successful or to "1" if an error occurs.

You can also delete a specific record without first retrieving it by specifying a key or relative record number. The syntax for this form of the Delete opcode is

```
....1....+....2....+....3....+....4....+....5....+....6....+....7....+
C*     Factor1+++++++Opcode(N)+Factor2+++++++                    NRER
C      search-arg    Delete   file-name                         yyxx
```

The search argument, file name, and resulting indicators are used in the same way as described earlier for the Chain opcode. With this type of Delete statement, DB2/400 first attempts to read the specified record (with a lock) and then delete it.

COBOL/400 Delete Statement

The Delete statement deletes either the most recently read record (for sequential access mode) or a record identified by RRN or key value. The Delete statement is allowed only with relative and indexed organization and requires that the file be opened for I-O. The form of the Delete statement is

```
Delete file-name
  Invalid Key statement
  Not Invalid Key statement
End-Delete
```

For a file declared as sequential access mode, a successful Read must be executed before the Delete, and you should not code the Invalid Key or Not Invalid Key phrase. For direct access files, you set up the RRN or key value as for a Read, and the Invalid Key and Not Invalid Key phrases have a similar meaning.

Using Multiformat Logical Files

In the preceding discussion of I/O operations, we dealt only with single-format files. With multiformat logical files, both RPG IV and COBOL/400 provide options to determine the format of a record just read or to specify the format of a record to be read, updated, added, or deleted.

Specifying a Format in RPG IV

In RPG IV, the Update and Write opcodes require a record format name. The Read, ReadP, Chain, ReadE, ReadPE, SetLL, SetGT, and Delete opcodes optionally allow a record format name instead of a file name.[34] For multiformat files, if a file name is specified, the next record of any format is returned for sequential reads; otherwise the first format defined in the DDS is used for the operation. Generally, for multiformat files, you should always specify an explicit format for any operation other than a sequential read.

[34] Note that in RPG IV, unlike in COBOL/400, the record format name cannot be specified as a variable. In RPG IV, to read different record formats, you need multiple statements.

The following statement provides an example of using a record format name instead of a file name. The statement reads the record (if one exists) with AUTOLOANR as its record format and with the key value in the LcKList key list. This type of Chain will not read a record other than one with the specified record format and a matching key value.

```
....1....+....2....+....3....+....4....+....5....+....6....+....7....+.
C*     Factor1+++++++Opcode(N)+Factor2++++++                   NRER
C      LcKList       Chain     AutoLoanR                       9899
```

Similar rules apply to the ReadP, ReadE, ReadPE, SetLL, SetGT, and Delete operations when you specify a record format name. The Read opcode — which always reads the next sequential record, regardless of its record format — is an exception. If you specify a record format on a Read statement and the next sequential record is a different format, you get an I/O error, and the resulting indicator in positions 73-74 will be set on.[35] This behavior means you should generally use a SetLL (or Chain) and subsequent ReadE operations to read a particular record format sequentially.

After any successful read (including Chain), positioning, update, write, or delete operation, the format of the record that was accessed is in bytes 261–272 of the file information data structure.[36] If you want to check this value, you can declare the information data structure as in the following example:

```
....1....+....2....+....3....+....4....+....5....+....6
D CsInfDs         DS
D   CsFileName       *File
D   CsFileSts        *Status
D   CsOpcode         *Opcode
D   CsRcdFmt           261     272A
```

COBOL/400 Format Phrase

For multiformat logical files declared with indexed mode, you can specify an optional Format phrase on the Read, Start, Rewrite, Write, and Delete statements. The Format phrase immediately follows the file or record name (or follows the Into or From phrase, if one is specified). The following examples show alternative ways to code the Format phrase:

```
Read LoanCust01
  Format "AUTOLOANR" ...

Read LoanCust01
  Format LoanCust01Fmt ...

Read LoanCust01 Into LoanCust01AutoLoan
  Format "AUTOLOANR" ...
```

[35] I have no explanation for the odd (and not very useful) way the Read opcode handles a record format. Neither DB2/400 internally nor COBOL/400 works this way.

[36] The record format name and other parts of the I/O Feedback Information are not updated automatically if the program contains a Post opcode with a non-blank program device (Factor 1). For more information on the Open and I/O Feedback Information contents, see the RPG IV reference manual.

The first example uses a literal format name, which must be an upper-case name of a record format that exists in the file. The second example uses a variable — a more flexible technique. This variable should be a 10-character variable (Pic X(10)) and should contain an uppercase record format name when the I/O operation is executed. If the variable contains all blanks, the operation occurs as if no format name were specified. The third example just shows where to code the Format phrase if the I/O statement also includes an Into (or From) phrase.

If no format name is specified, the next record of any format is returned for sequential reads; for other operations, the first format defined in the DDS is used. Generally, for multiformat files, you should always specify an explicit format for any operation other than a sequential read.

After any successful read, positioning, update, write, or delete operation, the format of the record that was accessed is in bytes 21–30 of the I-O-Feedback area. If you want to check this value, you can declare a group item to receive a copy of this area and use the Accept statement to update it after an I/O operation:

```
Environment division.
Configuration section.
Special Names.
    I-O-Feedback is IOFeedback.
    .
    .
    .

Data division.
    .
    .
    .

Working-Storage.
    .
    .
    .

01 LoanCust01IOFeedback.
    02 Filler           Pic X(20).
    02 LoanCust01RcdFmt Pic X(10).
    .
    .
    .

Procedure division.
    .
    .
    .

Read LoanCust01 ...
    .
    .
    .

Accept LoanCust01IOFeedback
  From IOFeedback for LoanCust01.
```

Identifying Which File Member to Open

Chapter 4 introduced the use of the OVRDBF (Override with Database File) command to tell DB2/400 which specific file member to open when a program runs. If you don't specify an OVRDBF command before running a program, DB2/400 searches the job's library list for a file with the same name as the external file name used in the program's file declaration. In RPG IV, this is the file name on the F-spec.[37] In COBOL/400, this is the file name that follows the Database- keyword on the Assign clause of the Select statement. If the file is found, the first member added to the file (chronologically) is the member that's opened. In many cases, this default behavior works adequately. However, if different files (including files with the same name but in different libraries) or different members need to be accessed, an OVRDBF command should be executed before the program is run.

The following example shows an OVRDBF to specify that DB2/400 should open the DEC member of the SALE96 file in the APPDTA library when the program opens the file with the external name of SALE. Note that the library, file, and member names aren't case sensitive.[38]

```
OVRDBF FILE( sale )
       TOFILE( appdta/sale96 )
       MBR( dec )
```

Although an OVRDBF command isn't required in many cases, it's a good idea to always code them for production applications. One reason is that the first member in a multimember file may change when you remove and add members.

Record Format Level Identifiers

When you create an externally described file, DB2/400 calculates a **level identifier** for each record format in the file. This level identifier is a long hexadecimal value that's calculated from the following elements:

- record format name
- total record length
- the number of fields in the record format
- field names and attributes, including data type, length, and decimal positions
- relative position of each field in the record format

---

[37] In RPG IV, the internal file name (used in the program's I/O statements) and the external file name are the same.

[38] In this text's code examples, I use uppercase for CL keywords and lowercase for command parameter values so the reader can easily see what parts can be changed by the user. For example, the MBR parameter name is required, but you can replace the parameter value dec with any valid member name.

For example, the record level identifier for the CUSTOMERR record format in Figure 7.6 is 3A5ABA1F95DF2 and the level identifier for the CUSTUPDR record format in Figure 7.7 is 3B988342D75CC. You can use the DSPFD (Display File Description) command to display the level identifiers for a file's record formats.

Figure 7.6
Abbreviated CUSTOMER
File DDS

```
................T.Name++++++RLen++XDcU......Keyword+++++++++++++++++
                                           UNIQUE

          R CUSTOMERR                      TEXT( 'Customers' )

            CUSTID       7P Ø              TEXT( 'Customer ID' )
            NAME         30A               ALIAS( CUSTOMERNAME )
                                           TEXT( 'Customer name' )

          K CUSTID
```

Figure 7.7
Abbreviated CUSTUPD
File DDS

```
................T.Name++++++RLen++XDcU......Keyword+++++++++++++++++
                                           UNIQUE
                                           REF( CUSTOMER )

          R CUSTUPDR                       TEXT( 'Customer updates' )

            CUSTID    R

            SEQNBR       7P Ø              ALIAS( SEQUENCENUMBER )
                                           TEXT( 'Sequence within +
                                                   customer' )
            NAME      R

            RCDACT       1A                ALIAS( RECORDACTION )
                                           TEXT( 'Record action' )
                                           VALUES( 'A' 'C' 'D' 'E' 'X' )
  *                                        Add, Change, Delete, Error,
  *                                        Completed

          K CUSTID
          K SEQNBR
```

When you create an HLL program that declares an externally described file, the HLL compiler stores the level identifiers for all record formats in the program. Subsequently, when you run the program and attempt to open a file, DB2/400 retrieves the record format level identifiers from the file that's to be opened and checks them against all the corresponding level identifiers stored in the program. If any one of the file's record format level identifiers doesn't match, the open fails and the file status is set to 1217 for RPG IV and to "39" for COBOL/400. This step, known as **level checking**, provides valuable protection against running a program with a file that's been modified since the program was last compiled.[39]

---

[39] You can direct DB2/400 to not check record format level identifiers on an open operation by specifying LVLCHK(*NO) on the CRTPF, CRTLF, or OVRDBF commands. This is generally a dangerous programming practice, and should not be used.

When you recompile a program, the latest level identifiers are incorporated into the program object. Thus, if you change a file's definition, such as increasing the length of one of the file's fields, you often need to do no more than recompile programs that use the file to incorporate the change. Of course, if you remove a field that a program uses or make other changes that affect the way a program works, you may have to make changes to the HLL source, as well.

Special Considerations for Files with Date, Time, Timestamp, and Floating Point Fields

RPG IV provides full support for date, time, and timestamp fields, but COBOL/400 does not.[40] In RPG IV, you can work with these fields using a variety of date/time-related opcodes, such as AddDur, SubDur, and Extrct. Although the CRTRPGMOD (Create RPG Module) or CRTBNDRPG (Create Bound RPG Program) commands let you specify a CVTOPT(*DATETIME) parameter to convert date, time, and timestamp database fields to character equivalents, this option is primarily for compatibility with older RPG/400 programs and isn't recommended for new RPG IV programs.

In COBOL/400, by default, the Copy DDS-All-Formats and Copy DDS-*format-name* directives generate Filler entries for date, time, and timestamp database fields. However, if you specify the CVTOPT(*DATETIME) parameter on the CRTCBLMOD (Create COBOL Module) or CRTBNDCBL (Create Bound COBOL Program) command, *character* (Pic X(n)) variables will be generated for date, time, and timestamp database fields. The size of each entry is determined by the format of the database field. For example, the compiler generates a Pic X(10) variable for a date field with *ISO date format. When database records are read into the program, the record's internal date value is converted to the field's date format (e.g., 1997-12-31 for *ISO). You can use any COBOL character manipulations on the value in a (converted) date field.[41] You must, however, be sure any converted date field has a valid value in the appropriate format before executing a Write or Rewrite statement.

Neither RPG IV nor COBOL/400 supports floating point database fields.[42] You can still declare and access files with floating point fields, but these fields can't be used in your programs. When you update an existing record, the value of floating point fields is unchanged. When you add a new database record, RPG IV automatically sets floating point fields to zero. In COBOL/400, to write a new record that has a floating point field, you should first move Low-Values to the record before assigning values to the non-floating point fields. This step initializes the floating point fields to zero.

---

[40] As of V3R2 and V3R6 of RPG IV and COBOL/400. See Chapter 2 for a discussion of date, time, and timestamp fields.

[41] COBOL/400 doesn't, however, provide any date-specific operations.

[42] As of V3R2 and V3R6 of RPG IV and COBOL/400.

Special Considerations for Files with Null-Capable Fields

Neither RPG IV nor COBOL/400 currently supports null values fully. You can still process files with null-capable fields, but with some limitations.[43]

In RPG IV, you can specify ALWNULL(*YES) on the CRTRPGMOD and CRTBNDRPG commands. Programs created with this option convert null values to the DDS-defined or system-defined default value when a record is read into your program. You cannot set any field to null for output or update operations. If you specify ALWNULL(*NO), you get a data mapping error when you attempt to read a record with any null values, and the read fails.

In COBOL/400, when you open a file that has null-capable fields, you get a warning file status of "0P." You should allow for this warning when you check the result of an open operation to a file with null-capable fields. You can read records from the file, and for records that don't have any null values, the file status will be the same as for a file without null-capable fields. However, if you attempt to read a record that has one or more null values, the read fails, and the file status will be set to "90." You should allow for this exception when you check the result of a read operation to a file with null-capable fields.

Sample Programs with Error Handling

We've covered all the I/O programming details; now let's put them together in a couple of sample programs that include the type of error handling a production application should use. The sample application is a batch update program that uses records in the CUSTUPD transaction file (Figure 7.7) to add, change, and delete records in the CUSTOMER file (Figure 7.6). The sample files include just a few fields so we can concentrate on the HLL I/O programming techniques. The CUSTOMER file has a unique key (CUSTID) and one non-key field (NAME). The CUSTUPD file has those two fields plus the SEQNBR field to sequence transactions within a particular customer ID and the RCDACT field that contains a one-letter code for the action (or the status after the action is attempted). The basic requirements for a valid CUSTUPD record are that together the CUSTID and SEQNBR values are unique within the file and that

- *To add a record*: RCDACT is A; CUSTID must be a key value that's not already in CUSTOMER; and NAME can be anything (it should be a valid name, but isn't checked)

- *To change a record*: RCDACT is C; CUSTID must be a key value that exists in CUSTOMER; NAME can be anything (it should be a valid name, but isn't checked)

---

[43] See Chapter 2 (DDS) and Chapter 13 (SQL/400) for a discussion of null-capable fields. This limitation is as of V3R2 and V3R6 of the compilers. I expect that IBM will add full support for null values in future versions of RPG IV and COBOL/400.

- *To delete a record*: RCDACT is D; CUSTID must be a key value that exists in CUSTOMER; NAME isn't used

After the application attempts to perform a transaction, it replaces the RCDACT field with X, if the transaction is successful, or E if there's an error. When the CUSTUPD file is read, records with X or E in the RCDACT field are just skipped.

The application handles all types of I/O errors. When a "key not found" or "duplicate key" error occurs, it's treated as a transaction error, a message is displayed, and the CUSTUPD record is flagged with an E in the RCDACT field. Other I/O errors cause a message to be displayed, and the application terminates.

The application doesn't reflect all the considerations you might have to cover in a real application, but it does illustrate a full range of I/O operations for the two most common types of file access: sequential access by key (for CUSTUPD) and direct access by key (for CUSTOMER). It also shows a production-level approach to error handling.

The RPG IV UPDCUST Program

Figure 7.8 (page 174) shows the RPG IV version of the sample application program. Both the CUSTOMER and CUSTUPD files are declared with the following attributes:

- Disk (database)
- used for update (U in position 17)
- full-procedural (F in position 18)
- externally described (E in position 22)
- keyed access (K in position 34)
- user-controlled open (UsrOpn keyword)

The CUSTOMER file is also declared to allow record additions (A in position 20). Both files have an InfDs keyword that specifies a file information data structure that's declared at the beginning of the D-specs. When any I/O operation is performed, the RPG runtime updates the file's information data structure. Both files are also declared with a Prefix keyword so their fields will be unique within the program. The resulting field names for the two files are

CUSTOMER
    CsCustID
    CsName

CUSTUPD
      UpCustID
      UpSeqNbr
      UpName
      UpRcdAct

The previous sections of this chapter covered the various I/O statements that are used in the program. The main thing to notice is that each I/O statement uses indicator 99 as a "dummy" for the resulting indicators. This is necessary to prevent compiler errors[44] and so that if an error occurs on an I/O statement, control will flow to the next statement, rather than to an exception-handling routine.

A standard approach is used for detecting and handling various conditions that can occur during execution of an I/O operation. After each statement, a Select or If statement checks the file's status code for successful completion of the operation, an anticipated condition (such as duplicate key), and unanticipated error conditions.[45] The complete set of file status values is documented in the RPG IV reference manual, but the four mnemonics declared in the UPDCUST program are the most common ones to anticipate.[46] If you want to handle any other file status explicitly, all you have to do is add another When condition to the appropriate Select statement.

Instead of the "indicator-less" error handling used in this example, you can use different indicators for the resulting indicators and test them, instead of the file status, after each I/O operation.[47] In any case, you should always

---

[44] The compiler requires an indicator for the EOF/BOF and invalid key resulting indicators.

[45] Note that the RPG IV compiler emits error message RNF0262 for indented opcodes, such as those the sample program uses. You can change this to an information message (so the compile completes) by issuing the following command:

```
CHGMSGD MSGID( RNF0262 ) MSGF( qrpgle/qrpglemsg ) Sev( 0 )
```

Indented code makes the control structure of a program much more obvious so this workaround is handy to know about.

[46] For simplicity, this example doesn't use the RPG IV /Copy compiler directive, nor does it call external programs, bound procedures, or subprocedures (introduced in V3R2). All these techniques are valuable for production applications. You can use a /Copy member to hold constant declarations for the complete set of file status values as well as any declarative or executable code that you need to use repeatedly. More sophisticated error handling can be put in a separate program or bound procedure and called with a Call or CallB opcode. Using a called program or procedure simplifies application coding and standardizes the way applications handle errors. See the annotated bibliography for RPG IV and other references that provide help with these techniques.

[47] Actually, the "indicator-less" technique uses one "dummy" indicator in the resulting indicator columns but never references this indicator in subsequent statements.

I mention the indicator-based technique mainly because it's a fairly common RPG programming practice. The indicator-less technique is much more flexible (because you can handle any file status), is just as easy (because you should use the file status in error

check for error conditions after each I/O operation — even those you're sure will never fail.

The error routines demonstrate how fields in the file information data structure can be used to provide precise information about the cause of an I/O error. The sample routines are just a starting point; you can provide much more information, if you want. You can also write error messages to a log file or send them to an OS/400 message queue so they're available for subsequent diagnosis. Thorough, informative handling of errors is a crucial part of production application development.

Figure 7.8
UPDCUST Sample
RPG IV Program

```
... 1 ...+... 2 ...+... 3 ...+... 4 ...+... 5 ...+... 6 ...+... 7
* - - - - - - - - - - - - - - - - - - - - - - - - - - - - -
* Program name: UpdCust
* Author.       Paul Conte
* Date-Written. 03/26/96
* Purpose:      Update Customer file from CustUpd file records
* - - - - - - - - - - - - - - - - - - - - - - - - - - - - -

FCustomer  UF A E           K Disk    InfDs( CsInfDs )
F                                      UsrOpn
F                                      Prefix( Cs )

FCustUpd   UF   E           K Disk    InfDs( UpInfDs )
F                                      UsrOpn
F                                      Prefix( Up )

 * File information data structures

D CsInfDs         DS
D   CsFileName        *File
D   CsFileSts         *Status
D   CsOpcode          *Opcode

D UpInfDs         DS
D   UpFileName        *File
D   UpFileSts         *Status
D   UpOpcode          *Opcode

 * Mnemonics

D True            C                    Const( '1' )
D False           C                    Const( '0' )
D FStsOK          C                    Const(    0 )
D FStsEOF         C                    Const(   11 )
D FStsNoKey       C                    Const(   12 )
D FStsDupKey      C                    Const( 1021 )
D AddAct          C                    Const( 'A' )
D ChangeAct       C                    Const( 'C' )
D DeleteAct       C                    Const( 'D' )
D CompltAct       C                    Const( 'X' )
D ErrAct          C                    Const( 'E' )
```

Figure 7.8 continued

messages, anyway), and results in much more readable code than the indicator-based technique. The main reason for the indicator-based technique is that before the addition of structured programming opcodes to RPG indicators were the only way to control program flow.

Figure 7.8
Continued

```
... 1 ...+... 2 ...+... 3 ...+... 4 ...+... 5 ...+... 6 ...+... 7
D InvActLbl        C                         Const( 'Invalid action' )
D NoKeyLbl         C                         Const( 'Key not found in file' )
D DupKeyLbl        C                         Const( 'Duplicate key in file' )

 * Program variables

D FileName         S                         Like( CsFileName )
D FileSts          S                         Like( CsFileSts )
D FileOpcode       S                         Like( CsOpcode )
D UpMoreRcds       S              1A         Inz( 'Ø' )
D CustIDText       S              7A
D FStsText         S              5A
D ErrText          S             5ØA
D Msg              S             52A

 * *In99 is used as "dummy" indicator where required on op. codes

 * - - - - - - - - - - - - - - - - - - - - - - - - - - - - -
 *     Main block
C                   ExSr      OpenFiles

C                   DoW       UpMoreRcds = True
C                     ExSr    PrcNxtCust
C                   EndDo

C                   ExSr      CloseFiles

C                   ExSr      ExitPgm

 * - - - - - - - - - - - - - - - - - - - - - - - - - - - - -
C     OpenFiles     BegSr

C                   Open      Customer                            99

C                   If        CsFileSts <> FStsOK
C                     ExSr    CsIOErr
C                   EndIf


C                   Open      CustUpd                             99

C                   If        UpFileSts <> FStsOK
C                     ExSr    UpIOErr
C                   Else
C                     Eval    UpMoreRcds = True
C                   EndIf

C                   EndSr
 * - - - - - - - - - - - - - - - - - - - - - - - - - - - - -
C     CloseFiles    BegSr

C                   Close     Customer                            99

C                   If        CsFileSts <> FStsOK
C                     ExSr    CsIOErr
C                   EndIf


C                   Close     CustUpd                             99

C                   If        UpFileSts <> FStsOK
C                     ExSr    UpIOErr
```

Figure 7.8 continued

Figure 7.8
Continued

```
      ... 1 ...+... 2 ...+... 3 ...+... 4 ...+... 5 ...+... 6 ...+... 7
C                       EndIf

C                       Eval      UpMoreRcds = False

C                       EndSr
 * - - - - - - - - - - - - - - - - - - - - - - - - - - - - - - - - - -
C     PrcNxtCust    BegSr

 * Read a CustUpd record, and dispatch on its action code.
 *
 * Each action-handling routine attempts to perform the action
 * and then changes the action code to indicate either
 * successful completion or an error. The modified CustUpd
 * record is then rewritten.

C                       Read      CustUpd                              9999

C                       Select
C                         When    UpFileSts = FStsOK
C                           ExSr  DoTransact
C                           ExSr  UpdCustUpd
C                         When    UpFileSts = FStsEOF
C                           Eval  UpMoreRcds = False
C                         Other
C                           ExSr  UpIOErr
C                       EndSl

C                       EndSr
 * - - - - - - - - - - - - - - - - - - - - - - - - - - - - - - - - - -
C     DoTransact    BegSr

C                       Select
C                         When    UpRcdAct = AddAct
C                           ExSr  AddCust
C                         When    UpRcdAct = ChangeAct
C                           ExSr  ChangeCust
C                         When    UpRcdAct = DeleteAct
C                           ExSr  DeleteCust
C                         When    UpRcdAct = CompltAct
 *                         Skip
C                         When    UpRcdAct = ErrAct
 *                         Skip
C                         Other
C                           Eval  ErrText = InvActLbl
C                           ExSr  ActionErr
C                       EndSl

C                       EndSr
 * - - - - - - - - - - - - - - - - - - - - - - - - - - - - - - - - - -
C     AddCust       BegSr

C                       Eval      CsCustID = UpCustID
C                       Eval      CsName   = UpName

C                       Write     CustomerR                            99

C                       Select
C                         When    CsFileSts = FStsDupKey
C                           Eval  ErrText   = DupKeyLbl
C                           ExSr  ActionErr
C                           Eval  UpRcdAct  = ErrAct
C                         When    CsFileSts = FStsOK
```

Figure 7.8 continued

Figure 7.8
Continued

```
... 1 ...+... 2 ...+... 3 ...+... 4 ...+... 5 ...+... 6 ...+... 7
C                           Eval  UpRcdAct  = CompltAct
C                           Other
C                             ExSr  CsIOErr
C                           EndSl

C                           EndSr
 * - - - - - - - - - - - - - - - - - - - - - - - - - - - - - - -
C      ChangeCust    BegSr

 * Attempt to read the specified Customer record, change its
 * data (i.e., name), and rewrite the record.

C      UpCustID      Chain     Customer                           9999

C                    Select
C                      When    CsFileSts = FStsNoKey
C                        Eval  ErrText   = NoKeyLbl
C                        ExSr  ActionErr
C                        Eval  UpRcdAct  = ErrAct
C                      When    CsFileSts = FStsOK
C                        Eval  CsName    = UpName
C                        ExSr  UpdateCust
C                      Other
C                        ExSr  CsIOErr
C                    EndSl

C                    EndSr
 * - - - - - - - - - - - - - - - - - - - - - - - - - - - - - - -
C      UpdateCust    BegSr

C                    Update    CustomerR                            99

C                    Select
C                      When    CsFileSts = FStsOK
C                        Eval  UpRcdAct  = CompltAct
C                      Other
C                        ExSr  CsIOErr
C                    EndSl

C                    EndSr
 * - - - - - - - - - - - - - - - - - - - - - - - - - - - - - - -
C      DeleteCust    BegSr

C      UpCustID      Delete    Customer                           9999

C                    Select
C                      When    CsFileSts = FStsNoKey
C                        Eval  ErrText   = NoKeyLbl
C                        ExSr  ActionErr
C                        Eval  UpRcdAct  = ErrAct
C                      When    CsFileSts = FStsOK
C                        Eval  UpRcdAct  = CompltAct
C                      Other
C                        ExSr  CsIOErr
C                    EndSl

C                    EndSr
 * - - - - - - - - - - - - - - - - - - - - - - - - - - - - - - -
C      UpdCustUpd    BegSr

C                    Update    CustUpdR                             99
```

Figure 7.8 continued

Figure 7.8
Continued

```
  ... 1 ...+... 2 ...+... 3 ...+... 4 ...+... 5 ...+... 6 ...+... 7
  C                    If        UpFileSts <> FStsOK
  C                      ExSr    UpIOErr
  C                    EndIf

  C                    EndSr
  * - - - - - - - - - - - - - - - - - - - - - - - - - - - - - - -
  C     CsIOErr        BegSr

  * Globals used as input parameters:   CsInfDs
  *
  * Globals used as arguments to IOErr: FileName
  *                                      FileSts
  *                                      FileOpcode

  C                    Eval      FileName  = CsFileName
  C                    Eval      FileSts   = CsFileSts
  C                    Eval      FileOpcode = CsOpcode

  C                    ExSr      IOErr

  C                    EndSr
  * - - - - - - - - - - - - - - - - - - - - - - - - - - - - - - -
  C     UpIOErr        BegSr

  * Globals used as input parameters:   UpInfDs
  *
  * Globals used as arguments to IOErr: FileName
  *                                      FileSts
  *                                      FileOpcode

  C                    Eval      FileName  = UpFileName
  C                    Eval      FileSts   = UpFileSts
  C                    Eval      FileOpcode = UpOpcode
  C                    ExSr      IOErr

  C                    EndSr
  * - - - - - - - - - - - - - - - - - - - - - - - - - - - - - - -
  C     IOErr          BegSr

  * Globals used as input parameters: FileName
  *                                    FileSts
  *                                    FileOpcode
  *
  * Globals used as work variables:   FStsText
  *                                    Msg

  C                    MoveL     FileSts      FStsText

  C                    Eval      Msg = 'I/O error '
  C                                  + FStsText
  C                                  + ' on '
  C                                  + FileOpcode
  C                                  + ' for '
  C                                  + FileName
  C                                  + ' file.'
  C     Msg            Dsply                              99
  C                    ExSr      ExitPgm

  C                    EndSr
  * - - - - - - - - - - - - - - - - - - - - - - - - - - - - - - -
```

Figure 7.8 continued

Figure 7.8
Continued

```
... 1 ...+... 2 ...+... 3 ...+... 4 ...+... 5 ...+... 6 ...+... 7
C     ActionErr     BegSr

* Globals used as input parameters: UpRcdAct
*                                    ErrText
*
* Globals used as work variables:   CustIDText
*                                    Msg

C                   MoveL     UpCustID      CustIDText

C                   Eval      Msg = 'Update error for customer '
C                             + CustIDText
C                             + ' on "'
C                             + UpRcdAct
C                             + '" action.'
C     Msg           Dsply                                          99

C                   Eval      Msg = %TrimR( ErrText ) + '.'
C     Msg           Dsply                                          99

C                   EndSr
* - - - - - - - - - - - - - - - - - - - - - - - - - - - - - - - -
C     *PsSr         BegSr

* Globals used as work variables: Msg

C                   Eval      Msg = 'Unexpected program error.'
C     Msg           Dsply                                          99
C                   ExSr      ExitPgm

C                   EndSr
* - - - - - - - - - - - - - - - - - - - - - - - - - - - - - - - -
C     ExitPgm       BegSr

* All files are automatically closed when LR is on at return point.

C                   Eval      *InLR = *On
C                   Return

C                   EndSr
* - - - - - - - - - - - - - - - - - - - - - - - - - - - - - - - -
```

The COBOL/400 UPDCUST Program

Figure 7.9 (page 181) shows the COBOL/400 version of the sample application. Both files are declared as Database files with keyed access (Organization Indexed). By using the Externally-Described-Key clause and the Copy DDS-All-Formats directive to declare the record structure under the FD entry, both files are treated as externally described.

Both files have a File Status clause in their respective Select statements to specify a file status variable that's declared in Working-Storage. When any I/O operation is performed, the COBOL/400 runtime updates the corresponding file status variable. Both files' record structures are also copied in using the Alias keyword so their fields have the long names from the DDS ALIAS keyword (if any) within the program. The resulting field names for the two files are:

CUSTOMER
    CustID
    CustomerName

CUSTUPD
    CustID
    SequenceNumber
    CustomerName
    RecordAction

The previous sections of this chapter covered the various I/O statements that are used in the program. The main thing to notice is that each I/O statement that can have an At End or Invalid Key phrase specifies Continue (which means "do nothing") as a "dummy" action for the conditions to avoid compiler errors. The result of specifying Continue is that if one of these conditions occurs on an I/O statement, control flows to the next statement. Control also flows to the next statement for successful completion of the I/O operation or any other error condition.

A standard approach is used for detecting and handling various conditions that can occur during execution of an I/O operation. After each statement, an Evaluate or If statement checks the corresponding file status code for successful completion of the operation, an anticipated condition (such as duplicate key), and unanticipated error conditions. The complete set of file status values is documented in the appendices of the COBOL/400 reference manual, but the four mnemonics declared in the UPDCUST program are the most common ones to anticipate.[49] If you want to handle any other file status explicitly, all you have to do is add another When condition to the appropriate Evaluate statement.

As an alternative to checking the file status, you can use (Not) At End and (Not) Invalid Key phrases, but these alone will not catch other I/O errors. COBOL/400 also allows Procedure Division Declaratives sections to trap I/O errors, but there's a Catch-22 involved. If you specify a File Status clause on a file's Select statement, the COBOL/400 runtime won't call the file's Declarative section when an error occurs. Because the file status is a highly useful piece of diagnostic information, you should always use the File Status clause, and thus, you're left with needing to check the file status after

---

[49] For simplicity, this example doesn't use the COBOL/400 Copy compiler directive (other than Copy DDS-All-Formats) nor does it call external programs or bound procedures. Both those techniques are valuable for production applications. You can use a Copy member to hold constant declarations for the complete set of file status values as well as any declarative or executable code that you need to use repeatedly. More sophisticated error handling can be put in a separate program or bound procedure and called with a Call statement. Using a called program or procedure simplifies application coding and standardizes the way applications handle errors. See the annotated bibliography for COBOL/400 and other references that provide help with these techniques.

each I/O statement anyway. However you decide to do it, just be sure you always check for error conditions after each I/O operation — even those you're sure will never fail.

The error routines are implemented as COBOL/400 nested programs[50] and demonstrate how you can provide precise information about the cause of an I/O error. The sample routines are just a starting point; you can provide much more information, if you want.[51] You can also write error messages to a log file or send them to an OS/400 message queue so they're available for subsequent diagnosis. Thorough, informative handling of errors is a crucial part of production application development.

Figure 7.9
UPDCUST Sample
COBOL/400 Program

```
Id division.

Program-Id.    UpdCust.
Author.        Paul Conte.
Date-Written.  03/26/96.
*  Purpose:      Update Customer file from CustUpd file records

* - - - - - - - - - - - - - - - - - - - - - - - - - - - - - -
Environment division.
Input-Output section.
File-Control.

    Select          CustomerFile
      Assign        Database-Customer
      Organization  Indexed
      Access        Random
      Record Key    Externally-Described-Key
      File Status   CustomerSts.

    Select          CustUpdFile
      Assign        Database-CustUpd
      Organization  Indexed
      Access        Sequential
      Record Key    Externally-Described-Key
      File Status   CustUpdSts.
* - - - - - - - - - - - - - - - - - - - - - - - - - - - - - -
* - - - - - - - - - - - - - - - - - - - - - - - - - - - - - -
Data division.

File section.

FD  CustomerFile.
01  CustomerRcd.
    Copy DDS-All-Formats of Customer with Alias.

FD  CustUpdFile.
01  CustUpdRcd.
    Copy DDS-All-Formats of CustUpd  with Alias.
```

Figure 7.9 continued

---

[50] These are an ANSI standard COBOL feature that was introduced in V3R1 ILE COBOL/400. You can use paragraphs and Perform's in earlier versions of COBOL/400.

[51] The COBOL/400 Open-Feedback and I-O-Feedback areas and the Accept verb provide a means to get extensive information on each I/O operation. These features are covered in the COBOL/400 reference manual.

Figure 7.9
Continued

```
Working-Storage section.

01   DataTypes              Global.
     02 AS400NameType       Pic X(10).
     02 BooleanType         Pic 1.
     02 CobolVerbType       Pic X(10).
     02 FileStsType         Pic X(02).
     02 TextType            Pic X(50).


01   FileSts.
     02 CustomerSts         Like FileStsType.
     02 CustUpdSts          Like FileStsType.


01   Mnemonics.
     02 FileStsOK           Like FileStsType     Value "00".
     02 FileStsEOF          Like FileStsType     Value "10".
     02 FileStsNoKey        Like FileStsType     Value "23".
     02 FileStsDupeKey      Like FileStsType     Value "22".

     02 CustomerFileName Like AS400NameType  Value "Customer".
     02 CustUpdFileName  Like AS400NameType  Value "CustUpd".

     02 IOErrPgm            Like AS400NameType   Value "IOERR".
     02 ActionErrPgm        Like AS400NameType   Value "ACTIONERR".

     02 AddAction           Like RecordAction of CustUpdRcd
                                                 Value "A".
     02 ChangeAction        Like AddAction       Value "C".
     02 CompletedAction     Like AddAction       Value "X".
     02 DeleteAction        Like AddAction       Value "D".
     02 ErrorAction         Like AddAction       Value "E".

     02 CloseLabel          Like CobolVerbType   Value "Close".
     02 DeleteLabel         Like CobolVerbType   Value "Delete".
     02 OpenLabel           Like CobolVerbType   Value "Open".
     02 ReadLabel           Like CobolVerbType   Value "Read".
     02 RewriteLabel        Like CobolVerbType   Value "Rewite".
     02 WriteLabel          Like CobolVerbType   Value "Write".

     02 InvActionLabel      Like TextType
                            Value "Invalid action".
     02 NoKeyLabel          Like TextType
                            Value "Key not found in file".
     02 DupeKeyLabel        Like TextType
                            Value "Duplicate key in file".

01   CustUpdNoMoreRcdsState Like BooleanType Value B"1".
     88 CustUpdMoreRcds                          Value B"0".
     88 CustUpdNoMoreRcds                         Value B"1".

* - - - - - - - - - - - - - - - - - - - - - - - - - - - -
* - - - - - - - - - - - - - - - - - - - - - - - - - - - -
Procedure division.

MainBlock.

    Perform OpenFiles.

    Perform ProcessNextCustomer Until CustUpdNoMoreRcds.

    Perform CloseFiles.

    GoBack.
```

Figure 7.9 continued

Figure 7.9
Continued

```
* - - - - - - - - - - - - - - - - - - - - - - - - - - - - -
  OpenFiles.

      Open I-O CustomerFile.

      If CustomerSts Not = FileStsOK
         Call IOErrPgm Using by Content
              OpenLabel
              CustomerFileName
              CustomerSts
      End-If.

      Open I-O CustUpdFile.

      If CustUpdSts Not = FileStsOK
         Call IOErrPgm Using by Content
              OpenLabel
              CustUpdFileName
              CustUpdSts
      Else
         Set CustUpdMoreRcds to True
      End-If.
* - - - - - - - - - - - - - - - - - - - - - - - - - - - - -
  CloseFiles.

      Close CustomerFile.

      If CustomerSts Not = FileStsOK
         Call IOErrPgm Using by Content
              CloseLabel
              CustomerFileName
              CustomerSts
      End-If.


      Close CustUpdFile.

      If CustUpdSts Not = FileStsOK
         Call IOErrPgm Using by Content
              CloseLabel
              CustUpdFileName
              CustUpdSts
      End-If.

      Set CustUpdNoMoreRcds to True.
* - - - - - - - - - - - - - - - - - - - - - - - - - - - - -
  ProcessNextCustomer.

* Read a CustUpd record, and dispatch on its action code.
*
* Each action-handling routine attempts to perform the action
* and then changes the action code to indicate either
* successful completion or an error. The modified CustUpd
* record is then rewritten.

      Read CustUpdFile
        At End Continue.

      Evaluate CustUpdSts
         When FileStsOK
                 Perform DoTransactionForCurCustomer
                 Perform RewriteCustUpdRcd
```

Figure 7.9 continued

Figure 7.9
Continued

```
                When FileStsEOF
                       Set CustUpdNoMoreRcds to True
                When Other
                       Call IOErrPgm Using by Content
                             ReadLabel
                             CustUpdFileName
                             CustUpdSts
        End-Evaluate.
*  - - - - - - - - - - - - - - - - - - - - - - - - - - - - - - - -
   DoTransactionForCurCustomer.

        Evaluate RecordAction of CustUpdRcd
            When AddAction        Perform AddCustomer
            When ChangeAction     Perform ChangeCustomer
            When DeleteAction     Perform DeleteCustomer
            When CompletedAction  Continue
            When ErrorAction      Continue
            When Other Call ActionErrPgm Using by Content
                            InvActionLabel
                            RecordAction of CustUpdRcd
                            CustID         of CustUpdRcd
        End-Evaluate.
*  - - - - - - - - - - - - - - - - - - - - - - - - - - - - - - - -
   AddCustomer.

        Move CustId of CustUpdRcd to
             CustId of CustomerRcd.

        Move CustomerName of CustUpdRcd to
             CustomerName of CustomerRcd.

        Write CustomerRcd
           Invalid Key Continue.

        Evaluate CustomerSts
            When FileStsOK
                    Move CompletedAction to RecordAction of CustUpdRcd
            When FileStsDupeKey
                    Perform DupeKeyErr
            When Other
                    Call IOErrPgm Using by Content
                           WriteLabel
                           CustomerFileName
                           CustomerSts
        End-Evaluate.

*  - - - - - - - - - - - - - - - - - - - - - - - - - - - - - - - -
   ChangeCustomer.

* Attempt to read the specified Customer record, change its
* data (i.e., name), and rewrite the record.

        Move CustId of CustUpdRcd to
             CustId of CustomerRcd.

        Read CustomerFile
           Invalid Key Continue.

        Evaluate CustomerSts
            When FileStsOK
                    Move CustomerName of CustUpdRcd to
                         CustomerName of CustomerRcd
```

Figure 7.9 continued

Figure 7.9
Continued

```
                              Perform RewriteCustomerRcd
                  When FileStsNoKey
                              Perform NoKeyErr
                  When Other
                         Call IOErrPgm Using by Content
                                ReadLabel
                                CustomerFileName
                                CustomerSts
          End-Evaluate.
* - - - - - - - - - - - - - - - - - - - - - - - - - - - - - - - - -
 RewriteCustomerRcd.

* Note that an Invalid Key condition indicates an unexpected
* error because the record was just read with the same key.

      Rewrite CustomerRcd
        Invalid Key Continue.

      Evaluate CustomerSts
          When FileStsOK
                  Move CompletedAction to RecordAction of CustUpdRcd
          When Other
                  Call IOErrPgm Using by Content
                         RewriteLabel
                         CustomerFileName
                         CustomerSts
      End-Evaluate.
* - - - - - - - - - - - - - - - - - - - - - - - - - - - - - - - - -
 DeleteCustomer.

      Move CustId of CustUpdRcd to
          CustId of CustomerRcd.

      Delete CustomerFile
        Invalid Key Continue.

      Evaluate CustomerSts
          When FileStsOK
                  Move CompletedAction to RecordAction of CustUpdRcd
          When FileStsNoKey
                  Perform NoKeyErr
          When Other
                  Call IOErrPgm Using by Content
                         DeleteLabel
                         CustomerFileName
                         CustomerSts
      End-Evaluate.
* - - - - - - - - - - - - - - - - - - - - - - - - - - - - - - - - -
 RewriteCustUpdRcd.

      Rewrite CustUpdRcd
        Invalid Key Continue.

      If CustUpdSts Not = FileStsOK
         Call IOErrPgm Using by Content
              RewriteLabel
              CustUpdFileName
              CustUpdSts
      End-If.

* - - - - - - - - - - - - - - - - - - - - - - - - - - - - - - - - -
```

Figure 7.9 continued

Figure 7.9
Continued

```
DupeKeyErr.

    Call ActionErrPgm Using by Content
         DupeKeyLabel
         RecordAction of CustUpdRcd
         CustID       of CustUpdRcd.

    Move ErrorAction to RecordAction of CustUpdRcd.

* - - - - - - - - - - - - - - - - - - - - - - - - - - - - - - - - -
* - - - - - - - - - - - - - - - - - - - - - - - - - - - - - - - - -
NoKeyErr.

    Call ActionErrPgm Using by Content
         NoKeyLabel
         RecordAction of CustUpdRcd
         CustID       of CustUpdRcd.

    Move ErrorAction to RecordAction of CustUpdRcd.

* - - - - - - - - - - - - - - - - - - - - - - - - - - - - - - - -
* - - - - - - - - - - - - - - - - - - - - - - - - - - - - - - - -

Id division.

  Program-Id. IOErr.
* Purpose:    Handle an unexpected I/O error
*             Emit an error message and end the run unit
*             Ending the run unit will close all open files

*----------------------------------------------------------------
Data division.

Linkage section.

01  CobolVerb Like CobolVerbType.
01  FileName  Like AS400NameType.
01  FileSts   Like FileStsType.

Procedure division Using CobolVerb
                         FileName
                         FileSts.

MainBlock.

    Display "I/O error " FileSts
            " on "       CobolVerb
            " for "      FileName  " file.".

    Stop Run.

End program IOErr.

* - - - - - - - - - - - - - - - - - - - - - - - - - - - - - - - -
* - - - - - - - - - - - - - - - - - - - - - - - - - - - - - - - -

Id division.

  Program-Id. ActionErr.
* Purpose:    Handle an action error
*             Emit an error message

*----------------------------------------------------------------
```

Figure 7.9 continued

Figure 7.9
Continued

```
Data division.

Linkage section.

01  ErrorText    Like TextType.
01  Action       Pic X(1).
01  CustID       Pic S9(7) Comp-3.

Procedure division Using ErrorText
                        Action
                        CustID.

MainBlock.

    Display "Update error for customer " CustID
            " on '"                       Action
            "' action: '"                 ErrorText "'.".

    GoBack.

End program ActionErr.

* - - - - - - - - - - - - - - - - - - - - - - - - - - - - - - - - - -
* - - - - - - - - - - - - - - - - - - - - - - - - - - - - - - - - - -

End program UpdCust.
```

Coding Suggestions

General

- For updating, use either a physical file or a single-format, non-join logical file whose member(s) do not span multiple physical file members. Update statements are much simpler for these types of files because only one physical file member is opened.

- For combining related information from different files for input, join logical files are generally simpler to work with than multiformat logical files.

- Always leave level checking in effect (don't use LVLCHK(*NO) on the CRTPF, CRTLF, or OVRDBF commands).

- Unless a program may subsequently update a record, do not place a lock on it when reading it. You can read records without a record lock by reading them through a file opened for input-only or by using the RPG IV (N) opcode extender or the COBOL/400 No Lock phrase when you read a record from a file opened for update.

RPG IV

- Use standard, two-character prefixes for all files. Always specify the Prefix keyword on the F-spec.

- Always specify the InfDs keyword on the F-spec, and always check the file status after each I/O operation.

- Generally, specify the UsrOpn keyword on the F-spec, and use explicit Open statements to provide better error handling and resource control.

- For a DB2/400 file for which you've declared the two-character prefix using the Prefix(*Xx*) keyword on the file's F-spec, use the following naming conventions:

*Xx*InfDs	for the file information data structure specified in the InfDs keyword on the F-spec and declared in the D-specs.
*Xx*FileName	for the *File subfield of the *Xx*InfDs file information data structure
*Xx*FileSts	for the *Status subfield of the *Xx*InfDs data structure
*Xx*Opcode	for the *Opcode subfield of the *Xx*InfDs data structure
*Xx*RcdFmt	for the record format subfield of the *Xx*InfDs data structure

- Use mnemonics (instead of literals) for file status values and other program constants. These can be coded in a source member that is /Copy'd into all programs.

- Be sure to close a file when you're done using it. A file can be closed either with an explicit Close statement, or by setting on the LR indicator before returning from a program.

- Generally, the "indicator-less" technique shown in the sample RPG IV program (Figure 7.8) provides more comprehensive error handling, reduces the potential for errors with indicators, and results in more readable code.

- If resulting indicators are used, always convert their value to a meaningfully named variable immediately after each I/O operation. Never use indicators directly (e.g., *In99) in subsequent conditional statements.

- Use standard routines for handling all I/O errors.

COBOL/400

- Always use the File Status clause on the Select statement, and always check the file status after each I/O operation.

- For a DB2/400 file with the name *filename*, use the following naming conventions:

*filename*File	for the internal file name (following a Select keyword and on the FD entry)
*filename*Rcd	for the 01-level name that follows the FD entry
*filename*Sts	for the File Status variable
*filename*Fmt	for a variable to hold the record format name supplied on the Format clause of I/O statements for multiformat logical files
*filename*IOFeeback	for the 01-level name into which the I-O-Feedback area is accepted

*filename*RcdFmt   for a variable to hold the format name in the I-O-Feedback area

For example: CustomerFile, CustomerRcd, CustomerSts, etc.

These conventions make it easy to know what name to use when referring to the file, the record, and the status.

- Use the Copy DDS-... compiler directive to declare the FD entry's record structure. Use Copy DDS-All-Formats for single-format files. Use either Copy DDS-All-Formats or Copy DDS-*format-name* for multiformat files.

    For Copy directive options, such as using alias names, use keywords (e.g., Alias), not the variations on Copy DDS-... (e.g., Copy DD-... and Copy DDR-...).

    Consider using the Alias option to enable the use of long field names in your program.

- Use mnemonics (instead of literals) for file status values and other program constants. These can be coded in a source member that is Copy'd into all programs.

- Be sure to close a file when you're done using it. A file can be closed either with an explicit Close statement or by executing a Stop Run.

- Use standard routines for handling all I/O errors.

Chapter Summary

To use a DB2/400 file from an HLL program, you must declare the file, open it, and then execute appropriate I/O operations, including positioning, read, update, write, and delete statements. You can declare a file for sequential or direct access, either by relative record number or by key. The file declaration and, in some HLLs, the type of file open, determine which operations are valid for the file. In RPG IV, a file is declared with an F-spec, and the compiler generates I-spec and O-specs to declare the fields in the file's record format(s). In COBOL/400, the Select statement declares a file and the Copy-DDS-All-Formats or Copy-DDS-*format-name* compiler directive generates record declarations for the file.

After an I/O operation is executed, DB2/400 (and the HLL runtime) update file status information for the file involved in the I/O operation. An RPG IV program can access this status information by using the F-spec InfDs keyword to specify a file information data structure, which is declared later in the program. A COBOL/400 program can access the file status by specifying the File Status clause on the Select statement and declaring a file status variable in Working-Storage.

Both RPG IV and COBOL/400 provide explicit Open and Close statements. RPG IV also opens files by default (if the UsrOpn keyword isn't specified on the F-spec), and closes all files when a program returns with the LR indicator set on. COBOL closes all files when a program executes a Stop Run.

RPG IV provides five opcodes to read a file (Read, ReadP, Chain, ReadE, and ReadPE) and two opcodes to position the file pointer before a subsequent read operation (SetLL, and SetGT). With one or more of these opcodes, you can read a file sequentially forward or backward starting from the beginning or end of the file or from a specific record. You can read sequentially by key or RRN, or you can read a specific record by specifying its key value or RRN.

COBOL/400 provides various options for the Read and Start statements, so you can read a file sequentially forward or backward starting from the beginning or end of the file or from a specific record. As with RPG IV, with COBOL/400 you can read sequentially by key or RRN, or you can read a specific record by specifying its key value or RRN.

With a file opened for update, you can replace or delete existing records. You can use the RPG IV Update or Delete opcodes, or the COBOL/400 Rewrite or Delete statements to update or delete the current record (the one that's just been read). In both languages, you can also delete a record (without first reading it) by specifying its key or RRN. COBOL/400 (but not RPG IV) also lets you update a record (without first reading it) by specifying its key or RRN.

You can add new records to a file opened for output or update using the RPG IV and COBOL/400 Write statements. Normally, a new record is added to the end of the file member to which it's written.

Both RPG IV and COBOL/400 support multiformat logical files. The various RPG IV I/O opcodes allow (or in some cases, require) the use of a record format name, rather than a file name. The COBOL/400 statements all allow an optional Format phrase to specify a particular record format.

By default, when a program opens a file, DB2/400 opens the first member of the file named on the RPG IV F-spec or the COBOL/400 Select statement. To open a different member in the same or different DB2/400 file, you code an OVRDBF command before calling the program.

DB2/400 and the HLL compilers use record format level identifiers to ensure that an externally described file's record descriptions haven't changed since a program that uses the file was compiled. The level identifiers are stored as part of both the file object and the program object, so they can be compared when a file is opened. Each time you compile a program, the file's current level identifiers are copied into the program object.

RPG IV, but not COBOL/400, supports date, time, and timestamp database fields. To access these fields in COBOL/400, you must specify the CVTOPT(*DATETIME) parameter when you compile the COBOL/400 program. Within the COBOL/400 program, date, time, and timestamp data is converted to character format. Neither RPG IV nor COBOL/400 support null values in database fields. Although you can open files that have null-capable fields, you must check various file status values to handle records with null values. Neither RPG IV nor COBOL/400 supports floating-point database fields.

Key Terms

General
access method
direct access
file pointer
level checking
sequential access

RPG IV
calculation specification
(C-spec)

definition specification
(D-spec)
file information data
structure
file description specification
(F-spec)
input specification (I-spec)
key list
output specification (O-spec)
partial key

COBOL/400
file description (FD) entry
select clause

Exercises

General

1. Explain four different ways a database file might be used in an application, then briefly explain how the application works with records from the file. Consider various combinations of the following:

   Sequential, direct, or both types of access

   Access by key or by RRN

   Types of I/O operations (e.g., read, positioning, update, write, and delete)

2. Describe five different specific results of attempted I/O operations. For each alternative, list the I/O operation (e.g., read), the type of access (e.g., direct by key), and the possible result (e.g., record successfully read).

3. Explain why it's important to check the file status after each I/O operation.

4. Identify at least two advantages of using externally described database files in HLL programs. Are there any disadvantages?

5. Briefly describe what must be done with HLL programs that use a file after the file's record format (i.e., its field definitions) is changed.

6. Briefly describe the advantages (if any) and disadvantages (if any) of using a multiformat logical file rather than a join logical file for input (only) applications. Consider various types of applications (e.g., retrieving customer sale information) you might develop that require data from multiple underlying physical files.

7. Briefly describe the advantages (if any) and disadvantages (if any) of using a multiformat logical file rather than multiple physical files or multiple single-format, non-join logical files for update applications. Consider various types of applications (e.g., updating customer sale information) you might develop that update data in multiple underlying physical files.

8. Although RPG IV and COBOL/400 I/O operations don't support null values, you can use embedded SQL/400 statements (discussed in Part III) in RPG IV and COBOL/400 to read and update records with null values. Discuss how you would decide when (if ever) a database field should be defined with the ALWNULL keyword. (Review the discussion on null-capable fields in Chapter 2.)

Exercises

9. Code an OVRDBF command so that DB2/400 opens the NYC member in the OFFICELOC file in the APPDTA library when a subsequently called program opens a file with a declared name (on the F-spec or Select statement) of Office.

RPG IV

10. Code the F-spec for a file with the following properties:

    DB2/400 filename is EMPLOYEE

    Access method is sequential and direct by key

    Read, update, write, and delete operations are allowed

    User controlled open

    Suitable field name prefix

    File information data structure

11. Code the D-specs for the file information data structure for the file declared in Exercise 10.

12. Code the F-spec for a file with the following properties:

    DB2/400 filename is PART

    Access method is sequential by RRN

    Only read operations are allowed

    User controlled open

    Suitable field name prefix

    File information data structure

13. For the file declared in Exercise 10, code the following operations and the appropriate code to handle any conditions that may occur on the operation:

    Read the record with a specific EMPID key value

    Update the record with a specific EMPID key value

    Write a new record

    Delete the current (previously read) record

14. For a file with two record formats: RCDFMT01 and RCDFMT02, code a statement to read the record with a specific key value (KEYVAL) and the RCDFMT02 record format.

COBOL/400

15. Code the Select statement, FD entry, and file status variable for a file with the following properties:

    DB2/400 filename is EMPLOYEE

    Access method is sequential and direct by key

16. Code the Open statement to open the file declared in Exercise 15 to allow read, rewrite, write, and delete operations.

17. Code the Select statement for a file with the following properties:

    DB2/400 filename is PART

    Access method is sequential by RRN

18. Code the Open statement to open the file declared in Exercise 17 to allow only read operations.

19. For the file declared in Exercise 15, code the following operations and the appropriate code to handle any conditions that may occur on the operation:

    Read the record with a specific EMPID key value

    Update the record with a specific EMPID key value

    Write a new record

    Delete the record with a specific EMPID key value

20. For a file with two record formats: RCDFMT01 and RCDFMT02, code a statement to read the record with a specific key value (KEYVAL) and the RCDFMT02 record format.

PART II

DATABASE MODELING AND DESIGN

Chapter 8

Introduction to Data Modeling and Database Design

Chapter Overview

This chapter introduces logical data modeling and physical database design, two important stages of a development project that should precede coding and creation of database files. We look at why these steps are necessary and what they produce. We also discuss how relational concepts are related to data modeling and database design. When you finish this chapter, you'll have a better understanding of the importance of the topics covered in the next four chapters as well as how data modeling and database design fit into the responsibilities of a professional application developer.

The Importance of Modeling and Design

It may seem obvious, but it's worth stating anyway: Before you use DDS, SQL/400, or any other facility for creating database files, you should know exactly *what* kinds of files you need to create. Consider how pointless it would be to create a customer file before you knew what information about its customers a company needs to have — some companies might need to know their customers' occupations, while other companies might not care about what their customers do for a living. The general requirement for database files, of course, is to store data that the business (or other kind of organization) needs so the data can be used effectively. And figuring out exactly what those needs are and how best to implement a database that meets the requirements clearly should happen *before* coding starts.

Figuring out and documenting business requirements — including both data and processes that use data — are tasks often collectively referred to as "modeling" because the result of the effort is a model (in words and diagrams) of the way the business works and the information it uses. The part of this effort that concentrates on the organization's data requirements is called **logical data modeling** (or data modeling, for short).[1] Once you have a **data model** for an organization, you have a specification of what data needs to be

---

[1] Modeling, or some parts of it, are also referred to by the following, overlapping terms: business requirements assessment, analysis, systems analysis, and design. The term "logical data modeling" is widely used and clearly states what this part of application development produces: a logical model of the organization's data. The terminology isn't all that crucial – as long as the job gets done.

stored and at least some of the ways in which the data is used. For example, the data model for a particular company might specify that the company needs to keep track of customers, including their names, shipping and billing addresses, voice and fax telephone numbers, and credit ratings. This data model might also document that the company needs complete customer lists, in order by the customers' names. From this model (or specification), you can then decide which data should be stored in computer files and which data should be stored in other ways — for instance, as paper documents in filing cabinets or on microfilm. It's important to realize that a data model might ultimately be implemented without *any* computer files at all. A data model says *what* the organization needs, not *how* a system will be implemented to address those needs.

A system to provide for storing, updating, and retrieving the information specified in a particular data model might be implemented in any number of ways. For example, all customer records might be stored in a single computer file, or customer records might be grouped by different countries, with customers from each country being stored in a separate file. The task of deciding how to implement a system for a particular data model is called **physical database design** (or database design, for short).[2] The result of a successful database design is a specification for the files, fields, and other related items to be created on a specific computer system, such as the AS/400. The final development step (i.e., the actual **implementation**) is the almost "cookbook" coding and compilation of the files and related items according to the database design specification. Of course, the design stage of a development project may also specify that certain parts of the data model are to be implemented with other facilities than computer files, and the implementation stage may involve other steps than coding and creating computer files. For example, the design specification may state that some data is to be kept only on paper forms in file cabinets, and the implementation would then involve laying out and printing the forms.

The successive stages of modeling, design, and implementation appear so rational that it would be easy to assume that these three stages are universally followed in *all* application development. Unfortunately, it's common practice among AS/400 development groups to spend a small amount of time jotting down a few notes from discussions with users and then jump straight into DDS and RPG or COBOL coding. Because of the widespread disparity between an apparently rational approach to application development and the actual practice among many application developers, it's worth examining why data modeling and database design are often neglected.

---

[2] The term "database design" is often used as an abbreviated way to refer to both the logical data modeling and the physical database design processes. The title of this book reflects that shorthand. In Part II of this book, however, the two processes are generally referred to by the distinct terms "data modeling" and "database design."

There are two probable reasons for this neglect:

- Many developers don't know how to go about data modeling and/or database design.
- In the minds of many developers, overly formal modeling and design methods take more time than they're worth.

The first barrier is easy to understand. Think about how hard it is to do something — even if you think it would be useful — if no one has ever shown you how to do it. Let's say you want to eat a low-fat, low-sodium diet because you've read that it's healthier. But if you don't have any simple, tasty recipes to start with, you may balk at even trying to change your diet or you may get discouraged and quit after a couple of bland meals. On the other hand, if an experienced cook offers some guidance or you find a good source of recipes, you're more likely to attempt — and succeed — at changing how you eat.

Some developers find themselves in the position of the person wanting to change diets who has no cookbook. They've received training only in how to write RPG or COBOL code, not in how to model data or design databases. An even larger group of developers has had some training in designing *programs,* but no comparable training in designing an integrated *database.* A person in either category may avoid data modeling and/or database design because he or she isn't sure how to go about it. This is the barrier that the introductory material presented in the rest of this part of the book is designed to remove.

The second barrier to more widespread use of data modeling and database design in "real world" application development is the perceived lack of value for the amount of time that it takes.[3] This perception probably stems from a certain all-or-none approach to the modeling and design tasks — that is, people may think design and modeling have to be done with a lot of formality (and overhead) or not at all. While rigorous, labor-intensive approaches that record every minute detail of a data model or database design might be useful in an organization with a hundred or more developers, for many small organizations, a simpler, less formal approach can work much better. Smaller organizations (especially the one- or two-person shops) may find that a few simple word processing documents, some hand-drawn diagrams, and a few spreadsheets or database files to track tabular design information (e.g., a list of files and their contents) are adequate. Such a "low-tech" solution can

---

[3] I've noticed that programmers who are insecure about their own lack of training or experience often claim that some well-proven design or programming practice isn't "practical" in the "real world." This claim has been made about structured programming, relational database, object-oriented programming, and a host of other practices that the highest-paid programmers in the industry use regularly. One has to wonder which group of programmers best reflects the "real world" of application development.

result in significantly less overhead and still produce the benefits of going through the modeling and design stages before coding.

One key to successful application development — including database programming and design — is to adapt your approaches to the specific goal and environment you work in. As you study the rest of this chapter and the other chapters in Part II, remember two points:

- The principles are what is most important.
- Each situation calls for applying the principles in ways that improve the quality of the resulting application database and don't add extreme amounts of effort to development projects.

Logical Data Modeling

We've already mentioned how logical data modeling produces a specification of what the organization needs. Now let's briefly consider some general aspects of data modeling.

First, what does a data model document? Among other things, it specifies the following items of interest to the organization:

- objects (e.g., customers, employees)
- events (e.g., placing an order, approving a loan)
- relationships among objects and events (e.g., a customer places an order, a loan officer approves a loan)
- details about objects, events, and relationships (e.g., customers' names, dates orders were placed)
- business rules or policies (e.g., a borrower must have an adjusted gross income at least half his or her total outstanding debt)

Your first reaction might be: "that's a *lot* of information to put into a data model" and to understand why people often skip the modeling process. Here are a couple of thoughts to counterbalance that reaction. First, many of an organization's rules are already documented in policy manuals, operating guides, or other documents. These documents can be referenced in a data model without re-documenting every detail. Second, if you are going to need a field or a file to track some piece of information, you'll be a lot better off if you clearly identify this requirement *before* you start coding DDS or SQL. Ignoring the modeling and design stages of a project doesn't make the need to fully understand the system go away; it just postpones that step and usually makes it more difficult to implement a correct and efficient system.

By now, I hope you have a good picture of why you (or someone in the development group) should tackle the job of creating a data model before starting the implementation. The natural question then is, when do we know we're *done* with the data model? The answer is, you know you're done with data modeling when you have one or more documents (and possibly diagrams) that provide a statement of the organization's data and how it's used. This statement should be

- clear
- comprehensible
- comprehensive
- correct
- consistent

A specification is clear and comprehensible if all the people who need to agree on what it says can readily understand it and understand it in essentially the same way. A comprehensive model is one that covers all the relevant aspects of the data that the organization needs; nothing is omitted. A correct specification provides an accurate representation of the organization's information. A consistent model has no ambiguous or contradictory specifications.

If you've created a clear and comprehensible data model, the end users — the people in the organization who actually use the data — can tell whether the model is also comprehensive and correct. Likewise, the people who have to do the physical database design (and that might be you) should be able to judge whether the data model is comprehensive and consistent.

In effect, a data model serves as a contract between the end users and the designers. As with any contract, both parties should have no question about its meaning. The data model, as a contract, specifies the *minimum* requirements for the database design. With that perspective, it's apparent that the person(s) producing the data model can't take for granted that the person(s) doing the database design will put anything in the final design unless the data model clearly calls for it.

Physical Database Design

With a good idea of what the organization needs to keep track of and how that data is used, a developer's next step is to decide how best to implement a system to support the organization's requirements. Suppose the business has customers — is it obvious that a CUSTOMER database file is required? What if the business builds custom yachts and has only three or four customers a year? Maybe a filing cabinet and file folders are adequate, and no computer database is necessary. Or what if the business has fairly independent divisions in different regions of the country; should there be a single customer file at the home office, or should there be separate files in each regional office? Questions such as these are answered in the database design stage, which follows the data modeling stage. The results of the data modeling efforts may answer some of these questions fairly well, but many others require closer consideration of the volume of data, types of data access, and the available hardware, software, and personnel.

Physical database design is the process that weighs the alternative implementation possibilities and carefully lays out exactly how files and other elements of the system will be set up. For the database implementation, the most important tangible result of the design is a set of file layouts, including detailed field specifications. As you'll learn in the next four chapters, other important elements of the database design are specific end-user views of the data and various integrity constraints that must be enforced. The database design details how these will be implemented with a particular database system, such as DB2/400.

You might wonder why an intermediate step between data modeling and coding DDS or SQL is necessary. At some point, you must consider alternative implementation approaches *and* document which ones you chose and why. A design document often includes information about such things as anticipated volumes and access paths as well as the rationale for choosing a particular implementation. You don't normally find this important information in either the data model or the source code used to create database files.

Earlier, we stressed that good modeling and design don't necessarily have to be overly formal. Keep this point in mind when considering how you might approach these tasks in a practical way. Nothing says that you can't combine a word processing document with actual DDS to produce a design specification. After all, DDS can be a fairly readable way to present a file layout. With this approach, an associated word processing document can include the other relevant information about the design so the parts that can't be expressed in DDS are still well documented. On the other hand, large organizations will probably find it more productive to use a computer-based database design tool that lets a team of developers work jointly on a design and have a shared set of machine-readable tables and diagrams on an AS/400 or LAN. A number of these tools can even generate DDS or SQL source code from a completed design so that part of the implementation step is automated. Whichever way the design is actually created, it should be specific enough so that a well-trained programmer can almost mechanically code and create the necessary database files and other associated application components.

To wrap up this introduction to data modeling and database design, let's look at how a system appears from several different perspectives. The following diagram shows three perspectives on a system.[4] At the top are various narrow and specialized end-user perspectives of the system. Note that any individual user "sees" only part of the overall data and its organization. Individual users also may have specialized ways of referring to various parts of the data. The middle layer shows the ideal, unified perspective of the data. At this level, the data and its organization are still understood in conceptual terms, but data that appears in multiple end-user perspectives (the top layer) is merged so there's not unnecessary redundancy in the middle

---

[4] This diagram is loosely based on the American National Standards Institute's "three-schema" architecture for DBMS.

layer's representation. The middle layer provides an integrated perspective and is what is documented in the data model. The bottom layer consists of files and other application objects that are part of an actual implementation of the concepts in the middle layer. This layer is what's specified as a result of the database design process.

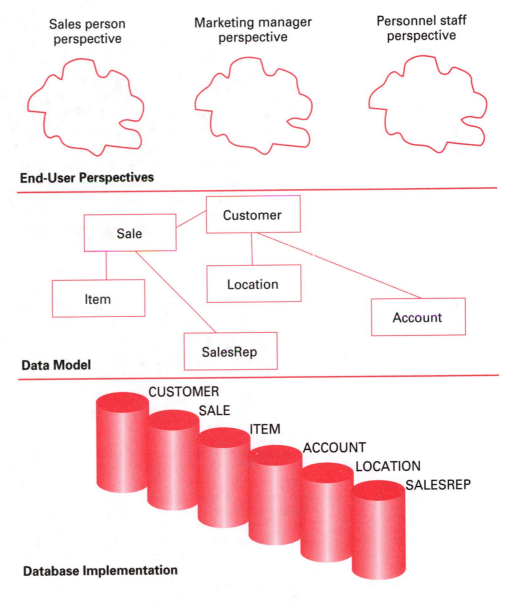

Sales person perspective   Marketing manager perspective   Personnel staff perspective

End-User Perspectives

Sale — Customer — Location — Account — SalesRep — Item

Data Model

CUSTOMER
SALE
ITEM
ACCOUNT
LOCATION
SALESREP

Database Implementation

Clearly, what matters to the organization is that the system deliver the functionality represented in the top layer — the layer that most closely represents the organization's day-to-day requirements. But meeting that objective requires that all three layers be consistent with one another; that is, the middle layer must faithfully represent the top layer (in an integrated structure), and the bottom layer must fully implement the middle layer. This point brings us again to the importance of data modeling and database design as essential parts of application development — these two processes are how you get an implementation that effectively supports the end users as they carry out the organization's work.

Relational Concepts as the Foundation

We've covered the purpose of data modeling and database design, as well as what these two processes produce in the way of specifications. Before we move on to subsequent chapters and a more detailed discussion of how these two tasks are done, you should understand the basis for the data modeling and database design methods presented in this book. In most good development methods, the specific techniques are based upon a general framework. For data modeling and database design, a widely used foundation is the **relational model**.[5] Chapter 9 describes the relational model in detail, and how it arose out of work with computer file and database systems. This section briefly discusses why the relational model is so suitable for data modeling and database design techniques.

This model has three main advantages:

- There's a wide body of mathematical research that's been done on the relational model. (It helps to know that this isn't just an idea some programmer cooked up in a Jolt-induced trance one weekend.)

- Despite the relational model's substantial mathematical underpinnings, many of the most useful concepts in the relational model have intuitive, informal representations. For example, a relation can be represented informally as a table. Both end users and developers without training in the formal mathematics of the relational model can develop a precise model using these informal representations. Because

---

[5] It may help to clarify the way the term "model" is used. When we speak of the relational model, we're speaking of a general conceptual model that isn't specific to a particular business or application. For example, the relational model incorporates the idea that a relation (informally, a table) is used to represent some type of entity, such as a customer. But the relational model doesn't say anything specific about customers, employees, or other particular entities.

When we talk about creating a data model before the design and implementation stages of a development project, however, we are referring to a particular model. For example, if we produce a data model for Ajax Plumbing, Inc., that data model will have some representation (e.g., a relation or table) of customers, employees, and other types of entities the company is interested in.

Note that there are other conceptual models (which we touch on in the next chapter), including hierarchical, and object-oriented. And, of course, there's an unlimited number of possible particular models besides Ajax Plumbing, Inc., including Picante Software, Inc., IBM, and the Eugene Department of Parks and Recreation. Like many words, model has several uses, so don't be tripped up by the two common ways that term is used in relation to database programming and design.

clear communication between the end user and the person working to produce a data model is essential, this strength of the relational model is very valuable. It's especially nice that this intuitive side of the relational model doesn't compromise the formal side at all. In fact, as there have been further developments on the research side, many of the results have found their way into the intuitive notations.

- Relational database management systems (DBMS) are the most widely used type of business-oriented DBMS today. Thus, a data model based on the relational model is the best starting point for developing a database design that targets a relational DBMS. If the data model is cast in terms of tables, primary keys, and other relational concepts, there's little problem translating these into similar implementation objects for a relational DBMS. For example, DB2/400 files are equivalent to relational tables (and vice versa) and can have primary keys. Using modeling, design, and implementation methods all based on the same conceptual model avoids some difficult problems that arise when different stages of development use fundamentally different conceptual models.

These advantages of the relational model have led to its widespread adoption as the basis for many modeling and design methods.

Chapter Summary

Before implementing database files, the developer needs to know what the files should contain and how they're related. This information is developed by two processes, logical data modeling and physical database design, that should occur before implementation.

Logical data modeling analyzes the organization's data requirements to develop a data model that's clear, comprehensible, comprehensive, correct, and consistent. This model integrates all the individual end-user perspectives. The data model documents objects, events, relationships, details about these items, and business rules and policy. The data model is a specification that says *what* information and capabilities the final database implementation must have, but the model doesn't state *how* the capabilities will be implemented.

Physical database design evaluates the anticipated volume of data, types of access, and available hardware, software, and personnel to decide the most effective way to implement the capabilities specified in the data model. The result of the database design is a specification for the database files, fields, and other related items. The design specification is used as the basis for coding DDS or SQL and creating the actual files.

Any system can be viewed from several perspectives: end-user, integrated conceptual model, and the actual implementation. One goal of data modeling and database design is consistence among all three perspectives. Data modeling assesses the end-user perspectives to produce an integrated perspective in the data model, and database design works with the data model and physical constraints to produce a specification for the implementation.

The formal, mathematical relational model underlies both the data modeling and database design techniques presented in this book and relational DBMS, such as DB2/400. The relational model is a good basis for all of these because it has an intuitive representation that's effective for communicating with end users, as well as a solid research foundation. When you as a developer use methods based on the relational model, the development process flows more smoothly from data modeling to database design to implementation.

Key Terms

data model
implementation
logical data modeling
    (data modeling)

physical database design
    (database design)
relational model

Exercises

1. Briefly explain the purpose of logical database modeling.

2. List at least five types of information that might be included in a logical data model. Can you think of any types of information — not mentioned in this chapter — that might be useful in a data model?

3. Briefly explain the purpose of physical database design.

4. Do you think it would be possible to combine logical data modeling and physical database design into a single stage of a development project? Explain the advantages and disadvantages of combining the two steps. If you think they might be combined, under what circumstances would it be appropriate to do so?

5. Give an example of two different end-user perspectives in a toy manufacturing business. Do the two perspectives involve any of the same data?

6. Briefly explain the advantages there might be to merging multiple end-user perspectives when you produce the data model. Can you think of any difficulties in merging end-user perspectives? [*Hint: Consider the cases in which two or more perspectives use the same data but in different ways.*]

Chapter 9

The Relational Database Model

Chapter Overview

This chapter covers the relational database model, the formal basis both for relational database management systems (DBMS), such as DB2/400, and for popular database design methods, such as entity-relationship diagramming. As background, we look at the purpose and advantage of a DBMS over a conventional computer file system. Understanding the role of a DBMS makes clearer the importance of the relational database model to database programming. Knowledge of the relational model and its three main parts — structure, integrity, and data manipulation — also provides the foundation for the design techniques discussed in the next chapter. Each of these areas is covered in a somewhat "formal" manner, but this chapter isn't filled with complex mathematics. Take the time to study the material in this chapter carefully because it will give you an invaluable basis for understanding DB2/400 and other relational DBMS, as well as various approaches to database design.

Background: Database Management Systems

Although the relational database model underlies both the architecture of relational DBMS and popular database design methods, its origin was in the research community that was studying how computer systems could better handle application data. Thus, it's appropriate to start with a discussion of the whole problem of computerized data storage and manipulation.

According to some estimates, more than 80 percent of a typical business application is taken up with code related to file access (including file definition, record selection, and I/O) and the editing of input data for valid values.[1] Less than 20 percent of program code is concerned with calculations and transformations of data after it is read as input and before it is written as output. The large proportion of code required just to get valid data for a computation and then to store the results is an expensive part of traditional application development, but when the same file access and editing code is repeated in different programs — as it often is — both coding errors and software maintenance costs increase too. Taken together, the large proportion of code not directly related to the main business function

---

[1] This proportion is reported for applications developed with an HLL and a traditional file system, not with an application generator or a DBMS.

of an application system and the repetition of this code throughout the system have historically been obstacles to higher productivity in application development.

This problem led computer systems designers around the late 1960s to look for ways to reduce the 80 percent chunk of non-problem-oriented application code by having the *system* software automatically handle many record specification, file access, and field editing functions, thus freeing application programmers to concentrate on the computations and data manipulation.[2] This effort led to what we now call **database management systems (DBMS)**. In the decades since their first appearance, DBMS have had a dramatic impact on data processing. As a result, more and more applications are being built on top of DBMS instead of more primitive conventional file systems. This requires, of course, that applications be designed with the use of DBMS facilities in mind — a subject we cover later in this chapter.

Conventional File System vs. DBMS

Conventional file systems provide a relatively primitive set of facilities to store and retrieve data. A conventional file is either a sequence of bytes (a **stream-oriented file**) or a sequence of records (a **record-oriented file**). In conventional file systems, a record is just some chunk of bytes, either fixed- or variable-length.[3] A conventional file system usually takes care of low-level device (e.g., disk) operations so the programmer can use HLL I/O statements (e.g. read, write) without being concerned with device-level programming. But conventional files systems don't usually do much more than that. In each program, the programmer has to code the layout of the data (i.e., field starting positions, lengths, and data types), as well as handle record sequencing and other file-related tasks. Although using RPG and COBOL COPY facilities (or a similar feature in other HLLs) can reduce some of the repetitive coding, it remains the programmer's responsibility to define a file and its contents within each program. Even more costly than the original coding of definitions is the effort required to change the source code in all programs that use a file if any change is made to its physical storage (i.e., adding a field, changing a field's length, or splitting files). Source code changes may be necessary even if a program doesn't use any of the modified items; for example, a change in one field's length may change the starting position of another field that the program uses.

A DBMS, on the other hand, attempts to free programs from physical data dependence and reduce the amount of code that must be repeated in multiple programs. Central to this goal is the ability to define to the DBMS

---

[2] With the introduction of graphical user interfaces (GUIs), programmers now have to spend considerable time coding the user interface — making it even more valuable for a DBMS to simplify I/O and other programming tasks.

[3] Conventional files typically don't have record format definitions, members, or access paths as DB2/400 files do.

some construct that represents an application entity type about which you want to store properties. In different types of DBMS, entity types are represented by different constructs, among them: record types, segments, relations, and tables.[4] In DB2/400, a physical file and its record format or an SQL table represent an entity type. Figure 9.1 shows some of the terminology you're likely to encounter in various contexts.

Figure 9.1

Comparative Terminology Used in Different Contexts

Relational Model	Table-Oriented DBMS	Conventional File Systems	Conceptually Represents
Relation	Table	File	Entity type
Tuple	Row	Record	Entity instance
Attribute	Column	Field	Property
Domain	Column type	Data type	Allowable values and meaning
Element	Column value	Field value	Property value

What these various constructs have in common is that they represent a set of distinguishable objects of some sort, whether the objects are concrete (e.g., customers) or abstract (e.g., AS/400 jobs). This is true of conventional file systems, as well — as far as it goes. What's important about DBMS is that you include as part of a file definition (or other construct) some representation of the entity type's properties. Properties are usually represented by fields or columns. For example, if we define a Customer entity type (e.g., as a file) in a DBMS, we would also define Customer ID, Name, Address, and other properties (e.g., as fields).[5] Conceptually, a property is simply some piece of information about an entity type.

So far it may appear that a DBMS offers no earth-shattering improvement over the records and fields of an ordinary file. But for a conventional (non-database) file, every program must contain the layout of fields in a record while a DBMS provides a **data definition language** (**DDL**) that's used to define constructs for both entity types and properties (including, for example, record layouts and fields) in a **system catalog** (also known as a **system dictionary**). DB2/400 has two alternative DDLs: DDS (covered in Part I) and SQL (covered in Part III). DB2/400 also has two ways that it implements a system dictionary: the record format definition plus other information that's stored as part of OS/400 file objects and a set of system files and SQL views that

---

[4] The closest representation of an entity type in a conventional file system is a file, but, as we'll see, a conventional file system doesn't know anything about what the file represents.

[5] The closest representation of a property in a conventional file system is a field, but see the previous footnote.

provide a database catalog. As you learned in Part I, once you define (and compile) a DB2/400 file, every program that references the file automatically has access to the file's definition. Thus, a DBMS lets a program reference a property by name (e.g., Name of Customer) without a programmer-coded specification (in the program) of how the actual field-level data is physically stored.[6] Defining entity types and their properties *in the DBMS* is just the first step toward representing more of the logical structure and meaning of application data in a central place.

With most DBMS, how a property (field) is stored can be changed and programs that use the property continue to execute properly with no revisions. For example, you can change the length or location (within the record) of a field in a DB2/400 file, and you only need to recompile programs that use the file for them to work properly with the changed definition.[7] Removing the physical storage aspects of a property from a program's code removes a significant amount of work, especially in system maintenance; it also removes a significant source of errors.

Besides requiring specification of the record layout in every program, a conventional file system also requires that every file-update program include code to check for legitimate values in the fields before a record is written. This validation is typically implemented by a series of conditional tests (e.g., If Age > 21 ..., If ActTyp = 'A' or 'B' or 'C' ...) on values entered on a display for interactive updating or on values in a transaction record read by a batch program. Not only is this code sometimes repeated (possibly with slight variations) in many programs, but also, when validity tests are directed at input values (i.e., before any program calculations or transformations) rather than at a record's output values at the time of a file update, it's still possible, due to a program error, to write a record containing invalid data to the file. Thus, most field-editing code in a conventional file system is both cumbersome to maintain and not wholly effective at guaranteeing the integrity of the data.

A DBMS can address this problem by providing DDL features you can use to specify **integrity constraints** in the system dictionary. The integrity constraints that can be specified vary among different DBMS. At a minimum they usually include range checks ("between 1 and 50") or allowable values ("equal to A or B or C").[8] More complex constraints may be specifiable as well. Examples include relationships between properties for the same entity type (e.g., an employee's hire date must be greater than his or her birth date) or inter-record relationships (a customer ID value in an order entity must exist as a

---

[6] Of course, the degree to which DB2/400 and other current DBMS achieve physical data independence, or any of the other concepts mentioned, varies greatly.

[7] In some cases, AS/400 programs that use SQL/400 don't even need to be recompiled.

[8] Note that DB2/400's COMP, RANGE, and VALUES DDS keywords, which can be specified for field definitions, do *not* apply to the database integrity. These attributes are used only when a *display file* defines an input-capable field based on a database file field with one of the keywords. Chapter 2 explains the use of these keywords.

customer ID value in exactly one customer entity). The DBMS, which handles all database updating, generally checks these constraints when database records are inserted, updated, or deleted. If a constraint is not met, the DBMS blocks the operation and signals an error. Specifying integrity in a central dictionary helps immensely in speeding implementation and in achieving improved quality of the organization's data.

Historically, efficient DBMS support for built-in integrity has been difficult to achieve. Recent developments in hardware power and more efficient DBMS software implementations have prompted a trend toward improved DBMS capabilities for ensuring data integrity. This is an area in which you can expect significant change over the next few years.

At a level above the field level, a conventional file system leaves it to each program to implement relationships between entity types. For example, every program that deals with customers or orders (or both) must be aware of the relationship between these two entity types. Thus, a customer file maintenance program must have code to ensure that a customer record isn't deleted if there are still order records for that customer. Likewise, a program that needs an order header record, a customer information record, and a set of order detail records must know which files to access and how to retrieve the related records. Applications implemented over conventional file systems typically use one of two methods to relate records: they use fields to store the relative record numbers (RRNs) of related records (in the same file or in different files), or they use matching values in common fields to associate records (e.g., having an order ID field in both the order header record and the order detail record). Whichever method is used in a conventional file system, the access strategy required to retrieve related records is reimplemented in every program that uses or affects a relationship between records.

But in many DBMS, relationships can be defined in the dictionary using the DDL. Thus, an order header entity type might be defined as the parent of an order detail entity type, which is the dependent. Ideally, the implementation details of this relationship are hidden from application programs. A program doesn't know whether RRN pointers or indexes are being used; for that matter, a program doesn't know whether one, two, or more files are used to store the data. The DBMS provides logical I/O operations such as "get first dependent," "get next sibling," "update current," and "get all records with specific property." In summary, a DBMS lets you define — *independently* from individual programs — entity types, properties, integrity constraints, and relationships . The DBMS can then enforce constraints and provide data access methods that hide the physical storage details.

DDL capabilities are only part of the story: a DBMS also provides a **data manipulation language** (**DML**) to retrieve and update the data. The DML may be provided through extensions to HLL I/O facilities (as is the case with DB2/400 and AS/400 HLLs) or through a distinct language, such as SQL (which DB2/400 also provides). The DML typically provides a superset of the conventional HLL I/O operations: read, write (or insert), delete, and update.

DML operations may operate on one or more records at a time, depending on the DBMS system. An important distinction between a DBMS DML and conventional file I/O operations is the way in which the target of the action is specified. In a conventional file system, the I/O operation must target a specific record in the file using either an explicit RRN (or relative byte position), an explicit key value, or a read next operation that implicitly targets a record based on the RRN or key of the previous record. Many DBMS, on the other hand, support access by field contents regardless of whether the field is a key (e.g., get next course with course status = "Open"). And, based on relationships in the dictionary, a DBMS can retrieve related records without explicit targeting (e.g., get first student for this course, or get first joined student and course). The power, consistency, and ease of use of a particular DBMS's DML helps determine how useful it will be in complex application systems. If the DML is well implemented in the DBMS, it can significantly reduce the number of source code statements necessary to implement application functions.

DBMS vary in how much they provide the application developer. The best are powerful, highly dynamic, and easy to use; most importantly, they succeed in substantially reducing the proportion of non-problem-oriented code. DBMS also vary in how they support the definition of entity types, properties, integrity constraints, and relationships between entity types and the types of manipulations that can be performed on the data. Most commercial DBMS have been based on one of four major database models: **hierarchic**, **network** (also known as **CODASYL**), **inverted list**, and relational.[9] Both the hierarchic and network models are based on explicit *physical* links (e.g., RRNs) between records of the same type (siblings) or between records of different types (where one is the parent and one is the dependent). The major difference between the two is that the hierarchic model allows a dependent to have only one parent just as in any familiar form of hierarchy (e.g., an organization chart), while the network model allows a record type to be the dependent of any number of parent record types (e.g., in the case in which a course record type can be the dependent of both an instructor record type and a student record type).

Both the hierarchic and the network DBMS approaches have fallen into disfavor because they, like conventional file systems, require a knowledge of how the entity types are physically structured — that is, which entity types have explicit links to each other. These explicit links not only require that the programmer write procedural code to navigate the database along the link pathways, but they also make the database structure cumbersome to change: new or modified link types are not always easy to incorporate once the database has gone into production.

A third alternative, the inverted list model, is really little more than a conventional file system with enhanced file index facilities to aid in record

---

[9] In recent years, a fifth model, **object-oriented**, has become more widespread. However, DBMS based on the relational model are still the most widely used.

retrieval. Records in different files are implicitly related by the values in key fields (rather than by pointers), but retrieval is still done by single-record read and write operations. As such, the inverted list is of interest not so much because of its particular approach but rather because a DBMS based on the inverted list model can be extended naturally to a relational DBMS by adding integrity rules and relational operators.[10]

The foundation of most commercial DBMS today is the **relational database model**, which was first introduced in the paper "A Relational Model of Data for Large Shared Data Banks," published by Edgar Codd in June 1970. Since the publication of this paper, the relational model has been developed extensively, and products such as IBM's DB2/400, Oracle Corporation's Oracle, and Microsoft's SQL Server provide many of the capabilities covered in the previous section.

Relational Model: Data Structure

The relational database model has three main parts: structure, integrity, and data manipulation. The data structure portion defines the form for representing data. Most basic to this form is the concept of a relation. Figure 9.2 shows an informal picture of a **relation**, which looks like what is commonly called a table. That is, a relation can be thought of as having columns that lay out properties (**attributes** in relational nomenclature) and rows (**tuples** in relational nomenclature) that hold specific instances of the entity type represented by the relation. This informal table representation is convenient for most purposes and is used in many parts of this book.

But to be more precise for the moment, a relation has two parts — the **relation heading** and the **relation body**. The heading is a set of attribute-and-domain pairs. For the Person relation represented informally by the table in Figure 9.2, the heading is the set of pairs {<SSN:SSNs>, <Name:Names>, <BthDat:Dates>}. Because a set has no specific ordering of its elements, I

Figure 9.2
Components of a Relation

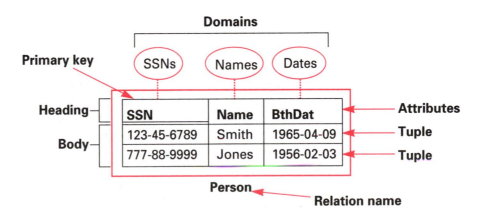

also could have said the heading is the set of attributes {<BthDat:Dates>, <SSN:SSNs>, <Name:Names>}.[11] The number of attribute-and-domain pairs in a relation is known as its **degree**; for example, the relation in Figure 9.2 is a degree 3 relation.

The body of the relation is a set of tuples (each tuple is represented as a row in Figure 9.2). Each tuple in the Person relation represents information about a single person; that is, each tuple represents an **instance** of the Person entity type. Formally, each tuple is a set of attribute-and-value pairs. The tuple in the Person relation identified by SSN value 123-45-6789 is actually the following set of pairs: {<SSN:123-45-6789>, <Name:Smith>, <BthDat:1965-04-09>}. Or again, because sets are not ordered, I could have said the tuple is the following set of pairs: {<Name:Smith>, <SSN:123-45-6789>, <BthDat:1965-04-09>}. Because the values in a tuple are not ordered, a value is always paired with the appropriate attribute that serves as a label; thus, you can keep track of the meaning of all the values in all the tuples in a relation. The number of tuples in a relation is known as its **cardinality**. For example, the relation in Figure 9.2 has a cardinality of 2.

At this point, you may wonder why something so simple as the row-column structure of a table must become as complex as a "set of attribute-and-value pairs." Because an unordered, labeled representation of data is used, the relational model can reference all values *by name* rather than by some physical mechanism, such as the position of the column in a table. This distinction is not a minor one — it's one of the breakthroughs in modeling data that the relational approach brought about. Nevertheless, in practical use of the relational model, it's perfectly adequate to use a table-like notation or other simplifications. It's important, however, not to make invalid inferences from the informal representation of a relation as a table. For example, although a table is depicted with a particular ordering of rows, relations do *not* have any particular ordering of tuples.

If tuples have no ordering — and thus can't be identified by row number, how can you refer to a particular tuple? Every tuple in a relation can be referenced by specifying values for **primary key** attributes. For example, in Figure 9.2, a tuple can be referenced by specifying its SSN attribute value, (SSN is thus a primary key attribute for the Person relation). This, of course, requires that a unique combination of attribute values exist for each tuple in a relation. This requirement is one of the integrity concepts covered later.

Referencing attributes by name and referencing tuples by primary key values provide a data model that has no physical storage concepts associated with the data organization. The same statement cannot be made about the hierarchic, network, or inverted list DBMS approaches. Thus, the relational database model is the only one that achieves complete **physical data independence**. Consider this: as long as the relational DBMS takes care of

---

[11] Notice how this differs from how we usually think of a table, where a column's relative position is important.

finding the right data when your program provides entity and attribute names along with primary key values, your program doesn't have to know *anything* about how the data is stored. The data could even be rearranged between program executions and it wouldn't matter (as long as the DBMS kept track of the data's physical location).[12]

Another fundamental part of data representation in the relational model is the concept of **domain**. Simply put, a domain combines two pieces of information: the set (possibly infinite) of allowable values and the semantics (or meaning) of the values.[13] A domain is not part of a relation, and it stores no particular values. Instead, a domain defines a pool of values that an attribute can have. Every attribute is specified as being "over" a domain. Two or more attributes can be over the same domain. Figure 9.3 shows some simplified examples of domains and attributes defined over those domains.

Figure 9.3

Sample Domains and Attributes

Domain:	Color Values {Red, Orange, Yellow, Green, Blue, Indigo, Violet, ...}	**Domain:**	Weight Range [0:100,000,000] Units Pounds
Attributes:	ProductColor HairColor	**Attributes:**	ShippingWeight EmpWeight
Domain:	Salary Range [0:100,000,000] Units Dollars/year	**Domain:**	Children Range Integers ≥ 0 Units People
Attributes:	EmpSalary ContractorSalary	**Attribute:**	ChildCnt
Domain:	Wages Range [0:1,000] Units Dollars/hour	**Domain:**	Cars Range Integers ≥ 0 Units Cars
		Attribute:	CarCnt
Attributes:	EmpWages ContractorWages	**Domain:**	Units Range Integers Units (none)
		Attribute:	ItemCnt

[12] Note that, internally, a relational DBMS generally uses RRNs or other physical references to keep track of data. These physical references may or may not be accessible to application programs — for example, in DB2/400, HLL I/O statements *can* use RRNs. The important thing for a relational DBMS is that it must at least allow applications to access data without physical references.

[13] The concept of a database domain is generally equivalent to the formal programming language concept of *data type*. The DDS field-level data type entry (position 35) is a less specific way of identifying a field's domain. Chapter 3 touches on how you can use a field reference file to incorporate the idea of more precise data types into your DB2/400 file definitions. DB2/400 doesn't currently support the explicit domain that we're discussing here.

These examples point out some interesting and important facets of domains. First, as I just mentioned, domains define allowable values; thus, the attribute EmpSalary can never be negative because it is defined over the domain Salary, which has no negative values. Second, a domain often specifies the units of measure. Attributes defined over domains with similar units of measure can be compared or added, but attributes defined over domains with dissimilar units of measure cannot be compared or added meaningfully. Thus, a statement such as "If HairColor = ProductColor," while perhaps an unlikely comparison, is at least possible, whereas "If HairColor = EmpSalary" is not allowed. This type of mismatched comparison may seem obvious, but domains help clarify in a data model and to the DBMS more subtle distinctions. For example, in most HLLs a field used to store the number of children in a household (ChildCnt) will be an integer, as will the field to store the number of cars owned by a household (CarCnt). Neither the RPG nor COBOL compiler balks at a statement such as "ItemCnt = ChildCnt + CarCnt." This statement is probably the result of bad coding, not a medieval social philosophy in which children and cars are both merely possessions, and should be prevented. In the relational database model, these two attributes could not be added because they are from different domains.[14]

What if you really do want to add such dissimilar units? In that case, you might use a mapping function — for example a function, UnitCvt, that is defined to convert (i.e., map) any integer value to a unitless value. The required statement then becomes "ItemCnt = UnitCvt(ChildCnt) + UnitCvt(CarCnt)." A more common example of a required mapping would be from annual salary values to hourly wages or vice versa. In this case, the numerator (e.g., dollars) for both units of measure is identical, but the denominators (year and hour) are different. This similarity (exacerbated by ambiguous field names) is precisely the cause of a typical HLL programming error in adding fields such as EmpSalary and EmpWages without converting either. The concept of domains allows system detection of invalid or questionable comparisons or computations.

Another point to be made about a relation is that a *database* relation (unlike the more general mathematical notion of relation) cannot have *sets* as values for an attribute.[15] Every attribute value in a tuple must be a single element drawn from the underlying domain.[16] Figure 9.4 shows the distinction between a mathematical relation (shown in table format) and a database relation.

---

[14] Not many commercial relational DBMS provide this level of support for domains, however.

[15] Actually, this restriction is part of the original relational model, but a variation known as the non-first normal form (NFNF) relational model *does* allow sets as attribute values. The reason for this restriction was that it greatly simplified the mathematical definitions of the relational operators. The NFNF model is also a step toward the object-oriented database model, which allows arbitrarily complex data attribute values.

[16] And, of course, the domain's values themselves must not be sets.

Figure 9.4
Mathematical Versus
Database Relations

Parent	Children
Smith	Bubba
Jones	Billy
	Susie
	Fred
Harris	Janice
	Tommy

Mathematical Relation

Parent	Children
Smith	Bubba
Jones	Billy
Jones	Susie
Jones	Fred
Harris	Janice
Harris	Tommy

Database Relation

Note that restructuring a mathematical relation that has sets of values into a database relation is a mechanical operation of adding additional tuples that repeat values for some attributes.

Normal Forms

Consideration of repeating values introduces another facet of the relational database model — **normal forms**. By definition, a database relation is in what is called **first normal form** (1NF), which simply means that there are no sets as attribute values. Because a relation is in 1NF, all the referencing and manipulative operations of the relational model can be performed on it. However, a 1NF relation may not always be the ideal form for representing data. A relation in 1NF may appear to represent information redundantly. And, if a database file or table is subsequently implemented that corresponds directly to the relation, actual redundant data may be updated inconsistently. Figure 9.5a shows a 1NF relation with apparent redundant storage of WarehouseAddress.

Figure 9.5a
First Normal Form (1NF)
Inventory Relation

ItemID	WarehouseID	Qty	WarehouseAddress
167	1	10	1511 Central Ave.
167	2	20	6803 Alder St.
448	1	26	1511 Central Ave.
302	2	18	6803 Alder St.

Inventory

Figure 9.5b shows the 1NF relation split into two relations that eliminate the WarehouseAddress redundancy.

Figure 9.5b

Inventory Relation Split
into Two Relations to
Eliminate Redundancy

ItemID	WarehouseID	Qty
167	1	10
167	2	20
448	1	26
302	2	18

Inventory

WarehouseID	WarehouseAddress
1	1511 Central Ave.
2	6803 Alder St.

Warehouse

The process of splitting relations with redundant representation of information into two or more relations without the redundancy is a process often called **normalization**. There are five main normal forms (1NF through 5NF) for relations, each normal form addresses the potential for a particular type of redundancy.

In a moment, we take a closer look at the various normal forms, but it's important to be clear about the meaning of redundancy. First, any nontrivial set of relations will have some values repeated more than once in the database. For example, in the relations in Figure 9.5b, the warehouse IDs that appear in the Inventory relation all appear in the Warehouse relation, as well. This is one of the central features of the relational model — tuples are related by values, not pointers or other physical means. So the three instances of warehouse ID 1 and warehouse ID 2 don't represent the type of redundancy we're concerned with.

The redundancy we want to avoid is repeated representation of the same fact.[17] For example, in Figure 9.5a, the fact that warehouse 1 is located at 1511 Central Ave. is repeated in two tuples. If we actually created a database file with this structure, we'd have to ensure that any change to the warehouse address was made consistently to *all* records that stored the address.

Now, let's look at an example that's not so obvious. Suppose we have a relation for the items that are included in customers' orders:

[17] Formally, the concept of facts is known as *functional dependence*. In a nutshell, if a relation has two attributes A and B, B is functionally dependent on A if-and-only-if whenever two tuples in the relation have the same value for A, they necessarily have the same value for B.

OrderID	ItemID	Qty	Price
9877	73	2	50.00
9878	52	1	10.00
9878	73	5	50.00
9879	73	1	50.00

This relation appears to redundantly represent the fact that the ItemID determines the Price. In many business systems, this might be true. But what if the price were negotiated on each order? Then it would be possible for the relation to have (at some point in time) the following contents:

OrderID	ItemID	Qty	Price
9877	73	2	50.00
9878	52	1	10.00
9878	73	5	45.00
9879	73	1	50.00

For the business model that this relation represents, there is no fact redundancy. This example brings us to a crucial point in understanding normal forms: If you want to *unambiguously* represent various facts in a (logical) database model that uses relations, you *must* structure the relations so they have no redundant representation of facts. The obvious consequence is that there's no mechanical method of normalizing relations. You first must know which facts you want to represent, and then you define the relations accordingly.

Despite these principles, some textbook and other presentations of normal forms convey the misconception that normalization is a process you apply when you *implement files*. Although informally you might consider some of the ideas related to nonredundant representation of facts when you implement files, normal forms are specifically a *design* concept. Chapter 10 takes up this issue more fully.

The misunderstanding probably stems from the conventional approach (which we more or less follow here) to introducing the normal forms and the examples that have obvious redundant representation of facts. Keep in mind as we go through the following examples, however, that each relation with apparent redundancy might, in some specific situations, be free of redundancy.

With that cautionary note, let's look at the main normal forms. To review, first normal form (1NF) requires that each attribute value be **atomic;** that is, it must not be a set (or other composite structure). The database relation in Figure 9.4 and the relation in Figure 9.5a illustrated first normal form. **Second normal form** (2NF), which is illustrated by the two relations in Figure 9.5b, requires that the relation be in (at least) first normal form and that each non-key attribute depend on the *entire* primary key. The primary key for the Inventory relation includes both the ItemID and WarehouseID (neither alone is unique). Because we assume that a warehouse's address depends only on the WarehouseID attribute, the relation in Figure 9.5a violates the 2NF requirement. Looking at the problem from the other direction, if we assumed incorrectly that Figure 9.5a was already in 2NF, we'd think that, for some reason, the WarehouseAddress values could be determined only by knowing both the ItemID and the WarehouseID.

Third normal form (3NF) requires that the relation be in (at least) second normal form and that each non-key attribute depend *only* on the primary key. In the following relation, each tuple represents a customer order:

OrderID	OrderCustID	CustCity	Amt
601	123	Portland	2,000
602	789	Eugene	50
603	123	Portland	500
604	198	Portland	1,000

If we assume that a customer's city depends only on the customer's ID, the proper 3NF structure is

CustID	City
123	Portland
198	Portland
789	Eugene

OrderID	OrderCustID	Amt
601	123	2,000
602	789	50
603	123	500
604	198	1,000

Fourth normal form (4NF) requires that the relation be in (at least) third normal form and that there be no more than one **multivalued fact** in the relation. A multivalued fact is one in which several values for an attribute might be determined by one value for another attribute (e.g., the children of an employee or the courses taken by an employee). The following relation represents two multivalued facts:

EmployeeID	Child	Course
576	Bonnie	Math 101
576	Janice	Psych 203
576	Sam	?
601	Abigail	Art 101

Look at the problem in this relation — when an employee has an unequal number of children and courses, what value should be used as a placeholder? You can't use null (discussed in the next section) because all three attributes are necessary in the primary key, and primary key attributes can't have null. The solution is to use two relations:

EmployeeID	Child
576	Bonnie
576	Janice
576	Sam
601	Abigail

EmployeeID	Course
576	Math 101
576	Psych 203
601	Art 101

So far, the rules for normal forms are pretty intuitive, which should be no surprise because the intent is to make clear the facts represented by a relation. The final normal form is a bit more involved to explain but also has an intuitive rule: A table in **fifth normal form** (5NF) cannot be split into two or more tables without loss of information. Suppose we know the following rule about sales agents, products, and companies:

If a sales agent sells a certain product and he represents a company that makes the product, then he sells that product for that company.

We might try to represent this with the following relation:

Agent	Company	Product
Boyd	Ford	Car
Boyd	Ford	Truck
Boyd	GM	Car
Boyd	GM	Truck
Harper	GM	Car

But we observe that, by definition, this relation isn't in fifth normal form. It can be split into the following three relations with no loss of information because we know (with the previously stated rule) exactly what agents sell from the contents in these three relations:

Agent	Company
Boyd	Ford
Boyd	GM
Harper	GM

Agent	Product
Boyd	Car
Boyd	Truck
Harper	Car

Company	Product
Ford	Car
Ford	Truck
GM	Car
GM	Truck

But even if we *can* split the original table, why would we *want* to? To answer that question, consider how we'd store the (new) fact that Harper sells Ford trucks. In the three-relation representation, the answer is simple: insert a <Harper, Ford> tuple into the Agent-Company relation and a <Harper, Truck> tuple into the Agent-Product relation. However, in the single-relation representation, we'd have to add the following tuples:

<Harper, Ford, Truck>
<Harper, Ford, Car>
<Harper, GM, Truck>

What's going on here is that the single relation redundantly stores some of the more elementary facts (which products an agent sells) to satisfy the rule stated earlier. By splitting the relation, as long as we also state the rule about which companies' products an agent sells, we don't redundantly represent the elementary facts. It's important to note, however, that *without* the rule, we *would* need a relation like the Agent-Company-Product one to know which companies' products an agent sells. Although fifth normal form may be a bit difficult to grasp at first, it illustrates the real purpose of normal forms — establishing a clear meaning for what a set of relations represents.

In summary, the data structures of the relational model provide data independence (a separation of the conceptual and physical aspects), and when viewed — as they normally are — as tables, relations are easy to understand and work with. Relations also put a firm theoretical footing under any DBMS based on them. This combination of the conceptual simplicity and formal definition of relations forms the foundation for the next two parts of the model: data integrity and data manipulation.

Data Integrity

While the data structure portion of the relational database model defines the form for representing data, the data integrity portion of the model defines mechanisms for ensuring that the stored data is valid. This requires, at a minimum, that the attribute values each be valid, that the set of values in a tuple be unique, and that relations known to be interrelated have consistent values within the tuples.

In discussing the concept of domains in the previous section, we essentially covered the first form of data integrity, known as **attribute integrity** — that values for attributes come only from their respective underlying domains. A widely accepted variation of the relational model also permits an attribute to contain a marker, referred to as **null**, that indicates a missing or unknown value.[18] Note that null is not a value per se — it's merely a placeholder.

---

[18] But some well-respected researchers believe the idea of null is a bad one and suggest default values instead. The C. J. Date book mentioned in the annotated bibliography provides a detailed discussion on the differing points of view.

The domain concept covers the common HLL implementation technique of checking a value to see that it's within an allowable range or that it's one of a list of allowable values; it also extends the concept to the meaning of the values (e.g., whether units are children or cars). What it does not address is a large group of validity constraints that involve other attribute values in the same tuple (e.g., QtyShip ≤ QtyOrdered) or other tuples (e.g., Sum(LoanAmt) ≤ 10000). These more comprehensive aspects of attribute integrity are included as part of extensions to the relational database model that have been developed since its inception.

The second form of integrity essential to the relational database model is **entity integrity**. This is a fairly straightforward concept — every tuple in a relation represents an entity (i.e., an instance of an entity type) that must exist in the real world; therefore, every tuple must be uniquely identifiable.[19] It follows that there can be no completely duplicate tuples (all attribute values identical) in a relation; otherwise, the unique existence of entities is not represented in the database. From this property of uniqueness is derived the principle that there exists in every relation some set of attributes (possibly all the relation's attributes) whose values are never duplicated entirely in any two tuples in the relation. If you don't include any superfluous attributes (i.e., ones not needed to guarantee uniqueness) in the set of attributes, the set of attributes can serve as the relation's primary key. (More than one possible set of attributes may meet the criteria for a primary key; each of these is referred to as a **candidate key**, and one is picked arbitrarily as the primary key.[20])

The primary key is a minimal set of attributes whose values are unique for all tuples in a relation. Because of this, the primary key forms the only means of addressing a specific tuple in the relational database model. A consequence of the requirement for unique primary key values is that none of the values in a tuple's primary key attributes can be null (i.e., missing or unknown). None of the primary key attributes can be null because then this tuple's primary key value couldn't be guaranteed to be unequal to some other tuple's primary key value.[21] Thus, if SSN is the attribute serving as the primary key in the Person relation and there exists a tuple with SSN = 123-45-6789, another tuple could not have SSN = null, because you couldn't tell whether

---

[19] Note that the "real world" includes both concrete and abstract entities.

[20] Formally, there's actually no absolute requirement that you pick any specific candidate key as the primary key because all that's really necessary for entity integrity is that all tuples are unique. But by convention, we usually select one candidate key to serve as the primary key for each relation.

[21] In the relational model, null isn't a value in the attribute's domain; null is essentially a placeholder that means "the value of this attribute is unknown — *and it might be any value in the domain.*" Because the actual attribute value, if it were known, could be any domain value, there's no way to know that the value isn't also present in the same primary key attribute of some other tuple.

the actual SSN value is equal to 123-45-6789. If you can't tell whether the two values are equal, you can't guarantee uniqueness. A similar argument holds for primary keys made up of more than one attribute (i.e., **composite** primary keys), which need all attribute values to guarantee uniqueness and hence cannot have null for any of the attributes in the primary key.

The third, and final, form of integrity fundamental to the relational database model is **referential integrity**. Simply put, referential integrity requires that tuples that exist in separate relations, but that are interrelated, be unambiguously interrelated by corresponding attribute values. Let's look at the warehouse example again to understand referential integrity. In Figure 9.5b, two relations are used so a warehouse address can be stored nonredundantly. The WarehouseID is stored as an attribute in both relations, so the WarehouseID value can be used in an Inventory tuple to reference (i.e., look up) the appropriate Warehouse tuple via the Warehouse relation's WarehouseID primary key. Thus, the tuples in the two relations are interrelated, based on matching values in the WarehouseID attributes in the two relations.

As I pointed out earlier, the WarehouseID attribute in the Warehouse relation serves as a primary key and can never be null. The WarehouseID attribute in the Inventory relation is referred to as a **foreign key** (it addresses "foreign" tuples that are usually outside the same relation). A foreign key value can be all null. That means that its related tuple is unknown. A foreign key value also can match exactly a primary key value in a related tuple. But a foreign key value cannot have some attribute values present (i.e., at least one attribute value is not null) and not match the primary key value of an existing tuple in the related relation. This requirement says nothing more than that if the foreign key points to a related tuple, the tuple must be there. A consequence of this rule is that composite foreign key values cannot be *partially* null because, by the entity integrity rule, no primary key attribute value can ever be null.

Together, the three integrity rules — attribute, entity, and referential — allow specification of important constraints that a relational DBMS can enforce automatically whenever a database update occurs. These rules protect not only the specific values in attributes, but also the identity and interrelationships of tuples as well. A DBMS that provides this level of integrity support lifts a large coding load off application programmers.

Data Manipulation

As I stated earlier, data representation and integrity do not make a complete model. There must be some means of manipulating the data as well. The relational database model defines data manipulations as the relational assignment operation and eight algebraic operations. The assignment operation simply allows the value of some arbitrary expression of relational algebra to be assigned to another relational variable. For example, the expression

RelationC ← RelationA JOIN RelationB

allows the relational variable RelationC to take on the value (set of tuples) resulting from the JOIN operation performed over tuples in the RelationA and RelationB relations. This is analogous to arithmetic assignment in HLL computations.

The eight relational algebraic operations include four standard set operations and four operations specific to database relations..[22] The four relational algebraic operations found in conventional set theory (and the syntax of the corresponding operators used in expressions in the examples in this chapter) are

- **union** (rel_1 UNION rel_2)
- **intersection** (rel_1 INTERSECT rel_2)
- **difference** (rel_1 MINUS rel_2)
- **product** (rel_1 TIMES rel_2)

Figures 9.6a through 9.6d show Venn diagrams of these operations.

Figure 9.6a
Union

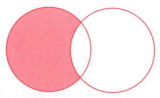

(Tuples in either)

Figure 9.6b
Intersection

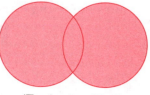

(Tuples in both)

Figure 9.6c
Difference

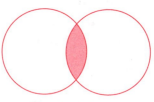

(Tuples in first, but not in second)

---

[22] In addition to these eight fundamental operations, various other operations have been proposed for relational algebra. Among these are *extend*, which adds a new, derived attribute to a relation, and *summarize*, which essentially creates a new relation by subtotaling groups of tuples (rows) in an existing relation. Rather than go into various extensions to the formal relational algebra, we cover more relational operations when we discuss SQL in Part III.

Figure 9.6d
Product

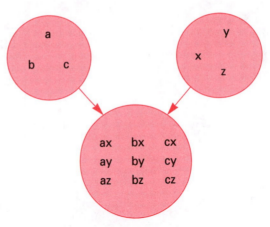

(All combinations of tuples)

The results of these four operations performed on the sample relations in Figure 9.7a are shown in Figures 9.7b through 9.7f.

Figure 9.7a
Three Relations Used
as Operands

SSN	Name
123-45-6789	Smith
601-11-9999	Wilson

RelA

SSN	Name
145-67-8888	Jones
601-11-9999	Wilson

RelB

Course	Instructor
Math 101	Aldridge
Psych 203	Ulrich

RelC

Figure 9.7b
RelA UNION RelB

SSN	Name
123-45-6789	Smith
601-11-9999	Wilson
145-67-8888	Jones

(Duplicate tuples are dropped)

Figure 9.7c
RelA INTERSECT RelB

SSN	Name
601-11-9999	Wilson

Figure 9.7d
RelA MINUS RelB

SSN	Name
123-45-6789	Smith

Figure 9.7e
RelB MINUS RelA

SSN	Name
145-67-8888	Jones

(Difference is not commutative)

Figure 9.7f
RelA TIMES RelC

SSN	Name	Course	Instructor
123-45-6789	Smith	Math 101	Aldridge
123-45-6789	Smith	Psych 203	Ulrich
601-11-9999	Wilson	Math 101	Aldridge
601-11-9999	Wilson	Psych 203	Ulrich

Note that union, intersection, and difference require the two relations to have the same attributes (i.e., they must be **union-compatible**). The product operation can work on dissimilar relations; if one relation has m attributes and the other has n attributes, the result is a relation with $m + n$ attributes. Also, union, intersection, and product are **commutative** operations — the order of operands does not matter (e.g., A UNION B is equal to B UNION A). The difference operation is not commutative as Figures 9.7d and 9.7e show.

The four special relational algebraic operations (and the syntax of the corresponding operators used in expressions in the examples in this chapter) are

- **projection** (PROJECT rel_1 [*attribute-list*])
- **selection** (SELECT rel_1 WHERE *predicate*)
- **division** (rel_1 DIVIDEBY rel_2)
- **join** (rel_1 JOIN rel_2 WHERE *predicate*)

Examples of these operations performed on the sample relations in Figure 9.8a are shown in Figures 9.8b through 9.8g.

Figure 9.8a

Sample Relations

CustID	City	Status	Credit
123	Portland	00	1,000
456	Portland	20	500
789	Eugene	10	10,000
304	Portland	00	2,000

Customer

OrderID	OrderCustID	Amt
601	123	2,000
602	789	50
603	123	500
604	198	1,000

Order

Company	Vehicle
Ford	Car
Ford	Truck
GM	Car
Nissan	Truck

AutoCompany

Vehicle
Car

CarsOnly

Vehicle
Car
Truck

CarsAndTrucks

Figure 9.8b
PROJECT Customer
[CustID, City]

CustID	City
123	Portland
456	Portland
789	Eugene
304	Portland

Figure 9.8c
PROJECT Customer
[City, Status]

City	Status
Portland	00
Portland	20
Eugene	10

(Duplicate tuples are dropped)

Figure 9.8d
SELECT Customer
WHERE City = "Portland"

CustID	City	Status	Credit
123	Portland	00	1,000
456	Portland	20	500
304	Portland	00	2,000

Figure 9.8e
AutoCompany DIVIDEBY
CarsOnly

Company
Ford
GM

Figure 9.8f
AutoCompany DIVIDEBY
CarsAndTrucks

Company
Ford

Figure 9.8g

Customer JOIN Order WHERE CustID = OrderCustID

CustID	City	Status	Credit	OrderID	OrderCustID	Amt
123	Portland	00	1,000	601	123	2,000
123	Portland	00	1,000	603	123	500
789	Eugene	10	10,000	602	789	50

Projection (Figures 9.8b and 9.8c) eliminates some attributes (columns) from a relation; any resulting duplicate tuples are then eliminated. Selection (Figure 9.8d) eliminates entire tuples (rows) if they don't satisfy a condition. Note that if you specify "WHERE CustID = 123," a specific tuple can be selected by its unique primary key value. The division operation (Figures 9.8e and 9.8f) results in tuples where all values of an attribute in the first relation match all values (in a different attribute) in the second relation.

The final special relational algebraic operation is join. Join is not a primitive operation (i.e., all join operations are equivalent to the product of two relations from which some tuples are then selected); however, its usefulness in interrelating two relations is so great that it's treated as one of the essential set of eight operations. Figure 9.8g provides an example of an **equijoin** in which the two relations (Customer and Order) are interrelated by equal values in the CustID and OrderCustID attributes. Conditions other than equality can be used to join tuples in two relations; for example, values of two attributes can be tested for greater than or unequal. In general, the test used can be any scalar comparison (=, >, ≥, ≤, <). This comparison operator is often referred to by the Greek symbol for theta (θ), and thus the generic version of the operation is often called a **theta-join**.

The result of an equijoin always has two attributes with identical values in every tuple (in Figure 9.8g, these attributes are CustID and OrderCustID). If one of these redundant attributes is dropped from the resulting relation, the equijoin is said to be a **natural join**. The natural join is the join most commonly meant when you see a nonspecific reference to a database join.

Other variants of join are possible. Figure 9.8g shows an **inner join**, one in which unmatched tuples are dropped. If instead of dropping unmatched tuples, you include them and put null in the attributes of the missing tuple, you have an **outer join**. If only the first relation's (the one on the left of the JOIN operator) unmatched tuples are paired with nulls, the result is a **left outer join**; a mirror image **right outer join** is also possible. A **full outer join** extends unmatched tuples from both relations with nulls.

This group of eight relational algebraic operations has the property of **algebraic closure**, which means that the result of any of the eight operations is a relation. Thus, the operations can be combined into complex, parenthesized expressions similar to the way ordinary arithmetic expressions can be built up; for example

(RelationA UNION RelationB) TIMES RelationC

is a valid relational algebraic expression. Because the operands and results in relational algebra are relations, not simple values or single tuples (i.e., rows or records), the manipulations provide a very powerful base for database operations, as well as a means of expressing subsets in complex integrity constraints. To relate this concept to a conventional file system, think of how much you could accomplish with operations that are expressed in algebraic form but that treat entire files (or record subsets) as the operands.

The eight relational algebraic operations provide a standard by which to measure any DBMS that claims to support relational data manipulations. While a particular DBMS may use a different syntax than is used here, it must provide equivalent power in manipulating relations without iteration (looping) or recursion.[23] The relational database model is unique among the various database models in that it provides for manipulations of entire *sets* of tuples. The following expression provides an example of using a set-at-a-time manipulation:

Update all Customers where AmtDue > 600, setting Status to "H"

Set-at-a-time operations provide a more powerful means of manipulating data than is possible with the record-at-a-time operations available with conventional file system I/O or with other types of DBMS. (Keep in mind that a set of tuples can contain a single tuple; and, thus, set-at-a-time operations provide both higher level manipulations and record-at-a-time operations.)

Expressions in relational algebra are used not only to retrieve data or create new relations, but also to define a scope for record-at-a-time retrieval and update. The result of a relational algebraic expression can be treated as a **view relation**[24] (rather than a **base relation** — one in which the data is actually stored). Figure 9.9 depicts (in table format) a view relation and the base relation over which it's defined.

---

[23] In fact, the most widely used relational DML is SQL, and it's based on *relational calculus*, another way of expressing relational operations that's equivalent to the relational algebra. In my experience, relational algebra is more intuitive than relational calculus for most people, so this introduction of the relational model uses that approach.

[24] A view is technically a named, derived (or virtual) relation. There are also unnamed, derived relations, and several other formal categories of relations. In this book, I keep things simple by using "view relations" somewhat loosely to cover various categories of relations other than base relations.

Also note that DB2/400 logical files are based on the concept of views, in that they don't contain actual data, but provide a way to access data in underlying physical files (which are like base relations). Recall from Part I how logical files support record selection, field projection, join, derived fields, and other relational-like operations.

Figure 9.9

View Relation and Its
Base Relation

View Relation

CustomerHighDebt

CustID	AmtDue	InterestRate	Status
663309	1250.00	0.12	B
802145	630.00	0.55	A
264502	800.00	0.10	B

SELECT Customer WHERE AmtDue > 600.00

CustID	AmtDue	InterestRate	Status
123886	500.00	0.07	A
663309	1250.00	0.12	B
802145	630.00	0.55	A
264502	800.00	0.10	B

Customer

Base Relation

Changes to a tuple in a view are treated as changes to the underlying tuple in the base relation. Thus the statement

Update all [tuples in] CustomerHighDebt, setting Status to "H"

is equivalent to the statement

Update all Customers where AmtDue > 600, setting Status to "H"

because the CustomerHighDebt view defines a subset[25] of the Customer relation for purposes of set-at-a-time operations, and the attribute update operation (setting Status to "H") is applied to all tuples in the base relation (Customer) that satisfy the view's predicate.

Those attributes in a view relation that are also in the base relation are known as **direct attributes**. Views can also have **virtual** (or **derived**) **attributes**, which are calculated from attribute values in the base relation. Figure 9.10 shows a simple example of a view that has one direct and one virtual attribute.

When we look at SQL views in Chapter 13, we'll see more ways to derive the contents of a view, as well as additional operations that use views.

Another important use of the relational algebra is to define complex integrity rules. For example, we could specify

For all Customers where AmtDue > 600, Status = "H"

[25] Possibly empty or containing all tuples.

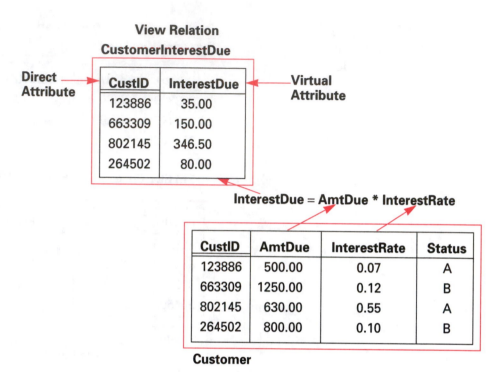

Figure 9.10

View Relation with a
Virtual Field

to require that the DBMS reject any update to the database that would violate this rule. We can use a full range of aggregation functions (e.g., SUM, AVERAGE) to specify many other integrity rules. For example, in a financial system we might express a borrower's maximum permissible outstanding debt as

> For each BorrowerID X in Borrowers,
> (SUM(AmtDue) in Loans where Loans.BorrowerID = X) < 1,000,000

This type of rigorous specification is useful for both database modeling and specifying integrity rules in a DBMS so the DBMS can enforce the rule across all applications.

Taken together, the data structure, data integrity, and data manipulation components of the relational database model provide the foundation for both DBMS facilities and database design methods. If you've already studied Part I, you no doubt recognize some of the relational concepts in DB2/400 physical and logical files. In Part III, you'll see even more of these concepts brought to life in SQL. Even more immediately, the next two chapters use relational concepts as part of a practical approach to database design.

Chapter Summary

Database management systems arose out of the need to reduce the amount of coding necessary to retrieve and update application data, as well as the desire to provide systemwide enforcement of integrity rules. DBMS provide a data definition language to define tables, files, etc. in a system catalog so their definitions and integrity constraints don't have to be repeated in the source code for multiple applications. DBMS also provide a data manipulation language to retrieve and update data. Typically the DML is more powerful than HLL I/O operations for conventional file systems.

Of the four major models for DBMS — hierarchic, network, inverted list, and relational — the relational database model has become the most widely accepted due both to the strong theoretical foundation that supports the relational model and its being the only model with physical data independence; that is, the relational model has no reference to physical storage characteristics such as pointers (links) or relative record numbers.

The relational database model has three major parts: data structure, data integrity, and data manipulation. Relations (often represented as tables) represent entity types. Each tuple in a relation (or row in a table) represents one instance of the relation's entity type. An attribute (or column in a table) represents some entity property. There is no particular ordering to the attributes or tuples. Each attribute is known by its name and is defined over a domain, which specifies the allowable values for the attribute. Each tuple is identified by a primary key value. The primary key is a minimal set of attributes that have unique values for all tuples. Tuples in one relation can be associated with tuples in another relation by foreign key values. A foreign key is a set of attributes in the referencing relation that correspond to the primary key attributes in the referenced relation.

Relations that satisfy the requirements for normal forms (1NF through 5NF) represent certain facts unambiguously and nonredundantly. The five major normal forms have the following requirements:

1NF — Attribute values are not sets

2NF — Each non-key attribute is dependent on the entire primary key

3NF — Each non-key attribute is dependent on nothing but the primary key

4NF — No more than one multivalued fact exists in a relation

5NF — No further splitting of a relation is possible without information loss

The relational model includes several important integrity constraints. Attribute integrity states that all values for an attribute must come from the underlying domain (or, in some cases an attribute may be null, meaning that the value is missing or unknown). Entity integrity states that there must be no duplicate tuples in a relation. As a consequence, every relation must have some minimal set of attributes that can serve as a primary key. If the relation has more than one such set of attributes, the alternatives are known as candidate keys, and one is picked arbitrarily as the primary key. To guarantee entity integrity, no primary attribute can be null. Referential integrity states that all foreign key values must either be null or match some existing tuple's primary key.

The relational model's DML is the relational algebra (or equivalent) that includes the assignment operator plus eight set-oriented operations: union, intersection, difference, product, projection, selection, division, and join. These operations are useful not just to manipulate data in a relational DBMS, but also to create expressions for defining the scope of data retrieval or update operations or to specify complex integrity constraints. A relational algebra expression can be used to define a view relation over a base relation (one that actually contains data). A view relation provides a way to access a derived set of tuples and attributes. Updates to a view relation affect the data in the underlying base relation.

The relational database model not only provides the foundation for DB2/400 and other relational DBMS, but it also is the basis for popular database design methods.

Key Terms

algebraic closure
atomic
attribute integrity
attribute
base relation
candidate key
cardinality
commutative
composite primary key
data definition language
     (DDL)
data manipulation language
     (DML)
database management
     system (DBMS)
degree
derived attribute
difference
direct attribute
division
domain
entity integrity
entity type

equijoin
fifth normal form (5NF)
first normal form (1NF)
foreign key
fourth normal form (4NF)
full outer join
hierarchic data model
inner join
instance
integrity constraint
intersection
inverted list data model
join
left outer join
multivalued fact
natural join
network (CODASYL) data
     model
normal form
normalization
null
outer join
physical data independence

primary key
product
projection
property
record-oriented file
referential integrity
relation
relation body
relation heading
relational database model
right outer join
second normal form (2NF)
selection
stream-oriented file
system catalog
system dictionary
theta-join
third normal form (3NF)
tuple
union
union-compatible
view relation
virtual attribute

Exercises

1. What advantages does a DBMS provide over a conventional file system? Are there any disadvantages?

2. Provide three specific examples of each of the following:

     — Entity type
     — Property
     — Integrity constraint

3. What is the purpose of the system catalog?

4. List three useful kinds of data retrieval that the ideal DBMS might provide in addition to reading a single record by key or by RRN. What (if anything) would be required so you could use these features from RPG IV or COBOL?

5. What problems might occur by storing one record's RRN in another record (as a link)?

6. What are the advantages and disadvantages of using attribute values as the only means to access data (as happens in the relational database model)? What might be done to alleviate some of the disadvantages?

Exercises Continued

Exercises continued

7. Explain the difference between a database relation and a database table. What advantage is there to the use of the table representation?

8. Explain the difference between an entity type and an instance of an entity. How is each represented in the relational database model?

9. Explain the difference between a relation's degree and its cardinality.

10. What purpose does the domain concept serve in the relational database model?

11. The null placeholder can be used instead of a domain value in an attribute when the actual value is unknown or missing. Describe an alternative scheme that doesn't use nulls. Be sure to consider the following issues:
    — calculating sums, averages, etc. over attributes with numeric domains
    — domains that include *all* values of a particular type (e.g., numbers)

12. Give an example of a foreign key that references the same relation that contains the foreign key.

13. Use table-like notation to show a relation (with data) that's in first normal form but not in second normal form. Along with your table, explain (in a few words) what the facts are that the table is representing redundantly. Show how to correct the problem by restructuring the relation.

14. Repeat Exercise 13 for third normal form.

15. Can you think of other types of redundancy that should be avoided that aren't covered by the normal forms? [*Hint: Reread the section on views.*]

16. Give the result of the following expressions, using the relations in Figure 9.7a:
    — RelA UNION RelC
    — RelA INTERSECT RelC
    — RelA MINUS RelC
    — RelA TIMES RelB

17. Give the result of dividing the relation shown in Figure 9.7f by RelC.

18. Using the relations in Figure 9.8a, give the result of
    — PROJECT Customer [City, Credit]
    — SELECT Customer WHERE Credit > 600

19. Describe how the concept of a view relation might be helpful in
    — A database design method in which you model a company's data and how it's used
    — A DBMS facility that HLL programs can use

Chapter 10

Logical Data Modeling

Chapter Overview

As we've learned in the previous two chapters, logical data modeling and physical database design are essential parts of business application development. The data modeling and database design processes produce a blueprint for implementation, whether the implementation uses a traditional language like COBOL and a conventional file system, an application generator for a relational DBMS, or an object-oriented language and an object-oriented database. This chapter begins our coverage of the data modeling process by presenting a step-by-step process you can use to produce a good data model.

Introduction

There are many approaches to data modeling, including variations based on the popular relational database model presented in Chapter 9. The relational model uses relations to represent things of interest, with relation attributes representing the particular properties of whatever the relation represents. As an example, a Part relation that represents parts used in a manufacturing business might include attributes for the part's identifying number, description, and cost. In this chapter, we use the table representation of relations because tables are familiar objects to end users and the terminology of tables and columns is usually easier for end users to work with. Chapter 9 explained the finer distinctions between relations and their representation as tables; as long as you understand these differences, you'll have no problems using relations and tables as more-or-less interchangeable data modeling concepts.

Relational concepts fit many business applications well and have proven useful in years of business application development — not only are the underlying mathematical foundations quite powerful and well defined, but both developers and end users seem comfortable with the concept of a table as an abstraction for things that businesses typically deal with. The 11-step process that's laid out in this chapter uses relational database concepts as a foundation, but many of the steps can be adapted to other methods, such as the fledgling object-oriented analysis and design.

Remember from Chapter 8 that there are three distinct stages to implementing a database: logical data modeling, physical database design, and database table or file implementation. Logical data modeling produces a description from the perspective of the business; physical database design produces a description from the perspective of the hardware and system software. Implementation converts the physical database specification to the proper source code and commands to create tables or files, programs, and other parts of an application. Conceptually, logical data modeling precedes physical database design, which precedes implementation. In practice, of course, there's often a lot of parallel activity.

Data modeling goes hand-in-glove with process modeling,[1] and the two occur together as a development project proceeds. Process modeling covers such aspects as how orders are entered and fulfilled and how customer credit limits are calculated. Obviously, the description of a process requires referring to the data model to identify where some of the values used in calculations come from and where user input and the results of calculations are stored. The data model may also refer to process definitions for actions that are triggered when some change occurs in the database (we'll look at DB2/400 trigger programs in Chapter 17). This book doesn't cover process modeling steps, but one commonly used method you might investigate is data flow diagrams (DFDs). DFDs dovetail nicely with relational data modeling methods. The annotated bibliography suggests several books on DFDs and other process modeling topics you may want to consult. A process model is the basis for a process design (often referred to as a system design), which in turn is the basis for implementing programs and accompanying manual procedures. Just as logical data modeling and process modeling occur together, so too do the two types of design (database and process) and implementation (tables or files and programs). Keep this in mind as you learn the following data modeling steps — they describe only part of what you must do when you tackle a complete development project.

The following sections present a series of 11 steps to produce a data model. Logically, they flow sequentially; however, in practice you skip around as you gather knowledge about the system you're developing. Much of the information is developed from interviewing end users or reading procedure manuals, forms, and other sources that explain how the business works. Thus, when you're talking to an end user or reading a procedure manual, you may learn things that are covered in several of the steps discussed below. For example, in a single conversation, you might learn about the existence of some entity types, about some of the entities' properties, including identifying properties (primary keys), and about relationships among the entity types. Rather than having a series of narrowly focused conversations — the first to discover the entity types, the next to discover entity properties, and so on — you try to learn as much as you can about all these dimensions when you discuss the system with an end user. Your first conversation may provide enough information to let you develop a broad overview of the most important entity types and their interrelationships, with details being filled in through further conversations and reading documents. As with all parts of data modeling and

---

[1] Process modeling is sometimes referred to as "systems analysis" or by various other terms.

database design, be adaptable and fit the following steps to the nature of the project and organization.

Step 1. Establish a Naming Standard and a Data Dictionary

Before you embark on a major data modeling project, you should get two things in order: your naming conventions and how you'll store the information you gather. Many business applications involve hundreds of names, and keeping them straight is half the battle in data modeling. Establish abbreviation and naming standards for data model and process objects such as tables, columns, relationships, domains, and programs. The "Naming Conventions" section in Chapter 3 explains the principles of a good naming system. Most importantly, names should be consistent and should express clearly what an item represents or stores.

Following your naming standard, create one table for valid abbreviations that can be used to form names and another table for valid names. In other words, before you start generating a bunch of names, know how you will form them and be ready to record them. You may need to record a lot of information about names — for example, short, standard, and long variations; synonyms; preferred usage; and a description.

Once you've established naming standards and have a place to track the names you use, you're ready to create a **data dictionary**.[2] A data dictionary isn't one thing; it's lots of things: all the containers you use to hold everything you record during the modeling process. These containers may be word-processing documents, database files, CASE[3] design tool project folders, or any other useful way to keep track of what you learn. In a typical project, you might have some word-processing documents that contain descriptions of business rules or processes, an AS/400 database file that contains table and column names and brief descriptions, and some entity-relationship diagrams produced using a CASE product. Together, all these records of your data model make up the data dictionary.

It's a good idea to set up your naming standards and tables before you create too many other computer-based data dictionary objects (e.g., documents and files) because as the data model progresses, you'll find it's important for your dictionary objects as well as your business objects to follow a rational naming standard. And be sure you've got a place to record *all* aspects of the data model. You don't necessarily need expensive, sophisticated CASE

---

[2] There are lots of alternative names for what we're referring to as the "data dictionary," including "model portfolio" and "repository." There's no widely accepted standard for what you call the totality of all the computer files, file folders, and other containers of specification information, so call it whatever you prefer — just be sure you've got some place to keep all the information you'll be recording.

[3] CASE stands for Computer Aided Software Engineering but has become an almost generic name for various kinds of application design and generator tools.

tools to produce an effective data dictionary, but do have some place to store information so you can retrieve and distribute up-to-date information about the current version of the data model. For many purposes, word-processing documents will suffice.

Step 2. Record End-Users' Views and Identify Entity Types

Think about who in the business best knows what needs to be implemented. Usually that's the end users — the people who carry out or manage the day-to-day operations of the organization. You might also need to work with top-level administrators, especially if the system is ultimately to implement major new ways of doing business. As you talk to end users, also collect manuals, documents, sample computer report listings, sample screen shots, and anything else that will help document the data the organization uses. Take care to make clear, written notes when you talk with an end user. Record a precise description of the various objects, events, relationships, and processes that individual users or departments are concerned with. Keep your notes and the materials you collect well organized.[4]

As we learned in the previous chapter, in relational terms, an object (e.g., a customer) and an event (e.g., placing an order) are two types of entities (things about which you want to record facts) and can be represented as base tables. Complex objects and events may be represented by a group of tables, so there's not necessarily only one table per object. In relational terms, a view or view table is the perspective that a user has on objects and events. For example, an order entry clerk's view of an order might include information about several distinct entities, such as a customer, the order itself, and the individual items ordered. Views are defined in terms of relational operations, such as join, over base tables. The difference between base and view tables is that base tables represent the essential, nonredundant facts about entities, and view tables represent a way of looking at these facts.

Because you're working at this stage with end-user perspectives, you won't be able to determine in every case whether something the user thinks of as an object or event should be represented as a base table or as a view over one or more base tables. Simply record the user perspective using base tables for objects and events, doing whatever structuring is obvious or required by the following steps in this chapter. For example, if the user describes an order, you can initially represent that as an Order base table that references the Customer table. When you identify the order's properties (in Step 3), you can split out a new table, OrderItem, to represent the multiple items that might be ordered on a single order. At this stage, don't become too concerned

---

[4] Do not return to your office after a conversation with an end user and throw the material in a pile on your desk. This may sound like obvious advice, but keeping project material well-organized is crucial to successful data modeling.

with the relational purity of what you record; we get to normalization and other refinements later.

When you discover an entity type, be sure to enter it in your data dictionary. Here are some of the things you should record about an entity type:

- The official name for the entity type, as used in the rest of the data model (e.g., Employee)

- Synonyms — other names for the entity type that end users use or that appear on such things as forms and screens (e.g., Worker)

- A short textual description (e.g., "Someone working for the organization under an Employment Contract, or recognized as an employee for purposes of tax reporting")

- Approximate or estimated yearly volumes (e.g., "Approximately 50 new employees are hired each year; approximately 40 employees leave employment")

This information can go into word-processing documents, spreadsheets, database tables you set up for the purpose, or into some CASE product's files.

As you identify entity types, also identify **entity type hierarchies**. For example, if some parts are produced on site and others are purchased, both are **subtypes** of the Part entity type. As another example, Manager and Nonmanager are subtypes of the Employee entity type. A subtype has all the properties and integrity rules of its supertype. For example, Manager and Nonmanager subtypes have all the properties (e.g., employee ID, name, department) of their Employee supertype.

Step 3. Determine the Most Important Entity Properties

In relational terms, an object's or event's properties are represented as attributes of a relation. As you learn about properties, determine which ones are single-valued (e.g., a person's birth date) and which are multivalued (e.g., a person's children). Multivalued properties are generally represented as a separate table in a normalized relational data model.

Also identify which properties are time-dependent. For example, if you need to know a part's cost on different dates, then cost is a **time-dependent property**. Also identify for each attribute whether there is a default value that should be used if no explicit value is supplied when a new instance is added.

As you learn about various properties that are important to the organization, list them in the data dictionary with at least the following information:

- The official name for the property, as used in the rest of the data model (e.g., AnnualSalary)

- Synonyms — other names for the property that end users use or that appear on such things as forms and screens (e.g., Salary)

- A short textual description (e.g., "The annual gross pay before taxes for an Employee")
- The source in the business process (e.g., "Defined in employee's Employment Contract")
- The domain that defines the allowable values for the property — discussed in Step 7 (e.g., Salary > 0)
- Whether a value for the property is required or optional
- The default value (if any) to be used when a new instance of the entity type is added and no explicit value is supplied for the property
- Whether the property is part of a primary key, candidate key, or foreign key — discussed in Steps 4, 5, and 6
- Whether the property is a *direct* or *derived* property. Direct properties cannot be derived from other properties. For example, an employee's name is a direct property. An employee's number of months in service is a derived property because it can be calculated from the starting and ending dates in the employee's employment history. An employee's annual salary might be direct, or it might be derived — for example, if there's also a monthly salary property from which the annual salary can be computed.

At this stage of the data model, don't worry about all the details of each property.[5] Mainly get some basic information into a list (which might be in a computer file, a word-processing document, or a CASE tool). As you go through the following steps, you'll learn more about the properties and the overall organization of the data model.

Step 4. Determine the Primary Key for Each Entity Type

In a proper data model, you must be able to identify each instance of an entity type (e.g., a particular Customer) by the values of one or more of its properties. In your data model, when you represent an entity type as a table, you specify the table's primary key, which is a column or group of columns that uniquely identify each row in the table (e.g., a CustomerID column). There may be several ways to identify rows uniquely, and any column or group of columns that could serve as a table's primary key is known as a candidate key.

---

[5] Some items that you at first consider properties might later turn out to be entity types. For example, a product's color might first be mentioned by a salesperson as a simple (atomic) type of value (e.g., red, green, blue). But someone in manufacturing might view color as an entity type, with its own properties, including chemical components or suppliers. With a data modeling technique based on the relational model, this kind of adjustment is straightforward; those tables that had Color as a column, now would have ColorID as a foreign key referencing the primary key of the Color table.

You should select one candidate key to serve as the table's primary key.[6] As you identify the candidate and primary keys, add them to the documentation for the respective entity type.

Each primary and candidate key must meet the following criteria:

- Candidate key values must be unique for each row in the table
- Candidate key values must never be missing or incomplete for a row
- Each candidate key must use no columns other than those necessary to identify a row uniquely

A primary key should also meet the following criteria:

- It should be meaningless (other than as an identifier)
- A row's primary key value should never change
- There should be no limit to the number of primary key values available
- Only one primary key should be specified for each table

Often, the best choice for a table's primary key is a large, meaningless, arbitrarily assigned, positive integer. This type of primary key may be something like an invoice number that's already part of the user's way of doing business, or you may have to introduce a new column as a **surrogate key**, when no naturally occurring columns meet the primary key criteria. Surrogate keys avoid problems that can sometimes occur with natural identifiers. For instance, a social security number, which might seem like a good candidate key for employees, in practice may change, may be missing, or may violate other rules for primary keys. A better choice might be an arbitrary employee ID that's assigned when a person is hired. To let users work with natural identifiers, you can include in the data model a table that maps surrogate keys to natural identifiers (when the natural identifier's value exists).

Because of their simplicity, primary keys consisting of just one column are preferable to keys with more than one column. However, there are two cases in which a composite primary key (i.e., a key consisting of more than one column) works satisfactorily in place of a single-column primary key. First, the primary key for a table that represents a many-to-many relationship (covered in Step 5) can be the combination of the foreign keys that designate the related tables. A foreign key is one or more columns whose values for a particular row match the primary key value of some other row (in the same or a different table). For example, an Order table might have a CustomerID column as a foreign key. Each order's CustomerID column would (normally) contain the value of some Customer row's primary key, thus identifying the customer

---

[6] You should use the same primary key for all subtypes of an entity type. For example, if the primary key of the Employee entity type is EmployeeID, then EmployeeID should be the primary key for the Manager and NonManager subtypes, as well.

who placed the order. As long as the foreign keys in a relationship are defined as never being null,[7] any combination of them will have the same desirable qualities as a single-column surrogate key. For example, in a PartSupplier table that represents the relationship between suppliers and parts, the primary key might be a combination of the PartID and the SupplierID foreign key columns.

A composite primary key also works satisfactorily for tables whose sole purpose is to define multivalued properties. For such tables, a sequence number that is unique within the same parent primary key value can be combined with the foreign key designating the parent. For example, an OrderItem table can have the combination of OrderID and SeqNbr columns as its primary key, where OrderID is a foreign key designating the OrderID of the parent Order table, and SeqNbr is the line sequence number within an order.

Step 5. Determine the Relationships Between Entity Types

The entity types you discover don't exist in isolation — they're interrelated. When you identify a **relationship**, document it, including giving it a name. You can record relationships in textual or table form, or use an entity relationship diagram (ERD). Chapter 11 provides a detailed explanation of ERD notation and advice on when its use is most appropriate. In addition, for each relationship, you should determine its *cardinality*. There are three major categories of cardinality:

- One-to-one (e.g., each company-owned car may have a single designated parking space, and each parking space may have a single authorized company car assigned to it)

- One-to-many (e.g., one customer may have many orders, but each order has only one customer)

- Many-to-many (e.g., many suppliers may supply a part, and a supplier may supply many parts)

In the relational model, you can represent a simple one-to-one or one-to-many relationship with a foreign key. You should represent a many-to-many relationship in a new table reflecting two (or more) one-to-many relationships. For example, you can represent a many-to-many relationship between parts and suppliers with a PartSupplier table. The Part and Supplier tables would then both have a one-to-many relationship with the PartSupplier table.

It helps to identify more specifically what a relationship's cardinality is. In general, after splitting your many-to-many relationships into one-to-many relationships, you need to determine

---

[7] Chapter 9 discusses the concept of a null placeholder instead of a column value.

- For all "one" sides of the relationships, whether the "one" means "zero-or-one" or "exactly one," and

- For all "many" sides of the relationships, whether the "many" means "zero-or-more" or "one-or-more"

If there are more specific cardinality rules (e.g., "there must be exactly five players on each team") record these, too. The most important reason for determining precise cardinality rules is so you know whether one side of a relationship is optional or required and so you know the maximum number (if any) of associated instances. (You wouldn't want to implement a basketball database that lets a user put six people on the court.)

As you identify relationships, also determine the degree of the relationship; that is, how many entity types are involved in the relationship. Most relationships will be binary (between two entity types). Others may be non-binary — that is, involve three or more entities. For example, a relationship for which suppliers supply particular parts for specific projects is a three-way relationship. A nonbinary relationship should also be represented as a new table, with one foreign key referencing each table that represents one of the entity types involved in the relationship.

Step 6. Determine the Foreign Key Rules for Each Relationship

For each relationship you include in the data model, one table must include a foreign key that designates the rows in the table for the target (referenced or parent) entity type that are associated with rows in the table for the designating (referencing or dependent) entity type. For example, an Order table might include a CustomerID column as a foreign key to designate the row in the Customer table that is associated with a particular order. For each relationship, you should identify which column(s) in the designating table make up the foreign key.

Also specify the nature of the relationship by specifying the **delete-update-insert rules** for the primary and foreign keys in each relationship.[8] This task involves two parts. First, determine the action to take if a primary key value in the target table is deleted or updated, potentially leaving orphan rows in the designating table that no longer reference an existing row in the target table. For example, you need to specify what should or should not happen when a row is deleted from the Customer table and there are rows in the Order table that reference the deleted Customer row (i.e., how should the system handle an attempt to delete a customer who has outstanding orders).

In this case, you can take several possible actions:

- Reject the delete or update (signal an error)

- Handle it with a custom procedure

[8] These rules define the specific way that referential integrity will be enforced.

- Cascade the delete or update to all the related dependent tables
- Set the related dependent foreign key column(s) to null or a default value (if allowed)

The end user's description of how the business operates is the basis for making this decision.

Next, determine the action to take if an insertion or update in the designating table creates an unmatched, non-null foreign key value in the designating table. For example, you need to specify what should or should not happen when a row is inserted into the Order table and there is no row in the Customer table that matches the customer ID in the new Order row (i.e., an attempt to insert an order with no matching customer). You can specify any of the following rules:

- Reject the insert or update (signal an error)
- Handle it with a custom procedure
- Create a default parent row in the target table and give it the same primary key value as the new foreign key value
- Reset the new or changed foreign key to null or to a default value (if allowed)

Note how the various rules can reflect different approaches to the structure of the organization's data and the way the organization operates. The delete-update-insert rules can be documented with the other information for the table that contains the foreign key to which the rules apply.

Step 7. Determine Additional Integrity Constraints

In Steps 4 and 6, you determined two important business rules: primary and foreign key integrity constraints. By describing the rules that the subsequent design and implementation must follow to ensure that the database always has valid primary and foreign key values, you can avoid ambiguous or incomplete identification of the entities your database stores and the interrelationships among those entities.

You should also identify several other categories of integrity constraints, including domains, **predicates**, and **transition constraints**. Business rules must be accurate and complete if you don't want the database to become a "garbage dump." Because end users often jumble their descriptions and even provide conflicting or incomplete rules, you must discuss and record them carefully — it's your neck out there when invalid or inconsistent data appears in the system. In this section, we look at some of the types of rules to record, starting with the simplest.

First, determine the domain of each property. A domain defines two aspects of a column: its allowable values and the allowable operations on the column. By explicitly defining domains, you establish guidelines for ensuring that your implementation won't let invalid values be put into a column and won't improperly use the column in an operation. For example, with clear definitions of the domains of HourlyWage and MonthlySalary, you can ensure that neither column ever contains negative values and that HourlyWage is not added to MonthlySalary without conversion.

You normally don't explicitly define the entire set of allowable operations on a domain because such a definition would require you to consider a very large number of cross-domain operations. Instead, define domains so their allowable values and meaning are clear, and the allowable operations can be inferred from the partial definition. Start by recording a concise, clear, verbal description of each domain, including its allowable values and constraints on operations. Once you have domains defined, you can add the appropriate domain name to each property definition.

Several characteristics of a domain can help further establish its meaning. You should express the domain's basic type (e.g., integer, string, date) in user-oriented terms, not computer-storage-oriented terms. For example, use "integer" or "decimal fraction with precision of 0.01" instead of "packed decimal." You can further restrict a domain's set of allowable values using various forms of set notation. For example, for integers you can use a range (e.g., Cost > 0); for enumerations, you can use a full or partial member list (e.g., DayOfTheWeek is {Sunday...Saturday}). For more complicated sets, it's best to use general set builder notation using logical predicates or use precise verbal set specifications.

When defining domains, you may encounter the need for a set that has values of a certain basic type plus one or more distinct values not of the same basic type. For example, to specify the beginning and ending dates for time-dependent data, you may want to use a domain that includes valid dates, plus distinct values for "open begin date" and "open end date" so you can store open-ended intervals. When you implement a column based on a domain with distinguished values such as these, you generally need to use two particular values (e.g., 0001/01/01 and 9999/12/31); but in the data model, the domain specification should identify the logical meaning of these distinguished values, not the specific implementation constants.

As you identify the domain for each property, you should also document whether either or both of the following possibilities are valid:

- The value of the property may be *unknown* for some rows
- The value of the property may be *not-applicable* for some rows

If it's valid for a row to exist with a particular column's value unknown (that is, the column doesn't contain a valid value), the column is said to allow *nulls*. Remember that null is a placeholder (not a value from the domain) that means "unknown, but may exist." For example, null might be used to represent an unknown customer phone number. Null does not mean 0, blank, or not-applicable.

Not-applicable means that no meaningful value exists for a column. For example, a Part table might have a Color column, so a part that has no color could contain a not-applicable placeholder in its Color column. It's important to specify in the data model whether a column can contain null or not-applicable so the implementation can support these cases (or enforce that a valid value is always present, if null and not-applicable are not allowed). The way these two placeholders are implemented depends on the DBMS or file system that's used for the implementation. For example, DB2/400 supports columns that allow nulls, but there's no direct support for a not-applicable placeholder. An application implemented in DB2/400 might use null for both cases, or the application might use special values to represent either or both cases.

Columns that allow a not-applicable placeholder are directly related to entity type hierarchies. You can always eliminate the need for a not-applicable placeholder in a column by splitting a table into separate tables representing the subtypes and omitting from the subtype tables columns where all rows would have not-applicable placeholders. For example, a Part table could be split into ColorPart and NoColorPart tables, representing subtypes of the Part entity type. The ColorPart table would have a Color column, but the NoColorPart would not. Whether to use subtypes or allow a not-applicable placeholder is a judgment call; pick the representation that is easier to work with. Use subtypes when there is a clear separation of the distinct subtypes in the business or end-user perspective. For example, you might use subtypes to distinguish between a part produced on site and an equivalent purchased part, whereas you might simply specify that a column allows the not-applicable placeholder to distinguish a part that doesn't have a color from others that do.

Units of measure or rate (e.g., kilograms or dollars per month) provide another way to clarify a domain's meaning. Also keep in mind that, just as you can define a hierarchy of entity types, you can define domains as a hierarchy. For example, Date is a very general domain. FirstOfMonth is a domain that is a subset of the Date domain, restricted to just those dates where the DayOfTheMonth is 1.

After defining domains to limit the allowable values for each column, you can represent other business rules by specifying row predicates to limit the combination of values present in any row in a table. A row predicate is a constraint that can be evaluated with just the values from a single row in a single table. For example, if an EmploymentHistory table has HireDate and TerminationDate columns; you might define a row predicate as

TerminationDate is null OR HireDate ≤ TerminationDate

Multirow and **multitable predicates** are even broader forms of integrity constraint. You can define these constraints using the general notation of **assertions** and **triggered procedures**. Assertions are logical expressions that must be true for a valid database. For example, your data model might state that in any fiscal year, an employee's incentive bonuses cannot exceed his or her total salary. Triggered procedures are actions that occur when a specified condition exists. For example, your model might state that whenever a customer places an order for more than $100,000, a notice must be sent to the sales manager. You can use pseudo-SQL[9] or simply precise narrative descriptions of multirow and multitable constraints. If you're familiar with any of the mathematical notations for formal logic, they can be useful in some cases. However, because many end users (and other developers) may not be familiar with this type of notation, you may find that a less rigorous, but more widely understood way of expressing constraints is the best technique.

You're also likely to encounter business rules that impose transition constraints on the data model. Transition constraints limit changes to the data. For example, the business rules may restrict a change to a customer's credit limit to either lowering the limit or increasing the limit a maximum of 100 percent in any one month. Assertions and triggered procedures provide good general mechanisms for specifying transition constraints.

Step 8. Determine Security Rules

Security rules are just a special case of integrity constraints that are dependent on the identity of the user. You can use the same notation for security rules that you use for other business rules. As you determine security rules, identify the following classes of constraints:

- *Value-independent* rules, which are restrictions on tables, views, and columns based solely on the type of data, not on particular values. For example, certain users may not be able to access customer data at all.

- *Value-dependent* rules, which are based on specific values. For example, a user may be authorized to see the Salary column in the Employee table only for rows with Salary $\leq$ 50,000.

- *Statistical* rules, which limit the types of inferences that can be made about values in the database using statistical functions such as SUM and COUNT. For example, users who are not authorized to individual employee salaries may also be restricted from running salary totals on subsets of employees, because by getting totals for two subsets they might be able to calculate a specific employee's salary.

---

[9] The term "pseudo-SQL" just means a SQL-like expression that doesn't have to conform strictly to any SQL standard or product's syntax.

- *Context-dependent* rules, which are defined in terms of functions or system values such as time of day. For example, users can be limited to updating the Employee rows of only the employees they supervise.

Step 9. Integrate Multiple Users' Views into an Overall Schema

After you determine the objects, events, relationships, properties, and integrity constraints for each user view, you should combine them into a single, consistent, nonredundant logical data model. The users' views are sometimes referred to as **subschemas** (or **external schemas**) and the integrated model as the **schema** (or **conceptual schema**). Integrating multiple views involves

- Identifying columns that are the same in multiple views
- Resolving domain and other integrity and security conflicts between multiple definitions of the columns and tables
- Synthesizing the schema's base tables from the multiple subschema tables and views

In practice, this integration process occurs as you record users' views. By working on the integrated schema, you uncover conflicts or ambiguities in users' views that you can (hopefully) resolve as you work with the end users.

The integration process demands a good naming convention and an effective data dictionary. Users often have many different synonyms for the same entity or property, and you'll want a single official name to use in all your table and integrity definitions. A synonym table in the data dictionary lets you relate end-user terminology to official names. The data dictionary should also let you record the original source(s) of an integrity constraint.

As an example of the type of synthesis that occurs during this step, you might find that one user perspective has a Customer table (representing a person who buys goods) and another user perspective has a Client table (representing a person who pays for services). If both tables represent a person who pays for goods and/or services, is billed, is sent marketing material, etc., then it's probably a good idea to have a single Customer or Client table (but not both) in the integrated data model. If there's a substantial amount of information that does not overlap for each role (customer or client) a person might play, then it may be a good idea to define a Customer table with CustomerOfService and CustomerOfProducts subtypes of Customer. If two or more tables have the same primary key and/or many of the same columns, the tables should probably be combined.

Another common situation in merging users' views is discovering that from one user's perspective a piece of information is a property represented as a column, and in another user's perspective, this same information is represented as a table with columns for more information about the item. Earlier, we discussed how a product's color might be viewed in different ways by a salesperson and someone in the manufacturing division. In cases like this, the more extensive perspective (i.e., representing the item with a table) belongs in the integrated data model.

As you integrate tables, you also must adjust foreign keys and tables that represent relationships accordingly. In addition, you may find (and need to revise the data model to document) that a column documented as a direct column in one user's view can actually be derived from columns that are documented in a different user's view. Another potential adjustment will be in the definition of underlying domains when two columns in different users' views are identified as representing the same property, but the different users' views perhaps document different ranges of values in the columns' respective domains. Similarly, whether a column can be null may need to be changed when column definitions are merged from different views.

As a note on the integration step: In many cases, your data modeling work will be for only part of the organization's overall information requirements. If a complete or partial data model already exists, any new modeling will need to be integrated with the existing data model, which may necessitate adjustments to the existing data model.

Step 10. Eliminate Redundancy in Schema Base Tables

This step is just a check on the result of the integration of multiple users' views. Make certain that the schema base tables do not contain redundant facts.[10] For example, a PartSupplier table shouldn't normally include a SupplierAddress column because each supplier's address is likely to appear in many rows in the table. In most cases, the SupplierAddress column would be part of a Supplier table, with one row per supplier.

One approach to eliminating redundancy is to check each table to see that it doesn't violate any of the rules of normalization. The "Normal Forms" section in Chapter 9 explains the most important normal forms for relations, and how each represents a way to avoid ambiguous representation of entity types and properties. Use that section as a guide to review your table definitions at this stage of the data modeling process. Your logical data model should be completely normalized (i.e., satisfy fifth normal form). This is the best way to communicate the business model accurately using tables as your notational tool. When you do the physical implementation design, you may choose to design files that do not correspond exactly to your data model's tables. Such controlled redundancy is perfectly acceptable but is part of the implementation design, not part of the logical data model.[11]

---

[10] Of course, much of the elimination of redundancy happens while you are working with the users' views, before final integration. As with most of the steps in this chapter, the order presented here isn't meant to be a rigid guideline.

[11] This is a frequently misunderstood point in data modeling. *Normal forms have nothing to do with physical database design.* Normal forms are a relational data modeling convention for representing a data model as tables that reflect functional dependencies (i.e., "facts").

Another way to eliminate redundancy is to check all columns to see whether they can be derived from other columns. If a column can be derived, it should not be in a base table, but rather in a view (see Step 11). For example, an order's TotalAmount usually can be derived from the set of associated OrderItem rows; thus, TotalAmount is a column that belongs in a view, not in a base table.

Step 11. Determine Subschema Views

Once you have an integrated schema, you should review the original users' views (subschemas) and determine how each is derived from the schema's base tables. This step produces a revised set of users' views defined over the schema's base tables. You may need to express the following types of derivation through the views:

- Restriction (subsetting) of rows
- Projection (elimination) of columns
- Combination of rows (joins or unions) from more than one table
- Derivation of virtual columns that are a function of columns in underlying base tables (e.g., OrderItemTotal = ItemUnitPrice * ItemQuantity)
- Ordering (sorting) of rows in a view

You can use expressions in relational algebra, as described in Chapter 9, or use a pseudo-SQL notation for describing views.

When you've successfully completed this step, the end users should all be able to validate that the data model reflects the type of information, its structure, and the necessary integrity constraints to support the organization's activities. When the end users first described their own requirements, these elements were modeled in isolation (i.e., without regard to other end users); at this stage of the data modeling process, an end user should be able to see how their data fits into the larger picture.

After making one iteration through these 11 design steps, you may need to repeat some of them several times to get the data model right. As the organization's business model changes, you'll also have to revise the logical data model. But using this set of steps, you'll have a framework for analyzing and recording both the original data model and subsequent revisions.

This chapter has only touched the surface of the 11 data modeling steps. The annotated bibliography suggests several excellent books to learn more about this approach. Keep in mind that data modeling isn't an exact science, and you must adapt a variety of methods and documentation techniques to produce a useful data model. In the next chapter, we look at entity relationship diagrams, which are one technique you'll find helpful in documenting a data model. Then, once you have a good data model, you have a solid basis for designing the database implementation. Chapter 12 takes you forward from the data model through physical database design.

Chapter Summary

Logical data modeling is an essential part of application development. A data model provides a description, from the business perspective, of an organization's information requirements. The data model provides the basis for subsequent physical database design, which in turn is the blueprint for implementing database tables or files and related items.

The following 11 steps are a guideline for developing a data model based on the relational database model described in Chapter 9:

Step   1   Establish a naming standard and a data dictionary

Step   2   Record end-users' views and identify entity types

Step   3   Determine the most important entity properties

Step   4   Determine the primary key for each entity type

Step   5   Determine the relationships between entity types

Step   6   Determine the foreign key rules for each relationship

Step   7   Determine additional integrity constraints

Step   8   Determine security rules

Step   9   Integrate multiple users' views into an overall schema

Step 10   Eliminate redundancy in schema base tables

Step 11   Determine subschema views

To complete a data model, you normally work on several steps at the same time, and you may need to repeat some steps to refine the model. A process model is also developed in parallel with the data model. The process model references the data model and vice versa.

Data modeling involves talking to end users and researching manuals, forms, and other documents that the organization uses. This information is first collected from the individual user or department perspective and then integrated into a unified, organization-wide data model. During the integration, conflicts, redundancy, and ambiguity need to be resolved. The completed logical data model should describe entity types, properties, relationships, and integrity constraints upon which all of the individual user perspectives can be based.

The data model is stored in a data dictionary, which is a collection of documents, tables or files, diagrams, etc. that contain all the descriptions that are part of the model. As with most application development processes, data modeling techniques must be adapted to the nature of the project and available resources.

Key Terms

assertion
conceptual schema
data dictionary
delete-update-insert rules
entity subtype
entity type

entity type hierarchy
external schema
multirow predicate
multitable predicate
predicate
relationship

schema
subschema
surrogate key
time-dependent property
transition constraint
triggered procedure

Exercises

1. Briefly describe and provide examples of five types of information that would be included in a logical data model.

2. For each item you described for Exercise 1, suggest one or more ways you could store the information in a data dictionary.

3. Give an example of how some part of the process model for an order entry system might need to refer to information in the data model.

4. Give an example of how some part of the data model might need to refer to information in the process model for an order entry system.

5. List five ways (or sources of information) to gather the information needed to develop a data model for an organization.

6. Why do you think a primary key value should be unchanging? *[Hint: Consider relationships.]*

7. Give an example of when you might specify that the "cascade" foreign key rule should apply when a row is deleted. (Describe two entity types and the nature of their relationship that makes the "cascade" rule appropriate.)

8. Specify four examples of multirow or multitable integrity rules. Try to make your descriptions as clear and precise as possible.

9. Provide two examples of cases in which two (or more) end users' views (subschemas) might have conflicts when you try to merge them into an integrated data model (i.e., in the schema).

Chapter 11

Entity Relationship Diagramming

Chapter Overview

This chapter describes entity relationship diagrams (ERDs), which are a way to represent parts of the logical data model in diagram form. You learn a standard set of symbols and other forms of notation that can be used in hand-drawn diagrams or with various computer-based diagramming tools. The chapter also provides guidance on when to use ERDs in your data model.

Introduction

In Chapter 10 we established a series of steps that occur during the data modeling stage of a development project. Many of these steps require some form of documentation to specify the data that the organization requires and how it's structured. Often, this documentation will be reviewed by the person creating the data model, the end user, and the person responsible for the physical database design. We noted in Chapter 8 that the data model must be clear and comprehensible. **Entity relationship diagrams** (**ERDs**) are a data modeling technique that can improve the clarity and comprehensibility of a data model.

ERDs describe data with pictures. For simple systems and high-level views of complex systems, an ERD's boxes, lines, and other symbols can be easier to understand than a textual description, which is what makes them a valuable data modeling tool for business systems. ERDs aren't suited for every data modeling task, however, and it's just as important to know when not to use ERDs as it is to know how to use them. We'll come back to that point at the end of the chapter.

There are many flavors of ERD notation and lots of religious wars about methodologies, most of which you can safely ignore, as this chapter does. The techniques described in this chapter are representative of a widely used ERD notation.

You can draw ERDs either by hand or using a variety of PC-based software tools. Usually, ER diagramming tools are part of a larger software package that may include other diagramming tools (e.g., for data flow diagrams), as well as dictionary facilities to store detailed definitions of various other elements of a complete data model. At the end of this chapter, we look at some of the advantages of both hand-drawn and tool-drawn ERDs; but first, let's get more familiar with how you construct ERDs.

Basic ERD Concepts and Symbols

In ERDs, boxes represent **entities**,[1] and lines connecting boxes represent **relationships** between entities — hence the name "entity relationship." An entity is some object, event, or association of interest in the data model. A relationship represents some dependency between two or more entities. The nature of relationships in an ERD tells us a lot about the structure of an organization's data.

The figure below shows a simple ERD with Customer and Order entities and a Places relationship between them.

This ERD is a clear, quickly digested depiction of an important aspect of a business: The system under consideration deals with customers and orders. This ERD's clarity and simplicity illustrate why ERDs are a popular technique that business analysts use to describe a business model (or at least some part of its data) to end users.

The line representing the relationship in the figure above indicates two other important aspects of the business model: Each order is placed by one customer, and a customer may place zero, one, or multiple orders.

The unbroken, single portion of the line attached to the Customer box specifies that each order has exactly one customer associated with it. The broken, crowsfoot portion of the line attached to the Order box specifies that each customer can have zero, one, or more associated orders. The figure below shows an easy way to remember what the crowsfoot means and on which end of the line you should place it. As you can see, the crowsfoot is shorthand for showing multiple boxes.

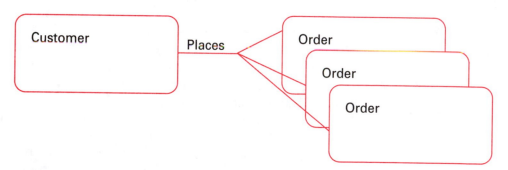

---

[1] More properly, boxes represent entity types. For simplicity, in this chapter we follow the common ERD terminology and use "entity" as shorthand for "entity type," except where the longer term is important for clarity.

A break at one end of a relationship line means the entity is optional (there can be zero or more), whereas a solid line on an end means it is required (there must be one or more). You can combine broken- or solid-line endings with single-line or crowsfoot endings to depict four possibilities on each end of a relationship, as shown below.

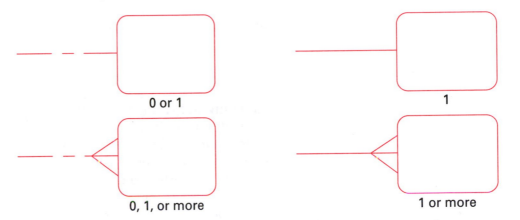

If you encounter a business situation that doesn't fit within these four possibilities, you can add your own annotation for the cardinality of the relationship (i.e., how many instances of one entity can be associated with an instance of the other entity). The following example shows one way to specify that an instance of a Team on court (e.g., a basketball team) must have exactly five instances of Player. The solid line ending next to Player states that Player is required, and the 5 above the crowsfoot specifies the number of Players that a Team on court must have.

You can also specify a range for the cardinality of a relationship, using annotation such as the following:

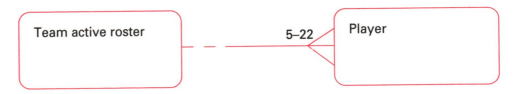

The 5–22 above the crowsfoot specifies that a team has at least 5, but no more than 22, players on the Team active roster.

One final addition completes the basic ERD notation. The line representing the relationship between two entities is often labeled at both ends so it's easier to talk about the relationship from the perspective of either entity. The example below adds "Shows" to the Order end of the relationship.

The entity and relationship labels, together with the way the relationship line is drawn, provide the pieces for verbal descriptions of the data model; for example, "Each customer places zero, one, or more orders, and each order shows exactly one customer."

The two relationship labels are alternatives for stating the same thing — there's still only one relationship — and the second label is optional. Don't clutter your diagrams with second labels that are merely passive voice constructions (e.g., "is placed by") for the relationship. While you're working on early versions of ERDs, you often don't need to label a relationship line at all, if the relationship is obvious. For example, in the Customer-Order diagram, it's pretty obvious that customers place orders. In your final diagrams, however, it's a good idea to label all relationship lines, even if the relationship is obvious.

Adding Properties to ERDs

A **property** is some identifying or descriptive piece of information for an entity.[2] For example, a Customer entity would likely have a Name property, and an Order entity would likely have an OrderDate property. You can list property names either inside an entity's box, as in the entity box below

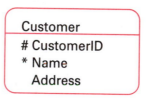

---

[2] For ERDs, the term "attribute" is frequently used instead of the term "property." We use the term "property" to avoid confusion with the specific meaning of attribute in the relational model discussed in Chapter 9. In actual practice, the terms can be used interchangeably.

or on an attached list, as in

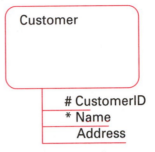

You place a # before properties that uniquely identify an entity (in relational terminology, the attributes that constitute the primary key). You place an * before properties that must have a value (and that are not part of the entity's identifier). Any remaining properties you list are for optional values (in relational terminology, the attribute can be null).

A relationship between two entities implies that one of them has one or more properties that contain identifier values from the other entity (in relational terminology, the foreign key). The following ERD shows that you can think of the box for the Order entity as implicitly specifying a CustomerID property that associates each order with a specific customer.

These properties don't need to be shown on an ERD because the relationship line tells us most of what we need to know about the logical relationship between the two entities and the required foreign key property. If a foreign key property is shown explicitly on an ERD, you may want to add some notation to indicate for which relationship it serves as a foreign key and with which property in the target entity it's paired, as shown below.

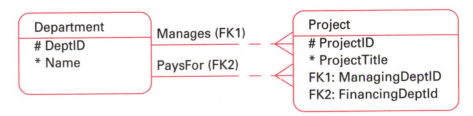

In this example, there are two relationships between the Department and Project entities. The Manages relationship represents which department is responsible for managing specific projects. The PaysFor relationship represents which department is responsible for funding specific projects. This ERD tells us that a project's managing and funding departments may be different. The FK1 and FK2 annotations specify which Project property is used as the foreign key for each of the respective relationships. Although the property names make this fairly obvious, the FK1 and FK2 annotations remove any doubt.

In practice, you may find that listing all of an entity's properties clutters your ERD and diminishes the value of presenting the data model pictorially. Nothing says you must use only ERDs to describe your entire data model. (In fact, that's not likely.) It's often easier to record and discuss entity properties with end users using a table-formatted list rather than working with all the properties on ERDs. Some computer-based analysis and design tool products let you display properties either way, which is especially helpful if the tool lets you mark a subset of an entity's properties for display on ERDs, helping keep the ERD readable. With hand-drawn ERDs, you should choose the level of detail to put on a diagram, depending on how you're using the diagram, and at what stage of data model development you are. Final drawings typically have more detail than early, working drafts.

You may also want to specify the details of foreign key rules (e.g., update and delete restrictions) separately from the ERD, using pseudo-SQL or some other specification language, as discussed in Chapter 10.

Multivalued Properties

A property may be single-valued or multivalued. For example, a customer would typically have a single name but might have several phone numbers. There are two ways to represent multivalued properties on ERDs.[3] You can simply list a multivalued property under an entity and describe the property as permitting a set of values by enclosing the property name in braces ({ }), as is done for PhoneNbr below.

```
┌─────────────────────┐
│ Customer            │
├─────────────────────┤
│ # CustomerID        │
│ * Name              │
│   Address           │
│ { PhoneNbr }        │
└─────────────────────┘
```

The other way is to show the multivalued property as another entity and associate it with the main entity in a many-to-one relation. (The vertical bar across the relationship line indicates that the CustomerID property is

---

[3] We learned in Chapter 9 that the basic relational model requires single-valued attributes, so it may at first seem like "relational heresy" to discuss ways to represent multivalued properties, but read on.

part of the CustomerPhoneNumber entity's primary key; this notation is explained later.)

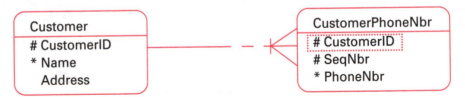

This latter method of specifying multivalued properties illustrates that, in ERDs, an entity can represent some "real" thing, such as a customer, or it can be a design artifact that represents a more abstract notion, such as the multivalued nature of a customer's telephone numbers.

Both techniques for showing multivalued properties can express the same underlying structure of the data. Although the basic, first-normal form (1NF) of the relational model forbids using multivalued attributes, there's really no reason not to use the { } notation on ERDs during your data modeling stage — if doing so makes your model's diagrams easier for the end user to understand. You can rest easy knowing you're on firm theoretical ground, too. There's an extension to the basic relational model, known as non-first normal form (NFNF), that deals with nonatomic attributes, including multivalued attributes. When you start to develop your physical database design, you want to show multivalued properties as separate tables, but remember the guideline we discussed in Chapter 8 — adapt various techniques to the situation at hand, and don't get hung up on dogma during the data modeling stage.

Representing Associations

You can also use an entity to represent an association between other entities. Take the case of describing a many-to-many association between suppliers and parts. You can show the many-to-many aspect of the association as follows:

The way this ERD is drawn, a supplier may supply no parts or one or more parts; and a part may have no supplier, or one or more suppliers. There's no place on this diagram, however, to place the price that a specific supplier charges for a particular part. The example on the following page splits the many-to-many relationship into two one-to-many relationships and adds a new SupplierOfPart entity to represent the association. This new entity provides a place to list the Price property. This type of entity is sometimes called an **intersection entity.**

In the example above, the SupplierOfPart entity's identifier consists of properties that contain ID values that match associated Supplier and Part instances' ID values. Remember that these two SupplierOfPart properties don't have to be listed explicitly because such foreign key properties are implied by the two relationships. However, you do need to specify that these implicit properties are part of the SupplierOfPart entity's identifier. In ERDs, you can explicitly represent the fact that one entity's identifier includes all its foreign key properties corresponding to the identifier properties of a parent entity by putting a bar across the dependent entity's end of the relationship line. The two bars across the relationship lines close to the crowsfeet connected to the SupplierOfPart entity mean that the identifier for SupplierOfPart contains all the foreign key properties that reference the identifier properties of the Supplier and Part entities.

The following example shows another case in which the bar notation is helpful:

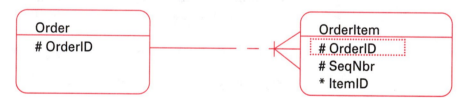

The OrderItem entity, which has a many-to-one relationship with the Order entity, uses an identifier comprising an order ID property and a sequence number unique within each order ID value. The only OrderItem identifier property that needs to be shown explicitly is SeqNbr.[4]

The formal meaning of the vertical bar is that the entity it's next to is a **weak entity**, one for which an instance cannot exist unless a corresponding entity on the other end of the relationship exists. For example, an instance of an OrderItem can't exist without a corresponding instance of an Order. An entity type that is not a weak entity is known as a **regular entity**.

---

[4] The examples in this chapter follow a naming convention wherein a property whose name ends with "ID" has values that are unique across all instances of an entity and a property named SeqNbr has unique values only within those instances that share a common value(s) for the other properties that compose the entity's complete identifier. For example, order ID values are unique across all orders, but an order item's sequence number is unique within a particular order.

Exclusive Relationships

There are lots of either-or situations in business, and ERDs provide a notation that helps identify them. The ERD below depicts the business situation in which an account is associated with either a person or a company, but not both.

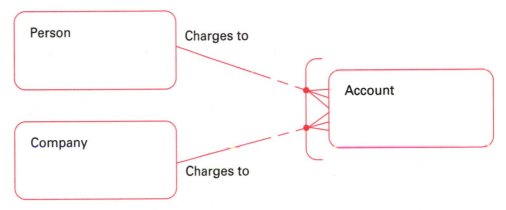

The **exclusive relationship** arc with connector dots (●) specifies that an instance of the entity having multiple relationship lines connected by the arc can participate in one and only one of the alternative relationships. For example, account number 123 might be associated with person Jones, and account 456 might be associated with company Ajax, Inc., but no account could be charged to by more than one person, more than one company, or both a person and a company.

Entity Subtypes

When you encounter two potential entity types that seem very similar but not quite the same, you can use ERD **entity subtype** boxes to represent them. The example below shows a Vehicle entity that has Car and Truck subtypes.

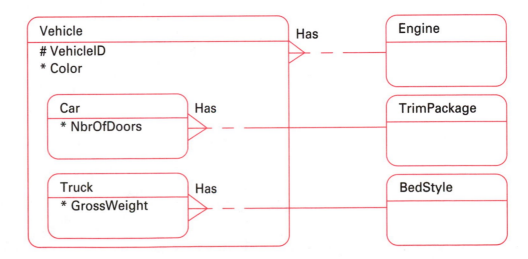

This diagram tells us that all cars are vehicles and all trucks are vehicles, and cars and trucks share some common properties of vehicles, such as color. Subtyping vehicles lets you show that there are properties of cars that don't apply to trucks, and vice versa. You can also show relationships between other entities and a Vehicle, Car, or Truck entity depending on how the organization's data is structured.

An implicit way to represent a subtype is to use a single entity with a "type" property, and specify optional properties for properties that don't apply to all instances of the type. The following ERD shows how the Vehicle entity might be represented:

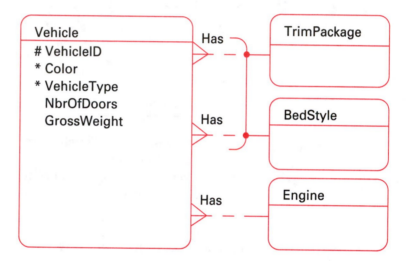

The two Has relationships that were connected to Car and Truck, respectively, in the previous example are now shown as exclusive relationships. The explicit depiction of subtypes gives a more precise view on the ERD of the underlying data model, but the simpler style of representing a subtype with a "type" property may be more appropriate for high-level diagrams on which it's not essential to show the subtype details. Note that while these alternative ERDs, in isolation, don't have identical semantics, they are consistent, and each ERD would be just part of a complete data model. Additional rules in the model specification would clarify details so that the same data model would be represented no matter which ERD was used.

When to Use ERDs

The ERD notation introduced in this chapter provides a simple but relatively powerful language for describing many important aspects of a business model. The following ERD provides one final, somewhat more complex, example of how you can represent a lot of information in a clear, concise manner using ERDs:

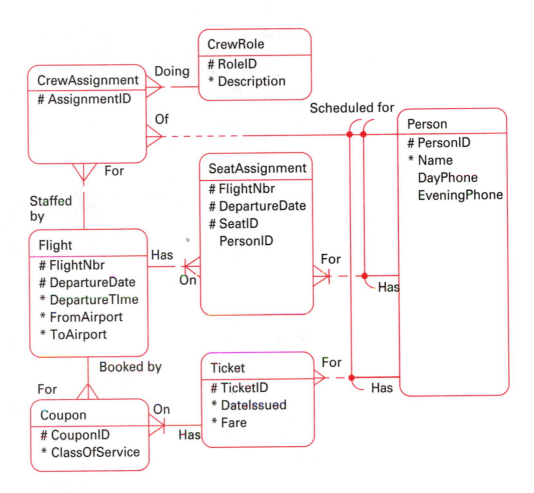

Here are a few of the things we know about this part of the business, just by looking at the ERD:

- A person either
  may be scheduled for *one or more* crew assignments, or
  may have *one or more* seat assignments

- A person either
  may be scheduled for *one or more* crew assignments, or
  may have *one or more* seat tickets

- A ticket *must* be for *exactly one* person

- A ticket *must* have *one or more* coupons

- A crew assignment *must* be of *exactly one* person

- A crew assignment *must* be for *exactly one* flight

- A crew assignment *must* do *exactly one* crew role

As you can see, this is an effective method for getting a high-level view of the entities and their interrelationships that are important to an organization.

Additional forms of notation are used in some versions of ERDs. You can explore these using the books listed in the annotated bibliography. Keep in mind, however, that ERDs are simply one of many possible means of expressing the structure and rules of your data model. The ERD notation is well suited for simple systems, parts of complex systems, or for high-level views of the most important entities and relationships of interest to a business.

On the other hand, ERDs may not be the best choice for expressing model details, such as the enumeration of all entities' properties, for a complex system. For a system of significant size, ERDs that include all entities, relationships, and properties become very difficult to read.[5] Further, ERDs may provide no way to express some business rules. For example, there's no standard ERD notation to represent a regulation that a construction company must use local subcontractors for projects funded by local government. Yet you can easily state and understand this business model rule in natural language, pseudo-SQL, or some other textual form. Researchers have expended a great deal of effort to add expressive capability to ERDs, but while these efforts may have academic value, practical applications for many of them are limited.

ERDs are almost always accompanied by textual and table-oriented specifications. Chapter 10 listed a number of important things to specify in a complete data model, including details about the entity types and their properties, integrity rules, and individual user's views. Some of this information can also be shown on an ERD, where adding the information enhances comprehensibility.

Remember two basic aspects of ERDs, however, before you go overboard learning dozens of arcane symbols in some extended ERD notation. First, ERD notations are based on formal logic and consequently do not add expressive power but offer an alternative means of expression. Second, ERDs are preferable as a means of expression when they are easier to understand than the alternatives, such as table- or text-oriented representations. In other words, ERDs are neither the only tool you need nor always the best. Yet when used for the right purpose, ERDs are a useful addition to your collection of analysis and design techniques. The best approach in most practical data modeling tasks is to use a mixture of ERDs, other diagrams, text, and tables to create the specification.

---

[5] A complex ERD may look more like the circuit diagram for a computer chip — hardly a good way to create a comprehensible data model.

Chapter Summary

Entity relationship diagrams represent entities, relationships, and their properties in pictorial form. Boxes represent entities, lines represent relationships, and properties are listed in the boxes with annotation to show required and optional values and identifier properties and referencing properties.

ERD notation can show alternative types of relationships, including one-to-one, one-to-many, or many-to-many relationships. ERDs also show whether one or more related instances are optional or required. You can also represent exclusive relationships (where only one or the other relationship exists for a particular instance), and entity subtypes (where an entity type that's a subtype of another entity type has all the properties and relationships of the other entity type).

ERDs are a good technique for showing high-level views of a data model or for small data models or parts of a larger data model. For complex data models, ERDs that include all details of the model can be difficult to read. Generally, ERDs are only part of the complete data model and are accompanied by text and table-format specifications.

Key Terms

entity
entity relationship diagram
    (ERD)
entity subtype

exclusive relationship
intersection entity
property
regular entity

relationship
weak entity

Exercises

1. Explain the advantages and disadvantages of ERDs.

2. Show an example of the ERD notation for the following:

    - Employee and department entity types

    - Employee properties: employee ID, name, office phone

    - A "works in" relationship between the employee and department entity types

    - A "manager" subtype of the employee entity type

    - A "manages" relationship between the manager and employee entity types

3. Draw the ERD for the agent, company, and product entity types and their inter-relationships based on the example presented in the discussion on fifth normal form in Chapter 9 (beginning on page 219). Are there any parts of the data model for this example that you can't represent on the ERD? If so, how could you include the necessary information in your data model?

4. What are the advantages and disadvantages of representing a many-to-many relationship with or without a separate box (for the intersection entity)? Consider the alternatives from the perspective of both the end user and the person who's responsible for the physical database design.

Chapter 12

Physical Database Design

Chapter Overview

Physical database design provides the bridge between logical data modeling and implementation. This stage of an application-development project determines how available hardware and system software resources will be used to implement an efficient set of files or tables and other application components that provide the capabilities specified in the data model. This chapter provides a series of steps you can follow to produce a database design from a logical data model that's developed using the methods described in Chapters 10 and 11.

Introduction

As we learned in Chapter 10, logical data modeling analyzes an organization's information requirements to produce a data model that specifies entity types, properties of entities, relationships among entity types, and integrity rules. These elements are represented as base and view tables, columns, foreign keys, domains, and other design objects based on the relational model. The data model provides a description of both individual end-user or department views, and an integrated set of tables and integrity rules. Both levels of description are from the business perspective and don't state particular implementation techniques.

If there were a DBMS that provided direct support for every concept we used in the data model (e.g., domains and multitable predicates) and the hardware and DBMS had infinite storage capacity and infinite speed, we could just use the data model as our finished database design. We wouldn't need to go through a distinct **physical database design** stage as part of our development process. In reality, current DBMS (including DB2/400) lack built-in features for many of the things found in a typical data model, and the performance of current hardware and software is still such that we must consider capacity and performance when deciding how to implement some part of the data model.

The limitations of facilities available for implementing a data model lead to the two major challenges of database design:

- How should we implement a data model concept for which the DBMS provides no direct support? For example, how should we enforce domain integrity with DB2/400, which has very limited support for domains?

- How should we implement a data model concept that may be a performance bottleneck if implemented in the most direct manner? For example, an end user view that includes selected records (rows) and presents them in a particular sequence can be specified directly in an SQL/400 view definition. However, for a large file or SQL/400 table, if we don't do any performance-related design, scanning the entire underlying file to select and sort records for the view may require an unacceptably long time. During database design, we can look at implementation options, such as creating an SQL/400 index, to speed record selection and ordering.

Of course, some concepts in a data model may have a direct and efficient implementation. For example, an entity type represented as a base table in the data model can be implemented as a physical file created from DDS or an SQL/400 table. These easy parts of database design nevertheless need to be documented explicitly in the final design document.

Database design is based on four major elements:

- The *logical data model* (and parts of the *process model*), which define what the implementation must do
- The expected *volumes* and *pattern of access* (e.g., numbers of customers and orders and frequency of retrieval and update of an order once it has been entered)
- The system software *functional characteristics* (e.g., whether the DBMS retrieval language supports date arithmetic)
- The hardware and system software *performance characteristics* (e.g., the relative cost of record retrieval by key versus sequentially)

Database design cannot be done properly without a complete logical data model, an estimate of the access patterns, and an understanding of the hardware and system software characteristics. For example, deciding how to enforce domain integrity requires knowing exactly what the DBMS provides in the way of domain support and other facilities. Consider fields or columns that must contain only dates within a specified range. The implementation is different with a DBMS (such as DB2/400) that provides a built-in date data type than with a DBMS that provides no date data type. Likewise, because DB2/400 doesn't provide field-level range checking for file insertions or updates, you must decide on some other mechanism, such as trigger programs, to enforce the constraint.

As an example of a performance-related design decision, determining which indexes to create requires estimating file sizes, the frequency of retrievals that might use the index, and the number of updates that might cause changes to the index.

Some design decisions have both a functional and a performance-related purpose. For example, to decide whether to include a redundant derived field in a file, you must know (or estimate) answers to the following questions:

- How frequently will the derived field be retrieved?
- Will it ever be retrieved using an end-user tool instead of an HLL program?
- Is it possible — and if so, how complex is it — to derive the field using an end-user tool?
- How frequently will the underlying source fields be updated?
- Will the underlying fields ever be updated using an end-user tool? If so, is it possible to calculate a new derived value automatically when this occurs?
- How fast can the system calculate the derived field during retrieval?

Specific database design decisions require a thorough understanding of the performance and complexity trade-offs. Separating logical data modeling and physical database design into two distinct stages is the best approach. You can concentrate on the conceptual aspects of the system during the data modeling stage. Then, as you work on the database design, you can concentrate on the numerous platform-specific details and design an efficient implementation without clouding your understanding of what the system needs to deliver.

Although physical database design tasks may proceed in parallel with logical data modeling tasks, conceptually the physical database design follows the logical data model: You must determine what you want to do before you decide how to do it. Here's a guideline to help keep the two processes distinct: Once you have a data model, you should be able to make all database design decisions based on the functionality and performance of the DBMS (and other system software) and the estimated pattern of data access. If you find yourself asking such conceptual questions as "What if there might be a nonstandard price of an item when it's sold?" you've got to go back to the data model and get the answer firmly established before you decide on an implementation — physical database design is not the time to address these types of questions.

The following sections lay out 10 steps you can follow to produce a database design. As with logical data modeling, you should establish naming standards and set up a data dictionary to hold your design specifications. Like the data dictionary used for the data model, the data dictionary used for database design is a set of containers, including documents, files or tables, spreadsheets, and possibly CASE tool repositories. We won't repeat all the advice from Chapter 10 about keeping the elements of your design specification well-organized and about adapting the techniques presented here to fit a particular organization and project. Be sure to review that material as you consider how to tackle a database design assignment.

Also note that many of the database design steps relate directly to implementation specifics that are covered in other chapters. The steps below refer you to the appropriate chapters for additional details related to the design issue.

Step 1. Specify a Physical File or Table for Each Entity Type

This first step is simple when you've used a data modeling technique based on the relational model and you intend to implement your applications with a relational DBMS such as DB2/400. Each entity type is represented in the data model as a base table with columns representing the entity's properties. The first cut at your design should be a direct one-to-one mapping to DDS-defined physical files and fields or SQL/400 tables and columns.[1] Other data model elements may not be as easy to handle. The table on the following page provides a summary of the most common implementation objects or techniques for various data model elements. We cover these in more detail in the rest of this chapter.

For a DB2/400 file or table, you should record the following design information:

- Name
- The name of the entity type in the related data model
- Descriptive text for the object (up to 50 characters)
- OS/400 library that will contain the object
- OS/400 user profile that will own the object
- Initial and incremental storage limits

For each field or column, record the following design information:

- Name of field or column
- File or table name that contains the field or column
- Descriptive text for field or column (up to 50 characters for DDS field definitions; up to 2000 characters for SQL/400 column comments)
- If you plan to use DDS: referenced field (if using a field reference file)[2]

[1] Recall that with DB2/400, an SQL/400 table is an OS/400 physical file object, an SQL/400 column is a field in a file, and an SQL/400 view is a logical file object. This chapter uses the terminology for the implementation objects interchangeably, except when there's an important distinction between SQL/400 and DDS techniques.

[2] If you use field referencing, you can simply record "from referenced field" for other field attributes in this list (e.g., data type) that are derived from the referenced field definition.

	Implementation Objects		
Model Elements	**DDS**	**SQL/400**	**HLL**
Entity type	Physical file	Table	
Property	Field	Column	
Domain	Field data type; optional field reference file	Column data type	Trigger program; file access routine
Primary key	Unique keyed access path or primary key constraint	Primary key	
Candidate key	Unique keyed access path or unique key constraint	Unique index or unique key constraint	
One-to-many relationship (as foreign key)	Referential integrity constraint	Foreign key	
Many-to-many relationship (as table)	Physical file with two or more referential integrity constraints	Table with two or more foreign keys	
Multirow and multitable predicates			Trigger program; file access routine
Security rules	Resource authorities; logical files with selected records and/or fields	Table and view privileges; views with selected rows and/or columns	Trigger program; program adopted authority
End-user view (subschema)	Logical file	View	OPNQRYF (Open Query File) command; embedded SQL/400 cursor; file access routine

- If you plan to use SQL/400: reference to the name of a standard data type[3]

---

[3] If you use standard data type names, you can simply record "from referenced data type" for other column attributes in this list (e.g., data type) that can be derived from the referenced data type.

- Default column heading(s) (up to 3 lines of 20 characters for DDS field definitions or SQL/400 column labels)
- Domain name (the domain definition itself should specify the field or column data type, length and decimal positions, and allowable values)
- Whether the null placeholder is allowed
- Value used for not-applicable (if allowed)
- Values used for special cases (e.g., open end date), if any
- Default value, if any
- Default display and print formats (e.g., for telephone numbers)

Later steps in this chapter suggest other information to add to the lists above. Most of the items listed are self-explanatory; however, a few require further discussion. Each OS/400 object must be contained in an OS/400 library and must have one user profile as its owner. Chapter 1 explains the OS/400 object-based architecture and the role of libraries and user profiles; Chapter 18 goes into more detail about OS/400 security, including object ownership and object authority.

AS/400 installations use various approaches to organizing objects into libraries. For database files, there are several considerations. Often, organizations group objects into multiple libraries. This approach helps manage objects, but be aware of the following aspects of multiple libraries:

- Backup and recovery is much simpler if all logical files and SQL/400 views that reference a physical file or SQL/400 table are in the same library as the file or table.
- An OS/400 job's library list can have a maximum of 25 user library entries. You don't want so many libraries that you can't include all the ones you need at a particular time in the library list.

Some installations also use libraries to group different types of OS/400 objects. For example, they put executable programs in one library and database files in another. In general, you should keep all database files related to an application in one library. If you have many different applications, you probably want to keep multiple, related applications in a single library to avoid an excessive number of libraries.

For object ownership, a common practice at many AS/400 installations is to have a single user profile (e.g., APPOWNER) that owns all database objects. Specific authority to access these objects is then granted to other user profiles, which are the user profiles that end users specify when they sign on to the AS/400. For large installations, there may be several user profiles whose purpose is to own application objects; for example, the PAYROLLOWN user profile may own the payroll application objects, and the SALESOWN user profile may own the order-entry and marketing application objects.

Chapter 2 explains how to specify explicit initial and incremental limits to the number of records that can be added to a physical file. These limits should be based on estimates for the initial number of records in the file and the expected growth over time.

Chapter 3 explains the use of DDS field reference files as a way to create standard field definitions. Chapter 13 explains a similar (but manual) approach to consider when using SQL/400 to create tables. Step 3 in this chapter discusses approaches to designing the implementation for domains, which aren't directly supported in DB2/400. Using one or more of these techniques can reduce the need to specify some of the column or field-level items. For example, by using a field reference, you don't need to specify explicitly the data type, length, or decimal positions for a field.

The implementation of special values or placeholders for a column or field requires careful consideration during design. One question is whether to specify an explicit default value to be used when a new record is added and no value is supplied for the field. The default value might also be used as the basis for the initial value put in an input field on a data-entry display. Chapter 2 discusses how DB2/400 handles explicit and system-defined defaults; generally, DB2/400 uses blank for character fields and zero for numeric fields. If some other value is appropriate, specify that value. In particular, you may want to use a value that represents unknown, not-applicable, or a special case such as "open end date."

Another fairly straightforward kind of value to consider is what we called a "distinguished value" in Chapter 10, Step 7. Recall the example of an ending date field for which we need some value that represents that the ending date is open ended. For these cases, you can generally pick a valid value that represents the special case; for example, 9999/12/31 might be used for "open end date."

Two more difficult exceptional cases are not-applicable and unknown. The first arises when a field might not always have a sensible value; for example, the COLOR field of a part that has no particular color. The second case is different in that a value for the field might make sense; we just don't know what the value is at some particular time. With DB2/400, you have two choices for either or both of these situations: use the null placeholder, or use some designated value to represent the condition(s).

Chapter 2 explains how DB2/400 supports null-capable fields, and Chapter 14 describes some special considerations with SQL/400 data manipulations. For example, when you add together several columns, the result will be null if any column is null. Also remember from Chapter 7 that the RPG IV and COBOL/400 support for null-capable fields is limited. Although null-capable fields have the advantage of being a system-supported way of identifying that a field contains no valid value, the use of nulls isn't problem-free. You should never allow null with primary key fields and rarely (if ever) with candidate key and foreign key fields.

Instead of null, you can designate a value that represents not-applicable and/or unknown. For example, for a field that contains the date an employee received his or her undergraduate degree, you might use 0001/01/01 for not applicable, if he or she doesn't have a degree and 0001/01/02 for unknown, if he or she has a degree but you don't know the date it was received. You need to consider a field's default value (if any) in conjunction with the way you represent not-applicable and unknown. In this case, you might specify the value for unknown (0001/01/02) as the default value.

When you design the implementation of views and processes that have computations involving numeric or date fields, be sure to consider the values used for default, not-applicable, and unknown. For example, to calculate the average age of employees, you must be sure to handle values that have the format of dates but aren't really valid birth date values. For example, if the field for an employee's birth date can be 0001/01/02 to represent unknown, then any summary routine should exclude employee records with this value. If you allow null for a field, be sure to consider the SQL/400 and HLL handling of null-capable fields.

Step 2. Specify Primary, Candidate, and Foreign Key Implementation

A primary key is one or more fields or columns that provide a means of uniquely identifying records or rows. Candidate keys are other field(s) that are also unique for each record. A foreign key is one or more fields in a dependent file that reference the primary key in some (usually different) parent file. Each of these types of keys requires some implementation technique to enforce the corresponding integrity constraints.

Files created from DDS and SQL/400 tables use different implementation techniques. DDS has no direct way of defining a primary, candidate, or foreign key. As a start, never specify the ALWNULL field-level keyword for a primary key field, and rarely should you specify this keyword for a candidate or foreign key field. To enforce unique values of primary and candidate keys, you can define a unique keyed access path. Typically, the physical file has a unique key that is the primary key. A logical file can be used to create a unique keyed access path for a candidate key.[4] In addition, you can use the ADDPFCST (Add Physical File Constraint) command to add a primary key

---

[4] Some sites also use a logical file to implement the primary key and don't specify any key for the physical file. They use this approach to reduce the recovery time if the keyed access path becomes damaged — something that happens so rarely in DB2/400 that the technique may not offer much benefit. Later in this chapter, we look at a broader approach to isolating the physical file — using a "master logical file" or view as the file that end users access instead of the physical file.

Note also how DB2/400 unique keyed access paths can serve two purposes: enforcing unique key values and providing an efficient way to access records sequenced by their key values. In SQL/400, these two functions are separate — primary key constraints enforce uniqueness, and indexes provide efficient keyed access.

and one or more unique key **constraints** to a single-member physical file. For example, the following command adds a primary key constraint to the CUSTOMER file using CUSTID as the primary key:

```
ADDPFCST FILE( customer )
         TYPE( *prikey )
         KEY( custid )
```

For files created with DDS, you can specify an ADDPFCST command to add a referential constraint for foreign keys, such as the following example that adds a constraint to the ORDER and CUSTOMER files. Chapter 16 explains in more detail how to create physical file constraints.

```
ADDPFCST FILE( order )
         TYPE( *refcst )
         KEY( custid )
         PRNFILE( customer )
         DLTRULE( *restrict )
         UPDRULE( *restrict )
```

For SQL/400, the Create Table statement provides the Constraint clause to specify primary, unique, and foreign keys. Candidate keys can also be implemented by specifying Not Null for the column definitions and creating a unique index over the candidate key.

The ADDPFCST command and the SQL/400 Create Table statement support only a limited set of actions for foreign key rules; for example, ADDPFCST supports only a reject rule when a record is inserted into the dependent file and the record's foreign key doesn't match an existing primary key in the parent file. For other rules, you can use one of three techniques:

- Attempt to prevent integrity violations by manual procedures
- Create a **trigger program** for the parent and/or dependent file
- Create a **file access routine** in an HLL, and use that exclusively to perform file updates

You might specify in your design that one or more of these methods are to be used in the implementation. Obviously, depending on users to follow manual procedures isn't a foolproof way to enforce integrity. But don't immediately reject this alternative. Although using programmatic means to enforce integrity is generally recommended, there may be cases in which the implementation and performance costs of a programmatic approach are high and the consequences of an orphan record aren't great. If you do use manual methods, consider writing a batch program that can be used periodically to scan the entire file(s) to check for integrity violations.

Trigger programs are HLL programs that DB2/400 calls when a file update is attempted. You write the trigger program in an HLL, such as RPG IV, and associate it with the appropriate physical file. When an update to the file is attempted, DB2/400 calls your program and passes it the before and after images of the updated record. Your program can analyze the pending file update and reject or accept it, as well as perform other actions. Chapter 17 explains more about writing and using trigger programs.

The final alternative is to write callable HLL file access routines that perform database updates. Such a routine can check the validity of the update before performing it and return an error condition (e.g., no parent record with matching primary key for foreign key) to the called program. This technique is similar to the use of triggers but offers more flexibility because the called routine can have any interface (i.e., the set of parameters) you need to be able to provide enough information to determine the validity of the file update. Trigger programs essentially get nothing more than the name of the file and the before and after record images. On the other hand, custom file access routines aren't called when a utility program is used to update the file,[5] but trigger programs are.

Step 3. Specify Domain Implementation

Unfortunately, DB2/400 (like many other relational DBMS) provides only limited support for domains. You can specify a field's or column's data type, length, and (if numeric) decimal positions. You can't specify a domain name (or data type name), any restriction (other than by type and length) on the allowable values, units of measure, or many other important aspects of a domain.

If you're using DDS, you should at least include a field reference file in your database design. Chapter 3 describes how to set up a field reference file and how to define fields in it that can be used to provide standard data types somewhat like domains.

There's no SQL/400 equivalent to a DDS field reference file. However, you should still follow the field definition principles discussed in Chapter 3 when you use SQL/400 to create tables — the general principle is to use a standard set of named data types to define columns. You must do this manually in SQL/400 or create a program that lets you use macros[6] for column definitions. Such a program would take as input an SQL/400 statement such as

```
Create Table AppDta.Customer
    ( CustID @IDType,
      Name   @NameType, ... )
```

---

[5] For this method to be effective, all application programs must call the file access routine to perform a file update. Any application that does file updates directly (e.g., with an RPG IV Update operation) will circumvent the integrity checks.

[6] In simple terms, a source code macro is an identifier that's replaced with some substitution text by a program that processes the source code. Many HLLs, including C and C++, support macro definition and substitution. ILE COBOL/400 has a very primitive Replace compiler directive that is somewhat like a macro facility. RPG IV doesn't have anything comparable.

and produce as output an SQL/400 statement such as

```
Create Table AppDta.Customer
  ( CustID Int      Not Null,
    Name   Char(50) Not Null, ... )
```

The macro-processing program would look for strings that begin with @ and replace them with the corresponding text. In the above example, the macro named @IDType would be replaced with the text "Int Not Null."

Providing the basic definitions of fields or columns is only the beginning of designing domain support. The more challenging part is determining how to enforce restrictions on values and operations with other columns. As they did with foreign key integrity, trigger programs and file access routines provide two alternatives. One consideration with either technique is how to avoid unacceptable impact on performance. For example, suppose you have a record format with 50 fields. If you check every field for every file update operation, you may add significant processing time to file updates.

Two programming techniques can help reduce the cost of checking domain integrity. First, you can design methods to temporarily disable field-level checks. Then, when a batch program or other program that updates lots of records runs, you can (hopefully) rely on the program to check the fields affected by its computations before performing a file update. Of course, there's some risk in this — the program must implement the necessary checks properly. But it's often better than avoiding trigger programs or file access routines altogether because of performance concerns.

Alternatively, you can use a programming technique that compares the before and after record images and checks only those fields whose values are different. This approach assumes that the before image values for unchanged fields are valid, which is a relatively safe assumption if this method has been used for all previous file updates.

In the database design specification, for each domain in the data model, you should list how it should be implemented (e.g., by field reference file and file access routine or by manually observed SQL/400 standards and a trigger program).

Step 4. Specify Implementation of Other Integrity Rules

DB2/400 doesn't provide more powerful integrity enforcing mechanisms than the ones we've already covered. For example, there's no direct way to specify a row predicate or a multirow or multitable predicate.[7] Essentially your alternatives are, again, trigger programs and file access routines.

---

[7] The SQL/400 Create View statement, discussed in Chapter 13, supports an optional With Check clause that can be used somewhat like a row predicate; however, the option is enforced only when the view itself is used to access the data.

One other alternative, of course, is to code the integrity constraints piecemeal in all the programs that might update a file. This is by far the most prevalent approach among AS/400 developers. The problem is that this approach is error-prone and hard to manage because rule enforcement is fragmented and often duplicated across many different programs. Even if you decide not to use trigger programs or file access routines in your database design, at least specify one callable program (or a small group of programs) that will implement all of the integrity checking for a file. Then specify that applications must call the appropriate validation routines before updating a file.

Step 5. Specify View Implementation

Once you have the initial database design for the integrated data model's base tables, it's time to specify how the database will provide for the necessary end users' views. Recall that end users may need to see only selected records or fields from data that is stored in base tables. Users also may need to see data from several base tables combined in a view (e.g., a CustomerOrder view may combine data from Customer, Order, OrderItem, and Part base tables).

Before we look at means to implement views that are different from base tables, we need to consider those views that correspond exactly to a single base table. Take the case of a Customer table in the data model, which will be implemented as a physical file or SQL/400 table. If the model also specifies that some user or application needs all the records and fields from this file, we can just specify that the physical file or table will implement the view. This solution works fine and is the most common way AS/400 organizations implement access to base table data.

There's an alternative approach, however, that may provide an implementation that can better handle subsequent changes to the base table definition. The technique is to create a "master" logical file or SQL/400 view over each physical file or table. The master logical file should select all records and fields of the base table so that it is equivalent, for retrieval and update purposes, to the physical file. The advantage to this technique is that when you must change the physical file definition (e.g., to add a new field or change a field's definition), the logical file can provide a layer that insulates programs and utilities from the physical file changes. For example, if a new field is added to the physical file, the master logical file can select only the original fields, excluding the new field. No immediate changes are necessary for applications that use the master logical file.[8] Obviously, the new field will have to be included in at least one existing or new logical file if the field is to be used by some application. And eventually, you need to create a new master logical file that incorporates all fields, including the newly added one. But the original

---

[8] Chapters 2 and 4 on physical and logical files created from DDS and Chapter 13 on SQL/400 tables and views provide more details about the steps necessary to create various objects discussed in this section.

master logical file buys time for you to revise applications to incorporate the physical file change.

For end users' views in the data model that aren't equivalent to a single base table, you have several design choices:

- A logical file or SQL/400 view
- File access routines
- The OPNQRYF (Open Query File) command or embedded SQL/400 cursor
- Interactive SQL/400 Select statements, and other data retrieval tools

A logical file or an SQL/400 view provides a way to select, transform, or combine data from one or more underling physical files or tables. Part I of this book describes the capabilities of logical files, and Part III describes the capabilities of SQL/400 views. Generally, logical files or views provide a good way to implement end users' views, as long as the required capabilities are supported.

In earlier steps, we saw how file access routines could be used to implement integrity constraints. For this purpose, these routines are called to perform file updates. You can also use file access routines to read one or more files and derive the type of data required in an end-user view. This technique is particularly useful when the capabilities of a DB2/400 logical file or SQL/400 view aren't adequate.

As part of a file access routine, or for use directly by an application, the OPNQRYF command or an embedded SQL/400 cursor provides another way to select, transform, and combine data. There are a few functional differences between these two facilities and logical files and views, the main one being that logical files and views are persistent DB2/400 objects, whereas an OPNQRYF invocation or an open SQL/400 cursor exists only during the job that uses them. Generally, if a logical file or view provides the functionality you need to implement an end-user view, it's the simplest alternative. In some cases, however, an OPNQRYF command or an SQL/400 cursor may avoid the need for DB2/400 to maintain an access path and, thus, be a desirable performance trade-off.

A final alternative for implementing end users' views is the use of interactive tools, such as the Interactive SQL (ISQL) component of IBM's DB2 Query Manager and SQL Development Kit for OS/400 product. This tool, as well as a number of PC-based data-retrieval tools, can provide methods of access that satisfy the requirements of some end users' views.

After selecting the appropriate design to provide the information specified in an end-user view, you should specify exactly how the view is implemented. This might take the form of the necessary definitions for a logical file or an SQL/400 Create View statement. Don't just stop at the general specification "use a logical file." Provide the full description so there's no ambiguity when the person responsible for implementation does his or her job. Note that Steps 8, 9, and 10 may revise some physical file or table designs, so you need to revisit this step when you make changes that affect the specification of a logical file, view, or other implementation method for an end-user view.

Step 6. Specify Security Implementation

Once you have the initial design for the implementation of base tables and end users' views, you have the objects necessary to design the implementation of security. This database design step specifies how read and update access will be controlled for physical and logical files or SQL/400 tables and views, as well as related objects such as programs that implement file access routines.

On the AS/400, the first step is to specify public and private (i.e., individual user profile) authority for file and program objects. You can use the GRTOBJAUT (Grant Object Authority) command or the SQL/400 Grant statement to grant authorities. Chapter 18 discusses DB2/400 security in detail. In general, you should grant only the resource-level authorities that you intend to be used in an unrestricted manner. For example, grant update rights to a physical file only if you intend the user profile to have the authority to update the file in any way — potentially changing any field in any record.

Logical files and SQL/400 views can implement access that's restricted to selected records or a subset of fields. This technique is especially useful for restricted read-only access. Trigger programs can provide some additional options for implementing specific update constraints based on the user profile.

For more context-sensitive control of database access, you can use HLL programs, either general-purpose file access routines or more specialized, task-specific routines. These routines can use program-adopted authority (discussed in Chapter 18) to provide controlled access beyond what a user profile normally has. For example, users who don't have general update authority to a file can still perform certain types of changes if they're authorized to use a program that adopts update authority to the file while the program is in use.

A final technique to consider in the database design is the implementation of an audit trail for some or all of the database access. OS/400 journaling (discussed in Chapter 17) or trigger programs provide two system-supported ways to record who accesses various data and what changes they make.

Step 7. Specify Additional
Indexes for Performance

Now we come to several performance-related database design steps. Before diving into the specific techniques, you should keep in mind a couple of general principles. First, there's only one way to know for certain the performance consequences of a particular implementation technique: measure the results. Although we look at some rules-of-thumb for alternative designs, any production-level approach to performance must include some means of measurement. OS/400 has several built-in performance measurements, and IBM provides the Performance Management/400 product to examine performance in more detail. Be sure to use these or similar tools to assess performance-related design decisions.

Another important principle is to avoid unnecessary effort trying to improve performance when there's no performance problem to begin with.[9] For example, if a file is accessed only once a month in a night shift batch job and the batch job completes in the allotted shift, it's probably not worth worrying about ways to improve the file design to reduce the time required for the batch job. Of course, if the situation changes and the job no longer finishes in its shift or there's some other significant reason to improve its performance, it may be worthwhile to work on the file design or program to improve performance.

Finally, keep in mind that performance is only one part of the overall cost equation. Consider that if it costs $10,000 in programmer time to improve a program's performance by 10 percent and it costs $9,000 for a CPU upgrade that improves the system's overall performance by 10 percent, it's better to tackle the performance problem by buying hardware than by working on the implementation.

With these general principles in mind, let's look at **indexes**, one of the most common options for improving DB2/400 performance. An index usually provides an efficient way to access a specific record by key value or to process some or all of a file in a particular sequence. You can create an index by either using DDS to create a logical file with a keyed access path or using the SQL/400 Create Index statement. Your database design will already include at least one index for each primary key, and potentially others for candidate and foreign keys. In most cases, the need to access individual records using the value of one or more fields will correspond to a primary or other candidate key; thus, you won't need many additional indexes for this purpose.

Instead, the two most common reasons to consider additional indexes are for retrieving groups of records in a particular sequence and as an efficient way to select a subset of records. For large files, indexes can speed these two types of retrieval. Indexes, however, add overhead to update operations because the system must keep index entries up to date when it adds, deletes, or changes records in a file with one or more indexes.

There are no hard and fast rules about which indexes to include in a database design. As a rule-of-thumb, you usually won't encounter serious update performance problems with 5 or fewer indexes over a physical file, but more than 20 indexes (and often even fewer) can cause unacceptably slow update performance. Within the range of 6 to 20 indexes, each index should be scrutinized carefully to ensure that it provides sufficient improvement in retrieval performance to warrant the additional update overhead.

One good candidate for an index is a field or column that's used frequently in either a join logical file or an SQL/400 view that defines a join. If

---

[9] This may sound obvious, but programmers sometimes expend time fine tuning their code or database implementation when the improvement will have a negligible effect.

sets of joined records are retrieved based on the one file's primary key, an index over the related field or column in the other file may significantly improve performance.

For selection purposes, an index provides the greatest performance improvement when the physical file contains a lot of records and the selection criteria selects a small percentage. For small files, or once the number of selected records reaches about 20 percent of the file, an index offers little, if any, performance improvement.

One type of index to avoid (unless it has a high payoff for retrieval) is an index over a frequently updated field. This type of index requires frequent updating and adds to the overhead of file updates.

When designing multiple indexes over the same file, consider DB2/400's ability to share indexes (access paths), as explained in Chapter 4. If possible, design multifield indexes so the major key fields are also the key fields for indexes with fewer key fields. For example, suppose you need to define an index to enforce uniqueness for a candidate key consisting of EmployeeID and ProjectID on a file that stores employee assignments to projects. To guarantee uniqueness, it doesn't matter whether the major key field in the index is EmployeeID or ProjectID. But if you also have a logical file that has a single-field key consisting of ProjectID (and you don't have a logical file keyed on EmployeeID), it may be better to define the composite key with ProjectID as the major key field. If you do that, DB2/400 can share the same index for both purposes. Also consider rebuild or delayed access path maintenance for logical files with non-unique keyed access paths, as described in Chapter 4. These types of access path maintenance reduce the overhead for file updates.

Permanent indexes aren't the only way to design record selection and sequencing using DB2/400. If no appropriate index exists when you use a logical file, SQL/400 view, OPNQRYF command, or embedded SQL/400 cursor, DB2/400 handles the request by creating a temporary index, sequentially scanning the file, or a variety of other on-the-fly methods. If these provide satisfactory retrieval performance, the update overhead of a permanent index may not be worth incurring.

Although your database design should plan the initial indexes, you also need to measure performance continually and consider adding or dropping indexes as conditions change or you get better production statistics. Designing the right indexes is part science, part black magic, and a lot of trial and error.

Step 8. Introduce Controlled Redundancy

In the data model, we avoided redundantly representing facts. We used a set of guidelines, normal forms, to ensure that the tables in our data model unambiguously conveyed the structure of the organization's data. It's not uncommon for normal form tables to give a fragmented appearance to the structure of the organization's data, breaking up tables with lots of columns and not in a fully normalized form into numerous, fully normalized tables.

This is the best way to approach the data model, but may need some restructuring when the actual file design occurs.

The reason some restructuring may be necessary is two-fold: It may be cumbersome (or impossible) for certain DBMS or utility programs to combine related data, and it may create an unacceptable performance impact to join related records that frequently are retrieved together. Fortunately, DB2/400 provides good support for combining related records with join logical files or SQL/400 views, so, in most cases, performance is the only issue.

For large, frequently accessed files, performance must be considered because it takes more time and system resources to return a joined record than to return a single record that has the combined information. As a result, you may decide to duplicate in related records some fields that could be retrieved by a join. Consider the case of a CUSTOMER file and an ORDER file that has a foreign key referencing the CUSTOMER file. In the data model, the normal form base tables for these two entity types would typically have the customer's name and phone number as columns in the Customer table. A view table that joined the Customer and Order base tables would provide a way for an end user to see the customer name and phone number for an order. If ORDER file records will be retrieved frequently and the end user needs the customer name and phone number, you may decide to design the files so the customer name and phone number are redundantly stored in the ORDER file, avoiding the need to join to the CUSTOMER file for this end-user view.

Controlled redundancy is a trade-off. As general principles

- Controlled redundancy usually makes retrieval faster and simpler
- Controlled redundancy usually makes updates slower and more complex

You can see from the previous example how controlled redundancy can reduce file I/O (thus improving speed) and potentially simplify working with the related data. You can understand why controlled redundancy often complicates file updates by considering what's necessary to update a customer's phone number. In addition to changing one CUSTOMER record, you must update all the ORDER records for the customer if they also have the customer phone number in them. As with many performance-related design issues, the best solution depends on the estimated or measured access pattern. If you expect or observe all the following

- Very frequent retrieval of orders requiring customer name and phone number
- Unacceptably slow retrieval using a join
- Unacceptable cost to upgrade hardware to meet response time criteria
- Infrequent updates to customer name and phone numbers

- Acceptable cost to modify CUSTOMER file update programs to handle redundant data in ORDER file

then a database design with this type of redundancy would be appropriate. If the first two items aren't both true, there's not likely to be justification for redundant storage of the customer name and phone number. If the first two items are true, but not all of the other items are, you must balance the various costs to decide on the best design.

Other types of controlled redundancy include storing derived fields, such as the total amount of an order, to avoid recalculating the value on each retrieval. As with the previous example, this type of redundancy complicates updates to values used in the computation of the derived field. The same kinds of trade-offs must be considered to determine the optimal design.

Another type of controlled redundancy is replicated data. Snapshot copies of all or part of a table can be created periodically to provide read-only access for data analysis and other purposes. The data may be combined or partially transformed to make it easier to work with, and it may be copied to other systems, such as PCs, so it can be used by additional tools (e.g., spreadsheet software). Because snapshot copies are intended as a view of the organization's data at some moment in time, the snapshot data usually doesn't have to be updated, except when the next snapshot is produced. Thus, this type of redundancy doesn't particularly complicate file updates; the only trade-off is that the data may be somewhat out of date.

One technique to improve consistency for redundant data is to use trigger programs to propagate changes. For example, a trigger program could be associated with the CUSTOMER file in our previous example so that when a CUSTOMER record's customer name or phone number is changed, the trigger program updates the corresponding records in the ORDER file. Using a trigger program guarantees that all changes to the redundantly stored fields will be propagated, no matter which HLL program or utility updates the CUSTOMER file.

Step 9. Merge Base Tables
Another performance-related design alternative is to merge two or more base tables from the data model into a single physical file or SQL/400 table in the implementation. This technique is motivated by similar concern for the speed of data retrieval. Consider the case in which a customer might have multiple phone numbers so your data model has a CustomerPhone table (as well as a Customer table) containing one row for each phone number. Implementing these two data model tables as two physical files works fine but requires retrieving one or more joined records to get a customer's phone number(s). An alternative database design could specify three phone fields (PHONE1, PHONE2, PHONE3) in the CUSTOMER file and eliminate the separate file for telephone numbers (or use it for customers with more than three phone numbers).

Repeating fields complicate updates because you must find an open "bucket" to store a new phone number, and you may (or may not) want to shift down values when a phone number (other than the last) is deleted. In some cases, you also must decide whether to limit the number of values to the number of "buckets" in the record, or use some (more complex) technique for handling the occasional overflow situation.

Although retrieval from a merged file may be faster than retrieving multiple records from multiple files, the use of repeating fields can also complicate some types of retrieval. For example, calculating a sum or average of numeric values stored in repeated fields requires summing both across the fields and across the records, and some method of excluding unused "buckets" must be part of the process. For an HLL program, this isn't particularly difficult, but using interactive SQL/400 or other query tools may pose problems. Be sure you consider how all retrieval and update access of repeating fields will be handled before using a merged file in your database design.

Another case in which base tables may be combined is for entity subtypes. For example, if the data model has an Employee entity type and two subtypes, Manager and NonManager, you can implement these as three physical files, all with a primary key field of EMPLOYEEID. Each employee will have one EMPLOYEE file record and either a MANAGER record or a NONMANAGER record. Retrieving the complete information for an employee requires retrieving two records. Some updates may also require changing or inserting two records. You can always combine subtypes and their supertype by designing a file that has all the fields that would be defined for all the separate files. You then need to specify in your database design how you'll represent the not-applicable placeholder for all the fields that would otherwise be defined for the subtype files. For example, if MANAGER records have a YEARSALARY field and NONMANAGER records have an HOURLYWAGE field, in a combined file there must be some way to represent not-applicable in the HOURLYWAGE field for MANAGER records and the YEARSALARY field for NONMANAGER records. In this case, you may simply specify that zero is used because zero would never (presumably) be a valid YEARSALARY or HOURLYWAGE value. When you combine subtypes into one file, you also need a field to identify which type a particular record is. For example, our combined EMPLOYEE file might have an EMPLTYPE field to hold this information.

We said in Chapter 10's discussion of data modeling that you can choose (based on how the organization views the entity types) whether to represent subtypes as separate tables or as columns that allow the not-applicable placeholder. In the database design stage, the decision has more to do with trade-offs among storage efficiency, retrieval and update performance, and implementation complexity. A combined file wastes storage for the unused fields, although in many cases, the amount of storage isn't a big issue. As mentioned, a combined file reduces retrieval and update I/O; it also generally simplifies retrieval and updates. For these reasons, it's fairly common to use a single, combined file for all the subtypes of an entity type.

Step 10. Adjust the Database Design to Anticipate Changes

Organizations and their information requirements change over time. You should anticipate changes in your database design and avoid rigid designs that will be expensive to modify. For example, we saw that one technique for merging tables was to use repeating fields. If, in the case of multiple phone numbers, you assume that the organization will never need to store more than three phone numbers for each customer, you might design your database (and the applications that use it) to depend on there being exactly three buckets for phone numbers in the CUSTOMER file. A better approach would be either not to merge the files or to specify that the CUSTOMER file will have MAXCUSTPHONE buckets for phone numbers. In other words, use a symbolic value for the limit. The actual value for MAXCUSTPHONE might be 3, 2, or 10, but all other items in the database design (e.g., file access routines) would be designed with the flexibility to handle different values for MAXCUSTPHONE.

Another tactic that can help protect against major disruption caused by changes in the data model is to use trigger programs, file access routines, or other similar techniques when you incorporate into your database design some technique that isn't a direct implementation of the data model. We've already explored how trigger programs can be used to maintain consistency when data is stored redundantly. File access routines can also be used to isolate performance-related techniques, such as repeating fields, to a routine that's called by all programs that need access to the data. This way, if you change the number of buckets or add the ability to handle overflow values, the programs calling the file access routine usually won't have to be changed. Only the file access routine will need to change to handle the modified file structure.

As part of your database design, you may want to document the dependencies among various implementation elements. For example, logical files are dependent on the underlying physical files, and fields are dependent on domains. This information can be presented so that you or another person can see the impact of a change to a physical file, a domain, or some other element. This type of **impact analysis** is important both during initial design work and for future revisions to the design. If you use files or CASE tools to keep track of design information, you may be able to produce the necessary "where referenced" lists automatically. After you create DB2/400 files and programs, some of this type of information is available from OS/400 commands (e.g., Display Database Relations) or from the system catalog tables.

As with logical data modeling, physical database design is an iterative process. After you make the first pass at your design, you'll probably have to revisit some of the steps. Remember that it's important to produce good documentation for both the specific implementation objects in your database design and the reason for any nonobvious design decision. Also try to keep your database design as simple and direct an implementation as possible of the data model as long as estimated or measured performance is acceptable. Avoid complex or tricky solutions because they increase the likelihood of errors and usually increase the cost of adapting to changing requirements. Once you have a well laid out database design, you have a good blueprint for the implementation.

Chapter Summary

Physical database design is the application development stage that produces a specification for the subsequent implementation. Database design uses the logical data model (produced in an earlier stage of the development project) and estimates of data volume and access patterns and frequency to plan an efficient database implementation that satisfies the requirements presented in the data model. The database design takes into account the functional capabilities of the DBMS and other systems software, as well as the hardware and software performance characteristics, to decide among alternative implementations for each element of the data model.

The major steps in database design are

Step 1   Specify a physical file or table for each entity type

Step 2   Specify primary, candidate, and foreign key implementation

Step 3   Specify domain implementation

Step 4   Specify implementation of other integrity rules

Step 5   Specify view implementation

Step 6   Specify security implementation

Step 7   Specify additional indexes for performance

Step 8   Introduce controlled redundancy

Step 9   Merge base tables

Step 10   Adjust the database design to anticipate changes

In some cases, DB2/400 provides a direct way of implementing an element of the data model. For example, DB2/400 supports physical files and SQL/400 tables to implement data model entity types. In other cases, you must design your own mechanism to implement some part of the data model. For example, DB2/400 doesn't offer much support for domains, so you must find alternatives (e.g., trigger programs) to provide the required capability.

During the design, you should keep an eye out for potential performance problems, keeping in mind that in many cases the only way to evaluate the significance of performance differences between alternative implementation techniques is to measure them. Use techniques that complicate the database design (e.g., repeating fields) only when there's a clear basis for expecting significant and necessary performance improvement.

Throughout the database design process, try to anticipate change and incorporate designs that provide flexibility to handle changes to the data model. At the end of the database design process, you should have a full specification that describes exactly how the database files and related items will be created. The actual coding and creation of files and other objects follows the completion of the database design stage.

Key Terms

constraint
file access routine

impact analysis
index

physical database design
trigger program

Exercises

1. List the essential information you need to have as the basis for a good physical database design.

2. Briefly describe and provide examples of five types of information that would be included in a database design (i.e., in the specification).

3. For each item you described for Exercise 2, suggest one or more ways you could store the information in a data dictionary.

4. From the following list, identify which data model items you think would be relatively easy to design an implementation for

   - Entity type
   - Property
   - Domain
   - Primary key
   - Candidate key
   - One-to-many relationship
   - Many-to-many relationship
   - Multirow and multitable predicates
   - Security rules
   - End users' views (subschema)

5. For the items you listed in Exercise 4, briefly describe how you would design their respective implementations.

6. List all the data model items (from the list in Exercise 4) for which a trigger program might be used in the implementation.

7. Explain the disadvantages of coding some or all of the validity checks for field values directly in each application that updates a file. Explain the advantages (if any) of this method.

8. Compare the advantages and disadvantages of trigger programs and file access routines. Can you think of any programming techniques that could be used to increase the flexibility of trigger programs?

9. Describe a case (other than the examples in the text) in which you might want to use controlled redundancy in the database design.

10. Describe a case (other than the examples in the text) in which you might want to use merged files in the database design.

PART III

SQL/400

Chapter 13

SQL/400 Data Definition Language

Chapter Overview

This part of the book covers Structured Query Language (SQL), specifically DB2 for OS/400 SQL (or SQL/400, for short).[1] SQL is an industry-standard language for defining and manipulating data contained in a relational database. This chapter introduces SQL/400 and covers the Data Definition Language parts of SQL/400. You learn how to create several kinds of SQL objects: collections, base tables, views, and indexes. In DB2/400, these SQL objects are implemented as OS/400 libraries and files, and we look at how SQL/400 fits into the overall DB2/400 picture. Chapter 14 covers the Data Manipulation Language parts of SQL/400. Many of the statements covered in this chapter and Chapter 14 can be embedded in HLL programs as well as entered interactively. Chapter 15 covers techniques for embedding SQL statements in HLL programs. In Chapter 15, you also learn how to use program variables in SQL statements.

Note that this book doesn't describe every available SQL/400 feature — SQL/400 is simply too large a product to be covered in complete detail in a single book (much less one section of a book). The annotated bibliography lists the IBM manuals and some other excellent books on SQL. This book does provide you sufficient information to create comprehensive, complex, and professional-quality SQL/400 databases. The details that have been omitted are ones you can pick up from the manuals as you gain more experience on the job.

Introduction to SQL

An IBM research lab developed Structured Query Language (SQL) in the 1970s to explore an implementation of the relational database model.[2] Since that time, SQL has become a widely used language that's included in most relational DBMS, including IBM's family of DB2 products. Several national

---

[1] This book uses "SQL" when discussing SQL in general (including DB2 for OS/400 SQL) and "SQL/400" when discussing DB2 for OS/400 SQL specifically.

[2] The original language was SEQUEL — Structured English Query Language — developed in 1974 by D. D. Chamberlin of IBM's San Jose lab. This lab developed several more versions of SEQUEL, and the language was renamed SQL in 1977 when it was included in IBM's System R relational DBMS prototype. In 1979, the first major commercial implementation of SQL was included in Relational Software, Inc.'s Oracle DBMS. The first version of SQL that was available for IBM's midrange computers was Advanced Systems Concepts' Sequel/38 product for the System/38 (the predecessor of the AS/400); Advanced Systems Concepts'

and international standards organizations have published SQL standards, which the major relational DBMS (including DB2/400) follow for their versions of SQL.[3]

SQL includes **Data Definition Language** (**DDL**) statements to create database objects based on the relational model covered in Chapter 9. SQL also includes **Data Manipulation Language** (**DML**) statements to retrieve and update the contents of a database. Figure 13.1 (page 295) lists all the available SQL/400 statements, including DDL, DML, dynamic SQL, and miscellaneous categories.

We look closely at most of the DDL statements later in this chapter; however, for now a simple example provides a preview of what SQL looks like. The following statement creates a simplified **base table**[4] to contain customer data:

```
Create Table AppDta/Customer
    ( CustID   Dec(    7, 0 ) Not Null,
      Name     Char(  30    ),
      ShpLine1 Char( 100    ),
      ShpCity  Char(  30    ),
      ShpState Char(   2    ),
      Status   Char(   1    ),
  Primary Key( CustID ) )
```

The Customer table can be used to store information about customers. Each customer-related item, such as Name, listed in the Create Table statement defines a table **column**. You may recognize this table as similar to the physical file defined by the Data Description Specifications (DDS) shown in Figure 1.7. In DB2/400, when you create an SQL base table, you create an AS/400 physical file object.[5] A base table's columns are simply fields in the file's record format.

Sequel/400 is still available on AS/400s. In 1988, IBM announced SQL/400 for the AS/400. IBM now uses the product name DB2 for OS/400 SQL, instead of SQL/400.

Due in part to the original name (SEQUEL), SQL for some time was usually pronounced "sequel." In recent years, especially among IBMers in the AS/400 community, the favored pronunciation is "S-Q-L" (the three letters) to avoid confusion with products with names that contain "sequel" (e.g., Advanced Systems Concepts' Sequel/400).

[3] As of releases V3R2 and V3R6, SQL/400 met most of the entry-level requirements of the following standards:
- ISO (International Standards Organization) 9075-1992
- ANSI (American National Standards Institute) X3.135-1992
- FIPS (Federal Information Processing Standards) publication 127-2

[4] In SQL terminology, a table is an object, made up of columns and rows, that stores data. A base table is a named persistent object created with the Create Table statement. A **result table** is an unnamed temporary set of rows that the DBMS generates from one or more base tables during database retrieval or update operations. In this book, the term "table" is used to mean "base table" when the context makes it clear that the term refers to a permanent object.

[5] As we see later, you can generally use SQL/400 tables and views interchangeably with physical and logical files created from DDS. There are some important differences, however, and we look at those aspects of SQL/400 tables and views, too.

Figure 13.1
Available SQL/400
Statements

Data Definition Language

Alter Table
Comment On
Create Collection
Create Index
Create Schema
Create Table
Create View
Drop Collection
Drop Index
Drop Package
Drop Schema
Drop Table
Drop View
Grant
Label On
Revoke

Dynamic SQL

Describe
Execute
Execute Immediate
Prepare

Data Manipulation Language

Close
Commit
Declare Cursor
Delete
Fetch
Insert
Lock Table
Open
Rollback
Select
Update

Miscellaneous

Begin Declare Section
Call
Connect
Create Procedure
Declare Procedure
Declare Statement
Declare Variable
Describe Table
Disconnect
Drop Procedure
End Declare Section
Include
Release
Set Connection
Set Option
Set Result Sets
Set Transaction
Whenever

As mentioned, SQL also includes statements to manipulate data in tables. For example, the following SQL statement inserts a customer's data into the table created above:

```
Insert Into Customer
 Values ( 10001,
          'Ajax Plumbing',
          '12 Main St.',
          'Seattle',
          'WA',
          'A' )
```

Each value supplied on the Insert statement corresponds positionally to a column in the Customer table. This Insert statement adds a new **row** to the Customer table — an SQL/400 row in a table is just a record in a file. If you're wondering how you can write application programs with Insert statements that handle a variety of customers and not just specific customers (e.g., Ajax Plumbing), don't worry — SQL/400 provides many features (which we cover in Chapter 15) that support writing complete RPG IV, COBOL/400, and other HLL programs using SQL. There's lots more flexibility than these first examples show.

As these simple examples suggest, SQL provides statements that can be used instead of DDS to create tables and **views** (the SQL counterpart to logical files). SQL also provides statements to read, insert, update, and delete individual rows within a table or view. If this were all SQL did, it's only claim to fame would be that it's a widely adopted standard for database definition and manipulation. But SQL also lets you manipulate *sets* of rows. For example, the following statement changes the status of all customers in Seattle that currently have a status of X:

```
Update   Customer
  Set    Status  = 'B'
  Where ShpCity = 'Seattle'
   And  Status  = 'X'
```

The Where clause selects only those rows that satisfy the specified condition, and the Set clause assigns the new value to the Status column in the selected rows. This statement can be entered interactively (using various DB2/400 tools); but more importantly, it can be placed in an HLL program and can use program variables for the values of the city and the old and new status. This provides powerful set-at-a-time data manipulation that's not found in conventional HLLs' database access. For example, without SQL, both RPG IV and COBOL/400 would require a read-write loop to carry out what SQL can do with a single Update statement.

The other significant capability that SQL offers is the capability to define very complex views. Like DB2/400 logical files, views don't store data but provide an alternative way to access data in one or more underlying base tables. Like logical files, views can select a subset of a base table's rows or can be defined with a subset of a base table's columns. Views can also derive new columns from other columns. But SQL views have a much richer language than DDS (as we shall see later in this chapter) for expressing both row selection and column derivation.

Learning SQL has many advantages. On the AS/400, it provides some important database capabilities not available through DDS and built-in HLL I/O operations. Because SQL is an industry standard, programming skills in SQL can also be used with many other relational databases, including Oracle, Microsoft SQL Server, and DB2 on other platforms (e.g., IBM mainframes, AIX, and Windows NT). This commonality also makes SQL a valuable cross-platform tool, especially with distributed database facilities, such as IBM's Distributed Relational Database Architecture (DRDA) and the widely used Open Database Connectivity (ODBC) interface between Microsoft Windows platforms and other operating systems.

As mentioned in Part II, SQL is also a good starting point for expressing many of the definitions, manipulations, and integrity constraints you need to document in the logical data modeling and physical database design stages of a project. When you use SQL as a design language, you can extend it with your own notation to cover conditions that aren't directly supported by any actual SQL implementation. Then, when you implement tables, views, and application programs, you can use the various techniques suggested in Chapter 12 to handle those cases in which SQL/400 (or the DBMS facility you use) doesn't provide a direct implementation of your pseudo-SQL design specification. Even though pseudo-SQL as a design language doesn't eliminate implementation challenges, it provides a very capable language for clearly expressing many database design concepts.

Entering SQL/400 Statements

In this and the following two chapters, we look at many SQL statements. You can use a variety of means to enter these statements, but for production development, you generally use either the **Interactive SQL (ISQL)** facility or the RUNSQLSTM (Run SQL Statement) command, both of which come as part of IBM's DB2 Query Manager and SQL Development Kit for OS/400. Figure 13.2 shows a typical ISQL display that's used to enter SQL statements.

Figure 13.2
Interactive SQL
(ISQL) Display

```
                          Enter SQL Statements

 Type SQL statement, press Enter.
 ===> Create Table AppDta/Customer
              ( CustID   Dec(    7, 0 ) Not Null,
                Name     Char(  30 ) Not Null,
                ShpLine1 Char( 100 ) Not Null,
                ShpLine2 Char( 100 ) Not Null,
                ShpCity  Char(  30 ) Not Null,
                ShpState Char(   2 ) Not Null,
                ShpPsCd1 Char(  10 ) Not Null,
                ShpPsCd2 Char(  10 ) Not Null,
                ShpCntry Char(  30 ) Not Null,
                PhnVoice Char(  15 ) Not Null,
                PhnFax   Char(  15 ) Not Null,
                Status   Char(   1 ) Not Null
                                     With Default ' ',
                CrdLimit Dec(    7, 0 ) With Default Null,
                EntDate  Date          Not Null,
                Primary Key( CustID ) )
                                                            Bottom

  F3=Exit    F4=Prompt    F6=Insert line    F9=Retrieve    F10=Copy line
  F12=Cancel              F13=Services      F24=More keys
```

Appendix E provides a brief introduction to using the ISQL interface. ISQL provides helpful prompting for most SQL/400 statements, so it's an especially good tool if you're just learning SQL. ISQL also lets you syntax check statements without actually executing them. Once you have the proper syntax for a statement, you can save it (from the ISQL session log) to a source file member. You can later execute statements in a source file using the RUNSQLSTM command. Saved source statements can also be copied to the source member of an HLL program and used as embedded SQL statements.

The RUNSQLSTM command processes the SQL statements contained in a source member,[6] as in the following example:

```
RUNSQLSTM SRCFILE( appsrc/sqltblsrc )
          SRCMBR( customer )
```

In this example, the CUSTOMER source member might contain a Create Table statement to create a base table. Putting SQL statements — especially statements to create production tables and views — in a source member is a good idea because you can subsequently revise and/or rerun the commands without having to re-create them. You can put one or more SQL statements in a source member by saving the session log from an interactive SQL session, as mentioned earlier. You can also enter SQL statements in a source file member using a source code editor, such as SEU.[7] If you're not already familiar with SEU and OS/400 source files, Appendix D provides an introduction.

Creating a Collection

As we covered in Chapter 1, a library is the type of OS/400 object that contains other objects, such as files and programs. In SQL terminology, this type of container is known as a **collection** or **schema**.[8] An SQL/400 collection is an OS/400 library. You create a collection with a statement such as the following:[9]

---

[6] Not all SQL statements can be executed with the RUNSQLSTM command. However, the most useful DDL statements to code in a source member — Create, Label On, Comment On, Drop, Grant, and Revoke — can be executed with RUNSQLSTM. You can also run Insert, Update, and Delete — but not Select — with RUNSQLSTM.

If you code multiple SQL statements in a source member, the RUNSQLSTM command requires that you end each statement with a semicolon (;).

Note also that you can code comments in a source member that's subsequently processed by the RUNSQLSTM command. To code a comment, begin the comment with two adjacent dashes (--) and use the rest of the line for the comment, as in the following example:

```
-- This is a comment in a RUNSQLSTM source member
```

[7] See also Footnote 1 in Chapter 2 regarding alternatives to SEU.

[8] SQL also has the concept of a **database** object. A database is a set of collections. On any AS/400, there's always just one SQL database — the entire local system. You can assign the name of this database using the ADDRDBDIRE (Add Relational Database Directory Entry) command.

[9] You can also create a collection with the Create Schema statement. Essentially, the Create Schema statement just combines a Create Collection and one or more Create Table, Create

```
Create Collection AppDta
```

This statement

- Creates an OS/400 library named APPDTA
- Creates a set of SQL views in the collection that reference the system catalog tables (discussed later in this chapter).
- Creates an OS/400 journal named QSQJRN and a journal receiver named QSQJRN0001 in the collection. By default, changes to SQL base tables in the collection are automatically journaled to this journal. (Chapter 17 discusses journaling.)

Once you create a collection, you can create SQL base tables, views, and indexes, as well as other types of OS/400 objects (e.g., non-SQL files and programs) in the collection.[10]

Creating a Table

In a relational database, a base table contains the actual data. To create a table with SQL/400, you enter a Create Table statement that specifies

- The collection to contain the table
- The table name, which must not be the same name as any other base table, view, index, or non-SQL file in the same collection
- Specifications for one or more columns
- An optional primary key constraint
- Optionally, one or more unique and/or foreign key constraints

Figure 13.3 shows a more complete version of a Create Table statement for a Customer table.

View, Create Index, Comment On, Label On, and Grant statements into a single statement. This can be an efficient way to transmit a single (usually program-generated) SQL statement to create an entire collection and all the SQL objects in it on a remote system. You can execute the Create Schema statement only by placing it in a source file member and entering the RUNSQLSTM command.

[10] As of V3R1 of OS/400, you can create any type of DB2/400 physical or logical file (e.g., using DDS and the CRTPF and CRTLF commands) in a collection as long as you don't specify the optional With Data Dictionary clause on the Create Collection statement. The With Data Dictionary clause is provided strictly for compatibility with earlier releases of SQL/400 and generally should not be used because it limits the types of files that can be placed in a collection to physical files with one member or source physical files.

You can also create SQL tables, views, and indexes in a non-collection library created with the CRTLIB command. Non-collection libraries don't have the set of views over the system catalog files, however. You also must explicitly create a journal and journal receiver if you want to journal tables in a non-collection library.

Figure 13.3
Create Table Statement
for Customer Base Table

```
Create Table AppDta/Customer
    ( CustID   Dec(    7, 0 ) Not Null,
      Name     Char(  30     ) Not Null,
      ShpLine1 Char( 100     ) Not Null,
      ShpLine2 Char( 100     ) Not Null,
      ShpCity  Char(  30     ) Not Null,
      ShpState Char(   2     ) Not Null,
      ShpPsCd1 Char(  10     ) Not Null,
      ShpPsCd2 Char(  10     ) Not Null,
      ShpCntry Char(  30     ) Not Null,
      PhnVoice Char(  15     ) Not Null,
      PhnFax   Char(  15     ) Not Null,
      Status   Char(   1     ) Not Null
                               With Default ' ',
      CrdLimit Dec(    7, 0 ) With Default Null,
      EntDate  Date            Not Null,
  Primary Key( CustID ) )
```

This statement creates a table with an identical layout to the physical file defined by the DDS shown in Figure 2.5.[11] When this statement is executed, DB2/400 creates an externally described physical file object in the AppDta collection with the following attributes:[12]

- It is tagged as an SQL table
- It has a maximum of one member
- It has no maximum size
- When a new record is inserted into the file, DB2/400 reuses record locations marked internally as "deleted" (if any)
- Both before and after record images are journaled
- The file's record format has the same name as the table, and the file has one member with the same name as the table
- The file has a keyed access path.[13] As part of the physical file object, DB2/400 creates an internal index on the CustID column, which is the table's primary key

When this statement is executed, DB2/400 also automatically starts journaling changes to rows in the table to the QSQJRN journal in the same

[11] Note that the Customer table created in Figure 13.3 doesn't have the alias names, column headings, or descriptive text of the Customer file defined by the DDS in Figure 2.5. Later in this chapter, we see how to add those field attributes.

[12] These file attributes correspond to the following CRTPF command parameters: MAXMBRS(1), SIZE(*NOMAX), REUSEDLT(*YES), and IMAGES(*BOTH). Note that SQL/400 base tables always have a single member; you cannot add members as you can with a physical file created from DDS.

[13] The physical file for a base table with no primary key or other constraint does not have a keyed access path, and the file object doesn't have an internal index.

collection.[14] As you can see from Figure 13.3, the Create Table statement first lists the table to be created and then lists the column and constraint definitions, separated by commas and enclosed in a set of parentheses. SQL is a free-format language, and you can use multiple lines for a statement as well as blanks between words. The example shows a coding style that puts each column definition and constraint on a separate line and aligns the similar parts of each column definition. Although this columnar style isn't required, it makes the statement much easier to read than an unaligned stream of text.

SQL isn't case sensitive: Create Table, CREATE TABLE, and CrEaTe TaBlE are all correct. Be aware, however, that string literals are case sensitive, and 'x' is not treated the same as 'X'. Also, when SQL/400 creates a DB2/400 file or field name, the name is generally stored as uppercase. Thus, if you display a list of the tables in the AppDta collection, the table created by the statement in Figure 13.3 will be listed as CUSTOMER. You can still refer to the table as Customer or customer in SQL statements and in HLLs that permit mixed-case names.

SQL/400 Naming Conventions

The table name used in Figure 13.3 is a qualified name, which includes the collection name (AppDta) before the unqualified table name (Customer). SQL/400 has two alternative approaches to names, including different rules for qualified names: the system naming convention and the SQL naming convention. The system naming convention generally follows the rules that apply to OS/400 objects, while the SQL naming convention conforms closely to the naming conventions established in several official SQL standards (e.g., the ANSI standard). When you use ISQL, execute a RUNSQLSTM command, or create an HLL program with embedded SQL, you must specify which form of name you're using. For example, you specify either *SYS (the default) or *SQL for the RUNSQLSTM command's OPTION parameter.

With system names, you use a slash (/) between the collection name and the table (or other object) name:

```
AppDta/Customer
```

With SQL names, you use a period (.) as the separator:

```
AppDta.Customer
```

---

[14] If the journal exists. The Create Collection statement automatically creates the QSQJRN journal, but you can delete the journal, or you can specify a non-collection library (without a QSQJRN journal) on the Create Table statement. You can use the STRJRNPF (Start Journaling Physical File) and ENDJRNPF (End Journaling Physical File) CL commands to control journaling explicitly on SQL/400 tables.

When you specify an unqualified name, SQL/400 determines the implicit collection based on the naming convention in effect and the type of statement being executed. If the statement is creating a new object (e.g., a Create Table statement), the rules for determining the collection are somewhat complex and you're better off always specifying a qualifier.[15] If the statement is not creating a new object (e.g., a Select or Drop Table statement) and system naming is in effect, DB2/400 searches the job's library list to find an object of the proper type with the specified name.[16] If SQL names are in effect, DB2/400 uses the current user profile name as the name of the collection to search for the object. Because collections on the AS/400 typically aren't given the same names as user profiles, you should use qualified names for most statements when the SQL naming convention is in effect.

Unless you plan to implement an application on systems other than an AS/400, you'll find the system naming convention more suitable for SQL/400 statements. This book uses the system naming convention, unless specifically noted otherwise.

Although SQL/400 has special features to allow long names (e.g., table names up to 128 characters) and names with special characters in them (e.g., !), your application implementation will be much simpler if you use only names that are a maximum of 10 characters, begin with a letter (A-Z), and contain only letters and digits (0-9).[17] If, as is likely, some SQL/400-created tables will be accessed from HLL programs using built-in I/O statements (e.g., an RPG IV or COBOL/400 Read statement), review Part I, especially Chapters 2 and 7, for important file- and field-naming considerations.

Also be aware that SQL has many reserved words, such as Create, Table, and Order, that have special meaning. If you want to use one of these reserved words as the name of a table, column, or other SQL object, you must use quotation marks around the names when they appear in an SQL statement. The following example shows how you would code an SQL Select statement that retrieves rows from a table named Order:

---

[15] The *DB2/400 SQL Reference* manual documents the rules for implicit qualifiers for all Create statements.

[16] Recall that a library list is the ordered list of library names associated with an OS/400 job.

[17] The "Identifiers" section of the *DB2/400 SQL Reference* describes various types of SQL names. One of the problems with long names or names with special characters is that DB2/400 generates an OS/400 object name that satisfies the OS/400 naming restrictions. For example, if you use Create table to create a table named CustomerInfo, DB2/400 creates a physical file object named something like CUSTO00001.

Although the underscore (_) is allowed in SQL names, OS/400 object names, and database field names, some HLLs don't allow the underscore in identifiers. Using only letters and digits avoids any chance of conflict between your database names and other facilities.

Special characters, such as the exclamation point (!), can cause problems with international applications because of the different characters represented in the character sets used by different countries.

```
Select *
  From "Order"
  Where CustID = 499320
```

Generally, you should not use SQL reserved words for names of objects. The *DB2/400 SQL Reference* manual lists SQL reserved words in an appendix.

Column Definitions

On the Create Table statement, after the new table name, you code one or more column definitions. Each column definition specifies the column name and a data type. Some data types have a length or precision (total number of digits). In addition, the Decimal and Numeric data types can have a scale (number of digits to the right of the decimal point). Figure 13.4 lists the SQL/400 column data types. (Review Chapter 2 for more information about the different data types.)

Figure 13.4
SQL Column Data Types

Character	
Char(*length*)	Fixed-length character string with a length from 1 to 32766. (If the length is omitted, it defaults to 1.)
VarChar(*max-length*)	Variable-length character string with a maximum length from 1 to 32740.
Graphic(*length*)	Fixed-length graphic string with a length from 1 to 16383. (If the length is omitted, it defaults to 1.)
VarGraphic(*max-length*)	Variable-length graphic string with a maximum length from 1 to 16370.
Numeric	
Dec(*precision, scale*)	Packed-decimal number. The precision is the number of digits and can range from 1 to 31. The scale is the number of digits to the right of the decimal point and can range from 0 to the value specified for precision. You can use Dec(*p*) for Dec(*p*,0). You can also use Dec by itself for Dec(5,0); however, always using an explicit precision with Dec provides clearer documentation.
Numeric(*precision, scale*)	Zoned-decimal number. The precision is the number of digits and can range from 1 to 31. The scale is the number of digits to the right of the decimal point and can range from 0 to the value specified for precision. You can use Numeric(*p*) for Numeric(*p*,0). You can also use Numeric by itself for Numeric(5,0); however, always using an explicit precision with Numeric provides clearer documentation.

Figure 13.4 continued

Errata

Page 303 in this text was printed incorrectly.

The correct version of the page is printed

on the reverse side of this sheet.

Create Table statement), the rules for determining the collection are somewhat complex and you're better off always specifying a qualifier.[15] If the statement is not creating a new object (e.g., a Select or Drop Table statement) and system naming is in effect, DB2/400 searches the job's library list to find an object of the proper type with the specified name.[16] If SQL names are in effect, DB2/400 uses the current user profile name as the name of the collection to search for the object. Because collections on the AS/400 typically aren't given the same names as user profiles, you should use qualified names for most statements when the SQL naming convention is in effect.

Unless you plan to implement an application on systems other than an AS/400, you'll find the system naming convention more suitable for SQL/400 statements. This book uses the system naming convention, unless specifically noted otherwise.

Figure 13.4
SQL Column Data Types

Character	
Char(*length*)	Fixed-length character string with a length from 1 to 32766. (If the length is omitted, it defaults to 1.)
VarChar(*max-length*)	Variable-length character string with a maximum length from 1 to 32740.
Graphic(*length*)	Fixed-length graphic string with a length from 1 to 16383. (If the length is omitted, it defaults to 1.)
VarGraphic(*max-length*)	Variable-length graphic string with a maximum length from 1 to 16370.
Numeric	
Dec(*precision, scale*)	Packed-decimal number. The precision is the number of digits and can range from 1 to 31. The scale is the number of digits to the right of the decimal point and can range from 0 to the value specified for precision. You can use Dec(*p*) for Dec(*p*,0). You can also use Dec by itself for Dec(5,0); however, always using an explicit precision with Dec provides clearer documentation.
Numeric(*precision, scale*)	Zoned-decimal number. The precision is the number of digits and can range from 1 to 31. The scale is the number of digits to the right of the decimal point and can range from 0 to the value specified for precision. You can use Numeric(*p*) for Numeric(*p*,0). You can also use Numeric by itself for Numeric(5,0); however, always using an explicit precision with Numeric provides clearer documentation.

Figure 13.4 continued

Figure 13.4

Continued

Numeric	
SmallInt	Two-byte, binary integer.
Integer	Four-byte, binary integer.
Real	Single-precision, floating-point number.
Double Precision	Double-precision, floating-point number.
Float(*precision*)	Floating-point number. The precision is the number of digits and can range from 1 to 53. The values 1 through 24 specify single precision, the values 25 through 53 specify double precision. You can use Float by itself for a double-precision number.
Date, Time, and Timestamp	
Date	Date.
Time	Time.
Timestamp	Timestamp.

Following the data type you can optionally code either or both of the following clauses:[18]

- Not Null

- Default *default-value*

If you specify Not Null, the column is not **null-capable**; otherwise, it is. For a null-capable column, you can set the column to null, which, as you'll recall from Chapter 2, is a placeholder that means "no value" or "not known." DB2/400 actually stores a hidden bit for each null-capable column. When the column is null, DB2/400 sets this hidden bit to 1; when the column has a normal value, DB2/400 sets this bit to 0. SQL and some HLLs have built-in tests to check whether a field is null.

In Figure 13.3, only the CrdLimit column is defined as null capable. Although SQL/400 has good support for null-capable columns, not all AS/400 HLLs have comparable support in their built-in I/O statements. Review Chapter 7 for the special considerations that apply to RPG IV and COBOL/400 programs that use built-in I/O operations to access files with null-capable fields.

The Default clause specifies a default column value. When you insert a row with an Insert statement that doesn't list all the base table columns or

---

[18] The following optional keywords can also be specified in column definitions: Allocate, For Bit Data, For SBCS Data, For Mixed Data, and CCSID. See the *DB2/400 SQL Reference* manual for details.

insert a row via a view that doesn't include all the columns in the underlying base table, DB2/400 puts a default value in those columns that aren't in the column list or view.[19] In Figure 13.3, the Status column has a default of blank, and the CrdLimit column has a default of null. The Default clause value must be a valid value for the data type and length of the column you're defining (the Null keyword is also valid if the column is null capable). If you don't specify either a Default clause or Not Null, DB2/400 uses null as the default. If you don't specify a default and you do specify Not Null, DB2/400 uses a default of blanks for fixed-length character and graphic fields, an empty string (length 0) for a variable-length character and graphic strings, zero for numeric fields, and the current date and time for date, time, and timestamp fields.

Using Standard Column Definitions

As we learned in Part II, in the relational model and with relational database design techniques, every base table column should be defined over a domain. The domain specifies the allowable values and operations for the column. We also saw in Chapter 3 that even though DDS doesn't support the domain concept, the DDS field reference feature does allow a set of standard field definitions to be used as the basis for all application field definitions. When used as described in Chapter 3, referenced fields can provide at least some of the benefits of domains. In addition, using a field reference file significantly increases the standardization of field definitions, which can reduce errors and simplify both new database implementations and revisions to existing database files.

Unfortunately, SQL/400 doesn't support the concept of user-defined domains or column data types, nor does SQL/400 provide anything equivalent to the DDS field reference feature. You must use ad hoc methods to implement the domains in your logical data model and achieve standardization in your SQL table definitions.

As a starting point, you can follow the guidelines in Chapter 3 to create a field reference file and a dictionary that lists standard field names and definitions. You can either create the field reference file using DDS, or use analogous SQL DDL statements to create an equivalent column reference table. In either case, the file or table is not used to contain application data. Instead, it's used as a reference for defining application fields and columns using standard names and definitions. In the case of SQL/400's Create Table statement, you must manually use the standard column definitions (or write your own tool to generate SQL DDL statements). Note that with either an SQL table or a file created from DDS, you can use SQL (interactively or in an HLL program) to retrieve column definitions from the SysColumns catalog table discussed near the end of this chapter.

Although it's beyond the scope of this text, it's also possible to write a program that reads a source member with a variation of the SQL Create Table syntax and that uses a field reference file to generate a complete SQL

---

[19] Default values are also used in join logical files, as discussed in Chapter 6.

Create Table statement. To give you the general idea, an input source line could be coded as

```
Name RefCol( TName ),
```

where Name is the column name for the new table and RefCol is the keyword that indicates the Name column should be defined based on the TName column definition. If the TName column is defined in the field reference file as Char(30) Not Null, the generated source line would be

```
Name Char( 30 ) Not Null,
```

which is a valid SQL/400 column definition. Whether you use manual methods or some automated tools, it's important to use a well-defined standard set of column definitions for your DB2/400 tables.

Constraints

When you create a table, you optionally can specify three types of **constraints**:

- Primary key
- Unique key
- Foreign key

DB2/400 enforces these constraints when rows in the table are inserted or updated (and in the case of a foreign key constraint, when rows in the referenced table are updated or deleted). Constraint clauses normally follow the last column definition, and are separated by commas.[20] You can optionally begin each constraint clause with the Constraint keyword followed by a constraint name:

```
Constraint CustomerPK Primary Key( CustID )
```

If you don't specify a constraint name, DB2/400 generates a name when the table is created. The constraint name can later be used in the Alter Table statement (discussed below) to drop the constraint. Because you don't need a constraint name to drop a primary key constraint with the Alter Table statement (you can specify just the keywords, Primary Key), constraint names are most useful for unique key and foreign key constraints.

None of the constraints are required, although most base tables will, by design, have a primary key that serves as the unique identifier for rows in the table. For example, in Figure 13.3, the CustID column is the primary key used to identify customers. The syntax of the **primary key constraint** (following the constraint name, if any is specified) is

---

[20] Alternatively, you can use a form of SQL syntax that lets you specify constraints on each column definition — e.g., by specifying Primary Key following Dec(7, 0) on the CustID column's definition. However, using separate clauses after the column definitions is a more readable way to code table constraints.

```
Primary Key(column-name, ... )
```

The definition of each primary key column must include Not Null. For a table with a primary key constraint, DB2/400 blocks any attempt to insert or update a row that would cause two rows in the same table to have identical value(s) for their primary key columns. A table definition can have no more than one primary key constraint.

A **unique key constraint** is similar to a primary key constraint; however, a column listed in a unique key constraint doesn't have to be defined with Not Null. The syntax is also similar:

```
Unique Key(column-name, ... )
```

A table can have multiple unique key constraints; however, the same set of columns (regardless of order) can be listed on only one primary or unique key constraint. For example, it's not valid to have the following two constraints on the same table:

```
Primary Key( ColA, ColB ),
Unique  Key( ColB, ColA )
```

Because a table can have more than one unique key constraint, you may want to include an explicit constraint name to make it easier to drop the constraint (if your database design changes) on a subsequent Alter Table statement. Here's an example of an explicitly named unique key constraint:

```
Constraint CustNameUK Unique Key( Name )
```

For each primary, unique, or foreign key constraint, DB2/400 creates an internal index in the physical file object.[21] Unlike the DDS key specifications for a physical file, however, neither a primary key nor a unique key defines any particular ordering for a table's rows.[22]

Recall from Chapter 10 that a foreign key is a set of columns in one table (the dependent table) whose column values match the values of a primary or unique key in another, usually different, table — the parent (or referenced) table. A **foreign key constraint** (also called a **referential constraint**) specifies the columns of the foreign key (in the same table as the constraint) and the columns of a primary or unique key in the parent table. Consider a Sale table that contains rows with information about sales, including a CustID column

---

[21] DB2/400 shares an existing index, rather than creating one, if an appropriate index exists.

[22] Nevertheless, if you plan to use an Order By clause in a Select statement or an embedded SQL cursor to retrieve rows in a particular sequence based on the same set of columns that are specified for a primary or unique key with multiple columns, it's a good idea to specify the constraint's columns in the same order you'll use in the Order By clause. That way, DB2/400 can use the same internal index for both guaranteeing unique key values and retrieving rows in a particular sequence. For example, if you use Order by ColA, ColB in a view, and you have a unique constraint over ColA and ColB, you should specify Unique Key(ColA, ColB) rather than Unique Key(ColB, ColA).

that contains the customer ID of the customer who placed the order. You might create the Sale table with the following constraints:

```
Constraint SalePK      Primary Key( OrderID ),
Constraint SaleCustFK Foreign Key( CustID  )
  References Customer ( CustID )
  On Delete Cascade
  On Update Restrict
```

This SaleCustFK foreign key constraint specifies that the CustID column in the Sale table is a foreign key that references the CustID primary key column in the Customer table. With this constraint, DB2/400 does not allow an application to insert a new row in the Sale table unless the row's CustID column contains the value of some existing CustID value in the Customer table.[23] This constraint also blocks any attempt to change the CustID column of a row in the Sale table to a non-null value that doesn't exist in any row in the Customer table. In other words, a new or updated Sale row must have a parent Customer row.

The On Delete clause specifies what action DB2/400 should take when an application attempts to delete a row in the Customer table and some row in the Sale table contains the CustID value of the row being deleted. The Cascade action causes DB2/400 to propagate the delete operation to all the Sale rows that have the same CustID as the Customer row being deleted.

The On Update clause specifies what action DB2/400 should take when an application attempts to update the CustID value in a row of the Customer table and some row in the Sale table contains the CustID value of the row being updated. The Restrict action causes DB2/400 to block the update operation and return an error to the application. The On Delete and On Update rules are intended to prevent orphan rows — rows in the dependent table that have a non-null foreign key that doesn't reference an existing parent row.

If you don't explicitly specify an On Delete or an On Update clause, the default action is the same as with the keywords No Action. The No Action alternative is similar to the Restrict action.[24] For the On Delete clause, you can also specify the Set Default action to have DB2/400 set all foreign key columns of dependent rows to their respective default values. If any foreign key column is null-capable, another On Delete alternative is Set Null which causes all null-capable foreign key columns to be set to null.

---

[23] If any column in the foreign key is null capable, DB2/400 allows a new row in the dependent table to be inserted if any foreign key column is null.

[24] There's a subtle difference between Restrict and No Action. With Restrict, the check for an unmatched foreign key is done *before* an "after event" database trigger program is called, whereas with No Action, the check is done *after* an "after event" trigger program is called. Trigger programs are discussed in Chapter 17. Also, with SQL/400 set-at-a-time statements (discussed in Chapter 14), DB2/400 checks the Restrict rule immediately after each record update (or delete), but checks the No Action rule only after the statement completes. In most cases, specifying Restrict (rather than No Action) provides the appropriate rule, but be sure you consider the finer points when you decide which to use.

Chapter 16 provides more details on DB2/400's support for referential integrity and foreign key constraints.

Long Column Names

In Figure 13.3, we used column names that conformed to the 10-character limit that DB2/400 has for field names. In fact, we used the same column names that we used for field names in the physical file DDS in Figure 2.5. With DDS, we could use the ALIAS field-level keyword to specify a longer field name that can be used by SQL/400 and COBOL/400. The Create Table statement has a similar capability to define long names (equivalent to the ALIAS name) for columns. Figure 13.5 shows the syntax for this option.

Figure 13.5

Create Table with Long Column Names

```
Create Table AppDta/Customer
    ( CustID                        Dec(    7, 0 ) Not Null,
      CustName          For Name     Char( 30    ) Not Null,
      CustShipLine1     For ShpLine1 Char( 100   ) Not Null,
      CustShipLine2     For ShpLine2 Char( 100   ) Not Null,
      CustShipCity      For ShpCity  Char( 30    ) Not Null,
      CustShipState     For ShpState Char(  2    ) Not Null,
      CustShipPostalCode1 For ShpPsCd1 Char( 10  ) Not Null,
      CustShipPostalCode2 For ShpPsCd2 Char( 10  ) Not Null,
      CustShipCountry   For ShpCntry Char( 30    ) Not Null,
      CustPhoneVoice    For PhnVoice Char( 15    ) Not Null,
      CustPhoneFax      For PhnFax   Char( 15    ) Not Null,
      CustStatus        For Status   Char(  1    ) Not Null
                                               With Default ' ',
      CustCreditLimit   For CrdLimit Dec(    7, 0 ) With Default Null,
      CustEntryDate     For EntDate  Date          Not Null,
  Primary Key( CustID ) )
```

All you have to do is code a long name followed by the For keyword before you code the shorter name. In SQL/400 terminology, the shorter name is the **system column name**.[25] In SQL/400 statements, you can use either the short or long name. In HLLs and utilities, the system column name is the standard field name, and the longer name is the ALIAS. (Review Chapter 7 for more information about how the ALIAS name can be used in COBOL/400 programs. Review Chapters 3 and 4 for the principles for creating good file and field names; the same principles apply to table, view, and column names.)

Descriptive Text and Column Headings

After you create a table, you can define descriptive text and longer comments for the table and its columns. You can also define column headings that ISQL and other utilities use to display or print data from the table.

---

[25] If you code a column name longer than 10 characters and you do not code a For clause with a shorter name, SQL/400 generates a system name. You should always include a For clause for long column names so the system column names are consistent and readable.

A Label On statement, such as the following, adds descriptive text to the OS/400 physical file object (as well as in the SQL catalog):

```
Label On Table AppDta/Customer Is 'Customers'
```

The Label On statement is equivalent to the TEXT parameter on the CRTPF command used to create a physical file from DDS. There is no SQL statement to add descriptive text to a table member, but you can use the CHGPFM command to accomplish this:

```
CHGPFM FILE( appdta/customer )
       MBR( customer )
       TEXT( 'Customers' )
```

To add descriptive text to columns (comparable to the TEXT field-level keyword in DDS), you use the form of the Label On statement shown in Figure 13.6.

Figure 13.6
Defining Descriptive Text for Columns

```
Label On AppDta/Customer
  ( CustID              Text Is 'Customer ID',
    CustName            Text Is 'Customer name',
    CustShipLine1       Text Is 'Customer shipping address line 1',
    CustShipLine2       Text Is 'Customer shipping address line 2',
    CustShipCity        Text Is 'Customer shipping address city',
    CustShipState       Text Is 'Customer shipping address state',
    CustShipPostalCode1 Text Is 'Customer shipping address postal code 1',
    CustShipPostalCode2 Text Is 'Customer shipping address postal code 2',
    CustShipCountry     Text Is 'Customer shipping address country',
    CustPhoneVoice      Text Is 'Customer voice phone number',
    CustPhoneFax        Text Is 'Customer Fax phone number',
    CustStatus          Text Is 'Customer status',
    CustCreditLimit     Text Is 'Customer credit limit',
    CustEntryDate       Text Is 'Customer info entry date' )
```

After the table name, there are one or more entries for the column text, separated by commas. Each column text entry has the form

column-name Text Is '*text-string*'

Column headings (comparable to the COLHDG field-level keyword in DDS) use another variation on the Label On statement (Figure 13.7).

The Text keyword is not used when defining column headings, and the text string is treated as three 20-character segments. The first 20 characters are used for the first line of the heading; characters 21 through 40 (if present) are the second heading line, and characters 41 through 60 (if present) are the third heading line. You must carefully align the contents of each string to get the right column headings.

SQL also lets you specify longer comments — up to 2,000 characters — for tables, views, and columns.[26] This comment is stored in the SQL catalog,

---

[26] As well as SQL packages, stored procedures, and stored procedure parameters. An SQL package is a type of object that contains control structures used to execute SQL

Figure 13.7
Defining Column
Headings

```
Label on AppDta/Customer
  ( CustID            Is 'Cust.         ID',
    CustName          Is 'Customer      Name',
    CustShipLine1     Is 'Customer      Shipping      Line 1',
    CustShipLine2     Is 'Customer      Shipping      Line 2',
    CustShipCity      Is 'Customer      Shipping      City',
    CustShipState     Is 'Customer      Shipping      State',
    CustShipPostalCode1 Is 'Customer    Shipping      Postal code 1',
    CustShipPostalCode2 Is 'Customer    Shipping      Postal code 2',
    CustShipCountry   Is 'Customer      Shipping      Country',
    CustPhoneVoice    Is 'Customer      Phone',
    CustPhoneFax      Is 'Customer      Fax',
    CustStatus        Is 'Cust.         Status',
    CustCreditLimit   Is 'Cust.         Credit        Limit',
    CustEntryDate     Is 'Cust.         Entry         Date' )
```

and has no counterpart in DDS or the CL commands for database files. To define a comment for a table, you use a Comment On statement such as the following. The Comment On statement for column comments is shown in Figure 13.8.

```
Comment On Table AppDta/Customer
        Is 'Customer master file ...'
```

Figure 13.8
Defining Long Comments
for Columns

```
Comment On AppDta/Customer
  ( CustID            Is 'Customer ID',
    CustName          Is 'Customer name',
    CustShipLine1     Is 'Customer shipping address line 1',
    CustShipLine2     Is 'Customer shipping address line 2',
    CustShipCity      Is 'Customer shipping address city',
    CustShipState     Is 'Customer shipping address state',
    CustShipPostalCode1 Is 'Customer shipping address postal code 1',
    CustShipPostalCode2 Is 'Customer shipping address postal code 2',
    CustShipCountry   Is 'Customer shipping address country',
    CustPhoneVoice    Is 'Customer voice phone number',
    CustPhoneFax      Is 'Customer Fax phone number',
    CustStatus        Is 'Customer status',
    CustCreditLimit   Is 'Customer credit limit',
    CustEntryDate     Is 'Customer info entry date' )
```

Notice the similarity to the Label On statement in Figure 13.6, except the statement name is different, and the Comment On statement doesn't use the Text keyword in the column entries. (This Comment On example uses

statements. Stored procedures are OS/400 program objects that can be called from a local or remote program that includes embedded SQL. Chapter 15 covers packages and stored procedures. The limit for comments was only 254 characters in V3R1 and earlier releases of SQL/400.

the same text as the Label On statement in Figure 13.6, but remember that long comments can be up to 2,000 characters while descriptive text is limited to 50 characters.)

When compared to DDS, SQL may at first seem more cumbersome because separate Label On statements must be executed for column text and column headings, whereas in DDS both are specified on the field definition itself. There's an important advantage to the SQL approach, however, because you can change a column's text or heading without having to re-create the physical file as is required with DDS. Although the SQL method requires a bit more source code, it provides important flexibility after a table is created.

Adding or Dropping Table Constraints and Columns

After you create a table, you may need to add or remove a primary, unique, or foreign key constraint. The Alter Table statement provides this capability:

```
Alter Table AppDta/Sale
   Drop Primary Key

Alter Table AppDta/Sale
   Drop Constraint SaleCustFK

Alter Table AppDta/Sale
   Add Constraint SaleCustFK Foreign Key( CustID  )
        References Customer ( CustID )
        On Delete Cascade
        On Update Restrict
```

The first example drops (i.e., removes) the table's primary key constraint, and the second example drops the foreign key constraint named SaleCustFK. The third example adds a foreign key constraint. You must specify a constraint name to drop a unique or foreign key constraint, but you need only the Primary Key keywords to drop a primary key constraint. The rules for specifying a constraint with the Alter Table statement are the same as those for the Create Table statement.

In V3R2 and V3R6[27] of DB2/400, IBM enhanced the Alter Table statement to allow adding, dropping, or changing base table columns. The following example shows how to add a column to the Customer table created in Figure 13.3:

```
Alter Table AppDta/Customer
   Add Discount Dec( 5, 3 ) Not Null Default 0
```

---

[27] As mentioned in the Preface, this book reflects Version 3 of DB2/400. At the time of publication, V3R2 and V3R6 were the current releases for the non-RISC and RISC systems, respectively. The significant differences between non-RISC and RISC hardware require two parallel releases.

For the most part, SQL/400 capabilities in V3R2 and V3R6 are the same as in V3R1 (an earlier release that runs only on non-RISC systems). However, the Alter Table statement in V3R1 and earlier releases does not support the ability to add, drop, or change the definition of columns.

The Alter Table statement provides flexibility for revising a database table without having to manually delete and re-create it (as is necessary with earlier releases of DB2/400). Note, however, that if you use the Not Null clause for a column added with the Alter Table statement, you must also specify a Default clause because all existing rows will have the new column set to the default value.

Creating a View

In SQL terms, a view is an object that appears like a table to application programs but doesn't contain any data. Instead, a view is defined over one or more base tables and provides an alternative way to access the data in the underlying base tables. You can use SQL views to

- Select a subset of the rows in a base table
- Include only a subset of a base table's columns
- Derive new view columns based on one or more underlying base table columns
- Join related rows from multiple base tables into a single row in the view
- Combine sets of rows from multiple tables into a single view

Views provide a way to simplify, as well as restrict, access to data. For example, to provide a view that contains only customers with a credit limit of at least 5000, you would execute the following statement:

```
Create View AppDta/CustCrd As
  Select  *
    From  AppDta/Customer
    Where CrdLimit >= 5000
```

Once you create this view, you can use it just like a table in other SQL statements. For example, you could execute the following Update statement

```
Update CustCrd
   Set Status   = 'B'
 Where ShpCity = 'Seattle'
   And Status  = 'X'
```

to change the Status column for the selected rows. Notice something important about the way this Update over a view works: Only those rows that meet all three conditions — CrdLimit >= 5000, ShpCity = 'Seattle', and Status = 'X' — will have their Status set to B. When the Update statement is processed, DB2/400 accesses only rows that satisfy the CustCrd view's selection criteria. To those rows, DB2/400 then applies the Update statement's selection criteria to determine which rows to update. As this example demonstrates, you can think of a view as if it were a table that contained just those rows with the specified criteria. You can also use views in HLL programs, as we'll see in Chapter 15.

When the Create View statement above is executed, DB2/400 creates an externally described, logical file object in the AppDta collection. The file has the following attributes:

- It is tagged as an SQL view
- It has a maximum of one member [28]
- The file's record format has the same name as the view, and the file has one member with the same name as the view
- The file does not have a keyed access path [29]

Other than the absence of a keyed access path, the view created from this statement is essentially the same as the logical file defined with DDS in Figure 4.8.

The Create View statement is the most complex DDL statement in SQL, and the best way to approach it is to look at one part at a time. Following the Create View keywords, you provide the view name, which is best coded as a qualified name that includes the collection in which the view is created.[30] A view name must not be the same name as any base table, other view, index, or non-SQL file in the same collection.

The next part of the Create View statement is an optional list of column names in the view. If you don't specify a list of names (as in this example), the view has the column names of the result table defined by the **subselect** specified after the As keyword. The subselect's result table determines which columns and rows from one or more underlying tables or views are encompassed by the view being defined. Keep in mind that a result table is an SQL *concept*, not necessarily a real table stored on disk or in memory. In the example above, the subselect,

```
Select  *
  From  AppDta/Customer
  Where CrdLimit >= 5000
```

defines a result table with all the columns from the Customer base table [31] and only those rows that have a credit limit of at least 5000. The subselect is

---

[28] SQL/400 views always have a single member; you cannot add members as you can with a logical file created from DDS. This file attribute corresponds to the MAXMBRS(1) parameter on the CRTLF command.

[29] Unlike some logical files created from DDS, logical files for SQL views never have keyed access paths.

[30] If you don't code a qualifier for the view name, DB2/400 determines the collection based on the naming convention in effect. For system naming, the default collection is the collection that contains the first table or view specified on the first From clause. For SQL naming, the default collection name is the user profile name associated with the job in which the Create View is executed.

[31] The * following the Select means "all columns."

probably the most important — and often most challenging — aspect of the SQL syntax to master. A subselect specifies a result table derived from the base tables and views listed in the From clause and is used in view definitions, SQL Select and Insert statements, and embedded SQL cursor declarations. In the next chapter we delve deeply into the structure of subselects (and some related parts of SQL). For now, we just look at a few of the simpler parts of a subselect to understand the basic way views work.

A subselect always begins with the Select keyword. For the simplest subselect, you follow the Select keyword with a list of column names (or * to use an implicit list of all columns) and a From clause that specifies a base table or view.[32] The following Create View uses a subselect that defines a result table with all the rows from the Customer table but only a subset of the columns:

```
Create View AppDta/CustShip As
   Select  CustID,
           ShpLine1,
           ShpLine2,
           ShpCity,
           ShpState,
           ShpPsCd1,
           ShpPsCd1,
           ShpCntry
     From  AppDta/Customer
```

Except for the absence of a keyed access path, the view created from this statement is essentially the same as the logical file defined with DDS in Figure 4.11. An SQL statement referencing the CustShip view can treat it as if it were a table with just the columns listed and with all the rows in the Customer table. The From clause can list a view as well as a table:

```
Create View AppDta/CustCrdStl As
   Select  *
     From  AppDta/CustCrd
    Where  ShpCity = 'Seattle'
```

DB2/400 combines (AND's) the Where clauses for a view defined over another view. Given the previous definition of the CustCrd view, this definition of the CustCrdStl view includes only rows from Customer that have CrdLimit ≥ 5000 *and* ShpCity = 'Seattle'.[33]

A From clause can also list multiple base tables and views. For example, the following statement defines a view that joins related rows in the Customer and Sale tables:

[32] You can also specify a non-SQL, externally described physical file in a view's subselect From clause. You can't specify a non-SQL logical file, however.

[33] With DDS, you can't define a logical file over another logical file. The SQL ability to define a view over another view is an important advantage over DDS.

```
Create View AppDta/CustSale As
  Select  Customer.CustID,
          Customer.Name,
          Sale.OrderID,
          Sale.SaleDate,
          Sale.SaleTot
    From  AppDta/Customer,
          AppDta/Sale
    Where Customer.CustID = Sale.CustID
```

This view is comparable to the join logical file specified with DDS in Figure 6.6, although DB2/400 doesn't actually create a join logical file object for this view. When you specify multiple tables and/or views in the From clause, conceptually, DB2/400 produces an intermediate result table that has all combinations of all rows from all the listed tables and views.[34] Each row has all the columns from all the tables, as well. From this complete set of combinations, only those rows that satisfy the condition specified in the Where clause are included in the subselect result table. And only those columns listed after the Select keyword are in the result table. In this example, only rows with matching CustID column values are in the result table. Consequently, the result table contains one row for each sale (with a matching customer), and each row has both sale data and customer data. Because an explicit list of columns is specified following the Select keyword, the result table has only the five columns listed. For a look at a sample of joining two tables, see Figure 6.3 (the sample Customer data), Figure 6.4 (the sample Sale data), and Figure 6.7 (the sample CustSale data). The contents of the CustSale join logical file, shown in Figure 6.7, are the same for the CustSale view defined above.

Notice how the subselect column names in this example are qualified with the table name from which the column is taken. For example, Customer.CustID specifies that this column in the result table is the CustID column from the Customer table. To qualify a column name, code the table or view name followed by a period (.) before the column name. You always use a period (.) — never a slash (/) — to qualify column names, regardless of whether the system or SQL naming convention is in effect.

In this example, no explicit names are specified for the view's columns, so DB2/400 uses the same unqualified names as in the result table (i.e., CustID, Name, OrderID, SaleDate, and SaleTot). If you were subsequently to refer to the CustSale view's column names using qualification, you would use CustSale.CustID, CustSale.Name, etc. If there are duplicate unqualified column names in the subselect result table (e.g., if both Customer.CustID and Sale.CustID were in the result table), you would have to use explicit and unique column names for the view's columns, as described below.

---

[34] DB2/400 usually takes a much more efficient approach to the actual implementation of a subselect that references multiple tables. What's described here is the logical definition of how a multitable subselect works.

The Where clause of a subselect is optional. If a Where clause isn't specified, the subselect includes all the rows from the underlying base table or view (if a single table or view is specified on the From clause) or all combinations of rows (if multiple tables and/or views are specified on the From clause),[35] A Where clause can specify a very complex **search condition** (i.e., test), which we explore in the next chapter.

A subselect can also group together rows with a common value (e.g., customers in the same city) and calculate an aggregate value, such as a total or average, over one or more columns (e.g., an average credit limit). The Group By and Having clauses specify aggregation and are covered in the next chapter. For now, the main thing you need to know is that any view that has an outer[36] subselect that uses Group By or Having is a read-only view. For example, the following view contains one row for each city in which there's at least one customer, and each row has the city name and average customer discount for customers in that city:

```
Create View AppDta/CustDscAvg
     ( ShpCity,
       AvgDsc )
     As Select      ShpCity,
                     Avg( Discount )
          From      AppDta/Customer
        Group By ShpCity
```

This view might have rows that look like those in the following table:[37]

ShpCity	AvgDsc
Seattle	00.056
Eugene	00.009
Portland	00.012
Richmond	00.011
Loveland	00.003
Denver	00.024

[35] It's highly unusual to specify multiple tables or views on the From clause and not specify a Where clause.

[36] Subselects can be nested (i.e., the search condition of a subselect can contain another subselect).

[37] Notice in this example how a view (unlike many logical files created with DDS) doesn't specify a particular order to the rows. Ordering of rows in SQL is always specified when the rows are retrieved (i.e., on a Select statement), never when a base table or view is defined.

With a view like this, it wouldn't make sense to allow rows to be inserted or updated through the view — if that were possible, which row(s) would DB2/400 change in the Customer base table, for instance, if you updated the AvgDsc value of the Eugene row in the CustDscAvg view?

There are other cases in which a view is read-only: those in which the main (i.e., first) From clause specifies multiple tables and/or views or specifies another read-only view; those in which the first Select (following the As keyword) specifies the Distinct keyword or a column function, such as Max(Discount); those in which a nested subselect specifies the same base table as the outer subselect; and those in which the first Select doesn't contain at least one column that is derived directly (i.e., without an expression) from a column of the underlying base table. You can't use a read-only view as the target of an SQL Insert, Update, or Delete statement.

The CustDscAvg example above also illustrates how to code view column names explicitly. The column list (if any) immediately follows the view name and is enclosed in parentheses, with commas used to separate each column's entry. The view column names correspond positionally to the columns in the subselect result table. In this example, the correspondence is

View column name	Result table column
ShpCity	ShpCity
AvgDsc	Avg(Discount)

As with the Create Table statement, you can optionally specify both a long column name (equivalent to the DDS ALIAS name) and a system column name (equivalent to the standard field name in DDS). The previous example could be coded, with both types of names, as

```
Create View AppDta/CustDscAvg
    ( CustShipCity        For ShpCity,
      CustAverageDiscount For AvgDsc )
  As Select      ShpCity,
                 Avg( Discount )
        From     AppDta/Customer
        Group By ShpCity
```

You can't specify column data types, Not Null, or For Default for view columns. The data type of a view column is determined by the data type of the result table column. SQL/400 includes several functions (e.g., Decimal, SubStr) to convert from one column data type or length to another in a derived column. (Chapter 14 covers these SQL functions.)

The final options for a Create View statement are With Check Option[38] or With Local Check Option. These options restrict row insert and update operations through an updateable view that selects a subset of rows.[39] For example, the following view definition

---

[38] You can also code With Cascaded Check Option, which is equivalent to With Check Option.
[39] You can't specify either check option with a read-only view or a view that has nested sub selects.

```
Create View AppDta/CustCrd As
  Select  *
    From  AppDta/Customer
    Where CrdLimit >= 5000
  With Check Option
```

will not allow an Insert or Update that would create a row with CrdLimit < 5000. This prevents so-called "phantom updates" in which a row is inserted or updated through a view, but can't subsequently be retrieved through the view. When a view specifies either With Check Option or With Local Check Option and another view is defined over the view with the check option, the check option restrictions also apply to the dependent view. For example, to insert a row into the following view

```
Create View AppDta/CustCrdStl As
  Select  *
    From  AppDta/CustCrd
    Where ShpCity = 'Seattle'
```

the row must have CrdLimit ≥ 5000, regardless of whether the CustCrdStl view definition specifies With Check Option or With Local Check Option (or neither check option).

If a view defined over another view specifies With Check Option, all the lower-level views' search conditions must be met (in addition to the search condition, if any, specified on the view being defined). If a view defined over another view specifies With Local Check Option, only the search conditions of the lower-level views that specify a check option must be met.

DB2/400 does some additional processing when you insert or update rows through a view that has a direct or indirect check option, so you should be careful about using such views for file updates when performance is critical. On the other hand, check options provide a way to have DB2/400 enforce some validity constraints on column values. For example, you could create a view that includes all columns from the base table and that has a subselect that lists all the column constraints you want DB2/400 to enforce for updates to the base table. A partial example of this type of view might be

```
Create View AppDta/CustChk As
  Select  *
    From  AppDta/Customer
    Where CustID        >  0
      And Length( Name ) >  0
      And CrdLimit       >= 0
      And EntDate         >= '1990-01-01'
  With Check Option
```

Notice how the Where clause expresses conditions that all Customer rows should satisfy (e.g., negative credit limits aren't allowed). If all applications that update the Customer table use the CustChk view or a view defined over the CustChk view, you can prevent rows that don't satisfy the specified conditions. And because all rows will satisfy the CustChk selection criteria, you can access all of the base table rows through this view.

Now that we've covered how you create an SQL view, we can look at some more examples and compare them to the logical files created with DDS in Chapters 4 through 6. Keep in mind that, as mentioned earlier, SQL views never specify an ordering to rows, so none of the DDS logical file examples that were used just to illustrate keyed access paths have an equivalent view. For the same reason, in the comparative examples below, none of the SQL views have a keyed access path.

The compound conditions expressed with multiple DDS select/omit specifications are implemented with a view's subselect. The following example corresponds to the logical file defined in Figure 4.9. (This example uses some SQL syntax features covered in Chapter 14, such as Between and In, that can improve the readability of search conditions):

```
Create View AppDta/CustCrd As
  Select  *
    From  AppDta/Customer
    Where ShpCity <> 'Richmond'
      And CrdLimit Between 1000 And 9999
      And Status   In ( 'A', 'B', 'C' )
```

You can reorder and rename columns, as in the following example, which corresponds to the logical file defined in Figure 4.13. Note that this example also creates six-character column names suitable for use in an RPG/400 program.

```
Create View AppDta/CustRpg
     ( CsStrt,
       CsCity,
       CsSt,
       CsZip,
       CsCrRt,
       CsAttn,
       CsCnry,
       CustID )
  As Select ShpLine2,
            ShpCity,
            ShpState,
            ShpPsCd1,
            ShpPsCd2,
            ShpLine1,
            ShpCntry,
            CustID
         From AppDta/Customer
```

The following example illustrates how you can derive columns in an SQL view using substring and concatenation operations, comparable to the DDS SST and CONCAT keywords described in Chapter 5.

```
Create View AppDta/EmpNamPhn
    ( EmpID,
      PfxVoice,
      FullName )
   As Select EmpID,
             SubStr( PhnVoice, 5, 3 ),
             FstNam ConCat MdlInl ConCat LstNam
         From AppDta/Employee
```

SQL, unlike DDS, provides a way to strip trailing blanks before you concatenate fixed-length character columns. The following expression strips both leading and trailing blanks and puts a single blank between each part of the name:

```
      Strip( FstNam ) ConCat ' '
ConCat Strip( MdlInl ) ConCat ' '
ConCat Strip( LstNam )
```

As with the DDS join logical file shown in Figure 6.10, an SQL view can join a table to itself:

```
Create View AppDta/EmpMgr
    ( EmpID,
      LstNam,
      MgrEmpID,
      MgrLstNm )
   As Select  Emp.EmpID,
              Emp.LstNam,
              Emp.MgrEmpID,
              Mgr.LstNam
        From  Employee Emp,
              Employee Mgr
       Where Emp.MgrEmpID = Mgr.EmpID
```

The From clause for the subselect in this view lists the Employee table twice. To have unambiguous references to the appropriate role of the table (that is, either the first role, which is as the whole set of employees, or the second role, which is the set from which matching manager rows are retrieved), each Employee table reference in the From clause is followed by a **correlation name**, Emp and Mgr, respectively. The unique correlation names are used as column qualifiers instead of the ambiguous table name. SQL correlation names serve a similar function to the relative file number in join logical file DDS. You can use correlation names in any subselect, not just ones that specify a join. For nested or other long, complex subselects, short correlation names can make the SQL code more readable.[40]

SQL/400 views can be created over a maximum of 32 base tables, including both tables listed directly on the view's first From clause, as well as tables upon which views listed in the From clause are based. As a final example,

---

[40] However, you should not use cryptic one- or two-letter correlation names just to save a few keystrokes.

consider the Customer table defined in Figure 13.3 and the three tables
defined in Figure 13.9.

Figure 13.9
Sale, Part, and SaleItem
Table Definitions

```
Create Table AppDta/Sale
    ( OrderID    Dec( 7, 0 ) Not Null,
      SaleDate   Date        Not Null,
      SaleTot    Dec( 7, 2 ) Not Null,
      CustID     Dec( 7, 0 ) Not Null,
  Primary Key( OrderID ),
  Constraint SaleCustFK Foreign Key( CustID  )
    References Customer ( CustID )
    On Delete Cascade
    On Update Restrict )


Create Table AppDta/Part
    ( PartID    Dec(   7, 0 ) Not Null,
      PartDesc  Char( 50    ) Not Null,
  Primary Key( PartID ) )


Create Table AppDta/SaleItem
    ( OrderID    Dec( 7, 0 ) Not Null,
      PartID     Dec( 7, 0 ) Not Null,
      Qty        Dec( 7, 0 ) Not Null,
  Primary Key( OrderID, PartID ),
  Constraint SlItmOrdFK Foreign Key( OrderID  )
    References Sale ( OrderID )
    On Delete Cascade
    On Update Restrict
  Constraint SlItmPrtFK Foreign Key( PartID )
    References Part ( PartID )
    On Delete Restrict
    On Update Restrict )
```

Based on the Customer table in Figure 13.3 and the three tables defined
in Figure 13.9, the view in Figure 13.10 provides an equivalent join capability
to the four-file join logical file shown in Figure 6.17.

Sample data for the underlying tables is shown in Figures 6.3 (Customer), 6.4 (Sale), 6.15 (Part), and 6.16 (SaleItem); Figure 6.18 shows how
the resulting rows in the CusSalPrt view would appear to an application.[41]

As you can see, SQL has many ways to define the contents of a view.
You will learn more of them when you study the subselect further in Chapter 14. As you work with SQL/400 views, here's a tip that can help you test
them. Using ISQL, enter a statement such as the following. This Select statement displays all columns and rows of the specified view. You can browse the
result to see whether it's what you want.

```
Select * From CusSalPrt
```

[41] Note, however, that the SQL view by itself would not guarantee a particular row ordering,
as does the join logical file defined in Figure 6.17.

Figure 13.10
CusSalPrt View Definition

```
Create View AppDta/CusSalPrt
     ( CustID,
       Name,
       SaleDate,
       PartDesc )
   As Select  Customer.CustID,
              Name,
              SaleDate,
              PartDesc
         From  Customer,
               Sale,
               SaleItem,
               Part
        Where Customer.CustID = Sale.CustID
          And Sale.OrderID    = SaleItem.OrderID
          And SaleItem.PartID = Part.PartID
```

To define column headings or descriptive text for views and view columns, you can use the Label On and Comment On statements exactly as described for base tables, just specifying a view name instead of a table name. You can also use the CHGLFM (Change Logical File Member) command to change the descriptive text of the logical file member created when you create a view.

Creating an Index

Although you don't specify a particular order of rows on either the Create Table or the Create View statement, DB2/400 does use internal **indexes** for efficient row selection and ordering. DB2/400 automatically selects which indexes to use when a DML statement, such as Select, is executed or when an SQL cursor embedded in an HLL program is opened. When you specify a primary, unique, or foreign key constraint, DB2/400 creates or shares an internal index as part of the physical file created for a base table. You can create additional indexes using the SQL Create Index statement.

The Create Index statement is fairly simple — you code an index name (which can't be the same name as any base table, view, other index, or non-SQL file in the same collection) and then specify a single base table[42] and the columns over which the index should be created. The following example creates an index over the ShpCity and CrdLimit columns of the Customer table:

```
Create Index AppDta/CustCtyX01
  On AppDta/Customer
   ( ShpCity,
     CrdLimit Desc )
```

This index corresponds to the index created as part of the logical file defined in Figure 4.7. When you create an SQL index, DB2/400 creates a logical file with a keyed access path. But unlike a view, you cannot access an

---

[42] You can also create an SQL/400 index over a non-SQL, externally described physical file.

SQL index directly with any SQL DML statement.[43] In SQL, indexes are solely for the internal use of DB2/400, and their purpose is generally related to performance.

As this example shows, you can optionally add the Desc keyword after any column name to specify a descending order. You also can optionally specify Unique or Unique Where Not Null in an index definition:

```
Create Unique Index AppDta/BldRoomX
  On AppDta/Building
  ( BldName,
    RoomNbr )
```

The Unique keyword enforces unique key values, *including null*, the same way as explained for a base table primary key constraint. If you specify Unique Where Not Null, DB2/400 enforces unique values, *except for null*, as explained for base table unique key constraints.[44] Generally, you should use a primary or unique key constraint on the Create Table for a base table — which causes DB2/400 to create an internal index — rather than create a separate index with Unique or Unique Where Not Null. In DB2/400, independent indexes are primarily useful for two cases:

- Non-unique indexes (as a performance aid)
- Unique indexes in addition to the primary key of a base table

Note that you can only specify a single primary key constraint for each base table, so if you need to enforce a second fully unique key for the table, you need a Create Unique Index statement. Because you can specify multiple unique key constraints on a base table, there's little reason to use a Create Unique Where Not Null Index statement in SQL/400.[45]

---

[43] The logical file for an SQL/400 index has attributes that correspond to the MAXMBRS(1) and MAINT(*IMMED) parameters on the CRTLF command. The logical file has the same record format as the physical file that it's created over. Note that you can change the index maintenance of non-unique indexes to delayed (*DLY) or rebuild (*REBLD) by using the CHGLF (Change Logical File) command.

You can also use the CHGLF and CHGLFM commands to set the descriptive text for the logical file and its member, respectively. In V3R2 (and in the forthcoming V3R7 release for RISC systems), the Comment On statement lets you specify an SQL index. The SQL Label On statement (and Comment On statement in earlier releases) is not valid with SQL indexes.

You can also use HLL built-in I/O statements, as described in Chapter 7, to access the logical file created for an SQL index.

[44] The SQL Create Index keywords can be confusing because Unique Index corresponds to the Create Table Primary Key constraint, while Unique Where Not Null Index corresponds to the Create Table Unique constraint. It would have been better for Create Index to use Primary Key Index instead of Unique Index to maintain consistency with the Create Table statement.

[45] Note that this advice may not apply to versions of SQL that are part of other relational DBMS.

Indexes affect database performance both positively and negatively. In brief, indexes can speed data retrieval, but may slow updates due to the time DB2/400 spends updating the entries in the index(es) over a base table. Review the discussion on the performance impact of DB2/400 indexes in Chapter 4 before creating many SQL indexes over the same base table.

Dropping Collections, Tables, Views, and Indexes

To delete a database object, you use one of the following statements:

- `Drop Collection` *collection-name*
- `Drop Table` *table-name*
- `Drop View` *view-name*
- `Drop Index` *index-name*

Be careful with these statements! When you drop a collection, all objects in the collection are also deleted. When you drop a table, all dependent objects, including views, indexes, and foreign key constraints defined in other base tables that reference the table being dropped are also deleted. And when you drop a view, all dependent views are also deleted.[46]

Granting and Revoking Table and View Privileges

OS/400 has extensive facilities for controlling access to all objects on the system, including database files. Most of these facilities are controlled through CL commands, as discussed in Chapter 18. SQL/400 has some limited — but useful — access control features, as well.

In SQL terminology, a **privilege** is the authorization to use a table or view[47] in a certain way. If you have the appropriate authority, you can grant and revoke privileges using the SQL Grant and Revoke statements. You grant privileges to an OS/400 user profile object, and then anyone who signs on to the AS/400 under that user profile has the authority you've granted.

Let's suppose you've created a Customer table (and are the table's owner) and you want to grant the user profile SmithJH the ability to retrieve rows from this table. You could enter a statement such as

```
Grant Select
  On  Customer
  To  SmithJH
```

---

[46] This is opposite to the way the comparable DLTF (Delete File) command works. DLTF requires that all dependent objects be deleted first. Note, however, that the DLTLIB (Delete Library) command works like Drop Collection and deletes all contained objects automatically.

[47] Or SQL **package**. Packages are a mechanism for executing SQL statements in a distributed application, and are discussed in Chapter 15.

In a Grant statement, you list the privileges (or the All keyword), then the On keyword followed by one or more table and/or view names, then the To keyword followed by one or more user profile names (or the Public keyword). Here's a more comprehensive example:

```
Grant Select,
      Insert
  On  Customer,
      CustCrd
  To  SmithJH,
      JonesRK
```

To revoke privileges, you use a Revoke statement that has a similar syntax to the Grant statement:

```
Revoke Select,
       Insert
  On   Customer,
       CustCrd
  From SmithJH,
       JonesRK
```

Figures 13.11 and 13.12 list the SQL privileges you can grant to tables and views, respectively, as well as the meaning of the privilege keywords and the corresponding OS/400 object authorities.

Figure 13.11

SQL Table Privileges

Keyword	SQL statement privileges that are granted or revoked	Corresponding OS/400 authorities to physical file
Alter	Alter Table, Comment On, and Label On	*OBJALTER
Delete	Delete	*OBJOPR and *DLT
Index	Create Index	*OBJALTER
Insert	Insert	*OBJOPR and *ADD
References	Add a foreign key constraint that references this table as parent	*OBJREF
Select	Select and Create View	*OBJOPR and *READ
Update	Update	*OBJOPR and *UPD
With Grant Option	Grant, Revoke, Alter Table, Comment On, Label On, Create Index, and add a foreign key constraint that references this table as parent	*OBJMGT

Figure 13.12
SQL View Privileges

Keyword	SQL statement privileges that are granted or revoked	Valid for views	Corresponding OS/400 authorities to logical file	Corresponding OS/400 authorities to referenced physical or logical files
Alter	Comment On and Label On	Yes	*OBJALTER	none
Delete	Delete	If not read-only	*OBJOPR and *DLT	*DLT
Index		Not valid	none	none
Insert	Insert	If view is not read-only, and allows inserts	*OBJOPR and *ADD	*ADD
References		Allowed, but ignored	*OBJREF	none
Select	Select and Create View	Yes	*OBJOPR and *READ	*READ
Update	Update	If not read-only	*OBJOPR and *UPD	*UPD
With Grant Option	Grant, Revoke, Comment On, and Label On	Yes	*OBJMGT	none

Note that authorities are granted to referenced logical and physical files only if the user profile doesn't already have explicit or public rights to the referenced file. Also note that the Revoke statement does not revoke any authorities to file objects referenced by the view (because the user profile might be intended to have these authorities regardless of the authorities to the referencing file). Chapter 18 explains the OS/400 object authorities in more detail.

The All keyword can be used instead of a list of privileges, and the implicit list contains those privileges that you're authorized to grant and that are relevant to the type of SQL object (e.g., the Index privilege applies to base tables but not views).

The Public keyword is an alternative to a user profile name and, if used, refers to the privileges that are available to all user profiles who don't have any other explicit authority (i.e., granted to their user profile by name) to the table or view.

On the Grant statement, you can optionally specify With Grant Option following the list of user profiles. This clause permits the user profiles (or

Public) listed on the Grant statement to themselves grant privileges on the listed tables and views, as well as to perform operations allowed with the Alter and References privileges.

The SQL Catalog

As described in Chapter 1, an OS/400 physical or logical file object contains descriptive information about the structure of the file. This information includes such things as a description of the file's record format (i.e., field definitions) and a list of the members in the file. Because DB2/400 creates a physical file for an SQL/400 table and a logical file for an SQL/400 view or index, much of the definition of a table or view is stored as part of the database file object. But DB2/400 also has several system files that store a copy of some of this information, as well as additional information about database files. For example, several DB2/400 system files contain the long names for SQL tables, views, indexes, and packages.

To conform with industry SQL standards, IBM supplies with DB2/400 a set of SQL views over the system files. Figure 13.13 lists these views, which are collectively referred to as the **catalog**.

Figure 13.13
SQL/400 Catalog Views

View	Contents
SysColumns	Column definitions
SysCst	Constraint definitions
SysCstCol	Information about columns referenced in a constraint
SysCstDep	Constraint table dependencies
SysIndexes	Index definitions
SysKeyCst	Primary, unique, and foreign key constraints
SysKeys	Information about index keys
SysPackage	Information about SQL packages
SysParms	Information about procedure parameters
SysProc	Information about procedures
SysRefCst	Referential (foreign key) constraint definitions
SysTables	Table and view definitions
SysViewDep	View table dependencies
SysViews	View definitions

Every AS/400 has one set of these views stored in the IBM-supplied QSYS2 library. The underlying system files (and consequently the views in the QSYS2 library) contain information about all SQL tables, views, indexes, constraints, and packages, as well as non-SQL physical and logical files on an

AS/400. Because the catalog views are just like any other SQL view, anyone with the proper authority can retrieve data from the catalog. For example, you can use ISQL to produce a list of all SQL/400 tables on the system by entering the following statement. This statement produces a display like the one shown in Figure 13.14.

```
Select     Sys_DName,
           Name,
           Label
  From     QSys2/SysTables
  Where    Type = 'T'
  Order By Sys_DName,
           Name
```

Figure 13.14

Sample Output From Querying the SysTables Catalog View

```
                                    Display Data
                                       Data width . . . . . . . :        75
    Position to line . . . . .   _____    Shift to column . . . . . .  _____
    ....+....1....+....2....+....3....+....4....+....5....+....6....+....7....+
    SYS_DNAME    NAME        LABEL
    APPDTA       BUILDING    Buildings
    APPDTA       COURSE      Courses
    APPDTA       CUSTOMER    Customers
    APPDTA       CUSTOMERBKP Customers -- Backup copy
    APPDTA       CUSTUPD     Customer updates
    APPDTA       CUSTUPDBKP  Customer updates -- Backup copy
    APPDTA       EMPLOYEE    Employees
    APPDTA       PART        Parts
    APPDTA       SALE        Sales
    APPDTA       SALEITEM    Sale items
    APPDTA       SUPPLIER    Suppliers
    QSYS2        SQL_LANGUAG
    QSYS2        SYSPARMS
    QSYS2        SYSPROCS
    ********  End of data  ********

                                                                    Bottom

    F3=Exit       F12=Cancel       F19=Left       F20=Right       F21=Split
```

When you use the Create Collection statement, DB2/400 also creates a similar set of catalog views in the new collection. The catalog views in a collection have the same view names and the same columns as those in the QSYS2 library but include only entries for objects in the same collection as the catalog. You can query these views to get information on the tables, views, and indexes in a particular collection. The *DB2/400 SQL Reference* manual lists all SQL catalog view definitions. You can also display or list the catalog view definitions by entering the following statement in ISQL. The Where clause selects only rows with a table name that begins with SYS, the common prefix of all the SQL catalog tables.[48]

---

[48] The Like 'SYS%' condition matches any character string that begins with SYS and has anything (represented by the % wild card) following SYS.

```
Select      *
  From      QSys2/SysColumns
  Where     DbName = 'QSYS2'
    And     TbName Like 'SYS%'
  Order By TbName,
```

Coding Suggestions

- Store most DDL statements to create production collections, tables, views, and indexes in source members and execute them using the RUNSQLSTM command.

  - Use a separate source file for each type of SQL object, and use meaningful source file names such as the following:
    SQLCLCSRC   — SQL statements to create collections
    SQLTBLSRC   — SQL statements to create tables
    SQLVIEWSRC — SQL statements to create views
    SQLIDXSRC   — SQL statements to create indexes

  - Use the name of the SQL object you're creating as the source member name

  - Enter a source member description that's the description of the SQL object

  - Place comments at the beginning of your SQL source to describe the object being created

  - Use a consistent order for statements such as Create, Label On, and Comment On in a source member

  - Use spaces, blank lines, and separator line comments to improve the readability of your source code

  - Align column names, data types, compound search conditions, etc, on multiline statements for readability

- Establish and follow a good naming convention for all SQL names. Review the "Naming convention" and "Coding Suggestions" sections in Chapter 3 for guidelines to follow when setting up a naming standard.

  - Use only letters (A-Z) and digits (0-9) in names of collections, tables, views, indexes, column names (both long and short), and constraints. Review the "Coding Suggestions" section at the end of Chapter 2 if any SQL object may be accessed using HLL built-in I/O operations.

  - Avoid SQL and COBOL reserved words (e.g., ORDER) as names

- Use the Label On and Comment On SQL statements to add descriptive text and column headings for tables, views, and columns

- Use the CHGLF command to add descriptive text for SQL indexes

- Use the CHGPFM and CHGLFM commands to add descriptive text for members of SQL tables, views, and indexes

- Code the *long-name* For *system-column-name* option on Create Table and Create View statements for any column whose short name isn't clear
- Use standard column definitions for the same type of column (e.g., use Char(50) for all columns that contain descriptive text). Review the discussion in Chapter 3 on field and column data types
    - Generally, for numeric columns, use Dec(p, s) where p is an odd number
- On the Create Table statement, code the Not Null option for all columns, except columns that should accept the system null value
    - Generally, code Not Null for unique and foreign key fields
- On the Create Table statement, code the Default clause for columns for which the DB2/400 defaults aren't acceptable
- For most tables, define one or more fields as a primary key constraint, and use the primary key as the main way you identify records
- Code any key constraints after all column definitions on the Create Table statement; use a consistent order — e.g., primary key, followed by unique key(s), followed by foreign key(s)
- Use the Constraint *constraint-name* option to assign a name to all unique and foreign key constraints; optionally assign names to primary key constraints, as well
    - Use a consistent suffix (e.g., PK for primary key, UK for unique key, and FK for foreign key) in constraint names
- To simplify object management, including save/restore operations, create views and indexes in the same collection as the based-on tables and views
- Consider the update, as well as retrieval, performance implications to decide which indexes to create (review Chapter 4)

Chapter Summary

SQL is an industry-standard language for defining and manipulating database objects. SQL/400 is the DB2/400 implementation of SQL. SQL includes a Data Definition Language (DDL) as well as a Data Manipulation Language (DML). You can enter most SQL statements interactively or embed them in HLL programs. SQL/400 statements can also be executed from a source file member using the RUNSQLSTM command.

The following table summarizes the correspondence between SQL/400 objects (and elements of objects) and their underlying OS/400 objects (and elements).

SQL/400 object or element	OS/400 object type or element	Attributes and notes
Collection	Library (*LIB)	• Contains: — QSQJRN journal — QSQJRN*nnnn* journal receiver — 12 view logical files for the collection's catalog
Base Table	Physical File (*FILE)	• Single member • Externally described • Has a keyed access path for each primary, unique, and foreign key constraint
View	Logical File (*FILE)	• Single member • Externally described • No keyed access path
Column (of a base table or view)	Field (in a file)	
Row (in a base table or view)	Record (in a file)	
Index	Logical File (*FILE)	• Single member • Externally described • Keyed access path over one physical file member
Catalog	Set of physical and (view) logical files	

The Create Collection statement creates an SQL collection, which is an OS/400 library object, to contain SQL tables, views, indexes, packages, and other, non-SQL objects.

The Create Table statement creates a base table, which is a DB2/400 externally described, physical file object. A base table contains the actual data for an application. Data in SQL tables is stored as rows. Each table definition specifies one or more columns, which represent different properties (e.g., customer name) of an application object. Each column has a name, data type, and explicit or implicit size. A column may optionally have a long name (alias) and explicit default value. A column can be defined to allow or prohibit the null placeholder.

A base table can optionally have one primary key constraint, one or more unique key constraints, and one or more foreign key (or referential) constraints. A primary key constraint defines the table's primary key column(s), which provide a unique, non-null value to identify each row in the table. A unique key is similar to a primary key, except a unique key permits a key column to be null. A foreign key constraint enforces the referential integrity rule that a row in a dependent table that specifies a non-null value for the primary key in another table must always specify a primary key value that actually exists in the parent (referenced) table.

The Label On and Comment On statements can be used to specify descriptive text for tables, views, and columns. Label On can also be used to specify column headings of up to three lines.

The Alter Table statement adds or drops a primary, unique, or foreign key constraint on a base table. In V3R2, V3R6, and later releases of DB2/400, the Alter Table also lets you add, drop, or change a base table column.

The Create View statement creates an SQL view, which is an externally described, logical file object. A view is a table-like object that doesn't actually contain data but that provides an alternative way to access data in underlying base tables. Views can be defined over base tables or other views. Among the ways a view can be used are to select a subset of rows, to select a subset of columns, to derive new columns, and to combine rows from multiple tables. A view definition explicitly or implicitly lists the columns in the view and optionally specifies a subselect expression to select the columns and rows to be included in the view. In most cases, a view can be used just as if it were a base table containing the selected rows and columns, although some views are read only.

A subselect is an SQL expression that defines a result table derived from one or more base tables or views. A subselect lists the columns of the result table and optionally specifies a search condition that determines the rows to be included in the result table. (A result table is a conceptual table and isn't stored as a separate table on disk or in memory.)

A view can optionally specify a check option to prevent row insert or update operations that would create a row that is not retrievable through the view. Check options can be used to enforce some types of data integrity.

The Create Index statement creates an SQL index, which is a logical file object with a keyed access path. An SQL index is created over a single base table and specifies one or more key columns. DB2/400 uses indexes to improve performance, and SQL DML statements cannot directly use an SQL index to access data.

The Drop Collection, Drop Table, Drop View, and Drop Index statements delete the respective SQL object and all dependent or contained objects.

The Grant and Revoke Statements grant and revoke authorization to specified user profiles to perform certain operations on tables and views. When you use a Grant or Revoke statement, you assign or remove OS/400 object authorities to the physical and logical files that are the DB2/400 objects for the specified tables and views.

DB2/400 maintains a set of system files that contain information about all SQL and non-SQL database files on the AS/400. SQL/400 provides a set of views over these files that is known as the SQL catalog. Each collection also has a similar set of views that include information about only the objects in the collection. You can use SQL/400 (or other means) to query any of the catalog files.

Key Terms

base table
catalog
collection
column
constraint
correlation name
Data Definition Language
    (DDL)
Data Manipulation Language
    (DML)

database
foreign key constraint
index
Interactive SQL (ISQL)
null capable
primary key constraint
privilege
referential constraint
result table
row

schema
search condition
subselect
system column name
unique key constraint
view

Exercises

1. For each of the following four SQL database objects, describe their purpose and the type of OS/400 object(s) created for each one:

   - Collection
   - Table
   - View
   - Index

2. Give one example of the appropriate Create statement to create each of the four SQL database objects listed in Exercise 1.

3. Code the Create Table, Label On, and Comment On statements for a base table to hold the following employee information:

   - Identification number
   - Name (last, first, middle initial)
   - Birth date
   - Address (street, city, state, postal code)
   - Identification number of employee's manager
   - Annual salary
   - Health insurance plan (coded)

Be sure to consider the following:

   - Appropriate table and column names
   - Column data types and lengths
   - Default values
   - The table's primary key
   - The table's unique and/or foreign key(s), if any
   - Good documentation

4. Explain the relationship between the following four database items:

   - A base table primary key constraint (specified with the Create Table or Alter Table statement)
   - A base table unique key constraint (specified with the Create Table or Alter Table statement)
   - An SQL Unique index (specified with the Create Index statement)
   - An SQL Unique When Not Null index (specified with the Create Index statement)

Exercises Continued

Exercises continued

5. Code the Create View for a view that contains a subset of the records in the Customer table (Figure 13.3). Selected rows should satisfy the following conditions:

   Status must not be X. Postal Code 1 must be 23225, 23227, or 23229, or the credit limit must be between 500 and 1000 (inclusive). The view should have the same columns as the Customer table.

6. Modify the definition of the CusSalPrt (join) view presented in Figure 13.10 so that

   a. only items that were ordered in quantities of two or more are included in the view's rows, and

   b. if an order doesn't include any items ordered in quantities of two or more, the order itself isn't in the view's rows, and

   c. if a customer doesn't have any orders that include items ordered in quantities of two or more, the customer isn't in the view's rows.

   Use the definitions in Figures 13.3 and 13.9 for the Customer, Sale, SaleItem, and Part tables.

   Hint: The required modifications may be simpler than you first think.

7. Explain why you think SQL/400 views that are based on more than one table are read only.

8. Code the Create Index for an index that SQL/400 can use to improve performance when retrieving rows from the Customer table (Figure 13.3) in order by state (major key) and city (minor key).

9. Why do you think SQL tables and views don't have explicit indexes to provide a particular ordering to rows? *Hint: Consider the principles of the relational database model discussed in Chapter 9.* List the advantages and disadvantages of the SQL approach versus the DDS approach (which does allow explicit indexes on physical and logical files).

10. Code the Grant statement to allow the user profile HarrisAK to read rows from and insert rows into the Customer and Employee tables.

11. Explain two ways you might use the SQL catalog to assist in application development and documentation.

Chapter 14

SQL/400 Data Manipulation Language

Chapter Overview

In the previous chapter we learned how to use SQL's data definition language (DDL) to create SQL base tables that contain data and SQL views that provide alternative ways to access data in base tables. In this chapter we begin our study of SQL's **data manipulation language (DML)**, which provides data retrieval and update capabilities for a relational database such as DB2/400. The four main DML statements we cover in this chapter are Select, Insert, Update, and Delete. We also delve deeply into SQL subselects, which are at the heart of SQL's set-at-a-time retrieval and update facilities. This chapter also introduces SQL Lock Table, Commit, and Rollback, three statements that can be used during data manipulation to help preserve database and transaction integrity.

Introduction to DML

As Chapter 13 explained, SQL lets you define and manipulate data represented in table-like form. SQL base tables contain actual data, and SQL views — which are structured like tables, with columns and rows — provide an alternative way to access the data. SQL's data representation and manipulation features are based on the relational model presented in Chapter 9. The relational model — and SQL — provide data manipulation capabilities that include not only row-at-a-time operations but also **set-at-a-time** operations. For example, you can retrieve and display a specific row using a Select statement such as the following:

```
Select  *
  From  Customer
  Where CustID = 499320
```

Or you can retrieve and display a set of rows with this statement:

```
Select  *
  From  Customer
  Where ShpCity = 'Seattle'
```

Both examples retrieve a set of rows; however, if CustID values are unique (e.g., CustID is the table's primary key), the first statement never returns more than a single row. (It might return no rows — the empty set — if there's no customer with the specified customer ID value.) The second example might return any of the following results:

- No rows — if there are no customers in Seattle
- One row — if there's exactly one customer in Seattle
- Multiple rows — if there are two or more customers in Seattle

As you can see, a set of rows can have zero, one, or more rows. The important thing is that SQL has the ability to express conditions (such as ShpCity = 'Seattle') that define a multirow set and then retrieve or update that set in a single statement.

Another important aspect of SQL is that previously defined column names (e.g., ShpCity) are used to identify the specific data that's retrieved, changed, or used in comparisons. With DB2/400, the information about tables and columns, such as a column's name, data type, and size, is stored in the OS/400 file object's header, as well as in the SQL catalog (as we discussed in Chapter 13). These stored descriptions enable SQL database routines to determine how to access the appropriate data without requiring further definition in a utility or HLL program.[1] This same information also supports DB2/400's ISQL facility and the RUNSQLSTM command so you can execute SQL DML statements without having to write an HLL program.

As we discussed in Chapter 13, you can execute SQL statements in a variety of ways. In this chapter we look at statements that can be executed dynamically. **Dynamic execution** of an SQL statement means that you construct a statement as a text string and have the SQL routines interpret and execute the text string. Probably the most common way to dynamically execute an SQL statement is to enter it on the ISQL display, as shown in Figure 13.2. Another means of dynamic execution is to put one or more SQL statements in a source member and process the source member as input to the RUNSQLSTM command. In Chapter 15, we look at a third method of dynamic SQL statement execution, in which you use HLL string operations to construct an SQL statement in a program variable and use the SQL Execute Immediate statement to execute the string contained in the variable. An important restriction of any dynamic method of execution is that the SQL statement itself can't contain references to HLL program variables.

An alternative way of executing SQL statements — known as **static execution** — lets you code HLL variables within an SQL statement, thus providing the ability to change some of the selection or other values (e.g., customer ID) between subsequent executions of the same statement.[2] Static execution

---

[1] DB2/400 is unique among DBMS in that the information about columns is stored in both the OS/400 physical or logical file object's header (as described in Chapter 1) and the SQL catalog. As a result, this information is also available to AS/400 utilities and HLL compilers, thus providing similar capabilities for non-SQL database files as the SQL catalog provides for tables and views. See Chapter 7 for more information about how the AS/400 HLL compilers use DB2/400 physical and logical files.

[2] The use of "static" and "dynamic" to describe the two ways you can execute an SQL statement may seem counterintuitive because static execution is the method that lets you use

is possible only when an SQL statement is **embedded** (i.e., coded) in an HLL program and then translated into executable form (i.e., machine language) as part of the program creation process.[3] When the compiled program runs, the translated SQL statement is executed as part of the program's execution. Because an SQL statement that you code for static execution is always translated before execution, you can include HLL variables in a static SQL statement — the translation takes care of the steps needed to get a variable's value into the SQL statement when it's executed. We'll defer the details of embedded SQL until Chapter 15; however, a simple example will make clear the difference between a dynamic and a static form of an SQL statement. The following statement shows the second Select example above, but uses the SlcCusCity HLL program variable (instead of a literal, such as 'Seattle') to hold the city value used in the Where clause.[4]

```
Select   *
  From   Customer
  Where ShpCity = :SlcCusCity
```

Notice the colon (:) at the beginning of SlcCusCity — that's what tells the SQL translator that SlcCusCity is a program variable name, not a column name.

Most types of SQL statements can be executed either as a dynamic or as a static statement.[5] It's easier to learn the basics of SQL DML by first using examples without program variables and without worrying about other aspects of embedding SQL statements in an HLL program. So in this chapter, we look at examples that can be executed dynamically, for instance by using ISQL. Keep in mind that in most places where a literal is used in an example,

program variables and perhaps appears to be the more flexible method. With static execution, however, a statement's structure is always the same (i.e., static). The only things that may change between executions of the statement are the values of program variables used in the statement. With dynamic execution, on the other hand, the entire statement can be constructed as a string, and thus, the structure of the statement is changeable (i.e., dynamic).

Note also that you can obviously change a selection or other value in a dynamically executed SQL statement by simply keying in another statement or constructing a new string in an HLL program. In an HLL program, however, coding dynamic SQL is often more complicated and less efficient than coding a static form of an SQL statement that includes program variables.

[3] With embedded SQL, the program creation process involves two steps. The first step is precompilation, which translates embedded SQL statements into HLL Call (and other) statements. The second step is compilation. This process is explained more fully in Chapter 15.

[4] Note that this example could be used only as part of an embedded SQL cursor, which is covered in Chapter 15. As we'll see in the next chapter, the Select Into statement is a similar embedded statement that is not part of a cursor. However, the Select Into statement must never return more than one row, and this example doesn't meet that restriction.

[5] Not all SQL statements can be executed either way, however. For example, the Connect statement can be executed only as a static statement or interactively, through ISQL; the Create Schema statement can be executed only dynamically with the RUNSQLSTM command.

the same statement could be embedded in an HLL program using a variable to provide more flexibility.

The four main (non-embedded) DML statements are

- **Select** — to retrieve rows from one or more tables
- **Insert** — to add new rows to a table
- **Update** — to update column values in a table's rows
- **Delete** — to delete rows in a table

All four statements can be used with base tables or views, although Insert, Update, and Delete require that a view be updatable (i.e., not read only). The Select statement can retrieve rows from one or more underlying base tables; however, the Insert, Update, and Delete statements can update only one underlying base table in a single statement.

Retrieving Rows with the Select Statement

The SQL Select statement retrieves rows from one or more tables or views. If you enter a Select statement using ISQL, the results are displayed at your terminal (or printed or written to database file). To use a Select statement, you list the columns you want in the result, identify the tables and views to access, and specify the selection criteria for returned rows. You also can group and order rows. SQL combines the information you specify on the Select statement with information in the file object headers and catalog to determine what to retrieve and how to carry out the retrieval. The basic structure of a Select statement is

```
Select     select-list
   From       table-list
   Where      search-condition
   Group By grouping-column-list
   Having     search-condition
   Order By order-by-column-list
```

Mastering the Select statement, which is powerful and can take quite complex forms, is the key to using SQL successfully. Many of the Select statement's forms are similar to forms of other SQL DML statements, such as Update and Declare Cursor. And as we saw in Chapter 13, the subselect (which is part of a complete Select statement) is central to defining SQL views.

The next series of examples work through each part of the Select statement. Many of the examples use the four tables shown in Figures 14.1 through 14.4.

Figure 14.1

Sample Customer
Base Table

```
Create Table AppDta/Customer
    ( CustID   Dec(   7, Ø ) Not Null,
      Name     Char( 30   ) Not Null,
      ShpCity  Char( 30   ),
      Discount Dec(   5, 3 ),
  Primary Key( CustID ) )
```

CustID	Name	ShpCity	Discount
133568	Smith Mfg.	Portland	.050
246900	Bolt Co.	Eugene	.020
275978	Ajax Inc.	Albany	\<null\>
499320	Adapto	Portland	.000
499921	Bell Bldg.	Eugene	.100
518980	Floradel	Seattle	.000
663456	Alpine Inc.	Seattle	.010
681065	Telez Co.	Albany	.000
687309	Nautilus	Portland	.050
781010	Udapto Mfg.	Seattle	.000
888402	Seaworthy	Albany	.010
890003	AA Products	Portland	.010
905011	Wood Bros.	Eugene	.010

We begin with an example of the simplest form of Select statement, which you've already seen in previous chapters.

```
Select *
  From Customer
```

The asterisk (*) that follows the Select keyword means "all columns."[6] The From clause specifies one or more base tables or views to be used — in this case, the Customer table. A table or view name in the From clause can optionally be qualified with a collection name (e.g., AppDta/Customer).[7] Because in this example no further restrictions are placed on what's retrieved (i.e., there is no Where clause), all columns for all rows are retrieved.

[6] The * represents all columns that exist at the time the statement is prepared. When an SQL statement is executed interactively, it's prepared and executed at essentially the same time. However, for static execution, the statement is prepared during the translation step (as part of program creation) and is executed some time later. If a column is added to a table or view after the statement is prepared (e.g., by an Alter Table statement), the new column will not be included in the implicit column list until the statement is prepared again.

[7] The examples in this chapter use unqualified table and view names to streamline the code and make it easier to digest.

Figure 14.2
Sample Sale Base Table

```
Create Table AppDta/Sale
    ( OrderID  Dec(  7, Ø ) Not Null,
      CustID   Dec(  7, Ø ) Not Null,
      TotAmt   Dec( 11, 2 ) Not Null,
      SaleDate Date          Not Null,
      ShpDate  Date,
   Constraint SalePK     Primary Key( OrderID ),
   Constraint SaleCustFK Foreign Key( CustID  )
     References Customer ( CustID )
     On Delete Cascade
     On Update Restrict )
```

OrderID	CustID	TotAmt	SaleDate	ShpDate
234112	499320	35.00	1996-05-01	1996-05-15
234113	888402	278.75	1996-05-01	1996-05-04
234114	499320	78.90	1996-05-03	\<null\>
234115	890003	1000.00	1996-05-04	1996-05-10
234116	246900	678.00	1996-05-04	1996-05-08
234117	133568	550.00	1996-05-05	1996-05-08
234118	905011	89.50	1996-05-05	1996-05-10
234119	499320	201.00	1996-05-05	\<null\>
234120	246900	399.70	1996-05-06	1996-05-08

Figure 14.3
Sample Employee
Base Table

```
Create Table AppDta/Employee
    ( EmpID    Dec(  7, Ø ) Not Null,
      FstNam   Char( 20     ),
      MdlInl   Char(  1     ),
      LstNam   Char( 3Ø     ) Not Null,
      MgrEmpID Dec(  7, Ø ),
    Constraint EmpPK Primary Key( EmpID ) )
```

EmpID	FstNam	MdlInl	LstNam	MgrEmpID
104681	Barb	L	Gibbens	898613
227504	Greg	J	Zimmerman	668466
668466	Dave	R	Bernard	709453
898613	Trish	S	Faubion	668466
899001	Rick	D	Castor	898613

Figure 14.4
Sample NullDate
Base Table

```
Create Table AppDta/NullDate
     ( NullDate Date )
```

Search Conditions and Predicates

The previous example retrieved all customers, but suppose you want only the customers from Seattle? As you've seen in previous chapters, this can be accomplished by adding a Where clause to restrict the retrieved rows:

```
Select  *
  From  Customer
  Where ShpCity - 'Seattle'
```

The simplest Where clause contains an SQL **search condition** that is a single SQL **predicate**, as above. All rows for which the predicate is true are retrieved.

When you need to retrieve a single, specific row with a Select statement, you can specify a search condition with a primary key value, as in the following statement:

```
Select  *
  From  Customer
  Where CustID = 499320
```

A Where clause with a primary key column lets you use SQL for single-row operations, comparable to an HLL built-in I/O operation, such as an RPG IV Chain or a COBOL/400 Read statement.

The Where clause also may contain a search condition that is two or more SQL predicates connected with And or Or. The following example shows a search condition with the conjunction (i.e., connected by And) of two predicates:

```
Select  *
  From  Customer
  Where ShpCity  = 'Seattle'
    And Discount > 0
```

To negate a predicate, you can specify the Not logical operator at the beginning of any predicate or before predicates connected by And or Or. To use Not to negate a compound condition, place parentheses around the condition. The following condition is true if ShpCity is not Seattle (and not null) or if Discount is 0 (and not null):

```
Not ( ShpCity = 'Seattle' And Discount > 0 )
```

You can also use parentheses to specify the order of evaluation for a compound condition that has both And's and Or's. In the following example

```
( ShpCity = 'Seattle' Or Discount > 0 ) And TotAmt > 100
```

SQL first evaluates the compound condition ShpCity = 'Seattle' Or Discount > 0. The result of the predicates connected by Or is then And'd with the value of the last predicate, TotAmt > 100. Without parentheses, SQL evaluates negated expressions first, then predicates connected by And, and finally predicates connected by Or. Thus, the following example

```
ShpCity = 'Seattle' Or Discount > 0 And TotAmt > 100
```

is evaluated as

```
ShpCity = 'Seattle' Or ( Discount > 0 And TotAmt > 100 )
```

Note that this is not equivalent to the previous example, where we put parentheses around the predicates connected by Or.

An SQL predicate is a logical condition that is true, false, or unknown for a given row. A predicate is unknown if it involves a comparison and one or both of the values being compared is null. (Recall from Chapter 13 that a null-capable column — one defined without the Not Null clause — may be set to null rather than contain a valid value.) For example, the value of the predicate ShpCity = 'Seattle' is unknown if ShpCity is null. In general, for any comparison

expression₁ = expression₂

the result is unknown if expression₁, expression₂, or both are null. This rule applies whether the comparison operator is not equal, greater than, or any of the other possibilities.

To negate a predicate with Not or to combine predicates with And and Or, SQL uses **three-valued logic** (Figure 14.5) rather than conventional two-valued logic.

This somewhat unusual form of logic is necessary to handle a predicate whose value may be unknown. As the table in Figure 14.5 shows, when you connect two predicates (p and q in the table) with And, if the value of either predicate is unknown, the conjunction is also unknown. A Select statement's result table contains only those rows for which the Where clause search condition is true. If the search condition is false or unknown, the row is omitted. So if a row had a null ShpCity column and its Discount column were 0.05, the search condition

```
Where ShpCity  = 'Seattle'
  And Discount > 0
```

would evaluate to unknown, and the row would not be selected.

A Select statement can retrieve rows using views as well as base tables in the From clause (recall from Chapter 13 that views are SQL objects that

Figure 14.5
SQL Three-Valued Logic

p	q	Not p	p And q	p Or q
True	True	False	True	True
True	False	False	False	True
True	Unknown	False	Unknown	True
False	True	True	False	True
False	False	True	False	False
False	Unknown	True	False	Unknown
Unknown	True	Unknown	Unknown	True
Unknown	False	Unknown	False	Unknown
Unknown	Unknown	Unknown	Unknown	Unknown

define a way to access data from one or more underlying base tables). When you specify a view in a Select statement, DB2/400 merges the view specifications with the Select statement specifications to produce the result table. For example, consider the view defined by the following Create View statement:

```
Create View  CustStl
  As Select  *
       From  Customer
       Where ShpCity = 'Seattle'
```

The CustStl view uses a form of the Select statement (known as a sub-select) to specify that the view contains only rows from the underlying Customer table that meet the specified condition: ShpCity = 'Seattle'. You can use this view in a DML Select statement that further restricts the returned rows to customers who get a discount.

```
Select  *
  From  CustStl
  Where Discount > 0
```

This Select statement's result table contains only rows from the Customer table for Seattle customers who get a discount. In general, when both the view and the Select statement contain Where clauses, SQL tests the conjunction (i.e., And) of the two search conditions.

Generally, a list of the columns you want in the result table follows the Select keyword. As mentioned earlier, when you specify * following the Select keyword, it means "all columns" in the result table. Rather than specifying *, you can list the columns you want, separated by commas.

```
Select  CustID,
        Name
  From  Customer
  Where ShpCity = 'Seattle'
```

When the select list doesn't include the primary key column(s), the result table may contain duplicate rows. For example, the following Select statement returns one row for each customer

```
Select  ShpCity
  From  Customer
```

but because only the ShpCity column is in the result table, there may be multiple rows with identical city values. To eliminate duplicate rows from the result table, you can follow the Select keyword with the Distinct keyword, as in

```
Select  Distinct ShpCity
  From  Customer
```

which displays a list of the cities (with no duplicates) in which there is at least one customer.

Literals, Expressions, and Scalar Functions

The select list that follows the Select keyword can also include literals, expressions, functions, and SQL **special registers**.[8] For example, the following Select statement uses both literals and an arithmetic expression

```
Select  Name,
        ' has a discount of ',
        Discount * 100,
        '%'
  From  Customer
 Where Discount > 0
```

to retrieve the result table shown in Figure 14.6.

Figure 14.6

Sample Retrieval Using Literals and Expressions

```
Smith Mfg.     has a discount of    5.000      %
Bolt Co.       has a discount of    2.000      %
Ajax Inc.      has a discount of    <null>     %
Adapto         has a discount of     .000      %
Bell Bldg.     has a discount of   10.000      %
Floradel       has a discount of     .000      %
Alpine Inc.    has a discount of    1.000      %
Telez Co.      has a discount of     .000      %
Nautilus       has a discount of    5.000      %
Udapto Mfg.    has a discount of     .000      %
Seaworthy      has a discount of    1.000      %
AA Products    has a discount of    1.000      %
Wood Bros.     has a discount of    1.000      %
```

SQL supports standard four-function arithmetic (+, −, *, and /), as well as exponentiation (**) for numeric values. You can also use addition and subtraction with date/time columns and literals, which we look at in a moment.

[8] SQL special registers are predefined values that you specify with the keywords Current Date, Current Server, Current Time, Current Timestamp, Current Timezone, and User.

The ConCat (or ||) operator can be used to concatenate (join together) two character strings. If an Employee table has three columns, FstNam, MdlInl, and LstNam, to contain different parts of a person's name, the following shows how they might be concatenated into a single string:

```
Select FstNam ConCat MdlInl ConCat LstNam
  From Employee
```

Note that this example produces a result table with a single column that is the concatenated result of the three base table columns.

SQL/400 also has a variety of **scalar functions**, listed in Figure 14.7, that can be used in expressions.

Figure 14.7

SQL/400 Scalar Functions

Data Type Conversion	
Char(*expression*)	Character string representing *expression*
Decimal(*expression, precision, scale*)	Packed-decimal value representing *expression*. The *precision* and *scale* arguments are optional. The default for *precision* is based on the type of the *expression*. The default for *scale* is 0.
Digits(*expression*)	String representing absolute value of *expression*
Float(*expression*)	Floating-point value representing *expression*
Hex(*expression*)	Hexadecimal value representing *expression*
Integer(*expression*) or Floor(*expression*)	Integer value representing *expression*
VarChar(*expression, max-length, ccsid*)	Variable character string of maximum length *max-length* (or default length) representing *expression*. The second and third arguments are optional. The Default keyword can be specified instead of a *max-length*. The third argument is an optional CCSID number.
VarGraphic(*expression, max-length, ccsid*)	Variable graphic character string of maximum length *max-length* (or default length) representing *expression*. The second and third arguments are optional. The Default keyword can be specified instead of a *max-length*. The third argument is an optional CCSID number.

Figure 14.7 continued

Figure 14.7
Continued

Zoned(*expression, precision, scale*)	Zoned-decimal value representing *expression*. The *precision* and *scale* arguments are optional. The default for *precision* is based on the type of the *expression*. The default for *scale* is 0.
Character String	
Character_Length(*expression*)	Returns length of string expression
Left(*string, length*)	Identical to SubStr(*string*, 1, *length*)
LTrim(*string*)	Identical to Strip(*string*, Leading)
RTrim(*string*)	Identical to Strip(*string*, Trailing)
Strip(*string, strip-type, character*) or Trim(*string, strip-type, character*)	Returns string with all leading and/or trailing *character*s removed from *string*. The *strip-type* argument is optional and can be B, Both, L, Leading, T, or Trailing. If not specified, Both is the default. The *character* argument is optional; if not specified the blank character is the default.
SubStr(*string, start-position, length*)	Substring of *string* beginning at *start-position* and having length *length*. The *length* argument is optional; default is to end of *string*.
Translate(*expression, to-string, from-string, pad-char*)	Translate characters in *expression* from characters in *from-string* to corresponding characters in *to-string*, using *pad-char* if *to-string* is shorter than *from-string*.
Upper(*expression*)	Uppercase string value in expression
Numeric	
AbsVal(*expression*)	Absolute value of *expression*
AntiLog(*expression*)	Anti-logarithm (base 10) of *expression*
Degrees(*expression*)	Number of degrees in an angle expressed by *expression* radians
Exp(*expression*)	Exponentiation; natural logarithm (base e) raised to power specified by *expression*
Ln(*expression*)	Natural logarithm (base e) of *expression*
Log(*expression*)	Common logarithm (base 10) of *expression*
Max(*expression, ...*)	Maximum value of set of one or more *expression*s
Min(*expression, ...*)	Minimum value of set of one or more *expression*s

Figure 14.7 continued

Figure 14.7
Continued

Mod(expression₁, expression₂)	Remainder of expression₁ divided by expression₂
Power(expression₁, expression₂)	Result of $expression_1 ** expression_2$
Sqrt(expression)	Square root of expression
Trigonometric	
ACos(expression)	Arc cosine of expression in radians
ASin(expression)	Arc sine of expression in radians
ATan(expression)	Arc tangent of expression in radians
ATanH(expression)	Hyperbolic arc tangent of expression in radians
Cos(expression)	Cosine of expression (as double-precision floating point number)
CosH(expression)	Hyperbolic cosine of expression (as double-precision floating point number)
Cot(expression)	Cotangent of expression (as double-precision floating point number)
Sin(expression)	Sine of expression (as double-precision floating point number)
SinH(expression)	Hyperbolic sine of expression (as double-precision floating point number)
Tan(expression)	Tangent of expression (as double-precision floating point number)
TanH(expression)	Hyperbolic tangent of expression (as double-precision floating point number)
Date, Time, and Timestamp	
CurDate()	Returns current date
CurTime()	Returns current time
Date(expression)	Date represented by expression
Day(expression) or DayOfMonth(expression)	For date and timestamps, day-in-month (1 to 31) part of expression; for date and timestamp durations, days (–99 to 99) part of expression
DayOfWeek(expression)	For date and timestamps, day-in-week (1 to 7) for expression
DayOfYear(expression)	For date and timestamps, day-in-year (1 to 366) for expression

Figure 14.7 continued

Figure 14.7
Continued

Days(*expression*)	Days from January 1, 0001 to date represented by *expression*
Hour(*expression*)	For time and timestamps, hour-of-day (0 to 24) part of *expression*; for time and timestamp durations, hours (–99 to 99) part of *expression*
Microsecond(*expression*)	For time and timestamps, microsecond-of-second (0 to 999999) part of *expression*; for time and timestamp durations, microseconds (–999999 to 999999) part of *expression*
Minute(*expression*)	For time and timestamps, minute-of-hour (0 to 59) part of *expression*; for time and timestamp durations, minutes (–99 to 99) part of *expression*
Month(*expression*)	For date and timestamps, month-in-year (1 to 12) part of *expression*; or for date and timestamp durations, months (–99 to 99) part of *expression*
Now( )	Returns timestamp for current time
Quarter(*expression*)	For date and timestamps, quarter-in-year (1 to 4) for *expression*
Second(*expression*)	For time and timestamps, second-of-hour (0 to 59) part of *expression*; for time and timestamp durations: seconds (–99 to 99) part of *expression*
Time(*expression*)	Time represented by *expression*
Timestamp(*expression₁*) or Timestamp(*expression₁, expression₂*)	Timestamp represented by *expression₁* (a string representation of a timestamp) or by *expression₁* (a string representation of a date) and *expression₂* (a string representation of a time)
Week(*expression*)	For date and timestamps, week-in-year (1 to 53) for *expression*
Year(*expression*)	For date and timestamps, year (1 to 9999) part of *expression*; for date and timestamp durations, years (–9999 to 9999) part of *expression*
Bitwise Operations	
LAnd(*expression*, ...)	Bitwise AND of two or more character (byte) string *expression*s
LNot(*expression*)	Bitwise NOT of character (byte) string *expression*

Figure 14.7 continued

Figure 14.7
Continued

LOr(*expression, ...*)	Bitwise (inclusive) OR of two or more character (byte) string *expression*s
Xor(*expression, ...*)	Bitwise XOR (exclusive or) of two or more character (byte) string *expression*s
Miscellaneous	
Coalesce(*expression, ...*) or Value(*expression, ...*)	First non-null value from list of *expression*s
IfNull(*expression, expression*)	Same as Coalesce(*expression, expression*)
Length(*expression*)	Length of *expression*
RRN(*table-or-view-name*)	Relative record number of a row in the underlying base table's physical file

A scalar function takes one or more arguments that can be literals, column names, or expressions. If a column name is used in a function, the function is applied to the column's value in each row in the result table and produces a value for the same row. The following statement shows how you could use the Strip function to better format the previous example:

```
Select      Strip( FstNam ) ConCat ' '
      ConCat Strip( MdlInl ) ConCat ' '
      ConCat Strip( LstNam )
   From Employee
```

In the example that doesn't use the Strip function, the three parts of the name are concatenated without stripping blanks and without ensuring that there is at least one blank between the parts of the name. With the column definitions in Figure 14.3, the resulting strings would look like

```
Janice        LGotchall
```

Using the Strip function and concatenating a couple of blank literals, the second example produces strings like

```
Janice L Gotchall
```

Date and Time Arithmetic

Another important use of expressions and scalar functions is to work with date and time values. Externally, SQL represents date values as character strings containing numbers for the year, month, day, and (in some formats) date separators. When you want to enter a literal date, you code the value as a string. The format of the string depends on the DATFMT and DATSEP values specified on the STRSQL, RUNSQLSTM, or CRTSQLxxx command.[9] For example, if you specify *ISO format, the following string represents May 1, 1996:

```
'1996-05-01'
```

With *USA format, the proper representation is

```
'05/01/1996'
```

SQL provides date addition and subtraction and date functions. The following example uses the Days function to get the number of days since January 1, 0001, and then uses the difference between the Days value for ShpDate and SaleDate to see how long after a sale the order was shipped. This Select statement produces the result table shown in Figure 14.8.

```
Select  CustID,
        OrderID,
        SaleDate,
        ShpDate,
        Days( ShpDate ) - Days( SaleDate )
  From  Sale
 Where ShpDate Is Not Null
```

Figure 14.8

Sample Retrieval Using Dates and Durations

CustID	OrderID	SaleDate	ShpDate	Days(ShpDate) - Days(SaleDate)
499320	234112	1996-05-01	1996-05-15	14
888402	234113	1996-05-01	1996-05-04	3
890003	234115	1996-05-04	1996-05-10	6
246900	234116	1996-05-04	1996-05-08	4
133568	234117	1996-05-05	1996-05-08	3
905011	234118	1996-05-05	1996-05-10	5
246900	234120	1996-05-06	1996-05-08	2

Notice how for the first row, the SaleDate is 1996-05-01 and the ShpDate is 1996-05-15, which results in a difference of 14 days between the Days function value for the two columns. If the SaleDate were 1995-05-01 (notice the year) and the ShpDate were 1996-05-15, the difference between the Days value for the two columns would be 380 days (366 + 14).

Note also how the search condition in this example excludes rows with a null ShpDate. Because the Sale table permits the ShpDate column to be null, we must consider the case in which a row has a null ShpDate. For arithmetic expressions, if one of the operands is null, the result of the expression is null. This rule makes sense, as you can see in this example, in which the difference between two dates is obviously unknown, if one or both of the dates is

---

[9] Review the "Date, Time, and Timestamp Data Types" section in Chapter 2 for the available date and time formats and separators. The online help for the STRSQL, RUNSQLSTM, and CRTSQLxxx commands also provides detailed information about the allowable values for the DATFMT, DATSEP, TIMFMT, and TIMSEP parameters.

unknown (i.e., null). The Is Not Null search condition lets us eliminate the cases where the ShpDate isn't known (e.g., the order hasn't shipped yet).[10]

You could alternatively use the following expression to calculate the difference between two dates as an SQL **date duration** value:

```
ShpDate - SaleDate
```

The result of this expression for sample column values would be

SaleDate	ShpDate	ShpDate – SaleDate
1996-05-01	1996-05-15	14
1995-05-01	1996-05-15	10014 (1 year, 0 months, 14 days)

SQL/400 represents a date duration as an eight-digit packed decimal number in the form yyyymmdd, not as a number of days. Be sure you don't get tripped up using a date duration instead of a days duration. You can also add a duration to or subtract one from a date. When SaleDate is 1996-05-01, the result of the following expression

```
SaleDate + 14 Days
```

is 1996-05-15. The term 14 Days is a **labeled duration**. You can use the following keywords to specify what a duration value represents: Years, Months, Days, Hours, Minutes, Seconds, or Microseconds.[11] To add 1 year, 2 months, and 14 days to a date, you would code

```
SaleDate + 1 Year + 2 Months + 14 Days
```

SQL supports time and timestamp columns, literals, and arithmetic similar to the way we've seen for date arithmetic. To code a time value with *ISO format, use a string representation like '13.30.10' for 10 seconds after 1:30 p.m. A time duration is a six-digit packed-decimal number with an hhmmss format. You also can use labeled time durations, as in the following expression, which adds labeled time duration values to a time column:

```
WrkBgnTime + 1 Hour + 30 Minutes
```

Column Functions

Scalar functions work on values from one row at a time. SQL also has **column functions** that you can specify in a select list to produce a value from a set of rows. Figure 14.9 lists the available SQL/400 column functions.

---

[10] Note that SQL requires ColA Is Null or ColA Is Not Null; you can't use ColA = Null or ColA <> Null.

[11] The singular form of these keywords is also allowed: Year, Month, Day, Hour, Minute, Second, and Microsecond.

Figure 14.9

SQL/400 Column Functions

Avg(*expression*)	Average of non-null *expression* values
Count(*) or Count(*expression*)	Count(*) returns the number of rows in the result table; Count(*expression*) returns the number of non-null *expression* values
Max(*expression*)	Maximum of non-null *expression* values
Min(*expression*)	Minimum of non-null *expression* values
StdDev(*expression*)	Biased standard deviation of non-null *expression* values
Sum(*expression*)	Sum of non-null *expression* values
Var(*expression*)	Variance of non-null *expression* values

As an example, the following Select statement results in a single row with the total number of customers and their average discount:

```
Select 'Average discount for ',
       Count( * ),
       ' customers is ',
       Avg( Discount )
  From Customer
```

The column function Count(*) returns the number of rows in a result table. The column function Avg(Discount) returns the numerical average of the set of non-null values for the specified column.

Be careful when you use column functions with columns that allow null. For example, suppose the Discount column allows nulls and that at least one row in the Customer table has a null Discount column. In this case, the following statement returns surprising results.

```
Select Count( * ),
       Avg( Discount ),
       Sum( Discount )
  From Customer
```

The sum is not equal to the average times the count! The Count(*) function includes all rows, but the Avg and Sum functions ignore rows with a null Discount column. There are two solutions to this problem. You can use an alternative form of the Count function, which does eliminate rows with a null Discount column:

```
Select Count( Discount ),
       Avg( Discount ),
       Sum( Discount )
  From Customer
```

Or you can use a more general solution: Use a Where clause to eliminate rows with null columns before the functions are applied:

```
Select  Count( * ),
        Avg( Discount ),
        Sum( Discount )
  From  Customer
 Where Discount Is Not Null
```

When you use a column function in the select list and you don't specify a Group By clause (discussed below), the column function applies to the entire set of records selected by the Where clause, and the Select statement's result table is always a single row. When you specify a Group By clause, the Select statement's result table contains one row for each group, or — if a Having clause (also discussed below) is also specified — the result table contains one row for each group that satisfies the Having clause's condition.

If the set of rows to which a column function is applied is empty (i.e., there are no rows), the result of any column function except Count(*) is null. Count(*) returns zero for an empty set.

You can optionally specify the Distinct keyword immediately after the opening parenthesis of a column function to eliminate duplicate expression values (as well as nulls) from the set of values to which the function is applied. The main practical use of this feature is with the Count function to count the number of different values for some column, as in

```
Select  Count( Distinct ShpCity )
  From  Customer
```

which produces a one-row, one-column result table that is the number of cities in which there's at least one customer.[12]

Group By and Having Clauses

You can use the Group By clause to apply column functions to (sub)groups of the rows you select. For instance, the following statement

```
Select      ShpCity,
            Count( * ),
            Avg( Discount )
  From      Customer
 Group By ShpCity
```

returns one row for each group of customers in a different city, as shown in Figure 14.10.

Figure 14.10

Sample Retrieval Using Group By Clause

ShpCity	Count(*)	Avg(Discount)
Albany	3	.005000
Eugene	3	.043333
Portland	4	.027500
Seattle	3	.003333

[12] Note that you can't use the Distinct keyword with the Count(*) form of the Count function.

In this example, ShpCity is the **grouping column** that partitions the rows in the Customer table into groups, one group for each different ShpCity value. The column functions Count and Avg are applied to each group in turn and produce one row in the result table for each group.[13] Normally, you list grouping columns' names in the select list as well as in the Group By clause so that each row in the final result table has the identifying column value(s) for the group. Any other columns that appear in the select list must be used as arguments of a column function.

You can use the Having clause to restrict rows in the result table after column functions have been applied to grouped rows.[14] The Having clause has a form similar to the form of the Where clause, which selects rows before they are grouped. For example, you could enter the following Select statement

```
Select      ShpCity,
            Count( * ),
            Avg( Discount )
   From     Customer
   Where    Discount Is Not Null
   Group By ShpCity
   Having   Avg( Discount ) > .01
```

to retrieve the information shown in Figure 14.11 for cities with an average discount above 1 percent.

Figure 14.11

Sample Retrieval Using
Having Clause

```
ShpCity            Count(*)        Avg(Discount)
Eugene                3               .043333
Portland              4               .027500
```

The search condition for a Having clause can include grouping columns (e.g., ShpCity) or column functions (e.g., Avg(Discount)).[15]

There's a conceptual ordering to a subselect (the part of a Select statement that we've been discussing up to this point) that helps clarify when the search conditions of the Where and Having clauses are tested as well as how the other clauses come into play. Each step produces a hypothetical result table from the intermediate result table of the previous step. The steps are

---

[13] In this example, rows with a null Discount column are intentionally not excluded, letting the result set have a complete count of the number of customers in each city. The average discount is for the customers with a non-null Discount column. For any null-capable grouping column, all nulls are considered in the same (null) group.

[14] Although you can specify a Having clause without a Group By clause, this is very unusual.

[15] In a subquery (i.e., a nested subselect), you also can specify a correlated column reference in the Having clause. A correlated reference is a reference to a column in an outer Select. Correlated references are discussed later in this chapter.

1. All combinations of all rows from all tables and views listed in the From clause are included in an intermediate result table produced by this step. (If only one table or view is specified in the From clause, the intermediate result table's columns and rows are the same as those in the specified table or view.)

2. If a Where clause is specified, the search condition is applied to each row in the result table produced by Step 1. Only those rows for which the search condition is true are included in the intermediate result table produced by this step. (If no Where clause is specified, all rows from the result table produced in Step 1 are included.)

3. If a Group By clause is specified, the rows from the result table produced in the previous steps are collected into separate groups such that all the rows in a group have the same values for all grouping columns. (If no Group By clause is specified, all the rows are considered as one group.)

4. If a Having clause is specified, the search condition is applied to each group. Only those groups of rows for which the search condition is true are included in the intermediate result table produced by this step. (If no Having clause is specified, all groups (and rows) from the result table produced in the previous steps are included.)

   If a Having clause is specified but no Group By clause is specified, the intermediate result table produced by this step is either empty or contains all rows produced in the previous steps.

5. If neither a Group By nor a Having clause is specified, the intermediate result table produced by this step includes the rows in the result table produced in Steps 1 and 2. Each row contains the direct and derived columns specified in the select list.

   If either a Group By or Having clause or both clauses are specified, the intermediate result table produced by this step includes one row for each group of rows produced in Steps 1 through 4. (If the previous result table was empty, the result table produced by this step is also empty.) Each row contains any grouping columns included in the select list as well as the result of applying any column function(s) in the select list to the group.

6. If the Distinct keyword is specified for the select list, duplicate rows are eliminated in the result table produced in the previous steps; otherwise, all rows are included in the final result table.

While this sequence of steps provides a way to understand the result of a subselect, it isn't necessarily how SQL/400 actually carries out a Select or other statement.

Because you can use either a Where clause or a Having clause for selecting rows based on the value of a grouping column, you can choose either of the following statements to display the average discount of customers in Portland or Seattle:

```
Select     ShpCity,
           Avg( Discount )
  From     Customer
  Where    ShpCity In ( 'Portland', 'Seattle' )
  Group By ShpCity
```

or

```
Select     ShpCity,
           Avg( Discount )
  From     Customer
  Group By ShpCity
  Having   ShpCity In ( 'Portland', 'Seattle' )
```

Using a Where clause is a clearer way to code this retrieval, and in many cases it performs significantly faster than using the Having clause because DB2/400 can eliminate rows before the grouping step and the calculation of the Avg column function values.[16]

The Order By Clause

You can use the Order By clause to sequence a Select statement's result table before it's displayed.[17] An Order By clause specifies a list of columns with ascending or descending (with the Desc keyword) sequence. For an unnamed column in the result table (e.g., one specified by an expression or function), you can use a relative column number instead of a column name to specify that the unnamed column is used to sequence the rows. The following statement retrieves shipped orders sequenced by customer ID and within customer ID, by the number of days (longest interval first) it took to ship the order:

```
Select     CustID,
           OrderID,
           SaleDate,
           ShpDate,
           Days( ShpDate ) - Days( SaleDate )
  From     Sale
  Where    ShpDate Is Not Null
Order By   CustID,
           5 Desc
```

In this case, the unnamed fifth column that results from the Days(ShpDate) – Days(SaleDate) expression is used to sequence rows within the same CustID value.

---

[16] Internally, the DB2/400 optimizer attempts to move Having conditions to the Where clause when it can. Nevertheless, it's a good idea to code tests in the Where clause when that provides the appropriate selection.

[17] An Order By clause is not part of the subselect and is valid only in a Select statement. Thus, you can use an Order By clause when you execute an interactive Select or in an Insert or Declare Cursor statement, but you can't use an Order By clause in a view definition.

As a more readable alternative to a relative column number, SQL lets you code a name for a derived column by following an expression or function with the As keyword and a column name.[18] Here's the previous example rewritten to use this technique:

```
Select   CustID,
         OrderID,
         SaleDate,
         ShpDate,
         Days( ShpDate ) - Days( SaleDate ) As DaysToShip
  From   Sale
  Where  ShpDate Is Not Null
Order By CustID,
         DaysToShip Desc
```

Complex Select Statements

The previous examples illustrate the basic parts of a Select statement. In the next examples, we look at more complex variations, starting with the From clause.

The From clause can list up to 32 tables and views. If you list more than one table or view in the From clause, the Select statement executes as if you had specified a single table that has all the columns from the specified tables and all possible combinations of rows from the tables (i.e., the Cartesian product of the two tables). This potentially large intermediate table isn't always created when you execute a multitable Select statement, but that's the simplest way to think about what happens. For example, the two tables in Figures 14.1 and 14.2 can be used in the following Select statement:

```
Select *
  From Customer,
       Sale
```

The result (Figure 14.12) isn't very useful because some rows combine information from unrelated customers and sales.

But if you use a select list and add a Where clause, you get a very useful table:

```
Select   Sale.OrderID,
         Sale.CustID,
         Customer.Name
  From   Customer,
         Sale
  Where  Sale.CustID = Customer.CustID
```

The resulting table (Figure 14.13) provides a list with the customer ID and name for each sale.

---

[18] You also can use this feature to create a synonym for a named column, but you should avoid a proliferation of synonyms because it leads to less consistent names. Even though you can give a column name to an expression in the select list, SQL/400 doesn't let you use this name in a Where, Group By, or Having clause.

Figure 14.12
Sample Retrieval Using
Cross Product

```
<------  Customer table columns ------>  <--------------- Sale table columns ------------>
CustID   Name         ShpCity    Discount OrderID CustID  TotAmt    SaleDate     ShpDate
133568   Smith Mfg.   Portland   .050     234112  499320      35.00 1996-05-01   1996-05-15
133568   Smith Mfg.   Portland   .050     234113  888402     278.75 1996-05-01   1996-05-04
133568   Smith Mfg.   Portland   .050     234114  499320      78.90 1996-05-03   <null>
133568   Smith Mfg.   Portland   .050     234115  890003   1,000.00 1996-05-04   1996-05-10
133568   Smith Mfg.   Portland   .050     234116  246900     678.00 1996-05-04   1996-05-08
133568   Smith Mfg.   Portland   .050     234117  133568     550.00 1996-05-05   1996-05-08
133568   Smith Mfg.   Portland   .050     234118  905011      89.50 1996-05-05   1996-05-10
133568   Smith Mfg.   Portland   .050     234119  499320     201.00 1996-05-05   <null>
133568   Smith Mfg.   Portland   .050     234120  246900     399.70 1996-05-06   1996-05-08
246900   Bolt Co.     Eugene     .020     234112  499320      35.00 1996-05-01   1996-05-15
246900   Bolt Co.     Eugene     .020     234113  888402     278.75 1996-05-01   1996-05-04
246900   Bolt Co.     Eugene     .020     234114  499320      78.90 1996-05-03   <null>
246900   Bolt Co.     Eugene     .020     234115  890003   1,000.00 1996-05-04   1996-05-10
246900   Bolt Co.     Eugene     .020     234116  246900     678.00 1996-05-04   1996-05-08
246900   Bolt Co.     Eugene     .020     234117  133568     550.00 1996-05-05   1996-05-08
246900   Bolt Co.     Eugene     .020     234118  905011      89.50 1996-05-05   1996-05-10
246900   Bolt Co.     Eugene     .020     234119  499320     201.00 1996-05-05   <null>
246900   Bolt Co.     Eugene     .020     234120  246900     399.70 1996-05-06   1996-05-08
275978   Ajax Inc.    Albany     Null     234112  499320      35.00 1996-05-01   1996-05-15
275978   Ajax Inc.    Albany     Null     234113  888402     278.75 1996-05-01   1996-05-04
275978   Ajax Inc.    Albany     Null     234114  499320      78.90 1996-05-03   <null>
275978   Ajax Inc.    Albany     Null     234115  890003   1,000.00 1996-05-04   1996-05-10
275978   Ajax Inc.    Albany     Null     234116  246900     678.00 1996-05-04   1996-05-08
275978   Ajax Inc.    Albany     Null     234117  133568     550.00 1996-05-05   1996-05-08
275978   Ajax Inc.    Albany     Null     234118  905011      89.50 1996-05-05   1996-05-10
275978   Ajax Inc.    Albany     Null     234119  499320     201.00 1996-05-05   <null>
275978   Ajax Inc.    Albany     Null     234120  246900     399.70 1996-05-06   1996-05-08
499320   Adapto       Portland   .000     234112  499320      35.00 1996-05-01   1996-05-15
499320   Adapto       Portland   .000     234113  888402     278.75 1996-05-01   1996-05-04
omitted rows ....
890003   AA Products  Portland   .010     234119  499320     201.00 1996-05-05   <null>
890003   AA Products  Portland   .010     234120  246900     399.70 1996-05-06   1996-05-08
905011   Wood Bros.   Eugene     .010     234112  499320      35.00 1996-05-01   1996-05-15
905011   Wood Bros.   Eugene     .010     234113  888402     278.75 1996-05-01   1996-05-04
905011   Wood Bros.   Eugene     .010     234114  499320      78.90 1996-05-03   <null>
905011   Wood Bros.   Eugene     .010     234115  890003   1,000.00 1996-05-04   1996-05-10
905011   Wood Bros.   Eugene     .010     234116  246900     678.00 1996-05-04   1996-05-08
905011   Wood Bros.   Eugene     .010     234117  133568     550.00 1996-05-05   1996-05-08
905011   Wood Bros.   Eugene     .010     234118  905011      89.50 1996-05-05   1996-05-10
905011   Wood Bros.   Eugene     .010     234119  499320     201.00 1996-05-05   <null>
905011   Wood Bros.   Eugene     .010     234120  246900     399.70 1996-05-06   1996-05-08
```

Figure 14.13
Sample Retrieval
Using Join

```
OrderID   CustID    Name
234112    499320    Adapto
234113    888402    Seaworthy
234114    499320    Adapto
234115    890003    AA Products
234116    246900    Bolt Co.
234117    133568    Smith Mfg.
234118    905011    Wood Bros.
234119    499320    Adapto
234120    246900    Bolt Co.
```

This two-table operation is an equijoin, one of the most common and useful relational database operations. An equijoin selects only those rows from the Cartesian product in which columns from separate tables have identical values; in this example, the equijoin selects columns in which the customer ID of the sale (Sale.CustID) matches the customer ID of the customer (Customer.CustID). In addition to the equijoin, SQL allows tables to be joined using other comparison operators, such as greater than or not equal. As this example illustrates, when a column with the same name exists in more than one table, you use a qualified column name of the form table.column.[19]

You also can join a table to itself. That is, a table can assume several roles in the From clause. To keep clear which table role you mean when you specify a column name in any of the other clauses, you must add a unique **correlation name** for any table listed more than once in a From clause. For example, you could enter the following statement

```
Select  Emp.EmpID,
        Emp.LstNam,
        Mgr.LstNam
  From  Employee Emp,
        Employee Mgr
 Where Emp.MgrEmpID = Mgr.EmpID
```

to produce the table shown in Figure 14.14, which includes both employees' names and their managers' names.

Figure 14.14
Sample Retrieval Using
Join of a Table with Itself

Emp.EmpID	Emp.LstNam	Mgr.LstNam
104681	Gibbens	Faubion
227504	Zimmerman	Bernard
898613	Faubion	Bernard
899001	Castor	Faubion

In this example, the Employee table is used in two roles: once to provide the set of employees (correlation name Emp) and once to provide a look-up table to find the name for each MgrEmpID value (correlation name Mgr). Using a qualified column name such as Emp.LstNam makes it clear from which role of the Employee table the column value is drawn.

As we've seen, the basic subselect syntax supports an inner join (i.e., where unmatched rows are dropped from the result). In the V3R2 and V3R6[20] releases of DB2/400, new SQL/400 syntax was introduced to support

---

[19] As the next example shows, the qualifier can be a correlation name rather than a table name. A period (.) is always used between the table or correlation name and the column name, regardless of whether the system or SQL naming convention is in effect.

[20] This new join support is also available as a PTF (Program Temporary Fix) for V3R1.

directly the left outer and other join variations described in Chapter 9. The new syntax for a left outer join looks like

```
Select  Customer.CustID,
        Customer.Name,
        Sale.SaleDate
  From  Customer
          Left Outer Join
        Sale
          On Customer.CustID = Sale.CustID
```

This Select statement's result is shown in Figure 14.15.

Figure 14.15

Sample Retrieval Using Left Outer Join

```
CustID      Name            SaleDate
133568      Smith Mfg.      1996-05-05
246900      Bolt Co.        1996-05-04
246900      Bolt Co.        1996-05-06
275978      Ajax Inc.       <null>
499320      Adapto          1996-05-01
499320      Adapto          1996-05-03
499320      Adapto          1996-05-05
499921      Bell Bldg.      <null>
518980      Floradel        <null>
663456      Alpine Inc.     <null>
681065      Telez Co.       <null>
687309      Nautilus        <null>
781010      Udapto Mfg.     <null>
888402      Seaworthy       1996-05-01
890003      AA Products     1996-05-04
905011      Wood Bros.      1996-05-05
```

In versions of SQL/400 before V3R1, you derive a left outer join by specifying the **union** of two sets: the set of matched (and hence joined) rows and the set that is the Cartesian product of the first (i.e., left) table's unmatched rows and a table with a single row that contains all null (or default) values for the columns drawn from the second table. For example, you could enter the following Select statement to retrieve the left outer join that contains all customers and their sale dates, if any:

```
Select  Customer.CustID,
        Customer.Name,
        Sale.SaleDate
  From  Customer,
        Sale
  Where Customer.CustID = Sale.CustID
Union
Select  Customer.CustID,
        Customer.Name,
        NullDate.NullDate As SaleDate
  From  Customer,
        NullDate
  Where Not Exists
        ( Select  *
            From  Sale
            Where Sale.CustID = Customer.CustID )
```

This example uses the SQL Union operator, which combines the rows from two subselects' result tables into a single result table. The first Select retrieves the Customer rows with at least one matching Sale row (i.e., the inner join). The second Select uses a nested Select (explained in the next section) to return only unmatched rows.[21] Essentially, the second set of rows includes one row for each Customer row where a matching row does not exist in the Sale table. The result of the complete Select statement (i.e., the union of the two subselects) is the same as for the left outer join example, as shown in Figure 14.15.

An SQL expression that contains a Union operator is known as a **fullselect**. A fullselect can specify a result table as the union of two or more intermediate result tables defined by subselects. Recall that a subselect is the form of SQL expression that starts with the Select keyword, has a From clause, and can optionally have Where, Group By, or Having clauses. A subselect does not have a Union operator or an Order By clause. (A Select statement, which can be a simple subselect or a fullselect, can have an Order By clause. When the Select statement contains a Union operator, the Order By clause is specified after the last subselect and determines the order of the resulting union of the rows in the subselects.)

To specify the union of two subselects, the subselects' result tables must be **union-compatible**, which means they must have the same number of columns and each pair of corresponding columns (by position in the respective select lists) must have compatible column definitions. Figure 14.16 lists the compatible column types and the column type of the resulting column in the fullselect's result table.

The other attributes of the fullselect's result table columns are determined as follows:

- If the two corresponding columns in the subselects' result tables have identical unqualified names, the fullselect's result table column has the same name; otherwise, the fullselect column is unnamed

- If neither of the corresponding columns in the subselects' result tables allows nulls, the fullselect's result table column doesn't allow nulls; otherwise, the fullselect column allows nulls

The preceding example also shows how the As option

```
NullDate.NullDate As SaleDate
```

can be used to provide a synonym for a column in the select list of one of the subselects so the fullselect column has a name.

When you specify the Union operator, duplicate rows are eliminated from the fullselect's result table. Two rows are duplicates if all columns in

---

[21] The second subselect by itself produces what is called an exception join in the V3R2 and V3R6 SQL/400 syntax.

Figure 14.16

Union-Compatible
Column Types

If one column is the following type	The other column can be the following type	The data type of the column in the result table is
Char(x)	Char(y)	Char(z) where $z = \max(x, y)$
VarChar(x)	Char(y) or VarChar(y)	VarChar(z) where $z = \max(x, y)$
bit data	bit, mixed, or SBCS data	bit data
mixed data	mixed or SBCS data	mixed data
SBCS data	SBCS data	SBCS data
Graphic(x)	Graphic(y)	Graphic(z) where $z = \max(x, y)$
VarGraphic(x)	Graphic(y) or VarGraphic(y)	VarGraphic(z) where $z = \max(x, y)$
Date	Date	Date
Time	Time	Time
Timestamp	Timestamp	Timestamp
Float (double)	any numeric type	Float (double)
Float (single)	Float (single)	Float (single)
Float (single)	Decimal, Numeric, Integer, or SmallInt	Float (double)
Decimal(w, x)	Decimal(y, z) or Numeric(y, z)	Decimal(p, s) where $p = \min(31, \max(x, z) + \max(w\text{-}x, y\text{-}z))$ $s = \max(x, z)$
Decimal(w, x)	Integer	Decimal(p, x) where $p = \min(31, x + \max(w\text{-}x, 11))$
Decimal(w, x)	SmallInt	Decimal(p, x) where $p = \min(31, x + \max(w\text{-}x, 5))$
Numeric(w, x)	Numeric(y, z)	Numeric(p, s) where $p = \min(31, \max(x, z) + \max(w\text{-}x, y\text{-}z))$ $s = \max(x, z)$
Numeric(w, x)	Integer	Numeric(p, x) where $p = \min(31, x + \max(w\text{-}x, 11))$
Numeric(w, x)	SmallInt	Numeric(p, x) where $p = \min(31, x + \max(w\text{-}x, 5))$

Figure 14.16 continued

Figure 14.16
Continued

If one column is the following type	The other column can be the following type	The data type of the column in the result table is
Integer	Integer	Integer
Integer	SmallInt	Integer
SmallInt	SmallInt	SmallInt
Nonzero scale binary	Nonzero scale binary	Nonzero scale binary (if either column is nonzero scale binary, both columns must be binary with the same scale)

the fullselect's result table have identical values. You can specify Union All to include duplicate rows in the fullselect's result table. The following example illustrates the use of Union All to get the last names of all employees and contractors:

```
Select   LstNam
  From   Employee
Union All
Select   LstNam
  From   Contractor
```

You also can add a tag column to each row of the fullselect's result table to show from which subselect the row came. The following Select statement retrieves the names (including people with the same name) of all employees and contractors, ordered by the person's name:

```
Select   'Employee',
         FstNam,
         MdlInl,
         LstNam
  From   Employee
Union All
Select   'Contractor',
         FstNam,
         MdlInl,
         LstNam
  From   Contractor
Order By LstNam,
         FstNam,
         MdlInl
```

As the sample results in Figure 14.17 show, each row includes a tag to indicate whether the person is an employee or contractor.

This example also shows how you code an Order By clause to sequence the rows in a Select statement (remember, the Order By clause is part of the Select statement, not part of a fullselect).

Figure 14.17
Sample Retrieval Using
the Union Operator

```
"Tag"       FstNam    MdlInl    LstNam
Employee    Dave      R         Bernard
Employee    Rick      D         Castor
Contractor  Bill      M         Dutcher
Employee    Trish     S         Faubion
Employee    Barb      L         Gibbens
Contractor  Cricket   S         Katz
Contractor  Tim       L         Murphy
Contractor  Richard   M         Rubin
Employee    Greg      J         Zimmerman
```

The previous examples have touched on most parts of the Select statement. In the next section we delve deeper into the search condition used in Where and Having clauses. The search condition is an important part of the subselect, which is at the heart of SQL's set-at-a-time facilities and must be well-understood to make effective use of views; the Select, Insert, Update, and Delete statements; and embedded SQL cursors.

Predicates and Subqueries

As we've seen, the Where and Having clauses of a subselect have a search condition that contains either a single predicate or multiple predicates connected by And or Or. Recall that a predicate specifies a condition that evaluates to true, false, or unknown. SQL has several kinds of predicates, including

- Basic predicate
- Null predicate
- Between predicate
- In predicate
- Like predicate
- Exists predicate
- Quantified predicate

A **basic predicate** compares two values, using one of the comparison operators listed in Figure 14.18.

Figure 14.18
SQL Comparison
Operators

Operator	Meaning
=	Equal
<>	Not equal
<	Less than
<=	Less than or equal
>	Greater than
>=	Greater than or equal

SQL/400 also allows the following equivalent operators

Operator	Equivalent to
¬=	<>
¬<	>=
¬>	<=

We've already seen several examples of the simpler form of basic predicate, which has the general syntax

$expression_1 \; \theta \; expression_2$

where each expression is a column name, literal, or some valid arithmetic, string, or other form of expression; and θ is one of the logical comparison operators in Figure 14.18. An example of this type of predicate is

```
Customer.CustID = Sale.CustID
```

A basic predicate also can take the form

$expression \; \theta \; (subselect)$

where *expression* and θ have the same meaning as above and the subselect specifies exactly one column and produces a result table with exactly one row. The following Select statement displays all customers who have an above average discount:

```
Select  CustID,
        Name
  From  Customer
  Where Discount > ( Select Avg( Discount )
                       From Customer )
```

A subselect that's used in a search condition is known as a **subquery**. In the preceding example, the subquery is

```
Select Avg( Discount )
  From Customer
```

This subquery produces a result table with a single row and one column, which contains the average discount for all customers. The search condition in the outer Select statement then compares each customer's discount to the average discount and includes in the Select statement's result table only those Customer rows with a Discount column value greater than the average.

Recall that a comparison between two values is unknown if either or both of the values is null. The **Null predicate** provides a way to test for null or not null, using syntax such as

```
Where ShpDate Is Null
```

or

```
Where ShpDate Is Not Null
```

SQL also has some shorthand forms for compound conditions. The **Between predicate** is an alternative to two inequality tests. The following search condition

```
Where Discount Between 0.01 And 0.02
```

is equivalent to

```
Where Discount >= 0.01
  And Discount <= 0.02
```

You also can use

```
Where Discount Not Between 0.01 And 0.02
```

which is equivalent to

```
Where Discount < 0.01
  Or Discount > 0.02
```

To simplify a series of equality tests, you can use the **In predicate**. A search condition such as

```
Where ShpCity In ( 'Eugene', 'Portland', 'Seattle' )
```

is equivalent to

```
Where ShpCity = 'Eugene'
  Or ShpCity = 'Portland'
  Or ShpCity = 'Seattle'
```

Another form of the In predicate lets you use a subquery to define the set of values to be compared.

```
Select  CustID,
        Name
  From  Customer
  Where ShpCity In ( Select Distinct City
                       From Warehouse )
```

In this example, the subquery produces a result table with one row for each city in which there's a warehouse. Each row from the Customer table is then selected only if the row's ShpCity column contains one of the cities in the subquery's result table. The Select statement's final result table has only those customers who are in the same city as a warehouse. Note that an In predicate's subquery must specify a result table with just one column. You also can specify the Not keyword before either form of In predicate to negate the test.

The **Like predicate** provides a rudimentary form of string pattern matching. A Select statement with a search condition such as

```
Select  CustID,
        Name
  From  Customer
  Where Name Like '%Steel%'
```

would display customers with the string Steel anywhere in the name. The following names would be included:

```
Ajax Consolidated Steel
Portland Steel Yards
Steel Fabricators of the Northwest
John Steeling Grocery Company
Umpqua Steelhead Fly Fishing Guides
```

The expression before the Like keyword must identify a string (e.g., a character column or a string function, such as SubStr). Following the Like keyword, you code a string literal.[22] This string provides the pattern to be matched. In the pattern, you can use the percent character (%) to represent a substring of zero or more occurrences of any character or the underscore character (_) to represent a substring of exactly one occurrence of any character. The following predicate tests for names that are exactly four characters long and end in "ick":

```
Name Like '_ick'
```

This pattern matches Dick, Rick, Mick, Nick, as well as dick, rick, mick, nick, kick, and !ick. The pattern doesn't match ick (too short), Ricky (too long), or RICK (wrong case).[23]

---

[22] You also can specify the User or Current Server special registers for the pattern, but there's not much point in doing so because these two special registers aren't likely to contain any wildcard characters. For embedded SQL statements, you can also use a host variable that contains a string pattern.

[23] With SQL/400, you can specify a sort sequence that treats uppercase and lowercase characters as identical for comparison purposes, in which case the pattern '_ick ' would match the string 'RICK'. The sort sequence is specified by the SRTSEQ parameter of the STRSQL, RUNSQLSTM, and CRTSQLxxx commands.

If you need to match a literal % or _ character, you can optionally define an escape character that's used in the pattern to specify that the escape character and the character following it are to be treated literally as the character following the escape character. For example, the following pattern matches any string that is at least two characters long and has an underscore in the second or later character:[24]

```
Name Like '_%\_%' Escape '\'
```

The first _ matches any one character. The first % matches zero or more of any character. The _ matches only an _. And the final % matches zero or more of any character.

The **Exists predicate** is another form of predicate that uses a subquery. The syntax is

```
Exists (subselect)
```

This predicate is true if the subselect's result table contains one or more rows; otherwise, it is false.[25] The subselect's select list can specify any number of columns, but the column values are ignored. You can specify the Not keyword before the Exists predicate, and the value of the negated predicate will be true only if the subselect's result table is empty. The following predicate is true if and only if there is at least one customer in Seattle:

```
Exists ( Select  *
         From  Customer
         Where ShpCity = 'Seattle' )
```

This example may not appear very practical because it just tells us whether there are any customers in Seattle, which won't be very useful as part of a search condition.[26] We saw a more useful form of the Exists predicate in the search condition of the example showing how to produce a left outer join.

```
Select  Customer.CustID,
        Customer.Name,
        NullDate.NullDate As SaleDate
  From  Customer,
        NullDate
  Where Not Exists
        ( Select  *
            From  Sale
            Where Sale.CustID = Customer.CustID )
```

---

[24] A matching string might also have an underscore in the first character as well as in a later character; thus, '_x_' would match the pattern.

[25] The value of the Exists predicate is never unknown.

[26] If we want an answer to how many customers are in Seattle, we can just use

```
Select  Count( * )
  From  Customer
  Where ShpCity = 'Seattle'
```

The subselect used in this search condition is known as a **correlated subquery** because the inner subselect (the one following Not Exists) refers to Customer.CustID, which is a reference to a column of a table specified in the outer subselect.[27] Thus, the evaluation of the inner subselect is correlated to the outer subselect's current row.

A close look at this example can help clarify both correlated subqueries and the usefulness of the Exists predicate. The example's Exists predicate answers the question "Do any sales exist for this customer?" If the answer is No, the search condition (Not Exists ...) is true and the customer is selected. (Recall that this Select was the second half of the left outer join and was intended to select unmatched Customer rows.) This Exists predicate tests whether the customer has any sales by (essentially) producing a temporary result table that contains all the Sale rows for the customer. If this set of rows isn't empty, the Exists predicate is true — the customer has one or more sales.

The temporary result table containing the customer's sales is produced by the subquery (the nested subselect)

```
Select   *
  From   Sale
  Where  Sale.CustID = Customer.CustID
```

Because we're interested only in the number of Sale rows, we use * to specify an implicit list of columns rather than listing explicit column names. The search condition we use for this subselect is quite simple: A Sale row is included in this subselect's result table if its CustID column contains the same customer ID as the current Customer row being tested in the outer subselect. You can think of SQL executing the following algorithm for the complete Select statement:

For all Customer rows
      Set CurCustID = Customer.CustID
      Set TmpSaleResultTable to Empty (remove all rows)
      For all Sale rows
          If Sale.CustID = CurCustID
             Add Sale row to TmpSaleResultTable
          EndIf
      EndFor
      If TmpSaleResultTable is Empty
          Add Customer row to final result table
      EndIf
EndFor

While SQL/400 doesn't necessarily use this algorithm to carry out the Select statement, the algorithm provides a logical way to understand a correlated subquery's result.

---

[27] This type of column reference is known as a **correlated reference**.

Subqueries can be quite complex, but they provide enormous power to express different search conditions. We're now ready to look at a more difficult, but practical, use of subqueries. Suppose you want to perform the following retrieval:

Retrieve the name and city for each customer who has placed any order with a total amount greater than the average total amount of orders placed by customers in the same city.

The following Select statement retrieves the desired list of customers:

```
Select  CurCust.Name,
        CurCust.ShpCity
  From  Customer CurCust
 Where Exists
     ( Select   *
         From  Sale BigSale
        Where BigSale.CustID = CurCust.CustID
          And BigSale.TotAmt >
            ( Select  Avg( AvgSale.TotAmt )
                From  Customer AvgCust,
                      Sale     AvgSale
               Where AvgCust.CustID  = AvgSale.CustID
                 And AvgCust.ShpCity = CurCust.ShpCity ) )
```

A detailed look at how this Select statement is structured illustrates many of SQL's advanced retrieval capabilities.

The first From clause specifies that the result table rows come from the Customer table and that correlation name CurCust is used elsewhere in the statement to qualify columns that come from this particular role of the Customer table.

The first Where clause uses the Exists predicate to see whether the customer has any orders that meet the specified criteria. The set of orders to be tested is specified by the first subquery (i.e., beginning with the second Select keyword). Remember, when you use a subquery, you can think of DB2/400 as executing the subquery for every row defined by the From clause in the outer Select statement. Thus, in this example, consider that for every row in Customer, the subquery is executed and then tested to see whether its result contains any rows.

The first subquery retrieves rows from the Sale table. Because the only test made on the result of this subquery is whether it contains any rows, all columns are retrieved (Select *). The From clause specifies that the rows from this use of Sale are qualified by the correlation name BigSale. The only rows retrieved in this subquery are those that are for the current customer and that have a total sale amount greater than the average total amount of orders placed by customers in the same city as the current customer.

The Where clause specifies the conjunction of two predicates that must be true for a Sale row to be in the subquery's result. The first predicate is that a Sale row must have the same customer ID as the current customer row's customer ID.

The second predicate is a basic predicate that uses another subquery. The total amount for each sale is compared to the average total amount of a set of sales. In this example, the greater than (>) test is used, and because both values in a basic predicate must be scalar, the set the subquery returns in this example must include no more than one value (i.e., one row with one column). By specifying only the Avg column function in the subquery's list of result columns, the subquery retrieves a single row with a single column that has the desired average value. This value is then compared to the column value BigSale.TotAmt.

The second subquery (i.e., the third Select statement) specifies the set of rows from which the average is calculated. The rows come from the equi-join of the Customer and Sale tables (AvgCust.CustID = AvgSale.CustID). But only those rows that have customers from the same city as the current customer are included in the average. To evaluate this condition, the city of each row in the innermost subquery (AvgCust.ShpCity) is compared to the city for the current customer in the main query (CurCust.ShpCity).

The final type of search condition predicate is a **quantified predicate**. These predicates have the syntax

expression θ *quantifier* (*subselect*)

The comparison operator can be any of those listed in Figure 14.18. The quantifier can be either of the keywords All or Any.[28] The following example selects customer rows that have a discount greater than all the Portland customers:

```
Select  CurCust.CustID
  From  Customer CurCust
  Where CurCust.Discount > All
      ( Select  CityCust.Discount
          From  Customer CityCust
          Where CityCust.ShpCity = 'Portland'
            And CityCust.Discount Is Not Null )
```

This > All quantified predicate is true if the subquery's result table is empty or if the current customer's discount is greater than all the values in the subquery's result table. The subselect used in a quantified predicate must have only one column, and the comparison test is applied to each value in the subselect's result table.

In general, a predicate with the All quantifier is

- True if the subselect's result table is empty or the comparison test is true for all values in the result table
- False if the comparison test is false for at least one value in the result table

[28] The Some keyword can be used as a synonym for Any.

- Unknown if the comparison test doesn't evaluate to false for at least one value in the result table and the comparison test is unknown for at least one value in the result table

A predicate with the Any quantifier is

- True if the comparison test is true for at least one value in the result table
- False if the subselect's result table is empty or the comparison test is false for all values in the result table
- Unknown if the comparison test doesn't evaluate to true for at least one value in the result table and the comparison test is unknown for at least one value in the result table

Be careful when you code a quantified predicate not to confuse informal ways of expressing a condition in English with the specific meanings of the All and Any quantifiers. For example, you might hear someone ask for a list of "customers who have a bigger discount than any of the Portland customers." But if you use the following Select statement

```
Select  CurCust.CustID
  From  Customer CurCust
 Where CurCust.Discount > Any
       ( Select  CityCust.Discount
           From  Customer CityCust
          Where CityCust.ShpCity = 'Portland'
            And CityCust.Discount Is Not Null )
```

the retrieved list would include all customers who have a discount greater than the lowest discount of any Portland customer. This list obviously might include some customers in Portland (those who have a discount that isn't the lowest among Portland customers). Using the All quantifier (as in the previous example) retrieves customers who have a discount greater than the highest discount of any Portland customer, which, of course, excludes all Portland customers.[29]

Using DML to Modify Table Data

SQL has three ad hoc DML statements that can be used to modify table data: Insert, Update, and Delete. All three statements can modify either a single row in a table or a set of rows in a table. None of the statements can modify

---

[29] A simpler approach to this Select statement would be to use the following basic predicate:

```
Select  CurCust.CustID
  From  Customer CurCust
 Where CurCust.Discount > ( Select  Max( CityCust.Discount )
                              From  Customer CityCust
                             Where CityCust.ShpCity = 'Portland' )
```

Using the Max column function also eliminates nulls automatically.

more than one table in a single statement. All three statements let you use a Where clause to specify the set of rows to be inserted, updated, or deleted. The general form of the Where clause in these statements parallels the form in the Select statement; however, there are restrictions, such as not referencing the table to be modified in an Update or Delete statement's Where clause.

You can specify an updatable view rather than a base table in an Insert, Update, or Delete statement. To be updatable, a view must be created over a single base table or updatable view and the outer Select cannot use column functions; the Distinct, Group By, or Having clauses; or a subquery that specifies the same base table as the outer subselect. An updatable view must also have at least one column that is derived directly (i.e., without an expression) from a column of the underlying base table.

The Insert Statement

To add a new row to a table, you use the Insert statement. For example, to add a new customer, you enter

```
Insert Into Customer
          ( CustID,
            Name,
            ShpCity,
            Discount )
   Values ( 678987,
            'Atlas Inc.',
            'Portland',
            Null )
```

A column list in parentheses follows the table name, and the Values clause specifies a list of new values, also in parentheses, for the columns that correspond positionally in the column list. You can omit the column list, in which case the implicit column list is all columns in the order they were defined by Create Table and Alter Table DDL statements. Omitting the column list is not generally a good practice, however, because it's error-prone and provides poor documentation.

You must insert a value for any column that doesn't have an explicit default (e.g., the Default clause was not specified on the Create Table statement). A column's default value (as described in Chapter 13) is used for any omitted column in the specified base table or in the underlying base table for a specified view.

The example above illustrates the use of the Null keyword to set the Discount column to null. Of course, a column that is set to null must have been defined without the Not Null clause.

A multirow Insert copies data from one table to another and implements the closest SQL equivalent to the relational assignment operation discussed in Chapter 9. For example, the following Insert copies all rows from an old version of a customer table to a new version that has an additional ShpState column:

```
Insert Into Customer
        ( CustID,
          Name,
          ShpCity,
          Discount,
          ShpState )
   Select CustID,
          Name,
          ShpCity,
          Discount,
          ' '
     From CustOld
```

Initially, all rows in the new table have a blank ShpState column because the result table for the Select includes the ' ' literal as the final element in its select list.

Although the Insert statement can add rows to only a single table, the inserted rows can be constructed from more than one table. For example, the following Create Table and Insert statements make a temporary copy of combined customer and sale information:

```
Create Table AppDta/TmpSale
  ( OrderID Decimal(  7, 0 ),
    TotAmt  Decimal( 11, 2 ),
    Name    Char(    30   ) )

Insert Into TmpSale
        ( OrderID,
          TotAmt,
          Name )
   Select  OrderID,
           TotAmt,
           Name
     From  Customer, Sale
     Where Customer.CustID = Sale.CustID
```

After the Insert statement is executed, changes to the data in the Customer or Sale tables are not reflected in the TmpSale table. A multirow insert, unlike a view, copies the data from the tables referenced in the From clause.

As the previous two examples show, you can use a form of the Select statement within an Insert statement to specify the rows to be inserted. This nested Select statement can use all the clauses and operators (e.g., From, Where, Having, Group By, Union, and Order By) discussed in the previous section.

If the target is a view, only insert-capable columns can be assigned values. A view column is not insert-capable if it's a literal, expression, or scalar function. You also can't insert values into more than one column derived from the same base table column. When you use a view, any base table column not present as an updatable column in the view must have been defined with a Default clause, and the new row gets this default value for the column.

The Update Statement

You can update a specific row by using its primary key value in the Where clause of an Update statement and assigning new values to one or more columns. For example, the following Update statement changes the name and adds 2 percent to a customer's current discount:

```
Update   Customer
  Set    Name     = 'Wood Products',
         Discount = Discount + .02
  Where CustID = 905011
```

You can update a set of rows by using a search condition that specifies more than one row.[30] The following statement gives all Portland customers a 10 percent discount. If you don't specify a Where clause, all rows in the specified table are updated.

```
Update   Customer
  Set    Discount = .10
  Where ShpCity = 'Portland'
```

You can set a null-capable column to null, using the Null keyword:

```
Update   Customer
  Set    Discount = Null
  Where ShpCity = 'Portland'
```

An Update statement can use a search condition with a subquery to select rows to be updated. The following statement increases to 10 percent the discount of customers who currently get less than a 10 percent discount and who have placed orders with a grand total amount greater than 1000:

```
Update   Customer
  Set    Discount = .10
  Where ( Discount < .10 Or Discount Is Null )
    And 1000 < ( Select  Sum( TotAmt )
                   From   Sale
                   Where Sale.CustID = Customer.CustID )
```

Optionally, you can specify a correlation name after the table name, as in

```
Update   Customer CurCust ...
```

and use the correlation name in the same way described for the Select statement.

In an Update statement's Where clause, you can use any of the search condition predicates discussed for the Select statement, except you can't use the table being updated as the base table of a subquery. Thus, the following Update statement is not valid:

---

[30] This type of Update is known as a **searched Update** because DB2/400 searches for the rows to be updated. Using an embedded SQL cursor, there's also a positioned Update, in which you first retrieve the row you want to update, and then specify Where Current Of *cursor-name* to update the current row. Chapter 15 covers positioned Update statements.

```
Update  Customer CurCust
  Set    Discount = .10
  Where CurCust.Discount Is Null
    Or CurCust.Discount <
      ( Select  Avg( DiscountCust.Discount )
          From   Customer DiscountCust
          Where DiscountCust.ShpCity = 'Portland' )
```

This invalid Update statement attempts to give a 10 percent discount to customers without a discount, or with a discount less than the average for customers in Portland. The problem is that the same statement would be updating some Portland customers' discounts while trying to compute an average.[31]

To update multiple tables, you must use more than one DML statement. For example, to increase the hourly rate of both employees and contractors, you would use two statements:

```
Update Employee
  Set  HourlyRate = HourlyRate * 1.05

Update Contractor
  Set  HourlyRate = HourlyRate * 1.05
```

When you update primary, unique, or foreign key columns, you must consider the key constraints that exist for a table. For example, to change a customer's ID, you must be sure the CustID column value is changed in the Customer table as well as in all tables that use CustID as a foreign key. If no foreign key constraints exist, you can just use multiple Update statements, such as

```
Update Customer
  Set   CustID = 123789
  Where CustID = 888402

Update Sale
  Set   CustID = 123789
  Where CustID = 888402
```

But if the Sale table has a foreign key constraint specified for the CustID column, both statements cause an error because either statement by itself

---

[31] Using embedded SQL in an HLL program, the desired change can be done in two SQL statements:

1. Retrieve the average discount into the PortAvgDsc program variable

```
Select  Avg( Discount )
  Into  :PortAvgDsc
  From  Customer
  Where ShpCity = 'Portland'
```

2. Use the PortAvgDsc program variable in the Update statement's search condition

```
Update  Customer
  Set   Discount = .10
  Where Discount Is Null
    Or Discount < :PortAvgDsc
```

would result in unmatched Sale rows.[32] DB2/400 doesn't support a Cascade option for the foreign key Update action (as it does for the Delete action), so you can't use that technique to automatically update the Sale table rows when a Customer row's CustID is updated. The best solution is the DB2/400 trigger program facility, which can be used to implement an ad hoc "cascade" for primary key updates. Trigger programs are discussed in Chapter 17.

The Delete Statement

To remove a row from a table, you enter a Delete statement such as

```
Delete
  From  Customer
  Where CustID = 905011
```

A set of rows can be deleted from a single table using a search condition that specifies more than one row.[33]

```
Delete
  From  Customer
  Where ShpCity = 'Portland'
```

The search condition for a Delete statement also can contain a subquery like the one in the previous Update statement example, with the same restriction: You can't use the table being modified as the base table of a subquery. And, as with the Update statement, you can specify a correlation name after the name of the table from which rows are being deleted.

You can clear all rows from a table — intentionally or accidentally — by entering a Delete statement with no Where clause.

```
Delete
  From Customer
```

Naturally, you may want to check interactive Delete statements carefully before you press the Enter key.[34] Note that after you clear all rows from a table, the table still exists; it's just an empty table. A table is cleared and deleted from the catalog using the Drop statement discussed in Chapter 13.

As discussed for the Update statement, if you want to delete rows from multiple tables, you must execute multiple Delete statements. You can use a foreign key constraint with a Delete Cascade rule to delete all dependent rows

---

[32] Technically, the update to Sale rows might not fail if there were already a Customer row with CustID = 123789. But the Customer row would normally be updated first to ensure that the new CustID value isn't a duplicate of some existing Customer row's CustID.

Of course, one way to accomplish this sequence is to insert a new Customer row that's identical to the current Customer row, except for a new CustID value. Then update the CustID value for all the associated Sale rows. Then delete the old Customer row.

[33] As with the Update statement, this type of Delete is known as a **searched Delete**. SQL also has a positioned Delete, discussed in the next chapter.

[34] ISQL requires that you confirm an Update or Delete statement without a Where clause.

along with a parent row. Thus, with the Customer and Sale table definitions in Figures 14.1 and 14.2, the statement

```
Delete
  From  Customer
  Where CustID = 499320
```

deletes one Customer row and three Sale rows.

Concurrent Updates and the Lock Table Statement

When two AS/400 jobs access the same base table, there's a possibility that one job's row updates might conflict with the other job's retrieval or update. For example, if one job executes the Select statement

```
Select  Avg( Discount )
  From  Customer
```

while another job is executing a statement to update the Discount column

```
Update  Customer
  Set    Discount = .10
  Where ShpCity = 'Portland'
```

the first job may get an average based on the old Discount value for some Portland customers and the new Discount value for others. DB2/400 (and other DBMS) don't automatically do anything to prevent these two jobs from interleaving the retrieval and update of individual rows.

The SQL Lock Table statement provides a way to explicitly **lock** a base table to prevent conflicting access. The Lock Table statement can provide a shared lock to let other jobs read, but not modify, the table. The following statement would protect the Select statement above from conflicting updates:[35]

```
Lock Table Customer In Share Mode
```

Alternatively, a Lock Table statement can provide an exclusive lock to prevent any type of access to the table by another job. The following statement would assure that no other access to the Customer table occurred during the Update statement above:[36]

```
Lock Table Customer In Exclusive Mode
```

A lock can be removed with a Commit or Rollback statement (with no Hold option), discussed below. Generally, you should keep a table locked for the briefest time necessary because a table lock may block other jobs from executing their normal access to a table. Chapter 17 discusses object locks in more detail and looks at another form of locking — individual record locks — that DB2/400 also uses to prevent conflicting updates.

---

[35] This statement places a *SHRNUP object lock on the physical file member for the table.

[36] This statement places a *EXCL object lock on the physical file member for the table.

Transaction Integrity and the Commit and Rollback Statements

Another consideration when updating a DB2/400 database is maintaining a consistent database when multiple rows are being modified. Suppose you enter the following Update statement to increase the discount for all customers with a non-null discount:

```
Update  Customer
  Set    Discount = Discount + 0.001
  Where Discount Is Not Null
```

To execute this statement, DB2/400 retrieves, tests, and updates each row. If the job in which this statement is being executed terminates abruptly (e.g., because of a power failure) after some — but not all — Customer rows have been processed, the Customer table will be in an inconsistent state. Some rows will have the increase, but others won't. The Update statement can't just be re-entered either, because that would add an additional discount to the customers who were updated in the previous, incomplete statement execution.

DB2/400 provides a facility called **commitment control**, which lets you specify all-or-none execution of multirow transactions. With this feature active, all row changes made by an update that fails before completion (and being committed) will automatically be backed out by DB2/400 — even if the system is shut down by a power failure. Under commitment control, after a failed update, all rows in the table are reset to their exact values before the update was started.[37]

To use commitment control, you first start a commitment environment by specifying either *CHG (change), *CS (cursor stability), *ALL (all), or *RR (repeatable read) for the COMMIT parameter on the STRSQL, RUNSQLSTM, or CRTSQLxxx commands. You can also use the SQL Set Transaction statement to establish (or end) a commitment environment. The statement has the syntax

```
Set Transaction Isolation Level level
```

where *level* is one of the following:

Level	Equivalent COMMIT parameter value
No Commit	*NONE
None	*NONE
NC	*NONE
Read Uncommitted, Read Write	*CHG
Chg	*CHG
UR	*CHG

[37] There's no magic to this DB2/400 capability. When a table is being updated under commitment control, DB2/400 simply stores in a journal receiver object (an OS/400 object designed for this purpose) a before image (copy) of each row just before the row is updated. If the whole update doesn't complete normally, DB2/400 uses these before images to change each row back to its pre-update values.

Level	Equivalent COMMIT parameter value
Read Committed	*CS
CS	*CS
Repeatable Read	*ALL
All	*ALL
RS	*ALL
Serializable	*RR
RR	*RR

In V3R2, V3R6, and later releases, you also can specify a With *isolation-level* clause on Select, Insert, Update, and Delete statements. The *isolation-level* is one of NC, UR, CS, RS, or RR, corresponding to the levels shown in the table above.

In V3R2, V3R6, and later releases, you can also code a Set Option as the first SQL statement in a program. The Set Option acts as a precompiler directive to set date and time formats, commitment control level, sort sequence, and other options that are available as parameters on the CRTSQLxxx commands. Chapter 17 discusses the different levels of commitment control in more detail.

When a commitment environment is active, you follow individual update statements or groups of update statements with a Commit or Rollback statement.[38] Because DB2/400 automatically backs out partially completed updates, you must explicitly indicate when all related updates are ready to be committed (i.e., made permanent). With the previous example, the Commit statement would immediately follow the Update statement, as in the following sequence:

```
Update  Customer
  Set   Discount = Discount + 0.001
  Where Discount Is Not Null

Commit
```

If the Update statement completes successfully, as soon as the Commit statement completes, the changes to the Customer table are permanent.[39]

Commitment control can be used to group multiple update statements into a single **transaction** (also called a **unit of work**). Commitment control guarantees that all or none of the database changes for all the update statements in a transaction are executed. Consider a classic banking transaction in which an amount is transferred from a savings account to a checking account. This transaction requires at least two Update statements, and it's essential that both complete or neither completes. Using commitment control, the sequence of statements would be

---

[38] You can use the optional Work keyword after Commit or Rollback (e.g., Commit Work or Rollback Work). The Work keyword has no effect on either statement.

[39] Essentially, DB2/400 just adds an entry to the journal that says the updates for the rows whose before images were previously saved have now been completed and committed.

```
Update  Saving
  Set    Balance = Balance - 100.00
  Where AcctID = 123987

Update  Checking
  Set    Balance = Balance + 100.00
  Where AcctID = 123987

Commit
```

If you decide you want to back out updates that have not yet been committed, you can execute a Rollback statement such as

```
Rollback
```

Both Commit and Rollback statements are typically used in HLL programs, rather than interactively. In particular, a Rollback statement is usually coded to back out uncommitted updates when an error is detected. We look at SQL error handling in the next chapter, but the basic logic where a Rollback might be used looks like the following. The transaction is committed only if both parts of the funds transfer complete successfully.

```
Update  Saving
  Set    Balance = Balance - 100.00
  Where AcctID = 123987
```
If Error
```
   Rollback
```
Else
```
  Update  Checking
    Set    Balance = Balance + 100.00
    Where AcctID = 123987
```
  If Error
```
     Rollback
```
  Else
```
     Commit
```
  EndIf

EndIf

You can optionally specify the Hold keyword after Commit or Rollback, as in the following example:

```
Commit Hold
```

When you specify Hold, all prepared statements (discussed in the next chapter) are kept (without Hold, they're discarded when you execute a Commit or Rollback statement). Also, the Hold keyword avoids releasing a table lock (as discussed in the previous section).[40]

---

[40] You can also use the Hold keyword to avoid closing embedded SQL cursors, as discussed in the next chapter. But a better solution for most situations is to code the With Hold option on the Declare Cursor statement.

Note that the CL Commit and Rollback commands are equivalent to the SQL/400 Commit Hold and Rollback Hold statements.

Notice that there isn't a "begin transaction" SQL statement. DB2/400 always begins a transaction implicitly — either when you start a commitment environment or when you end the previous transaction with a Commit or Rollback statement.

Coding Suggestions

- Store most DML statements to perform production (dynamic) Insert, Update, and Delete statements in source members and execute them using the RUNSQLSTM command.
  - Use a source file with a meaningful source file name, such as SQLDMLSRC.
  - Use the name (or abbreviation) of the SQL table or view you're updating as part of the source member name (e.g., DLTOLDCUST).
  - Enter a source member description that's the description of the action taken and the name of the table or view.
  - Place comments at the beginning of your SQL source to describe the action taken.
  - Use spaces, blank lines, and separator line comments to improve the readability of your source code.
  - Indent the From, Where, Group By, and Having clauses under the Select clause.
  - Align the beginning and continuation of each clause (e.g., the select list, the from table list, the search condition).
  - Align column names, expressions, compound search conditions, etc. on multiline statements for readability.
- Use an As clause to give a meaningful column name to an expression or function in the select list.
- Consider using the SubStr scalar function to shorten long character fields for Select statements entered with ISQL. Also consider using a combination of the SubStr and Digits scalar functions to return only the meaningful part of long numeric fields. These techniques can make the results easier to view.
- Use meaningful correlation names (e.g., CurCust, not C1).
- Consider null-capable columns when specifying expressions, functions, or search conditions.
- Be sure that a subquery used in a basic predicate can never have more than one row in the result table.
- Be careful to use the proper Any or All keyword in quantified predicates.
- Generally, when a Group By clause is specified, include all grouping columns in the select list so that each row in the result table has the identifying information for the group.

- When a Union operator is used and the two subselects have corresponding columns with different names, use the As clause in one or both of the subselects to give the columns the same name. This technique ensures that the column has a name in the fullselect's final result table.
- Use an explicit list of columns in the Insert statement to make clear which column each new value corresponds to.
- Be careful to include a Where clause in an Update or Delete statement, unless you intend to update or delete all rows in the table.
- Be sure to consider the effect of primary, unique, and foreign key constraints when updating a primary, unique, or foreign key column or when deleting a row in a table referenced by a foreign key.
- Be sure to consider the potential for conflicting access by other jobs when you execute multirow retrieval or update statements. Consider the Lock Table statement or other DB2/400 facilities to prevent conflicts.
- Use commitment control when you need to guarantee all-or-none execution of a multirow transaction.
- Performance-related suggestions:
  - When possible, use a Where clause rather than a Having clause to select rows.
  - In some cases, a search condition without a subquery is faster than an equivalent search condition that uses a subquery.
  - Avoid conversion between different numeric data types in predicates. For example, if a column's data type is Integer, use a comparison such as ColA = 1, rather than ColA = 1.0.
  - If possible, avoid patterns that begin with % or _ in the Like predicate so the DB2/400 optimizer can use an index to select rows.

Chapter Summary

SQL's DML provides a way to retrieve and update data with either record-at-a-time operations or with set-at-a-time operations. The four main DML statements are Select, Update, Insert, and Delete. These statements can be executed dynamically (e.g., by entering them using ISQL) or statically by embedding them in an HLL program.

The Select statement retrieves rows from one or more base tables and/or views. The Select statement can be broken down further as follows:

- A Select statement is a fullselect, with an optional Order By clause. The Order By clause specifies the column(s) whose value(s) are used to sequence the rows in the result table.

  A Select statement can be used interactively or as part of an embedded cursor definition. A nested form of the Select statement can also be used in an Insert statement.

- A fullselect is a single subselect or two or more subselects connected by the Union operator. The Union operator combines rows from the intermediate result tables of two subselects to produce the result table for the fullselect.

  A fullselect is part of a Select statement.

- A subselect is a specification of a result table with the following structure:

```
Select     select-list
  From     table-list
  Where    search-condition
  Group By grouping-column-list
  Having   search-condition
```

The purpose of the parts of a subselect are

Select *select-list*	specifies the columns in the subselect's result table
From *table-list*	specifies 1 to 32 base tables and/or views from which the result table data comes
Where *search-condition*	specifies a logical condition that must be true for a row to be included in the result table
Group By *grouping-column-list*	specifies the column(s) whose values are used to group the rows
Having *search-condition*	specifies a logical condition that must be true for a group to be included in the result table

A subselect is part of a fullselect and can be used in the Create View statement. A subselect can be used in the search condition of another subselect, in which case the nested subselect is known as a subquery. (Neither a fullselect with a Union operator nor a Select statement with an Order By clause can be used in a search condition.) A correlated subquery is a subquery that references a column in a table listed on the From clause of an outer subselect.

The select list for a subselect can specify either asterisk (*) — for all columns — or an explicit list of column names, literals, expressions, and scalar or column functions. SQL supports arithmetic, string, and date/time expressions. Scalar functions operate on a single value for each argument and a value is produced for each row. Column functions operate on a set of values, one value from each selected row.

The From clause can specify one or more tables and views. If multiple tables and views are specified, the subselect containing the From clause is based on an intermediate table that has all combinations of all rows from the listed tables and views.

A search condition is a single predicate or multiple predicates connected by the And or Or logical operators. Simple or compound predicates can be negated with the Not operator. A predicate is a condition that's true, false, or unknown. A predicate may be unknown if one or more operands are null. SQL uses three-valued logic to combine predicates (see Figure 14.5). A row is selected only if the search condition is true for the row.

There are several kinds of predicates:

- Basic predicate — a comparison between two expressions or an expression and a subquery that returns a single value (a result table with one row and one column)

- Null predicate — tests whether an expression is null

- Between predicate — tests whether an expression is within a range of values

- In predicate — tests whether an expression is in a set of values, which can be specified as a list or as a single-column subquery

- Like predicate — a string comparison using pattern matching

- Exists predicate — tests whether a subquery contains any rows

- Quantified predicate — compares an expression against all the values in a single-column subquery

When a Group By clause is specified, the final result table consists of one row for each group. All rows in a group have the same value(s) for the specified grouping column(s). The result table columns can include the grouping column(s) and any column functions.

The search condition of a Having clause is applied either to each (sub)group of rows — if a Group By clause is also specified — or to the entire set of rows in the intermediate result table — if a Group By clause is not specified. The final result table includes only those rows for groups for which the Having clause's search condition is true.

The Insert statement can insert one or multiple rows into a single base table or updatable view. A single-row Insert specifies a list of values. A multirow Insert specifies a nested Select statement to define the rows that will be copied from one or more tables or views into the target table.

A searched Update can update one or more rows in a single base table or updatable view. The rows to be updated are specified by a Where clause with a search condition similar to the Where clause used in a Select statement. The new column values are specified as a list of *column-name = expression* entries in the Update statement.

A searched Delete can delete one or more rows in a single base table or updatable view. The rows to be deleted are specified by a Where clause with a search condition similar to the Where clause used in a Select statement.

The Lock Table statement places a lock on a base table to prevent either update access or all access to the table by other jobs. A table lock is one technique for preventing conflicting table access by two different jobs.

Commitment control is a DB2/400 facility that provides transaction integrity by guaranteeing that a multirow update operation completes in an all-or-none fashion. You can use the COMMIT parameter on the STRSQL, RUNSQLSTM, or CRTSQLxxx commands to establish a commitment environment. The Set Transaction statement also serves this purpose. The Commit statement commits (makes permanent) all updates within the current transaction (i.e., since the last Commit or Rollback). The Rollback statement backs out all uncommitted updates within the current transaction.

Key Terms

basic predicate
Between predicate
column function
commitment control
correlated subquery
correlation name
data manipulation language
    (DML)
date duration
Delete statement
dynamic execution
embedded SQL statement
Exists predicate

fullselect
grouping column
In predicate
Insert statement
labeled duration
Like predicate
Null predicate
predicate
quantified predicate
scalar function
search condition
searched Delete
searched Update

Select statement
set-at-a-time operation
SQL special register
static execution
subquery
table lock
three-valued logic
transaction
union
union-compatible
unit of work
Update statement

Exercises

1. Show the Select statement to retrieve the entire Employee table (all rows and columns).

2. Show the Select statement to retrieve from the Customer table in Figure 14.1 the customers in Eugene who haven't yet been assigned a discount (i.e., their discount is unknown).

3. Show the Select statement to retrieve customers that have a name ending in "Inc." and with "Oregon" anywhere in the name.

4. Show the Select statement to retrieve a list of the different discount rates assigned to any customer. For this retrieval, do the following:
    - Eliminate duplicate discount values from the list
    - Calculate the percent discount from the fractional value
    - Include the text "percent" following the values

5. Show the Select statement to retrieve the minimum and maximum customer discount, and the difference between them, for each city. Include the city name in your retrieval. What will be the result if all customers in a particular city have an unknown (i.e., null) discount?

6. Modify the Select statement you created for Exercise 5 so that a city must have different minimum and maximum discounts to be included in the result table. Show two different solutions and state which you think is preferable and why.

7. Using the following partial definition for a Warehouse table

```
Create Table AppDta/Warehouse
    ( WhseID   Dec( 7, 0 ) Not Null,
      City     Char( 30   ),
   Primary Key( WhseID ) )
```

show the Select statement to retrieve the list of cities in which there's either a customer or a warehouse (or both). Sequence the result table by the city.

8. Using the Warehouse table defined in Exercise 7, show the Select statement to retrieve customers who are in a city without a warehouse.

Exercises Continued

Exercises continued

9. Show the Select statement to retrieve customers who have a discount identical to at least one customer in Portland. Will all customers in Portland necessarily be included in this retrieval? Why or Why not?

10. Modify the Select statement you created for Exercise 9 to include the following additional criteria:

    • A Portland customer must have a discount identical to at least one *different* customer in Portland.

    • A customer with a null discount *is* included in the result table if and only if at least one different customer in Portland also has a null discount. (The "different customer" restriction is relevant only to customers in Portland.)

    Hint: This problem may be harder than it looks; consider a fullselect.

11. Show the Insert statements to add to the Customer table in Figure 14.1 two new customers with the following values:

Customer ID:	906785	907744
Name:	Humble Bagel	New Frontier Market
ShpCity:	Oakridge	Pendleton
Discount:	0.010	Null

12. Show the Create Table and Insert statement to create a table that has one column (City) and contains a list of cities in which there is either a customer or warehouse or both. Use the Customer table in Figure 14.1 and the Warehouse table defined in Exercise 7. *Hint: This only requires one Insert statement.*

13. Show the Update statement to reduce all customers' discounts to half of their current rate.

14. Using the sample data in Figure 14.1, show the Update statement to change the name of the Alpine Inc. customer to Rocky Mountain Sports Inc. *Hint: As a general solution, be sure you consider the unlikely — but possible — case in which two customers might have the same name.*

15. Show the Delete statement to delete all customers with a null discount. Given the definition of the Sale table in Figure 14.2, what will happen to rows in the Sale table for the deleted customers?

16. Using the Warehouse table defined in Exercise 7, show the Delete statement to delete customers who are in a city without a warehouse.

17. Show the Lock Table statement to protect the Sale table from updates by other jobs (but allow other jobs to still retrieve data from the Sale table). What statement(s) can be used to release the table lock?

18. Describe two situations (other than those presented in this chapter) that might arise in a business application in which DB2/400 commitment control would be useful in preserving transaction integrity.

Chapter 15

Embedded SQL/400

Chapter Overview

This chapter builds on Chapter 14's introduction to SQL data manipulation language (DML) and shows how to embed SQL DML statements in a program written in an HLL, such as RPG IV or COBOL/400. It covers how to use host variables in SQL statements, how to create and execute entire SQL statements dynamically, and how to use an SQL cursor for row-at-a-time retrieval and update similar to database programming with an HLL's built-in I/O statements. We also look at SQL error handling and some additional SQL/400 features that can be used in HLL programs.

Introduction to Embedded SQL

In Chapter 14, we saw how dynamic, ad hoc SQL (e.g., a statement entered in the ISQL display) could be used to update a set of rows. For example, the following statement sets all Portland customers' discount to 10 percent:

```
Update   Customer
  Set    Discount = .10
  Where ShpCity = 'Portland'
```

Interactive entry of an SQL statement is quite useful for ad hoc retrieval and updates. However, there are a number of reasons you might want to control the execution of SQL statements from within an HLL program rather than using them interactively:

- Unrestricted dynamic execution of Insert, Update, or Delete statements lets the user make *any* change to the data. This may not be something you want to allow.

- Ad hoc entry of statements can be error-prone. For example, if a user mistypes the > symbol for the < symbol, an Update statement will change the wrong set of rows.

- Ad hoc entry of statements can be complex. For example, constructing the proper quantified predicates or subqueries may be difficult for end users not trained in SQL.

- SQL alone may not provide adequate computational or logic capabilities to perform a required operation. For example, SQL's Update statement doesn't allow a subselect in the Where clause to reference the table being updated. Such operations can be implemented with multiple SQL statements using program variables.

- SQL doesn't provide user interface (e.g., display file) programming capabilities. To present retrieved results or to prompt for input for updates in other ways than provided by ISQL, you need HLL (or other utility) capabilities.

Fortunately, SQL statements can be **embedded** (i.e., coded) in HLL programs. And you can use program variables to receive retrieved values as well as to supply values used in a statement's search condition or as the input values for an Insert or Update statement. The following example shows how the Update statement above could be coded as an embedded statement, using two program variables:

```
Update   Customer
  Set    Discount = :NewDisc
  Where ShpCity  = :SlcCusCity
```

Before this statement, the program would set the values of the NewDisc and SlcCusCity variables. If these two variables were set to .10 and Portland, respectively, the effect of the Update statement would be exactly the same as in the previous example. With the use of program variables in this SQL statement, an application can both simplify and control the update action. For example, the user could be presented with a simple interface into which he or she enters the discount amount and city. The program could even provide a list of cities from which the user selects. The program could also check the discount the user enters, making sure it's not negative and not over some maximum allowed discount.

To create an HLL program with embedded SQL, you code SQL statements along with HLL statements in a source member. You then execute an appropriate CL command to create a program object[1] from the source member. For example, to create an RPG IV program from a source member with embedded SQL, you use a CRTSQLRPGI (Create SQL ILE RPG Object) command, such as the following:

```
CRTSQLRPGI OBJ( appexc/updcust )
           SRCFILE( appsrc/qrpglesrc )
           SRCMBR( updcust )
```

Although it takes only one CL command to create a program, the underlying process involves two major steps, as shown in Figure 15.1.

---

[1] For RPG IV, ILE COBOL/400, and other Integrated Language Environment (ILE) languages, you can create an OS/400 module or service program object instead of a program object. If you create a module object, you can subsequently bind one or more modules to create a program or service program object. "The SQL/400 Translation Process" section later in this chapter discusses different aspects of program creation.

Figure 15.1
Creation Steps for
HLL Program with
Embedded SQL

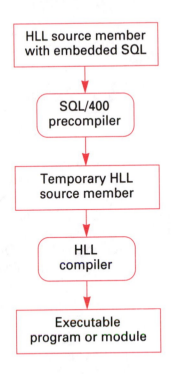

The first step is called **precompilation** and translates the input source member with the embedded SQL statements into a temporary output source member with all the embedded SQL statements translated into HLL declarations and procedural statements. The second step is the normal HLL compilation process, which translates the temporary source member input into an executable program object. The details of the process are more complex than this overview, but we'll defer discussion of the details until later in the chapter.

The SQL precompiler requires some way to differentiate embedded SQL statements from HLL statements. For example, SQL, RPG IV, and COBOL/400 all have a Delete statement; without some way to differentiate between an SQL Delete statement and an HLL Delete statement, the precompiler wouldn't know whether to translate the statement or pass it on (untranslated) as an HLL statement.

The solution is quite simple — you code a pair of **precompiler directives** around each embedded SQL statement. In RPG IV, you code all embedded SQL statements in the C-specs, which requires a C in position 6. Before each SQL statement, you code /Exec SQL in positions 7 through 15. After each SQL statement, you code /End-Exec in positions 7 through 15. Any lines (other than blank lines and comments) between the /Exec SQL and /End-Exec delimiters must have a plus (+) in position 7 (this marks an

SQL continuation line).[2] Here's the previous example as it would be coded in RPG IV:

```
....1....+....2....+....3....+....4....+....5.
C/Exec SQL
C+ Update  Customer
C+    Set   Discount = :NewDisc
C+    Where ShpCity  = :SlcCusCity
C/End-Exec
```

A similar approach is used in COBOL/400. Most SQL statements, including all the DML statements, must be coded in the Procedure Division. All parts of an embedded SQL statement must be coded in positions 12 through 72.[3] Before each SQL statement, you code Exec SQL; after each SQL statement, you code End-Exec. End-Exec can optionally be followed by a period to end a COBOL sentence that includes the SQL statement. Here's the previous example as it would be coded in COBOL/400:[4]

```
....1....+....2....+....3....+....4....+....5.
    Exec SQL
      Update  Customer
        Set   Discount = :NewDisc
        Where ShpCity  = :SlcCusCity
    End-Exec
```

Between the Exec SQL and End-Exec delimiters, you can use blank lines or HLL comment lines. You can also code SQL comments by beginning a comment anywhere in a line with two dashes (--); the comment then includes the rest of the line. The following example shows blank lines, an RPG IV comment, and SQL comments as they're coded in RPG IV:

```
....1....+....2....+....3....+....4....+....5....+
C/Exec SQL

 * Change the discount for all customers in a city

C+ Update  Customer
C+    Set   Discount = :NewDisc     -- New discount
C+    Where ShpCity  = :SlcCusCity  -- Selected city

C/End-Exec
```

In SQL, a program variable coded in an embedded SQL statement is referred to as a **host variable**. You always put a colon (:) at the beginning of a

---

[2] You can also begin an SQL statement in position 17 of the line containing the /Exec SQL directive. The examples in this book always begin the SQL statement on the line following the /Exec SQL directive.

[3] The SQL/400 precompiler actually allows the Exec SQL and End-Exec directives to begin in position 8 of a COBOL/400 source line.

[4] This COBOL/400 example shows the ruler to indicate where the statement is coded. Subsequent COBOL/400 examples don't use a ruler because, other than being coded in positions 12-72, SQL statements embedded in COBOL/400 have no positional requirements.

host variable name within an SQL statement. You can see how this is done for the NewDisc and SlcCusCity host variables in the example above. Note that you do not use the : with the host variable when coding normal HLL statements. Here's how a sequence of two RPG IV Eval statements and the embedded Update statement would look:[5]

```
....1....+....2....+....3....+....4....+....5....+...
C                     Eval      NewDisc    = InpDisc
C                     Eval      SlcCusCity = InpCusCity
C/Exec SQL
C+                    Update  Customer
C+                       Set    Discount = :NewDisc
C+                       Where ShpCity  = :SlcCusCity
C/End-Exec
```

In SQL/400, you don't need to do anything special to declare a host variable that's used in an SQL statement, although there are some restrictions as to the types of host variables that can be used. Host variables, however, should be declared before their first use in an SQL statement.[6]

In COBOL/400, you code qualified host variable names within an SQL statement using an SQL-like syntax such as

```
CustomerRow.CustID
```

rather than the standard COBOL syntax

```
CustID of CustomerRow
```

You can also use an RPG data structure name to qualify an RPG subfield used in an SQL statement, but this serves only a documentation purpose because the unqualified names of all RPG subfields must be unique within a source member.

Each HLL has its own variations on variable data types, and SQL has its set of column data types, as well. Figures 15.2 and 15.3 show the correspondence between the SQL, RPG IV, and COBOL/400 data types.

Generally, when you use a host variable to receive a column value, compare a host variable to a column in a predicate, or use a host variable as a

---

[5] This example shows a recommended coding style for embedding SQL statements in an RPG IV program. The SQL statement is aligned with the opcodes so the code layout flows smoothly rather than jumping to the left for SQL statements. In this chapter, when SQL examples do not include RPG IV statements, they're shown left-justified.

[6] This is required in COBOL/400 but not in RPG IV or RPG/400. It's good programming practice in all HLLs.

In COBOL/400 (but not RPG IV or RPG/400), you can optionally code the SQL Begin Declare Section and End Declare Section statements in the Working-Storage and Linkage sections to identify host variables that will be used in SQL statements. You code normal COBOL/400 variable declarations between the Begin Declare Section and End Declare Section statements. If you code Begin Declare Section and End Declare Section statements, only variables declared between the two statements can be used in SQL statements. You can have multiple SQL declare sections within a program.

Figure 15.2
SQL/400 Column Data
Types and Corresponding
RPG IV Host Variable
Data Types

SQL/400	RPG IV Definition Specification (D-spec)
Character	
Char(*nnnnn*)	`....1....+....2....+....3....+....4..` `D              S           nnnnnA`
VarChar(*max-length*)	No exact equivalent (use character variable large enough to hold largest expected string)
Graphic(*nnnnn*)	`....1....+....2....+....3....+....4..` `D              S           nnnnnG`
VarGraphic(*max-length*)	No exact equivalent (use graphic variable large enough to hold largest expected string)
Numeric	
Dec(*pp, ss*)	`....1....+....2....+....3....+....4..` `D              S           ppPss`
Numeric(*pp, ss*)	`....1....+....2....+....3....+....4..` `D              S           ppSss`
SmallInt	`....1....+....2....+....3....+....4..` `D              S           4B Ø`
Integer	`....1....+....2....+....3....+....4..` `D              S           9B Ø`
Real	No exact equivalent (use packed decimal)
Double Precision	No exact equivalent (use packed decimal)
Float(*precision*)	No exact equivalent (use packed decimal)
Date, Time, and Timestamp	
Date	`....1....+....2....+....3....+....4..` `D              S           D`
Time	`....1....+....2....+....3....+....4..` `D              S           T`
Timestamp	`....1....+....2....+....3....+....4..` `D              S           Z`

value assigned to a column in an Insert or Update statement, it's preferable to declare the host variable with a data type and size that matches the associated column's data type and size exactly. SQL/400 also allows host variables that are structures (e.g., RPG IV data structures and COBOL/400 group items) as well as arrays of structures. The "Host Structures and Arrays" section later in this chapter covers the use of these types of variables.

Recall from Chapters 13 and 14 that SQL supports null-capable columns. With interactive SQL, a column may be null when you retrieve data using the Select statement, and you can use the Null keyword to set a column to null on

Figure 15.3
SQL/400 Column Data Types and Corresponding COBOL/400 Host Variable Data Types

SQL/400	COBOL/400
Character	
Char(*length*)	`Pic X(`*length*`)`

VarChar(*max-length*)	Varying length string, declared as follows:
	`Ø1` *host-variable-name*.
	   `49` *string-length* `Pic S9(4) Binary.`
	   `49` *string-identifier* `Pic X(`*max-length*`).`

Graphic(*length*)	Not supported
VarGraphic(*max-length*)	Not supported
Numeric	

Dec(*precision, scale*)	`Pic S9(`*precision – scale*`)V9(`*scale*`)`
	    `Packed-Decimal`
	Maximum *precision* is 18.

Numeric(*precision, scale*)	`Pic S9(`*precision – scale*`)V9(`*scale*`) Display` Maximum *precision* is 18.
SmallInt	`S9(4) Binary`
Integer	`S9(9) Binary`
Real	No exact equivalent (use packed decimal)
Double Precision	No exact equivalent (use packed decimal)
Float(*precision*)	No exact equivalent (use packed decimal)
Date, Time, and Timestamp	
Date	No exact equivalent (use character string with at least 6 characters for *JUL format, 8 characters for *YMD, *DMY, or *MDY formats, and 10 characters for *USA, *JIS, *EUR, or *ISO formats)
Time	No exact equivalent (use character string with at least 6 characters for hours and minutes, and 8 characters for hours, minutes, and seconds)
Timestamp	No exact equivalent (use character string with 19 to 26 characters)

an Insert or Update statement. SQL also has provisions for handling nulls with embedded statements that include host variables. Wherever you can specify a host variable, you can optionally code an **indicator variable** following the host variable. The following example shows the use of the NewDiscNul indicator variable in an Update statement:

```
....1....+....2....+....3....+....4....+....5.
C                   If        InpDiscNul = 'Y'
C                     Eval    NewDisc    = Ø
C                     Eval    NewDiscNul = -1
C                   Else
C                     Eval    NewDisc     = InpDisc
C                     Eval    NewDiscNul = Ø
C                   EndIf
C                   Eval      SlcCusCity = InpCusCity
C/Exec SQL
C+                  Update  Customer
C+                    Set   Discount = :NewDisc :NewDiscNul
C+                    Where ShpCity  = :SlcCusCity
C/End-Exec
```

To understand the use of the NewDiscNul indicator variable, first notice how this example sets it. If the user input indicates that the discount should be set to null (i.e., InpDiscNul = 'Y'), the NewDisc host variable is set to 0 and the NewDiscNul indicator variable is set to –1. Otherwise, the NewDisc host variable is set to the user input (InpDisc) and the NewDiscNul indicator variable is set to 0. For an indicator variable, a negative number means null and a non-negative number means not null.

Next look at the Update statement's Set clause — the indicator variable is coded after the host variable.[7] When the indicator variable is negative, the value of the host variable is ignored and the result is the same as if the Set clause were

```
Set Discount = Null
```

If the indicator variable isn't negative, the result is the same as if the Set clause were

```
Set Discount = :NewDisc
```

An indicator variable must be a declared as a 2-byte, binary integer. In RPG IV, the D-spec for NewDiscNul would be

```
....1....+....2....+....3....+....4....+....5.
D NewDiscNul      S              4B Ø
```

In COBOL/400, the declaration would be

```
Ø1  NewDiscNul  Pic S9(4) Binary.
```

Indicator variables are also used for other purposes (e.g., to hold the length of a truncated string) in embedded SQL Select and Fetch statements, discussed on the following page.

---

[7] You can optionally code the Indicator keyword between the host variable and the indicator variable. This example's Set clause would look like

```
Set Discount = :NewDisc Indicator :NewDiscNul
```

Embedded SQL Error Handling

When an embedded SQL statement is executed, DB2/400 sets several program variables to provide feedback about any exceptional conditions that may occur during execution. You should always check these variables to handle both anticipated conditions (e.g., no row found) and unexpected errors (e.g., invalid data).[8] The SQL-related program variables, known as the **SQL communication area** (**SQLCA**), are automatically generated by the SQL precompiler for RPG IV programs. For COBOL/400 programs, you should always code the following statement in the Working-Storage section to have the SQL precompiler generate the SQLCA group and elementary items:

```
Exec SQL
  Include SQLCA
End-Exec.
```

Later in this chapter, we look more closely at the SQLCA, but for now the main variables of interest are

RPG IV	COBOL/400	Purpose
SQLCod	SQLCode	Error code
SQLWn0	SQLWarn0	Warning flag

Note that the RPG IV names are shortened to the six-character length imposed by RPG/400. The COBOL/400 names are the industry-standard SQL names and are used in all AS/400 HLLs except RPG/400, RPG IV, and FORTRAN. The explanations that follow use the longer names, except when RPG IV is discussed specifically.

The possible conditions that can result from executing an embedded SQL statement can be categorized as follows:

Condition	SQLCode	SQLWarn0
Error	< 0	Blank or W
No row found	100	Blank or W
Warning	1-99 or 101	Blank or W
Warning	0	W
No exception	0	Blank

You can use RPG IV code such as the following to cover all categories:

```
....1....+....2....+....3....+....4....+....5....+....6....+
C/Exec SQL
C+                 Update   Customer
C+                    Set   Discount = :NewDisc
C+                  Where ShpCity  = :SlcCusCity
C/End-Exec
```

[8] SQL also has a Whenever statement that generates tests and GOTOs based on the value of the SQLCode and SQLWarn0 variables. You should never use Whenever, however, because it's error prone (simply rearranging source code can inadvertently change the way exceptions are handled), and Whenever provides only a GOTO as a way to handle an exception.

```
....1....+....2....+....3....+....4....+....5....+....6....+
C                   Select
C                     When     SQLCod < 0
C                       ExSr   SQLError
C                     When     SQLCod = 100
C                       ExSr   SQLNoRow
C                     When     ( SQLCod > 0 ) Or ( SQLWn0 <> *Blank )
C                       ExSr   SQLWarning
C                   EndSl
```

In COBOL/400, you can use the following code:

```
Exec SQL
  Update  Customer
    Set    Discount = :NewDisc
    Where ShpCity  = :SlcCusCity
End-Exec

Evaluate True
  When SQLCode < 0
    Perform SQLError
  When SQLCode = 100
    Perform SQLNoRow
  When ( SQLCode > 0 ) Or ( SQLWarn0 Not = Space )
    Perform SQLWarning
End-Evaluate
```

It might seem cumbersome to code these eight lines of error-handling code after each embedded SQL statement, but you can place the code in a source member and use an RPG IV /Copy or COBOL/400 Copy directive to have the compiler automatically copy the code into the source input during compilation.[9] In RPG IV, this more concise approach looks like the following:

```
....1....+....2....+....3....+....4....+....5....+....6....+
C/Exec SQL
C+                  Update  Customer
C+                    Set    Discount = :NewDisc
C+                    Where ShpCity  = :SlcCusCity
C/End-Exec
C/Copy AppSrc/RpgCpySrc,SQLErrChk
```

There are several common conditions that can result from executing an embedded SQL statement. One of these, "No row found" (SQLCode = 100), occurs when no rows satisfy the search condition of a Select, Update, or Delete statement or when a Fetch statement has already retrieved the last available row from an open cursor. Another case is a duplicate value for a

---

[9] Alternatively, you could use an SQL Include statement to include the error-checking code. In COBOL/400, this could be coded as

```
Exec SQL
  Include SQLErrChk
End-Exec
```

The member specified on an SQL Include statement (e.g., SQLErrChk) must exist in the source file specified on the INCFILE parameter of the CRTSQLxxx command used to create the program.

primary or unique index on an Insert or Update operation, in which case SQLCode is set to –803. The complete set of SQLCode values is listed in an appendix of the *DB2/400 SQL Programming* manual. To handle a specific exception, you can add a condition to the sample error-handling code shown above, or you can check for the condition in the routines you invoke to handle errors and warnings (e.g., in an RPG IV SQLError subroutine).

Static Statements

Most of the DDL statements we discussed in Chapter 13 and all the DML statements we explored in Chapter 14, including Select, Insert, Update, and Delete, can be embedded in an HLL program. When you code an SQL statement directly in the source code (as in the Update examples we've been looking at), the statement is known as a **static statement** — static because the structure of the statement doesn't change; only the values supplied by host variables used in the statement may change. DDL statements (e.g., Create Table) aren't typically coded in HLL application programs. It is valid to use them when appropriate, however, as shown by the following example, which creates and later deletes a temporary table:

```
....1....+....2....+....3....+....4....+....5....+....6....+
C/Exec SQL
C+ Create Table AppDta/TmpSale
C+     ( OrderID Decimal(  7, Ø ),
C+        TotAmt  Decimal( 11, 2 ),
C+         Name    Char(    3Ø    ) )
C/End-Exec

C*    Use TmpSale as temporary table ....

C/Exec SQL
C+ Drop Table AppDta/TmpSale
C/End-Exec
```

Static Select Into Statement

As embedded statements in HLL programs, DML statements are more common than DDL statements. One DML statement, the Select statement, has a special form when coded as a static statement. This form, known as the Select Into statement, retrieves a single row into host variables. For example, using the Customer base table defined in Figure 15.4, the following code segment shows how a specific customer could be retrieved:

```
....1....+....2....+....3....+....4....+....5....+....6....+
D CustomerR       DS
D  CsCustID                       7P Ø
D  CsName                        3ØA
D  CsShpCity                     3ØA
D  CsDiscount                     5P 3
D  CsCityNull     S               4B Ø
D  CsDiscNull     S               4B Ø

D  SlcCustID      S                        Like( CsCustID )
```

```
....1....+....2....+....3....+....4....+....5....+....6....+
C* Get the selected customer ID from user input and place
C* the value in the SlcCustID variable.
        .
        .
        .
C/Exec SQL
C+                   Select  CustID,
C+                           Name,
C+                           ShpCity,
C+                           Discount
C+                   Into :CsCustID,
C+                        :CsName,
C+                        :CsShpCity  :CsCityNull,
C+                        :CsDiscount :CsDiscNull
C+                   From  Customer
C+                   Where CustID = :SlcCustID
C/End-Exec
```

Figure 15.4

Sample Customer
Base Table

```
Create Table AppDta/Customer
    ( CustID   Dec(   7, 0 ) Not Null,
      Name     Char( 30    ) Not Null,
      ShpCity  Char( 30    ),
      Discount Dec(    5, 3 ),
   Primary Key( CustID ) )
```

In addition to the From, Where, Group By, Having, and Order By clauses, a Select Into statement has an Into clause that follows the list of columns in the result table. The Into clause must list one host variable (and optionally, an indicator variable) for each column in the select list.[10] When the Select Into statement is executed, the result table must have no more than one row. If exactly one row is retrieved, its column values are assigned to the corresponding host variables listed in the Into clause. If no row is retrieved, DB2/400 sets the SQLCode variable to 100. If the result table contains two or more rows, DB2/400 sets SQLCode to −811 and the host variables' values are undefined.

A Select Into statement can't retrieve more than one row at a time for each execution of the statement because there's no straightforward way to provide the right amount of storage — such as an array with enough elements — to hold an indeterminate number of rows. The SQL cursor, which we look at later in this chapter, provides a way to specify a set of rows and then retrieve them one at a time using a Fetch statement.

In the example above, if the row that's retrieved has a null ShpCity or Discount column, the respective null indicator (CsCityNull or CsDiscNull) is set to −1 (or −2, if the retrieved value is null because of a data mapping error). If a column is non-null (i.e., has a valid value), the corresponding

---

[10] An appropriate host structure variable can be used instead of listing each variable individually, as discussed later in this chapter.

indicator variable is set to 0 (unless the value is a truncated string, in which case the null indicator holds the original length of the string[11]). On a Select Into statement, you should always code an indicator variable for a null-capable column because if no indicator variable is specified and the column is null, an exception occurs and SQLCode is set to –407.

In addition to retrieving a single row by supplying its primary key value (as in the example above), another standard use of the Select Into statement is to retrieve the count, average, etc. of a set of rows using a column function. The following statement retrieves the average discount for all customers into the AvgDisc host variable:

```
....1....+....2....+....3....+....4....+....5....+....6....+
D AvgDisc         S              5P 3
D AvgDiscNul      S              4B 0

C/Exec SQL
C+                        Select  Avg( Discount )
C+                          Into :AvgDisc :AvgDiscNul
C+                          From  Customer
C/End-Exec
```

This Select Into statement retrieves one row with one column. An indicator variable (AvgDiscNul) is coded to handle the unlikely cases in which there are no customers or all customers have a null discount — in either case, the Avg column function returns null.

Other Static DML Statements

The Insert, searched Update, and searched Delete statements[12] are exactly the same in both static and dynamic SQL, except for the use of host variables. We've already seen examples of the Update statement. A static Insert statement to add a new customer looks like the following:

```
....1....+....2....+....3....+....4....+....5....+....6....+
D CustomerR       DS
D  CsCustID                      7P 0
D  CsName                       30A
D  CsShpCity                    30A
D  CsDiscount                    5P 3
D  CsCityNull     S              4B 0
D  CsDiscNull     S              4B 0
```

[11] Or, if the value is a time value with the seconds portion truncated, the indicator variable holds the seconds.

[12] Recall that a searched Update or Delete is an Update or Delete statement with a Where clause that specifies a search condition.

```
....1....+....2....+....3....+....4....+....5....+....6....+
C* Get the values for the customer from user input and
C* place in the host variables CsCustID, etc.
C* Also set the CsCityNull and CsDiscNull indicator
C* variables to 0 if a value is supplied for the column,
C* or to -1 if the column should be set to null.
            .
            .
            .
C/Exec SQL
C+                      Insert Into Customer
C+                              ( CustID,
C+                                Name,
C+                                ShpCity,
C+                                Discount )
C+                      Values ( :CsCustID,
C+                               :CsName,
C+                               :CsShpCity   :CsCityNull,
C+                               :CsDiscount  :CsDiscNull )
C/End-Exec
```

The main thing to be aware of when you use a static Insert statement is that you must set any indicator values to the proper setting, depending on whether the column should be set to a valid value (use 0 for the indicator variable) or set to null (use −1 for the indicator variable). When the indicator variable is negative, the associated host variable value is ignored. Note that an indicator variable isn't required and is only useful when you need to set a column to null. If no indicator variable is specified, the host variable value is always considered a valid value. You also can specify an appropriate host structure instead of a list of host variables, as well as an array of structures to insert a set of rows with one operation. Both techniques are covered later in this chapter.

A static Delete statement can be used to delete a single row or a set of rows from a table. The following example shows how to delete a row using the primary key value a user enters:

```
....1....+....2....+....3....+....4....+....5....+....6....+
D SlcCustID       S              7P 0

C* Get the selected customer ID from user input and place
C* the value in the SlcCustID variable.
            .
            .
            .
C/Exec SQL
C+                  Delete
C+                    From  Customer
C+                    Where CustID = :SlcCustID
C/End-Exec
```

If no row exists with the specified customer ID, the SQLCode is set to 100 (no row found).

Other SQL DML statements, such as Lock Table, Commit, and Rollback can also be coded as static statements and have the form described in Chapter 14.

Dynamic Embedded Statements

As we've seen, static statements have a hard-coded structure, and host variables provide the ability to execute the same statement using different values in a search condition or as values assigned to a column on an Insert or Update statement. A static statement can't, however, change its structure from one execution to the next. For example, the same static Update statement can't use a particular search condition, such as ShpCity = :SlcShpCity, in one execution and a different search condition, such as Discount > :SlcDisc, in a subsequent execution. Of course, you can code two static Update statements and use HLL program logic to decide which one is to be executed on a particular iteration through the program. But **dynamic embedded SQL statements** provide even greater flexibility and let you construct entire SQL statements on the fly in an HLL program.

The simplest form of dynamic SQL uses HLL string operations to construct an SQL statement as a string in a host variable and then executes the string using the SQL Execute Immediate statement. Here's a (not very practical) example:

```
....1....+....2....+....3....+....4....+....5....+....6....+....7.
D SQLStmtStr      S             256A

C                 Eval      SQLStmtStr = 'Delete From Customer +
C                                       Where ShpCity Is Null'
C/Exec SQL
C+                Execute Immediate :SQLStmtStr
C/End-Exec
```

The SQLStmtStr variable is assigned a string that's a complete SQL Delete statement. The host variable is then specified on an Execute Immediate statement that executes the string contained in the variable. If the string in SQLStmtStr doesn't contain a syntactically valid SQL statement, or if an exception occurs when the statement is executed, DB2/400 sets the SQLCode and other SQLCA variables.

A slightly more complex example shows how dynamic SQL can be used to add flexibility to embedded SQL. This example lets the user input any valid SQL search condition as a string that's stored in the InpSrchCnd host variable:

```
....1....+....2....+....3....+....4....+....5....+....6....+....7.
D SQLStmtStr      S             256A
D InpSrchCnd      S             256A
```

```
....1....+....2....+....3....+....4....+....5....+....6....+....7.
C* Get a search condition (as a string) from user input
C* and place the string in the InpSrchCnd variable.
      .
      .
      .
C                  Eval      SQLStmtStr = 'Delete From Customer +
C                                         Where '
C                  Eval      SQLStmtStr = SQLStmtStr + InpSrchCnd
C/Exec SQL
C+                 Execute Immediate :SQLStmtStr
C/End-Exec
```

In this example, only the first part of the statement (i.e., Delete From Customer Where) is coded as a literal in the program. The user input is then concatenated to the literal to complete the statement. Thus, the user could enter "ShpCity Is Null", "Discount < .01", or any other valid search condition, and the Delete statement would delete the rows that satisfied the search condition.[13]

You can break dynamic execution of a statement into two steps, preparation and execution, as in the following example:

```
....1....+....2....+....3....+....4....+....5....+....6....+....7.
D SQLStmtStr      S             256A
D InpSrchCnd      S             256A

C* Get a search condition (as a string) from user input
C* and place the string in the InpSrchCnd variable.
      .
      .
      .
C                  Eval      SQLStmtStr = 'Delete From Customer +
C                                         Where '
C                  Eval      SQLStmtStr = SQLStmtStr + InpSrchCnd
C/Exec SQL
C+                 Prepare DynSQLStmt
C+                   From :SQLStmtStr
C/End-Exec
C                  If        ( SQLCod = Ø ) And ( SQLWnØ = *BLANK )
C/Exec SQL
C+                 Execute DynSQLStmt
C/End-Exec
C                    If      ( SQLCod <> Ø ) Or ( SQLWnØ <> *BLANK )
C                      ExSr  SQLError
C                    EndIf
C                  Else
C                    ExSr    SQLError
C                  EndIf
```

[13] You probably wouldn't create an application exactly like this because the potential for deleting the wrong rows would still be great. However, the example serves to show how SQL statements can be created with string operations.

As another way to understand how dynamic SQL can be used, consider that ISQL is essentially an application that gets user input in the form of complete SQL statements and stores the input in a string variable that is then used on an Execute Immediate

Here the HLL statements to create a string with an SQL statement are the same. But the string is first prepared for execution by the SQL Prepare statement. The Prepare statement has the syntax

```
Prepare statement-name From :host-variable
```

where *host-variable* is a string variable containing an SQL statement and *statement-name* is any name you choose; it doesn't have to be the name of a host variable (in fact, it generally shouldn't be the same to avoid confusion).[14] The statement name serves to identify an internal SQL structure that has the translated form of the statement. Be sure to check for successful completion of a Prepare statement, as the example above does, before a subsequent Execute statement. After an SQL statement has been successfully prepared from a string, the statement can be executed by the Execute statement. Note how Execute specifies a statement name, whereas Execute Immediate specifies a host string variable — don't confuse the two forms.

Separate Prepare and Execute statements allow the relatively time-consuming process of translating an SQL statement from a string into an executable form to be done just once,[15] and then the statement can be executed more efficiently multiple times during the same program execution.

Figure 15.5 lists the statements that can be executed using either Execute Immediate or Prepare and Execute. Notice that you can't use either method to execute a Select statement; however, you can prepare a Select statement and use the prepared form in a cursor declaration, a technique discussed later in this chapter.

Figure 15.5
SQL/400 Statements that Can Be Executed Dynamically

Alter Table
Call
Comment On
Commit
Create Collection
Create Index
Create Procedure
Create Table
Create View
Delete

Drop
Grant
Insert
Label On
Lock Table
Revoke
Rollback
Set Transaction
Update

statement. The actual internals of ISQL are slightly different, but the point is still valid, and you could write your own replacement for ISQL using dynamic SQL.

[14] The Prepare statement also has an optional Into *descriptor* clause that places information about the statement in an SQL descriptor area. SQL descriptors are discussed briefly in Footnote 40.

[15] That is, once per program execution. The Prepare statement does not save a permanent copy of the executable form of the prepared statement after the program ends. The copy is also destroyed when a subsequent Prepare is executed for the same statement name or when a Commit or Rollback statement — without Hold — is executed or other actions (e.g., ending commitment control) cause a unit of work to be ended.

When a statement is prepared for subsequent execution, you can use one or more question marks (?) as **parameter markers** in the statement to designate a place in the statement where a host variable (or a host variable and indicator variable) will supply a value when the prepared statement is executed. This approach makes it possible to prepare a statement and still change search condition values or values assigned to columns when the statement is executed, providing flexibility similar to that gained by using host variables in static statements.[16] The following example shows how a parameter marker can be placed in a statement string and how a host variable is subsequently specified to supply the value at the location of the parameter marker.

```
....1....+....2....+....3....+....4....+....5....+....6....+....7
D SlcShpCity       S             30A
D SQLStmtStr       S             256A

C                    Eval      SQLStmtStr = 'Delete From Customer +
C                                           Where ShpCity = ?'
C/Exec SQL
C+                      Prepare DynSQLStmt
C+                        From :SQLStmtStr
C/End-Exec

C                    If        ( SQLCod = 0 ) And ( SQLWn0 = *BLANK )

C* Get the selected city from user input and place
C* the value in the SlcShpCity variable.
     .
     .
     .
C/Exec SQL
C+                      Execute DynSQLStmt
C+                        Using :SlcShpCity
C/End-Exec
C                    If        ( SQLCod <> 0 ) Or ( SQLWn0 <> *BLANK )
C                      ExSr    SQLError
C                      EndIf
C                    Else
C                      ExSr    SQLError
C                    EndIf
```

The Using clause of the Execute statement specifies one host variable for each ? in the statement string that was prepared.[17] The host variables in the Using clause correspond positionally to the parameter markers in the string. When the Execute statement is executed, the value of the first host variable is used in place of the first ?, and so on. An indicator variable can follow the host variable in the Using clause, but only one ? should be used in the statement

---

[16] The difference, of course, is that static statements are hard-coded in the source whereas dynamic statements are constructed as string values during program execution.

[17] Or a host structure can be used, as discussed later.

string (i.e., don't include one ? for the host variable and another ? for the indicator variable).

We end this section by looking at a more complex, but more realistic, example. The following code segment lets a user enter a search condition to select a category of customers to be updated (e.g., the customers in Portland). Then for this category, the user can repeatedly enter a pair of old and new discount values. The resulting Update statement is executed once for each pair of old and new discount values and sets the discount for customers who meet the search condition and who have the specified old discount value.

```
....1....+....2....+....3....+....4....+....5....+....6....+....7
D OldDisc         S               5P 3
D NewDisc         S               5P 3
D SQLStmtStr      S               256A
D InpSrchCnd      S               256A

C* Get a search condition (as a string) from user input
C* and place the string in the InpSrchCnd variable.
    .
    .
    .
C                     Eval      SQLStmtStr = 'Update Customer +
C                                             Set Discount = ? +
C                                             Where Discount = ? And ('
C                     Eval      SQLStmtStr = SQLStmtStr + InpSrchCnd
C                     Eval      SQLStmtStr = SQLStmtStr + ')'
C/Exec SQL
C+                    Prepare DynSQLStmt
C+                      From :SQLStmtStr
C/End-Exec
C                     If        ( SQLCod = 0 ) And ( SQLWn0 = *BLANK )
C                       ExSr    ExcSQLStmt
C                     Else
C                       ExSr    SQLError
C                     EndIf

C       ExcSQLStmt    BegSr

C* Repeat the following until done or error . . .
C*
C*      Get old and new discount values from user
    .
    .
    .
C*
C                     Eval      NewDisc = InpNewDisc
C                     Eval      OldDisc = InpOldDisc
C/Exec SQL
C+                    Execute DynSQLStmt
C+                      Using :NewDisc,
C+                            :OldDisc
C/End-Exec
C                     If        ( SQLCod <> 0 ) Or ( SQLWn0 <> *BLANK )
C                       ExSr    SQLError
C                     EndIf
C* . . . End of repeated loop
C                     EndSr
```

SQL Cursors

As mentioned earlier, a static Select Into statement can retrieve no more than one row. SQL has another form of embedded statements — those that use **cursors** — to input rows from a result table containing more than one row. In highly simplified terms, an SQL cursor declaration serves a purpose similar to a conventional database file declaration in an HLL program. As we look more closely at SQL cursors, however, we'll see that there are important differences between cursor operations and conventional, built-in database file I/O (as discussed in Chapter 7). The main programming steps to use a cursor are

- Declare the cursor

- Open the cursor

- Fetch (i.e., read) rows from the cursor

- (Optionally) update or delete the most recently fetched row

- Close the cursor

The Declare Cursor statement declares an SQL cursor. Like an RPG F-spec or a COBOL/400 Select statement to declare a file, the Declare Cursor statement is a declaration, not an executable statement. Although the SQL precompiler requires Declare Cursor statements to be coded in the procedural part of a program (e.g., RPG C-specs), nothing happens when the program's execution flows through a Declare Cursor statement.[18] Only when an SQL Open statement is executed does the cursor get opened.

The Declare Cursor statement uses a nested SQL Select statement to specify the table(s) and/or view(s) that are accessed when the cursor is opened. The following example shows a very simple form of the Declare Cursor statement that provides access to all rows and columns of the Customer table, in order by customer ID:

```
Declare CustomerCursor Cursor
   For Select      *
        From     Customer
        Order By CustID
```

The cursor name (which you choose) follows the Declare keyword. Following the For keyword, you specify a Select statement, which can have all the clauses we discussed in Chapter 14 — From, Where, Group By, Having, and Order By — as well as the Union operator. (There are several other optional clauses, which we cover later.) Unlike HLL file declarations, a cursor declaration can specify row selection, derived columns, aggregation (e.g., the Sum

---

[18] The SQL/400 precompiler converts all Declare Cursor statements to HLL comments. The precompiler uses the information you specify on the Declare Cursor to properly translate subsequent statements and to set up internal tables used by DB2/400 when the program executes.

column function), union, and other data manipulations.[19] Notice that you specify the order in which rows are retrieved in the cursor declaration — not in the base table or view definitions.

The following sequence of embedded statements provides a preview of how you use a cursor in an HLL program (for simplicity, this example omits error handling):

```
....1....+....2....+....3....+....4....+....5....+....6....+
D CustomerR       DS
D  CsCustID                       7P Ø
D  CsName                        3ØA
D  CsShpCity                     3ØA
D  CsDiscount                     5P 3
D CsCityNull      S               4B Ø
D CsDiscNull      S               4B Ø
       .
       .
       .

C/Exec SQL
C+ Declare CustomerCursor Cursor
C+    For Select      *
C+          From      Customer
C+          Order By CustID
C/End-Exec
C/Exec SQL
C+                    Open CustomerCursor
C/End-Exec
C* Repeat the following Fetch until no more rows or error...
C/Exec SQL
C+                    Fetch Next
C+                      From  CustomerCursor
C+                      Into :CsCustID,
C+                           :CsName,
C+                           :CsShpCity   :CsCityNull,
C+                           :CsDiscount :CsDiscNull
C/End-Exec
C/Exec SQL
C+                    Close CustomerCursor
C/End-Exec
```

We cover more details of the Open, Fetch, and Close statements later. For now, notice how the Open makes the result table defined by the cursor's Select statement available and how the Fetch retrieves the next available row (if any) into host variables much the same way the static Select Into statement does.

As the example above shows, the Declare Cursor statement (like all other embedded SQL statements) must be coded in the C-specs in RPG IV and RPG/400 programs. In COBOL/400 programs, a Declare Cursor statement must be coded in the Procedure Division. In all HLLs, the Declare Cursor

---

[19] On the AS/400, the closest facility available with HLL built-in I/O operations is the OPNQRYF (Open Query File) feature of DB2/400. OPNQRYF lets a CL program set up runtime record selection, derived fields, etc., for a query file that is then declared and accessed with HLL built-in I/O statements, just like a physical or logical file. OPNQRYF is covered in Chapter 17.

statement must be coded before any embedded SQL statement that references the cursor. A good coding practice is to place cursor declarations at the beginning of the C-specs or Procedure Division.[20]

A cursor's Select statement can include host variable references, which provides the ability to determine the selection criteria for rows when the cursor is opened rather than when the program is created.[21] The following example shows how to code a cursor so that the rows available through it are from a city that's specified when the program is run:

```
....1....+....2....+....3....+....4....+....5....+....6....+
D SlcShpCity      S             30A

C/Exec SQL
C+ Declare CustomerCursor Cursor
C+    For Select     *
C+         From      Customer
C+         Where     ShpCity = :SlcShpCity
C+         Order By CustID
C/End-Exec

C* Get the selected city from user input and place
C* the value in the SlcShpCity variable.
    .
    .
    .
C/Exec SQL
C+                     Open CustomerCursor
C/End-Exec
```

When the Open statement is executed, DB2/400 evaluates the SlcShpCity host variable and uses its value in the search condition of the cursor's Select statement. If SlcShpCity contains Portland when the cursor is opened, subsequent Fetch operations retrieve only customers with a ShpCity value of Portland. Host variables used in a cursor declaration are evaluated only when the Open statement opens the cursor; changing the value of a host variable has no effect on the cursor until the cursor is closed and reopened. By closing and reopening a cursor, you can use the same cursor to retrieve different sets of rows (e.g., Portland customers, then Seattle customers) in the same program execution.

---

[20] It's somewhat anomalous that the Declare Cursor statement, which is a declaration, must be coded in the procedural part of an HLL program. The coding practice recommended here follows the principle that all declarations should be made at the beginning of the source code that's within the same scope. Because SQL cursors are scoped to the whole program (rather than to a subroutine or internal procedure), the beginning of the program's main block of procedural code is the appropriate location.

[21] You can also use host variables in expressions in the select list. These host variables are also evaluated only when the cursor is opened.

A cursor can be declared as either a read-only or an updatable cursor. If you add the For Read Only clause to the cursor's Select statement,[22] the cursor is read only:

```
Declare CustomerCursor Cursor
  For Select  *
       From  Customer
       Where ShpCity = :SlcShpCity
  For Read Only
```

It's good practice to declare read-only cursors explicitly with the For Read Only clause because doing so provides better documentation and can sometimes improve performance.

A cursor that is declared with a single subselect (no Union operator) over a single base table or updatable view and that has a Select statement that satisfies the restrictions on updatable views (discussed in Chapter 13) can be used for Update and Delete, as well as Fetch, operations. To use a cursor for Update operations, you should add a For Update Of clause to the cursor's Select statement. Following the For Update Of keywords, you list one or more columns that will be referenced in a subsequent Update statement's Set clause.[23] Here's an example of a cursor that allows updates of a customer's city and discount:

```
Declare CustomerCursor Cursor
  For Select  *
       From  Customer
  For Update Of ShpCity,
                Discount
```

For an updatable cursor without a For Update Of clause, a subsequent Update statement can reference any updatable column (i.e., one not derived using an expression, constant, or function). Limiting the columns that can be updated through a cursor provides some protection against coding mistakes and can also improve performance.

If the cursor's Select statement includes an Order By clause and you want to use the cursor for updates, you must specify a For Update Of clause

---

[22] For Fetch Only is synonymous with For Read Only. Technically, the For Read Only, For Update of, and Optimize For clauses are part of the Select statement. In practical terms, they're used almost exclusively in cursor declarations.

[23] If you specify the For Update Of clause without any columns, all updatable columns in the cursor's base table or view are updatable. A column listed in the For Update Of clause does not have to be included in the select list. That is, you can update a column even if it's not in the result table defined by the cursor's Select statement.

If the cursor will be used for Delete operations, but not for Update operations, you should not specify the For Update Of clause. As long as the cursor meets the requirements for an updatable cursor and the program contains a Delete statement that references the cursor, the cursor is opened as a delete-capable cursor. Specifying a For Update Of clause may cause poorer performance and causes a cursor open error if the user doesn't have Update privileges to the table.

that doesn't include any of the columns listed in the Order By clause.[24] The following example adds a valid Order By clause to the example above:

```
Declare CustomerCursor Cursor
  For Select        *
        From        Customer
        Order By CustID
  For Update Of ShpCity,
               Discount
```

If you don't specify a For Read Only or a For Update Of clause and the cursor satisfies the restrictions on updatable cursors, the cursor is opened as an updatable cursor if the program contains an Update or Delete statement that references the cursor or an Execute or Execute Immediate statement.[25] It's much better, however, to explicitly code the For Read Only or For Update Of clause so you don't rely on the default open mode. This practice also avoids unintentionally changing the nature of a cursor when you revise the SQL statements in a program.

When a commitment control environment is active, you generally should code a With Hold clause on cursor declarations so the cursor remains open when a Commit or Rollback statement that does not have a With Hold clause is executed. The With Hold clause follows the Cursor keyword, as shown below:

```
Declare CustomerCursor Cursor
  With Hold
  For  Select        *
        From        Customer
        Order By CustID
  For  Update Of ShpCity,
               Discount
```

For most AS/400 applications, you should code the With Hold clause on the Commit and Rollback statements, as well as on the cursor declaration, to hold other resources (such as prepared statements).

The SQL Open statement has a simple syntax

```
Open cursor-name
```

where *cursor-name* is the name specified on a Declare Cursor statement.[26] A cursor must be closed when the Open statement is executed. As mentioned earlier, the cursor's Select statement — including any host variables — is

---

[24] This is an understandable requirement — you can't update one of the columns used to sequence the rows; otherwise, the row's relative position in the cursor might change.

[25] However, the cursor is read only if the program is created with the ALWBLK(*ALLREAD) parameter and does not contain an Update or Delete statement that references the cursor — regardless of whether the program contains an Execute or Execute Immediate statement.

[26] For cursors that use a dynamically prepared Select statement with parameter markers, the Open statement includes a Using clause to identify the values for the parameter markers. Dynamically prepared Select statements are discussed later in the chapter.

evaluated when the Open statement is executed. If the Open is successful, the cursor is positioned before the first row in the result table.[27]

The SQL Close statement is equally simple:

```
Close cursor-name
```

A cursor must be open when the Close statement is executed.[28] Generally, you should close a cursor as soon as you're done using it.

The Fetch statement provides two capabilities: setting the position of the SQL cursor for subsequent input or update operations and reading one or more rows into host variables. There are several variations of the Fetch statement, providing forward and backward positioning and input operations. In this section, we look at only single-row input; later in this chapter we look at multiple-row input.

We've already seen an example of a simple Fetch statement that reads the next row in the result table defined by a cursor. The following example shows how this Fetch might be used in a loop to read the Customer table sequentially by customer ID and process all rows:

```
....1....+....2....+....3....+....4....+....5....+....6....+
D CustomerR       DS
D  CsCustID                      7P 0
D  CsName                       30A
D  CsShpCity                    30A
D  CsDiscount                    5P 3
D  CsCityNull     S              4B 0
D  CsDiscNull     S              4B 0
         .
         .
         .

C/Exec SQL
C+ Declare CustomerCursor Cursor
C+    For Select      *
C+          From      Customer
C+          Order By CustID
C+    For Read Only
C/End-Exec
C/Exec SQL
C+                  Open CustomerCursor
C/End-Exec
C                   If        ( SQLCod <> 0 ) Or ( SQLWn0 <> *BLANK )
C                     ExSr    SQLError
C                     Return
C                   EndIf
```

---

[27] If the result table is empty, the cursor is effectively positioned after the last row. In this case, the first Fetch operation will fail with a "no row" condition (SQLCode = 100).

[28] DB2/400 implicitly closes SQL cursors in several cases, including when a job, activation group, program, or module ends — depending on the CLOSQLCSR parameter value of the CRTSQLxxx command used to create the program. A Commit or Rollback statement without a With Hold clause closes a cursor declared without a With Hold clause. A Disconnect statement also closes cursors associated with the connection to a remote database.

```
....1....+....2....+....3....+....4....+....5....+....6....+
C                         Eval      MoreRows = *On

C                         DoW       MoreRows = *On
C/Exec SQL
C+                  Fetch Next
C+                    From  CustomerCursor
C+                    Into :CsCustID,
C+                         :CsName,
C+                         :CsShpCity  :CsCityNull,
C+                         :CsDiscount :CsDiscNull
C/End-Exec
C                         Select
C                         When    SQLCod < 0
C                           ExSr SQLError
C                           Eval MoreRows = *Off
C                         When    SQLCod = 100
C                           Eval MoreRows = *Off
C                         When    ( SQLCod > 0 ) Or ( SQLWn0 <> *Blank )
C                           ExSr SQLWarning
C                         Other
C                           ExSr ProcessRow
C                         EndSl
C                         EndDo
C/Exec SQL
C+                  Close CustomerCursor
C/End-Exec
C                         If        ( SQLCod <> 0 ) Or ( SQLWn0 <> *BLANK )
C                           ExSr    SQLError
C                           Return
C                         EndIf
```

The basic algorithm for sequentially processing all rows of an SQL cursor is

Open cursor
If error
    Handle error
    Quit
EndIf
While more rows and no error
    Fetch next row
    If error
        Handle error (end loop)
    Else If "no row" condition
        Do nothing (end loop)
    Else If "other" warning
        Handle warning (continue or end loop)
    Else
        Process current row
    EndIf
EndWhile
Close cursor

If error
> *Handle error*
EndIf

Remember that an SQLCode value of 100 indicates that there are no more rows to be read.[29]

In addition to the Next keyword, you can specify any of the alternatives shown in Figure 15.6, if you add the Scroll or Dynamic Scroll option to the cursor declaration.

Figure 15.6
Fetch Statement
Positioning Keywords

Keyword	Positions Cursor
Next	On the next row after the current row
Prior	On the row before the current row
First	On the first row
Last	On the last row
Before	Before the first row
After	After the last row
Current	On the current row (no change in position)
Relative *n*	$n < -1$ Positions to *n*th row before current $n = -1$ Same as Prior keyword $n = 0$ Same as Current keyword $n = 1$ Same as Next keyword $n > 1$ Positions to *n*th row after current

The following example shows the required Declare Cursor and Fetch statements to read the row before the current row:

```
....1....+....2....+....3....+....4....+....5....+....6....+
C/Exec SQL
C+ Declare CustomerCursor Scroll Cursor
C+    For Select      *
C+         From     Customer
C+            Order By CustID
C+    For Read Only
C/End-Exec
         .
         .
         .
C/Exec SQL
C+                    Fetch Prior
C+                       From  CustomerCursor
C+                       Into :CsCustID,
C+                             :CsName,
```

[29] This is comparable to the end-of-file condition for an HLL sequential read operation.

```
....1....+....2....+....3....+....4....+....5....+....6....+
C+                              :CsShpCity  :CsCityNull,
C+                              :CsDiscount :CsDiscNull
C/End-Exec
```

The Scroll and Dynamic Scroll options define a **scrollable cursor**, which is one that lets you use Fetch operations other than Fetch Next. The Scroll option (without the Dynamic keyword) implicitly defines the cursor as a read-only cursor, and because DB2/400 may make temporary copies of the result table's rows, changes to a row in the underlying table made by another job or another SQL statement in the same program may not be reflected immediately in the data retrieved by a Fetch. The Dynamic Scroll option can be used with an updatable cursor; and in most cases, a dynamic scrollable cursor does immediately reflect changes to a row made by another job or SQL statement.[30]

When you use Fetch without an Into clause, the operation positions the cursor but doesn't input anything. The Into clause cannot be used with the Before and After positioning keywords and is optional with all other positioning keywords. The Before and After options' purpose is to reset the cursor position to the beginning or end of the result table.

SQL/400 cursors don't provide an exact equivalent to HLL direct, keyed positioning and read operations, such as RPG IV SetLL and Chain opcodes and COBOL/400 Start and Read statements. As we've seen earlier, a static Select Into statement can be used to read a single row based on a primary or unique key value, which provides comparable function to an HLL direct read by primary or unique key value.

Another common sequence of HLL I/O operations is to position to the first record in a set of records with a common partial key value (e.g., the first order in the set of orders for a customer[31]) and then read sequentially by full key through the set. In RPG IV or COBOL/400, this task requires that the file be opened once and that repeated positioning and read operations be executed. In SQL, this type of task is normally implemented by repeated cursor open/close operations, with each cursor open selecting the desired subset, based on host variable values (e.g., the customer ID).[32] For example, the

---

[30] The Dynamic keyword is ignored when DB2/400 produces a temporary table to implement the cursor or when the cursor's Select statement includes certain types of subqueries. The *DB2/400 SQL Reference* manual's Declare Cursor documentation provides a complete list of the cases in which the Dynamic keyword is ignored.

[31] A typical approach would be to use a logical file with a keyed access path that had CustID as the major key field and OrderID as the minor key field. Chapter 7 shows an example of the technique with RPG IV Chain and ReadE opcodes.

[32] When an SQL cursor is opened and closed multiple times in the same program execution, DB2/400 attempts to avoid repeated internal file opens and closes. Thus, the performance of repeated cursor open and close statements may be much faster than repeated HLL open and close operations on a physical or logical file.

following cursor could be used to access, in order ID sequence, only those Sale table[33] rows for a particular customer:

```
Declare SaleForCustCursor Cursor
   For Select      *
         From      Sale
         Where     CustID = :SlcCustID
         Order By OrderID
   For Read Only
```

Before the cursor is opened, the appropriate customer ID must be assigned to the SlcCustID host variable.

Positioned Update and Delete Statements

You can use a **positioned Update** or **Delete** statement to update or delete the current row of an updatable cursor.[34] A successful Fetch must be executed before a positioned Update or Delete statement. Positioned Update and Delete statements use a Where clause with the syntax

```
Where Current of cursor-name
```

instead of a Where clause that specifies a search condition. The following example shows a Declare Cursor, Fetch, and subsequent positioned Update statement:

```
....1....+....2....+....3....+....4....+....5....+....6....+
C/Exec SQL
C+ Declare CustomerCursor Cursor
C+    For Select      CustID,
C+                    Name,
C+                    Discount
C+         From       Customer
C+           Order By CustID
C+    For Update of   Discount
C/End-Exec
      .
      .
      .
C/Exec SQL
C+                Fetch Next
C+                   From  CustomerCursor
C+                   Into :CsCustID,
C+                        :CsName,
C+                        :CsDiscount :CsDiscNull
C/End-Exec
```

---

[33] See Figure 14.2 for the Sale table definition.

[34] In those cases in which the necessary cursor definition forces the cursor to be read only, you can still update or delete a retrieved row by using a searched Update or Delete statement that specifies the retrieved row's primary key.

Note that you should not use a searched update with Where RRN(*table-name*) = :RowRRN to try to execute a direct by RRN retrieval or update because this causes a sequential scan of the table to find the specified row. The performance would be extremely slow for large tables.

```
....1....+....2....+....3....+....4....+....5....+....6....+
        .
        .
        .
C/Exec SQL
C+                      Update Customer
C+                         Set  Discount = :NewDisc
C+                         Where Current of CustomerCursor
C/End-Exec
```

Other than the Where clause, the syntax of positioned Update and Delete statements is the same as for searched Update and Delete statements. You code the cursor name in the Where clause of a positioned Update or Delete statement, but you code the table or view name that's specified in the From clause of the cursor's Select statement after the Update or Delete From keywords. Any columns that are assigned values in the Set clause must either be listed in a For Update Of clause on the cursor's Select statement or be an updatable column included in the cursor's select list, if no For Update Of clause is specified.

A positioned Update doesn't change the cursor's position — the updated row remains the current row.[35] A positioned Delete changes the current position to before the row (if any) following the current row.

There is no cursor-related Insert statement; the static Insert covered earlier in the chapter provides the SQL mechanism to add new rows to a base table regardless of whether a cursor is also opened for the table.

Host Structures and Arrays

SQL/400 provides an option to code an HLL structure variable, such as an RPG IV data structure or a COBOL/400 group item, anywhere that a list of individual (i.e., scalar) host variables is allowed. For example, you can use a **host structure variable** in the Into clause of a Select Into or Fetch statement or the Values clause of an Insert statement. The SQL/400 precompiler generates the list of individual host variables from the variables declared as elements (e.g., RPG subfields or COBOL elementary items) of the structure. You can optionally specify a second host structure from which the SQL/400 precompiler generates a list of indicator variables.

The following example illustrates the use of the CustomerR and CustomerI host structure variables in a Select Into statement:

---

[35] If the cursor is declared with the Dynamic Scroll option and has an Order By clause, and an update by a different job (or through a different cursor in the same job) changes one of the current row's Order By column values such that the relative position of the current row changes within the result table, a subsequent attempt to use Fetch Current . . . will fail.

```
....1....+....2....+....3....+....4....+....5....+....6....+
D CustomerR        DS
D   CsCustID                      7P Ø
D   CsName                       3ØA
D   CsShpCity                    3ØA
D   CsDiscount                    5P 3
D CustomerI        DS
D   CsIDNull                      4B Ø
D   CsNameNull                    4B Ø
D   CsCityNull                    4B Ø
D   CsDiscNull                    4B Ø
         .
         .
         .
C/Exec SQL
C+                  Select  CustID,
C+                          Name,
C+                          ShpCity,
C+                          Discount
C+                  Into :CustomerR :CustomerI
C+                  From  Customer
C+                  Where CustID = :SlcCustID
C/End-Exec
```

The resulting Select Into statement is equivalent to

```
....1....+....2....+....3....+....4....+....5....+....6....+
C/Exec SQL
C+                  Select  CustID,
C+                          Name,
C+                          ShpCity,
C+                          Discount
C+                  Into :CsCustID    :CsIDNull,
C+                       :CsName      :CsNameNull,
C+                       :CsShpCity   :CsCityNull,
C+                       :CsDiscount :CsDiscNull
C+                  From  Customer
C+                  Where CustID = :SlcCustID
C/End-Exec
```

The four individual host variables (e.g., :CsCustID) come from the subfields of the first host structure that follows the Into keyword, and the four individual indicator variables (e.g., :CsIDNull) come from the subfields of the second host structure.

This feature is especially convenient when you use an RPG IV externally described data structure or a COBOL/400 Copy directive to create the host structure.[36] The previous example can be coded in a simpler and less error-prone way:

[36] There's no automatic way to generate a host structure for a list of indicator variables. A helpful programming practice is to create an SQL Include source member with the structure declarations for the indicator variables. With RPG IV or RPG/400, you can also use the /Copy compiler directive, which the SQL/400 precompiler processes. You can't use COBOL/400 Copy source members for this purpose because the host indicator structure must be included during the precompile phase, and the COBOL/400 Copy directive operates only during the compile phase.

```
....1....+....2....+....3....+....4....+....5....+....6....+
D CustomerR      E DS                       ExtName( Customer )
D                                           Prefix( Cs )
D CustomerI        DS
D  CsIDNull                        4B Ø
D  CsNameNull                      4B Ø
D  CsCityNull                      4B Ø
D  CsDiscNull                      4B Ø
        .
        .
        .
C/Exec SQL
C+                 Select  *
C+                   Into :CustomerR :CustomerI
C+                   From  Customer
C+                   Where CustID = :SlcCustID
C/End-Exec
```

Notice the use of the asterisk (*) to specify an implicit list of columns in the result table. When an externally described host structure is used in the Into clause, both the implicit column list and the generated host variables include all columns in the table, in the same order. This example also uses the Prefix keyword on the CustomerR data structure definition. This RPG IV keyword adds Cs to the beginning of all the column names so the resulting subfield names will be unique within the program.

In COBOL/400, the equivalent statements to define both the host structure for a list of host variables and a host structure for a list of indicator variables are

```
Ø1  CustomerRow.
    Copy DDS-All-Formats of Customer With Alias.
Ø1  CustomerInd.
    Ø2 CustIDNull    Pic S9(4) Binary.
    Ø2 NameNull      Pic S9(4) Binary.
    Ø2 ShpCityNull   Pic S9(4) Binary.
    Ø2 DiscountNull  Pic S9(4) Binary.
        .
        .
        .
    Exec SQL
      Select  *
        Into :CustomerRow :CustomerInd
        From  Customer
        Where CustID = :SlcCustID
    End-Exec
```

In COBOL/400, you can use either the DDS-All-Formats or the DDS-All-Formats . . .With Alias form of the Copy directive; DDS-All-Formats generates the short column names, and DDS-All-Formats . . .With Alias generates the long column names.

As a performance enhancement, SQL/400 also lets you retrieve multiple rows into a **host structure array** with a single Fetch operation, as well as add multiple rows to a base table by specifying a host structure array on an Insert statement.

To declare a host structure array in RPG IV, you use a multiple-occurrence data structure (the Occurs keyword in positions 44–80). In COBOL/400, you use the Occurs clause on the declaration of the group item for the host structure.

A **multiple-row Fetch** uses a For *n* Rows clause, as in the following example:

```
....1....+....2....+....3....+....4....+....5....+....6....+
D CustomerR      E DS                          ExtName( Customer )
D                                              Prefix( Cs )
D                                              Occurs( 10 )
D CustomerI        DS                          Occurs( %Elem( CustomerR ) )
D  CsIDNull                       4B 0
D  CsNameNull                     4B 0
D  CsCityNull                     4B 0
D  CsDiscNull                     4B 0
D CsAryElem       S               7P 0 Inz( %Elem( CustomerR ) )
D CsTopRow        S               7P 0
   .
   .
   .

C/Exec SQL
C+                Fetch Next
C+                   From  CustomerCursor
C+                   For   :CsAryElem Rows
C+                   Into :CustomerR :CustomerI
C/End-Exec
C                 Eval      CsTopRow = SQLErrD( 3 )
```

The For *n* Rows clause specifies the maximum number of rows to be fetched. As the example above shows, you can specify the number of elements in the host structure array (in this case, in the CsAryElem host variable) to retrieve a full array's worth, if that many rows are available. After a multiple-row Fetch statement, the SQLErrCode(3) variable (part of the SQLCA, mentioned earlier) has the number of rows returned. If no rows are returned because no more were available and if no other exception occurs, the SQLCode variable is set to 100. If one or more rows are returned and the last available row was returned by the Fetch, the SQLErrD(5) variable is set to 100. Be sure to check the SQLCode before doing any processing and use SQLErrD(3) to determine how many elements in the array hold rows returned by the most recent Fetch.

A successful multiple-row Fetch operates in two steps:

First, the cursor is positioned according to the positioning keyword (Next, Relative, etc.)

Second, the row on which the cursor is positioned is fetched and up to *n* − 1 (where *n* is the number specified on the For *n* Rows clause) additional rows are fetched as if a Fetch Next were specified

The first row fetched is placed in the first element of the host structure array, the next row fetched into the second array element, and so on. Fetching stops when *n* rows have been fetched or there are no more available rows in the cursor. Fetching is always forward from the position set by the positioning keyword. If you wanted to fetch the previous three rows in one operation, you could use

```
C/Exec SQL
C+                      Fetch Relative -3
C+                          From  CustomerCursor
C+                          For   3 Rows
C+                          Into :CustomerR :CustomerI
C/End-Exec
```

You shouldn't use a Fetch Prior . . . For 3 Rows statement for this purpose because that would fetch the previous row, the current row, and the next row — not the previous row, the one before the previous row, and the one before that. In other words, Fetch Prior . . . For n Rows does not mean "fetch the previous n rows."

A **blocked Insert** lets you specify that multiple elements from a host array structure are inserted into a table. The following example shows how to use this form of Insert statement:

```
....1....+....2....+....3....+....4....+....5....+....6....+
D CustomerR      E DS                      ExtName( Customer )
D                                          Prefix( Cs )
D                                          Occurs( 10 )
D CustomerI        DS                      Occurs( %Elem( CustomerR ) )
D  CsIDNull                      4B 0
D  CsNameNull                    4B 0
D  CsCityNull                    4B 0
D  CsDiscNull                    4B 0
D  CsRowCnt        S             7P 0
     .
     .
     .
C* Fill n rows of the CustomerR and CustomerI multiple
C* occurrence data structures, and set CsRowCnt to n
     .
     .
     .
C/Exec SQL
C+                      Insert Into Customer
C+                          :CsRowCnt Rows
C+                          Values( :CustomerR :CustomerI )
C/End-Exec
```

The first through the nth elements of the host structure array, where n is the value of the Rows clause, are inserted into the table, just as if n Insert statements had been specified, one for each element of the host structure array. Notice that this example uses an implicit column list in the Insert statement. As mentioned earlier, when an externally described host structure is used instead of a list of individual host variables, an implicit column list provides a perfectly corresponding list of columns.

Multiple-row Fetch statements and block Insert statements can provide significant performance improvement, especially for batch jobs that process large numbers of rows.

SQL Error Handling

As mentioned earlier, DB2/400 sets various values in a set of variables known as the SQLCA. In RPG IV programs that contain embedded SQL, data structure and subfield declarations for this set of variables are automatically generated. Figure 15.7 shows the layout of the RPG IV SQLCA data structure.

Figure 15.7
RPG IV SQLCA
Data Structure

```
....1....+....2....+....3....+....4....+....5
D*     SQL Communication Area
D SQLCA
D  SQLAID                 1      8A
D  SQLABC                 9     12B 0
D  SQLCod                13     16B 0
D  SQLErL                17     18B 0
D  SQLErM                19     88A
D  SQLErP                89     96A
D  SQLErrD               97    120B 0 Dim(6)
D  SQLErr                97    120A
D   SQLEr1               97    100B 0
D   SQLEr2              101    104B 0
D   SQLEr3              105    108B 0
D   SQLEr4              109    112B 0
D   SQLEr5              113    116B 0
D   SQLEr6              117    120B 0
D  SQLWrn               121    131A
D   SQLWn0              121    121A
D   SQLWn1              122    122A
D   SQLWn2              123    123A
D   SQLWn3              124    124A
D   SQLWn4              125    125A
D   SQLWn5              126    126A
D   SQLWn6              127    127A
D   SQLWn7              128    128A
D   SQLWn8              129    129A
D   SQLWn9              130    130A
D   SQLWnA              131    131A
D  SQLStt               132    136A
```

In COBOL/400 programs, you use an Include SQLCA statement in the Working-Storage section to generate the group and elementary items shown in Figure 15.8.

Figure 15.8
COBOL/400 SQLCA
Structure

```
01  SQLCA Global.
    05 SQLCAID    Pic  X(8).
    05 SQLCABC    Pic S9(9) Binary.
    05 SQLCode    Pic S9(9) Binary.
    05 SQLErrM.
       49 SQLErrML Pic S9(4) Binary.
       49 SQLErrMC Pic  X(70).
    05 SQLErrP    Pic  X(8).
    05 SQLErrD    Occurs 6 Times
                  Pic S9(4) Binary.
    05 SQLWarn.
       10 SQLWarn0 Pic X(1).
       10 SQLWarn1 Pic X(1).
       10 SQLWarn2 Pic X(1).
       10 SQLWarn3 Pic X(1).
       10 SQLWarn4 Pic X(1).
       10 SQLWarn5 Pic X(1).
       10 SQLWarn6 Pic X(1).
       10 SQLWarn7 Pic X(1).
       10 SQLWarn8 Pic X(1).
       10 SQLWarn9 Pic X(1).
       10 SQLWarn0 Pic X(1).
       10 SQLWarnA Pic X(1).
    05 SQLState   Pic X(5).
```

Figure 15.9 provides a description of the contents of the SQLCA.

Figure 15.9
SQLCA Structure Contents

SQLCAID	Char(8)	Structure identifying literal: "SQLCA"
SQLCABC	Integer	Length of SQLCA
SQLCode	Integer	Return code: < 0 Error 0 Successful execution > 0 Successful execution with warning
SQLErrML	SmallInt	Length of SQLErrMC
SQLErrMC	Char(70)	Message replacement text
SQLErrP	Char(8)	Product ID literal: "QSQ" for DB2/400
SQLErrD	Array of Integer	SQLErrD(1) — treated as Char(4); last 4 characters of CPF or other escape message, if any SQLErrD(2) — treated as Char(4); last 4 characters of CPD or other diagnostic message, if any SQLErrD(3) — for Fetch, Insert, Update, or Delete, number of rows retrieved or updated.

Figure 15.9 continued

Figure 15.9

Continued

		SQLErrD(4) — for Prepare, relative number indicating estimated resources required for execution SQLErrD(5) — for multiple-row Fetch, contains 100 if last available row is fetched; for Delete, number of rows affected by referential constraints; for Connect or Set Connection, contains –1 if connection is unconnected, 0 if connection is local, 1 if connection is remote SQLErrD(6) — when SQLCode is 0, contains SQL completion message identifier
SQLWarn	Char(11)	Set of 11 warning indicators; each is blank, W, or N
SQLWarn0	Char(1)	Blank if all other SQLWarnX warning indicators are blank, W if any warning indicator contains W or N
SQLWarn1	Char(1)	W if a string column was truncated when assigned to host variable
SQLWarn2	Char(1)	W if null values were eliminated from a function
SQLWarn3	Char(1)	W if number of columns is larger than number of host variables
SQLWarn4	Char(1)	W if prepared Update or Delete statement doesn't include a Where clause
SQLWarn5	Char(1)	Reserved
SQLWarn6	Char(1)	W if date arithmetic results in end-of-month adjustment
SQLWarn7	Char(1)	Reserved
SQLWarn8	Char(1)	W if result of character conversion contains the substitution character
SQLWarn9	Char(1)	Reserved
SQLWarnA	Char(1)	Reserved
SQLState	Char(5)	Return code; "00000" if no error or warning

We've already looked at several of the variables in the SQLCA, including SQLCode and SQLWarn0. As you can see, the other variables provide additional information about exceptions. The main purpose of these variables is to provide better diagnosis and reporting of exceptional conditions. You can also use variables like SQLErrD(3) — number of rows Fetched, Inserted, Updated, or Deleted — to provide user feedback for normal operations.

The SQLState variable provides an alternative way to check for exceptional conditions. Whereas SQLCode values may vary among different products (e.g., DB2/400 vs. DB2 on IBM mainframes), all products in the IBM DB2 family use the same SQLState value for the same condition. Also, SQLState is all zeros ("00000") only when SQLCode is 0 and SQLWarn0 is blank; thus, it enables a more concise test for no exceptions. An appendix in the *DB2/400 SQL Programming* manual lists all SQLCode values and the corresponding SQLState values.

Transaction Integrity

In Chapter 14, we looked at transaction integrity and the use of DB2/400's commitment control facility to provide an all-or-none guarantee for multirow transactions. You can use the Commit and Rollback statements as embedded statements to provide the same kind of transaction integrity for embedded updates that we discussed for interactive updates. The commitment control level for a program is set with the COMMIT parameter of the CRTSQLxxx commands (discussed later) or with a Set Transaction statement. The following statement sets the commitment control level to the equivalent of COMMIT(*ALL):

```
Set Transaction Isolation Level Repeatable Read
```

The corresponding levels are

Set Transaction Option	Alternative Keyword(s)	COMMIT parameter
No Commit	None or NC	*NONE
Read Uncommitted, Read Write	Chg or UR	*CHG
Read Committed	CS	*CS
Repeatable Read	All or RS	*ALL
Serializable	RR	*RR

The main thing to consider with embedded Commit and Rollback statements is where in your program logic to place these statements and the impact of a commit or rollback on other resources, such as open cursors. In Chapter 17, we look more closely at the issue of program logic with commitment control; but in brief, you should try to code Commit and Rollback at the point(s) in your application where you have completed (successfully or not) all the DML statements that are involved in a transaction. By checking for errors after each DML statement, you can quit performing further update operations when an unrecoverable error occurs. At that point, your program flow should return control to a higher-level statement (e.g., by returning from a subroutine or procedure call) where a Rollback can be executed. The main mistake to avoid is coding lots of Rollback statements at each point where an error might be detected. A program should have few Commit and Rollback statements, and these should be executed at the appropriate point where the overall transaction is started and ended.

Putting It All Together — Sample Programs

We've covered most of the programming details related to embedded SQL; now let's put them together in a couple of sample programs that include the type of error handling a production application should use. The sample application is a batch update program that uses rows in the CustUpd transaction table (Figure 15.10) to add, change, and delete rows in the Customer table (Figure 15.11).

Figure 15.10
CustUpd Table

```
Create Table AppDta/CustUpd
    ( CustID                      Dec(   7, 0 ) Not Null,
      SequenceNumber For SeqNbr Dec(   7, 0 ) Not Null,
      CustomerName   For Name   Char( 30    ) Not Null,
      RowAction      For RowAct Char(  1    ) Not Null,
    Primary Key( CustID,
                 SeqNbr ) )
```

Figure 15.11
Customer Table

```
Create Table AppDta/Customer
    ( CustID                    Dec(   7, 0 ) Not Null,
      CustomerName For Name Char( 30    ) Not Null,
    Primary Key( CustID ) )
```

The sample tables include just a few columns so we can concentrate on the embedded SQL programming techniques. The Customer table has a unique key (CustID) and one non-key column, CustomerName (Name). The CustUpd table has those two columns plus the SequenceNumber (SeqNbr) column to sequence transactions within a particular customer ID and the RowAction (RowAct) column, which contains a one-letter code for the action (or the status after the update is attempted). The basic requirements for a valid CustUpd row are that together the CustID and SequenceNumber values are unique within the table and that

- *To add a row*: RowAction is A; CustID must be a key value that's not already in the Customer table; and CustomerName can be anything (it should be a valid name, but isn't checked)
- *To change a row*: RowAction is C; CustID must be a key value that exists in the Customer table; CustomerName can be anything (it should be a valid name, but isn't checked)
- *To delete a row*: RowAction is D; CustID must be a key value that exists in the Customer table; CustomerName isn't used

After the application attempts to perform a transaction, it replaces the RowAction column with X if the transaction is successful or E if there's an error. When the CustUpd table is read, rows with X or E in the RowAction column are skipped.

The application handles all types of SQL exceptions. When a "row not found" or "duplicate key" error occurs, it's treated as a transaction error; a message is displayed, and the CustUpd row is flagged with an E in the RowAction column. Other errors cause a message to be displayed, and the application terminates. Regardless of whether the application terminates normally or because of an unanticipated exception, it always explicitly closes any open SQL cursor because program termination may not automatically close cursors (it depends on the value of the CLOSQLCSR parameter on the CRTSQLxxx command that created the program).

The application doesn't reflect all the considerations you might have to cover in a real application, but it does illustrate a full range of embedded SQL operations for the two most common types of table access: sequential access by key (for CustUpd) and direct access by key (for Customer). It also shows a production-level approach to error handling.

This same application was the basis for Chapter 7's sample RPG IV and COBOL/400 programs that used built-in database I/O statements. You may find it helpful to compare the programs in these two chapters. The main structural difference between the two pairs of examples is that the SQL programs explicitly close the SQL cursors when an exception occurs, whereas the non-SQL programs let the HLL runtime handle closing files by default.

Because SQL/400 is used to access the database, the RPG IV version (Figure 15.12, page 433) and the COBOL/400 version (Figure 15.13, page 441) have almost identical I/O code. The coding for host variables and non-SQL procedural code is, of course, language dependent. In both versions, the Customer and CustUpd tables are accessed through updatable cursors declared with Declare Cursor statements. The CustomerTable cursor's For Update clause specifies that only the CustomerName column is updated. The CustUpdTable cursor specifies that only the RowAction column is updated. In the RPG IV version, within SQL statements, long identifiers can be used for things like cursor and column names; however, host variables are still limited to RPG IV's 10-character maximum because they're used outside SQL statements. The COBOL/400 version uses long names both in SQL and HLL statements.

For each table, an externally described host structure variable is declared to provide variables to fetch a row into. The host structure variable for the Customer table is also used to insert a new row.

In the RPG IV version, the data structures are declared with the Prefix keyword so their subfield names will be unique within the program. The subfield names for the two data structures are

CustomerR
    CsCustID
    CsName
CustUpdR
    UpCustID
    UpSeqNbr
    UpName
    UpRowAct

In the COBOL/400 version, Copy-DDS-All-Formats . . . With Alias directives are used to generate two group items. Each generated group item has the same name as a table (e.g., Customer and CustUpd). Because the With Alias option is specified on the Copy directives, the elementary items in each group have long column names, as follows:

Customer
    CustID
    CustomerName
CustUpd
    CustID
    SequenceNumber
    CustomerName
    RowAction

One coding technique to point out is the use of implicit column lists in the cursors' Select statements (i.e., the use of * instead of a list of columns) and in the Insert statement (i.e., no column names follow the table name). As suggested in Chapter 14, when individual host variables are used for a Select or Insert statement, you should also use explicit column names. That way you know you have the right number and correspondence of host variables and columns, even if the table definition changes. But with externally described host structure variables, each time you compile the program, you get an exact match of the generated column list and the generated host variable list, so implicit column lists are simpler and less error prone.

The sample programs also illustrate how you handle update and delete operations somewhat differently with SQL than with HLL built-in I/O operations. The two SQL examples show two alternatives: a positioned Update using repeated opens and closes of a cursor and a searched Delete. In both cases, a primary key value is used to select the record to be updated or deleted.

In both the RPG IV and COBOL/400 versions, the CustomerTable cursor isn't opened once at the beginning of the program, as was done with the Customer file in Chapter 7's sample programs. Instead, when an update action is processed, the CsCustID (in the RPG IV example) or the CustID of Customer (in the COBOL/400 example) host variable is set and the cursor is opened. If a row with the specified customer ID exists, the cursor's result table contains that row; otherwise, the cursor's result table is empty. A single Fetch

Next operation retrieves the row to be updated (or if no row exists, SQLCode is set to 100). If the row is Fetch'd successfully, a positioned Update statement changes the CustomerName column. After the update action (whether successful or unsuccessful), the CustomerTable cursor is closed. Although this might seem like a slow approach to updating a single row, DB2/400 doesn't actually open and close the underlying physical file repeatedly. Instead, the first time the cursor is opened, DB2/400 opens the physical file, and subsequently DB2/400 just changes the rows that are made available through the cursor using the already open physical file.

The delete action uses an alternative approach, a searched Delete that specifies the primary key value of the row to be deleted. This same technique could have been used for the update action. Even though the Delete statement doesn't reference the CustomerTable cursor, DB2/400 uses the same open physical file for the Delete statement as it uses for the cursor.

Using a searched Update or Delete is a little simpler coding for an application such as this. However, if you already have an updatable cursor open to retrieve rows, a positioned Update to the current row may be equally simple and slightly faster (if you don't have to reposition the cursor).[37]

A standard approach is used for detecting and handling various conditions that can occur during execution of an SQL statement. After each statement, a Select (RPG IV), Evaluate (COBOL/400), or If statement checks the SQLCode (SQLCod in RPG IV) and SQLWarn0 (SQLWn0 in RPG IV) variables for one of the following:

- Successful completion of the operation
- An anticipated condition (such as duplicate key)
- An unanticipated error condition

The complete set of SQLCode values is documented in an appendix of the *DB2/400 SQL Programming* manual, but the two mnemonics declared in both versions of the UPDCUST program are the most common ones to anticipate.[38] If you want to handle any other SQLCode value explicitly, all you have to do is add another When condition to the appropriate Select or Evaluate statement.

---

[37] Another consideration is row locking, discussed in Chapter 17. You may want to minimize locks on rows that the user is browsing (and thus, use a read-only cursor) until the user indicates he or she wants to perform an update. For an update, you can use a single-row, updatable cursor such as the one in the sample programs to re-retrieve the row with a lock. A subsequent positioned Update can then update the locked row.

[38] For simplicity, this example doesn't use the SQL Include, RPG IV /Copy, or COBOL/400 Copy directives, nor does it call external programs or bound procedures. All these techniques are valuable for production applications. You can use an Include, /Copy, or Copy member to hold constant declarations for the complete set of SQLCode values as well as any declarative or executable code that you need to use repeatedly. More sophisticated error handling can be put in a separate program or bound procedure and called with a Call (or

The error routines demonstrate how you can provide precise information about the cause of an SQL error.[39] The sample routines are just a starting point; you can provide much more information, if you want. You can also write error messages to a log table or send them to an OS/400 message queue so they're available for subsequent diagnosis. Thorough, informative handling of errors is a crucial part of production application development.

Figure 15.12

RPG IV UpdCust Program

```
....1....+....2....+....3....+....4....+....5....+....6....+....7
* - - - - - - - - - - - - - - - - - - - - - - - - - - - - - -
* Program name: UpdCust
* Author.      Paul Conte.
* Date-Written. Ø5/Ø1/96.
* Purpose:     Update Customer table from CustUpd table rows.
* - - - - - - - - - - - - - - - - - - - - - - - - - - - - - -

* Externally described host structure variables

D CustomerR      E DS                    ExtName( Customer )
D                                        Prefix( Cs )

D CustUpdR       E DS                    ExtName( CustUpd )
D                                        Prefix( Up )

 * Mnemonics

D True           C                       Const( '1' )
D False          C                       Const( 'Ø' )
D SqCdOK         C                       Const(    Ø )
D SqCdNoRow      C                       Const(  1ØØ )
D SqCdDupKey     C                       Const( -8Ø3 )
D CsTblName      C                       Const( 'Customer' )
D UpTblName      C                       Const( 'CustUpd'  )
D AddAct         C                       Const( 'A' )
D ChangeAct      C                       Const( 'C' )
D DeleteAct      C                       Const( 'D' )
D CompltAct      C                       Const( 'X' )
D ErrAct         C                       Const( 'E' )
D CloseLbl       C                       Const( 'Close'  )
D DeleteLbl      C                       Const( 'Delete' )
D OpenLbl        C                       Const( 'Open'   )
D FetchLbl       C                       Const( 'Fetch'  )
D UpdateLbl      C                       Const( 'Update' )
D InsertLbl      C                       Const( 'Insert' )
D InvActLbl      C                       Const( 'Invalid action' )
D NoKeyLbl       C                       Const( 'Key not found in table' )
D DupKeyLbl      C                       Const( 'Duplicate key in table' )
```

Figure 15.12 continued

CallB) statement. Using a called program or procedure simplifies application coding and standardizes the way applications handle errors. See the annotated bibliography for RPG IV, COBOL/400, and other references that provide help with these techniques.

[39] In the COBOL/400 version, the error routines are implemented as COBOL/400 nested programs. These are an ANSI standard COBOL feature that was introduced in V3R1 ILE COBOL/400. You can use paragraphs and Perform's in earlier versions of COBOL/400.

Figure 15.12
Continued

```
....1....+....2....+....3....+....4....+....5....+....6....+....7
 * Program variables

D PgmErr          S              1A   Inz( 'Ø' )
D CsOpen          S              1A   Inz( 'Ø' )
D UpOpen          S              1A   Inz( 'Ø' )
D UpMoreRows      S              1A   Inz( 'Ø' )
D TblName         S             10A
D SqlStmt         S             10A
D CustIDText      S              7A
D SqlCodSign      S              1A
D SqlCodDec       S              5P Ø
D SqlCodText      S              5A
D ErrText         S             50A
D Msg             S             52A

 * *In99 is used as "dummy" indicator where required on opcodes


 * - - - - - - - - - - - - - - - - - - - - - - - - - - - - - - -
 * Table cursor definitions

C/Exec SQL
C+
C+ Declare CustomerTable Cursor
C+    With Hold
C+    For  Select          *
C+          From          Customer
C+          Where         CustID = :CsCustID
C+          For Update of CustomerName
C/End-Exec

C/Exec SQL
C+
C+ Declare CustUpdTable Cursor
C+    With Hold
C+    For  Select          *
C+          From          CustUpd
C+          Order by      CustID,
C+                        SequenceNumber
C+          For Update of RowAction
C/End-Exec


 * - - - - - - - - - - - - - - - - - - - - - - - - - - - - - - -
 *     Main block
C                 ExSr      OpnTables

C                 DoW       ( UpMoreRows = True ) And ( PgmErr = False )
C                   ExSr    PrcNxtCust
C                 EndDo

C                 ExSr      ClsTables

C                 ExSr      ExitPgm
 * - - - - - - - - - - - - - - - - - - - - - - - - - - - - - - -
```

Figure 15.12 continued

Figure 15.12
Continued

```
....1....+....2....+....3....+....4....+....5....+....6....+....7
C     OpnTables     BegSr

 * Don't open the CustomerTable cursor here because it is
 * opened and closed for each update.

C                   ExSr      OpnCustUpd

C                   EndSr
 * - - - - - - - - - - - - - - - - - - - - - - - - - - - - -
C     OpnCust       BegSr

C/Exec SQL
C+                  Open CustomerTable
C/End-Exec
C                   If        ( SqlCod = SqCdOK ) And ( SqlWn0 = *Blank )
C                     Eval    CsOpen = True
C                   Else
C                     Eval    CsOpen  = False
C                     Eval    SqlStmt = OpenLbl
C                     ExSr    CsSqlErr
C                   EndIf

C                   EndSr
 * - - - - - - - - - - - - - - - - - - - - - - - - - - - - -
C     OpnCustUpd    BegSr

C/Exec SQL
C+                  Open CustUpdTable
C/End-Exec
C                   If        ( SqlCod = SqCdOK ) And ( SqlWn0 = *Blank )
C                     Eval    UpOpen      = True
C                     Eval    UpMoreRows = True
C                   Else
C                     Eval    UpOpen      = False
C                     Eval    UpMoreRows = False
C                     Eval    SqlStmt     = OpenLbl
C                     ExSr    UpSqlErr
C                   EndIf

C                   EndSr
 * - - - - - - - - - - - - - - - - - - - - - - - - - - - - -
C     ClsTables     BegSr

 * Close table(s) that are currently open.

C                   If        CsOpen = True
C                     ExSr    ClsCust
C                   EndIf

C                   If        UpOpen = True
C                     ExSr    ClsCustUpd
C                   EndIf

C                   EndSr
 * - - - - - - - - - - - - - - - - - - - - - - - - - - - - -
```

Figure 15.12 continued

Figure 15.12
Continued

```
....1....+....2....+....3....+....4....+....5....+....6....+....7
C     ClsCust      BegSr

* Set the Customer table state to "closed" in all cases, so the
* error handling for an error on the close doesn't attempt
* another close.

C                    Eval      CsOpen = False
C/Exec SQL
C+                   Close CustomerTable
C/End-Exec
C                    If        ( SqlCod = SqCdOK ) And ( SqlWn0 = *Blank )
 *                     Skip
C                    Else
C                      Eval    SqlStmt = CloseLbl
C                      ExSr    CsSqlErr
C                    EndIf

C                    EndSr
 * - - - - - - - - - - - - - - - - - - - - - - - - - - - - -
C     ClsCustUpd   BegSr

* Set the CustUpd table state to "closed" in all cases, so the
* error handling for an error on the close doesn't attempt
* another close.

C                    Eval      UpOpen     = False
C                    Eval      UpMoreRows = False
C/Exec SQL
C+                   Close CustUpdTable
C/End-Exec
C                    If        ( SqlCod = SqCdOK ) And ( SqlWn0 = *Blank )
 *                     Skip
C                    Else
C                      Eval    SqlStmt = CloseLbl
C                      ExSr    UpSqlErr
C                    EndIf

C                    EndSr
 * - - - - - - - - - - - - - - - - - - - - - - - - - - - - -
C     PrcNxtCust   BegSr

* Read a CustUpd row, and dispatch on its action code.
*
* Each action handling routine attempts to perform the action
* and then changes the action code to indicate either
* successful completion or an error.  The modified CustUpd
* row is then rewritten.

C/Exec SQL
C+                   Fetch Next
C+                     From  CustUpdTable
C+                     Into :CustUpdR
C/End-Exec
C                    Select
C                      When    ( SqlCod = SqCdOK ) And ( SqlWn0 = *Blank )
C                        ExSr  DoTransact
```

Figure 15.12 continued

Figure 15.12
Continued

```
....1....+....2....+....3....+....4....+....5....+....6....+....7
C                           If      PgmErr = False
C                              ExSr UpdCustUpd
C                           EndIf
C                           When    SqlCod = SqCdNoRow
C                              Eval UpMoreRows = False
C                           Other
C                              Eval SqlStmt = FetchLbl
C                              ExSr UpSqlErr
C                           EndSl

C                           EndSr
 * - - - - - - - - - - - - - - - - - - - - - - - - - - - - - -
C     DoTransact    BegSr

C                           Select
C                              When    UpRowAct = AddAct
C                                 ExSr AddCust
C                              When    UpRowAct = ChangeAct
C                                 ExSr ChangeCust
C                              When    UpRowAct = DeleteAct
C                                 ExSr DeleteCust
C                              When    UpRowAct = CompltAct
 *                               Skip
C                              When    UpRowAct = ErrAct
 *                               Skip
C                              Other
C                                 Eval ErrText = InvActLbl
C                                 ExSr ActionErr
C                           EndSl

C                           EndSr
 * - - - - - - - - - - - - - - - - - - - - - - - - - - - - - -
C     AddCust       BegSr

C                           Eval    CsCustID = UpCustID
C                           Eval    CsName   = UpName
C/Exec SQL
C+                          Insert Into Customer
C+                            Values(  :CustomerR )
C/End-Exec
C                           Select
C                              When    ( SqlCod = SqCdOK ) And ( SqlWn0 = *Blank )
C                                 Eval UpRowAct = CompltAct
C                              When    SqlCod = SqCdDupKey
C                                 Eval ErrText = DupKeyLbl
C                                 ExSr ActionErr
C                                 Eval UpRowAct = ErrAct
C                              Other
C                                 Eval SqlStmt = InsertLbl
C                                 ExSr CsSqlErr
C                           EndSl

C                           EndSr
 * - - - - - - - - - - - - - - - - - - - - - - - - - - - - - -
C     ChangeCust    BegSr
```

Figure 15.12 continued

Figure 15.12
Continued

```
....1....+....2....+....3....+....4....+....5....+....6....+....7
* Attempt to fetch the specified Customer row, change its
* data (i.e., name), and update the row.
*
* It would be as fast or faster to use a searched Update
* (instead of a Fetch and positioned Update), similar to the
* way the DeleteCust subroutine (below) is implemented.
* This example uses a positioned Update to demonstrate the
* technique.

C                     Eval       CsCustID = UpCustID

C                     ExSr       OpnCust

C                     If         CsOpen = True
C/Exec SQL
C+                       Fetch Next
C+                         From  CustomerTable
C+                         Into :CustomerR
C/End-Exec
C                        Select
C                        When   ( SqlCod = SqCdOK ) And ( SqlWn0 = *Blank )
C                          ExSr UpdateCust
C                        When   SqlCod = SqCdNoRow
C                          Eval ErrText = NoKeyLbl
C                          ExSr ActionErr
C                          Eval UpRowAct = ErrAct
C                        Other
C                          Eval SqlStmt = FetchLbl
C                          ExSr CsSqlErr
C                        EndSl

C                     ExSr       ClsCust
C                     EndIf

C                     EndSr
* - - - - - - - - - - - - - - - - - - - - - - - - - - - - - - -
C     UpdateCust      BegSr

* Note that a No Row Found condition indicates an unexpected
* error because the row was just fetched with the same key.

C/Exec SQL
C+                     Update  Customer
C+                       Set    CustomerName = :UpName
C+                       Where Current of CustomerTable
C/End-Exec
C                     If         ( SqlCod = SqCdOK ) And ( SqlWn0 = *Blank )
C                        Eval    UpRowAct = CompltAct
C                     Else
C                        Eval    SqlStmt = UpdateLbl
C                        ExSr    CsSqlErr
C                     EndIf

C                     EndSr
* - - - - - - - - - - - - - - - - - - - - - - - - - - - - - - -
```

Figure 15.12 continued

Figure 15.12

Continued

```
....1....+....2....+....3....+....4....+....5....+....6....+....7
C       DeleteCust     BegSr

 * Use a positioned Delete.

C/Exec SQL
C+                     Delete From Customer
C+                       Where     CustID = :UpCustID
C+
C/End-Exec
C                      Select
C                        When    ( SqlCod = SqCdOK ) And ( SqlWn0 = *Blank )
C                          Eval  UpRowAct = CompltAct
C                        When    SqlCod = SqCdNoRow
C                          Eval  ErrText = NoKeyLbl
C                          ExSr  ActionErr
C                          Eval  UpRowAct = ErrAct
C                        Other
C                          Eval  SqlStmt = DeleteLbl
C                          ExSr  CsSqlErr
C                      EndSl

C                      EndSr
 * - - - - - - - - - - - - - - - - - - - - - - - - - - - - - - - -
C       UpdCustUpd     BegSr

C/Exec SQL
C+                     Update   CustUpd
C+                       Set   RowAction = :UpRowAct
C+                       Where Current of CustUpdTable
C/End-Exec
C                      If          ( SqlCod = SqCdOK ) And ( SqlWn0 = *Blank )
 *                       Skip
C                      Else
C                        Eval    SqlStmt = UpdateLbl
C                        ExSr    UpSqlErr
C                      EndIf

C                      EndSr
 * - - - - - - - - - - - - - - - - - - - - - - - - - - - - - - -
C       CsSqlErr       BegSr

C                      Eval    TblName = CsTblName
C                      ExSr    SqlErrRtn

C                      EndSr
 * - - - - - - - - - - - - - - - - - - - - - - - - - - - - - - -
C       UpSqlErr       BegSr

C                      Eval    TblName = UpTblName
C                      ExSr    SqlErrRtn

C                      EndSr
 * - - - - - - - - - - - - - - - - - - - - - - - - - - - - - - -
C       SqlErrRtn      BegSr

 * Handle an unexpected SQL error.
 * Emit an error message, close tables, and exit.        *Figure 15.12 continued*
```

Figure 15.12
Continued

```
....1....+....2....+....3....+....4....+....5....+....6....+....7
* Globals used as input parameters: TblName
*                                    SqlCod
*                                    SqlWrn
*                                    SqlStmt
*
* Globals used as work variables:    SqlCodSign
*                                     SqlCodDec
*                                     SqlCodText
*                                     Msg

C                   If        SqlCod < 0
C                     Eval    SqlCodSign = '-'
C                     Eval    SqlCodDec  = SqlCod * -1
C                   Else
C                     Eval    SqlCodSign = *Blank
C                     Eval    SqlCodDec  = SqlCod
C                   EndIf

C                   MoveL     SqlCodDec      SqlCodText

C                   Eval      Msg = 'SQL error '
C                               + SqlCodSign
C                               + SqlCodText
C                               + ' on '
C                               + %TrimR( SqlStmt )
C                               + ' for '
C                               + %TrimR( TblName )
C                               + ' table.'
C     Msg           Dsply                                      99

C                   If        SqlWrn <> *Blank
C                     Eval    Msg = 'Warning Flags = "' + SqlWrn + '".'
C     Msg           Dsply                                      99
C                   EndIf

C                   Eval      PgmErr = True

C                   EndSr
* - - - - - - - - - - - - - - - - - - - - - - - - - - - - - - -
C     ActionErr     BegSr

* Globals used as input parameters: UpCustID
*                                    UpRowAct
*                                    ErrText
*
* Globals used as work variables:    CustIDText
*                                     Msg

C                   MoveL     UpCustID       CustIDText

C                   Eval      Msg = 'Error for customer '
C                               + CustIDText
C                               + ' on "'
C                               + UpRowAct
C                               + '" action.'
C     Msg           Dsply                                      99
```

Figure 15.12 continued

Figure 15.12
Continued

```
....1....+....2....+....3....+....4....+....5....+....6....+....7
C                       Eval       Msg = %TrimR( ErrText ) + '.'
C         Msg           Dsply                                              99

C                       EndSr
 * - - - - - - - - - - - - - - - - - - - - - - - - - - - - - -
C         *PsSr         BegSr

 * Globals used as work variables: Msg

C                       Eval       Msg = 'Unexpected program error.'
C         Msg           Dsply                                              99

 * To avoid recursive call to *PsSr, don't attempt to close tables.

C                       ExSr       ExitPgm

C                       EndSr
 * - - - - - - - - - - - - - - - - - - - - - - - - - - - - - -
C         ExitPgm       BegSr

C                       Eval       *InLR = *On
C                       Return

C                       EndSr
 * - - - - - - - - - - - - - - - - - - - - - - - - - - - - - -
```

Figure 15.13
COBOL/400 UpdCust
Program

```
Id division.

    Program-Id.    UpdCust.
    Author.        Paul Conte.
    Date-Written.  05/01/96.
 *  Purpose:       Update Customer table from CustUpd table rows.

 * - - - - - - - - - - - - - - - - - - - - - - - - - - - - -
 * - - - - - - - - - - - - - - - - - - - - - - - - - - - - -
 Data division.
 Working-Storage section.

     Exec SQL
       Include SQLCA
     End-Exec.

 * Externally described host structure variables

   01  CustomerRow.
       Copy DDS-All-Formats of Customer With Alias.

   01  CustUpdRow.
       Copy DDS-All-Formats of CustUpd With Alias.


   01  DataTypes             Global.
       02 AS400NameType      Pic X(10).
       02 BooleanType        Pic 1.
```

Figure 15.13 continued

Figure 15.13
Continued

```
            02 SqlStmtType         Pic X(10).
            02 SqlCodeType         Like SqlCode.
            02 SqlWarnType         Like SqlWarn.
            02 TextType            Pic X(50).

        01  Mnemonics.
            02 SqlCodeOK           Like SqlCodeType     Value     0.
            02 SqlCodeNoRowFnd     Like SqlCodeType     Value   100.
            02 SqlCodeDupeKey      Like SqlCodeType     Value  -803.

            02 CustomerTableName Like AS400NameType Value "Customer".
            02 CustUpdTableName  Like AS400NameType Value "CustUpd".

            02 SqlErrPgm           Like AS400NameType  Value "SQLERR".
            02 ActionErrPgm        Like AS400NameType  Value "ACTIONERR".

            02 AddAction           Like RowAction of CustUpd
                                                      Value "A".
            02 ChangeAction        Like AddAction      Value "C".
            02 CompletedAction     Like AddAction      Value "X".
            02 DeleteAction        Like AddAction      Value "D".
            02 ErrorAction         Like AddAction      Value "E".

            02 CloseLabel          Like SqlStmtType    Value "Close".
            02 DeleteLabel         Like SqlStmtType    Value "Delete".
            02 OpenLabel           Like SqlStmtType    Value "Open".
            02 FetchLabel          Like SqlStmtType    Value "Fetch".
            02 UpdateLabel         Like SqlStmtType    Value "Update".
            02 InsertLabel         Like SqlStmtType    Value "Insert".

            02 InvActionLabel      Like TextType
                                   Value "Invalid action".
            02 NoKeyLabel          Like TextType
                                   Value "Key not found in table".
            02 DupeKeyLabel        Like TextType
                                   Value "Duplicate key in table".

        01  ProgramErrorState      Like BooleanType Value B"0".
            88 NoProgramError                        Value B"0".
            88 ProgramError                          Value B"1".

        01  CustomerOpenState      Like BooleanType Value B"0".
            88 CustomerNotOpen                       Value B"0".
            88 CustomerOpen                          Value B"1".

        01  CustUpdOpenState       Like BooleanType Value B"0".
            88 CustUpdNotOpen                        Value B"0".
            88 CustUpdOpen                           Value B"1".

        01  CustUpdNoMoreRowsState Like BooleanType Value B"1".
            88 CustUpdMoreRows                        Value B"0".
            88 CustUpdNoMoreRows                      Value B"1".

        * - - - - - - - - - - - - - - - - - - - - - - - - - - - -
        * - - - - - - - - - - - - - - - - - - - - - - - - - - - -
```

Figure 15.13 continued

Figure 15.13
Continued

```
Procedure division.

* Table cursor definitions

      Exec SQL

        Declare CustomerTable  Cursor
          With Hold
          For  Select           *
                  From          Customer
                  Where         CustID = :Customer.CustID
                  For Update of CustomerName
      End-Exec.

      Exec SQL

        Declare CustUpdTable Cursor
          With Hold
          For  Select           *
                  From          CustUpd
                  Order by      CustID,
                                SequenceNumber
                  For Update of RowAction
      End-Exec.

* - - - - - - - - - - - - - - - - - - - - - - - - - - - - - -
 MainBlock.

     Perform OpenTables.

     Perform ProcessNextCustomer
       Until CustUpdNoMoreRows Or ProgramError.

     Perform CloseTables.

     GoBack.
* - - - - - - - - - - - - - - - - - - - - - - - - - - - - - -
 OpenTables.

* Don't open the CustomerTable cursor here because it is
* opened and closed for each update.

     Perform OpenCustUpdTable.

* - - - - - - - - - - - - - - - - - - - - - - - - - - - - - -
 OpenCustomerTable.

     Exec SQL
       Open CustomerTable
     End-Exec.

     If ( SqlCode = SqlCodeOK ) And ( SqlWarn0 = Space )
       Set CustomerOpen to True
     Else
       Set CustomerNotOpen to True

       Call SqlErrPgm Using by Content
             OpenLabel
```

Figure 15.13 continued

Figure 15.13
Continued

```
                      CustomerTableName
                      SqlCode
                      SqlWarn
                      ProgramErrorState
          End-If.
*  - - - - - - - - - - - - - - - - - - - - - - - - - - - - - - - -
   OpenCustUpdTable.

       Exec SQL
         Open CustUpdTable
       End-Exec.

       If ( SqlCode = SqlCodeOK ) And ( SqlWarn0 = Space )
          Set CustUpdOpen      to True
          Set CustUpdMoreRows to True
       Else
          Set CustUpdNotOpen     to True
          Set CustUpdNoMoreRows to True

          Call SqlErrPgm Using by Content
                OpenLabel
                CustUpdTableName
                SqlCode
                SqlWarn
                ProgramErrorState
       End-If.
*  - - - - - - - - - - - - - - - - - - - - - - - - - - - - - - - -
   CloseTables.

*  Close table(s) that are currently open.

       If CustomerOpen
         Perform CloseCustomerTable
       End-If.

       If CustUpdOpen
         Perform CloseCustUpdTable
       End-If.


*  - - - - - - - - - - - - - - - - - - - - - - - - - - - - - - - -
   CloseCustomerTable.

*  Set the Customer table state to "closed" in all cases, so the
*  error handling for an error on the close doesn't attempt
*  another close.

       Set CustomerNotOpen to True.

       Exec SQL
         Close CustomerTable
       End-Exec.

       If ( SqlCode = SqlCodeOK ) And ( SqlWarn0 = Space )
          Continue
       Else
          Call SqlErrPgm Using by Content
                CloseLabel
                CustomerTableName
```

Figure 15.13 continued

Figure 15.13
Continued

```
                        SqlCode
                        SqlWarn
                        ProgramErrorState
              End-If.

* - - - - - - - - - - - - - - - - - - - - - - - - - - - - - -
  CloseCustUpdTable.

* Set the CustUpd table state to "closed" in all cases, so the
* error handling for an error on the close doesn't attempt
* another close.

      Set CustUpdNotOpen    to True.
      Set CustUpdNoMoreRows to True.

      Exec SQL
        Close CustUpdTable
      End-Exec.

      If ( SqlCode = SqlCodeOK ) And ( SqlWarn0 = Space )
         Continue
      Else
         Call SqlErrPgm Using by Content
                 CloseLabel
                 CustUpdTableName
                 SqlCode
                 SqlWarn
                 ProgramErrorState
      End-If.

* - - - - - - - - - - - - - - - - - - - - - - - - - - - - - -
  ProcessNextCustomer.

* Read a CustUpd row, and dispatch on its action code.
*
* Each action-handling routine attempts to perform the action
* and then changes the action code to indicate either
* successful completion or an error. The modified CustUpd
* row is then rewritten.

      Exec SQL
        Fetch Next
          From  CustUpdTable
          Into :CustUpd
      End-Exec.

      Evaluate True
          When ( SqlCode = SqlCodeOK ) And ( SqlWarn0 = Space )
               Perform DoTransactionForCurCustomer
               If NoProgramError
                  Perform UpdateCustUpd
               End-If
          When SqlCode = SqlCodeNoRowFnd
               Set CustUpdNoMoreRows to True
          When Other
               Call SqlErrPgm Using by Content
                   FetchLabel
                   CustUpdTableName
```

Figure 15.13 continued

Figure 15.13
Continued

```
                                                SqlCode
                                                SqlWarn
                                                ProgramErrorState
        End-Evaluate.
* - - - - - - - - - - - - - - - - - - - - - - - - - - - - - - - - - - -
  DoTransactionForCurCustomer.

        Evaluate RowAction of CustUpd
            When AddAction        Perform AddCustomer
            When ChangeAction     Perform ChangeCustomer
            When DeleteAction     Perform DeleteCustomer
            When CompletedAction  Continue
            When ErrorAction      Continue
            When Other Call ActionErrPgm Using by Content
                                InvActionLabel
                                RowAction of CustUpd
                                CustID    of CustUpd
        End-Evaluate.
* - - - - - - - - - - - - - - - - - - - - - - - - - - - - - - - - - - -
  AddCustomer.

        Move CustId of CustUpd to
            CustId of Customer.

        Move CustomerName of CustUpd to
            CustomerName of Customer.

        Exec SQL
          Insert Into Customer
            Values(  :Customer )
        End-Exec.

        Evaluate True
            When ( SqlCode = SqlCodeOK ) And ( SqlWarn0 = Space )
                    Move CompletedAction to RowAction of CustUpd
            When SqlCode = SqlCodeDupeKey
                    Perform DupeKeyErr
            When Other
                    Call SqlErrPgm Using by Content
                        InsertLabel
                        CustomerTableName
                        SqlCode
                        SqlWarn
                        ProgramErrorState
        End-Evaluate.

* - - - - - - - - - - - - - - - - - - - - - - - - - - - - - - - - - - -
  ChangeCustomer.

* Attempt to fetch the specified Customer row, change its
* data (i.e., name), and update the row.
*
* It would be as fast or faster to use a searched Update
* (instead of a Fetch and positioned Update), similar to the
* way the DeleteCustomer paragraph (below) is implemented.
* This example uses a positioned Update to demonstrate the
* technique.
```

Figure 15.13 continued

Figure 15.13
Continued

```
        Move CustId of CustUpd to
            CustId of Customer.

        Perform OpenCustomerTable.

        If CustomerOpen

            Exec SQL
              Fetch Next
                From  CustomerTable
                Into :Customer
            End-Exec

            Evaluate True
              When ( SqlCode = SqlCodeOK ) And ( SqlWarn0 = Space )
                    Move CustomerName of CustUpd to
                        CustomerName of Customer

                    Perform UpdateCustomer
              When SqlCode = SqlCodeNoRowFnd
                    Perform NoKeyErr
              When Other
                    Call SqlErrPgm Using by Content
                        FetchLabel
                        CustomerTableName
                        SqlCode
                        SqlWarn
                        ProgramErrorState
            End-Evaluate

            Perform CloseCustomerTable
        End-If.
* - - - - - - - - - - - - - - - - - - - - - - - - - - - - - - - -
  UpdateCustomer.

* Note that a No Row Found condition indicates an unexpected
* error because the row was just read with the same key.

        Exec SQL
          Update  Customer
            Set   CustomerName = :Customer.CustomerName
            Where Current of CustomerTable
        End-Exec.

        If ( SqlCode = SqlCodeOK ) And ( SqlWarn0 = Space )
            Move CompletedAction to RowAction of CustUpd
        Else
            Call SqlErrPgm Using by Content
                UpdateLabel
                CustomerTableName
                SqlCode
                SqlWarn
                ProgramErrorState
        End-If.
* - - - - - - - - - - - - - - - - - - - - - - - - - - - - - - - -
  DeleteCustomer.

* Use a positioned Delete.
```

Figure 15.13 continued

Figure 15.13
Continued

```
Exec SQL
  Delete From Customer
     Where      CustID = :CustUpd.CustID
End-Exec.

Evaluate True
   When ( SqlCode = SqlCodeOK ) And ( SqlWarn0 = Space )
        Move CompletedAction to RowAction of CustUpd
   When SqlCode = SqlCodeNoRowFnd
        Perform NoKeyErr
   When Other
        Call SqlErrPgm Using by Content
             DeleteLabel
             CustomerTableName
             SqlCode
             SqlWarn
             ProgramErrorState
   End-Evaluate.
* - - - - - - - - - - - - - - - - - - - - - - - - - - - - - - -
UpdateCustUpd.

   Exec SQL
     Update   CustUpd
       Set    RowAction = :CustUpd.RowAction
       Where Current of CustUpdTable
   End-Exec.

   If ( SqlCode = SqlCodeOK ) And ( SqlWarn0 = Space )
      Continue
   Else
      Call SqlErrPgm Using by Content
           UpdateLabel
           CustUpdTableName
           SqlCode
           SqlWarn
           ProgramErrorState
   End-If.

* - - - - - - - - - - - - - - - - - - - - - - - - - - - - - - -
DupeKeyErr.

   Call ActionErrPgm Using by Content
        DupeKeyLabel
        RowAction of CustUpd
        CustID    of CustUpd.

   Move ErrorAction to RowAction of CustUpd.

* - - - - - - - - - - - - - - - - - - - - - - - - - - - - - - -
NoKeyErr.

   Call ActionErrPgm Using by Content
        NoKeyLabel
        RowAction of CustUpd
        CustID    of CustUpd.

   Move ErrorAction to RowAction of CustUpd.
```

Figure 15.13 continued

Figure 15.13
Continued

```
* - - - - - - - - - - - - - - - - - - - - - - - - - - - - - - -
* - - - - - - - - - - - - - - - - - - - - - - - - - - - - - - -

Id division.

  Program-Id. SqlErr.
*  Purpose:    Handle an unexpected SQL error.
*              Emit an error message, close tables,
*              and set ProgramErrorState to True.

*---------------------------------------------------------------
Data division.
Working-Storage section.

01  SqlCodeDisplay  Pic ---------9 Display.

Linkage section.

01  SqlStmt            Like SqlStmtType.
01  TableName          Like AS400NameType.
01  SqlCode            Like SqlCodeType.
01  SqlWarn            Like SqlWarnType.
01  ProgramErrorState  Like BooleanType.
    88 ProgramError    Value B"1".

Procedure division Using SqlStmt
                         TableName
                         SqlCode
                         SqlWarn
                         ProgramErrorState.

MainBlock.

    Move SqlCode to SqlCodeDisplay.

    Display "SQL error " SqlCodeDisplay
            " on "        SqlStmt
            " for "       TableName  " table.".

    If SqlWarn Not = Space
      Display "Warning flags = '" SqlWarn "'."
    End-If.

    Set ProgramError to True.

    GoBack.

End program SqlErr.

* - - - - - - - - - - - - - - - - - - - - - - - - - - - - - - -
* - - - - - - - - - - - - - - - - - - - - - - - - - - - - - - -

Id division.

  Program-Id. ActionErr.
*  Purpose:    Handle an action error.
*              Emit an error message.
```

Figure 15.13 continued

Figure 15.13
Continued

```
*----------------------------------------------------------------
 Data division.

 Linkage section.

 01  ErrorText    Like TextType.
 01  Action       Pic X(1).
 01  CustID       Pic S9(7) Comp-3.

 Procedure division Using ErrorText
                          Action
                          CustID.

 MainBlock.

     Display "Error for customer " CustID
             " on '"              Action
             "' action: '"        ErrorText "'.".

     GoBack.

 End program ActionErr.


*  - - - - - - - - - - - - - - - - - - - - - - - - - - - - - - -
*  - - - - - - - - - - - - - - - - - - - - - - - - - - - - - - -

 End program UpdCust.
```

Other Embedded SQL Features

Embedded SQL has a few other features that we'll look at briefly.

Include Statement

The Include statement lets you include SQL and HLL source statements from a source member other than the one you're coding. Suppose you have the following standard error-checking code in a source member SQLERRCHK:

```
....1....+....2....+....3....+....4....+....5....+....6....+
C                   Select
C                     When     SQLCod < 0
C                       ExSr   SQLError
C                     When     SQLCod = 100
C                       ExSr   SQLNoRow
C                     When     ( SQLCod > 0 ) Or ( SQLWn0 <> *Blank )
C                       ExSr   SQLWarning
C                   EndSl
```

You can specify that the SQL precompiler include this code after an SQL statement by using an Include statement:

```
....1....+....2....+....3....+....4....+....5....+....6....+
C/Exec SQL
C+                      Update  Customer
C+                        Set   Discount = :NewDisc
C+                        Where ShpCity = :SlcCusCity
C/End-Exec
C/Exec SQL
C+ Include SQLErrChk
C/End-Exec
```

The source member name follows the Include keyword. The INCFILE parameter on the CRTSQLxxx command used to create the program specifies the library and source file containing the member.

Dynamic Cursors

SQL lets you combine the capabilities of dynamic execution and a cursor by dynamically preparing the Select statement that's used for a cursor declaration. The following shows a simplified example of the statements used for this type of dynamic cursor:

```
....1....+....2....+....3....+....4....+....5....+....6....+
D CustomerR       DS
D  CsCustID                      7P Ø
D  CsName                        3ØA
D  CsShpCity                     3ØA
D  CsDiscount                    5P 3
D  CsCityNull     S              4B Ø
D  CsDiscNull     S              4B Ø
D SQLStmtStr      S            256A
D InpSrchCnd      S            256A


C/Exec SQL
C+ Declare CustomerCursor Cursor
C+   For   DynSQLStmt
C/End-Exec
           .
           .
           .
C* Get a search condition (as a string) from user input
C* and place the string in the InpSrchCnd variable.
           .
           .
           .
C                      Eval      SQLStmtStr = 'Select * +
C                                              From Customer +
C                                              Where '
C                      Eval      SQLStmtStr = SQLStmtStr + InpSrchCnd
C/Exec SQL
C+                     Prepare DynSQLStmt
C+                       From :SQLStmtStr
C/End-Exec
C/Exec SQL
C+                     Open CustomerCursor
C/End-Exec
C/Exec SQL
C+                     Fetch Next
```

```
....1....+....2....+....3....+....4....+....5....+....6....+
C+                      From   CustomerCursor
C+                      Into  :CsCustID,
C+                            :CsName,
C+                            :CsShpCity   :CsCityNull,
C+                            :CsDiscount  :CsDiscNull
C/End-Exec
```

The Declare Cursor statement's For clause specifies the DynSQLStmt statement name rather than a nested Select statement as we saw earlier in the chapter. The DynSQLStmt statement is prepared from a Select statement that's contained in the SQLStmtStr host variable. The statement must be successfully prepared before the Open statement opens the cursor. At the time the Open statement is executed, DB2/400 uses the Select statement that's been prepared to determine which rows are in the cursor's result table. You can use question marks (?) as parameter markers in the Select statement string and then specify a Using clause with corresponding host variables on the Open statement. The host variables' values are used in place of the parameter markers, as we saw with the dynamic execution of other DML statements using the Execute statement.[40]

Stored Procedures

Embedded SQL provides the ability to call an executable procedure, known as a **stored procedure**. On the AS/400, a stored procedure is simply an HLL program with or without embedded SQL statements.[41] Because you can always use an AS/400 HLL's built-in Call statement to call another AS/400 program on the same system, stored procedures are mainly useful for distributed applications.

SQL/400 provides a Call statement to call a stored procedure. The following example calls the Proc1 procedure with two host variables, Arg1 and Arg2, passed as arguments:

---

[40] SQL provides an even more flexible facility for dynamic cursor definitions. You can use the Describe statement to retrieve information about a prepared statement (e.g., the columns in a Select statement's result table). You can use a Describe Table statement to retrieve information about a table or view (e.g., a table's column definitions). The information retrieved by a Describe or Describe Table statement is stored in an SQL structure known as an SQL descriptor area (SQLDA). You can also place addresses of program variables (i.e., pointers) in an SQLDA and then use the descriptor name instead of a list of host variables on an Open, Fetch, or Execute statement. The combination of these two uses of the SQLDA provides a way to construct and execute any DML statement without having to hard code any host variable names or parameter markers. Using descriptors is an advanced level of SQL programming and is more typically used in general-purpose utilities than in application programs. The *DB2/400 SQL Programming* manual provides a more detailed explanation and examples of these techniques.

[41] Some other DBMS implement stored procedures by using extensions to SQL rather than HLL procedures or programs.

```
....1....+....2....+....3....+....4....+....5....+....6....+
C/Exec SQL
C+ Call Proc1 ( :Arg1,
C+              :Arg2 )
C/End-Exec
```

A stored procedure should be declared before it's called (if you don't create a permanent definition in the catalog, as discussed below). You can declare a procedure in the same program that calls it, as in the following example:

```
....1....+....2....+....3....+....4....+....5....+....6....+0
C/Exec SQL
C+ Declare Proc1 Procedure
C+
C+ ( In    Arg1 Char(    1    ),
C+   InOut Arg2 Decimal( 7, 2 ) )
C+
C+   External Name AppExc/Proc1
C+   Language RPGLE
C+   General with Nulls
C/End-Exec
```

The Declare Procedure statement specifies the procedure's parameter types and whether they're used for input, output, or both (from the perspective of the called procedure). The Declare Procedure statement also can specify the library, program name, and language used for an AS/400 HLL program. The final clause specifies whether null indicators are valid for the arguments used on a Call statement.

You can store a permanent definition of a stored procedure's interface in the SQL system catalog by using a Create Procedure statement:

```
Create Procedure AppExc/Proc1
   ( In    Arg1 Char(    1    ),
     InOut Arg2 Decimal( 7, 2 ) )
   External Name AppExc/Proc1
   Language RPGLE
   General with Nulls
```

Unlike the Declare Procedure statement, which must be embedded in an HLL program, a Create Procedure statement can be executed interactively or from a source member using the RUNSQLSTM command. The procedure definition stored in the SQL catalog by a Create Procedure statement is available to all applications, whereas the definition on a Declare Procedure statement is available only within the program that contains the declaration. To remove a procedure definition from the SQL catalog, you execute a Drop Procedure statement:

```
Drop Procedure AppExc/Proc1
```

The *DB2/400 SQL Programming* manual provides more details and examples for using stored procedures.

Distributed Database

In addition to letting you call a stored procedure on a remote system, SQL/400 lets you perform other operations. Distributed database is also covered in Chapter 17; here we look briefly at several related SQL statements that can be embedded in an HLL program.

Normally, all SQL statements in an AS/400 HLL program operate on base tables, views, and other SQL objects that are on the same system as the program that is executing. If you want to operate on objects on a different system, you first establish a connection to that system using the Connect statement,[42] which names the database server (i.e., the remote database):

```
Connect To EugBrnch
```

Any statements executed after this connection is established operate on objects on the EugBrnch database. The Connect statement allows an optional user profile and password to be specified:

```
Connect To EugBrnch User :UserName Password :UserPassWd
```

To end a connection, you can execute either a Disconnect statement or a Release statement followed by a Commit or Rollback statement. The Disconnect statement is used when commitment control is not in effect for transactions involving the remote system. On the Disconnect statement, you can specify a currently connected system, the Current keyword to disconnect from the currently active connection, or the All keyword to disconnect from all connections. The following example disconnects the current connection:

```
Disconnect Current
```

When commitment control is in effect, a connection can't be ended until any pending database updates on the remote system are either committed or rolled back. Thus, you use a Release statement to indicate the connection is no longer needed (except to complete the current transaction) and should be ended on the next Commit or Rollback operation or other implicit end to the current unit of work. The Release statement has the same options as the Disconnect statement; the following example shows how you would release all connections:

```
Release All
```

To switch among connections when several connections have been established, you use the Set Connection statement with the name of the connection you want to make current. As with the other connection-related SQL statements, you can use a host variable for the database name:

```
Set Connection :CurDtaBase
```

---

[42] You can also have a program automatically establish a connection when it starts execution.

To switch from a remote database to the local database, you use a Set Connection statement with the local database name.

To obtain information about the current connection, you can execute a Connect statement with no keywords or other arguments, and information is returned in the SQLCA (see Figure 15.9).

The following statements show how you could use DB2/400's distributed database capability to delete a customer row that's stored in the Customer table on an AS/400 identified as the EugBrnch database (error handling for the Delete and Disconnect statements is omitted to simplify the example):

```
....1....+....2....+....3....+....4....+....5....+....6....+
C/Exec SQL
C+                      Connect To EugBrnch
C/End-Exec
C                       If        ( SQLCod = 0 ) And ( SQLWn0 = *Blank )
C                         ExSr    ExcSQLDlt
C                         ExSr    DisCnctEug
C                       Else
C                         ExSr    SQLError
C                       EndIf

C       ExcSQLDlt       BegSr
C/Exec SQL
C+                      Delete
C+                        From  Customer
C+                        Where CustID = :SlcCustID
C/End-Exec
C                       EndSr

C       DisCnctEug      BegSr
C/Exec SQL
C+                      Disconnect EugBrnch
C/End-Exec
C                       EndSr
```

Note how this example checks for a successful connection before executing the Delete statement. Also note that this example is not using commitment control.

Creating SQL/400 Programs

Once you've entered your HLL and embedded SQL source code, you execute one of the commands listed in Figure 15.14 to create the program, module, or service program object from the source code.

You enter the CRTSQLxxx command from any display screen that lets you enter CL commands. Or, if you're using PDM (discussed in Appendix C), you enter option 14 (Compile) or 15 (Create Module) beside the source member name to execute the CRTSQLxxx command. In either case, you can press the F4 key to prompt for the command's parameter values. Figure 15.15 lists commonly used parameters and their default values for the CRTSQLxxxI commands that create ILE objects.

Figure 15.14
CL Commands to Create
Programs or ILE Modules
and Service Programs

Command	Language
Non-ILE Programs	
CRTSQLCBL	COBOL/400
CRTSQLFTN	FORTRAN
CRTSQLPLI	PL/I
CRTSQLRPG	RPG/400
ILE Programs, Modules, and Service Programs	
CRTSQLCI	ILE C/400
CRTSQLCBLI	ILE COBOL/400
CRTSQLRPGI	RPG IV

Figure 15.15
Commonly Used
Command Parameters for
CRTSQLxxxI Commands

Parameter	Purpose	Default (other values)
OBJ	Name of program, module, or service program to be created	
SRCFILE	Source file that contains HLL and embedded SQL source	*LIBL/QCLESRC, *LIBL/QCBLLESRC, or *LIBL/QRPGLESRC
SRCMBR	Source member that contains HLL and embedded SQL source	*OBJ
OPTION	Naming convention (and other options)	*SYS (*SQL)
OBJTYPE	Type of object to create (program, module, or service program)	*PGM (*MODULE, *SRVPGM)
INCFILE	Source file to use for embedded Include statements	*LIBL/*SRCFILE
COMMIT	Level of commitment control environment for program execution	*CHG (*NONE, *CS, *ALL, *RR)
CLOSQLCSR	When SQL cursors are implicitly closed	*ENDACTGRP (*ENDMOD)
RDB	Database name for distributed program	*LOCAL
TEXT	Description of the created object	*SRCMBRTXT

Online help provides a full description of all CRTSQLxxx command parameters; this section briefly discusses the parameters you need to be familiar with.

The following example shows a typical command to create the RPG IV version of the UPDCUST program:[43]

```
CRTSQLRPGI OBJ( appexc/updcust )
           SRCFILE( appsrc/qrpglesrc )
           OPTION( *sys )
           OBJTYPE( *pgm )
           INCFILE( appsrc/sqlincsrc )
           COMMIT( *none )
```

The CRTSQLRPGI command's OBJ parameter specifies the object you're creating. Normally, you should provide a qualified name to ensure that the new object is placed in the correct library. The SRCFILE parameter identifies the source file in which the object's source code is stored. By default, all the CRTSQLxxxI commands use the same source member name as the object name you specify in the OBJ parameter.

This example explicitly specifies that the system naming convention is used (i.e., the slash (/) is used between a collection name and the object it qualifies). The object to be created is a program, and any members specified on an Include statement will be found in the APPSRC/SQLINCSRC source file. The last parameter specifies that no commitment control environment is used (our sample program omitted Commit and Rollback statements for simplicity). One of the most important decisions to make when creating a program is the level (if any) of commitment control to use. Chapter 17 delves more deeply into commitment control.

For programs that access tables or views with date or time columns, be sure to use the same DATFMT, DATSEP, TIMFMT, and TIMSEP values on the CRTSQLxxx command as were used when the tables and views were created. Normally, your installation will have set system and command defaults to the same formats (e.g., *ISO). But, for example, if you inadvertently use *MDY as the date format when you create a program and the program uses embedded SQL to access a table with a column that has *ISO date format, you get either unnecessary data conversions or (if you use multiple-row Fetch or block Insert) data errors. Problems caused by mismatched date and time formats can be hard to diagnose.

The CRTSQLxxx commands include some, but not all, of the parameters available with the various HLL compiler commands (e.g., CRTBNDRPG). If you want to use one of the compiler command options that's not available on a CRTSQLxxx command, you can specify OPTION(*NOGEN) on the CRTSQLxxx command. Doing so produces a temporary member in the

---

[43] To create the COBOL/400 version of the UPDCUST program, you could enter a CRTSQLCBLI command with the same parameters, except naming the appropriate source file.

QTEMP/QSQLTEMP source file (or QTEMP/QSQLTEMP1 for RPG IV) with the same name as the object name specified in the CRTSQLxxx command's OBJ parameter. You can then execute any compiler command specifying this source member as the input file and adding other compiler command parameters, as needed. You should not edit the temporary source member. If you do, any subsequent attempt to compile the modified source member will fail.[44]

As we learned in Chapter 13, SQL/400 base tables are DB2/400 physical files and SQL/400 views are DB2/400 logical files. In most cases, you can use SQL/400 DML statements, including those embedded in an HLL program, on either tables and views created with SQL DML statements or physical or logical files created from DDS. You can also use the OVRDBF (Override with Database File) commands before executing an HLL program with embedded SQL, and the overrides apply to tables and views (as well as physical and logical files) accessed by the program. The OVRDBF command, which is discussed in Part I and Chapter 17, and whose parameters are documented in Appendix B, can be used to redirect an embedded table or view reference to a specific table, view, physical file, or logical file object at runtime. DB2/400 recognizes the following OVRDBF parameters for SQL/400 access:

- TOFILE (file containing member to open)
- MBR (member to open)
- SEQONLY (process rows sequentially)
- INHWRT (inhibit write operations)
- WAITRCD (seconds to wait for a row lock)

All other OVRDBF parameters are ignored for SQL/400 access.

The SQL/400 Translation Process

At the beginning of the chapter, we looked at a simplified view of the steps involved in creating a program object from a source member that contains embedded SQL. The process consists of two major steps: translating embedded SQL statements to HLL statements and creating a program from the combined original HLL and translated SQL statements. Figure 15.16 shows a more detailed picture of the complete process for RPG IV, COBOL/400, or other ILE languages.

The SQL/400 precompiler initiates the overall process. A component of the precompiler performs the first step, in which embedded SQL statements are translated into HLL statements. For most embedded SQL statements,

---

[44] This restriction is built in to compiler commands to prevent inconsistencies between the source member's HLL code and the application plan information that the SQL precompiler generates.

Figure 15.16
Detailed SQL/400
Translation Process

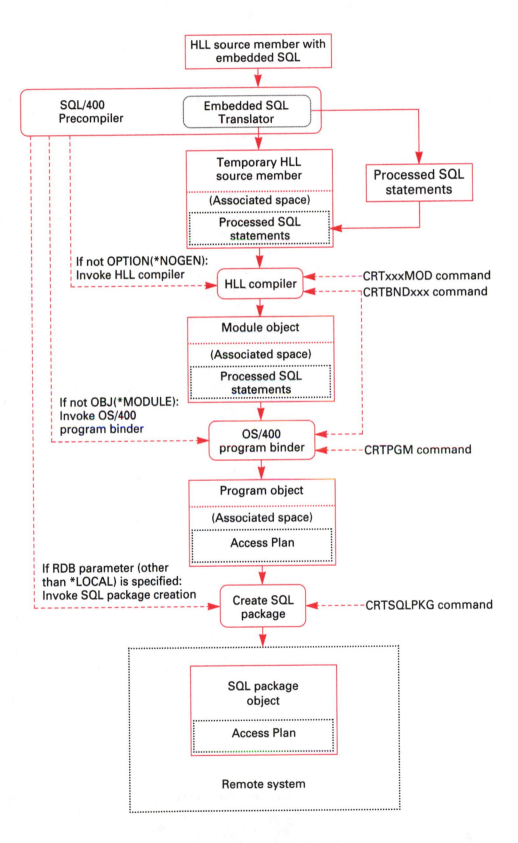

this precompiler component generates some or all of the following HLL statements:

- Variable declarations for temporary work variables
- Assignment operations (e.g., RPG IV Move) that copy programmer-defined host variable values to temporary precompiler-generated variables
- A Call statement that calls QSQROUTE or other IBM-supplied program
- Assignment operations (e.g., RPG IV Move) that copy some of the temporary variables' values back to the programmer-defined host variables

The precompiler writes the generated HLL code and the original, untranslated HLL statements to a member of a temporary source file in the job's QTEMP library.

In addition, the precompiler processes the embedded SQL statements to produce a set of internal structures that will be used later in the translation process to create an access plan. An access plan is another set of internal tables and executable code used by DB2/400 when the QSQROUTE or other program is called to perform an embedded SQL operation. The processed SQL statements are stored in the associated space of the temporary source member.[45]

After the initial translation of embedded SQL statements, unless you specified OPTION(*NOGEN), the precompiler invokes the appropriate HLL compiler, which reads the temporary source file member and produces a module object. If this step is successful, the compiler copies the processed SQL statements (which were built during the first step) from the temporary source file member's associated space to the associated space of the module object.

After a module is created, the precompiler invokes the OS/400 program binder (unless you specified OPTION(*MODULE)), which combines or links modules into a program object. The binder invokes a set of system routines that translate the processed SQL statements in the modules' associated spaces into the access plan, which is stored in the associated space of the program object. If OBJTYPE(*MODULE) is specified on the CRTSQLxxxI command, the precompiler doesn't invoke the OS/400 program binder, and

---

[45] Recall from Figure 1.2 that an OS/400 object has a header, a part that contains the main contents of the object, and an associated space that's used for miscellaneous data. In a database file object, each member also has an associated space that can be used for miscellaneous data. The associated space is not where the member's records are stored, and the contents of the associated space are not accessible by I/O operations.

you must subsequently use a CRTPGM command to create a program from one or more module objects.[46]

DB2/400 supports distributed database access by programs with embedded SQL. A distributed database program is one that accesses data on a remote database. A distributed database program requires an SQL package object on the remote system. The package contains the access plan to perform the program's SQL operations on the remote system's tables, views, and other objects. As Figure 15.16 shows, a package is created from a program object. The SQL precompiler invokes this step automatically when you specify a relational database name on the RDB parameter (other than *LOCAL) on a CRTSQLxxxI command. Or you can use the CRTSQLPKG (Create SQL Package) command to create a package from a program object.

Coding Suggestions

- Always check SQLCode and SQLWarn0 or SQLState after each executable SQL statement to check for exceptions. Use standard error-handling routines to handle exceptions.

- Follow the applicable SQL coding suggestions (e.g., alignment) listed in Chapters 13 and 14.

- In RPG programs, align SQL statements (other than Declare Cursor and Include, which aren't executable statements) with the opcode column.

- For RPG IV, use externally described data structures with the Prefix keyword to generate host variables.

- For COBOL/400, use Copy DDS-All-Formats . . . With Alias (for long column names) or simply Copy DDS-All-Formats (for short column names) to generate host variables.

- Generally, declare host variables so they have the same data type and size as any column with which they're used.

- Use an Include, /Copy, or Copy to include commonly used declarations, mnemonics, SQL source code, or HLL source code in programs. Remember that the Include statement and RPG /Copy compiler directive include a source member during precompilation; a COBOL/400 Copy includes source during the compile phase.

- For a search condition that's used in multiple embedded SQL statements (within the same or multiple programs), consider creating a view and referencing that in embedded SQL statements rather than repeating the search condition in multiple statements.

---

[46] You can also create service program objects by specifying OBJTYPE(*SRVPGM) on the CRTSQLxxxI commands. An ILE service program is somewhat like a dynamic link library (DLL) under Windows or OS/2. If you create module objects with the CRTSQLxxxI command, you can subsequently bind them into a service program using the CRTSRVPGM command.

- For an explicit select list (i.e., a list of columns) used in multiple Select Into statements or cursor definitions, consider creating a view that's referenced by the statements.

- For any SQL statement executed in more than one place in a program, place the statement in a subroutine, paragraph, or internal procedure and execute that routine rather than coding the statement multiple times in the program.

- For any SQL statement that's used in multiple programs, consider putting the statement in a source member by itself and using an Include statement to include it during the precompilation phase.

- When you use an externally described host structure in a Select Into, Fetch, or Insert statement, use an implicit column list rather than explicitly listing each column. When you use individual host variables, use an explicit column list.

- Never use a Select Into statement with a search condition that might be satisfied by more than one row (unless the select list contains a column function). Generally, use Select Into only to retrieve individual rows by primary or unique key or to retrieve column functions.

- In a Select Into or Fetch statement, always use an indicator variable for a null-capable column.

- On cursor declarations
    - For a read-only cursor always specify the For Read Only clause
    - For a cursor that will be referenced in an Update statement, always specify the For Update Of clause
    - For a cursor that will be referenced in a Delete statement — but not an Update statement — don't specify either a For Read Only or a For Update Of clause
    - Generally, use the With Hold option on cursor declarations.

- Explicitly close all open cursors when the cursor is no longer needed or an unrecoverable exception occurs. Be careful not to recursively execute SQL error handling when you're closing a cursor while still handling another SQL error.

- Use commitment control to guarantee the all-or-none execution of multi-row transactions.

- Be sure to specify the correct COMMIT parameter value on the CRTSQLxxx command used to create a program.

- Execute a Disconnect or Release statement as soon as you no longer need access to a remote database.

- Use the OVRDBF command to redirect an embedded SQL table or view reference to a different table, view, or physical or logical file.

- Other, performance-related suggestions:
    - To get additional information about how DB2/400 performs embedded SQL operations, run the HLL program in debug mode against production tables and views (or with comparable test tables, views, and indexes). When a program with embedded SQL runs in debug mode, DB2/400 puts informational messages in the job log. The *DB2/400 SQL Programming* manual provides a guide to these messages. The STRDBG (Start Debug) command begins debug mode for a job.
    - List only the columns you need to retrieve on a Select Into statement or cursor declaration. (If you need to retrieve all but a few columns, it may be simpler to specify an asterisk (*) for an implicit column list along with an externally described host structure variable.)
    - For sequentially retrieving large numbers of rows, use a multiple-row Fetch statement.
    - For inserting large numbers of rows, use a blocked Insert statement.
    - Add the Optimize For *n* Rows clause to a cursor declaration when you know approximately how many rows you intend to fetch and when the number of rows is significantly fewer than the expected number of rows in the result table.
    - Don't use expressions in the Set clause of a positioned Update. (DB2/400 does an open for the first execution of a positioned Update when the Set clause has an expression.) Calculate the new column value in a host variable, and use just the host variable in the Set clause assignment.
    - When a particular dynamic SQL statement will be executed only once in a program, use Execute Immediate. If a statement may be executed more than once, use Prepare and Execute statements.
    - Consult the *DB2/400 SQL Programming* manual for additional performance tips for the DB2/400 release you're using. Be sure to check the latest version of the manual when you install a new release of DB2/400 because performance characteristics can change significantly in a new release.

Chapter Summary

Embedded SQL statements are SQL statements coded in HLL programs. You can code most DDL and DML statements as embedded statements. Each embedded statement is coded between an Exec SQL and an End-Exec precompiler directive. The SQL precompiler translates embedded SQL statements into HLL declarations and procedural code, which an HLL compiler then compiles.

You can use host variables in embedded SQL statements. A host variable can be used to supply a value in a search condition or expression in the select column list. A host variable can also receive data returned by a Select Into or

Fetch statement or can provide a value to be assigned to a column on an Update or Insert statement. Wherever you can use a host variable, you may follow it with an indicator variable, which is used to handle columns that are null (on the Select Into and Fetch statements) or that should be set to null (on the Update and Insert statements). With SQL/400, you can use a host structure variable instead of a list of host variables or a list of indicator variables. An externally described HLL structure can be used as a host structure variable. SQL/400 also lets you use host structure arrays on multiple-row Fetch and block Insert statements.

There are three major categories of embedded SQL statements: static statements, dynamic statements, and statements that involve cursors. Static statements have a fixed structure and use host variables and literals to supply new column values and search condition values. The Select Into is the static form of the Select statement and can retrieve a single row's values into host variables. Static Select, Update, and Delete statements that specify a search condition on a table's primary or unique key provide direct access by key for input and update operations. The static Insert statement provides a means to add new rows to a base table.

Dynamic embedded statements are contained in a host string variable and are prepared and executed at runtime. The Execute statement prepares and executes an SQL statement all in one step. The Prepare statement prepares an SQL statement from a string for subsequent execution by an Execute statement. The question mark (?) can be used as a parameter marker in a string that's prepared as an SQL statement. When the statement is executed, host variables can be used on the Execute statement to provide values that are substituted for the parameter markers.

An SQL cursor provides a result table through which a program can perform input, update, and delete operations. A cursor uses a nested Select statement to define the result table. This Select statement can have a From, Where, Group By, Having, and Order by clause, as well as a Union operator. The Where and Having clauses can contain host variables that are evaluated when the cursor is opened. Thus, a cursor can be used to access different sets of rows depending on the value of host variables. A cursor can also have a For Read Only clause, to specify it as read only, or a For Update Of clause, to specify it as an updatable cursor.

After a cursor is opened, the Fetch statement is used to retrieve one or more rows into host variables. The Fetch Next statement reads rows sequentially in the order (if any) specified on the Order By clause of the cursor's Select statement. A positioned Update or Delete statement can be used to update the column values in an updatable cursor's current row or to delete the current row.

A scrollable cursor is one defined with the Scroll option (for read-only access) or Dynamic Scroll option (which allows updates). A scrollable cursor allows other Fetch statement positioning options in addition to Next. With these positioning options, the cursor's current position can be moved forward or backward from the current position or set to the beginning or end of the result table.

After execution of every SQL statement, DB2/400 sets the SQLCode variable and (in some cases) other variables that are part of the SQL communication area (SQLCA). A program should always check SQLCode and SQLWarn0 (or SQLState) after each SQL statement.

HLL programs with embedded SQL statements can use DB2/400's commitment control facility. Multirow transactions can be committed with the Commit statement or rolled back with the Rollback statement.

SQL provides several additional features for embedded SQL programming. The Include statement lets you include a source member into the program during the precompile phase. Dynamic cursors let you use dynamically prepared Select statements with parameter markers. Stored procedures let you call a procedure or program on a remote system. With distributed database support, embedded SQL statements can be executed and operate on tables, views, and other objects on a remote system.

Embedded SQL combines HLL logic, procedural, and user interface capabilities with SQL's data access capabilities to provide better control, greater functionality, and a better user interface than interactive, dynamic SQL by itself.

Key Terms

blocked Insert
cursor
dynamic embedded
    statement
host structure array
host structure variable
host variable

indicator variable
multiple-row Fetch
    statement
parameter marker
positioned Delete statement
positioned Update statement
precompilation

precompiler directive
scrollable cursor
SQL communication area
    (SQLCA)
static statement
stored procedure

Exercises

Note: In all the following exercises that require HLL or embedded SQL statements, use any suitable AS/400 HLL (e.g., RPG IV or COBOL/400).

1. Describe two examples of application operations in which embedded SQL would be necessary to perform database updates that couldn't be done with interactive SQL.

2. Using the Customer table defined in Figure 15.4, show a static Update statement to change the discount to .05 for customer 707899. Use host variables instead of literals in the Update statement. Show the necessary HLL host variable declarations and the HLL statements to set the host variables before the Update statement and to detect and handle the following conditions after the Update statement:

    • No customer exists with a customer ID of 707899

    • Some other error or warning occurred on the Update statement

    • The update completed successfully

(You can use ExSr, Perform, or Call statements to indicate what action is taken for each condition. It's not necessary to show the code for the actual routines that handle each condition.)

3. Modify the code you created for Exercise 2 to let the discount be set either to a valid value or to null. Show the required variable declarations as well as the essential program logic. Assume there are two variables set from the user interface:

    • InpDiscNul, which is Y if the discount should be set to null, or N if the discount should be set to the value in the InpDisc variable

    • InpDisc, which contains the new discount value if InpDiscNul is N

4. Show the HLL variable declarations and Select Into statement to get the maximum discount of any customer into a host variable. Be sure to consider all possible contents of the Customer table (e.g., an empty table). (Use the table defined in Figure 15.4. You don't need to show error-handling code.)

5. Show the HLL variable declarations and Select Into statement to get the number of customers in a selected city into a host variable. Also use a host variable for the city. (Use the Customer table defined in Figure 15.4. You don't need to show error-handling code.)

    Are indicator variables required or useful for this statement? Explain why you would or would not use indicator variable(s) in either or both the Into and Where clauses.

Exercises Continued

Exercises continued

6. Show the HLL code and static Insert statement to insert a single new row into the Customer table, using an externally described host structure variable as well as a host structure variable for indicator variables. (Use the table defined in Figure 15.4. You don't need to show error-handling code.)

7. Show the HLL code and static Delete statements to let an end user select which customers to delete based on the city the customer is in. Implement your solution so the end user can specify either a specific city name (as a string) or that rows with a null city should be deleted. (Use the Customer table defined in Figure 15.4. You don't need to show error-handling code.)

   Explain why a solution that uses static Delete statements requires two Delete statements.

8. Show two alternative solutions to Exercise 7 that use a single Execute statement to dynamically execute an appropriate Delete statement. For the first solution, use a parameter marker in the statement string (when a valid city is specified). For the second solution, do not use any parameter markers. What are the advantages and disadvantages of the two approaches?

9. Show the HLL code and cursor-related statements (including cursor declaration, Open, Close, and Fetch statements) to sequentially read all customers with a non-null discount. For each row, execute a ListCust routine (e.g., an RPG IV subroutine or COBOL/400 paragraph — you don't need to show the routine's code). Read the rows in order by city and within city by descending discount. Include the necessary option to make the cursor a read-only cursor. Include appropriate error-handling code. (Use the Customer table defined in Figure 15.4.)

10. Revise your solution to Exercise 9 to use a multiple-row Fetch that reads 50 rows at a time. Include

the necessary HLL loop structures to process all rows and terminate when there are no more rows or an unanticipated error occurs.
Hint: You'll need nested loops.

11. Revise your solution to Exercise 9 to use an updatable cursor and a positioned Update statement to insert one blank character at the beginning of each customer's name. (Use a single-row Fetch for this problem.)

    Tip: The RPG IV statement to append a blank to the beginning of a string in a character variable is

```
....1....+....2....+....3....+....4....+....5....+.
C                Eval       StrVar = ' ' + StrVar
```

12. Explain why the technique used for a multiple-row Fetch wouldn't be a complete solution to the problem of retrieving multiple rows for a static Select Into statement.

    Describe an approach that might make the Select Into more flexible for retrieving sets of rows. Would this have any advantages over a cursor?

    Describe how the static Update statement might be enhanced to support multiple-row updates. If this feature were available, would it make a multiple-row Select Into more useful?

13. Show the CRTSQLRPGI (or CRTSQLCBLI) command to create a program object APPEXC/LISTCUST from a source member LISTCUST in source file APPSRC/QRPGLESRC (or APPSRC/QCBLLESRC). The program object should have the following attributes:

    - System naming convention
    - The source file used for Include statements should be APPSRC/SQLINCSRC
    - Change-level commitment control environment
    - Implicit close of SQL cursors when the module ends

PART IV

ADDITIONAL DB2/400 FEATURES

Chapter 16

Database Constraints

Chapter Overview

In DB2/400, database constraints provide a way to guarantee that records in the database have valid primary or unique key values and that records in a dependent file have valid foreign key values that reference records in a parent file. This chapter covers how to use CL commands to define primary key, unique, and referential constraints for physical files created with either DDS or SQL. We also look closely at the way DB2/400 implements referential constraints.

Introduction to Database Constraints

In general terms, database **constraints** are restrictions on the contents of the database or on database operations. As we discussed in Chapter 10, the logical data model documents a variety of constraints, or integrity rules, that reflect the organization's requirements for valid data and valid operations. DB2/400 uses the term "constraint" in a narrower sense that covers three specific integrity rules:

- Primary key constraint (to enforce existence integrity)
- Unique constraint (to enforce candidate key integrity)
- Referential constraint (to enforce referential, or foreign key, integrity)

In DB2/400, these constraints can be defined for single-member, externally described physical files. With SQL/400, you can include any of these constraints on a Create Table statement. For an existing table, you can use the Alter Table statement to add or remove a constraint. DB2/400 also provides a set of CL commands to work with constraints. You can use the ADDPFCST command to add any of the three types of constraints to an existing SQL/400 base table or non-SQL single-member physical file. The RMVPFCST command removes a constraint from either an SQL/400 base table or other physical file. Later in this chapter we look at other commands related to constraints.

If you use SQL/400, you probably want to use the Create Table and Alter Table statements for working with constraints. Chapter 13 provides a detailed discussion of these statements, as well as some basic information about constraints. The following sections explain the use of the ADDPFCST and RMVPFCST commands and provide more detailed information about

DB2/400 constraints. This information is applicable to both SQL/400 base tables and non-SQL physical files because DB2/400 constraints are the same regardless of how you define them.

Primary Key and Unique Constraints

Recall that in relational database terms, a primary key is a combination of attributes that provide a unique identifier for every tuple in a relation. For DB2/400 physical files, this means a combination of fields whose values are unique for every record in the file.[1] To add a **primary key constraint**, you use the ADDPFCST command.

```
ADDPFCST FILE( appdta/customer )
         TYPE( *prikey )
         KEY( custid )
         CST(  customerpk )
```

The *PRIKEY special value designates the constraint as a primary key type. The KEY parameter lists one or more fields that comprise the primary key. The CST parameter supplies an optional name that can be used to reference the constraint. If you don't specify a constraint name, DB2/400 generates one. A constraint name must be unique within the library containing the physical file.

A primary key field must not allow nulls; that is, the field must not have been created with the DDS ALWNULL keyword specified, or, for SQL tables, the column definition must have included the Not Null phrase. You can define only one primary key constraint for a physical file. For DDS-based physical files, if the file was created with a keyed access path, the file must have a unique key, and the primary key fields on the ADDPFCST command must match exactly the names and relative key positions of the DDS key field specifications. For SQL base tables, DB2/400 creates a unique keyed access path for the physical file to enforce the primary key constraint and subsequently treats the file as having a keyed access path.[2]

For most single-member physical files, a primary key constraint is a good idea because there should almost always be some system-enforced unique identifier for every record. (Chapter 10 discusses the properties that a good primary key should have, e.g., key values should be meaningless.)

---

[1] Note that DB2/400 allows physical files to have more than one member, and the DDS UNIQUE keyword (discussed in Chapter 2) requires only that records within the same member have unique key field values. Thus, a multimember file might have records with the same key values, as long as the records are in different members. However, DB2/400 allows constraints only on single-member physical files, so primary key values are unique across the entire file.

[2] As explained in Chapter 13, DB2/400 implements an SQL/400 base table as a single-member, externally described physical file. When you don't specify any constraints on the SQL Create Table statement, the physical file has an arrival sequence access path. Adding a primary key constraint makes the file a keyed file.

A DB2/400 **unique constraint** provides a way to enforce unique values for fields other than those in the primary key. To add a unique constraint, you use a command similar to that for a primary key but with the *UNQCST special value for the constraint type.

```
ADDPFCST FILE( appdta/customer )
         TYPE( *unqcst )
         KEY( name )
         CST( custnameuk )
```

A key field listed for a unique constraint can allow nulls, and the file can contain multiple records with equal key values as long as one key field is null (i.e., all null values are treated as unique). You also can have multiple unique constraints on a single physical file; however, the same set of fields (regardless of order) can be listed on only one primary key or unique constraint. For example, it's not valid to have the following two constraints on the same table:

```
ADDPFCST FILE( appdta/filex )
         TYPE( *prikey )
         KEY( field1  field2 )
         CST( filexpk )

ADDPFCST FILE( appdta/filex )
         TYPE( *unqcst )
         KEY( field2  field1 )
         CST( filexuk )
```

Because a file can have more than one unique constraint, it's good practice always to specify an explicit constraint name for the CST parameter. This approach makes it easier to recognize the constraint in displays and to reference the constraint later, if necessary.

For DDS-based files, you don't have to define any DDS key fields to subsequently add a unique constraint to the file. For files created with either DDS or an SQL Create Table statement, DB2/400 creates a keyed access path, or shares an appropriate existing access path, for each unique constraint. The access path for a unique constraint does not affect whether DB2/400 treats the file as having an arrival sequence or keyed access path.[3] If you already have a keyed access path (e.g., a keyed logical file or an SQL index) defined over the physical file, using the same key fields, you should specify the constraint key fields in the same order as the key fields of the access path, enabling DB2/400 to share the existing access path.

When you execute an ADDPFCST command for either a primary key or a unique constraint, DB2/400 checks the key values for existing records (if any) to ensure that they satisfy the constraint. If there are duplicate key values,

---

[3] That is, if the physical file doesn't have a keyed access path, either from DDS key field specifications or because of a primary key constraint on an SQL base table, DB2/400 treats the file as arrival sequenced. This nuance is important only when you want to use HLL built-in I/O operations to access an SQL base table. Whereas defining a primary key constraint allows opening the table for keyed access, a unique constraint by itself doesn't.

the command fails. When you attempt a record insert or update that would create a record with a duplicate key value, DB2/400 rejects the operation and returns a status code that you can check in your program. (Review Chapter 7 for information about handling I/O errors with HLL built-in I/O statements, and review Chapter 15 for information about handling errors with embedded SQL statements.)

Referential Constraint

A DB2/400 **referential constraint** specifies how records in different files are related and how DB2/400 should handle record insert, delete, and update operations that might violate the constraint. For example, sales records are generally related to the customers who place the orders. While it might be valid for a customer record to exist without any corresponding sales records, it would normally be invalid for a sale record not to have a reference to a valid customer. With relational DBMS, the relationship between records in two files is expressed by a **foreign key** in the **dependent file**. A foreign key is one or more fields that contain a value identical to a primary key value in some record in the **parent file** (i.e., the referenced file).

With DB2/400, we might set up the CUSTOMER and SALE files so they have the following partial definitions:

CUSTOMER file (parent)

- Primary key field: CUSTID

SALE file (dependent)

- Primary key field: ORDERID
- Foreign key field: CUSTID

The CUSTID field in the SALE file should contain the same value as some CUSTID field of a CUSTOMER record because this value tells which customer placed the order. The purpose of specifying a referential integrity constraint is to have DB2/400 ensure that the SALE file never has a record with a non-null value in the CUSTID field that has no matching CUSTOMER record.

Because a foreign key is a means of identifying a related record, generally the foreign key field(s) definition should be identical to the definition of the primary key field(s). DB2/400 provides some flexibility (for example, a foreign key can reference the key fields of a unique constraint, rather than the primary key). But unless you've got a good reason (such as retrofitting referential integrity to previously created files that don't meet this criteria), you should define a foreign key and referential constraint to reference the parent file's primary key. Of course, this suggestion implies that you should define a primary key constraint for the parent file before you define referential constraints for any dependent files.

Assuming that a primary key constraint has been defined for the CUSTOMER file (using the CUSTID field as the primary key field), the following command defines a referential constraint for the CUSTOMER and SALE files:

```
ADDPFCST FILE( appdta/sale )
         TYPE( *refcst )
         KEY( custid )
         CST( salecustfk )
         PRNFILE( appdta/customer )
         PRNKEY( *prnfile )
         DLTRULE( *restrict )
         UPDRULE( *restrict )
```

You add referential constraints to the dependent file and specify the parent file in the PRNFILE parameter. The KEY parameter specifies the foreign key field(s) (from the dependent file), and the PRNKEY parameter specifies the **parent key** fields. In this example, the *PRNFILE keyword specifies that the key fields in the parent file's keyed access path (e.g., the primary key fields) are used as the parent key. As an alternative to the *PRNFILE keyword, you can specify one or more fields in the parent file; however, as mentioned earlier, using the parent file's primary key as the target for a foreign key is the best approach.

When a referential constraint exists for a dependent file and a parent file, DB2/400 blocks the following operations and returns an error to your program:

- Attempts to insert a record in the dependent file with a non-null foreign key value that doesn't match a parent key value in a record in the parent file
- Attempts to update a record in the dependent file by setting the foreign key to a non-null value that doesn't match a parent key value in a record in the parent file

Both operations, if allowed, would create a dependent file record with an invalid reference to a nonexistent parent.

If any field in the foreign key is null capable, DB2/400 allows a record in the dependent file to have a foreign key that contains at least one null field, in which case, DB2/400 considers the entire foreign key null (i.e., unknown). Conceptually, a null foreign key represents an unknown parent record rather than an invalid reference to a nonexistent parent record.[4]

The UPDRULE and DLTRULE parameters of the ADDPFCST command determine the rules DB2/400 enforces when an attempt is made to update or delete a parent file record in such a way as to leave dependent file

---

[4] For many cases in which you need to handle dependent records without a real parent record, using a default parent, as discussed later under the Set Default delete rule, is preferable to using null foreign keys.

records that have invalid foreign key references. Both rules apply in those cases in which one or more dependent file records have a foreign key value that matches the parent key of the parent file record being deleted or updated. The *RESTRICT value used in the example above provides a simple rule for both cases: don't allow such updates or deletes to parent file records.

The update rule governs the case in which an update operation attempts to change a parent key value. The only two DB2/400 options for this rule are *NOACTION (the default) and *RESTRICT. With either choice, DB2/400 blocks the update to the parent file record if it would result in unmatched foreign key values. The difference between the two options is when DB2/400 checks to see whether the update would leave any dependent file records with unmatched foreign key values. For the *NOACTION rule, DB2/400 checks *after* any after-update-event trigger program is executed (triggers are discussed in Chapter 17). For the *RESTRICT rule, DB2/400 checks *before* any after-update-event trigger program is executed. There's no effective difference between the two options unless an after-update-event trigger exists for the parent file. For most situations, the *RESTRICT rule is the appropriate choice.[5]

The delete rule governs the case in which a delete operation would eliminate a parent key value that's referenced by some dependent file record(s). The *NOACTION and *RESTRICT options block such operations and have the same timing differences as discussed for the update rule. The DLTRULE parameter supports three additional options:

---

[5] Because DB2/400 provides no *CASCADE option for the update rule, you might consider two techniques to propagate parent key field changes to the foreign key fields in dependent records.

The first approach would be to insert a new parent record with the new parent key values, then update the dependent records so their foreign keys contain the new parent key value, then delete the old parent record.

Alternatively, you could add an after-update-event trigger to the parent file and have the trigger program change the foreign key values of the dependent records. Note that a before-update-event trigger wouldn't work because DB2/400 wouldn't allow the trigger program to change the foreign key values to a nonexistent parent key value. Only after the parent record is updated can the trigger program make this change to the dependent records. This technique is one that requires UPDRULE(*NOACTION). In most cases, UPDRULE(*RESTRICT) is the appropriate choice because it blocks an invalid update before subsequent operations are performed by any after-update-event triggers. Except for the propagation of parent key updates, after-update-event triggers usually are intended only for valid updates.

There's another subtle consideration with SQL/400 set-at-a-time statements (discussed in Chapter 14). DB2/400 checks the *RESTRICT rule immediately after each record update (or delete) but checks the *NOACTION rule only after the statement completes. It's possible (though not common) to have an update statement that changes a set of records' parent key values (e.g., by adding 1 to each parent key value) such that as each record is changed, some foreign key value has no match, but when all the parent records have been changed, all foreign key values are once again matched. In the unlikely event you need to allow this kind of update, *NOACTION may be the appropriate update rule. (You can also temporarily disable a referential constraint, as discussed later in the chapter.)

- *SETDFT sets the matching foreign key values to their default values. A parent file record must exist that has a parent key that matches this default foreign key value. This parent record becomes the new parent of the dependent records.

- *SETNULL sets all null-capable foreign key fields to null in those dependent records with a matching foreign key. The foreign key fields that aren't null capable are unchanged.

- *CASCADE deletes all the matching records in the dependent file.

The *SETDFT option lets you have a default parent record for all dependent records without their own real parent record. As an example of how you might use this, suppose you want to allow inactive customers to be deleted, but you want to keep their old sales records for statistical purposes. You could define the default value for the CUSTID field in the SALE file as 0, then create one CUSTOMER file record with a CUSTID (primary key) value of 0. With DLTRULE(*SETDFT) for the previous example's referential constraint, when you deleted a CUSTOMER record, its SALE records would be updated to have 0 for their CUSTID (foreign key) value.

The *SETNULL option is similar to *SETDFT, except it sets the matching dependent file records' null-capable foreign key fields to null. At least one foreign key field must be null capable to use this rule. As mentioned earlier, DB2/400 allows a dependent record that has at least one null foreign key field. No matching parent record is required for dependent records with a null foreign key field.

The *CASCADE option deletes all the matching dependent records, along with the parent. You might use this rule, for example, if you want to delete all of a customer's sales records when you delete the customer record.

A dependent file in one referential constraint can be the parent file in another referential constraint. For example, the SALE file might be the parent file in a referential constraint that exists for the SALEITEM dependent file. This raises the possibility that a cascaded delete might delete dependent records that are also parent records for some other file. For example, if DLTRULE(*CASCADE) were specified for the previous example, deleting a CUSTOMER record could delete some SALE records that were parents of SALEITEM records. If a referential constraint for the SALEITEM file specifies *NOACTION or *RESTRICT and DB2/400 blocks the deletion of the SALE records, DB2/400 also blocks the attempted deletion of the CUSTOMER record. In general, with *CASCADE, if DB2/400 blocks any operation caused by the cascading delete, all operations are blocked.[6] Similar rules apply when DLTRULE(*SETDFT) or DLTRULE(*SETNULL) are specified and a resulting change in a foreign key value would violate some other constraint.

---

[6] DB2/400 may actually perform some of the operations and then use commitment control facilities (discussed in Chapter 17) to roll back the operations.

A referential constraint can specify the same file as the dependent and parent files. Suppose you have an EMPLOYEE file with an EMPID primary key field and a MGREMPID field that holds the employee ID for the person's manager. The referential constraint to express this relationship could be specified by the following command:

```
ADDPFCST FILE( appdta/employee )
         TYPE( *refcst )
         KEY( mgrempid )
         CST( empmgrfk )
         PRNFILE( appdta/employee )
         PRNKEY( *prnfile )
         DLTRULE( *restrict )
         UPDRULE( *restrict )
```

To handle the case of an employee who had no real manager (e.g., the president of the company), a dummy employee record could be inserted with the name "No manager," and EMPID and MGREMPID values could be set to 0 (or any other value not used by real employees). The MGREMPID for any employee with no manager could be set to 0 to satisfy the referential constraint.

Depending on how you wanted to implement the removal of an employee (who might be a manager), you could define the MGREMPID field with a default value of 0 and use DLTRULE(*SETDFT).[7] Alternatively, you might define MGREMPID as null capable and consider a null MGREMPID to mean "no manager." In this case, you could use DLTRULE(*SETNULL) to handle the deletion of a manager's record.

A file can have multiple referential constraints, including overlapping foreign keys. If a referential constraint specifies DLTRULE(*SETDFT) and the constraint's foreign key has a field that's in another constraint's foreign key, deleting a record from the parent file of the first constraint may change the value of a foreign key field in the second constraint. If this happens and the new foreign key value for the second constraint doesn't match a parent key in the parent file of the second constraint, DB2/400 blocks the dependent record updates and the parent record delete.

A file can also be the parent file for multiple referential constraints. DB2/400 enforces all constraints when a record in such a file is updated or deleted. DB2/400 checks the constraints based on the order of the rules. For an update action, DB2/400 checks *RESTRICT rules and then *NOACTION rules. For a delete action, the order of checking is

- *RESTRICT
- *CASCADE
- *SETNULL

[7] Or you could change all the records for the manager's employees so they had a new, valid MGREMPID value before you deleted the old manager's record.

- *SETDFT
- *NOACTION

If any rule fails, DB2/400 blocks the operation and ends the constraint checking.

When a referential constraint has both UPDRULE(*RESTRICT) and DLTRULE(*RESTRICT), DB2/400 can check the constraint before doing any actual file update or delete operations. With any other rules, DB2/400 must perform some operations and then, if the constraint check fails, DB2/400 must back out the partial changes to the file(s). As a result, you must journal both the dependent and parent file in any referential constraint other than one with *RESTRICT specified for both the update and delete rules. Both files must be journaled to the same journal. However, you don't have to explicitly start commitment control. When necessary, DB2/400 implicitly uses a commitment control cycle to ensure that file changes occur on an all-or-none basis, as described in Chapter 17.

Referential Constraint States

We mentioned earlier that when you execute the ADDPFCST command to define a primary key or unique constraint, DB2/400 checks the key values and establishes the constraint or the command fails. Thus, a primary key or unique constraint is either in effect or it doesn't exist. With referential constraints, there are several intermediate states that must be considered. The six possible states are shown in the following chart.

		Disabled	Enabled
Defined		1	2
Established	Check pending	3	4
	No check pending	5	6

1. Defined and disabled
2. Defined and enabled
3. Established and disabled with check pending
4. Established and enabled with check pending
5. Established and disabled without check pending
6. Established and enabled without check pending

When you use the ADDPFCST command to define a referential constraint, the constraint is defined (but not established) if the dependent or parent file doesn't yet have a member or if the foreign key attributes don't match the parent key attributes. When both files have a member and the foreign and parent key attributes match, the constraint is established. In either case, the constraint is initially enabled.

When a referential constraint is first established, DB2/400 checks to ensure that all non-null foreign key values have a matching parent key value. As part of this process, DB2/400 also creates a new access path for the foreign key if there's not an appropriate existing access path that can be shared. If the foreign key check is satisfied, the constraint becomes established and enabled and has no checks pending. If there's an unmatched foreign key value, the constraint becomes established and enabled with check pending.

To remove the check pending, you must disable the referential constraint (which becomes established and disabled), correct the records in the dependent and/or parent file(s), and then re-enable the constraint. The CHGPFCST command lets you change the enabled/disabled state of a referential constraint. The following command disables the SALECUSTFK constraint:

```
CHGPFCST FILE( appdta/sale )
         CST( salecustfk )
         STATE( *disabled )
```

To re-enable the constraint, use the STATE(*ENABLED) parameter.[8] While a referential constraint is in the established and enabled with check pending state, no I/O operations are allowed on the dependent file and only read and insert operations are allowed for the parent file. (In the established and disabled state, all I/O operations are allowed.)

DB2/400 includes several other commands to help manage constraints. The DSPCPCST command displays dependent file records without a matching parent key for a constraint that is in established and disabled with check pending state. The WRKPFCST command displays a list of physical file constraints and (for referential constraints) their states. From this display, you can

- Remove primary key, unique, or referential constraints
- Enable or disable referential constraints
- Issue the DSPCPCST command for referential constraints

The EDTCPCST command lets you edit a list of referential constraints that have a check pending status. You can use the list to schedule the order in which DB2/400 rechecks the foreign key values after you make corrections. Appendix B lists the parameters for all the constraint-related commands.

---

[8] To reduce system overhead, you can also use the CHGPFCST command to disable referential constraints before starting a long running batch job. The system must recheck foreign keys when you use the CHGPFCST command to re-enable the constraint. Be sure your processing will not create invalid foreign key values.

Chapter Summary

DB2/400 provides three types of database constraints: primary key, unique, and referential. You can define these constraints with the SQL/400 Create Table or Alter Table statements or with the ADDPFCST command. These three constraints can be defined only for single-member, externally described physical files.

A physical file can have one primary key constraint, which defines the set of fields that will always have unique, non-null values and thus can be used as the identifier for individual records in the file.

A physical file can have multiple unique constraints. Each unique constraint defines a set of fields that must have unique values. Unique constraints allow a key field to be null.

A physical file can have multiple referential constraints. Referential constraints define a parent-dependent relationship between two physical files. A referential constraint defines the dependent file's foreign key fields, which reference the parent key (usually the primary key) of the parent file. Each record in the dependent file must have a foreign key value that is the same as the parent key value in a record in the parent file or that is fully or partially null.

When you define a referential constraint, you specify the action DB2/400 should take when an update or delete operation to a parent file record would leave dependent file records with invalid foreign key values. For an update operation, you can specify *NOACTION or *RESTRICT, both of which block an invalid update; but they differ in when DB2/400 makes the check. For a delete operation, you can specify *NOACTION, *RESTRICT, *SETDFT, *SETNULL, or *CASCADE. The *SETDFT and *SETNULL actions set dependent records' foreign key fields to their default value or null, respectively. The *CASCADE action deletes matching dependent records.

A delete action may lead to other constraint checks. DB2/400 uses an implicit commitment control cycle to ensure that all record updates and deletes satisfy the database constraints, or no records are updated or deleted. When a referential constraint is defined, DB2/400 checks the validity of all foreign key values and sets the constraint in a check-pending status until all foreign key values are valid.

Key Terms

constraint   parent file   referential constraint
dependent file   parent key   unique constraint
foreign key   primary key constraint

Exercises

1. Show the command to add a primary key constraint to the APPDTA/LOAN physical file that is defined with a DDS unique key consisting of the LOANID field.

2. Show the command to add a unique constraint to the APPDTA/LOAN physical file based on the CUSTID and LOANDATE fields.

3. Explain why you think DB2/400 limits database constraints to physical files.

    Give an example of a situation in which you might use a unique constraint for a logical file. Does DB2/400 provide any equivalent mechanism to enforce this type of constraint? If so, what is it?

    Give an example of a situation in which you might use a referential constraint that specifies a logical file as the parent file. Does DB2/400 provide any equivalent mechanism to enforce this type of constraint? If so, what is it?

4. Show the command to define a referential constraint between the EMPLOYEE file, which has a DEPTID field to identify the department an employee belongs to, and the DEPT file, which has a primary key of DEPTID. Describe (in general terms) how you would implement the EMPLOYEE and DEPT files and the referential constraint to handle an employee not yet assigned to a department.

5. For the EMPLOYEE and DEPT files in Exercise 4, describe (in general terms) how you would implement the necessary record updates to handle an organizational change in which a department's name and department ID change, but all employees remain in the department.

6. Considering the files in Exercise 4, describe the changes to the database file structure that would be necessary to handle employees who belonged to multiple departments.

7. Show the commands to add all necessary primary key and referential constraints for the files in your answer to Exercise 6.

Chapter 17

DB2/400 Advanced Features

Chapter Overview

This chapter covers a variety of DB2/400 features that you need to be familiar with to develop production database applications:

- *File overrides* — we delve more deeply into the use of the OVRDBF (Override with Database File) command that was introduced in earlier chapters
- *The OPNQRYF (Open Query File) command* — for HLL built-in I/O operations, this command provides many of the data access features available with SQL/400 cursors
- *Object and record locks* — this section covers both implicit system locks to prevent conflicting file access and commands to control locking explicitly
- *Journaling* — you learn how to set up and manage journals and journal receivers to provide enhanced recovery for database files
- *Commitment control* — we look at potential problems with multirecord transactions and concurrent database access and how commitment control provides solutions
- *Trigger programs* — you learn how to use this DB2/400 feature to add additional database constraints or to perform other actions when a file is updated
- *Distributed database* — this section introduces three facilities for accessing data on a system other than the system on which an application runs: Distributed Data Management (DDM), Distributed Relational Database Architecture (DRDA), and Open Database Connectivity (ODBC)
- *Query tools* — we look briefly at how two IBM utilities, Query/400 and Query Manager/400, provide data retrieval facilities for end users and programmers

This material covers both configuration and programming topics. As you develop more complex database applications, you need to master all these areas.

File Overrides

In Chapter 4, we looked at how an OVRDBF command's TOFILE and MBR parameters let you specify that DB2/400 should open a particular physical or logical file member when you run an HLL program (see Figures 4.2, 4.3, and 4.4 for the complete example). Part of that example used the following two commands:

```
OVRDBF FILE( customer )
       TOFILE( appdta/custname )
       MBR( custname )

CALL listcust
```

The OVRDBF command specifies that DB2/400 should open the CUSTNAME member of the APPDTA/CUSTNAME file when the LISTCUST program opens the CUSTOMER file. As this example shows, an important use of file overrides is to let a single program work with a variety of files and file members. For multimember files, overrides provide the only way for an RPG IV, RPG/400, or COBOL/400 program to open a member other than the first one added to the file. (By default, DB2/400 opens the first member when no override is in effect.) For sequential processing either by key or in arrival sequence, you can also use a file override to open a member of any file with an identical record format as the file declared in the program executing the open. For direct access by key, the file specified in the TOFILE parameter generally should have an identical record format and the same key field definitions as the file declared in the program executing the open.

A file override also lets you temporarily change a file's attributes when it's opened. For example, the following command specifies that DB2/400 should ignore record insert, update, and delete operations to the CUSTOMER file when the file is opened while the override is in effect:

```
OVRDBF FILE( customer )
       TOFILE( apptst/customer )
       INHWRT( *yes )
```

The INHWRT(*YES) file attribute lets you run a program that makes changes to the CUSTOMER file without the changes actually occurring.[1] Appendix B lists all the OVRDBF command's parameters; in this section, we look more closely at a few of these.[2]

Unlike the CHGPF, CHGLF, CHGPFM, and CHGLFM commands that permanently set the attributes of a file or one of its members, the OVRDBF command causes only temporary effects. The attributes on a file override apply only for file access in the job in which the override is executed; other jobs running concurrently are not affected by a different job's overrides. All

---

[1] With INHWRT(*YES), DB2/400 lets your program execute any insert, update, and delete operations to the file, but DB2/400 just throws the changes in the "bit bucket," letting you test a program without changing the target file. I would not advise using INHWRT(*YES) as a means to run tests on production files. The danger is you may omit the INHWRT parameter on the OVRDBF command or the attribute may be changed by another level of override (discussed later). Notice how this example specifies the APPTST (test) library as the library containing the file that's opened. You can also use the job's library list to control which version — test or production — of a file is opened by a program when *LIBL is specified for the file's library.

[2] Chapter 15 discusses which OVRDBF parameters apply when a program uses embedded SQL to access database files.

the overrides still in effect when a job ends are deleted when the job ends (they may be deleted sooner).

Although you can use an OVRDBF command interactively, for most production applications, OVRDBF commands are coded in CL programs before calling an HLL application program that opens the file specified in the FILE parameter (as in the example above). An OVRDBF command applies only to files opened after the command is executed; files already opened are not affected, even if their name is the same as the one specified on the OVRDBF command's FILE parameter.

Override Scope

When you execute an OVRDBF command, you can specify one of the following values for the OVRSCOPE (**override scope**) parameter:

- *CALLLVL
- *ACTGRPDFN (the default scope)
- *JOB

A *CALLLVL (call level) scope means that the override is in effect for any files subsequently opened by the same program or any program at a higher call level.[3] OS/400 deletes a call level override when the program that executed it returns to its caller or when you execute an appropriate DLTOVR to explicitly delete it. To illustrate, the following diagram shows the call level scope of the CUSTOMER file override.

APPPGMCL

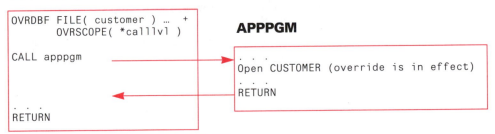

```
OVRDBF FILE( customer ) … +
       OVRSCOPE( *calllvl )

CALL apppgm
```

APPPGM
```
. . .
Open CUSTOMER (override is in effect)
. . .
RETURN
```

```
. . .
RETURN
```

Override is deleted when APPPGMCL returns

You can see from this diagram why you normally execute an OVRDBF command in a CL program and then call an HLL application program that opens the file that you've overridden. Don't make the mistake of having the

---

[3] The first program in a job's invocation stack has call level 1, the next program in the stack has call level 2, and so on. Thus, if a job's current program stack starts with PGMA, which calls PGMB, which calls PGMC, the three programs' call levels would be 1, 2, and 3, respectively.

HLL program call a CL program to execute the override before you open a file in your HLL program, as in the following diagram:

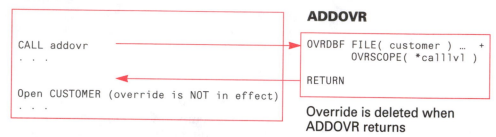

APPPGM

```
CALL addovr
. . .

Open CUSTOMER (override is NOT in effect)
. . .
```

ADDOVR

```
OVRDBF FILE( customer ) …  +
        OVRSCOPE( *calllvl )

RETURN
```

Override is deleted when
ADDOVR returns

This approach won't do any good with call level scope because the override established by the ADDOVR CL program is deleted when ADDOVR returns to the application program.[4]

The *ACTGRPDFN (activation group definition) option for the OVRSCOPE parameter determines the override scope based on the type of ILE (Integrated Language Environment) activation group.[5] If you execute an OVRDBF command with OVRSCOPE(*ACTGRPDFN) while in the job's default activation group, the effect is the same as with OVRSCOPE(*CALLLVL). If you execute the OVRDBF command while in a non-default activation group, the override is in effect for any files subsequently opened by any program in the same activation group. OS/400 deletes the override when the activation group ends or when you execute an appropriate DLTOVR to delete it explicitly.

The *JOB option specifies that the override is in effect for any files subsequently opened by any program in the same job. OS/400 deletes the override when the job ends or when you execute an appropriate DLTOVR to delete it explicitly.

---

[4] To override a file from within an HLL program, you can call the IBM-supplied QCMDEXC program and pass it a string with an OVRDBF command. OS/400 treats the QCMDEXC program as a special case and leaves a call level scoped override in effect until the program that called QCMDEXC returns. This is the same as if the program that called QCMDEXC executed the OVRDBF command directly.

[5] An activation group is an ILE substructure of a job. All jobs have a default activation group. You can also create programs to run in other, named activation groups (non-default activation groups). One purpose of activation groups is to insulate file opens in an application running in its own activation group from file opens in a different application running in a different activation group. When you specify OVRSCOPE(*ACTGRPDFN), the attributes on overrides in a non-default activation group won't affect opens in a different activation group.

Merging Overrides

For each file name specified on the FILE parameter, OS/400 limits the overrides to the following:

- One override per file at each call level in the job
- One override per file for each non-default activation group in the job
- One job scope override per file

This means there may be multiple overrides that apply when a file is opened. If there are, OS/400 merges the overrides for the file as follows:

1. Call level overrides starting at the current call level and working back to the lowest call level in the same activation group
2. Activation group level overrides
3. Call level overrides for all call levels below the lowest call level in the activation group (from highest to lowest)
4. Job level overrides

As each additional override is processed, any parameter values specified on the override's OVRDBF command replace the corresponding parameter values (if any) specified on previously merged overrides.

You can specify the SECURE(*YES) parameter on an OVRDBF command to stop OS/400 from merging further overrides after processing the override on which SECURE(*YES) is specified. This guarantees that the parameters you specify on the OVRDBF command won't be replaced by some previously entered OVRDBF command.

As OS/400 checks for the next override to merge, it looks for the most recent name specified on the TOFILE parameter, if any. To see how this can affect which overrides are merged, consider an application program that opens the CUSTOMER file. OS/400 begins by looking for an override that was specified with FILE(CUSTOMER). If OS/400 finds an override added with the following command

```
OVRDBF FILE( customer )
       TOFILE( custname ) ...
```

from that point on in the merging process described above, OS/400 checks for overrides for the CUSTNAME file — that is, overrides specified with an OVRDBF FILE(CUSTNAME) ... command, not with FILE(CUSTOMER).

In most cases, applications require nothing more complicated than a single override scoped to the call level or activation group. If you get into more complex situations, be sure you carefully analyze the way overrides are merged.

Open Data Path Scope and Sharing

When a program opens a file, DB2/400 creates or shares an internal system control structure known as an **open data path** (**ODP**). This structure holds information needed by DB2/400, such as the actual file member opened, the type of record operations for which the file was opened (e.g., read and insert), and the current file position. An ODP is associated with only one job, and a job may have multiple ODPs for the same or different files.

When an ODP is created, OS/400 establishes a scope for the ODP.[6] An **ODP's scope** determines when the file is implicitly closed as well as what other open operations can share the ODP. Don't confuse the scope of an override with the scope of an ODP — an override's scope determines which file opens it affects. An override might have a job scope, which means it affects all opens, but the opens themselves might have call level or activation group scope.

By default, when a program in the default activation group opens a file, the ODP has call level scope; when a program in a nondefault activation group opens a file, the ODP is scoped to the same activation group.[7] You can use the OPNSCOPE(*JOB) parameter of the OVRDBF command to specify that a file should be opened with job scope.

A program can execute an explicit close operation to close a file. In addition, OS/400 implicitly closes a file with call level scope when the program that opened the file is deactivated (e.g., by setting on the LR indicator before returning from an RPG program or by a COBOL Cancel statement).[8] OS/400 implicitly closes a file with activation group scope when the activation group ends. All files are closed when the job ends.

By default, a new ODP is created each time a program opens a file; the ODP is deleted when the file is closed. Thus, if a file is opened by more than one program in the same job,[9] the job may have multiple ODPs for the same file at the same time. You can cause DB2/400 to share an existing ODP within the same job by setting the file's share attribute to *YES, either permanently with the CRTPF, CRTLF, CHGPF, or CHGLF commands, or temporarily by executing an OVRDBF command before the file is first opened. The following command

```
OVRDBF FILE( customer )
       SHARE( *yes )
```

specifies that when the CUSTOMER file is opened, DB2/400 should open the first member (by default) and mark the member's ODP as shared. If this

---

[6] The ODP's scope is also known as the file's "open scope."

[7] This behavior is the same as that for the default OPNSCOPE(*ACTGRPDFN) parameter option for the OVRDBF command.

[8] Also, a RCLRSC (Reclaim Resources) command closes files with a call level scope that were opened by an HLL (not CL) program at the same or higher call level as the program executing the RCLRSC command.

[9] Or by separate open operations in the same program.

sharable ODP exists when another shared open occurs for the same file member and the second open has a compatible open scope as the ODP (e.g., they both have the same activation group scope), DB2/400 shares the ODP created for the first open.[10] DB2/400 deletes a **shared ODP** only when a close has been executed for all of the respective opens.[11] Keep in mind that an ODP can be shared only within the same job; different jobs opening the same file concurrently always have separate ODPs. Remember also that the default DB2/400 behavior is to create separate ODPs for each open operation; for most circumstances, this is the appropriate approach.

While two programs in a job share an ODP, subsequent record positioning operations by either program affect the current file position for both programs. For example, using an RPG SETLL opcode changes the current record for both programs. If you use a shared open, be careful about conflicting I/O operations.

The most important use for a shared open is to access data with a query file that you define using the OPNQRYF command (discussed in a later section). This specialized use of a shared ODP isn't actually intended to let multiple programs simultaneously access a file member through the same ODP.

Another common — but not necessarily advisable — use of a shared open is to improve performance for applications that follow a particular design structure.[12] In these applications, a controlling program, such as a CL menu program, calls an application program that performs some function by opening a file, accessing one or more records, and closing the file, as depicted in Figure 17.1a.

If the APPPGM program is called frequently, the repeated opening and closing of the FILEX file may cause some performance degradation. The situation would be even worse if APPPGM were called in a loop in a batch program. One way to try to improve the performance in this situation is to pre-open the file with a shared ODP in the menu program and leave it open until the menu program ends, as in Figure 17.1b.

---

[10] Note that for an open to share an existing ODP, the following must be true:
- The existing ODP must have been created by a shared open.
- The current open must be for the same file member.
- The current open must be a shared open.
- The current open must not be for any operations (read, insert, update, or delete) that were not also specified on the open operation that created the ODP.
- The current open must have a scope that's identical to, or within the scope of, the ODP's scope.

[11] Or some other action, such as a RCLACTGRP (Reclaim Activation Group), implicitly closes the file.

[12] I cover this technique because many IBM trainers and others advise the use of this technique, despite its disadvantages. You should be familiar with the concept so you can decide when (if ever) it's an appropriate technique.

Figure 17.1a
Sample Application

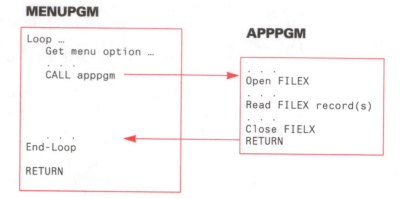

Figure 17.1b
Sample Application with
Pre-Opened File

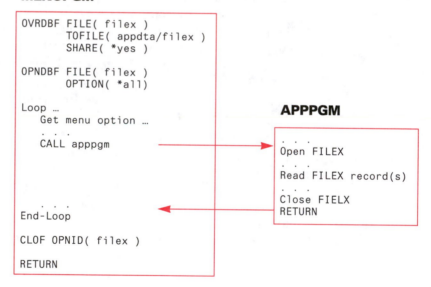

The OVRDBF command establishes an override with the SHARE(*YES) attribute, and the OPNDBF command opens the FILEX file for any type of I/O operation. As a result of the override, when the OPNDBF command is executed, DB2/400 creates a sharable ODP for the file. The FILEX file stays open until the MENUPGM program executes a CLOF command to close the file. Also as a result of the override, the opens done by the APPPGM program are shared opens and use the existing ODP. A shared open that uses an existing ODP is significantly faster than an open that has to create an ODP.

Although this technique may improve performance, there are several better solutions. The most obvious is to leave the FILEX file open when APPPGM returns, thus avoiding a file open in APPPGM altogether except the first time MENUPGM calls APPPGM. Just before MENUPGM itself returns, a final call to APPPGM can pass a parameter to indicate that APPPGM should close the FILEX file.[13] This solution is faster than the shared open technique; it is also simpler because the MENUPGM doesn't require code to open the FILEX file and handle errors that might occur on the open.

The DLTOVR command deletes overrides. The following command deletes the override for the CUSTOMER file:

```
DLTOVR FILE( customer )
```

Instead of a specific file name, you can specify *ALL to delete all file overrides. The DLTOVR command has an optional LVL parameter that parallels the OVRDBF command's OVRSCOPE parameter. As it is for the OVRDBF command, the default value for this parameter is *ACTGRPDFN, which limits the deleted overrides to those scoped to the current call level or to the current activation group (as explained for OVRSCOPE(*ACTGRPDFN). The other values are asterisk (*) (overrides scoped to the current call level) and *JOB (job scope overrides).

The DSPOVR command displays the overrides currently in effect. You can look at overrides individually, as well as see the net effect of OS/400's merging of multiple overrides. For more information about file overrides, see the *Data Management* manual.

The Open Query File Command

DB2/400 provides many dynamic database functions that are accessible with SQL/400 but not through DDS and HLL built-in I/O operations alone. The OPNQRYF (Open Query File) command, however, extends the capabilities of HLL built-in I/O operations so they can take advantage of dynamic record selection, mapped fields, dynamic join, record aggregation, and several other useful database functions.[14]

Before exploring what the OPNQRYF command does, let's dispose of some confusion that arises from the command's name. The OPNQRYF command has nothing to do with the AS/400 Query report-generator utility, other than that both OPNQRYF and Query use the same underlying DB2/400 support for such functions as dynamic record selection and field mapping. In addition, although the OPNQRYF command creates an ODP, an HLL shared-file open must follow the OPNQRYF command before an application program can use the selected records. Thus, the OPNQRYF command doesn't replace your HLL database file opens; rather it's used, much as an OVRDBF command, to modify the results of an HLL file open.

---

[13] There are a number of alternative ways the FILEX file could be closed, including by executing a RCLRSC command in MENUPGM. The essential point is that it's not generally necessary to open and close a file repeatedly within a limited part of an application.

[14] You may find it helpful to review the discussion of the SQL Select statement in Chapter 14 because many of the capabilities discussed in that chapter are also applicable to OPNQRYF.

Dynamic Record Selection

The OPNQRYF command — which is executed before an HLL file open — changes what the HLL program views much the way a logical file changes what an HLL program views of underlying physical file(s). The major difference is that the OPNQRYF command lets you specify record selection, record ordering, field mapping, and other access options when the OPNQRYF command is executed, whereas the specifications for a logical file are set when the file's DDS is compiled. For example, an OPNQRYF command can use the contents of a CL program variable to limit the customer records read by an HLL program to those customers in a specific city. With a logical file, the name of a city used in select/omit specifications must be hard coded in the DDS.

Figure 17.2 shows how the OPNQRYF command can be used to provide such execution-time (i.e., dynamic[15]) record selection. The CL variable &CityInp must be assigned the name of a city (e.g., Portland); the city name might come from a program parameter, a data entry display, or some other source. The OVRDBF command is used to specify that the CUSTOMER file will be opened as a shared file; the shared open enables the HLL program to subsequently access the file through the ODP established by the OPNQRYF command and thus take advantage of the record selection specified by the OPNQRYF command's QRYSLT (Query Select) parameter.

Figure 17.2
Dynamically Selecting Customers with the OPNQRYF Command

```
DCL &CityInp *Char 30

/* Get customer city, using HLL program or other method, and store */
/* the city name in the &CityInp variable.                         */
      .
      .
      .
OVRDBF  FILE( customer ) SHARE( *yes )

OPNQRYF FILE( customer )                                        +
        QRYSLT( 'shpcity = "' *CAT &CityInp *CAT '"' )

/* Call HLL program to open CUSTOMER file and display all records  */
/* selected by the OPNQRYF statement's QRYSLT parameter.           */

CALL dspcust

CLOF    OPNID( customer )

DLTOVR  FILE( customer )
```

[15] In Chapter 4, we discussed the DYNSLT DDS keyword, which provides another form of "dynamic" record selection. The DYNSLT keyword controls whether DB2/400 applies select/omit selection criteria when a record is updated or when a record is retrieved. Even with the DYNSLT keyword, however, the selection criteria is static. With OPNQRYF, the selection criteria can be changed at runtime (i.e., is dynamic).

The OPNQRYF command's FILE parameter specifies one or more database files that provide the underlying data for the command.[16] The QRYSLT parameter specifies record selection as a string up to a maximum of 5,000 characters that contains a free-format logical expression with field names, relational operators, and arithmetic or embedded-character-string expressions. The logical, arithmetic, and embedded-character-string expressions can be fully parenthesized.

In the example in Figure 17.2, the QRYSLT argument is created by concatenating (*CAT) the field name (SHPCITY) and the equal sign (=) with the contents of CL variable &CityInp. If the &CityInp variable contains the string "Portland", the resulting selection expression would be

```
shpcity = "Portland"
```

This type of concatenation lets you create selection criteria dynamically. When the OPNQRYF command is executed, DB2/400 parses the QRYSLT argument and appropriate code is generated and stored with the ODP's access routines. When an HLL program retrieves records through the shared ODP, the generated code tests and selects the records.

The following QRYSLT parameter illustrates how a more complex selection expression can be coded:

```
QRYSLT( '(%XLATE( name qsystrntbl ) *CT "' *CAT &ProdInp *CAT '")' +
          *CAT ' *AND ' *CAT                                       +
        '(acctbal > crdlimit * ' *CAT &FracInp *CAT ')' )
```

In this example, the QRYSLT parameter value is used to select all customers who have a specific product in their customer name and who have an account balance (ACCTBAL) that exceeds a specified fraction of the customer's credit limit (CRDLIMIT). If the &ProdInp variable contains the string "SOFTWARE", and the &FracInp variable contains the string "0.3", the resulting selection expression would be

```
(%XLATE( name qsystrntbl ) *CT "SOFTWARE") *AND (acctbal > crdlimit * 0.3)
```

This use of the QRYSLT parameter demonstrates the %XLATE function, used to translate lowercase to uppercase for string matching, and the *CT (contains) operator, used to look for a string value anywhere within a character field. The QRYSLT parameter also demonstrates the use of arithmetic expressions and compound logical tests. Figure 17.3 lists other functions that can be used in selection and field mapping expressions.

Under the OPNQRYF command description, the CL reference manual lists the complete documentation for the operators and functions listed in Figure 17.3. Many of these functions are identical to the SQL/400 functions listed in Figure 14.7.

---

[16] If multiple files (or file members) are specified, the result is a dynamic join. Only physical files, join logical files, and SQL views can be specified for a dynamic join.

Figure 17.3

Operators and Functions
Available for Selection
Expressions and
Mapped Fields

Arithmetic operators: +, −, *, /, ** (exponentiation), // (remainder)

String operators: *CAT or ‖ (concatenation), *CT (contains)

Relational operators: *LT (<), *LE (<=), *EQ (=), *GE (>=), *GT (>), *NE (¬=), *NL (¬<), *NG (¬>)

Logical operators: *AND (&), *OR (|), *XOR or && (exclusive OR), *NOT (¬)

Functions:

%ABSVAL	%DURHOUR	%SECOND
%ACOS	%DURMICSEC	%SIN
%AND	%DURMINUTE	%SINH
%ANTILOG	%DURMONTH	%SQRT
%ASIN	%DURSEC	%SST
%ATAN	%DURYEAR	%STDDEV
%ATANH	%EXP	%STRIP
%AVG	%HEX	%SUBSTRING
%CHAR	%HOUR	%SUM
%COS	%LEN	%TAN
%COSH	%LN	%TANH
%COT	%LOG	%TIME
%COUNT	%MAX	%TIMESTP
%CURDATE	%MICSEC	%USER
%CURTIME	%MIN	%VALUES
%CURTIMESTP	%MINUTE	%VAR
%CURTIMEZONE	%MONTH	%WLDCRD
%DATE	%NONNULL	%XLATE
%DAY	%NOT	%XOR
%DAYS	%NULL	%YEAR
%DIGITS	%OR	
%DURDAY	%RANGE	

Keep in mind two important rules for creating a QRYSLT parameter value:

- Any CL variables you use to create the selection expression string must be character variables. Even values you use to supply numeric literals must be in string form, as the &FracInp example above illustrates.

- You must properly use double quotes to delimit string literals, but not numeric literals, in the resulting selection expression.

    If the contents of a CL variable are to be used as a character literal, you must code double quotes to delimit the value, as shown for the &CityInp and &ProdInp variables in the two previous examples. If the contents of a CL variable are to be used as a numeric literal, you must not code delimiters, as shown for the &FracInp variable in the previous example.

One CL programming technique you may find helpful is to construct the complete QRYSLT string and assign it to a CL variable, then use this variable in the OPNQRYF command:

```
CHGVAR &QrySltStr ( 'shpcity = "' *CAT &CityInp *CAT '"' )

OPNQRYF FILE( customer )
       QRYSLT( &QrySltStr )
```

This technique not only simplifies the OPNQRYF command, but it also lets you use OS/400's interactive debug facility to inspect the string to see whether you have all the concatenations and delimiters right.

Dynamic Sequencing

An OPNQRYF command also can be used to resequence selected records dynamically. For example, if the CUSTOMER physical file has CUSTID as its key, but you want to retrieve and display the selected records by NAME, you can do so by using the KEYFLD parameter in the OPNQRYF command, as in the following statement:

```
OPNQRYF FILE( customer )
       QRYSLT( 'shpcity = "' *CAT &CityInp *CAT '"' )
       KEYFLD( name )
```

It's not necessary to have a logical file over the CUSTOMER physical file that provides an access path on the NAME field. If no appropriate access path exists, DB2/400 selects the records and builds a temporary access path on the selected records.

As you can see, the flexibility of the OPNQRYF command allows you to build a single retrieve/display program for the CUSTOMER file and use that program to select and sequence records in countless ways — without making any program modifications. To provide an easy-to-use interface, you can front-end the OPNQRYF QRYSLT and KEYFLD parameters with menus and fill-in-the-blank displays.

Mapped Fields

Dynamic record selection and sequencing are only two of the capabilities that the OPNQRYF command provides. Appendix B includes a list of other OPNQRYF parameters and a brief description of their use. Chapter 6 of the *DB2/400 Database Programming* manual explains the major OPNQRYF command functions and provides further examples.

One of the most useful features of the OPNQRYF command is its ability to map fields using the MAPFLD parameter. Field mapping lets you derive new fields from one or more fields in the file(s) specified on the FILE parameter.[17] For example, you can derive a mapped field for the cost of an item on an order from the underlying physical file fields for the item quantity, unit price, and discount percentage for the item. The OVRDBF and OPNQRYF commands in Figure 17.4 result in the automatic calculation of the COST

---

[17] In relational database terminology, the derived fields are known as virtual attributes, and the underlying fields are known as direct attributes. Chapter 9 explains the relational concepts upon which many of the OPNQRYF command's features are based.

Figure 17.4
Field Mapping

```
/* Override the HLL program's declared file (SALDTLCST) to the   */
/* underlying file (SALEITEM).                                   */

OVRDBF  FILE( saldtlcst ) TOFILE( saleitem) SHARE( *yes )

/* Open the underlying physical file, but specify that the record */
/* format to be used when records are read is the HLL program's   */
/* declared format (with the derived field COST).  Also specify   */
/* how to compute the derived field.                              */

OPNQRYF FILE( saleitem )                                         +
        FORMAT( saldtlcst )                                     +
        MAPFLD( ( cost 'qty * unitprc * ( 1 - ( discpct / 100 ) )' ) )

/* Call HLL program to open SALDTLCST file and display order ID,  */
/* item ID, and net cost for item on this sale.                   */

CALL dspsalcst

CLOF    OPNID( saleitem )

DLTOVR  FILE( saldtlcst )
```

mapped field when the DSPSALCST program reads a record from the SALDTLCST file.

To use field mapping, you normally define a new record format that includes all the underlying fields you want visible to the HLL program and any new mapped fields you want automatically computed by the OPNQRYF field mapping specifications. This new record format is defined by creating a physical file. Figure 17.5 shows the DDS for SALDTLCST, a physical file that defines a record format with two fields (ORDERID and PARTID from the SALEITEM file — Figure 17.6) and one mapped field (COST).

The SALDTLCST file is not used to contain any data and can be created without any members. The DSPSALCST program, used to display sale item net cost, must declare SALDTLCST (not SALEITEM) in the RPG IV file specification or COBOL/400 Select statement. The compiler then uses the record format from SALDTLCST to declare the appropriate fields (ORDERID, PARTID, and COST) and their layout in any record that the program reads.

Because two files are involved in field mapping — the file that contains the data and the file that defines the resulting record format — you must relate these two files correctly with the OVRDBF and OPNQRYF commands. Thus, in Figure 17.4 the OVRDBF command specifies in the FILE parameter the file that defines the resulting record format, including mapped fields (i.e., the file declared in the HLL program). The OVRDBF command specifies in the TOFILE parameter the file that contains the data. The OVRDBF command also specifies SHARE(*YES) so ultimately the HLL file open operation is redirected to the shared ODP created by the OPNQRYF command.

The OPNQRYF command defines the relationship between the fields in the file containing the data and the fields, including mapped fields, in the

Figure 17.5
SALDTLCST Physical File

```
...1....+....2....+....3....+....4....+....5....+....6....+....7.
            R SALDTLCSTR                       TEXT( 'Sale detail costs' )

              ORDERID    R                      REFFLD( ORDERID SALEITEM )
              PARTID     R                      REFFLD( PARTID  SALEITEM )
              COST              7P 2            TEXT( 'Cost' )
```

Figure 17.6
SALEITEM Physical File

```
...1....+....2....+....3....+....4....+....5....+....6....+....7.
                                               UNIQUE

            R SALEITEMR                         TEXT( 'Sale items' )

              ORDERID    R                      REFFLD( ORDERID SALE )
              PARTID     R                      REFFLD( PARTID  PART )
              QTY               7P 0            TEXT( 'Quantity ordered' )
              UNITPRC           7P 2            TEXT( 'Unit price' )
              DISCPCT           7P 5            TEXT( 'Discount percent' )

            K ORDERID
            K PARTID
```

resulting record format. Thus, the OPNQRYF command specifies in the FILE parameter the file containing the data and in the FORMAT parameter the file that defines the resulting record format. Note that the OVRDBF and OPNQRYF commands use opposite values in their respective FILE parameters; a general rule is that the OVRDBF FILE parameter's value should be the same as the OPNQRYF FORMAT parameter's value, and the OVRDBF TOFILE parameter's value should be the same as the OPNQRYF FILE parameter's first (and possibly only) value.

The field mappings, as I mentioned earlier, are defined by the MAPFLD parameter on the OPNQRYF command. If a field in the resulting format has the same name and meaning as a field in the file containing the data, it doesn't need to be included in the MAPFLD parameter (e.g., fields ORDERID and PARTID). But the computations to derive a mapped field, such as COST, must be included in the MAPFLD parameter, as shown in Figure 17.4. The computation can use standard arithmetic or character-string expressions and the functions listed in Figure 17.3.

After an OPNQRYF command is executed to access a format with mapped fields, you should follow the normal practice of closing the file and deleting the file override. As Figure 17.4 shows, the CLOF OPNID and DLTOVR FILE parameters' values correspond to the OPNQRYF and OVRDBF FILE parameters, respectively.

When you use numeric mapped fields, you may encounter a potential problem with division by zero. For example, if a derived field to calculate "income-per-child = gross-income / number-of-children" were specified as

```
MAPFLD( ( incperchl 'grsinc / childcnt' ) )
```

a division-by-zero error would occur for those records with zero children. But if you use a simple trick, you can avoid this common error with mapped fields. If you use the expression

```
'( grsinc * childcnt ) / %MAX( ( childcnt * childcnt ) 0.1 )'
```

in the MAPFLD parameter, a default result of zero for INCPERCHL can be calculated and you won't trigger an error.

If CHILDCNT is zero, CHILDCNT * CHILDCNT in the divisor is also zero, and the %MAX function returns 0.1, a valid divisor. In this case, GRSINC * CHILDCNT in the dividend is also zero and the final result is 0.0 / 0.1, or zero. If CHILDCNT is not zero, the %MAX function returns CHILDCNT * CHILDCNT, which is divided into GRSINC * CHILDCNT. The result is the desired value of GRSINC / CHILDCNT. When you use this method, the constant (e.g., 0.1) must be less than the smallest possible non-zero value for the divisor squared. A safe value is 0.*nnnn*1, where *nnnn* represents the number of leading zeros, and is determined as two times the number of decimal places in the divisor.[18] For example, assuming CHILDCNT has zero decimal places, the constant is 0.1; for a field with two decimal places, you should use 0.00001.

Dynamic Join

OPNQRYF also can be used to create a dynamic join file that takes advantage of mapped fields and dynamic sequencing. Consider an application that joins sale item, sale, customer, and part records (files SALEITEM, SALE, CUSTOMER, and PART in Figures 17.6, 17.7, 17.8, and 17.9). The record selection is based on a customer city value input by the user (&CityInp); the sequencing is by customer name, order ID, and part ID (a mixture of primary and secondary file fields); and a mapped field (COST) is calculated from fields in the SALEITEM file.

With the OPNQRYF command, a dynamic join file is set up much like a single file with mapped fields. First you create a physical file (not a join logical file) to define the resulting record format (see SALFULDTL in Figure 17.10). Then you can write an HLL program that references this physical file.

---

[18] In other words, the constant should be $10^{-(2d+1)}$, where d is the number of decimal places of the divisor.

Figure 17.7
SALE Physical File

```
...1....+....2....+....3....+....4....+....5....+....6....+....7.
                                      UNIQUE

           R SALER                    TEXT( 'Sales' )

             ORDERID        7P Ø      TEXT( 'Order ID' )
             SALEDATE       L         TEXT( 'Sale date' )
             CUSTID      R            REFFLD( CUSTID CUSTOMER )

           K ORDERID
```

Figure 17.8
CUSTOMER Physical File

```
...1....+....2....+....3....+....4....+....5....+....6....+....7.
                                      UNIQUE

           R CUSTOMERR                TEXT( 'Customers' )

             CUSTID         7P Ø      TEXT( 'Customer ID' )
             NAME           30A       TEXT( 'Customer name' )
             SHPCITY        30A       TEXT( 'Customer shipping +
                                            address city' )

           K CUSTID
```

Figure 17.9
PART Physical File

```
...1....+....2....+....3....+....4....+....5....+....6....+....7.
                                      UNIQUE

           R PARTR                    TEXT( 'Parts' )

             PARTID         7P Ø      TEXT( 'Part ID' )
             PARTDESC       5ØA       TEXT( 'Part description' )

           K PARTID
```

Figure 17.10
SALFULDTL Physical File

```
...1....+....2....+....3....+....4....+....5....+....6....+....7.
           R SALFULDTLR               TEXT( 'Sale full detail' )

             ORDERID     R            REFFLD( ORDERID  SALE     )
             CUSTID      R            REFFLD( CUSTID   SALE     )
             SALEDATE    R            REFFLD( SALEDATE SALE     )
             PARTID      R            REFFLD( PARTID   SALEITEM )
             QTY         R            REFFLD( QTY      SALEITEM )
             UNITPRC     R            REFFLD( UNITPRC  SALEITEM )
             DISCPCT     R            REFFLD( DISCPCT  SALEITEM )
             COST           7P 2      TEXT( 'Cost' )
             NAME        R            REFFLD( NAME     CUSTOMER )
             SHPCITY     R            REFFLD( SHPCITY  CUSTOMER )
             PARTDESC    R            REFFLD( PARTDESC PART     )
```

To use the dynamic join file, the code in Figure 17.11 uses an OVRDBF command to redirect the physical file that defines the resulting format (i.e., SALFULDTL) to the primary (i.e., first) file in the dynamic join (SALE). Next the OPNQRYF command specifies all the underlying physical files in the FILE parameter; the first of these is the primary file. The JFLD parameter defines the field correspondence between pairs of files that are joined.[19]

Figure 17.11
Dynamically Joining
Four Files

```
DCL &CityInp *Char 30

/* Get customer city, using HLL program or other method, and store */
/* the city name in the &CityInp variable.                         */
         .
         .
         .

/* Override the HLL program's declared file (SALFULDTL) to the      */
/* primary physical file (SALE).                                    */

OVRDBF  FILE( salfuldtl ) TOFILE( sale ) SHARE( *yes )

/* Open all the underlying physical files that are involved in the */
/* join, but specify that the record format to be used when records*/
/* are read is the HLL program's declared format (with all the      */
/* joined fields and the derived field COST). Also specify how to  */
/* join the records, how to select and order them, and how to       */
/* compute the derived field.                                       */

OPNQRYF FILE( sale saleitem customer part )                         +
        FORMAT( salfuldtl )                                         +
        QRYSLT( 'shpcity = "' *Cat &CityInp *Cat '"' )              +
        KEYFLD( name orderid partid )                               +
        JFLD( ( sale/orderid     saleitem/orderid )                 +
              ( sale/custid       customer/custid  )                +
              ( saleitem/partid part/partid        ) )              +
        MAPFLD( ( orderid 'sale/orderid'     )                      +
                ( custid  'sale/custid'      )                      +
                ( partid  'saleitem/partid' )                       +
                ( cost    'qty * unitprc * ( 1 - ( discpct / 100 ) )' ) )

/* Call HLL program to open SALFULDTL file and display full sale   */
/* details by customer name and city.                              */

CALL dspfulsal

CLOF    OPNID( sale )

DLTOVR  FILE( salfuldtl )
```

---

[19] Review Chapter 6's detailed explanation of join logical files. Many join logical file concepts apply to dynamic joins, as well.

Note that join field names are qualified with a file name by using the syntax

file-designator/field-name

A similar syntax is used in the definition of mapped fields — both those mapped without modification (but that must be specified if the field name occurs in more than one underlying physical file) and those that are mapped fields. Note an important difference between the syntax used in the JFLD and MAPFLD parameters. Fields in the JFLD parameter are never delimited with quotes; however, a qualified name or an expression must be quoted in the MAPFLD parameter.

As with mapped fields, an HLL program opens the file that defines the resulting record format for a dynamic join file. The shared ODP established by the OPNQRYF command joins and resequences the records at execution time. Field mapping and resequencing on secondary file fields can result in a temporary copy of the data, but the DB2/400 routines that the OPNQRYF command uses attempt to minimize both file accesses and duplication of data.

After the dynamic join file has been used, it's closed with a CLOF command that references the primary file. Last, a DLTOVR command should be executed for the file that defines the resulting format (in this case, SALFULDTL).

Group Fields

Another way that mapped fields add flexibility to applications is with group fields, a special type of mapped field set up by using the GRPFLD (Group Field) parameter. Group fields provide data aggregation such as counts, totals, and averages. The process for using group fields is similar to that for other mapped fields; a physical file is used to define the resulting format and the OPNQRYF MAPFLD parameter is used to define how the group fields are calculated.

Figure 17.12 shows the DDS for physical file SALITMSUM, which defines a format that contains a count of the different items sold on each order, the total number of items ordered, and the average unit price for the items ordered. The OPNQRYF command in Figure 17.13 includes a MAPFLD parameter that uses the functions %COUNT, %SUM, and %AVG to specify how the group fields are calculated. The GRPFLD keyword specifies how the aggregation is done. In this case, the grouping is done for each order ID. When HLL program DSPITMSUM reads records from the SALITMSUM file, each record contains the desired aggregate values for a single sale.

Figure 17.12
SALITMSUM Physical File

```
...1....+....2....+....3....+....4....+....5....+....6....+....7.
        R SALITMSUMR                       TEXT( 'Sale item summary' )

          ORDERID    R                      REFFLD( ORDERID SALEITEM )
          ITEMCNT        7P 0               TEXT( 'Item count'      )
          QTYTOT         7P 0               TEXT( 'Quantity total'  )
          UNTPRCAV       7P 2               TEXT( 'Unit price avg.' )
```

Figure 17.13
Group Fields

```
/* Override the HLL program's declared file (SALITMSUM) to the   */
/* underlying physical file (SALEITEM).                          */

OVRDBF  FILE( salitmsum ) TOFILE( saleitem) SHARE( *yes )

/* Open the underlying physical file, but specify that the record */
/* format to be used when records are read is the HLL program's   */
/* declared format (with the group fields). Also specify how to   */
/* compute the group fields.                                      */

OPNQRYF FILE( saleitem )                              +
        FORMAT( salitmsum )                           +
        GRPFLD( orderid )                             +
        KEYFLD( orderid )                             +
        MAPFLD( ( itemcnt   '%COUNT'         )  +
                ( qtytot    '%SUM( qty )'     )  +
                ( untprcav '%AVG( unitprc )' ) ) +
        GRPSLT( 'itemcnt >= 3' )

/* Call HLL program to open SALITMSUM file and display order ID,  */
/* item count, total quantity, and average unit price for each    */
/* sale.                                                          */

CALL dspitmsum

CLOF    OPNID( saleitem )

DLTOVR  FILE( salitmsum )
```

The GRPSLT (Group Select) keyword allows record selection after an aggregate record is calculated; in this example, only aggregates with three or more items on an order are selected. GRPSLT operates like QRYSLT, but QRYSLT selects records before aggregation and GRPSLT selects records after aggregation.[20]

Additional Considerations
However you use the OPNQRYF command, note that it must be executed before the HLL file open. But it's not necessary to go in and out of your HLL application program to change selection or ordering specifications

---

[20] The Chapter 14 discussion on the SQL Select statement's Group By and Having clauses provides additional information that explains how grouping and group selection works.

because QCMDEXC can be called to execute the OPNQRYF command from an HLL program.

Note also that the file that the OPNQRYF command opens should be closed with a CLOF (Close File) command when the current use is over. Because the file is shared, it can inadvertently affect subsequent file opens if it is left open. By using the following four-step cycle, you can let a user retrieve records with different selection and sequencing without ever exiting the application.

1. Get the selection and sequencing requirements
2. Execute the OPNQRYF command
3. Execute an HLL program to process the current view
4. Execute CLOF

Object and Record Locks

The AS/400 lets multiple users access application objects simultaneously. To prevent one job's operations from interfering with another job's operations, OS/400 provides object- and record-locking facilities. When one job holds an **object** or **record lock**, it restricts what other jobs can do with the locked object or record. DB2/400 uses OS/400 object and record locking to avoid conflicting database updates from multiple jobs. For many situations, DB2/400's default locking is adequate; however, in some cases you may need to add explicit locks to your applications to prevent conflicts.

For example, if one user starts end-of-day batch transaction processing and another user, not knowing this, calls an interactive program to add a few last-minute transactions, unless your program is designed to handle this situation, transactions entered by the interactive job may be lost as they're added behind those already processed by the batch job. DB2/400's default object locking would let both jobs have update access to the file. However, you can use the ALCOBJ (Allocate Object) command to let the batch job place a lock on the file so no other job can perform any updates until the lock is released.

When you allocate an object during a job, OS/400 places an object lock on the object. This lock serves two purposes: It guarantees to your job specific types of access to the object, and it prevents other jobs from having specific types of access to the object. The lock is released when a program executes a DLCOBJ (Deallocate Object) command, when the routing step ends,[21] or when the object is deleted by the job holding the lock.

The type of lock placed on an object governs the way the object is shared among different jobs. This mechanism allows the AS/400 to provide different

---

[21] A routing step is one part of an AS/400 job. Most jobs have a single routing step that starts when the job starts and ends when the job ends. For one-step jobs, it might be simpler to think of allocating an object to a job rather than to a routing step. Where this chapter uses the term "routing step," you can read "job" for most situations.

users a high degree of concurrent access to programs, data, and other objects. While sharing is allowed, the object is protected against simultaneous uses that would conflict; for example, a job cannot delete a file member if another job is currently reading it.

Object allocation differs from object authorization, which is used to protect the security of shared objects (see Chapter 18). Object authorization allows a user profile specific types of access to an object; this authority generally remains in effect even when no job is active (the exception is the authority that may be adopted while a program is executing).

Object allocation, on the other hand, is used to protect the integrity of shared objects. Object allocation grants a specific type of lock to the routing step that requests the allocation; objects are allocated only by active jobs. The allocation remains in effect only while the routing step is active. The ALCOBJ command can be used to

- Prevent a program from being deleted while someone is executing it
- Allow only one job at a time to execute a program
- Obtain database file locks that aren't available when you use the default locks obtained by HLLs
- Guarantee access to a group of required objects before using any one of them
- Set aside a data area to provide an unduplicated sequence number for control purposes (such as sequencing transactions)

Types of Object Locks

Suppose the automatic allocation that an HLL provides has not obtained restrictive enough locks in one of your applications and you've decided you need to explicitly allocate an object. In doing so, you lock, to some degree, other jobs out of the object — the degree depends upon the kind of lock you obtain. You have five types of locks from which to choose:

- *Exclusive (*EXCL)* — only the routing step holding the lock can use the object; routing steps in other jobs cannot access the object.
- *Exclusive-allow-read (*EXCLRD)* — the routing step that holds the lock can read or update the object, while routing steps in other jobs can only read it.
- *Shared-for-update (*SHRUPD)* — the routing step that holds the lock, as well as routing steps in other jobs, can read or update the object.
- *Shared-no-update (*SHRNUP)* — the routing step that holds the lock is guaranteed only read access to the object;[22] routing steps in other jobs can only read the object.

---

[22] With this lock, the routing step may also be able to update the object, as long as no other job holds a conflicting lock. But this lock doesn't guarantee update access.

- *Shared-for-read (*SHRRD)* — the routing step that holds the lock is guaranteed only read access to the object; routing steps in other jobs can read or update it.

The table in Figure 17.14 summarizes these locks. You can use the table to quickly determine the type of lock to obtain in a given instance. Suppose you've decided to update a file and while you're updating it you want other jobs or routing steps to be able to read the file but not update it. In the left column of the table in Figure 17.14, find "Update." Move across the Update row to the "Read Only" column for routing steps in other jobs. The type of lock you need in this instance is *EXCLRD.

Fig 17.14

Object Lock Type to Use for Required Access Control

Your routing step needs this type of access:	And you want to allow a routing step in another job the following access		
	No access	**Read only**	**Update**
None, but restrict other jobs	*EXCL	*SHRNUP	(no lock)
Read only	*EXCL	*SHRNUP	*SHRRD
Update	*EXCL	*EXCLRD	*SHRUPD

Although a lock provides the routing step that holds it a guarantee of access to an object and limits access by routing steps in other jobs, it does not limit subsequent access in the same routing step that holds the lock. For example, a CL program can execute an ALCOBJ command to obtain an *EXCLRD lock on a database file member. A CL program in another job cannot call an HLL program that opens the locked file member for updating. However, it's possible for the CL program holding the *EXCLRD lock to call an HLL program that updates the file.[23]

When a routing step attempts to obtain a lock, it gets the lock unless a routing step in another job already holds a conflicting lock on the same object. The AS/400 ensures proper sharing of an object by preventing conflicting locks. Figure 17.15 shows the types of locks that are allowed if a routing step in another job already holds a lock.

A routing step, at different times in its processing, can obtain multiple locks of the same or different type on an object. The system keeps a count of each type of lock placed on an object. Eventually, each lock must be released individually, even if they are of the same type. Thus, if at two different points

---

[23] This is, of course, the whole point of object locking.

Fig 17.15

Allowable Object Lock
Combinations

If a routing step already has this lock:	A routing step in another job can obtain this lock:				
	*EXCL	*EXCLRD	*SHRUPD	*SHRNUP	*SHRRD
*EXCL					
*EXCLRD					Yes
*SHRUPD			Yes		Yes
*SHRNUP				Yes	Yes
*SHRRD		Yes	Yes	Yes	Yes

in a routing step a *SHRRD lock is placed on an object, at some point both *SHRRD locks must be released on that object to return the system lock count to zero. Not until the count returns to zero is the *SHRRD lock totally removed from the object.

A routing step can use a single ALCOBJ command to obtain a lock on more than one object. Therefore, a group of objects required to complete an operation can be allocated at one time. Often an HLL program requires several files, some for read-only access, others for updating. By allocating the files before calling the HLL program, you can simplify error handling. If explicit allocation is not used, you must either open all files before processing begins so you're assured of access to them all, or you must use a restart procedure to continue at an interruption point (if one of the files turns out to be unavailable).

The statement below shows an ALCOBJ command that allocates the following objects: a daily transaction input file that no other job will be allowed to update, a customer name file that will be read, a customer account file that will be updated, and a data area with the last transaction number processed that will be updated and can be read by other jobs.

```
ALCOBJ OBJ( ( dailytran *file   *shrnup dailytran )
            ( custname  *file   *shrrd  custname  )
            ( custact   *file   *shrupd custact   )
            ( lsttrnnbr *dtaara *exclrd           ) )
      WAIT( 10 )
```

If any one of the locks cannot be obtained, none of the objects will have locks placed on them by this ALCOBJ command. This all-or-none approach makes it easy to allocate the set of objects you need before you start to use any of them.

An ALCOBJ command succeeds if all the requested locks can be obtained. If any of the locks cannot be granted, an escape message (CPF1002) is sent to the program executing the ALCOBJ command. If the command is in a CL program, you can monitor for this message using the MONMSG command. If an HLL program's operation (e.g., a file open) cannot allocate an object, the HLL program's exception procedures must handle the problem.

The WAIT(10) parameter in the example above specifies that the ALCOBJ command can wait up to 10 seconds for the locks. This wait may be necessary if a routing step in another job has one or more of the objects allocated with a lock that conflicts with the requested lock. If such a conflict exists and the conflicting locks are released within 10 seconds, this routing step gets the locks it has requested unless a job with a higher dispatching priority also has requested locks on any of the objects.

A routing step also can release more than one lock with a single DLCOBJ command. When the objects in the example above are no longer needed, they can be deallocated with the following command:

```
DLCOBJ OBJ( ( dailytran *file    *shrnup dailytran )
            ( custname  *file    *shrrd  custname  )
            ( custact   *file    *shrupd custact   )
            ( lsttrnnbr *dtaara *exclrd           ) )
```

Generally, for every ALCOBJ command in your CL program, there should be a corresponding DLCOBJ command with the same object list.[24] However, if the job ends when the objects are no longer needed, no DLCOBJ command is necessary. The routing step ends when the job ends, and all objects are deallocated automatically.

Within a routing step, you may need to change the type of lock you have on an object. You should first obtain the new lock and then release the old lock. This technique prevents a routing step in another job from obtaining a conflicting lock before you obtain the new lock. For example, if you want to use a file first for updating and then just to read, execute the following sequence of commands:

```
ALCOBJ OBJ( ( customer *file *shrupd customer ) )
  .
  . Call a program that updates the file.
  .
ALCOBJ OBJ( ( customer *file *shrrd  customer ) )
DLCOBJ OBJ( ( customer *file *shrupd customer ) )
  .
  . Call a program that reads the file.
  .
DLCOBJ OBJ( ( customer *file *shrrd  customer ) )
```

Allocation of Objects by Type

Only certain object types can be allocated using the ALCOBJ command. Figure 17.16 shows these objects and the valid lock types for each. Different purposes are served by allocating each of the object types.

---

[24] The use of DLCOBJ for an object that has not been allocated by an ALCOBJ can be dangerous. Deallocating objects that you have not specifically allocated can release locks on device descriptions or internal system locks and cause system malfunctions.

Fig 17.16
Supported Object Locks

Object Type	Lock Type				
	*EXCL	*EXCLRD	*SHRUPD	*SHRNUP	*SHRRD
Authorization List	Yes	Yes	Yes	Yes	Yes
Data Area	Yes	Yes	Yes	Yes	Yes
Data Dictionary	Yes	Yes	Yes	Yes	Yes
Data Queues	Yes	Yes	Yes	Yes	Yes
Device Description		Yes			
File	Yes	Yes	Yes	Yes	Yes
Forms Control Table	Yes	Yes	Yes	Yes	Yes
Library		Yes	Yes	Yes	Yes
Message Queue	Yes				Yes
Menu	Yes	Yes	Yes	Yes	Yes
Panel Group	Yes	Yes	Yes	Yes	Yes
Program	Yes	Yes			Yes
Search Index	Yes	Yes	Yes	Yes	Yes
Session Description	Yes	Yes	Yes	Yes	Yes
Subsystem Description	Yes				

Several database-related objects require special consideration when using the ALCOBJ command:

Data areas: Data areas can be used to provide a unique control number for shared programs. When a program needs a control number, it calls a CL program such as GETCTLNBR, shown in Figure 17.17. The CL program first places an *EXCL lock on the data area so that no other job can access it. If the data area can't be allocated within 60 seconds, the program returns 0 to signal an error. Once the data area is locked, the CL program receives the data area to get the last number used, increments it by one and puts the new number in the return parameter, updates the data area, and releases the lock. ALCOBJ must be used to place the *EXCL lock on the data area because the RCVDTAARA (Receive Data Area) command places only a *SHRRD lock on the data area. Without the *EXCL lock, another job could read the same control number from the data area before the first job has a chance to update it.

Fig 17.17
GETCTLNBR CL Program

```
PGM        PARM( &CtlNbrArg )

/* Return next control number. Return 0 if error. */

DCL        &CtlNbrArg  *dec ( 9 0 )
DCLDTAARA  DTAARA( ctlnbr )


ALCOBJ     OBJ( ( ctlnbr *dtaara *excl ) ) WAIT( 60 )
MONMSG     cpf0000  EXEC( DO )
           CHGVAR &CtlNbrArg 0  /* Signal error */
           RETURN
           ENDDO

RCVDTAARA  DTAARA( ctlnbr )

CHGVAR     &CtlNbrArg ( &CtlNbr + 1 )
CHGVAR     &CtlNbr    ( &CtlNbrArg )

SNDDTAARA  DTAARA( ctlnbr )

DLCOBJ     OBJ( ( ctlnbr *dtaara *excl ) )

RETURN
ENDPGM
```

Database Files: An open operation executed on a database file by CL or an HLL program obtains default locks determined by the type of open operation (input, output, input-output). When an open operation is executed on a file, a lock is placed on the file itself, but the locking does not end there. If the file is a physical file, a lock is also placed on the member of the file you're opening, on the access path of the opened member (if it's a keyed file), and on the data of the opened member. If the file is a logical file, a lock is placed on the member of the file you're opening, and a lock is placed on one or more of the following: the access path of the opened member, the access path of a member that's sharing its access path with the member you're opening, and the data of all physical file members included in the scope of the logical file member you're opening. If all this seems a bit complex, just remember that when you open a file, you lock the data that's accessed through a member and anything else that's necessary to protect the integrity of related files and members.

By default, CL and HLL programs place a *SHRRD lock on the data in input-only physical file members and place a *SHRUPD lock on the data in output-only and input-output physical file members. You can cause locks other than these defaults to be obtained when a database file is opened by using the OVRDBF command's RCDFMTLCK (Record Format Lock) parameter to specify that a more restrictive lock be placed on a record format when the file is opened. When used with a logical file, this parameter places more restrictive locks on the underlying data in the physical file member. The

RCDFMTLCK parameter affects the allocation of the file only when it's opened, not when an ALCOBJ command is used.

If the control provided by CL or HLL opens is not sufficient, you can explicitly allocate a file before you open it by executing an ALCOBJ command such as

```
ALCOBJ OBJ( ( appdta/customer *file *shrupd customer ) )
```

When this command is executed, if CUSTOMER is a physical file, the file will get a *SHRRD lock, the CUSTOMER member will get a *SHRRD lock, and the data will get a *SHRUPD lock. Then, when CUSTOMER is opened, its access path will get a *SHRRD lock, the default lock of an open operation. Default locks on the file, the member, and the data also will be obtained by the open operation. If CUSTOMER is a logical file, many other locks may be placed on it. The important consideration about these other locks is their effect on jobs trying to access different logical files that may be sharing the same underlying data.

Locks placed on a database file member through the ALCOBJ command or a file open operation should not be confused with record locks. File member locks establish, for the entire file member, allowable access methods by routing steps in different jobs. Record locks, on the other hand, restrict access to individual records within a physical file member. A record lock usually is obtained at the beginning of an input-output statement and is held until the next input-output statement begins, at which time the first record lock is released. If you use commitment control, which allows processing a group of database records as a single unit, record locks are generally held from the I/O operation until the next commitment boundary (e.g., the next commit or rollback operation).

Without commitment control, an *UPDATE type record lock is held by an ODP and is similar to the *EXCLRD object lock in that it lets a locked record be read, but not updated or locked, through another ODP. If all ODPs for a file are in use under commitment control, the record lock is held by the commitment control environment. With commitment control, there are two types of record locks: *READ and *UPDATE. The type of lock obtained and the allowable operations by other jobs depends on the lock level for the commitment control environment in effect (which is explained in a later section).

An important point to keep in mind is that record locks held by an ODP can conflict within the same routing step (unlike object locks). This conflict can occur if the same physical file record is accessed for updating through separate ODPs — for example, by having opened two logical files at the same time that are over the same physical file member.

Programs: When a program is called, normally no locks are placed on it, which means that a job can execute or delete the program while it's being executed by another job. Often, this is not a desirable situation. Using allocation, you can prevent a program from being deleted while it's in use or let only one job at a time execute the program.

To prevent a program from being deleted, obtain a *SHRRD lock on it. A convenient place to do this is in CL menu programs just before the CALL command is executed. After the program returns to the calling program, it should be deallocated using the DLCOBJ command.

If you want only one job at a time to execute a program, you can implement a controlling CL program that attempts to obtain an *EXCL lock on the desired program before calling it.[25] Because no two jobs can hold an *EXCL lock on the same object at the same time, you can have the calling program monitor for failed allocation of the restricted program and execute a GOTO to branch to a label after the CALL command. At that label you can send a message informing the user that the program is in use and then exit the controlling program.

Displaying Locks

A time may come when you need to see how objects and database file records are being locked. At that point three commands are available to you:

- WRKOBJLCK (Work with Object Locks) — to see the locks held on an object by all jobs
- DSPRCDLCK (Display Record Locks) — to see the records in a physical file that have locks on them
- DSPJOB (Display Job) — to see all external locks for a job, both those already held and those for which the job is waiting

These commands can help you understand what OS/400 and the HLLs are doing automatically and also can identify the cause of any failed allocation. The *CL Reference* manual provides full descriptions of the displays for each command.

If you want to see the locks on file members, press F6 from the Work with Object Locks display, and the Work with Member Locks display is presented. This display shows the data locks for the physical file members. The Lock Type column on this screen can have the following values: MBR for the member control block, DATA for the actual data in a physical file member, or ACCPTH for the access path of a keyed file. The lock held for DATA is generally the most useful in determining how the member is being shared.

For logical file members only, use option 9 — Shared member locks — on the Work with Member Locks display to move to the Work with Shared Member Locks display. The Work with Shared Member Locks display shows

---

[25] Note that holding an *EXCL lock on a program object does not prevent other jobs from executing the program. For the suggested technique to work, all jobs that call the program must attempt to get an *EXCL lock.

one or more lists of the other logical or physical file members that have had a lock placed on them because of the locks on the logical file member that you're displaying. This information always includes the data of physical file members within the scope of the logical file member. It also includes logical file members that share an access path with the logical file member you're displaying.

The third command, DSPJOB, leads you to the Display Job Menu. From there, option 12 — Display Locks — displays the Job Locks display. From this display you can get further information about object locks through displays similar to those displayed by the WRKOBJLCK command. In addition, you can display information about record locks through displays similar to those displayed by the DSPRCDLCK command.

You also can use the System Request key to interrupt an interactive program and then select System Request Menu option 3 — Display Current Job — to get to the Display Job Menu and from there to the Job Locks display. This display can provide insight into how OS/400 and HLLs are locking objects. When you see that they are not providing the exact type of sharing you want, it's time to try the ALCOBJ and DLCOBJ commands.

While OS/400 and HLL compilers take care of most of the necessary object allocation on the AS/400, many complex applications require specific control of data and program sharing. A traditional solution is to provide written procedures to tell the operator to make sure that the program about to be run will not interfere with other jobs on the system. But with an understanding of object allocation, you can automate this control, writing it into the program instead of including it in run books or other operations documentation.

Journaling

If a hardware or software malfunction damages an AS/400 physical file that an online application uses, you want to be able to restore the file to the last valid state before the failure occurred. You can use the save commands described in Chapter 19 to make a tape copy of a physical file, and you can use this copy to restore members of the physical file should they become damaged. But a save command provides only a partial backup because it creates a static snapshot of the file's data; that is, it captures the state of the file at one point in time. As soon as subsequent updates are made to the file's data (records are added, deleted, or changed), the snapshot is out of date. Other data protection methods, such as mirrored disk and device parity protection (also discussed in Chapter 19), can provide additional protection from hardware failure. But these facilities require additional disk storage and don't protect you from malfunctioning application software.

OS/400 journal management provides an important data recovery facility that can help you recover most data up to the last transaction that was entered before a failure. When a physical file is journaled, DB2/400 automatically creates a separate copy of file changes and, if necessary, you can use this copy along with save tapes to recover data in the file.

Journaling Basics

Before we discuss how to use journal management for enhanced database file recovery, let's look at how a journal works. A **journal** is an AS/400 object used primarily to record changes to data in a physical file member and, optionally, changes to a logical file's access path.[26] To help you during recovery, a journal also records file opens, file closes, system IPLs, user-generated entries, and other types of activity related to physical files.

A journal does not discriminate when it records changes made to data in a physical file member; it doesn't matter whether the data is changed by a general-purpose utility, an RPG IV program accessing a logical file over the physical file member, or a CPYF (Copy File) command accessing the member. In all cases, if the data in the physical file member is changed, the journal records the changes in the exact sequence in which they occur to the member. That is, if two programs are simultaneously updating the same physical file member, the journal records any changes these two programs cause in the same order in which DB2/400 processes the changes to the physical file member. Because a journal records all changes to a physical file member in precise time sequence, these changes can be used later to recover the physical file member to an exact point in time.

In addition, a single journal can be (and usually is) used for a group of files, in which case the journal records in proper time sequence the changes to all members of all files in the group. This sequencing allows synchronization of a group of files during recovery, either under explicit user control or automatically if commitment control (discussed in the next section) is in use.

A journal records a change to the data in a physical file member by placing a **journal entry** into an object known as a **journal receiver**. Although access to a journal receiver is not the same as access to a database file, you can think of the journal receiver as the container for journal entries in the same sense that a file member is a container for file records.

The distinction between the journal and the journal receiver is important. The journal is the control mechanism — it maintains information about which physical files it's journaling and about which journal receiver is being used. It also maintains a directory of journal receivers it has used. The journal receiver is the actual repository of the entries that record the changes to the data in a physical file member.

Each entry a journal places into a journal receiver contains system-generated information, including a journal code and an entry-type code that identifies the type of entry, a sequence number, and a date-time stamp. For changes to a file's data, the system-generated portion of an entry includes job name, job user, job number, program name, file name, library name, member name, and relative record number. Journal entries for changes to data also contain a complete copy of the physical file member's affected record. This

---

[26] OS/400 doesn't provide built-in support for journaling changes to the contents of other types of objects such as data areas or message queues.

copy is bit for bit the same as the record, either before it was changed (known as a before image) or after it was changed (known as an after image).

When data is changed, a journal always puts after image journal entries into a journal receiver. Optionally, you can specify that the journal should put both before images and after images into the journal receiver. A journal entry's after image for an add operation to a physical file member contains the new record's data. A journal entry's after image for a change to an existing record contains the revised version of the data. When an existing record is deleted, an after image is a meaningless concept; the journal entry type code that indicates a delete operation and the relative record number provide adequate record-specific information.

Because the journal receiver contains properly sequenced after images for every change made to the data, it's straightforward for journal management to recover a file member to a point in time just before a failure occurred. First, the file member is restored from a previous save tape. Then journal management steps through the after images beginning with the first one after the time of the file save. Each after image has the relative record number of the affected record as well as every bit of the record after a change, so journal management simply replaces, adds, or marks as deleted the record to which the relative record number points. As the affected record is updated, any access path over the physical file member also is updated.

So that the journal reflects all changes made to the data, journal entries are forced to auxiliary storage (disk) before the change is made to the database record. Thus, if a system failure occurs during a database operation, the journal receiver may contain the change, but the database file may not. At IPL (Initial Program Load), the AS/400 always attempts to synchronize the file member and journal by applying any changes recorded in the journal receiver but not recorded in the file. This approach provides almost fool-proof recovery — unless the disk on which your journal receiver resides suffers a head crash and is damaged irretrievably. Later in this section, we look at ways to survive such a head crash.

Setting Up Journaling

Now that we have covered the basics of how a journal works, let's look at some guidelines for setting up journaling to provide enhanced database file recovery. First, you must decide which files to journal and how to group them. Some of your files may be small, inactive, or easily recoverable without journaling. If these files are not involved in transactions that use the files you decide to journal and if they are not related to journaled files by logical files, they need not be journaled. Periodic saves of these files provide adequately for recovery. However, you should journal files that are large, active, have critical transactions applied, or are related to files with these characteristics.

After you identify files to be journaled, you need to decide how to group them. A single journal can be used for a single physical file, or one journal can be used for a group of physical files. You can create as many journals on your system as you need using the CRTJRN command. Each journal covers one or more physical files. However, a physical file can use only one journal at a time.

If a journal is used for a group of files, the journal covers all members of those physical files using the journal. Generally, you should group files so that a single journal is used by all physical files that are related closely in an application system, have members included in the same logical file, or may be open at the same time by a job using commitment control. Although in some situations performance can be improved in concurrent jobs by using multiple journals, the simplest approach is to use a single journal for all physical files within an application system.

Second, establish for each file to be journaled whether to keep after images or both before and after images. Only after images are required for journal management recovery operations. However, if you want to be able to back out changes or to analyze specific changes to records using journal management, you need both before and after images. In addition, when a file is in use under commitment control, the system always keeps both before and after images, regardless how you've set up the physical file to be journaled, so you do not need to specify that both images be kept just to use commitment control.

Also consider that keeping both before and after images increases the disk space requirement but does not necessarily double it. Add and delete operations always generate a single journal entry; the add always contains an after image, and the delete contains a before image. Only a change operation generates two journal entries, one for the before image and one for the after image. Keeping both images has a negligible impact on runtime performance.

Third, decide whether you need a single journal receiver or dual journal receivers. A journal can be set up so that instead of just one receiver for journal entries, there are two. Every entry is duplicated and placed in both receivers. Dual receivers provide extra protection against damaged receivers because if one receiver is damaged, the other one still can be used for recovery. The disk space required for dual receivers is twice that for a single receiver; however, the runtime performance with dual receivers is only slightly slower than with a single receiver and should not be an impediment to using dual receivers. If disk space isn't a constraint, you can start with dual receivers and revert to a single receiver if disk space becomes more limited.

Finally, you should decide onto which user ASP (Auxiliary Storage Pool) unit you want to place each journal receiver.[27] The CRTJRNRCV (Create Journal Receiver) command's default parameter value of ASP(*LIBASP) allocates storage for the journal receiver in the same auxiliary storage pool as the library that contains the journal receiver. If you use dual receivers and are using multiple user ASPs, you probably want to assign each journal receiver to a different ASP to reduce the chance of a disk malfunction damaging both journal receivers.

---

[27] ASPs are discussed in Chapter 19.

The Journaling Process

Having made these decisions, you're ready to enable journaling. The following steps describe how to create the objects you need for journaling, how to start journaling your files, and how to save journal management objects to tape periodically for offline backup.

Your first steps are to create the journal receivers and then the journals. When you do so, you should create both receivers and journals in the same library as the physical files that use them. This practice simplifies backup/restore operations. If a journaled physical file is in a different library from its journal and the journal is not in existence when the physical file is restored, journaling of the physical file ends. Putting the journal and the journal receivers into the same library as the physical file is simpler and more reliable.

With that in mind, you first create one or both receivers needed for each journal. Journal receivers should be given generic receiver names with one to six characters and then a four-digit number (e.g., RCVA0001). A generic receiver name enables the system to build new receiver names automatically when you want to detach one receiver and attach a new one. (We cover detaching and attaching receivers later in this section.) With generic receiver names, the system increments the numeric portion of the currently attached receiver to form the name of the next receiver in the chain. Generic names also make it easier for you to see the order in which receivers have been used. To create a single receiver, you use a command such as the following:

```
CRTJRNRCV JRNRCV( appdta/rcva0001 )
          ASP( 2 )
          TEXT( 'Primary receiver' )
```

To create a second receiver for dual receivers:

```
CRTJRNRCV JRNRCV( appdta/rcvb0001 )
          ASP( 3 )
          TEXT( 'Secondary receiver' )
```

After you've created the journal receivers, you create the journal. If you use a single journal receiver, you use a command such as the following:

```
CRTJRN JRN( appdta/appjrn )
       JRNRCV( appdta/rcva0001 )
       TEXT( 'Production File Journal: single receiver' )
```

If you use dual receivers:

```
CRTJRN JRN( appdta/appjrn )
       JRNRCV( appdta/rcva0001 appdta/rcvb0001 )
       TEXT( 'Production File Journal: dual receivers' )
```

When you create the journal, the first receiver or pair of dual receivers is attached to the journal and ready for use.

With the journal receivers and journals created, you can begin journaling physical files by using one or more STRJRNPF (Start Journal Physical File) commands. Each STRJRNPF command includes 1 to 50 physical files and specifies for them the type of images to keep.

To keep only after images, you use a command such as the following:

```
STRJRNPF FILE( appdta/customer )
         JRN( appdta/appjrn )
         IMAGES( *after )
```

To keep both before and after images for several files:

```
STRJRNPF FILE( appdta/sale appdta/saleitem appdta/part )
         JRN( appdta/appjrn )
         IMAGES( *both )
```

You can keep only after images for some of the files using a journal and keep both before and after images for other files using the same journal. For example, both preceding STRJRNPF commands could be used with the APPJRN journal.

During recovery, journal entries can be applied only to a version of the physical file that was being journaled. Thus, to provide recovery capability for a physical file, you must save a file immediately after you begin journaling it. In addition, you must save a physical file immediately after adding a member to it so the new member also can be recovered. (You can use any of the save commands discussed in Chapter 19.) Recovery of logical files over the physical file is faster if you save their access paths at the same time you save the physical file; however, saving logical file access paths is not required for recovery.

After you begin journaling a physical file, the journal records any changes made to the data in the file's members. The file itself has the name of the journal stored in its description. You can find out which journal, if any, a physical file is using with the DSPFD (Display File Description) command.

Finally, you need to establish the frequency for saving the physical files, journal, and journal receivers. Many approaches to making periodic saves offer you adequate recovery capability. One commonly used guideline is to follow procedures that produce one disk copy for recovering up-to-the-minute, one disk and one tape copy for recovering to the beginning of the current day, one disk and two tape copies for recovering to the beginning of the previous day, and three tape copies for recovering to the beginning of two days previous. If you follow this guideline, you have redundant coverage with more copies available for older versions of the data. Maintaining online copies makes recovery more convenient, while additional tape copies provide coverage in case of disk damage.

The following procedures provide this graduated level of backup:

- At the end of each workday, before the daily save of the journal and journal receivers, detach the current receiver and attach a new receiver. (Instead of changing receivers at the end of the day, you may choose to do it before the beginning of the next workday. You also would want to do the daily save then.) With generic receiver names, you can do this with a single CHGJRN (Change Journal) command. For journals with a single receiver, you use a command such as the following:

```
CHGJRN JRN( appdta/appjrn )
       JRNRCV( *gen )
```

For journals with dual receivers:

```
CHGJRN JRN( appdta/appjrn )
       JRNRCV( *gen *gen )
```

If you use dual receivers, be sure to include two *GEN values for the JRNRCV parameter, as shown in the command above. If you use only one *GEN, the command succeeds, but the journal is switched to using a single receiver.

- At the end of each workday, after you've changed receivers, save the journal and the journal receivers for the current day and the past two days. Do not omit the daily save on the last day of the workweek, even though you also do a weekly save on that day. This last day's save tape is a necessary element in the redundant backup coverage. Do not free storage with the save command.

  To save the journals and journal receivers, you can use any of the save commands discussed in Chapter 19; a SAVCHGOBJ (Save Changed Object) command such as the following does not require that you identify the journal receiver names (*mm/dd/yy*, is the current date minus two work days.):

```
SAVCHGOBJ OBJ( *all )
          LIB( appdta )
          OBJTYPE( *jrn *jrnrcv )
          REFDATE( mm/dd/yy )
```

  Instead, this command saves the journal that was changed by the CHGJRN command and the journal receivers used during the current and previous two days. Cycle 10 to 14 sets of tapes (two times the number of workdays in a week).

- At the end of the workweek, after the last workday's daily save, save all files, journals, and journal receivers (as well as other objects you may want to save weekly). Do not free storage. Again, you can use any of the save commands discussed in Chapter 19. Cycle three or more sets of tapes.

- After the weekly save, save a second copy of all journals and journal receivers. Free the storage of the journal receivers. Use a SAVOBJ (Save Object) command similar to the following one. Cycle two or more sets of tapes.

```
SAVOBJ OBJ( *all )
       LIB( appdta )
       OBJTYPE( *jrn *jrnrcv )
       STG( *free )
```

Although you specify that storage is freed, the save does not free storage for the journal or for any attached receiver, which is precisely what you want because the journal and the attached receiver remain usable while the disk space used by detached journal receivers is made available.

- After making this second copy, delete detached, saved journal receivers more than two weeks old. You can determine which journal receivers these are by using the WRKJRNA (Work with Journal Attributes) command to display the journal receiver directory. Let the date on which each journal receiver was attached guide you in selecting the journal receivers to delete. Use DLTJRNRCV (Delete Journal Receiver) commands similar to the following:

```
DLTJRNRCV JRNRCV( appdta/rcva0015 )
```

If you used dual receivers, you must delete both sets; for example, you would use

```
DLTJRNRCV JRNRCV( appdta/rcvb0015 )
```

in addition to the previous DLTJRNRCV command. You can use a generic form of the receiver name in the DLTJRNRCV command; for example,

```
DLTJRNRCV JRNRCV( rcva001* )
```

deletes all journal receivers with names that begin with RCVA001. You should exercise care when you use a generic receiver name to ensure that you do not inadvertently delete the wrong receivers.

You won't reduce your coverage if you delete all detached, saved journal receivers at this time, rather than just the ones that are more than two weeks old. However, when you delete a receiver, it's removed from the journal's receiver directory. By leaving receivers on the system for up to three weeks, you can take advantage of journal management's use of the receiver directory to control recovery. Little extra disk space is used because the storage is freed for the detached, saved receivers.

Many variations on this approach are workable. The key aspects are that the procedures should be clearly documented and carefully followed; the entire file should be saved periodically (weekly, biweekly, or monthly); the journal and journal receivers should be saved daily; the journal receivers should be changed daily; and saves should be done in a way to produce multiple copies for recovery.

If your disk constraints are severe, a similar level of backup can be obtained by making multiple copies of the journal and journal receivers daily. After these daily saves, delete detached, saved journal receivers to free disk space.

Handling Critical Recovery Requirements

When you complete all the preceding steps, you'll have the additional recovery protection of journal management. All the journal entries except those for the current workday will be on tape. Thus, if a disk malfunction damages both the file and the journal receiver, you can use an offline copy to restore the file and any damaged receivers before using journal management recovery. If the currently attached receiver is damaged, though, journal management cannot recover beyond the last saved journal receiver's entries. Transactions entered during the current workday would be lost. Installations that cannot afford to lose part of a day's transactions must take additional measures to protect against this type of damage.

One alternative is to detach and save the current receiver more frequently than once a day. Because the CHGJRN command can be executed while journaled files are being updated, changing journal receivers has no impact, other than performance, on application systems that update the files. As soon as a receiver is detached, it should be saved. Appropriate procedures for freeing storage of detached, saved receivers or for deleting them should be followed. This strategy covers most critical recovery situations. Also consider other AS/400 data protection and recovery facilities, such as auxiliary storage pools, mirrored disk, and device parity protection, as discussed in Chapter 19.

Journaling Considerations

One of the main reasons separate objects (journals and journal receivers) are used in journal management is to facilitate disk-space management. As journal entries are put into a journal receiver, the receiver consumes increasing amounts of disk space. At some point, you need to make a tape copy of the accumulated journal entries and free the disk space for new ones. Journal management provides this capability by using a chain of journal receivers. A journal receiver into which a journal is currently putting entries is considered an attached receiver. Using the CHGJRN command, you can change the receiver the journal is using. The current receiver is detached, and the journal no longer uses it to store journal entries. A new receiver is attached in its place. Journal management synchronizes this change so no journal entries are lost even if you change receivers while journaled files are being updated. A sequence of journal entries spans the two receivers without interruption.

Once a receiver is detached, it can be saved with its storage freed, thus releasing the disk space it was using. The journal maintains a journal receiver directory that includes all receivers a journal used and that still exist on the system, even if their storage has been freed. This directory includes information about when journal receivers were saved. Journal management uses this directory during recovery operations to restore journal receivers containing the journal entries necessary for the recovery. Because journal management tracks the order in which the journal receivers were used (i.e., the names of previous and next receivers) you can perform recovery operations based on date/time periods or events (file opens and closes); journal management finds the necessary journal entries in the chain of journal receivers, which greatly simplifies recovery.

Journal management also provides several commands to obtain information about a journal. The DSPJRN (Display Journal) command is used to display the journal entries in online journal receivers used by the journal. The receivers can be either attached or detached, as long as they exist on the system and their storage has not been freed. If you want to find out which files are covered by a journal or which receivers have been used by a journal, use the WRKJRNA command. To see how many entries are in a journal receiver, what the previous and next receivers are in the current receiver chain, or other related information, use the DSPJRNRCVA (Display Journal Receiver Attributes) command. These and other journal management commands are included on the Journal Commands and Journal Receiver Commands menus, which you can get to with the commands GO CMDJRN and GO CMDJRNRCV, respectively.

Using Journal Management for Recovery

Hopefully, after you've taken the time to set up journaling, you'll never need to use it for recovery. If you're not that fortunate, however, journal management provides a menu-driven recovery facility.

To use this facility, you execute a WRKJRN command and specify the journal (or journals) you want to work with. On the Work with Journals display you select option 2 for the journal to show the Work with Forward Recovery display. The options on the Work with Forward Recovery display step you through any RSTOBJ (Restore Object) and APYJRNCHG (Apply Journaled Changes) commands necessary to recover the desired file members. Using the menu-driven facility is simpler than entering individual commands, especially because you probably will not have to enter them often. The menu-driven recovery also makes certain that important recovery functions, such as recovering all damaged physical file members used by a logical file, are done. If you follow the guidelines laid out in this chapter for setting up journaling, most recoveries should be straightforward using just the WRKJRN command.

Recovery of an individual file normally involves restoring the most recently saved version of the file and then using the APYJRNCHG command to bring it up to the most recent change. If you choose to use individual commands (rather than the menu-driven facility) to do this, you first must use one of the restore commands discussed in Chapter 19 to restore the file. Then you use a command similar to the following:

```
APYJRNCHG JRN( appdta/appjrn )
          FILE( appdta/customer *all)
```

This example uses default values for most APYJRNCHG command parameters. Among the parameters for which default values are used, the RCVRNG(*LASTSAVE) default specifies that the system should determine which journal receivers to use by using system-stored information about when the file was saved. The FROMENT(*LASTSAVE) default specifies that the first journal entry to be applied to the file is the first one after the file was last saved. The TOENT(*LASTRST) default specifies that the last journal entry to be applied is the last one occurring before the date and time the file was last restored. These defaults result in the file being fully recovered.

If you want to recover the file up to a specific file update, you can use an explicit journal entry sequence number for the TOENT (To Entry) parameter rather than taking the default. The journal entry sequence numbers are displayed by the DSPJRN command. If you want to recover the file up to some particular time, you can specify the date and time in the TOTIME parameter rather than using a TOENT parameter. In addition to these options, the APYJRNCHG command provides other alternatives for specifying the first and last journal entries to be applied.

If the journal or a journal receiver is damaged or if the last saved version of the file is unusable, other steps (such as restoring the journal or receivers) are necessary. Most of these are incorporated in the menu-driven recovery facility mentioned earlier.

Journal management used with save/restore functions can significantly increase your recovery capabilities with a minimum of programmer effort. Journal management also reduces the time you must dedicate to saving physical files. The key to successful use of journal management is careful planning of the journals and receivers that you use and developing written procedures for saving files, journals, and journal receivers. With these in place, your data will have up-to-the-minute protection.

Commitment Control

Two situations present special problems in database applications: transactions that update multiple records and concurrent updating of database files by multiple jobs. Without an appropriate implementation, you can end up with invalid or lost updates. In the previous sections we looked at three facilities to help with these problems: object and record locking help avoid conflicting database access, and journaling helps avoid lost updates. **Commitment control** is another important tool to protect the integrity of your database and help you recover from abnormal system termination.[28]

To begin our look at commitment control, let's consider a common application task that requires commitment control. Figure 17.18 shows a typical funds transfer **transaction**. Normally, the total funds for one person's checking and saving accounts is the same before and after the transfer of funds from one account to the other. But if there's a power or other failure

---

[28]Although this section focuses on how commitment control is used with database access, OS/400 has built-in commitment control support for some other types of objects as well as provisions for user-defined rollbacks for object types not included in the built-in support. The *Backup and Recovery — Advanced* manual describes these additional commitment control facilities.

between time *t5* and time *t6*, the total will be invalid. In this example, the transferred amount gets posted to the SAVACT file, but not taken out of the CHKOUT file if the system fails before the CHKACT record is rewritten. Reordering the updates won't solve the problem because you can still have a failure between the two required updates.

Figure 17.18
Typical Funds
Transfer Transaction

Time	Action	CHKACT File	SAVACT File
t0	"Transfer 500 from checking to savings"	500.01	0
t1	Read SAVACT file for update	500.01	0
t2	Read CHKACT file for update	500.01	0
t3	Add 500 to SAVACT amount	500.01	0
t4	Subtract 500 from CHKACT amount	500.01	0
t5	Update SAVACT file	500.01	500.00
t6	Update CHKACT file	.01	500.00

Transaction Rollback

What's needed to prevent this error is a facility that guarantees all-or-none execution of a multiple-record update transaction. Another way to phrase this is that the system must consider a multiple-record transaction as an atomic (i.e., indivisible) **unit of work**. Commitment control provides just such a mechanism. Figure 17.19 shows what happens when commitment control is used and a transaction is interrupted.

Figure 17.19
Interrupted Transaction
with Commitment Control

Time	Action	CHKACT File	SAVACT File
t0	Commitment boundary established	500.01	0
t1	"Transfer 500 from checking to savings"	500.01	0
t2	Read SAVACT file for update	500.01	0
t3	Read CHKACT file for update	500.01	0
t4	Add 500 to SAVACT amount	500.01	0
t5	Subtract 500 from CHKACT amount	500.01	0
t6	Update SAVACT file	500.01	500.00
t7	"Pull power plug"	500.01	500.00
t8	IPL — automatic system rollback of uncommitted transactions	500.01	0

The AS/400 automatically rolls back (i.e., backs out) any file updates that were performed as part of an uncommitted (i.e., incomplete) transaction. If an abnormal system termination occurs, the rollback is performed at the next IPL and is completed before the affected records can be accessed. If an abnormal routing step termination (such as an immediate job cancellation) occurs, the AS/400 performs the rollback during routing-step termination processing.

Conflicts with Concurrent Updates

Figure 17.20 illustrates the other type of problem that commitment control can help with. In this example, two jobs concurrently access the PARTINV file, which has parts inventory by warehouse and part number. Job A updates the quantity on hand for a part in two warehouses and Job B sums the total quantity on hand for the part, using an HLL program. The file ends up at time *t10* with two as the quantity on hand for part XYZ at each warehouse. But the HLL program reports a total of five because the HLL program adds the quantity on hand for warehouse 678 after it's been updated but adds the quantity on hand for warehouse 123 before it's been updated.

Figure 17.20

Invalid Totaling Caused by
Concurrent Updating

Time	Job A	Job B	PARTINV file Whse 123	Whse 678
t0	"Transfer 1 part XYZ from Whse 123 to Whse 678"		3	1
t1	Read Whse 678, Part XYZ record for update		3	1
t2	Read Whse 123, Part XYZ record for update		3	1
t3	Add 1 to Whse 678, Part XYZ amount		3	1
t4	Subtract 1 from Whse 123, Part XYZ amount		3	1
t5	Update Whse 678, Part XYZ record	"Total part XYZ"	3	2
t6		Read Whse 678, Part XYZ record for input	3	2
t7		Add 2 to total (2)	3	2
t8		Read Whse 123, Part XYZ record for input	3	2

Figure 17.20 continued

Figure 17.20
Continued

Time	Job A	Job B	PARTINV file Whse 123	Whse 678
t9	Update Whse 123, Part XYZ record	Add 3 to total (5)	2	2
t10		Print total: 5	2	2

Even if the two jobs access the PARTINV file under commitment control, the default low **lock level** (*CHG) of commitment control lets this error slip by because the record locks obtained by Job A at time *t1* and *t2* do not normally prevent a read-for-input such as the ones by Job B at time *t6* and time *t8*. You can use the commitment control high lock level (*ALL), however, to prevent the incorrect total. Figure 17.21 shows the Figure 17.20 operations with Job A using the low lock level (*CHG) of commitment control and Job B using the high lock level (*ALL) of commitment control. Under the *ALL level of commitment control, Job B acquires a record lock even

Figure 17.21
Correct Totaling with
Commitment Control
Level *ALL

Job A Time	Job B Lock level *CHG	Lock level *ALL	PARTINV file Whse 123	Whse 678
t0	Commitment boundary established		3	1
t1	"Transfer 1 part XYZ from Whse 123 to Whse 678"		3	1
t2	Read Whse 678, Part XYZ record Part XYZ record for update (obtain record lock)		3	1
t3	Read Whse 123, Part XYZ record for update (obtain record lock)		3	1
t4	Add 1 to Whse 678, Part XYZ amount		3	1
t5	Subtract 1 from Whse 123, Part XYZ amount	Commitment boundary established	3	1
t6	Update Whse 678, Part XYZ record	"Total part XYZ"	3	2

Figure 17.21 continued

Figure 17.21
Continued

Job A Time	Job B Lock level *CHG	Lock level *ALL	PARTINV file Whse 123	Whse 678
t7		Read Whse 678, Part XYZ record for input (begin wait for record lock)	3	2
t8		Wait for record lock	3	2
t9	Update Whse 123, Part XYZ record	Wait for record lock	2	2
t10	Commit transaction (release record locks)	Wait for record lock		
t11		Read completes (obtain record lock)	2	2
t12		Add 2 to total (2)	2	2
t13		Read Whse 123, Part XYZ record for input (obtain record lock)	2	2
t14		Add 2 to total (4)	2	2
t15		Commit transaction (release record locks)	2	2
t16		Print total: 4	2	2

when it reads a record for input. Thus, Job B begins waiting for the record lock at time *t7* and completes the read only after Job A has completed its transaction and released its record locks (after time *t10*).

With commitment control, your programs can handle both failed transactions and potential conflicts caused by other jobs if you follow these six steps:

1. Identify which files to place under commitment control.
2. Specify in your CL and HLL programs those files that are opened under commitment control.
3. Add commit and rollback statements to your application programs to define **commitment boundaries** for both successful and unsuccessful transactions.
4. Journal physical files that are accessed under commitment control.
5. Start a commitment control environment for a job or activation group before opening any files under commitment control.
6. End the commitment control environment when it's no longer needed for a job or activation group.

Identifying Which Files to Place Under Commitment Control

Identifying which physical and non-join logical files to access under commitment control requires looking at each application program's use of database files. If a file is updated in a multiple-record transaction, it should be opened under commitment control. This guarantees that no partial update is left in the database because of an abnormal termination and assures that recovery can begin with the first transaction that was not completed.[29]

A file should also be opened under commitment control when you do not want to allow records from the file to be read if the records are involved in an incomplete transaction in a different job (as in the totaling program in Figures 17.20 and 17.21).[30] Finally, a file must be opened under commitment control if it's opened as a shared file and another shared open places the file under commitment control.

It's possible in a single program to have some files that are opened under commitment control and other files that are not. Such a mixture of files opened for update is inadvisable, however, because if a file is not placed under commitment control when it's opened for update, the commitment control environment does not encompass updates to the file (i.e., updates are permanent; they cannot be rolled back). Similarly, record locks for files not opened under commitment control are not held for the duration of a transaction; they are released by the next read-for-update or update operation to the file. Commitment control doesn't affect input-only files unless the intermediate (*CS) or high (*ALL) lock level is in effect; so in many cases, input-only files can be left outside the commitment control environment, except when they're opened as a shared file and the other open is for update under commitment control.

Specifying Files Under Commitment Control in HLL and CL Programs

The second step in using commitment control is to specify in HLL and CL programs those files that will be opened under commitment control. A key point to remember is that in RPG/400 and COBOL/400 programs, you must

---

[29] As an alternative for standalone batch jobs that use small files, you might get better performance than with commitment control by creating a backup copy of all files updated with multiple-record transactions and by allocating the file members exclusive-allow-read (*EXCLRD), using the ALCOBJ command, before executing the program. Recovery is then possible by re-creating the files from the backup copy and restarting the program with the first transaction.

[30] Another way to prevent a job from reading records from a partially completed transaction is to allocate the file member exclusive-read (*EXCLRD) or share-no-update (*SHRNUP). Either of these object locks will prevent other jobs from updating the files; thus, no transactions can occur in other jobs. Allocating a file member to prevent updates is feasible only when there is no requirement for multiple jobs updating the member concurrently.

decide how the file will be opened before you compile the program; an execution-time option to open a file under commitment control is available only in CL, RPG IV, and C/400. To specify that a file will be opened under commitment control in RPG IV, you code a COMMIT keyword in positions 44-80 of the F-spec:

```
... 1 ...+... 2 ...+... 3 ...+... 4 ...+... 5 ...+... 6
FCustomer  UF A E            K Disk    Commit
```

Optionally, you can specify a 1-byte character variable as an argument to the Commit keyword and set this variable to "0" (no commitment control) or "1" (commitment control) before you open the file, as in Figure 17.22.

Figure 17.22
Conditional Commitment
Control in RPG IV

```
... 1 ...+... 2 ...+... 3 ...+... 4 ...+... 5 ...+... 6 ...+... 7 ...
FCustomer  UF A E            K Disk    Commit( CsCommit )
          .
          .
          .
C                       Eval      CsCommit = '1'
          .
          .
          .
C                       Open      Customer                              99
          .
          .
C                       Update    CustomerR                            99
          .
          .
C                       If        CsCommit = '1'
C                         If      TransOK
C                           Commit
C                         Else
C                           Rolbk
C                         EndIf
C                       EndIf
```

If you use conditional commitment control when you open files in an RPG IV program, you must execute the Commit and Rolbk operations (discussed later) only if a commitment environment has been started.

In COBOL/400 you must include the internal file name in the Commitment Control clause of an I-O-Control paragraph entry, as in Figure 17.23.

In CL, you must specify COMMIT(*YES) on the OPNDBF (Open Data Base File) command, as follows:

```
OPNDBF FILE( customer )
       OPTION( *all )
       COMMIT( *yes )
```

Figure 17.23
Specifying Commitment
Control in COBOL/400

```
Environment division.
Input-Output section.
File-Control.

    Select      CustomerFile
      Assign      Database-Customer
      Organization Indexed
      Access      Random
      Record Key  Externally-Described-Key
      File Status CustomerSts.

I-O-Control.
    Commitment Control for CustomerFile.
```

Adding Commit and Rollback Statements to Application Programs

The third step is to place commit and rollback statements in your programs to define commitment boundaries. Before examining the statements' syntax, let's look briefly at the concept of a transaction and a commitment boundary. Figure 17.24 shows a sequence of events in a job using commitment control.

Before time $t1$, the job doesn't use commitment control. At $t1$ the job establishes a commitment control environment, but no transaction has begun. When the first database file is opened under commitment control ($t2$), the beginning commitment boundary of the first transaction is established. This first transaction includes all activity on files opened under commitment control ($t3$) that occurs before the next commitment boundary. Any database file updates are temporary until the next commitment boundary is reached. A new commitment boundary is established when either a commit ($t4$) or rollback ($t6$, $t8$) operation occurs. The rollback may be explicit ($t6$), or it may occur because the commitment control environment ends ($t8$) or because the routing step abnormally terminates.

When a commit or rollback operation establishes a new commitment boundary, the current transaction ends and a new transaction begins. Execution of the commit operation causes all database file updates executed during the transaction to be made permanent, whereas a rollback — whatever its cause — removes all database file updates performed since the previous commitment boundary. In addition, a rollback resets all file pointers (i.e., the current record pointer for sequential access) to their values at the last successful commitment boundary. Both the commit and rollback operations cause all record locks within the scope of the commitment control environment to be released.

The commit statements should be placed in your programs before you worry about rollbacks. Place commit statements at those points in your program logic where a transaction is successfully completed (e.g., in the funds transfer example in Figure 17.19, after both the checking and savings account files have been updated). There may be more than one place where you should place a commit statement, and there is no significant disadvantage to

Figure 17.24
Transaction and
Commitment Boundaries

Time	Action
t0	— —
t1	Begin commitment control (BGNCMTCTL)
	— —
	— —

— — — — — — — — — — — — — — *Commitment boundary* — —

t2	Open first file under commitment control
	— —
	— —
t3	Other opens, closes, reads, updates
	— —
	— —
t4	Commit

Transaction 1

— — — — — — — — — — — — — — *Commitment boundary* — —

	— —
	— —
t5	Other opens, closes, reads, updates
	— —
	— —
t6	Rollback

Transaction 2

— — — — — — — — — — — — — — *Commitment boundary* — —

	— —
	— —
t7	Other opens, closes, reads, updates
	— —
	— —
t8	End commitment control (ENDCMTCTL)
	(implicit rollback)

Transaction 3

— — — — — — — — — — — — — — *Commitment boundary* — —

having multiple commit statements in a program.[31] Also, there is no harm in executing a commit (or a rollback) when there are no uncommitted file updates; the only action that occurs is placement of a commit entry in the journal and establishment of a new commitment boundary. On the other hand, if you execute a commit (or rollback) in an RPG IV or CL program and a commitment control environment has not been established, an exception occurs. In COBOL/400, a commit (or rollback) statement is ignored if it's executed in a noncommitment control environment, and no error occurs.

Keep two points in mind when you add the commit statements. First, neither closing a file nor ending a program establishes a new commitment boundary. Thus, you must make certain that the last successfully completed transaction in an update program is followed by a commit operation. Second, a transaction encompasses all activity on files opened under commitment control within a job or activation group; if separate programs and separate ODPs are used to update files, the updates still are included in the same transaction. (You can have only one transaction in progress at a time for each commitment control environment.) Therefore, you must be sure that a commit statement is not executed too soon (i.e., before all files involved in the transaction have been updated) or too late (i.e., after file updates occur that are not involved in a completed transaction).

After adding the commit statements, you must add the rollback statements. Within an HLL program, you need to code a rollback statement only if the program logic determines that the transaction cannot be completed successfully. Occasions for using rollback include handling database file I/O errors and applications in which multiple records in the same file must be updated before the validity of the transaction can be determined.

A good practice to follow in CL shell programs that call HLL programs is to place a ROLLBACK command within a MONMSG (Monitor Message) command after the CL CALL command that invokes an HLL program. The sample code below shows a generic MONMSG command that traps RPG IV and ILE COBOL/400 program abnormal terminations:[32]

```
CALL     updcust
MONMSG   MSGID( rnq0000 rnx0000 lnr7000 cpf9999 ) EXEC( DO )
         ROLLBACK
         /* Other error handling goes here */
         ENDDO
```

The ROLLBACK command avoids leaving a partially completed transaction, which might accidentally be committed if a commit operation were subsequently executed later in the same job.

---

[31] However, it's often better to organize your code so that the commit/rollback decision occurs at a single point of control.

[32] RPG IV runtime messages begin with RNQ or RNX, ILE COBOL/400 runtime messages begin with LNR, and the CPF9999 message ID is a "safety net" to catch escape messages not covered by the other three generic message IDs.

In addition, if commitment control is ended or the routing step is terminated and partial uncommitted updates exist, an error condition occurs, and OS/400 sends the CPF8356 escape message. Executing a rollback after abnormal program termination helps prevent this error. The *Backup and Recovery — Advanced* manual and the HLL programmer's guides provide detailed examples of programs using the commit and rollback statements.

Journaling Physical Files

The fourth step in implementing commitment control is to journal the physical files that will be opened under commitment control or that are within the scope of a logical file that will be opened under commitment control. Although as of V3R1 it's not required, the simplest approach is to journal to the same journal all physical files accessed under commitment control in the same commitment control environment (i.e., after a STRCMTCTL command and before an ENDCMTCTL command or the end of the routing step). If you're considering multiple journals, check the *Backup and Recovery — Advanced* manual for several restrictions. Keep in mind that there are save/restore, as well as commitment control, considerations in setting up your journals, as discussed in the previous section.

To perform rollback operations, commitment control requires that both the before and the after record images be placed in the journal. You can still specify IMAGES(*AFTER) on the STRJRNPF command, however, because DB2/400 automatically switches to journaling both images while a file is open under commitment control. Besides journaling before and after record images, commitment control also places an entry in the journal for each commit and rollback operation.

Establishing a Commitment Control Environment in a Job or Activation Group

The fifth step is to establish, by executing the STRCMTCTL command, a commitment control environment in a job or activation group before you open database files under commitment control. The STRCMTCTL command's LCKLVL (Lock Level) parameter specifies the type of record locking that occurs when files under commitment control are accessed. The low lock level, specified by the *CHG parameter value, causes locks to be placed on records read for update and records that are updated, added, or deleted. The intermediate lock level, specified by *CS, causes locks to be placed on all records accessed, even those read for input; but records that are not updated or deleted are locked only until another record is read. The high lock level, specified by *ALL, causes locks to be placed on all records accessed and holds all locks until the next commitment boundary.[33]

---

[33] In SQL/400 applications, you can use one other lock level, *RR (repeatable read). This level provides the same record locking as *ALL and also places an exclusive (*EXCL) object lock on all tables referred to in Select, Update, Delete, and Insert statements until the end of the transaction.

By default, the STRCMTCTL command establishes a commitment control environment that encompasses all programs and files accessed in the same activation group (either the default activation group or a named activation group). You can specify CMTSCOPE(*JOB) to establish a commitment control environment that encompasses all programs and files accessed in the same job (and that aren't already covered by an activation group level commitment control environment). All programs in each activation group are associated with only one commitment control environment, either for that activation group or for the job. If you use named activation groups and commitment control, be sure you either use a job scope commitment control environment or properly start and end the appropriate activation-group-level commitment control environments, as needed.

The commitment control lock level applies only within the commitment control environment for the job or activation group executing the STRCMTCTL command; record locking in a different job or activation group's commitment control environment is determined by whether the job or activation group has established its own commitment control environment and, if it has, which lock level is in effect. Also keep in mind that the lock level doesn't affect files that are not opened under commitment control. One further consideration is that the lock level applies to all files under commitment control; you cannot lock input-only records in some files and not in others. To change the lock level, you must end commitment control and start it again with a different lock level.[34]

Ending the Commitment Control Environment in a Job or Activation Group

The final step in implementing commitment control is to end commitment control. Because commitment control protects you from partially completed transactions, it requires an orderly end to processing. First, you must complete the last transaction with a commit or rollback operation. Next, you must close all files that were opened under commitment control (this may be done automatically by ending an RPG IV program or COBOL/400 run unit). Finally, you must end the commitment control environment. The ENDCMTCTL command can be used explicitly or you can end commitment control by terminating the routing step (e.g., by ending the job).

If any uncommitted updates remain when you end commitment control, OS/400 sends an escape message and the updates are rolled back. Also, if you execute the ENDCMTCTL command when no commitment control environment exists, an escape message is sent.

Record Locking with Commitment Control

The preceding six steps put commitment control to work for you; but to use commitment control effectively, you must consider how record locking

---

[34] Recall from Chapter 15 that SQL/400 lets you set the lock level dynamically.

operates under commitment control. Otherwise, you may experience problems with conflicting record locks arising from concurrent access of the database by multiple jobs. Commitment control introduces additional locking rules beyond those discussed earlier in this chapter. Most importantly, while record locks for files not under commitment control are always held by individual ODPs, record locks under commitment control are held by ODPs when the records are first read for update and then transferred to the job or activation group's commitment control environment control block when the records are updated.

Though subtle, this difference is important. It means that without commitment control, when a record is locked by an ODP and a different ODP in the same job attempts to lock the same record before the first ODP's lock is released, the second lock is not granted and the read fails. To better understand this concept, consider two logical files, FILEX and FILEY, that are defined over the same physical file, FILEP, and that are both opened for update without commitment control in the same program. The following sequence of operations results in a failed read operation:

1. READ record 123 from FILEX — lock is obtained by ODP for FILEX
2. READ record 123 from FILEY — lock request by ODP for FILEY fails

Under the same conditions, an update operation between the two reads releases the first lock and lets the second read obtain the required lock:

1. READ record 123 from FILEX — lock is obtained by ODP for FILEX
2. UPDATE record 123 in FILEX — lock held by ODP for FILEX is released
3. READ record 123 from FILEY — lock is obtained by ODP for FILEY

With commitment control, the handling of locks is more complex. As a result, the outcome of I/O operations that involve record locks may be different. Within a transaction, when a record is read for update, its lock is held by the ODP. Until the lock is released or transferred to the commitment control environment control block, the same record cannot be read with a lock through a different ODP in the same job. Using FILEX and FILEY again, but with commitment control (any lock level), the following sequence of operations still results in a failed read operation because the lock for record 123 is not transferred to the commitment control environment control block before the second READ is attempted. In this case, the result is the same as without commitment control.

1. READ record 123 from FILEX — lock is obtained by ODP for FILEX
2. READ record 123 from FILEY — lock request by ODP for FILEY fails

Under lock level *CHG, if the first lock is released explicitly (e.g., by an RPG IV Unlock operation) or implicitly by a read to FILEX for a different record, the FILEY read succeeds. Under lock level *CS, the lock can be released by a subsequent read to FILEX (but the lock can't be explicitly released). As the following sequence demonstrates, locks are not retained by commitment control lock level *CHG or *CS unless an update (or add or delete occurs). The result of this sequence of operations is also the same as it would be without commitment control.

1. READ record 123 from FILEX — lock on 123 is obtained by ODP for FILEX

2. READ record 987 from FILEX — lock on 123 is released; lock on 987 is obtained by ODP for FILEX

3. READ record 123 from FILEY — lock on 123 is obtained by ODP for FILEY

Now let's look at a case where commitment control does make a difference. When a record is updated, its record lock is transferred from the ODP to the commitment control environment control block. As long as a record lock is held by the control block — but not by any ODP — the same record can be reread in the same commitment control environment:

1. READ record 123 from FILEX — lock on 123 is obtained by ODP for FILEX

2. UPDATE record 123 in FILEX — lock on 123 is transferred to job or activation group's commitment control environment control block

3. READ record 123 from FILEY — lock on 123 is held by job or activation group's commitment control environment control block but not by any ODP, so read succeeds; lock on 123 is obtained by ODP for FILEY

Unlike what happens without commitment control, a lock is still held on record 123 after step 2; but the lock is held by the commitment control environment control block, thus allowing the READ in step 3. Note that at the end of this sequence of operations, the ODP for FILEY holds a lock on record 123, and this lock prevents any other ODP in the same job (including the ODP for FILEX) from reading record 123 with a lock until the FILEY ODP lock is released or transferred.[35]

The commitment control handling of locks is necessary because locks on updated records are held until the next commit or rollback operation, rather than released when the update occurs, as happens without commitment control. To be able to re-access records that were previously updated in the same transaction (and therefore still locked), it must be possible to satisfy a second lock request within the same job or activation group.

Another important aspect of record locking under commitment control is the duration of the record locks. For each I/O operation, Figure 17.25 shows when a record is locked and when the lock is released. As the last three rows of the figure show, all lock levels of commitment control hold record locks on updated, added, and deleted records until the next commitment boundary. In a noncommitment control environment, the record lock is released after the update, add, or delete occurs. The first two rows illustrate the differences between the three lock levels.

Figure 17.25
Record Lock Duration

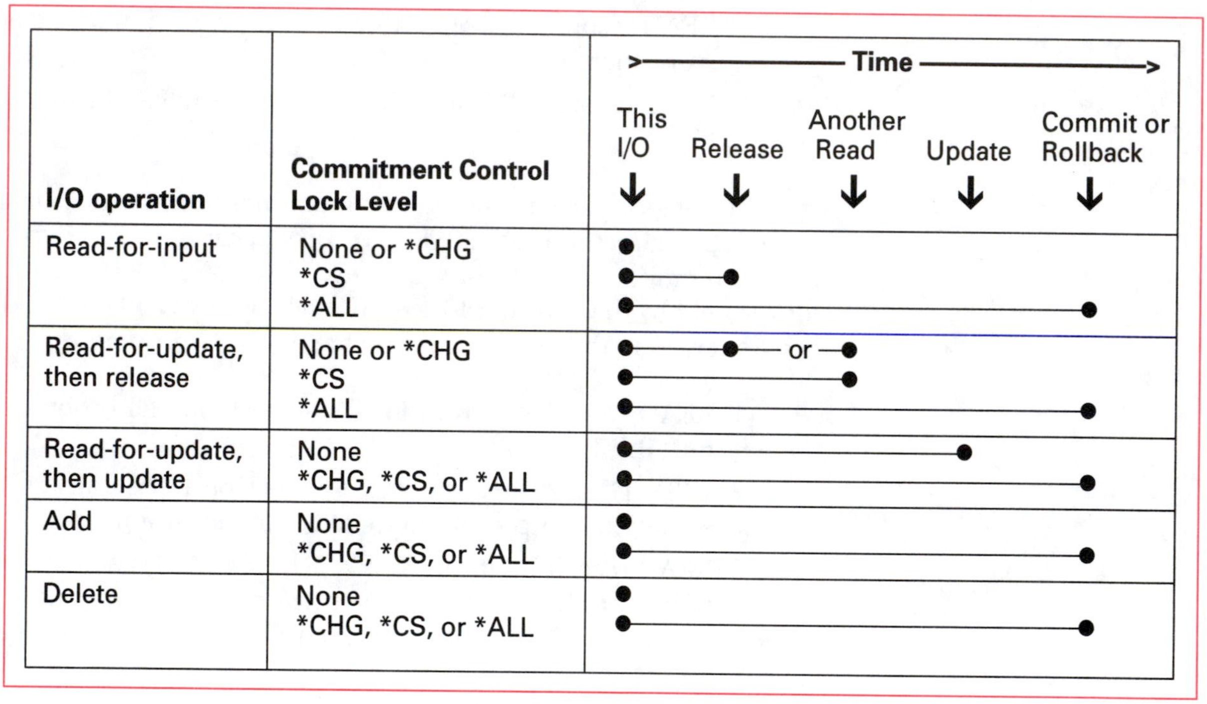

Records read for input are locked only when the intermediate or high lock level (*CS or *ALL) is used. The *ALL lock level — but not *CS — holds a record lock on input-only records until the next commitment boundary.

For the *CHG lock level, records read for update — but explicitly released without being updated[36] — are unlocked when the release occurs.

[35] The *CS and *ALL lock levels also cause *READ locks to be placed on records read for input. These locks don't interfere with attempts to read the same record for update within the scope of the same commitment control environment. The role of the ODP and commitment control environment control block in holding *READ locks depends on the lock level (*CS or *ALL) and whether record blocking is in effect when the file is read.

[36] For example, with the RPG IV Unlock operation.

With the *CS lock level, however, the lock is retained until the next read to the file (or the next commitment boundary). With the *ALL lock level, the lock is retained until the next commitment boundary. With no commitment control or the *CHG or *CS lock levels, the lock on a record that has been read for update can be released in an HLL program by performing, before any update of the record, another read-for-update via the same ODP.

Figure 17.26 shows the allowable access of a record by a second job (Job B) when a job (Job A) has already read the record but has not yet released or updated it. As you may have determined from the lock duration rules of Figure 17.25, the rules for a second job's access are the same for a non-commitment control environment and for the *CHG lock level of commitment control.[37] The *CS and *ALL lock levels, on the other hand, require a *READ type record lock to perform a read-for-input. Two jobs can hold *READ type record locks on the same record, but there can't be simultaneous *READ and *UPDATE locks on a record.

Figure 17.26

Allowable Record Access

Job A		Allowed type of read by Job B		
Commitment environment	Read record for	Non-Commitment environment	Lock level *CHG	Lock level *CS or *ALL
None	Input Update	Update Input	Update Input	Update None
Lock level *CHG	Input Update	Update Input	Update Input	Update None
Lock level *CS or *ALL	Input Update	Input Input	Input Input	Input None

Because the use of commitment control is likely to increase both the number and duration of record locks, you must design your applications, particularly interactive applications, to avoid holding record locks for long periods of time. The best design for concurrent interactive database updating avoids long-duration record locks by not locking records when they're first read. Instead, records are read without a lock, a copy of each record is made in program variables, and the records are displayed for update. If the workstation user changes the records, the update proceeds by re-retrieving the records *with* a lock, validating the records by comparing the re-retrieved records with their respective original copies, and, if the re-retrieved records

[37] For simplicity, the figures and discussion refer to two different jobs, each with a job scope commitment control environment. The same principles apply to any two commitment control environments, whether they have job scope or activation group scope.

are the same as the originals, performing the update operations. If any record was changed during the interval between the original retrieval and the re-retrieval, the update is rejected and the workstation user notified.

To extend this algorithm to a commitment control environment, you must declare a program variable for the record(s) from each file involved in a multiple-file transaction. If a transaction can involve more than one record from a single file, the program variable for that file's record copies must be an array. In addition, with multiple records from the same file, you cannot simply re-retrieve and validate all records from the file before beginning the update phase. Unless you're using the high lock level, a sequence of read-for-update operations to the same file releases the lock on the previously read record if it's not updated. The proper way to handle this condition is to re-retrieve, validate, and update each record in turn. If a record is re-retrieved that does not match its original copy, a rollback must be executed and the update rejected.

Other techniques, such as maintaining an "in use" flag in a field of a retrieved record, may offer a partial solution to the problem of record lock conflicts. But these methods do not work well in all environments, particularly with large numbers of interactive users. The read-copy-validate-update technique, on the other hand, always minimizes lock contention.

Handling record locks with a high lock level is a further challenge. The first thing to determine is when to use the high lock level. If you require a summary report on a file and want to be certain no record updates occur that will make the report inconsistent, consider using object allocation instead of a high lock level to prevent all updates while the report application runs. If object allocation cannot be used for a read-only (i.e., report) application, make certain that the locks on input records are held only while the input phase executes. Once that phase ends, execute a commit operation to release record locks, and then analyze and display or print the results. Keep in mind that a job can hold a maximum of 500,000 record locks during any one commitment cycle (i.e., between commitment boundaries). When you attempt an input-output operation that would exceed this limit, DB2/400 signals an exception, and the operation fails. The current transaction is not rolled back or committed, and all updates and record locks remain pending. You should monitor for this error and execute a rollback or commit operation to free the locks and restart or cancel the transaction. If you have transactions that approach the record-lock limit, use object allocation instead of record locking.

Although it takes some planning to set up properly, commitment control offers substantial benefits in improved database integrity and recovery. Most production-level AS/400 applications should be designed to run under commitment control.

Trigger Programs

A **trigger**, in general database terms, is a condition that causes some procedure to be executed. In DB2/400, a **trigger program** is a program that

DB2/400 calls when an application program attempts to insert, update, or delete a database record. You write and compile a trigger program just as you do any other HLL program, then use the ADDPFTRG (Add Physical File Trigger) command to associate the trigger program with a physical file.

DB2/40 supports six trigger conditions for a physical file:

- Before insert
- Before update
- Before delete
- After insert
- After update
- After delete

The ADDPFTRG command associates a trigger program with one or more of these conditions for a physical file. When a trigger condition is true (i.e., right before or after an insert, update, or delete event), DB2/400 automatically calls the trigger program you specify for the associated file and condition.

The advantage of trigger programs is that you can be sure the actions of the trigger program occur regardless of which application or system utility attempts to change the file. You can use trigger programs to block file updates that don't meet specified conditions, to propagate file updates to other files, or to log changes to specific fields. Thus, trigger programs provide an important tool to extend DB2/400 capabilities for enforcing database integrity and providing other database functions.

Implementing triggers is a two-step process: You code the trigger program and then associate it with one or more trigger conditions for a file. (The same trigger program can be used for multiple conditions or even for multiple files.) Because the second step is simpler, we cover that first.

Suppose you've written a trigger program named CUSTCHK to make additional integrity checks before allowing a record insert or update and you want to associate the trigger program with the CUSTOMER file. The following commands make the proper association:

```
ADDPFTRG FILE( appdta/customer )
         TRGTIME( *before )
         TRGEVENT( *insert )
         PGM( appexc/custchk )
         RPLTRG( *yes )
ADDPFTRG FILE( appdta/customer )
         TRGTIME( *before )
         TRGEVENT( *update )
         PGM( appexc/custchk )
         RPLTRG( *yes )
```

You can specify either *BEFORE or *AFTER for the TRGTIME parameter. A trigger program that's called before file changes occur can perform actions before DB2/400 checks other constraints, such as referential integrity constraints. Because a trigger program can itself perform file I/O, a before trigger program can take necessary actions to ensure that the constraints are satisfied. When you specify TRGTIME(*AFTER), DB2/400 calls the trigger program after the file is updated.[38]

The choices for the TRGEVENT parameter are *INSERT, *UPDATE, and *DELETE. You can specify any one of the six combinations of TRGTIME and TRGEVENT on an ADDPFTRG command. To associate the same program with multiple conditions, you use several ADDPFTRG commands, as in the example above.

The RPLTRG parameter determines whether the trigger program replaces an existing trigger program for the same file and condition. If you specify *NO for this parameter, the ADDPFTRG command fails if the specified condition already has an associated trigger program. Each of the six possible trigger conditions for a file can have only one trigger program.

An optional TRGUPDCND parameter lets you specify *CHANGE so that DB2/400 calls a trigger program for an update event only if the update is changing the contents of the record. Or you can specify *ALWAYS (the default) to have DB2/400 call a trigger program for an update event whether or not the record is changed.

Another optional parameter, ALWREPCHG (Allow Repeated Change), determines whether an after insert or after update trigger program can directly update (i.e., by file I/O) the record that the application program is inserting or updating. With ALWREPCHG(*NO), the default, the trigger program can't perform I/O to the same record; with ALWREPCHG(*YES), it can. In V3R2 and later releases, specifying ALWREPCHG(*YES) for a before insert or before update trigger program lets the program change the contents of the after image in the trigger buffer. DB2/400 then uses the modified after image for the actual insert or update operation on the associated physical file.

A trigger program must exist when you execute the ADDPFTRG command, as well as when DB2/400 attempts to call it for subsequent file operations.[39] However, after associating a trigger program with a physical file, you can delete and re-create the program without having to re-execute the ADDPFTRG command. You can use the RMVPFTRG command to remove a trigger program

---

[38] Recall from Chapter 16 that the *NOACTION option for a referential integrity (foreign key) constraint causes DB2/400 to check the constraint after any after event trigger program has been called. Later in this section we look at the details of how DB2/400 sequences database actions, including calling trigger programs and checking constraints.

[39] If you omit the library or specify *LIBL for the library on the TRGPGM parameter, the library list is searched for the program at the time the ADDPFTRG command is executed. The name of the library in which the program is found is stored in the physical file's description so that subsequent calls to the trigger program are explicitly qualified. If you move a trigger program from one library to another, you must execute the ADDPFTRG command to replace the trigger program with the program in the new library.

for one or more trigger conditions. The following example shows how to remove the before insert trigger program for the CUSTOMER file:

```
RMVPFTRG FILE( appdta/customer )
         TRGTIME( *before )
         TRGEVENT( *insert )
```

The RMVPFTRG command's TRGTIME and TRGEVENT parameters allow the same values as the parameters for the ADDPFTRG command, as well as *ALL for all times and/or events. Trigger programs can't be added or removed while the file is open.

Coding a Trigger Program

You can code a trigger program in RPG IV, COBOL/400, or other AS/400 HLLs. The only requirement for a trigger program is that it have two parameters that conform to the IBM-defined interface for DB2/400 trigger programs. These two parameters provide the trigger buffer and the trigger buffer length. When DB2/400 calls a trigger program, it fills the trigger buffer with the before and/or after image of the database record along with some control information. DB2/400 also places the length of this buffer in the trigger buffer length parameter. The trigger program can use these parameters to inspect and — for V3R2 and later releases, if ALWREPCHG(*YES) is specified for the trigger program — modify the record's contents.

Figure 17.27 shows the layout of the trigger buffer. The buffer starts with fixed-length fields that name and describe the physical file and the trigger condition (event and time). The buffer ends with four variable-length fields that contain the before and after images of the record and null field maps for the images. Each null field map is a series of one-character flags that indicate whether the corresponding field (in the before or after image) is null (1) or not null (0).

Because different files' record formats can have different numbers of fields and field sizes and thus, the before and after image fields in the trigger buffer can vary in length, the starting positions of the images and the null field maps can vary, as well.[40] The fixed part of the trigger buffer provides eight fields that contain the offsets and lengths of the four variable fields. An offset is the number of bytes from the start of the trigger buffer to the first byte of the field; you add one to an offset to get the beginning position of a subfield in an RPG IV data structure. Figure 17.28 shows the trigger buffer layout and the relationship of the offset and length fields that describe the variable part of the buffer.

---

[40] One implication is that when a physical file's record format changes, you must be sure to keep any trigger programs associated with the file up to date. In particular, the layout of the trigger buffer parameter must accurately reflect the physical file's record format. You can use RPG externally described data structures or COBOL/400 Copy-DDS-. . . compiler directives to help keep your trigger programs synchronized with your physical files. Later in the chapter, we look at a technique for soft coding the trigger buffer's before and after image layouts.

Figure 17.27
Trigger Buffer Layout

Field	Description	Codes	Type	Length	Starting Position
TbFile	File name		Char	10	1
TbLib	Library name		Char	10	11
TbMbr	Member name		Char	10	21
TbTrgEvt	Trigger event	1 — Insert 2 — Delete 3 — Update	Char	1	31
TbTrgTime	Trigger time	1 — After 2 — Before	Char	1	32
TbCmtLvl	Commit lock level	0 — *NONE 1 — *CHG 2 — *CS 3 — *ALL	Char	1	33
	Reserved		Char	3	34
TbCcsId	Coded character set ID		Binary	4	37
	Reserved		Char	8	41
TbBfrOfs	Before record image offset		Binary	4	49
TbBfrLen	Before record image length		Binary	4	53
TbBfrNulOf	Before null field map offset		Binary	4	57
TbBfrNulLn	Before null field map length		Binary	4	61
TbAftOfs	After record image offset		Binary	4	65
TbAftLen	After record image length		Binary	4	69
TbAftNulOf	After null field map offset		Binary	4	73
TbAftNulLn	After null field map length		Binary	4	77
	Reserved		Char	16	81
TbBfrRcd	Before record image (update and delete events)		Char	Varies (physical file record length)	Varies (TbBfrOfs)

Figure 17.27 continued

Figure 17.27
Continued

Field	Description	Codes	Type	Length	Starting Position
TbBfrNul	Before null field map (update and delete events)	0 — Not null 1 — Null	Char	Varies (equal to number of fields in record format)	Varies (TbBfrNulOf)
TbAftRcd	After record image (insert and update events)		Char	Varies (physical file record length)	Varies (TbAftOfs)
TbAftNul	After null field map (insert and update events)	0 — Not null 1 — Null	Char	Varies (equal to number of fields in record format)	Varies (TbAftNulOf)

Figure 17.28
Trigger Buffer Layout

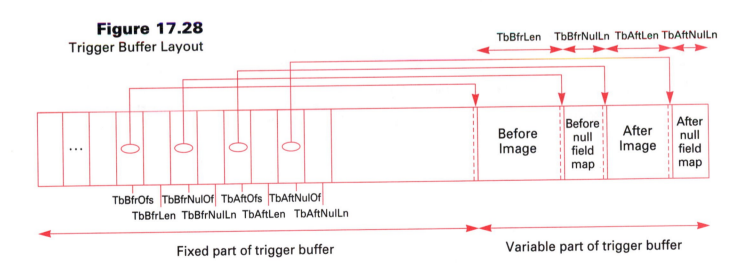

For a simplified CUSTOMER file, such as that shown in Figure 17.29, the starting positions and lengths are as follows:

Field	Starting Position	Length
Before image	97	38
Before null field map	135	3
After image	138	38
After null field map	176	3

Figure 17.29
CUSTOMER File DDS

```
....1....+....2....+....3....+....4....+....5....+....6....+....7....+
                                      UNIQUE

      R CUSTOMERR                     TEXT( 'Customers' )

        CUSTID          7P Ø          TEXT( 'Customer ID' )
        NAME            3ØA           TEXT( 'Customer name' )
        CRDLIMIT        7P Ø          TEXT( 'Customer credit limit' )

      K CUSTID
```

Using this information, we can code the definition of the trigger buffer parameter. Figure 17.30 shows a simple RPG IV trigger program (CUSTCHK) that prevents setting a customer's credit limit to a negative value.

Figure 17.30
CUSTCHK RPG IV
Trigger Program

```
....1....+....2....+....3....+....4....+....5....+....6....+....7..
* CUSTCHK --   Sample trigger program to check for non-negative
*              values in the CRDLIMIT field in the CUSTOMER file.

* Requirements: This trigger program must be associated only with
* before insert and before update conditions. If associated with
* other conditions (e.g., a delete event), errors may occur.

* Data structure for trigger buffer parameter, including:
*    The trigger buffer header fields (bytes 1-96)
*    Before image fields    (prefix Bf)
*    Before null field map (prefix Bn)
*    After  image fields    (prefix Af)
*    After  null field map (prefix An)

D TrgBuf          DS
D  TrgBufHdr                    96A
D  BfCustID                      7P Ø
D  BfName                       3ØA
D  BfCrdLimit                    7P Ø
D  BnCustID                      1A
D  BnName                        1A
D  BnCrdLimit                    1A
D  AfCustID                      7P Ø
D  AfName                       3ØA
D  AfCrdLimit                    7P Ø
D  AnCustID                      1A
D  AnName                        1A
D  AnCrdLimit                    1A
```

Figure 17.30 continued

Figure 17.30
Continued

```
....1....+....2....+....3....+....4....+....5....+....6....+....7..
 * Trigger buffer length parameter

D TrgBufLen       S               9B 0

 * Constant

D CrdLmtMsg       C                       Const( 'CRDLMTMSG' )


 * - - - - - - - - - - - - - - - - - - - - - - - - - - - - - -
 * Main block

C     *Entry      PList
C                 Parm                    TrgBuf
C                 Parm                    TrgBufLen

 * Check after image value; valid only for insert and update events.

C                 If         AfCrdLimit < 0
C                   ExSr     CrdLmtErr
C                 EndIf

C                 Return

 * - - - - - - - - - - - - - - - - - - - - - - - - - - - - - -
 * Credit limit error

C     CrdLmtErr   BegSr

 * Call program to send escape message to caller of this trigger program.

C                 Call       CrdLmtMsg                              99
C                   Parm                    AfCrdLimit

C                 EndSr
```

In this example, the only trigger buffer fields defined are the before and after image fields and null field maps. (The AfCrdLimit field is the only essential field; the others are coded to illustrate the trigger buffer layout.) This trigger program should be associated with the before insert and before update conditions. Figure 17.31 shows the comparable COBOL/400 program.

Figure 17.31
CUSTCHK COBOL/400
Trigger Program

```
...1....+....2....+....3....+....4....+....5....+....6....+....7..
 Id division.

    Program-Id.   CustChk.
    Author.       Paul Conte.
    Date-Written. 05/01/96.
*   Purpose:      Sample trigger program to check for non-negative
*                 values in the CRDLIMIT field in the CUSTOMER file.

*   Requirements: This trigger program must be associated only with
*   before insert and before update conditions. If associated with
*   other conditions (e.g., a delete event), errors may occur.

* - - - - - - - - - - - - - - - - - - - - - - - - - - - - - - - -
 Data division.

 Working-Storage section.

 01   Mnemonics.
      02 CrdLmtMsgPgm      Pic  X(10)  Value "CRDLMTMSG".

 Linkage section.

 01   TriggerBuffer.
      02 Header            Pic  X(96).
      02 BeforeImage.
         03 CustId         Pic S9(7) Packed-Decimal.
         03 Name           Pic  X(30).
         03 CrdLimit       Pic S9(7) Packed-Decimal.
      02 BeforeNullFieldMap.
         03 CustId         Pic 1.
         03 Name           Pic 1.
         03 CrdLimit       Pic 1.
      02 AfterImage.
         03 CustId         Pic S9(7) Packed-Decimal.
         03 Name           Pic  X(30).
         03 CrdLimit       Pic S9(7) Packed-Decimal.
      02 AfterNullFieldMap.
         03 CustId         Pic 1.
         03 Name           Pic 1.
         03 CrdLimit       Pic 1.

 01   TriggerBufferLength Pic S9(9) Binary.


* - - - - - - - - - - - - - - - - - - - - - - - - - - - - - - - -
```

Figure 17.31 continued

Figure 17.31
Continued

```
Procedure division Using TriggerBuffer
                        TriggerBufferLength.

MainBlock.

* Check after image value; valid only for insert and
* update events.

    If CrdLimit of AfterImage < 0
       Perform CrdLimitErr
    End-If.

    GoBack.
* - - - - - - - - - - - - - - - - - - - - - - - - - - - - - - - -
  CrdLimitErr.

* Call program to send escape message to caller of this
* trigger program.

    Call CrdLmtMsgPgm Using by Content
         CrdLimit of AfterImage.

  End program CustChk.
```

Both examples of the CUSTCHK trigger program test the after image's credit limit field and if it's less than zero, call the CRDLMTMSG CL program shown in Figure 17.32.[41] The CRDLMTMSG program sends an escape message to the program that called the CUSTCHK trigger program. DB2/400 handles this message and returns an error to the application program that attempted the I/O operation. In RPG IV and RPG/400, the error resulting indicator (positions 73-74) for the I/O operation is set on and the file status (positions 11-15 in the RPG IV file information data structure) is set to 1023 for before-event trigger programs and to 1024 for after-event trigger programs. In COBOL/400, the file status is set to 90. In SQL/400, the SqlCode is set to −443. DB2/400 also updates the I/O feedback area and sets the exception identifier to CPF502B. For RPG IV programs, CPF502B is placed in positions 46-52 of the file information data structure. Your application program should be designed to handle errors signaled by a trigger program just like other I/O errors, as described in Chapters 7 and 15.

---

[41] The CRDLMTMSG program is intentionally shown as a single-purpose program to simplify this example. For a production application, you should use a more general-purpose approach. You can either use a CL program with appropriate parameters or call the OS/400 system API program QMHSNDPM to send program messages.

Any messages sent by the trigger program normally appear in the job's message queue and can be received by the application program, using the RCVMSG command or QMHRCVPM system API. Sending messages from trigger programs involves a number of issues beyond the scope of this book. For details, see the IBM publication, *DB2/400 Advanced Database Functions*.

Figure 17.32
CRDLMTMSG CL Program

```
/* CRDLMTMSG -- Send escape message to caller of CUSTCHK trigger program*/

PGM PARM( &CrdLmt )

DCL &CrdLmt      *Dec  ( 7 0 )     /* Input parameter                 */
DCL &CrdLmtChr   *Char  8          /* Credit limit in character format */
DCL &MsgDta      *Char 256         /* Message data for escape message  */
DCL &Blank       *Char  1          VALUE( ' ' )   /* Mnemonic          */

/* Convert credit limit to character, leave room for minus sign.      */
/* If error occurs, just use blank for the value in the message.      */

CHGVAR     &CrdLmtChr  &CrdLmt
           MONMSG ( CPF9999 ) EXEC( DO )
                 CHGVAR &CrdLmtChr &Blank
           ENDDO

CHGVAR     &MsgDta ( 'Invalid credit limit value: ' *CAT &CrdLmtChr )

SNDPGMMSG MSGID( CPF9898 )                   +
          MSGF( qcpfmsg )                    +
          TOPGMQ( *prv ( custchk ) )         +
          MSGDTA( &MsgDta )                  +
          MSGTYPE( *escape )

          MONMSG MSGID( CPF0000 MCH0000 ) /* Ignore error            */

RETURN
ENDPGM
```

Soft Coding the Trigger Buffer[42]

The example above provides an introduction to how a trigger program works, but in production applications, you can benefit from a somewhat more advanced set of programming techniques. The basic idea in the example we look at next is that the trigger buffer is soft coded so that changes to the physical file's record can be incorporated by simply recompiling the trigger program. This example also shows how RPG IV /Copy source members let you reuse standard source code for parts of your trigger programs.[43]

The sample trigger program uses three /Copy source members. The DTATYPE member (Figure 17.33) declares a set of RPG IV variables of various data types. These are used as the basis for other declarations in the program.

[42]The technique shown in this section was originally suggested by Julian Monypenny and published in "Before Pulling the Trigger in RPG IV," *NEWS/400*, April 1996. The material here is derived from that article and is used with permission.

[43]Although space limitations prevent showing a COBOL/400 program that uses the same techniques, COBOL/400 has all the necessary language elements: the Copy compiler directive, pointers, and based variables. The implementation in COBOL/400 corresponds closely to the example shown here.

The TRGDCL member (Figure 17.34) declares an RPG IV data structure for the trigger buffer parameter along with several other variables used with this technique. The TRGENTRY member (Figure 17.35) declares the trigger program's parameter list and includes some initial setup code.

Figure 17.33
DTATYPE RPG IV /Copy
Source Member

```
....1....+....2....+....3....+....4....+....5....+....6....+....7..
 * DTATYPE -- Standard data type definitions
 *
 * Note that the Based keyword is just a technique to
 * avoid any storage being allocated for the variables
 * because they're never referenced during execution.

D NulTypePtr      S                     *

D TypeBin2        S              4B 0 Based( NulTypePtr )
D TypeBin4        S              9B 0 Based( NulTypePtr )
D TypeChr         S              1A   Based( NulTypePtr )
D TypeIdx         S              7P 0 Based( NulTypePtr )
D TypeLgl         S              1A   Based( NulTypePtr )
D TypeSysNam      S             10A   Based( NulTypePtr )
D TypePtr         S                 * Based( NulTypePtr )
D TypeQlfNam      S             20A   Based( NulTypePtr )
D TypeTxt         S             50A   Based( NulTypePtr )
```

Figure 17.34
TRGDCL RPG IV /Copy
Source Member

```
....1....+....2....+....3....+....4....+....5....+....6....+....7..
 * TRGDCL -- Trigger program standard declarations
 *
 * Requires copy modules: DtaType

D TbBufDs         DS
D  TbFile                               Like( TypeSysNam )
D  TbLib                                Like( TypeSysNam )
D  TbMbr                                Like( TypeSysNam )
D  TbTrgEvt                             Like( TypeChr )
D  TbTrgTime                            Like( TypeChr )
D  TbCmtLvl                             Like( TypeChr )
D  TbReserve1                    3A
D  TbCcsId                              Like( TypeBin4 )
D  TbReserve2                    8A
D  TbBfrOfs                             Like( TypeBin4 )
D  TbBfrLen                             Like( TypeBin4 )
D  TbBfrNulOf                           Like( TypeBin4 )
D  TbBfrNulLn                           Like( TypeBin4 )
D  TbAftOfs                             Like( TypeBin4 )
D  TbAftLen                             Like( TypeBin4 )
D  TbAftNulOf                           Like( TypeBin4 )
D  TbAftNulLn                           Like( TypeBin4 )
```

Figure 17.34 continued

Figure 17.34
Continued

```
....1....+....2....+....3....+....4....+....5....+....6....+....7..
D  TbBufChr                      1    32767A
D  TbBufAry                            1A        Overlay(    TbBufChr )
D                                                Dim( %Size( TbBufChr ) )
D* -- End of TbBufDs --

D  TbBufLen          S                           Like( TypeBin4 )

D  TbBfrPtr          S                           Like( TypePtr )
D  TbAftPtr          S                           Like( TypePtr )

D  TbBufSiz          C                           Const( %Size( TbBufChr ) )

D  TbEvtIns          C                           Const( '1' )
D  TbEvtDlt          C                           Const( '2' )
D  TbEvtUpd          C                           Const( '3' )
D  TbTimeBfr         C                           Const( '1' )
D  TbTimeAft         C                           Const( '2' )
```

Figure 17.35
TRGENTRY RPG IV /Copy
Source Member

```
....1....+....2....+....3....+....4....+....5....+....6....+....7..
* TRGENTRY -- Trigger program standard entry and setup code
*
* Requires copy module: TrgDcl
*
* Requires subroutine:  BufAryErr
*   Handles case where after TbBufAry (the array that overlays the trigger
*   buffer) is too small for the trigger buffer that's actually passed in.
*
* Side effects:
*   Sets TbBfrPtr   Pointer to before image in trigger buffer
*   Sets TbAftPtr   Pointer to after  image in trigger buffer

* - - - - - - - - - - - - - - - - - - - - - - - - - - - - - - - - -
C     *Entry        PList
C                   Parm                          TbBufDs
C                   Parm                          TbBufLen

C                   If          TbBufLen > TbBufSiz
C                     Exsr      BufAryErr
C                     Return
C                   Endif

C                   Eval        TbBfrPtr = %Addr( TbBufAry( TbBfrOfs + 1 ) )
C                   Eval        TbAftPtr = %Addr( TbBufAry( TbAftOfs + 1 ) )
```

The CUSTLOG trigger program (Figure 17.36) uses three /Copy
directives to incorporate the standard code into the program. CUSTLOG is
a simple program that checks to see whether the value of the customer
credit limit has been changed and, if it has, calls another program (not
shown) to write the change to a log file.

Figure 17.36
CUSTLOG RPG IV
Trigger Program

```
....1....+....2....+....3....+....4....+....5....+....6....+....7..
* CUSTLOG --    Sample trigger program to log changes to
*              CRDLIMIT field in the CUSTOMER file.

* Standard data types and trigger program declarations

/Copy DtaType
/Copy TrgDcl

* Data structures to provide templates for before and after images

D BfCustomer    E DS                    ExtName( Customer )
D                                       Prefix ( Bf )
D                                       Based( TbBfrPtr )

D AfCustomer    E DS                    ExtName( Customer )
D                                       Prefix ( Af )
D                                       Based( TbAftPtr )

 * Mnemonics and constants

D CrdLimit0     S                       Like( BfCrdLimit )
D                                       Inz( 0 )

D LogCrdChg     C                       Const( 'LOGCRDCHG' )


* - - - - - - - - - - - - - - - - - - - - - - - - - - - - - - -
* Entry point and setup code

/Copy TrgEntry

* Dispatch on event (insert, update, or delete).

C                    Select
C                       When    TbTrgEvt = TbEvtIns
C                         ExSr  InsRcdEvt

C                       When    TbTrgEvt = TbEvtUpd
C                         ExSr  UpdRcdEvt

C                       When    TbTrgEvt = TbEvtDlt
C                         ExSr  DltRcdEvt
C                    EndSl

C                    Return


* - - - - - - - - - - - - - - - - - - - - - - - - - - - - - - -
C    InsRcdEvt       BegSr

* Log first credit limit assigned to new customer.
* Use after image (new record) for customer ID and
* zero for "before" credit limit.
```

Figure 17.36 continued

Figure 17.36
Continued

```
....1....+....2....+....3....+....4....+....5....+....6....+....7..
C                       Call      LogCrdChg                              99
C                         Parm                    AfCustId
C                         Parm                    CrdLimit0
C                         Parm                    AfCrdLimit

C                       EndSr

* - - - - - - - - - - - - - - - - - - - - - - - - - - - - - - - - -
C     UpdRcdEvt         BegSr

* Log changed credit limit for customer.
* Use before image (old record) for customer ID.

C                       If        AfCrdLimit <> BfCrdLimit
C                         Call    LogCrdChg                              99
C                           Parm                  BfCustId
C                           Parm                  BfCrdLimit
C                           Parm                  AfCrdLimit
C                       EndIf

C                       EndSr

* - - - - - - - - - - - - - - - - - - - - - - - - - - - - - - - - -
C     DltRcdEvt         BegSr

* Log last credit limit assigned to customer being deleted.
* Use before image (old record) for customer ID and
* zero for "after" credit limit.

C                       Call      LogCrdChg                              99
C                         Parm                    BfCustId
C                         Parm                    BfCrdLimit
C                         Parm                    CrdLimit0

C                       EndSr

* - - - - - - - - - - - - - - - - - - - - - - - - - - - - - - - - -
* Trigger buffer array too small

C     BufAryErr         BegSr

C* --- Put code here to emit message, log error, etc. ---
C                       EndSr
```

The CUSTLOG trigger program declares two externally defined record structures (BfCustomer and AfCustomer) with the format of the CUSTOMER file. Notice that the Prefix keyword is used on the declarations to provide a unique two-character prefix for every field name (e.g., Bf for the before image fields and Af for the after image fields). The trigger program picks up the layouts for the trigger buffer's before and after images from these declarations. For any file's trigger program, you must code similar declarations that refer to the file with which the trigger program is associated.

Both declarations use the Based keyword, which specifies that a declaration is a template for storage that begins at the address contained in the pointer variable coded as the Based keyword argument. As a result, the compiler won't allocate storage for the BfCustomer data structure but instead treats whatever storage starts at the address in TbBfrPtr as if it were the data structure. Obviously, this requires the program to place an appropriate address in the TbBfrPtr variable before referencing any of the data structure's subfields. The same considerations apply to the AfCustomer data structure and the TbAftPtr variable. In a moment, we look at how these two pointer variables are set.

Following the data structure declarations, two /Copy directives incorporate the DTATYPE and TRGDCL source members. The declarations in the TRGDCL member (Figure 17.34) include the TbBufDs data structure, which has subfields for the fixed portions of the trigger buffer. This declaration corresponds to the layout described in Figure 17.27. The subfield declarations use RPG IV's Like keyword to specify each subfield's data type using one of the standard data types declared in the DTATYPE source member (Figure 17.33). The TbBufChr subfield is declared as a single-character field that's the maximum size allowed by RPG IV (32,767 bytes). The TbBufChr subfield provides a basis to redefine the trigger buffer as an array of bytes using another subfield, TbBufAry. Later we look at how this array is used to set the TbBfrPtr and TbAftPtr pointer variables upon which the BfCustomer and AfCustomer data structures are based.

The rest of the declarations in TRGDCL include the trigger buffer length parameter (TbBufLen), the two pointers discussed earlier, a constant initialized to the actual declared size for the trigger buffer (TbBufSiz), and constants for the codes DB2/400 uses for the trigger event and time fields in the trigger buffer.

Looking back at Figure 17.36, the next /Copy directive incorporates the code from the TRGENTRY source member (Figure 17.35). This code declares the program's entry point with the two parameters — TbBufDs and TbBufLen — required by DB2/400. An initial defensive check ensures that the trigger buffer passed in when DB2/400 calls the trigger program isn't larger than the declared size (to avoid array reference errors). Then the copied code sets the two pointers. The TbBfrPtr pointer variable is set to the address of the first byte in the before image part of the trigger buffer parameter. This is done by getting the address (using the %Addr built-in function) of the corresponding byte in the array that we declared to correspond to the trigger buffer. The array index for the before image's first byte is simply the offset (TbBfrOfs) supplied as one of the fixed fields in the trigger buffer plus one. A similar calculation is done to set the TbAftPtr pointer variable. After these two pointers are set, subsequent statements in the trigger program can refer to the subfields of the BfCustomer and AfCustomer data structures and the references will be to the appropriate fields in the trigger buffer.

The statements in the UpdRcdEvt subroutine of the CUSTLOG program illustrate this technique. If the after image credit limit isn't the same as the before image credit limit, the before image customer ID and the before and after image credit limit values are passed to the LOGCRDCHG program (not shown) to log the change.

With the techniques illustrated in this trigger program, when the physical file's record format changes, you need only recompile the trigger program to synchronize its declarations with the new record format. This approach substantially reduces maintenance effort and the possibility of errors when you change a physical file's definition.

Considerations for Using Trigger Programs

You should create trigger programs that perform their own I/O so they execute within the same ILE activation group and use the same commitment control environment as the application program.[44] With this approach, the application program executes all commit and rollback operations and any I/O that the trigger program performs is included in the transaction managed by the application program.

Keep in mind that any I/O performed by a trigger program may in turn cause another trigger program to be called. You should carefully design your trigger programs so they don't result in infinite recursive calls of the same trigger program. Also be sure to properly handle all errors that might occur when a trigger program performs its own I/O.

Another consideration with trigger programs is the timing of their calls when referential integrity constraints are also defined for the physical file. Figure 17.37 shows the sequence of events for insert, update, and delete operations.

Figure 17.37

How DB2/400 Sequences Trigger Programs and Referential Integrity Constraints

Insert

1. Calls *BEFORE trigger
2. Inserts record and performs checks (e.g., member full) other than referential integrity constraints
3. Calls *AFTER trigger
4. Checks referential integrity constraints for dependent file
5. Checks primary and unique key constraints

Update

1. Calls *BEFORE trigger
2. Updates record and performs checks (e.g., invalid data) other than referential integrity constraints

Figure 17.37 continued

[44] For ILE HLLs (RPG IV, ILE COBOL/400, and ILE/C), specify ACTGRP(*CALLER) when you create the program.

Figure 17.37
Continued

3. Checks all *RESTRICT referential integrity constraints for parent file
4. Calls *AFTER trigger
5. Checks all *NOACTION referential integrity constraints for parent file
6. Checks all referential integrity constraints for dependent file
7. Checks primary and unique key constraints

Delete
1. Calls *BEFORE trigger
2. Deletes record and performs checks other than referential integrity constraints
3. Checks all *RESTRICT referential integrity constraints for parent file
4. Calls *AFTER trigger
5. Performs all *CASCADE referential integrity constraints for parent file
6. Performs all *SETNULL and *SETDFT referential integrity constraints for parent file
7. Checks all *NOACTION referential integrity constraints for parent file

You should also be aware of the performance implications of trigger programs. Each call to a trigger program adds some overhead, of course. If you run trigger programs in the caller's activation group and don't deactivate them (e.g., you leave the RPG IV LR indicator off when you return from a trigger program), the call overhead isn't large compared to the time the system takes for a database I/O operation. The biggest impact comes because DB2/400 doesn't use record blocking when you access a file with a trigger. This restriction is enforced so that the trigger program is called for each file update, not just when the database attempts to write a block of records to the file. For batch jobs that sequentially access large numbers of records, unblocked access may be significantly slower than blocked access. You may want to consider locking a file and removing its trigger program(s) before executing a long-running batch job. After the batch job completes, the trigger program(s) can be added to the file again and the file unlocked. Of course, you must be very careful that any program that runs while trigger programs are not in effect performs all the integrity checks or other operations that the trigger program(s) normally carry out. Because this technique complicates your application design, you should consider using it only when performance is critical.

Distributed Database

DB2/400 provides several ways to access data that's located on a system other than the one on which an application program runs. The most important distributed database facilities are

- **Distributed Data Management (DDM)**
- **Distributed Relational Database Architecture (DRDA)**
- **Open Database Connectivity (ODBC)**

To use any of these facilities, you must first configure the appropriate communications between the systems involved in the distributed database access. AS/400 communications is beyond the scope of this book, so consult the appropriate IBM manuals for more information on that topic.

DDM

DDM lets you define a DB2/400 file on one AS/400 and access it from another AS/400 as if it were a local file.[45] There are four steps to using DDM:

- Create the database file on the target (remote) system.
- Create a DDM file on the source (local) system.
- Configure a communications link between the source and target systems.
- Open the DDM file from an application on the source system.

You can create the target system database file using DDS or SQL/400. This file is a normal DB2/400 physical or logical file and doesn't require any special coding.

To create a DDM file on the source system, you enter a command such as the following:

```
CRTDDMF FILE( appdta/salehq )
        RMTFILE( appdta/sale )
        RMTLOCNAME( hdqtr )
        TEXT( 'Headquarter''s SALE file' )
```

The CRTDDMF command creates a *FILE object on the source system and associates it with a database file on the target system. On the CRTDDMF command, you identify the target system by using the RMTLOCNAME parameter.[46] The remote location name is defined when you configure communications between systems.

When an application program on the source system opens the APPDTA/SALEHQ file, OS/400 connects via DDM to the APPDTA/SALE database file on the HDQTR remote system. The application program requires no special coding and can read and write to the SALEHQ file as if it were a local database file.

You can use the OVRDBF command to override a program's database file so it opens a DDM file. Override processing is the same as described earlier in this chapter, with one exception. If you specify an override with a MBR parameter, but not a TOFILE parameter, OS/400's data management routines

---

[45] DDM provides facilities other than those discussed in this section, including the ability to access files from or on systems other than an AS/400. See the *Distributed Data Management* manual for more information.

[46] In some cases, you may also need to use the CRTDDMF command's DEV, MODE, and RMTNETID parameters to fully specify the appropriate connection to the remote system.

first search the job's library list for a *database* file that contains the member. Only when no such database file is found does OS/400 look for a *DDM* file. Always specifying the TOFILE parameter guarantees that you open the correct file (database or DDM) and member. A DDM file can also be specified in the FILE parameter of an OPNQRYF command.

DDM supports commitment control transactions (units of work) that span file operations on remote systems. When the application updates files on just a single remote system, you need to ensure that the files are being journaled on the remote system before starting commitment control. For applications that update records in files on multiple systems (local or remote), you also need to specify PTCCNV(*YES) on the CRTDDMF command(s) to establish a protected conversation between the source and target systems. DB2/400 uses a two-phase commit protocol with protected conversations to ensure that a communications failure doesn't result in some file updates being committed on one system while others are rolled back on another system.

DRDA

DRDA is IBM's standard for interoperation among the DB2 family of DBMS, including DB2/400 and DB2 on the mainframes, OS/2, Windows NT, and AIX. In addition to IBM's relational DBMS, many other vendors' relational DBMS products also use DRDA.

To use DRDA from the AS/400, you must use SQL/400 because SQL is the common DRDA database access language. Part III describes SQL/400, and Chapter 15 covers several specific SQL statements (e.g., Connect) used with DRDA.

An essential step in using DRDA is to identify remote databases to the system on which the application program runs. On the AS/400, you do this with an ADDRDBDIRE (Add Relational Database Directory Entry) command that adds an entry in the local system's relational database directory. The following example adds an entry for the EUGBRNCH database:

```
ADDRDBDIRE RDB( eugbrnch )
           RMTLOCNAME( eugbrnch )
           TEXT( 'Eugene branch office' )
```

Entries in the relational database directory identify the communications link and other optional attributes of the remote database.[47]

Within an application program, executing a statement on a remote system is simply a matter of executing a successful Connect statement to connect to that system before executing the SQL statement, as shown in Chapter 15.

DRDA supports commitment control transactions that span operations on remote systems. There are two levels of this support available with DB2/400. DRDA-1 (remote unit of work support) lets a single transaction be

---

[47] In some cases, you may also need to use the ADDRDBDIRE command's DEV, MODE, and RMTNETID parameters to fully specify the appropriate connection to the remote system.

on any one system, local or remote. You specify RDBCNNMTH(*RUW) on the CRTSQLxxx command to have the application program establish this type of remote connection when an SQL Connect statement is executed.

DRDA-2 (distributed unit of work support) lets a single transaction perform table updates on multiple systems, including the local system and/or remote systems. You specify RDBCNNMTH(*DUW) on the CRTSQLxxx command to have the application program establish this type of remote connection when an SQL Connect statement is executed.

You should create SQL/400 application programs with the appropriate RDBCNNMTH value for the types of transactions the program performs. The *DB2/400 Advanced Database Functions* manual provides additional information and an example of an AS/400 application that uses DRDA.

ODBC

ODBC is a standard developed primarily by Microsoft for access to relational databases from Windows-based applications. The ODBC architecture is based on SQL but uses function calls rather than embedded SQL statements. Figure 17.38 shows the main components of a Windows application that accesses a DB2/400 file using ODBC.

The ODBC driver manager is supplied by Microsoft and is a Windows dynamic link library (DLL) that contains functions that the application calls to connect to a database. Microsoft also supplies a program that lets you configure the ODBC driver manager and add one or more ODBC driver entries to the list of databases that the driver manager makes available.

The target DBMS vendor[48] supplies an ODBC driver (which is also a Windows DLL) that implements functions the ODBC driver manager calls to carry out the application's requests. For example, IBM provides an ODBC driver for DB2/400 as part of the Client Access/400 product.

When an application uses ODBC, the first step is to call a function of the driver manager to connect to a specified database. The driver manager uses a list of available databases, each with a unique name. The application can supply one of these names for the connection, or the driver manager can display a list of available DBMS and the end user can select one at runtime. After a connection is established, the application calls driver manager functions to perform SQL Insert, Update, and Delete operations, as well as to open cursors and perform Fetch operations. ODBC also supports dynamic SQL statements, calls to stored procedures, and other database functions.

The advantage of using ODBC is that an application can be written with calls to standard ODBC functions and then used with a variety of DBMS, just by configuring the ODBC driver manager and selecting an available DBMS for the connection.

A number of Windows-based applications (e.g., Excel, Word) provide built-in support for ODBC. With such applications, the end user can request

[48] And possibly other vendors.

Figure 17.38
Structure of an
Application that Uses
ODBC to Access a
DB2/400 File

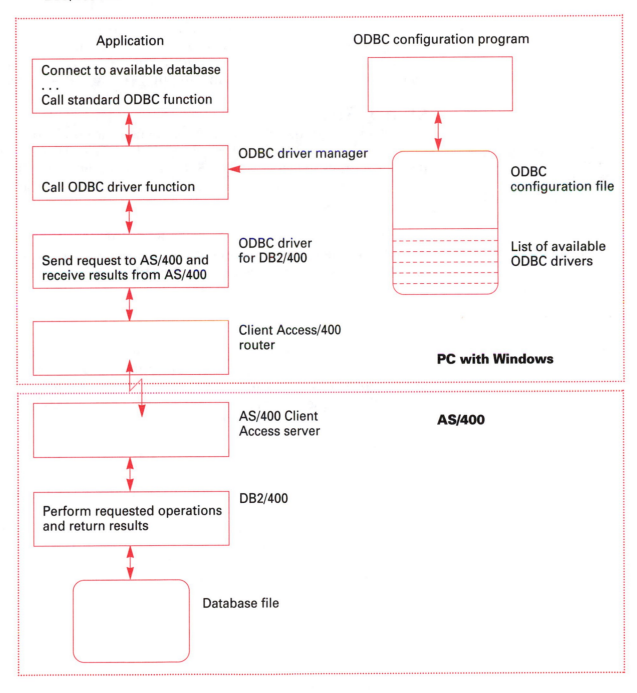

a connection to an available DBMS and the application treats the DBMS in a manner similar to the way it treats a local relational database, such as Microsoft's Access product. This facility lets the user perform application operations such as loading an Excel spreadsheet from a table or running a Word document mail merge with data from a table. The data can come from any available ODBC connection.

The *Microsoft ODBC 2.0 Programmer's Reference and SDK Guide* provides comprehensive information about the standard ODBC functions. IBM's *Client Access Windows 3.1 Client for OS/400 ODBC User's Guide* manual provides additional information about ODBC and IBM's ODBC driver for Windows.

Query Tools

OS/400 provides two commands that can be used (mainly by programmers) to browse the contents of database files. The following RUNQRY command displays or prints all fields for all CUSTOMER records in a simple format that allows browsing. The output uses default formatting for noncharacter fields.

```
RUNQRY QRYFILE( appdta/customer )
```

The following DSPPFM command displays the CUSTOMER physical file's CUSTOMER member in an unformatted (no field labels or separation of field contents) layout. The resulting display lets you choose a hexadecimal format for examining numeric fields.

```
DSPPFM FILE( appdta/customer )
       MBR( customer )
```

Neither command is intended for end users or for programmers to use to develop more complex reports. For that purpose, IBM offers two AS/400 utilities that can be used to produce interactive or printed reports from DB2/400 files: Query/400 and Query Manager/400. Both products must be purchased in addition to OS/400.

Query/400

Query/400 is an IBM licensed program that was derived from a similar report-generator product on the IBM System/36. Both programmers and end users can use Query/400's menus and fill-in-the-blank prompts to design ad hoc or permanent reports. After designing a report, you can save a **query definition** that can be run periodically.

You start the Query/400 definition process by entering the STRQRY or QUERY command.[49] The Query/400 interface lets you perform the following functions:

---

[49] If you don't have the Query/400 product installed, you can't use the QUERY command. Also, without the product, the STRQRY command displays the Query Utilities menu without the "Work with queries" menu option.

- Select 1 to 32 physical and/or logical files for input
- Join records from related files
- Select records to be included in the report
- Specify the ordering of records in the report
- Select fields to include in the report
- Derive new report fields from calculations on existing database fields
- Format the layout of the report
- Define subtotal and pagination control breaks
- Calculate summary information by subgroups of records

Query/400 displays lists of files and fields from which the user can select. Query/400 also includes a WYSIWYG (what-you-see-is-what-you-get) layout editor to design the report.

The Query/400 record selection capability is comparable to the logical file select/omit specifications discussed in Chapter 4. As that chapter explains, the simple AND/OR combination of tests for field values is somewhat limited. Record selection is one of the weaker areas of Query/400 compared to other utilities, such as Query Manager/400. Query/400 supports both inner and left outer joins, as described in Chapter 6.

The reports you define with Query/400 can be displayed or printed. In addition, you can specify that the retrieved data, including any derived fields, should be written to a database file, rather than displayed or printed. Thus, Query/400 can be used to extract data from existing files into new files for subsequent processing.

When you save a query definition, Query/400 creates a *QRYDFN OS/400 object. You can later run the same query with a command such as the following:

```
RUNQRY QRY( appqry/custlist )
```

The QRY parameter must identify an existing query definition object. The RUNQRY command also has optional parameters to specify different record selection criteria; output to a display, printer, or database file; and other options for the query's execution.

Query Manager/400

Query Manager/400 is a component of IBM's DB2 Query Manager and SQL Development Kit for OS/400 licensed program.[50] This is the same

---

[50] Don't confuse Query Manager/400 with Query/400 (a different product) or OS/400 Query Management. Query Management is part of OS/400 and provides a set of APIs that programmers can use to create queries and forms and execute queries. The OS/400 Query Management API corresponds closely to the features in Query Manager/400 but is intended only for programmer use. Query Manager/400 is designed for end users.

product that contains the SQL/400 tools, including Interactive SQL and the SQL precompilers. With this product installed, you can retrieve data either by entering Select statements in ISQL or by designing and running reports via Query Manager/400. ISQL is suitable only for programmers, whereas Query Manager/400 is suitable for both programmers and end users.

You start the Query Manager/400 utility with the STRQM command. Like Query/400, Query Manager/400 lets you specify the data to be retrieved and lay out the format of a report. Query Manager/400 takes a somewhat different approach, however, by separating the process into two steps:

- Specify a result table with an SQL Select statement. In Query Manager/400, this is called a query, and is stored as a *QMQRY OS/400 object.

- Specify the report format for the result table. In Query Manager/400, this is called a form, and is stored as a *QMFORM OS/400 object.

This approach lets you mix and match queries and forms. Thus, you might produce multiple reports from the same data or produce similarly formatted reports from different sets of data.

Chapter 14 describes the SQL Select statement, which is the basis for Query Manager/400 queries. For end users, Query Manager/400 provides menus, fill-in-the-blank prompts, and selection lists to construct the appropriate Select statement without an intimate knowledge of SQL.

Like Query/400, Query Manager/400 also provides a WYSIWYG report layout editor to define forms. Query Manager/400's formatting capabilities are fairly primitive (compared to third-party report products), and Query Manager/400 forms offer fewer layout options than Query/400.

One strength of Query Manager/400 is that a query can be defined to accept user-supplied values at runtime. For example, you can define a query that prompts for a city name that's then used to select records from only the specified city.[51]

The data from a Query Manager/400 query can be displayed or printed, using either a default format or a specified form. You can also output the results of a query to another file. Query Manager/400 also supports DRDA and lets you run queries on distributed data.

The STRQMQRY command runs existing queries.[52] The following example illustrates running a query with a specified form and a user-supplied character-string value:

---

[51] Chapter 15 describes how to use host variables in embedded SQL statements. The Query Manager/400 support for variables is similar, except the values are supplied from the STRQMQRY command's SETVAR parameter or from interactive prompts rather than from program variables.

[52] The STRQMQRY is normally used to run queries created with Query Manager/400 but can also run query definitions created with Query/400.

```
STRQMQRY QMQRY( appqry/custcity )
         QMFORM( appqry/custdtl )
         SETVAR( ( SHPCITY '''Eugene''' ) )
```

Instead of requiring that a user enter the SETVAR parameter to supply a value, you can define Query Manager/400 queries to display an interactive prompt for the value.

Chapter Summary

DB2/400 has a variety of advanced features that support production-level database applications. Some of these are programming facilities (e.g., file overrides) that are coded in the complete application, others are system configuration facilities (e.g., journaling) that provide support for running applications, and still others involve some of both programming and configuration (e.g., commitment control).

The OVRDBF (Override with Database File) command lets you specify file overrides. An override can direct your application program to open a specific database member and can specify which attributes should be used when the system creates an ODP (open data path) that the program uses to access a file. File overrides have an override scope and an ODP (or open) scope. The override scope determines which subsequent opens are affected by the override. The ODP scope affects which program file operations use an ODP and when the system automatically closes the file and deletes the ODP. OS/400 merges overrides based on the file name and override scope specified on the OVRDBF commands.

The OPNQRYF (Open Query File) command provides to HLL built-in I/O operations many of the data access features available with SQL/400 cursors. To use OPNQRYF, you establish a shared ODP (with the OVRDBF command) and then execute an OPNQRYF command to specify dynamic record selection, mapped fields, dynamic join, record aggregation, or other access features. After the OPNQRYF command is executed, an HLL program can open a file using an ODP shared with the OPNQRYF command, and to the program the file appears as a standard database file with the record format and selection defined by the OPNQRYF command.

OS/400 uses object and record locks to control the allocation of resources so that simultaneous object or record access by different jobs won't result in conflicting operations. OS/400 provides many automatic object and record locks, but you can also place additional locks explicitly. The ALCOBJ (Allocate Object) and DLCOBJ (Deallocate Object) commands let you place and remove object locks. OS/400 has five types of object locks and prevents conflicting types of locks from being obtained by different jobs. DB2/400 places record locks automatically when you open a file for update or when commitment control is in effect. Commitment control lock levels let you specify that DB2/400 should place additional record locks beyond those normally placed without commitment control.

OS/400 journal management provides a data recovery facility that can be used to recover damaged database files up to the most recent transaction. A journal object is the controlling OS/400 object. When you start journaling a physical file, the system writes an after image of all new and changed records and an entry for deleted records to the journal. When commitment control is in effect, or when a before image is specified when a physical file is journaled, the system also writes a before image for each file operation. A journal stores all changes for a physical file regardless of which application or utility updates the file. The journal uses a series of journal receiver objects to store journal entries. You can attach new journal receivers to a journal and save the detached journal receivers to tape for improved database backup. If a file is damaged, you can use the journal to reapply lost database changes to a restored copy of the file.

Commitment control provides an all-or-none facility for transactions that involve multiple database records. Under commitment control, an application must execute a commit operation to make permanent those database changes performed since the last complete transaction. If the application or system fails before file changes are committed, the system subsequently backs out all uncommitted changes. An application can also explicitly execute a rollback operation to remove uncommitted changes. There are several commitment control lock levels, which provide different levels of isolation for transactions in different jobs.

DB2/400 trigger programs are HLL programs that DB2/400 calls before and/or after a physical file insert, update, or delete operation. DB2/400 passes a copy of the old and/or new record image to the trigger program. The trigger program can examine and optionally change the record image. The trigger program can also signal an exception to prevent the operation. Another use of trigger programs is to perform other file operations or to log specific changes to file data.

DB2/400 supports several facilities for accessing data on a system other than the system on which an application runs. Distributed Data Management (DDM) lets you define a DDM file on one system and associate it with a communications link to another system and a database file on the other system. An application can open a DDM file and perform I/O operations to it as if it were a local database file. DB2/400 also supports Distributed Relational Database Architecture (DRDA) through SQL/400. To support DRDA, each AS/400 has a relational database directory that associates a database name with a communications link to another system. An application program can use an embedded SQL Connect statement to connect to a remote database, and subsequent SQL statements in the program are then executed on the remote system. Both DDM and DRDA support commitment control for transactions that involve file operations on one or more remote systems. Open Database Connectivity (ODBC) is a Microsoft standard for accessing a relational database from a Windows application. An application makes calls to standard

ODBC functions, which are then routed to the target database system by an ODBC driver. IBM and other vendors supply ODBC drivers for DB2/400.

IBM offers two query utilities: the Query/400 product and the Query Manager/400 component of the DB2 Query Manager and SQL Development Kit for OS/400 product. Both utilities provide data retrieval facilities for end users, as well as programmers. Both products allow you to define a query and save it for subsequent execution.

Key Terms

commitment boundary
commitment control
Distributed Data
    Management (DDM)
Distributed Relational
    Database Architecture
    (DRDA)
journal
journal entry

journal receiver
lock level (commitment
    control)
object lock
ODP scope (open scope)
Open Database Connectivity
    (ODBC)
open data path (ODP)
override scope

Query/400
query definition
Query Manager/400
record lock
shared ODP
transaction
trigger
trigger program
unit of work

Exercises

1. Suppose the you have the following sequence of program calls, file overrides, and a file open:

    PGMA executes:
    ```
    OVRDBF FILE( filex )
    MBR( mbrx )
    OVRSCOPE( *calllvl )

    CALL pgmb
    ```

    PGMB executes:
    ```
    OVRDBF FILE( filey )
    TOFILE( filex )
    MBR( mbry )
    OVRSCOPE( *calllvl )

    CALL pgmc
    ```

    PGMC opens FILEY

    Which file and member does DB/400 open for PGMC?

2. Describe two practical uses of file overrides besides directing DB2/400 to open a specific file member.

3. Show the sequence of CL commands (including OPNQRYF) so that when an application subsequently opens the EMPLSLCT database file, DB2/400 opens a query file that selects only records from the APPDTA/EMPLOYEE file with a DEPTID field value of 4455 and LSTNAM field value of "SMITH." Assume DEPTID is a numeric field and LSTNAM is a character field.

4. Modify your answer to Exercise 3 to use two CL variables to hold the selection values. The CL variables should be declared as

    ```
    DCL &DeptId *Dec (7 0)

    DCL &LstNam *Char 30
    ```

    Hint: You may need additional CL variable(s). Be careful working with &DeptId — remember that CL's concatenation (*CAT) operator works only with character variables.

5. Which type of object lock should you get if you want to be sure that a job can have update access to an object and no other job can update the object?

6. List the types of object locks that another job can get if a job already holds a *SHRNUP lock on an object.

7. Explain why record locks are necessary. Would record locks ever be necessary if only one person used the AS/400 at a time? Why or why not?

8. Explain the differences between a journal and a journal receiver.

9. What is a major purpose of before image journal entries?

Exercises Continued

Exercises continued

10. Describe an example of a multiple-record transaction (other than the funds transfer example used in this chapter). Explain why commitment control is necessary with this type of transaction.

11. Describe a situation in which the *ALL commitment control lock level is necessary. Is there an alternative solution to the problem? If so, describe the advantages and disadvantages of each approach.

12. Describe two uses of a trigger program.

13. Show the commands needed to establish the following trigger programs for the APPDTA/EMPLOYEE file:

    Before inserts and updates: `APPEXC/CHKEMPL`

    After inserts, updates, and deletes:
    `APPEXC/LOGEMPL`

14. Describe a technique that would let an application program optionally pass information to a trigger program. Indicate how the application program would supply the information and how the trigger program would access the information. Be sure to cover the case in which the trigger program is called and the program performing the update has not supplied any information.

15. Describe the comparative advantages and disadvantages of DDM and DRDA.

16. Describe two significant differences between Query/400 and Query Manager/400.

Chapter 18

Database Security

Chapter Overview

OS/400 provides a wide variety of security mechanisms to control access to the contents of a DB2/400 database. This chapter introduces the way OS/400 implements security and how you can set up user profiles and authorities to restrict the types of operations people can perform. In addition to user profiles, we also focus on libraries, database files, and programs, which are the central objects in database security.

Security Basics

As we discussed in Chapter 1, OS/400 is organized so that everything is an object. OS/400 objects include several types that are central to DB2/400 operations:

- User profiles (*USRPRF)
- Libraries (*LIB)
- Database files (*FILE)
- Programs (*PGM)
- Authorization lists (*AUTL)

As the name implies, a **user profile** object represents a user of the AS/400. A user profile has a name, password, and set of values that control various aspects of security and the AS/400 interactive and batch job environments. Typically, when a person who's not already authorized to use the AS/400 needs access to AS/400 data, the organization's security officer or authorized representative uses the CRTUSRPRF command to create a user profile object for the person. The user profile is created with a unique password that the person uses to sign on to the AS/400. The security officer or someone in charge of the organization's applications then grants the user profile appropriate **authority** to various OS/400 objects so the person can work with application programs and data.

When someone signs on to the AS/400, he or she must supply a valid combination of user profile name and password.[1] After a person has signed on with a particular user profile, that user profile governs all access to other objects, including libraries, programs, and files. When a person submits a batch job, the job normally runs under the submitter's user profile, and that user profile also governs data access in the batch environment.[2]

In concept, OS/400 security is simple: When an operation is attempted, OS/400 checks to ensure that the job's user profile has adequate authority to perform the operation on the target object. For example, when someone tries to run a program to display employee records, OS/400 first checks that the user profile the person signed on with has authority to execute the program, and then OS/400 checks that the user profile has authority to read records from the employee file.

In practice, OS/400 security can become quite complex because a user profile might obtain authority to an object in many different ways. In this chapter, we explore many details of OS/400 security as it relates to libraries, database files, and programs, but keep in mind the following simple picture:

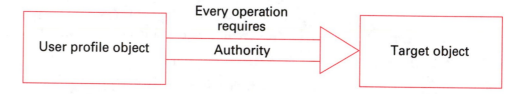

Every operation on the AS/400 (e.g., running a program or opening a file to read records) requires appropriate authority to the target object. If you want a person to be able to perform a particular operation on an object, you must ensure that he or she has the required authority. If you want to prevent a person from performing a particular operation on an object, you must ensure that he or she does not have the required authority.

OS/400 Authorities

There are two major categories of OS/400 authority:

- Special authorities
- Specific authorities

---

[1] A password is not required when the QSECURITY system value is set to 10. Level 10, the lowest allowable value for QSECURITY, essentially specifies that the AS/400 operates with no security. Levels 20 and higher require a user profile and password to sign on.

[2] You can configure some batch jobs so they run under a different, prespecified user profile, in which case, the prespecified user profile's authority governs the access allowed the batch job.

Special authorities are assigned to a user profile (e.g., by the security officer) using the SPCAUT parameter of the CRTUSRPRF or CHGUSRPRF (Change User Profile) command. Special authorities generally have a system-wide scope and aren't associated with specific objects. The special authorities that are directly relevant to database security include

- All object authority (*ALLOBJ) — allows the user unlimited access to all objects on the system
- Save system authority (*SAVSYS) — lets the user save and restore all objects on the system

In general, no one on the system should have *ALLOBJ special authority unless he or she is responsible for system-wide security. In typical installations, trained and trusted system operators are usually given *SAVSYS authority so they can do regular backups. The user profiles for most end users have neither of these special authorities; thus, they need specific object authorities to work with the database.

Specific authorities are assigned to one or more user profiles to use one or more objects.[3] Specific authorities are further subdivided into two groups, **object authorities** and **data authorities,** as shown in Figure 18.1.

Figure 18.1
Specific Authorities

Authority Special Value	Type of Authority	Sample Functions Allowed
Object Authorities		
*OBJOPR	Object operational	• Retrieve an object's description • Use an object as determined by the user's data authorities to the object
*OBJMGT	Object management	• Grant and revoke authorities for an object • Rename or move an object to another library • All *OBJALTER and *OBJREF functions

Figure 18.1 continued

[3] The terminology here can be somewhat confusing. "Specific authorities" include the subcategory "object authorities." Informally, "object authority" is often used synonymously with "specific authority." Where there's little chance for confusion, this book also uses "object authority" for "specific authority."

Figure 18.1
Continued

Authority Special Value	Type of Authority	Sample Functions Allowed
*OBJEXIST	Object existence	• Delete an object • Free an object's storage on a save operation • Transfer ownership of an object to another user profile
*OBJALTER	Object alter	• Add, clear, initialize, and reorganize members of a database file • Change and add attributes of a database file, including adding and removing triggers for physical files • Change the attributes of an SQL package object
*OBJREF	Object reference	• Specify a physical file as the parent file in a referential constraint
*AUTLMGT	Authorization list management	• Add and remove users and their authorities from an object's authorization list
Data Authorities		
*READ	Read	• Read the contents of an object (e.g., read records from a file)
*ADD	Add	• Add entries to an object (e.g., insert new records into a file)
*UPD	Update	• Update the entries in an object (e.g., update records in a file)
*DLT	Delete	• Delete entries from an object (e.g., delete records from a file)
*EXECUTE	Execute	• Run a program, service program, or SQL package • For library objects, locate objects in the library

OS/400 also has several special values for sets of specific authorities, as shown in Figure 18.2.

Figure 18.2
Special Values for Sets of
Specific Authorities

Special Value	Equivalent Specific Authorities	Notes
*ALL	All object and data authorities listed in Figure 18.1	
*CHANGE	*OBJOPR and all data authorities	Lets a user have full read and update access to a database file
*USE	*OBJOPR, *READ, and *EXECUTE	Lets a user execute a program or have read-only access to a database file
*EXCLUDE		Explicitly denies all access to the object

You can grant object authority with the GRTOBJAUT command or by using the EDTOBJAUT command to edit a displayed list of user profiles and their authorities to an object.[4] To enable a user named Betty Smith with the user profile BSMITH to display customer records, you could use a command such as

```
GRTOBJAUT OBJ( appdta/customer )
          OBJTYPE( *file )
          USER( bsmith )
          AUT( *use )
```

If you wanted Betty to be able to read and add customer records but not delete or update them you could use the following command:

```
GRTOBJAUT OBJ( appdta/customer )
          OBJTYPE( *file )
          USER( bsmith )
          AUT( *objopr *read *add )
```

You can revoke object authority with the RVKOBJAUT command or by using the EDTOBJAUT command. To revoke Betty's authority to add customer records, you could use a command such as

```
RVKOBJAUT OBJ( appdta/customer )
          OBJTYPE( *file )
          USER( bsmith )
          AUT( *add )
```

This command leaves intact any other authorities that the BSMITH user profile has to the CUSTOMER file object.

---

[4] With SQL/400, you can also use the Grant and Revoke statements to grant and revoke specific authority. Chapter 13 explains the correspondence between the SQL statements and the OS/400 specific authorities.

To grant or revoke authority to an object, your user profile must satisfy one or more of the following conditions:

- Own the object (typically as a result of creating it)
- Be the system security officer (QSECOFR)
- Have *ALLOBJ special authority
- Have *OBJMGT authority to the object

The *OBJMGT authority by itself lets you grant and revoke only those authorities your user profile has to the object, and *OBJMGT authority (again, by itself) doesn't let you grant another user profile *OBJMGT authority.

Authorities for Libraries, Programs, and Database Files

Later in this chapter, we look at more options for providing the appropriate authority to a user. But first, we need to examine more closely how authorities control user access to libraries, programs, and database files.

To access any object, a user profile must have *EXECUTE authority to the library that contains the object. Without this authority, the user profile can't do anything with objects in the library. If you want to enable a user to access one or more of the objects in a library, you should normally grant the person's user profile *USE authority (which includes *EXECUTE authority) to the library. If any authorized application creates temporary or permanent objects in the library, you should also grant the user profile *ADD authority to the library.

To run a program, a user profile must have *OBJOPR and *EXECUTE authorities to the program. This includes programs and ILE service programs called from application menus or other programs.[5] As we'll see later, programs can provide an important means of controlling database access, so you should be careful to grant authority to programs only to those users who should be allowed to run them.

Application programs can access the data in a physical file member either directly by opening the physical file member or indirectly by opening a member of a logical file defined over the physical file. To access data through an open physical file member, a user profile must have *OBJOPR authority to the file and one or more of the *READ, *ADD, *UPD, or *DLT data authorities to the physical file. The data authorities control which record operations — read, add, update, and delete — are allowed.

---

[5] When a job on another system makes a remote SQL request to an AS/400, the remote job's user profile must have *OBJOPR and *EXECUTE authorities to the SQL package (*SQLPKG object type) on the target AS/400. The SQL package contains control information and the access plan for remote access of files and stored procedures.

To access data in a physical file member by opening a logical file member, a user profile must have *OBJOPR authority and one or more of the *READ, *ADD, *UPD, or *DLT data authorities to the logical file. In addition, the user profile must have the required data authorities to the physical file. For example, to read and update records through a logical file, the user profile must have *OBJOPR, *READ, and *UPD authorities to the logical file and *READ and *UPD authorities to the physical file.[6] This dual check on data rights provides the basis for a field-level approach to database security, which we explore later in the chapter.

Public Authority

So far, we've considered only individual user profiles. OS/400 has two features — public authority and group profiles — that let you grant authority to more than one user profile at a time. Every object has **public authority**, which controls access by user profiles that aren't otherwise authorized to the object. An object's public authority may include any of the object authorities listed in Figures 18.1 and 18.2, which you can grant and revoke using the *PUBLIC special value instead of a user profile name on the GRTOBJAUT and RVKOBJAUT commands. For example, to grant public authority to read data from the customer file, you could use the following command:

```
GRTOBJAUT OBJ( appdta/customer )
          OBJTYPE( *file )
          USER( *public )
          AUT( *use )
```

On the CRTLIB, CRTPGM, CRTPF, and CRTLF commands, you also can specify one of the special values listed in Figure 18.2 for the respective command's AUT parameter.[7] The following command creates the CUSTOMER file with public authority to read the file:

```
CRTPF FILE( appdta/customer )
      SRCFILE( appsrc/qddssrc )
      AUT( *use )
```

The default value for the CRTxxx commands' AUT parameter is *LIBCRTAUT, which means that the object's public authority is set from a value associated with the library in which the object is created. This value is specified on the CRTAUT parameter of the CRTLIB and CHGLIB

---

[6] This approach to logical file data authorities was introduced in V3R1. In earlier releases, you couldn't grant data authorities to logical files, and the rules for accessing data were different.

[7] If you want some combination of authorities other than those provided by the special values listed in Figure 18.2, you should specify *EXCLUDE for the AUT parameter on the CRTxxx commands, then use the GRTOBJAUT command to grant the appropriate specific authorities to *PUBLIC.

commands.[8] For example, if a library is created with CRTAUT(*CHANGE), new objects created in the library will have public authority *CHANGE, unless you specify an AUT parameter value other than the default, *LIBCRTAUT, on the CRTxxx command.[9]

Although it's common practice in many AS/400 installations to allow *USE public authority to most application objects, you should be sure you want everyone to be able to run a program or read data from a file before you grant *USE public authority. A more cautious approach is to specify *EXCLUDE for library, program, and database file objects' public authority unless there's a clear reason for allowing some higher level of access to everyone.

Group Profiles

Group profiles provide a way to identify an individual user profile as a member of one or more groups. You can then grant authority to the group rather than to the individual user profiles. This approach can greatly simplify the administration of authority.

To establish a group, the security officer or someone with appropriate authority creates a user profile that serves as the group profile. This user profile should be created with no password (i.e., use the PASSWORD(*NONE) parameter on the CRTUSRPRF command) so no individual actually uses the profile to sign on.[10]

To assign an individual user profile to a group, you specify the group profile name for the GRPPRF or SUPGRPPRF (supplemental group profiles) parameter on the CRTUSRPRF or CHGUSRPRF command. A user profile

---

[8] A new object's public authority is set when it's created. A subsequent change to the containing library's CRTAUT value does not affect existing objects.

[9] CRTAUT(*SYSVAL) is the default parameter for the CRTLIB command, which means that a new library's CRTAUT value is taken from the QCRTAUT system value. IBM ships AS/400s with QCRTAUT set to *CHANGE. As a result, if you use the default CRTAUT parameter for CRTLIB commands and use the default AUT parameter for other CRTxxx commands, new objects will have *CHANGE as their public authority. This is *not* generally a good practice because it allows too much access.

Unfortunately, IBM also ships some OS/400 system libraries (e.g., QSYS) with CRTAUT(*SYSVAL) so changing the QSYSVAL system value to a more restrictive setting, such as *EXCLUDE, may cause problems with objects created in these system libraries. For example, workstation devices created in QSYS using a default AUT parameter might not be accessible by end users.

For most installations, application libraries should be created with a CRTAUT value of *EXCLUDE or *USE. To simplify this practice, you can change the CRTLIB command's default CRTAUT parameter value to something other than *SYSVAL, as in the following example:

```
CHGCMDDFT CMD( CRTLIB ) NEWDFT( 'CRTAUT(*EXCLUDE)' )
```

You can use the CHGLIB command to change the CRTAUT attribute of existing libraries.

[10] This isn't a requirement of a group profile, but it's good administrative practice not to use the same profile for an individual and for a group profile.

implicitly becomes a group profile when it's referenced as a group profile for any other user profile.[11] A group profile cannot itself be a member of another group; that is, you cannot specify anything other than GRPPRF(*NONE) and SUPGRPPRF(*NONE) — the defaults — for a group profile.

An individual user profile can have up to 16 group profiles. The first group profile must be specified on the GRPPRF parameter, and up to 15 additional group profiles can be specified on the SUPGRPPRF parameter.[12] The following command assigns Betty Smith the group profiles GRPSALES and GRPACCOUNT:

```
CHGUSRPRF USRPRF( bsmith )
          GRPPRF( grpsales )
          SUPGRPPRF( grpaccount )
```

When OS/400 checks for a user profile's authority to an object, and the individual user profile has no explicit authority (including not having *EXCLUDE authority) to the object, OS/400 then checks the user profile's group profile(s), if any, to see whether they have any authorities to the object. If they do and the combination of authorities granted to the group profile(s) is adequate, OS/400 permits the operation.[13] If there are no group profiles or they have no authorities to the object, OS/400 next checks the object's public authority.[14] If the group profile(s) have any authorities (including *EXCLUDE) to the object, but the combination of authorities isn't adequate for the operation, OS/400 skips the check for public authority and continues with the check for program adopted authority (discussed below).

There are a couple of important aspects to the way OS/400 checks authority. First, notice that the search for sufficient authorities stops with the individual user profile if the profile has any authority to the object. This means you can use the *EXCLUDE authority or any other specific authority to "short circuit" the authority an individual user profile derives from its group profiles and public authority because OS/400 won't check either

---

[11] A user profile is explicitly designated a group profile if you specify a value other than *NONE for the GID (group ID) parameter on the CRTUSRPRF or CHGUSRPRF commands. Group ID numbers are used for accessing files in the hierarchical part of the AS/400 Integrated File System, not DB2/400 files.

[12] The significance of the group profile specified in the GRPPRF parameter is that the OWNER, GRPAUT, and GRPAUTTYP attributes of the individual user profile (i.e., the one that belongs to the group profile) apply just to the group profile specified in the GRPPRF parameter, not to any group profile specified in the SUPGRPPRF parameter.

[13] If any group profile has the *ALLOBJ special authority, this provides the group profile with adequate authority for any operation, regardless of the group profile's specific authorities to the object.

[14] The actual steps OS/400 goes through to check for authority are more complex than this; however, this is the basic mechanism that lets you use group profiles or public authority to simplify granting authority. The *Security — Reference* manual includes a complete flowchart for OS/400's authority search algorithm.

group profile authority or public authority if the individual user profile has any authority to the object. A similar principle applies for group profile authorities to an object — if there are any, OS/400 doesn't check the object's public authority.[15]

This approach means OS/400 doesn't add together the individual, group, and public authorities. Consider the following authorities:

- The BSMITH individual user profile has *OBJOPR authority to the CUSTOMER file
- The GRPSALES group profile has *UPD authority to the CUSTOMER file
- The CUSTOMER file has *READ public authority

Even if the GRPSALES profile is the group profile for BSMITH, a job running under BSMITH would not be able to open the CUSTOMER file for read and update or any other operations. What's required is one of the following conditions:

- The BSMITH user profile has *OBJOPR, *READ, and *UPD authorities to the CUSTOMER file
- The BSMITH user profile has no authorities (not even *EXCLUDE) to the CUSTOMER file, and the GRPSALES user profile has *OBJOPR, *READ, and *UPD authorities to the CUSTOMER file
- Neither the BSMITH nor the GRPSALES user profile has any authorities to the CUSTOMER file, and CUSTOMER file has *OBJOPR, *READ, and *UPD authorities public authorities

---

[15] IBM originally introduced this approach as a tool for security management by exception. The idea was that you could grant more group or public authority than some individuals should have and use *EXCLUDE or other limited authorities for just those individual profiles you wanted to restrict. In my opinion, however, using this technique is dangerous and difficult to manage because you can't easily see the net effect of changes to group or public authorities. Unfortunately, there isn't a foolproof solution because granting an individual user profile more authorities than its group profiles could unintentionally leave authorities in place for an individual when you reduce a group's authorities. The dilemma results from the fact that you have to grant all the group profile's authorities plus any additional ones for an individual user profile because OS/400 doesn't add individual and group profile authorities together when determining authority to an object. My advice is to use group profiles as the primary way you grant authority but don't assign any individual user profile to a group that has more authority than the individual profile should have. That way, you won't have to grant a more limited set of authorities to the individual profile to short circuit the authority the individual profile would get from the group profile. Instead, when an individual profile must have more authority than provided by any of the individual profile's group profiles, grant the necessary authority to the individual user profile directly.

OS/400 does add together the group profile authorities when an individual user profile has more than one group profile with some authority to the target object. But this combination of authorities applies only for the group profile step of the authority check.

As a performance tweak, you can use the CHGOBJPGP command to set or change an object's **primary group**. The following command sets the CUSTOMER file's primary group profile to GRPSALES:

```
CHGOBJPGP OBJ( appdta/customer )
          OBJTYPE( *file )
          NEWPGP( grpsales )
```

This command doesn't change the GRPSALES group profile's or any other profile's authority to the CUSTOMER file. All it does is store some information about the GRPSALES profile's authority to the CUSTOMER file in the file object itself,[16] thus speeding up OS/400's authority checking in some cases. As a rule of thumb, you may get some improvement in performance if you set up group profiles so that individual user profiles that frequently access an object have as their first group profile (i.e., as specified on the CRTUSRPRF command's GRPPRF parameter) a group profile that's also been made the primary group for the frequently accessed object. Obviously, there may be objects that are frequently accessed by user profiles that belong to different groups, and only one of the group profiles can be designated as an object's primary group.

Authorization Lists

Group profiles provide a way to organize groups of individual user profiles so authorities can be granted to a single group profile and thus indirectly made available for the individual user profiles that belong to the group. **Authorization lists** provide a somewhat comparable feature that lets you organize sets of objects for which identical authorities are granted.

An authorization list is an OS/400 object that represents a list of objects. If you associate other objects with an authorization list object, when you grant a user profile or public authority to the authorization list, you indirectly grant authority to the objects associated with the authorization list. To create an authorization list, you use a command such as the following:

```
CRTAUTL AUTL( salesobj )
        AUT( *exclude )
        TEXT( 'Sales objects' )
```

This command creates the SALESOBJ authorization list and does not provide any public authority to the authorization list or the objects subsequently associated with it. All authorization lists are created in the QSYS

---

[16] This information is stored in the object header part of the object (as described in Chapter 1), not in the file's records.

library, so you cannot specify a qualified name on the AUTL parameter of any command.

To take advantage of an authorization list, you associate two lists with the authorization list:

- A list of objects that are in the scope of the authorization list
- An implicit list of individual user profiles and/or group profiles that are authorized to the authorization list

An object is put under the scope of an authorization list by using a command such as the following:

```
GRTOBJAUT OBJ( appdta/sale )
          OBJTYPE( *file )
          AUTL( salesobj )
```

As an alternative, you can use the EDTOBJAUT command to edit a display of the authorities that exist for an object. This display contains an entry field for the object's associated authorization list (if any). An object can be associated with only one authorization list at a time, and you can't nest authorization lists (i.e., you can't specify OBJTYPE(*AUTL) along with the AUTL parameter on the GRTOBJAUT command).

To grant a user profile authority to an authorization list, and hence to the associated objects, you can use a GRTOBJAUT command, such as the following:

```
GRTOBJAUT OBJ( salesobj )
          OBJTYPE( *autl )
          USER( bsmith )
          AUT( *use )
```

OS/400 has an ADDAUTLE (Add Authorization List Entry) command to slightly simplify granting a user profile authority to an authorization list. The following example is equivalent to the GRTOBJAUT command above:[17]

```
ADDAUTLE AUTL( salesobj )
         USER( bsmith )
         AUT( *use )
```

When you grant a user profile authority to an authorization list, you effectively provide the specified authorities to the user profile for all the objects associated with the authorization list.[18] Notice that each user profile

---

[17] The ADDAUTLE command may confuse more than simplify the understanding of the relationship between user profiles and authorization lists, especially because the security manuals sometimes give the impression that adding an authorization list entry is somehow different from just granting a user profile authority to the authorization list. The GRTOBJAUT and ADDAUTLE commands with comparable parameter values achieve identical results.

[18] For the USER parameter, you can specify the *PUBLIC special value, instead of a user profile name. Public authority to an authorization list provides public authority only to those

has its own set of authorities, which are the same for all associated objects. You can specify any of the values in Figures 18.1 and 18.2 for the AUT parameter on a GRTOBJAUT or ADDAUTLE command. A user profile can be granted authority to more than one authorization list.

If an object is associated with an authorization list, OS/400 performs another round of authority checks when an operation is attempted. In simple terms, OS/400

1. Checks the individual user profile's authority to the target object

2. Checks the individual user profile's authority to the target object's associated authorization list object

3. Checks the group profiles' (if any) authority to the target object or to the target object's associated authorization list object. If there are multiple group profiles, their authorities are added together for the test.

    Each group profile is first checked for authority to the target object. If the group has any authorities (including *EXCLUDE) to the target object, then the group contributes these authorities to the combined total for all groups. If the group has no authority to the target object, then the system checks the group's authority to the target object's associated authorization list object, and, if there are any authorities, adds them to the combined total for all groups. (Note that each group contributes either its authorities to the object or its authorities to the authorization list, but not both.)

4. Checks the public authority either for the target object or for the target object's associated authorization list object

At the completion of each of these steps, if OS/400 finds any authority to the target object, either directly or to its associated authorization list, OS/400 stops checking.

As Step 4 implies, an object's public authority can also be controlled with an authorization list. To do this, you use the name of the authorization list as the value for the AUT parameter on the CRTxxx command, as in the following command:

```
CRTPF FILE( appdta/sale )
    SRCFILE( appsrc/qddssrc )
    AUT( salesobj )
```

objects associated with the list that have their public authority set to use the authorization list (i.e., the object has PUBLIC(*AUTL) specified).

After this command is executed, the public authority to the SALE file is defined by the SALESOBJ authorization list's public authority (which may be *EXCLUDE or any of the authorities in Figures 18.1 and 18.2).[19]

Authorization lists can reduce the number of specific authorities you have to grant to individual and group profiles. But because authorization lists add additional steps to OS/400 authority checking, they may adversely affect performance. As a rule of thumb, if you have several objects for which the same set of authorities are frequently granted, consider an authorization list. It's not uncommon to have sets of application programs and files for which *USE authority is frequently granted en masse (and public authority is *EXCLUDE). Such sets are good candidates for authorization lists.

Program Adopted Authority

With all the different ways you can specify authority under OS/400, you might think every possible situation could be covered. In fact, there are many types of database access rules that can't be directly specified with what we've looked at so far. The problem stems from the broad meaning of the four kinds of data authorities: *READ, *ADD, *UPD, and *DLT. If a user profile has *OBJOPR and *UPD authorities to a physical file, any type of update to any field in any record in any member is allowed. This level of access is not usually desirable. Instead, most applications are intended to let a user make only valid changes to some fields, often for only a subset of the records in the file.

Logical files provide a more fine-tuned solution for some situations. With a logical file, you can limit access to a subset of records and fields (as explained in Chapter 4). If you grant a user profile appropriate data authorities to both the logical file and underlying physical file, but grant *OBJOPR authority only to the logical file, the user profile is limited to accessing only those fields and records accessible through the logical file. (The lack of *OBJOPR authority to the physical file prevents opening the physical file

---

[19] In this example, when you specify AUT(SALESOBJ), the SALESOBJ authorization list must already exist. Specifying AUT(SALESOBJ) associates the SALE file with the SALESOBJ authorization list, so it's not necessary to execute a subsequent GRTOBJAUT command to make the association, as shown in the earlier example. As mentioned, the AUT parameter also sets the object's public authority to *AUTL.

For an object created without an authorization list specified for the AUT parameter, you can use the GRTOBJAUT or EDTOBJAUT commands to set the object's public authority to *AUTL so OS/400 will check the public authority of the object's associated authority list. Before doing this, the object must first be associated with an authorization list (also using either a GRTOBJAUT or EDTOBJAUT command).

Note that OS/400 checks public authority by first looking at the object's public authority setting. If this is *AUTL, OS/400 then looks at the associated authorization list object's public authority setting. Otherwise, OS/400 uses the target object's specific authorities for the public (if any). This either-or approach is different from the way OS/400 checks individual and group profile authorities. In both those cases, OS/400 first checks the user profile's authorities to the target object and, if there are none, then checks the user profile's authorities to the authorization list (if any).

directly.) You can even define logical file fields as input-only to control read/update capabilities on a field-by-field basis.

This field-level approach to access is fairly limited, however. The biggest problem is that it provides no way to control the values that are put in fields that can be updated. Thus, a payroll clerk authorized to update the salary field in employee records can put in any value for the salary. Another problem is that the logical file record selection criteria available through DDS is quite limited. (SQL/400 views are more powerful but still can't express many application constraints.)

Ultimately, you'll find you must use application program logic to control access and to limit updates to valid values. OS/400 provides an excellent tool for this purpose: **program adopted authority**.

Normally when you create a program, any operations it performs (e.g., updating records in a file) require the job's user profile to have adequate authority (either directly or via a group profile, public authority, or an authorization list). You can optionally, however, create a program that can perform any operation that the program's owner has authority to perform (in addition to operations the job's user profile has authority to perform).

Let's look at a simple example. Suppose there's a user profile (created expressly for this purpose) named PRFCHGEMP (profile — change employee). This user profile is made the owner of the CHGEMPSAL (change employee salary) program — we'll discuss how in a moment. The PRFCHGEMP user profile is also granted *CHANGE authority to the EMPLOYEE file. Finally, the CHGEMPSAL program is designated as a program that adopts the authority of its owner when the program runs (again, we'll see how in a moment). With this arrangement, any user profile that has *EXECUTE authority to the CHGEMPSAL program can run it. And while that user profile is running the CHGEMPSAL program, the program can perform any retrieval or update operations to the EMPLOYEE file, regardless of the authority of the user profile running the program.

What this setup lets you do is not grant individual user profiles full *CHANGE authority to the EMPLOYEE file. Instead, you can grant them *USE or no specific authority to the EMPLOYEE file and *EXECUTE authority to the CHGEMPSAL program. Then the only way they can update the EMPLOYEE file is through operations provided by the CHGEMPSAL program — which, presumably, enforces the appropriate business rules for the application.[20]

---

[20] There's another approach — often called "menu-based security" or "menu access control" — that's used in many AS/400 organizations. This approach grants extensive private or public authority to files and then tries to limit how the user can get at files by confining them to selecting options from application menus. Typically, the user profile is also set up with LMTCPB(*YES) to limit the user profile's ability to run commands from interactive jobs.

The theory is that the user will never be able to perform any operation except those made available from an application menu. This approach is ineffective and should never be used as a substitute for resource security (as we've been discussing in this chapter). There

The user profiles that own programs that adopt authority don't represent end users, programmers, or security personnel. These user profiles should be created with names that reflect their purpose and with PASSWORD(*NONE) specified so no one can sign on with the user profile.

Using a command such as the following makes a special-purpose user profile the owner of a program:

```
CHGOBJOWN OBJ( appexc/chgempsal)
          OBJTYPE( *pgm )
          NEWOWN( prfchgemp )
```

Then the appropriate security person or application administrator changes the program so it adopts the authority of the program owner's user profile:

```
CHGPGM PGM( appexc/chgempsal)
       USRPRF( *owner )
```

The **PRFCHGEMP** special-purpose user profile can be granted authority, just like any other user profile:

```
GRTOBJAUT OBJ( appdta/employee )
          OBJTYPE( *file )
          USER( prfchgemp )
          AUT( *change )
```

With programs that adopt authority, you have available a method to control access in precisely the way applications require.

Programs that adopt authority normally propagate their authority to programs they call. OS/400 adds together all the adopted and propagated authority for programs in the job's program call stack[21] when authority is checked. You can create programs with the USEADPAUT(*NO) parameter to prevent the program from inheriting any adopted authority from the program that calls it.[22]

A user profile created to own a program that adopts authority should own only one program and should have the minimum authorities needed to perform the operations it implements. Do not use a user profile that owns application files (as discussed in the next section) as the owner of programs

---

are many ways to circumvent application menus, and someone serious about breaching security will not be deterred by this approach. Furthermore, this approach leaves data exposed to improper access when PCs are connected to the AS/400 (because remote access doesn't flow through AS/400-based menu programs). There are additional AS/400 security features not covered in this chapter that might appear to provide adequate mechanisms to make menu-based security viable, but they don't. IBM's own security specialists, as well as the leading AS/400 security experts, agree that menu-based security by itself is not an adequate approach to database security.

[21] The job's call stack is essentially the list of programs that have been called but have not yet returned to the program that called them.

[22] This isn't a particularly useful capability because the problem isn't inheriting too much adopted authority; rather the problem is propagating authority unnecessarily. (See Footnote 23.)

that adopt authority. This practice provides too much authority for a job while the program is executing. Although a full discussion of security risks and program adopted authority is beyond the scope of this chapter, you want to be sure that if a user is able to circumvent constraints that are part of the program, the scope of the harm the user can do is as limited as possible.[23]

Object Ownership

We've been considering in detail how OS/400 controls object access by checking the authority a user profile has to an object. User profiles play another essential role in OS/400 — every object is owned by a user profile.[24] Thus, it's important to plan which user profiles will own application objects, such as libraries, files, and programs.

The owner of an object normally has all authorities to an object. For that reason, once you put application files and programs into production, you shouldn't leave the programmer who created them as the owner. Instead, there should be one or more special-purpose user profiles created to own production versions of application objects. In small organizations, a single user profile — e.g., PRFAPPOWN (profile — application owner) — may suffice. For larger organizations, there may be several user profiles, each owning objects of a particular application (e.g., PRFSALEOWN, PRFEMPOWN). The CHGOBJOWN command (which we saw earlier) can be used to transfer ownership from a programmer's user profile to a special-purpose profile. Or, after testing, the source code may be used to re-create the objects in a job that runs under the special-purpose user profile. (Different approaches to managing application objects use different methods.)

We've already discussed how programs that adopt authority should be owned. Programs that don't adopt authority can be owned by the same special-purpose user profiles that own application database files. Similarly, application libraries can be owned by these special-purpose user profiles.

---

[23] For example, let's say PGMA adopts authority and calls PGMB. If the person who calls PGMA can introduce a different version of PGMB (e.g., by changing the job's library list so OS/400 finds the program object named PGMB in a different library), then he or she can perform operations in the "impostor" PGMB (which he or she may have written for this purpose) using the authority adopted (and propagated) by PGMA. As this example points out, you must carefully control program calls from programs that adopt authority.
As a side note, at the operating system level, you can specify on a program CALL operation whether to propagate adopted authority. This option isn't available in any of the major AS/400 HLLs. At the time this book went to press, IBM was considering adding this option to HLL CALL operations. This would be a highly valuable feature because it would enable a program to make calls without propagating authority.

[24] User profile objects themselves are normally owned by the user profile that created them. IBM-supplied user profiles, such as QPGMR, are normally owned by the IBM-supplied QSYS user profile. The QSYS user profile owns itself.

Database Security Principles and Guidelines

OS/400 security is an important and extensive topic. This section provides some principles and guidelines to help you lay a solid foundation for your DB2/400 database security. The annotated bibliography lists several references that provide more detailed discussions and advice.

General

- Security is a business function of protecting an organization's resources and operations; computer systems security should be designed within the context of the organization's overall security plan.

- Security rules cover different levels of threat — the more vital a security policy is to your organization's well-being, the more thoroughly you must enforce the policy.

- Assume that people who will intentionally try to breach your security understand the technical aspects of the AS/400 as well as you do. Don't rely on an attacker's ignorance of the AS/400 to protect your system. What they shouldn't know are the passwords.

- If the implementation of a security mechanism fails, the error should result in unintended restrictions on access rather than unintended additional access.

AS/400 Specific

- Set your AS/400's QSECURITY system value to 30 or higher. This setting enforces password protection and resource-level security, as we've discussed in this chapter.

  Level 40 is recommended and provides all the security enforcement of level 30 plus additional checks to see that various features of the operating system aren't tampered with or used improperly to circumvent security.

- Assign a unique user profile and password to each individual who uses your system.

- Consider changing the CRTLIB command's CRTAUT parameter default to *EXCLUDE (see Footnote 9).

- Carefully consider how much public authority (if any) each application file and program should have.

- Use group profiles to organize user profiles into groups that can be granted identical authority for many objects.

- Use authorization lists to organize sets of objects for which identical authorities are frequently granted.

- Be aware of how OS/400's authority search works and the way granting any authority to an individual user profile short circuits the search of group profile and public authorities. Avoid using this short-circuit technique unless it's necessary.

- Grant the minimum authority necessary for any operation. This principle applies for individual and group profiles, authorization lists entries, and adopted authority.

- Use program adopted authority to provide required authority under control of a program when you don't want to give the full capabilities of a specific authority (e.g., *UPD) to a user profile.

- For the user profile that owns a program that adopts authority, do not have a user profile that owns other application objects or that has more authority than the program needs for its operations.

- Have special-purpose user profiles (not programmer or end-user user profiles) own application objects.

- Be sure to consider PCs attached to your AS/400 and other types of remote access when setting up security and granting authorities.

Chapter Summary

OS/400 controls access to objects by checking the authority a user profile has to the target object. A user profile is an AS/400 object with a name, password, and other attributes. Generally, each person that uses the AS/400 should have a unique user profile.

The two main categories of OS/400 authorities are special authorities and specific authorities. The *ALLOBJ special authority provides all access to all objects on the AS/400 and is usually assigned only to user profiles for people responsible for system-wide security. The *SAVSYS special authority lets the user profile save and restore objects and is usually assigned to the user profiles for some members of the systems operation staff.

Specific authorities are granted to a user profile or the public to provide various levels of access to a specific object. Specific authorities are subdivided into object authorities and data authorities. Object authorities control general use of the object, including basic access, changing object attributes, management operations (e.g., renaming), and existence. Data authorities control read, add, update, and delete operations on an object's contents, as well as the ability to find objects in a library and to run a program.

To use an object in a library, a user profile must have *EXECUTE authority to the library. To run a program, a user profile must have *OBJOPR and *EXECUTE authorities to the program. To open a database file, a user profile must have *OBJOPR authority and one or more of the *READ, *ADD, *UPD, and *DLT data authorities to the file. When you open a physical file member, the user profile's data authorities to the file control the types of record operations allowed. When you open a logical file, the user profile must have the appropriate data authorities to both the logical file and the underlying physical file. You can use logical files as a means of limiting access to selected fields and/or a subset of records in a physical file.

Group profiles provide a way to simplify authority management by organizing individual user profiles into groups and granting authority to the group profiles. A user profile can have up to 16 group profiles. A group profile is just a user profile object referenced as the group profile by some individual (i.e., non-group) user profile. When an individual user profile has no authority to an object, OS/400 checks the individual user profile's group profiles (if any) for sufficient authority. If the individual user profile has more than one group profile with any authority to the object, all of the group profiles' authorities are added together.

An object's public authority governs access to the object when an individual user profile has no specific authorities to the object and the individual user profile's group profiles (if any) also have no specific authorities to the object.

An authorization list object provides a way to organize objects for which the same set of authorities is frequently granted. The GRTOBJAUT command (or the AUT parameter on a CRTxxx command) associates an object with an authorization list. All authorities granted to a user profile for an authorization list then apply to all objects that are associated with the authorization list.

Program adopted authority provides a way to control access under program logic, for example, to allow only certain types of updates to a file. A program that has the USRPRF(*OWNER) attribute can perform any operation for which the user profile that owns the program has sufficient authority. A special-purpose user profile can be made the owner of a program that adopts authority and can be granted the required authorities to perform the program's functions. Subsequently, any user profile authorized to run the program can use it to perform the operations the program implements, regardless of the authority the job's user profile has for the target object.

Special-purpose user profiles should be created to own application objects. One or more of these special-purpose user profiles can own files and programs that don't adopt authority. Each program that adopts authority should be owned by a separate user profile that is not one of the user profiles that own other application objects. A user profile that owns a program that adopts authority should have no more than the necessary authorities to perform the operations the program implements.

Key Terms

authority	object authority	special authority
authorization list	primary group	specific authority
data authority	program adopted authority	user profile
group profile	public authority	

Exercises

1. Explain why each person who uses the AS/400 should have his or her own user profile and password.

2. Discuss the reasons production application objects should not be owned by programmers' user profiles. Can you think of any problems this rule might cause?

3. Assume that the APPDTA/CUSTSHP logical file is defined over the APPDTA/CUSTOMER physical file and that the CUSTSHP file's record format has only the shipping address fields defined as updatable (B in position 38 of the DDS field definition.). Also assume that the BSMITH user profile has no authorities to either file and that both files have *EXCLUDE public authority. Show the commands necessary to allow the following capabilities:

   - Anyone can read the information in the shipping address fields

   - BSMITH can read and update the information in the shipping address fields

4. Considering the CUSTSHP and CUSTOMER files in Exercise 3 and the authority you granted to the public and BSMITH, describe the necessary steps to let BSMITH also read all the customer information and add new customers (but still not be able to update any information other than shipping address).

   Hint: This isn't as simple as it might appear. Consider carefully the access rules when using physical and logical files.

5. Why do you think IBM doesn't allow a group profile to be a member of another group? What would be the advantages for managing security if you could create nested group profiles? How does the current limitation affect your design for setting up security for an organization?

6. Show how you would authorize the RJONES user profile to have *USE authority to the APPDTA/EMPLOYEE and the APPDTA/TRAINING files with the following constraints:

   - RJONES should have GRPEMP as a group profile

   - Neither RJONES nor GRPEMP should have specific authorities to the EMPLOYEE or TRAINING files

   - The public should have *EXCLUDE authority to the EMPLOYEE and TRAINING files

   - No programs that adopt authority are used

   - The same authorities are always granted for the EMPLOYEE and TRAINING files

7. Assume the following conditions:

   - There's an APPDTA/CUSTOMER physical file that has no public authority.

   - The APPEXC/CHGCUST program provides the ability to read, change, and delete (but not add) records in the CUSTOMER file. This program is currently owned

Exercises Continued

Exercises continued

by the APPOWN profile that owns all application database files.

- The BSMITH user profile currently has *OBJOPR, *READ, *UPD, and *DLT authorities to the CUSTOMER file and no authorities to the CHGCUST program.

- The security officer will create any new user profile you need.

Show the necessary commands so the BSMITH user profile can read, update, and delete records in the CUSTOMER file under control of the CHGCUST program, but no other way. Be sure your actions don't potentially give BSMITH more than the specified authority.

Chapter 19

Backup and Recovery

Chapter Overview

This chapter describes the AS/400's facilities for backing up database files and related objects and for restoring these objects if they become lost or damaged because of a hardware or software failure or due to a human error. We look at several approaches to saving database-related objects that can reduce the amount of time needed for daily backups and/or simplify the recovery process. A final section provides a brief overview of several other AS/400 features that can help improve the availability of your database.

Introduction to Backup and Recovery Strategies

If nothing ever went wrong with computer hardware or software, we wouldn't have to worry about database **backup** and **recovery**. But things do sometimes go wrong; among the potential problems are

- A power failure that causes the system to halt
- A disk drive or other piece of hardware that fails
- A system software failure
- An application error
- A mistake by a user

When one of these events happens, database files may be lost or corrupted and need to be recovered. The most basic means of recovery is to use a backup copy of data to restore files to a valid state. In the simplest terms a backup consists of a complete copy of one or more database files written to magnetic tape or other media. When recovery is necessary, the copy is rewritten to disk to completely replace lost or corrupted files. Figure 19.1 shows this simple cycle of backup and recovery. Keep in mind that in typical operations, backups are made regularly so the tape copies of database files are relatively current, but recovery is usually a rare event.

The AS/400 has extensive facilities for backing up everything on the system, including the operating system, user profiles and authorities, device configurations, programs, database files, and all the other IBM-supplied and user

Figure 19.1
The Backup and
Recovery Process

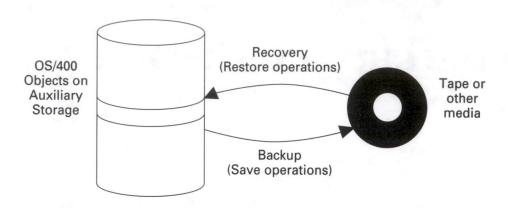

objects. In this chapter, we look at only the OS/400 **save/restore facilities** for database files and associated objects, such as journals and journal receivers.

Saving Database Objects

A full backup and recovery strategy must periodically save everything on the system, including IBM-supplied software, user programs, database objects, and other types of user-created objects. The *AS/400 Backup and Recovery — Basic* and *AS/400 Backup and Recovery — Advanced* manuals provide step-by-step instructions for a complete system backup and recovery plan. The database-related objects that you need to save are

- Physical and logical files
- Logical file access paths (optional)
- Journals
- Journal receivers

You can save these objects by entering an appropriate CL command or by selecting one of the options from the interactive Save or Backup Tasks menus.[1] When you use a Save or Backup Tasks menu option, you're generally prompted for one or more CL commands, so we focus here on the CL commands to understand how to save database objects.

The three commands that save database objects are [2]

- SAVLIB   Saves one or more libraries and all objects in them
- SAVOBJ   Saves one or more specific objects in one or more libraries

---

[1] To display the Save menu, enter Go Save at any command prompt. To display the Backup Tasks menu, enter Go Backup at any command prompt.

[2] There are other SAVxxx commands to save non-database objects.

- SAVCHGOBJ   Saves one or more objects that have been changed since the last time they were saved by a SAVLIB command or since a specified date and time

The SAVLIB command is the simplest way to save database files and related objects. To save the entire APPDTA library, including all the files, programs, journals, journal receivers, and other objects, you could use a command such as the following:

```
SAVLIB LIB( appdta )
       DEV( tap01 )
```

The DEV parameter specifies the name of a storage device, usually a tape drive, to which the save operation writes the backup copy of the objects.[3]

A SAVLIB command can save more than one library in a single operation (i.e., one command execution). The LIB parameter takes a list of libraries. Each item in the list can be a specific library name or a generic library name, such as APP*, which means all libraries that have a name beginning with APP. The following command would save all libraries that begin with APP, as well as the TSTPGM and TSTDTA libraries:

```
SAVLIB LIB( app* tstpgm tstdta )
       DEV( tap01 )
```

There are also several special values you can specify for the LIB parameter instead of a list of libraries:

*ALLUSR	All user (non-IBM) libraries
*NONSYS	All user libraries, the QGPL and QUSRSYS libraries, and IBM licensed program libraries such as QSQL[4]
*IBM	All IBM-supplied libraries

If you specify *ALLUSR, *NONSYS, or *IBM, you can also specify the OMITLIB parameter with one or more library names to exclude from the restore operation, as in the following command:

```
SAVLIB LIB( *allusr )
       DEV( tap01 )
       OMITLIB( tmplib )
```

---

[3] You can also create a disk copy of saved objects by specifying DEV(*SAVF) and SAVF(*save-file-name*) on one of the SAVxxx commands. This lets you create a backup copy to disk and later save the copy to tape. A backup tape produced this way can be used in a subsequent restore operation just as if the tape had been created directly by a save operation.

[4] If you specify LIB(*NONSYS), you must end all other operations on the system before the save operation. You end operations by entering either an ENDSBS SBS(*ALL) or an ENDSYS command.

The big advantage of saving entire libraries is that OS/400 takes care of properly sequencing the order in which objects are restored to the library, in case you need to recover the entire library. As we'll see later in this chapter, the order in which you restore objects is important to a successful recovery.

For large libraries, however, the SAVLIB command has two disadvantages:

- Because the SAVLIB command saves all objects in a library, even those that haven't changed, it may require more tape capacity and time than necessary or available.
- Depending on how the save operation is run, the SAVLIB command may keep objects unavailable for use for longer than desired.

The SAVOBJ command provides an alternative to the SAVLIB command and lets you save specific objects. For example, you can save only the journals and journal receivers in a library — a process that may require much less time and tape capacity than saving the entire contents of the library. The following command saves all journals and journal receivers in the APPDTA library:

```
SAVOBJ OBJ( *all )
       LIB( appdta )
       DEV( tap01 )
       OBJTYPE( *jrn *jrnrcv )
```

For the OBJ parameter, you can specify a list of individual or generic object names instead of *ALL. You can also specify up to 300 individual libraries in the LIB parameter (generic library names aren't allowed on the SAVOBJ command). There's essentially no limit to the number of object types you can specify in the OBJTYPE parameter.

The SAVOBJ command also has an optional FILEMBR parameter that lets you specify specific database file members to save. The following command saves all the members in the SALE95 file but only the JAN and FEB members of the SALE96 file:

```
SAVOBJ OBJ( sale95 sale96 )
       LIB( appdta )
       DEV( tap01 )
       OBJTYPE( *file )
       FILEMBR( ( sale96 ( jan feb ) ) )
```

For each file from which you want to select specific members to save, you code a FILEMBR parameter entry within parentheses. The first item is the file name; the second item is a list of members, also enclosed in parentheses.[5]

---

[5] Don't be intimidated by the way nested parentheses are used for the FILEMBR parameter — the CL command prompter makes it quite easy to enter the file name and member names in the right places.

The SAVOBJ command has two disadvantages:

- You must be sure you explicitly include all objects that should be saved.
- If you need to recover objects, you must manually execute restore commands in the proper sequence (this requirement is discussed later in the chapter).

Another alternative for saving some, but not all, objects in one or more libraries is the SAVCHGOBJ command. This command checks the system-maintained last-changed date that is stored in every object. Based on the SAVCHGOBJ command parameters you specify, only selected objects are saved. For example, to save all objects in the APPDTA library that have been changed since they were last saved by a SAVLIB command, you would use

```
SAVCHGOBJ OBJ( *all )
          LIB( appdta )
          DEV( tap01 )
          OBJTYPE( *all )
          OBJJRN( *yes )
          REFDATE( *savlib )
```

The OBJ parameter can be *ALL or a list of individual and generic object names. The LIB parameter can be *ALLUSR (with the same meaning as for the SAVLIB command) or a list of up to 300 individual library names.

The OBJJRN(*YES) parameter specifies that a changed file should be saved even if it's being journaled. The alternative, OBJJRN(*NO), specifies that a journaled file should not be saved. The purpose of this parameter is to let you avoid saving large, active files that are being journaled because saving the journal and its journal receivers can provide adequate backup (as discussed below).

The REFDATE(*SAVLIB) parameter specifies that any object changed since it was last saved by a SAVLIB command should be saved.[6] You can also specify a date for the REFDATE parameter, along with a time in the REFTIME parameter. If a specific date and time are used, objects that have been changed since that point are saved.

The advantage of the SAVCHGOBJ command is that, like the SAVOBJ command, it saves only some of the objects in the specified libraries, yet it automates the selection of objects so you don't have to explicitly identify them as the SAVOBJ command requires.

As mentioned, for a simple backup strategy, you can use the SAVLIB command regularly (e.g., daily) to make a copy of everything in application libraries. A more complex set of backup procedures can be used to reduce the time and tape capacity required for daily backups. One approach is to do

---

[6] Note that an object changed since it was last saved by a SAVLIB command will be saved even if it has not been changed since it was last saved by a SAVOBJ or SAVCHGOBJ command.

a complete backup every weekend and to execute the following command every night:

```
SAVCHGOBJ OBJ( *all )
         LIB( *allusr )
         DEV( tap01 )
         OBJTYPE( *all )
         OBJJRN( *yes )
         REFDATE( *savlib )
```

This isn't much more complicated than doing a SAVLIB every night, but it avoids repeated backups of unchanged objects. On the other hand, if large application files change every day, this approach may not reduce the size of the daily backups as much as necessary.

Reducing the Time Required for Backups

To minimize the size of daily backups, you can use journaling to avoid backing up production files even if they're changed every day. (Journaling is discussed in Chapter 17.) With this strategy, you still do weekly or other periodic full backups, but on a daily basis you do the following steps:

- Change journals so the current journal receiver is detached and a new journal receiver is used
- Use the following command to save changed journals and journal receivers as well as changed, unjournaled files and other (non-file) changed objects

```
SAVCHGOBJ OBJ( *all )
         LIB( *allusr )
         DEV( tap01 )
         OBJTYPE( *all )
         OBJJRN( *no )
         REFDATE( *savlib )
```

After a full backup is completed, the detached journal receivers can be deleted because they are all on at least two backup tapes: the daily and full backup.[7]

If you use any approach other than saving all your application libraries daily, you should frequently review your procedures to ensure that you're saving all the necessary files and associated objects, such as journal receivers. When you create new application libraries or files or you change which files are being journaled, you may need to revise the commands you use to save selected objects.

If your backup operations are lengthy, the files being saved may be unavailable to applications for too long an interval. You can use the SAVACT parameter on the SAVLIB, SAVOBJ, and SAVCHGOBJ commands to specify

---

[7] Review the section on journaling in Chapter 17 for more detail about a backup strategy using journals.

that applications can access the objects being saved before the save operation completes. The simplest way to use the **save-while-active** feature is to ensure that all applications that update files you want to save are ended before you begin a save operation. Then start the backup using a command such as

```
SAVLIB LIB( appdta )
       DEV( tap01 )
       PRECHK( *yes )
       SAVACT( *synclib )
       SAVACTMSGQ( qsysopr )
```

When you specify SAVACT(*SYNCLIB), the system first establishes a checkpoint for all files in all libraries being saved.[8] When a checkpoint is established, the system sends a message to the message queue specified in the SAVACTMSGQ parameter (in the command above, the system sends a message to QSYSOPR, the system operator's message queue). After the checkpoint for a library is established, applications can update the files in that library while the save process for the library completes. During any overlap of the time the save operation takes to back up a library and the time applications are updating files in the library, OS/400 keeps two separate copies (in memory or on disk) of any changed records: the old version, which gets copied to tape by the save operation, and the new version, which applications see when they access the file.[9] When the save operation completes, the system discards any copies of old versions of changed records.

The optional PRECHK(*YES) parameter, which can be used on any of the three save commands, specifies that the system should make certain all objects specified to be saved exist, are available (i.e., not locked by an application), and aren't damaged before any objects are saved. This option is useful if you want to ensure that a save operation backs up all the objects you specify. Without PRECHK(*YES), the system simply skips any object that can't be saved (e.g., because it's in use) and issues diagnostic messages describing the

[8] Other options for the SAVACT parameter are

*NO, the default

*LIB, which synchronizes the checkpoint for files in each individual library being saved rather than synchronizing the checkpoint across all libraries

*SYSDFN, no synchronization of checkpoints

The *SYNCLIB option is generally the best choice because it assures the saved copies of all files are synchronized, thus simplifying recovery.

[9] The save-while-active feature also lets you start a save while applications are updating the files. This capability can be used when you can't end applications that update the file for any length of time. Some businesses run their operations 24 hours a day, 7 days a week, and need nonstop availability of application files. There's a significant disadvantage to beginning a save operation while an application is updating one or more files, however. The necessary recovery steps may be much more complex to bring all the files back to a consistent state because some application updates may be on the backup tape and others may not. If you end applications until a checkpoint is established, you don't have this problem because none of the file updates that occur after the checkpoint are included in the save operation.

problem. If you don't use PRECHK(*YES), be sure you check all messages after a save operation to ensure that no objects you expected to be saved were skipped.

Figure 19.2 lists commonly used parameters on the SAVLIB, SAVOBJ, and SAVCHGOBJ commands. The *CL Reference* manual and on-line Help provide detailed explanations of these and other save commands.

Figure 19.2
Commonly Used Save
Command Parameters

Parameter	SAVLIB	SAVOBJ	SAVCHGOBJ	Purpose
Selection parameters				
OBJ		✔	✔	Objects to save
OBJTYPE		✔	✔	Object types to save
OBJJRN			✔	Save journaled objects
REFDATE			✔	Save objects changed since this date (or since object was saved with the SAVLIB command)
REFTIME			✔	Save objects changed since this time
LIB	✔	✔	✔	Libraries to save
OMITLIB	✔		✔	Libraries to omit from save
FILEMBR		✔		Database file members to save
ACCPTH	✔	✔	✔	Whether to save logical file access paths
SAVFDTA	✔	✔	✔	Whether to save contents of save file objects
Other parameters				
DEV	✔	✔	✔	Device on which data is saved
VOL	✔	✔	✔	Tape volume identifiers

Figure 19.2 continued

Figure 19.2
Continued

Parameter	SAVLIB	SAVOBJ	SAVCHGOBJ	Purpose
SEQNBR	✔	✔	✔	Which tape file sequence number to start writing saved data to
SAVF	✔	✔	✔	Name of save file to write saved data to
UPDHST	✔	✔	✔	Whether to update the last saved date attribute of saved objects
PRECHK	✔	✔	✔	Whether to check that all requested objects can be saved before beginning the save operation
SAVACT	✔	✔	✔	Whether to allow applications to access objects while they're being saved
SAVACTMSGQ	✔	✔	✔	Message queue to which checkpoint messages should be sent
STG	✔	✔		Whether to free system storage for the contents of saved objects after they're saved
DTACPR	✔	✔	✔	Whether to perform data compression on the saved data

Handling Dependent Database Objects

Various database-related objects have dependencies on one another that you must take into account when you back up your database. These dependencies include

- Access paths for physical and logical files
- Record formats shared by multiple files
- Logical files defined over physical files
- SQL/400 views defined over other views
- Journals in use for physical files

- Journal receivers attached to journals
- Trigger programs associated with a physical file
- Primary, unique, and foreign key constraints associated with a physical file

The simplest way to deal with dependencies is to observe three rules:

1. Place all dependent objects in the same library as the referenced object (e.g., place logical files, journals, journal receivers, and trigger programs in the same library as the associated physical file).
2. Save the library containing all related objects using a SAVLIB command.
3. If necessary, use the RSTLIB command to restore the entire library.

When all dependent objects are in the same library and all are saved together with the SAVLIB command, a subsequent RSTLIB command automatically sequences the restore steps so all dependencies are preserved.

Even if your save procedures don't use a SAVLIB command for all save operations (e.g., you use a SAVCHGOBJ command for daily backups), it's much simpler to manage backup and recovery if you keep dependent objects in the same library. When you follow that guideline, the basic rule for full recovery is to make sure a referenced object exists in the library before you restore a dependent object. For example, make sure a physical file exists before you restore any dependent logical files. Figure 19.3 lists the order to follow in restoring database objects.

Figure 19.3
Order to Restore Objects

1. A journal before its journal receivers
2. A journal before physical files that use the journal
3. A physical file before logical files defined over it
4. A file whose record format is shared by another file before the file that shares the format
5. A trigger program before physical files that use the trigger program

Restoring Objects

There are two commands to restore database objects: RSTLIB (Restore Library) and RSTOBJ (Restore Object).[10] You can use these commands with backup copies produced by the three save commands as shown in the following table:

---

[10] There are other RSTxxx commands to restore non-database objects.

Save Command	Valid Restore Commands
SAVLIB	RSTLIB, RSTOBJ
SAVOBJ	RSTOBJ
SAVCHGOBJ	RSTOBJ

For recovery purposes, you generally restore objects (including entire libraries) to the same library from which they were saved. The following command shows how you would restore the entire APPDTA library from a backup tape created with the SAVLIB command:

```
RSTLIB SAVLIB( appdta )
       DEV( tap01 )
```

However, you can specify the RSTLIB parameter with a library name different from the original, if you want to create a new library or restore individual objects to a different library, as in the following command:

```
RSTLIB SAVLIB( appdta )
       DEV( tap01 )
       RSTLIB( newappdta )
```

The RSTLIB command restores entire libraries.[11] With the RSTLIB command, you can specify a value for the SAVLIB parameter that's one of the following:

library-name	An explicit library name
*ALLUSR	All user (non-IBM) libraries
*NONSYS	All user libraries, the QGPL and QUSRSYS libraries, and IBM licensed program libraries such as QSQL
*IBM	All IBM-supplied libraries

For application database recovery, you typically specify an explicit library name or *ALLUSR.[12] If you specify *ALLUSR, *NONSYS, or *IBM, you can also specify the OMITLIB parameter with one or more library names to exclude from the restore operation.

The RSTOBJ command lets you select which objects are restored from a single library.[13] The RSTOBJ command's OBJ parameter lets you specify *ALL, to restore all saved objects, or a list of objects to restore. If you specify

---

[11] Note that all three save commands let you save objects from multiple libraries in one operation. The RSTLIB command lets you restore multiple libraries, but you can't explicitly specify a list of objects to restore.

[12] If you specify SAVLIB(*NONSYS) or SAVLIB(*IBM), you must end all other operations on the system before the restore operation. As noted in Footnote 4, you end operations by entering either an ENDSBS SBS(*ALL) or an ENDSYS command.

[13] The RSTOBJ command lets you explicitly specify which objects to restore, but all the specified objects must be in a single library. There is no command to explicitly specify a list of

a list, each item in the list can be an object name (e.g., SALE96) or a generic object name (e.g., CUST*, which indicates that all objects whose name begins with CUST should be restored). To restore the SALE96 file to the APPDTA library, you could use the following command:

```
RSTOBJ OBJ( sale96 )
       SAVLIB( appdta )
       DEV( tap01 )
       OBJTYPE( *file )
```

Both the RSTLIB and RSTOBJ commands have an OPTION parameter that lets you specify how to restore objects based on whether the objects already exist on the system. The four values for the OPTION parameter are

*ALL	All objects on the backup tape and selected for restoring are restored. If an object on the backup tape has the same object type and name as an existing object in the target library, the existing object is replaced by the saved version. This is the default parameter value.
*NEW	Only objects on the backup tape that do not exist in the target library are restored. This option adds new objects to the target library or restores objects that were deleted after they were saved.
*OLD	Only objects on the backup tape that do exist in the target library are restored. This option replaces existing objects with a previously saved version.
*FREE	Only objects on the backup tape that exist in the target library and had their storage freed (i.e., with the STG(*FREE) parameter) on a previous save operation are restored. This option replaces existing objects that had their storage freed with a previously saved version.

For recovery purposes, OPTION(*ALL) is most commonly used. Be careful when using one of the other OPTION parameter values that you get all the objects you want — and no others — restored. Generally, if only some database objects need to be recovered, you can use the RSTOBJ command to select exactly which objects to restore.

When you're restoring to an existing database file, you can use the MBROPT parameter to select which file members are restored. The available options are

objects to restore from multiple libraries in a single operation. This task requires one RSTOBJ command for each library.

*MATCH	If the saved copy of the file and the existing file don't have exactly the same set of members, the restore fails. This is the default option.
*ALL	All members of the saved copy of the file are restored.
*NEW	Only members of the saved copy of the file that are not members of the existing file are restored.
*OLD	Only members of the saved copy of the file that are members of the existing file are restored.

The RSTOBJ command's FILEMBR parameter lets you list specific members to restore. It has the same syntax as the FILEMBR parameter on the save commands described earlier.

When you restore a database file that already exists on the system, the system restores the file's data and access paths but keeps the existing file's file attributes. To restore the file attributes of the saved copy of the file, you should delete the existing file before you restore the saved copy. The same rules apply for member attributes.[14]

Figure 19.4 shows commonly used RSTLIB and RSTOBJ command parameters.

Saving and Restoring Access Paths

When you save a nonsource physical file, the system automatically saves any access paths associated with it, including a DDS-defined key or the access paths for primary, unique, or foreign key constraints. Access paths for logical files are saved only when you specify the ACCPTH(*YES) parameter on a save command. Note that logical file access paths are saved when you save the physical file because the access path is dependent on the contents of the physical file.[15]

When you restore a physical file, the system always restores rather than rebuilds the physical file's access paths (if any). Logical file access paths are restored only if all the following conditions are met:[16]

---

[14] If a file exists with the same name and library as a saved file, but the two versions have different creation dates, the system can't tell whether these are the same file or whether they're different files with the same name. By default, the saved copy of the file won't be restored in this situation. If you specify the ALWOBJDIF(*ALL) parameter on a RSTLIB or RSTOBJ command, the system renames the existing file before it restores the saved file. The same principles apply to a member of a file that has the same name but different creation dates on the existing and saved versions of the member

[15] It wouldn't make sense to save a logical file's access path separately from the physical file data because they could easily get out of synch. Even with the ACCPTH(*YES) parameter, a logical file access path will not be saved if it's defined with MAINT(*REBLD) or if the logical file spans physical files that aren't in the same library or that aren't being saved on the same command.

[16] In addition, there are some special considerations for shared access paths. These are covered in the *AS/400 Backup and Recovery — Basic* manual.

Figure 19.4

Commonly Used Restore
Command Parameters

Parameter	RSTLIB	RSTOBJ	Purpose
Selection parameters			
OBJ		✔	Objects to restore
OBJTYPE		✔	Object types to restore
SAVLIB	✔	✔	Libraries to restore
OMITLIB	✔		Libraries to omit from restore
OPTION	✔	✔	Whether to restore old, new, or all objects
MBROPT	✔	✔	Whether to restore old, new, or all members
FILEMBR		✔	Database file members to restore
Other parameters			
DEV	✔	✔	Device that holds data to be restored
VOL	✔	✔	Tape volume identifiers
SEQNBR	✔	✔	Which tape file sequence number to start reading saved data from
SAVF	✔	✔	Name of save file to read saved data from
RSTLIB	✔	✔	Library to which objects should be restored

- The logical file's access path was saved (i.e., ACCPTH(*YES) was specified on the save command).
- If the logical file already exists, it doesn't have the MAINT(*REBLD) file attribute.
- All the logical file's based-on physical files are in the same library and are being restored by the same command as the logical file.

For large physical files, saving and restoring logical file access paths can save significant time because the system doesn't have to rebuild the access path. Be sure to consider both where you place logical and physical files (in the same library simplifies things considerably) and how you save groups of files (saving dependent files together lets you save logical file access paths, if you want).

Required Authority for Save and Restore Operations

To save and restore objects, you need either the *SAVSYS special authority defined in your user profile or adequate authority to the saved libraries and objects as well as other objects. The following list describes the basic requirements for database-related objects:[17]

> *For save and restore operations:*
>> *USE authority to the tape or other device description and device file specified on the DEV parameter[18]
>
> *For save operations:*
>> *EXECUTE authority to or ownership of the specified libraries containing saved objects
>>
>> *OBJEXIST authority to or ownership of any objects that are saved
>
> *For restore operations:*
>> *ADD and *EXECUTE authority to or ownership of the specified libraries containing restored objects.
>>
>> *OBJEXIST authority to or ownership of any existing objects that will be replaced by a restore operation
>>
>> *ADD authority to the user profile that owns any (new) objects that don't already exist at the time of a restore operation

In most AS/400 installations, the user profile for the person responsible for performing save/restore operations is assigned the *SAVSYS authority. This assures that all objects can be saved.

Other AS/400 Recovery Facilities

In addition to the save/restore facilities we've looked at, the AS/400 has several other features that can be used to increase system (including database) availability and recovery. These features include

- Auxiliary storage pools
- Mirrored disk protection
- Device parity protection

On the AS/400, disk storage is referred to as auxiliary storage. When IBM ships an AS/400, all disk storage is organized as one **auxiliary storage pool (ASP)**, known as the system ASP. By default, OS/400 spreads all stored objects, including programs, database files, and other types of objects more or

---

[17] In addition, on a restore command, if the VOL(*SAVVOL) parameter is specified, you must have *USE authority to the library from which the object was originally saved.

[18] Or, to the save file specified on the SAVF parameter, if DEV(*SAVF) is specified.

less evenly across all the disk drives on the system. This approach improves performance because the system can be retrieving data from multiple drives simultaneously. But if one disk drive fails, the entire system becomes unusable because pieces of many objects may be stored on the damaged drive. On AS/400s that have multiple disk drives, you can organize one or more disk drive units into user ASPs and specify on which ASP an object, such as a database file, will be stored. Then if one disk drive in an ASP fails, only objects stored in the ASP need to be recovered after the drive is replaced. Organizing AS/400 disk storage into ASPs doesn't prevent loss due to disk failure, but it can help limit the scope of the damage when a drive failure occurs.

Mirrored disk protection is a way to configure AS/400 hardware so there are duplicates of one or more of the following disk-related components:

- Disk units
- Disk controllers
- Disk I/O processors
- A data bus

If an AS/400 is configured with duplicates of a particular component and that component fails, the system keeps running using the remaining component. The failed component can be replaced while the system continues running. This facility provides substantial increase in availability but, of course, requires buying extra hardware.

Device parity protection is an optional hardware feature that uses arrays of disks to hold data and redundant parity bytes that can be used to reconstruct data if one of the disks in an array fails. Device parity protection offers similar benefits to fully mirrored disk protection but doesn't require full duplication of disk units. Unlike mirrored disk protection, however, device parity protection can't protect against disk controller, I/O processor, or data bus failures.

The *AS/400 Backup and Recovery — Basic* manual provides additional information about these features.

Chapter Summary

Making regular backup copies of database files and other objects is necessary so that recovery is possible when an unexpected event loses or corrupts database files. The SAVLIB, SAVOBJ, and SAVCHGOBJ commands are the commands to save a backup copy of DB2/400 database files, journals, journal receivers, and other related objects. These commands make a copy of entire libraries or selected objects.

Regularly saving entire libraries with the SAVLIB command provides the simplest approach to backup but may require more time and tape capacity than desired. The SAVOBJ and SAVCHGOBJ commands can be used along with journaling to reduce the amount of data that has to be saved for daily backups. The save commands' SAVACT parameter lets you run applications during part or all of a save operation for files used by the applications, thus reducing the amount of time files are unavailable during the backup process.

When recovery is necessary (or to make a new copy of a saved object), you can use the RSTLIB and RSTOBJ commands to restore saved libraries or selected objects from a previous backup tape. The restore commands let you select whether to restore all saved objects and file members or whether to restore only existing or new objects and members.

For a complete recovery, related objects must be restored in the proper sequence. When related objects are in the same library and the SAVLIB and RSTLIB commands are used, the system automatically restores them in the proper sequence. In other cases, a referenced object (such as a physical file) must be restored before a dependent object (such as a logical file) to get a complete recovery.

Logical file access paths can be saved and restored along with a physical file. Although this practice requires more time during save operations, it can significantly reduce the time needed for a complete recovery because the system may not have to rebuild the saved access paths.

Proper authority is required to save and restore objects. Generally this authority is the *SAVSYS authority assigned to the user profile of the person responsible for backup and recovery operations.

The AS/400 has additional facilities to increase database availability and recovery. These include user-defined auxiliary storage pools, mirrored disk protection, and device parity protection.

Key Terms

auxiliary storage pool (ASP)
backup
device parity protection

mirrored disk protection
recovery
save/restore facilities

save-while-active

Exercises

Note: For all exercises below that require you to code a save or restore command, assume the tape device is named TAP01.

1. Describe three events that might cause a database file to be lost or become corrupted.

2. Rank the following items by how serious it would be to lose them. Explain your reasons for the rankings.

   - A database file object
   - A logical file object
   - The DDS source code for a physical file
   - The DDS source code for a logical file
   - The only backup tape you have for a physical file

3. For each column in the following table, rank each of the three save commands according to the criteria listed in the column heading. Briefly explain your reasons for each column's rankings.

4. Show two different save commands to save all the objects in library PRDDTA.

5. For each command you created in Exercise 4, code the valid restore commands to restore all the objects you saved. If more than one restore command is valid, show both alternatives.

6. Show the save command to save all *FILE, *JRN, *JRNRCV, and *PGM objects in libraries LIBA, LIBB, and LIBC that have been changed since they were last saved by a SAVLIB command. Do not include files that are being journaled.

7. Why do you think the SAVCHGOBJ command doesn't have an option to save only objects that have been changed since they were saved by any save command, not just the SAVLIB command?

   Hint: Consider how frequently different types of production database files might change.

Command	Simplest backup (1=simplest; 3=most complex)	Simplest restore (1=simplest; 3=most complex)	Reduces time for daily backups (1=requires shortest time; 3=requires longest time)
SAVLIB			
SAVOBJ			
SAVCHGOBJ			

Exercises Continued

Exercises continued

8. Show the restore command to restore only existing file objects and their members in the APPDTA library.

9. What do you think is the minimum number of tape backup copies of a physical file you should have at all times? In your answer, consider the possibility that while you are restoring a file from a backup tape, the tape drive malfunctions and damages the tape. What impact would your answer have on regular backup procedures?

Appendix A

Data Description Specification Keywords

Using the DDS Keyword Descriptions

The keywords for each file type (physical and logical) are listed in alphabetical order. Each entry includes a brief description of the keyword's function and its parameters (if any). For each keyword, Level and Group categories are specified. The Level category refers to the section of DDS source in which the keyword is used:

Physical Files	Logical Files
File	File
Record	Record
Field	Field
Key	Key
	Join
	Select/Omit

The Group category indicates the general purpose of the keyword:

- Validity Check
- Edit
- Join
- Miscellaneous
- Access path
- Naming and referencing
- Select/omit
- Text definition

Parameters that require one of several values show the choices separated by a vertical bar (|). For example

```
CHECK(AB | ME | MF | M10 | M10F | M11 | M11F | VN | VNE)
```

The CHECK keyword allows AB or ME or MF, et cetera, as a parameter value. Parameters that are optional are enclosed in square brackets ([ ]). For example

```
COLHDG('line-1' ['line-2' ['line-3']])
```

The COLHDG keyword requires at least one string value (for line 1), and allows one or two additional lines of text to be specified.

Physical File DDS Keywords

ABSVAL	**Absolute value**
	Causes the sign of the key field to be ignored when sequencing values (use absolute values).

Level	Group
Key field	Access path

Example: ABSVAL

ALIAS	**Alternative name**
	Provides an alternative name to be used for a field. The alias name must be 1 to 30 characters. The first character must be A through Z. Subsequent characters must be A–Z, 0–9, or underscrore (_).

ALIAS(alternative-name)

Level	Group
Field	Naming and referencing

Example: ALIAS(CUSTOMERNAME)

ALTSEQ	**Alternative collating sequence**
	Uses the specified alternate collating sequence table for key fields when sequencing records.

ALTSEQ([library-name/] table-name)

Level	Group
File	Access path

Example: ALTSEQ(APPDTA/TABLE01)

ALWNULL	**Allow nulls**
	Allow nulls for field.

Level	Group
Field	Miscellaneous

Example: ALWNULL

CCSID	**Coded character set identifier**
	Specifies a coded character set identifier for character fields.

CCSID(value)

Level	Group
File	Miscellaneous
Field	Miscellaneous

Example: `CCSID(501)`

CHECK   ## Check

CHECK has no effect in physical files. If the field you are describing is referenced as an input-capable field at display file creation time, CHECK is duplicated into the display file. In the display file, CHECK tests the validity of data entered into the input-capable field.

```
CHECK(AB | ME | MF | M10 | M10F | M11 | M11F | VN
     | VNE)
```

Value	Meaning
AB	Allow blank
ME	Mandatory enter
MF	Mandatory fill
M10	IBM modulus 10 self-check algorithm
M10F	IBM modulus 10F self-check algorithm
M11	IBM modulus 11 self-check algorithm
M11F	IBM modulus 11F self-check algorithm
VN	Validate name
VNE	Validate name extended

Level	Group
Field	Validity check

Example: `CHECK(AB)`

CHKMSGID   ## Check message identifier

CHKMSGID has no effect in physical files. However, if the field you are describing is referenced during the display file creation time, CHKMSGID identifies an error message that is issued when a validity-checking error is detected on fields that contain the following keywords:

Keyword	Meaning
CHECK(M10)	IBM modulus 10 self-check algorithm
CHECK(M11)	IBM modulus 11 self-check algorithm
CHECK(VN)	Validate name
CHECK(VNE)	Validate name extended

Keyword	Meaning
CMP, COMP	Comparison
RANGE	Range
VALUES	Values

```
CHKMSGID(message-id [library/] message-file
         [message-data-field])
```

Level	Group
Field	Validity check

Example:
```
CHKMSGID(USR1357 APPDTA/USRMSGF &MSGFLD1)
```

CMP

Comparison

See COMP (the preferred spelling).

COLHDG

Column heading

Specifies a column heading for a field (used by Query, SDA, DFU, and other utilities).

```
COLHDG('line-1' ['line-2' ['line-3']])
```

Level	Group
Field	Text definition

Example: `COLHDG('Customer' 'Name')`

COMP

Comparison

For physical files, COMP has no effect. If the field you are describing is referenced by an input-capable field at display file creation time, COMP is duplicated into the display file, where it tests the validity of data keyed into the input-capable field.

For COMP, the test is a comparison between the value of the field specified in positions 19-28 and the value on the COMP keyword.

```
COMP(relational-operator  value)
```

Valid relational operators are

Operator	Meaning
EQ	equal
NE	not equal
LT	less than
NL	not less than

Operator	Meaning
GT	greater than
NG	not greater than
LE	less than or equal
GE	greater than or equal

Level	Group
Field	Validity check

Example: `COMP(GE 5000)`

DATFMT   **Date format**

Specifies the format of the date field.

`DATFMT(date-format)`

Format description	Parameter	Format
Job default	*JOB	
Month/Day/Year	*MDY	mm/dd/yy
Day/Month/Year	*DMY	dd/mm/yy
Year/Month/Day	*YMD	yy/mm/dd
Julian	*JUL	yy/ddd
ISO	*ISO	yyyy-mm-dd
IBM USA	*USA	mm/dd/yyyy
IBM Europe	*EUR	dd.mm.yyyy
Japanese Industrial Standard Christian Era	*JIS	yyyy-mm-dd

Level	Group
Field	Miscellaneous

Example: `DATFMT(*ISO)`

DATSEP   **Date separator**

Specifies the separator character for a date field.

`DATSEP(*JOB | 'date-separator')`

Valid date separator values are slash ('/'), dash ('-'), period ('.'), comma (','), or blank (' ')

Level	Group
Field	Miscellaneous

Example: `DATSEP('/')`

DESCEND	**Descend**
	Values in a key field are retrieved in descending sequence.

Level	Group
Key field	Access path

Example: `DESCEND`

DFT	**Default**
	Specifies a default value for the field.

```
DFT('value' | X'hexadecimal-value' |
    numeric-value | *NULL)
```

Level	Group
Field	Miscellaneous

Example: `DFT('XYZ')`

DIGIT	**Digit**
	Only the digit portion (low-order 4 bits) of each byte of the key field is used to build a key value.

Level	Group
Key field	Access path

Example: `DIGIT`

EDTCDE	**Edit code**
	Specifies the edit code by which field values are to be displayed. EDTCDE does not affect the physical file you are describing, but can be duplicated into display or printer file descriptions when the field is referenced during display or printer file creation.

```
EDTCDE(edit-code [* | floating-currency-symbol])
```

Level	Group
Field	Edit

Example: `EDTCDE(K  $)`

EDTWRD   **Edit word**

Specifies an edit word that describes the form in which values are to be displayed. EDTWRD does not affect the physical file you are describing, but can be duplicated into display or printer file descriptions when the field is referenced during display or printer file creation.

```
EDTWRD('edit-word')
```

Level	Group
Field	Edit

Example: `EDTWRD('$     0.  &CR')`

FCFO   **First-changed first-out**

Specifies that records retrieved from same physical file member and which have duplicate key values are retrieved in a first-changed first-out order.

Level	Group
File	Access path

Example: `FCFO`

FIFO   **First-in first-out**

Specifies that records retrieved from same physical file member and which have duplicate key values are retrieved in a first-in first-out order.

Level	Group
File	Access path

Example: `FIFO`

FLTPCN   **Floating point precision**

Specifies the precision of a floating-point field.

```
FLTPCN(*SINGLE | *DOUBLE)
```

Level	Group
Field	Miscellaneous

Example: `FLTPCN(*SINGLE)`

FORMAT	**Format**
	Uses previously described record format.

```
FORMAT([library-name/] database-file-name)
```

Level	Group
Record	Naming and referencing

Example: `FORMAT(APPDTA/CUSTOMER)`

LIFO	**Last-in first-out**
	Specifies that records retrieved from same physical file member and which have duplicate key values are retrieved in a last-in first-out order.

Level	Group
File	Access path

Example: `LIFO`

NOALTSEQ	**No alternative collating sequence**
	The alternative collating sequence is not to be used for the key field.

Level	Group
Key field	Access path

Example: `NOALTSEQ`

RANGE	**Range**
	For physical files, RANGE has no effect. If the field you are describing is referenced by an input-capable field at display file creation time, RANGE is duplicated into the display file, where it tests the validity of data keyed into the input-capable field.

For RANGE, the test is that the value of the field specified in positions 19-28 must be greater than or equal to the low value and less than or equal to the high value specified on the RANGE keyword.

```
RANGE(low-value  high-value)
```

Level	Group
Field	Validity check

Example: `RANGE(1000  5000)`

REF	**Reference**

The system refers to the specified database file (and optionally the specified record format) for referenced field specifications.

```
REF([library-name/] database-file-name
    [format-name])
```

Level	Group
File	Naming and referencing

Example: REF(APPDTA/FIELDDFN)

REFFLD	**Referenced field**

The field being defined refers to the definition of the field specified on the REFFLD keyword. If a record format name and/or a database file name are also specified on the REFFLD keyword, they qualify the referenced field's location.

```
REFFLD([record-format-name/]
       referenced-field-name
       [*SRC | [library-name/]
       database-file-name])
```

Level	Group
Field	Naming and referencing

Example: REFFLD(SHPCITY)

REFSHIFT	**Referenced shift**

For physical files, REFSHIFT has no effect. If the field you are describing is referenced by an input-capable field at display file creation time, REFSHIFT is duplicated into the display file, where it specifies a keyboard shift.

```
REFSHIFT(keyboard-shift)
```

The valid keyboard shift codes are

Code	Meaning	Data Types
X	Alphabetic only	Character
A	Alphanumeric	Character
N	Numeric shift	Character or numeric
S	Signed numeric	Numeric
Y	Numeric only	Numeric

Code	Meaning	Data Types
W	Katakana	Character
I	Inhibit keyboard entry	Character or numeric
D	Digits only	Character or numeric
M	Numeric only character	Character
F	Floating point	Numeric

Level	Group
Field	Naming and referencing

Example: `REFSHIFT(X)`

SIGNED

Signed

The sign of a field is considered when sequencing values.

Level	Group
Key field	Access path

Example: `SIGNED`

TEXT

Text

Specifies descriptive text for the record format or field.

`TEXT('description')`

Level	Group
Record	Text definition
Field	Text definition

Example: `TEXT('Customer name')`

TIMFMT

Time format

Specifies the format of a time field.

`TIMFMT(time-format)`

Format description	Parameter	Format
Hours:Minutes:Seconds	*HMS	hh:mm:ss
ISO	*ISO	hh.mm.ss
IBM USA	*USA	hh:mm am or pm
IBM Europe	*EUR	hh.mm.ss
Japanese Industrial Standard Christian Era	*JIS	hh:mm:ss

Level	Group
Field	Miscellaneous

Example: `TIMFMT(*ISO)`

TIMSEP

Time separator

Specifies the separator character used in a time field.

`TIMSEP(*JOB | 'time-separator')`

Valid time separator values are: colon (':'), period ('.'), and blank (' ') .

Level	Group
Field	Miscellaneous

Example: `TIMSEP(':')`

UNIQUE

Unique

Specifies that key values must be unique. (No duplicate key values allowed.)

If the optional parameter is specified, it determines whether nulls in key field(s) of multiple records cause duplicates. *INCNULL is the default and includes records with nulls for a key field when determining whether two records have the same key value. *EXCNULL excludes all records with nulls when checking for duplicates.

`UNIQUE[(*INCNULL | *EXCNULL)]`

Level	Group
File	Access path

Example: `UNIQUE`

UNSIGNED

Unsigned

The field is sequenced as unsigned binary data.

Level	Group
Key field	Access path

Example: `UNSIGNED`

VALUES

Values

For physical files, VALUES has no effect. If the field you are describing is referenced by an input-capable field at display file creation time, VALUES is duplicated into the display file, where it tests the validity of data keyed into the input-capable field.

For VALUES, the test is that the value of the field specified in positions 19-28 must be equal to one of the values specified on the VALUES keyword.

```
VALUES(value-1 [value-2 ... [value-100]])
```

Level	Group
Field	Validity check

Example: `VALUES( 'A'  'B'  'C')`

VARLEN

Variable-length field

Defines a character field as a variable-length field.

For a physical file, you can specify the optional allocated-length parameter, which determines the number of bytes allocated for the field in the fixed portion of the file. If you do not specify the allocated-length parameter, all data for the field is stored in the variable length portion of the file.

The allocated-length parameter (if any) must be between 1 and the maximum length of the field specified in positions 30 - 34.

```
VARLEN[(allocated-length)]
```

Level	Group
Field	Miscellaneous

Example: `VARLEN(100)`

ZONE

Zone

Only the zone portion (high-order 4 bits) of each byte of the key field is used to build a key value.

Level	Group
Key field	Access path

Example: `ZONE`

Logical File DDS Keywords

ABSVAL	**Absolute value**

Causes the sign of the key field to be ignored when sequencing values (use absolute values).

Level	Group
Key field	Access path

Example: `ABSVAL`

ALIAS	**Alternative name**

Provides an alternative name to be used for a field. The alias name must be 1 to 30 characters. The first character must be A through Z. Subsequent characters must be A–Z, 0–9, or underscrore (_).

`ALIAS(alternative-name)`

Level	Group
Field	Naming and referencing

Example: `ALIAS(CUSTOMERNAME)`

ALL	**All**

Selects or omits all records not meeting the previously specified select/omit rules.

Level	Group
Select/omit	Select/omit

Example: `ALL`

ALTSEQ	**Alternative collating sequence**

Specifies alternate collating sequence for key fields.

`ALTSEQ([library-name/] table-name)`

Level	Group
File	Access path

Example: `ALTSEQ(APPDTA/TABLE01)`

CHECK	**Check**

CHECK has no effect in logical files. However, if the field you are describing is referenced as an input-capable field at display file creation time, CHECK is duplicated into the display file. In the display file,

CHECK tests the validity of data entered into the input-capable field.

```
CHECK(AB | ME | MF | M10 | M10F | M11 | M11F | VN
      | VNE)
```

Value	Meaning
AB	Allow blank
ME	Mandatory enter
MF	Mandatory fill
M10	IBM modulus 10 self-check algorithm
M10F	IBM modulus 10F self-check algorithm
M11	IBM modulus 11 self-check algorithm
M11F	IBM modulus 11F self-check algorithm
VN	Validate name
VNE	Validate name extended

Level	Group
Field	Validity check

Example: CHECK(AB)

CHKMSGID — Check message identifier

CHKMSGID has no effect in logical files. If the field you are describing is referenced during the display file creation time, CHKMSGID identifies an error message that is issued when a validity-checking error is detected on fields that contain the following keywords:

Keyword	Meaning
M10	IBM modulus 10 self-check algorithm
M11	IBM modulus 11 self-check algorithm
VN	Validate name
VNE	Validate name extended
CMP, COMP	Comparison
RANGE	Range
VALUES	Values

```
CHKMSGID(message-id [library/] message-file
         [message-data-field])
```

Level	Group
Field	Validity check

Example:

```
CHKMSGID(USR1357 APPDTA/USRMSGF &MSGFLD1)
```

CMP	**Comparison**
	See COMP (the preferred spelling).

COLHDG	**Column heading**

Specifies a column heading for a field (used by Query, SDA, DFU, and other utilities).

```
COLHDG('line-1' ['line-2' ['line-3']])
```

Level	Group
Field	Text

Example: `COLHDG('Customer' 'Name')`

COMP	**Comparison**

When specified at the field level, COMP has no effect. If the field you are describing is referenced by an input-capable field at display file creation time, COMP is duplicated into the display file, where it tests the validity of data keyed into the input-capable field.

When specified at the select/omit level, this entry selects or omits records retrieved from the physical file(s) on which the logical file is based if they pass the specified test.

For COMP, the test is a comparison between the value of the field specified in positions 19-28 and the value or field on the COMP keyword.

Field-level syntax:

```
COMP(relational-operator  value)
```

Select/omit-level syntax:

```
COMP(relational-operator  value | field name
    | *NULL)
```

Valid relational operators are

Operator	Meaning
EQ	equal
NE	not equal
LT	less than
NL	not less than
GT	greater than
NG	not greater than
LE	less than or equal
GE	greater than or equal

Level	Group
Field	Validity check
Select/omit	Select/omit

Example: COMP(GE 5000)

CONCAT — **Concatenate**

Concatenates fields from the physical file on which this logical file is based into this logical file field.

CONCAT(field-1 field-2 ...)

Level	Group
Field	Naming and referencing

Example: CONCAT(FSTNAM MDLINL LSTNAM)

DATFMT — **Date format**

Specifies format of the date field.

DATFMT(date-format)

Format description	Parameter	Format
Job default	*JOB	
Month/Day/Year	*MDY	mm/dd/yy
Day/Month/Year	*DMY	dd/mm/yy
Year/Month/Day	*YMD	yy/mm/dd
Julian	*JUL	yy/ddd
ISO	*ISO	yyyy-mm-dd
IBM USA	*USA	mm/dd/yyyy
IBM Europe	*EUR	dd.mm.yyyy
Japanese Industrial Standard Christian Era	*JIS	yyyy-mm-dd

Level	Group
Field	Miscellaneous

Example: DATFMT(*ISO)

DATSEP — **Date separator**

Specifies the separator character for a date field.

DATSEP(*JOB | 'date-separator')

Valid date separator values are slash ('/'), dash ('-'), period ('.'), comma (',') or blank (' ').

Level	Group
Field	Miscellaneous

Example: `DATSEP('/')`

DESCEND

Descend

Values in a key field are retrieved in descending sequence.

Level	Group
Key field	Access path

Example: `DESCEND`

DIGIT

Digit

Only the digit portion (low-order 4 bits) of each byte of the key field is used to build a key value.

Level	Group
Key field	Access path

Example: `DIGIT`

DYNSLT

Dynamic select

Specifies that dynamic record selection is to be used.

Level	Group
File	Select/omit

Example: `DYNSLT`

EDTCDE

Edit code

Specifies the edit code by which field values are to be displayed. EDTCDE does not affect the logical file you are describing, but can be duplicated into display or printer file descriptions when the field is referenced during display or printer file creation.

`EDTCDE(edit-code [* | floating-currency-symbol])`

Level	Group
Field	Edit

Example: `EDTCDE(K  $)`

EDTWRD **Edit word**

Specifies an edit word that describes the form in which values are to be displayed. EDTWRD does not affect the logical file you are describing, but can be duplicated into display or printer file descriptions when the field is referenced during display or printer file creation.

```
EDTWRD('edit-word')
```

Level	Group
Field	Edit

Example: `EDTWRD('$    Ø.    &CR')`

FCFO **First-changed first-out**

Specifies that records retrieved from same logical file member and which have duplicate key values are retrieved in a first-changed first-out order.

Level	Group
File	Access path

Example: `FCFO`

FIFO **First-in first-out**

Specifies that records retrieved from same logical file member and which have duplicate key values are retrieved in a first-in first-out order.

Level	Group
File	Access path

Example: `FIFO`

FLTPCN **Floating point precision**

Specifies the precision of a floating-point field.

```
FLTPCN(*SINGLE | *DOUBLE)
```

Level	Group
Field	Miscellaneous

Example: `FLTPCN(*SINGLE)`

FORMAT	**Format**
	Uses previously described record format.

```
FORMAT([library-name/] database-file-name)
```

Level	Group
Record	Naming and referencing

Example: `FORMAT(APPDTA/CUSTOMER)`

JDFTVAL	**Join default values**
	Specifies that the system is to provide default values for fields when a join to a secondary file produces no records.
	This keyword is valid only with join logical files.

Level	Group
File	Join

Example: `JDFTVAL`

JDUPSEQ	**Join duplicate sequence**
	Specifies the field to use for sequencing records when duplicates are found in secondary files.
	This keyword is valid only with join logical files.

```
JDUPSEQ(sequencing-field-name [*DESCEND])
```

Level	Group
Join	Join

Example: `JDUPSEQ(EFCDATE)`

JFILE	**Joined files**
	Identifies 2 to 32 physical files containing data to be accessed through the join logical file you are describing.
	This keyword is valid only with join logical files.

```
JFILE([library-name/] physical-file-name [...32])
```

Level	Group
Record	Join

Example: `JFILE(CUSTOMER  ORDER)`

JFLD	**Joined fields**

Identifies the join fields in a join specification. This keyword is valid only with join logical files.

`JFLD(from-field-name  to-field-name)`

Level	Group
Join	Join

Example: `JFLD(CUSTID  CUSTID)`

JOIN	**Join**

Identifies the pair of files joined by a join specification. This keyword is valid only with join logical files.

`JOIN(from-file-name  to-file-name)`

Level	Group
Join	Join

Example: `JOIN(CUSTOMER  ORDER)`

JREF	**Join reference**

Identifies the file to use for a field name if the field name occurs in more than one based-on physical file. This keyword is valid only with join logical files.

`JREF(file-name | relative-file-number)`

Level	Group
Field	Join

Example: `JREF(1)`

LIFO	**Last-in first-out**

Specifies that records retrieved from same logical file member and that have duplicate key values are retrieved in a last-in first-out order.

Level	Group
File	Access path

Example: `LIFO`

NOALTSEQ	**No alternative collating sequence**
	The alternative collating sequence is not to be used for the key field.

Level	Group
Key field	Access path

Example: `NOALTSEQ`

PFILE	**Physical file**
	Names 1 to 32 physical file(s) on which the logical file record format is to be based.
	This keyword is valid only with non-join logical files.

`PFILE([library-name/] database-file-name[...32])`

Level	Group
Record	Naming and referencing

Example: `PFILE(CUSTOMER)`

RANGE	**Range**
	When specified at the field level, RANGE has no effect. If the field you are describing is referenced by an input-capable field at display file creation time, RANGE is duplicated into the display file, where it tests the validity of data keyed into the input-capable field.
	When specified at the select/omit level, this entry selects or omits records retrieved from the physical file(s) on which the logical file is based if they pass the specified test.
	For RANGE, the test is that the value of the field specified in positions 19-28 must be greater than or equal to the low value and less than or equal to the high value specified on the RANGE keyword.

`RANGE(low-value   high-value)`

Level	Group
Field	Validity check
Select/omit	Select/omit

Example: `RANGE(1000   5000)`

REFACCPTH	**Reference access path definition**

Specifies that the keyed-sequence access path definition from a previously created logical or physical file is to be copied to the file you are creating.

This keyword is valid only with non-join logical files.

```
REFACCPTH([library-name/] database-file-name)
```

Level	Group
File	Access path

Example: `REFACCPTH(APPDTA/CUSTCITY)`

RESHIFT	**Reference shift**

For logical files, REFSHIFT has no effect. If the field you are describing is referenced by an input-capable field at display file creation time, REFSHIFT is duplicated into the display file, where it specifies a keyboard shift.

```
REFSHIFT(keyboard-shift)
```

The valid keyboard shift codes are

Code	Meaning	Data Types
X	Alphabetic only	Character
A	Alphanumeric	Character
N	Numeric shift	Character or numeric
S	Signed numeric	Numeric
Y	Numeric only	Numeric
W	Katakana	Character
I	Inhibit keyboard entry	Character or numeric
D	Digits only	Character or numeric
M	Numeric only character	Character
F	Floating point	Numeric

Level	Group
Field	Naming and referencing

Example: `REFSHIFT(X)`

RENAME	**Rename**
	Renames a physical file field for a logical file record format.

RENAME(field-name)

Level	Group
Field	Naming and referencing

Example: RENAME(PARTID)

SIGNED	**Signed**
	The sign of a field is considered when sequencing values.

Level	Group
Key field	Access path

Example: SIGNED

SST	**Substring**
	Specifies a character or hexadecimal field is a substring of an existing character, hexadecimal, or zoned field.

SST(field-name starting-position [length])

Level	Group
Key field	Naming and referencing

Example: SST(NAME 22 50)

TEXT	**Text**
	Specifies descriptive text for the record format or field.

TEXT('description')

Level	Group
Record	Text
Field	Text

Example: TEXT('Customer name')

TIMFMT — Time format

Specifies the format of a time field.

```
TIMFMT(time-format)
```

Format description	Parameter	Format
Hours:Minutes:Seconds	*HMS	hh:mm:ss
ISO	*ISO	hh.mm.ss
IBM USA	*USA	hh:mm am or pm
IBM Europe	*EUR	hh.mm.ss
Japanese Industrial Standard Christian Era	*JIS	hh:mm:ss

Level	Group
Field	Miscellaneous

Example: `TIMFMT(*ISO)`

TIMSEP — Time separator

Specifies the separator character used in a time field.

```
TIMSEP(*JOB | 'time-separator')
```

Valid time separator values are colon (':'), period ('.'), and blank (' ') .

Level	Group
Field	Miscellaneous

Example: `TIMSEP(':')`

TRNTBL — Translation table

On input to your program, the field is translated using the specified translation table. This keyword is valid only for character fields with a field usage (position 38) of I (input-only) or N (neither input nor output).

```
TRNTBL([library-name/] translate-table-name)
```

Level	Group
Field	Miscellaneous

Example: `TRNTBL(QSYS/QSYSTRNTBL)`

UNIQUE	**Unique**

Specifies that key values must be unique. (No duplicate key values allowed.)

If the optional parameter is specified, it determines whether nulls in key field(s) of multiple records cause duplicates. *INCNULL is the default and includes records with nulls for a key field when determining whether two records have the same key value. *EXCNULL excludes all records with nulls when checking for duplicates.

```
UNIQUE[(*INCNULL | *EXCNULL)]
```

Level	Group
File	Access path

Example: `UNIQUE`

UNSIGNED	**Unsigned**

The field is sequenced as unsigned binary data.

Level	Group
Key field	Access path

Example: `UNSIGNED`

VALUES	**Values**

When specified at the field level, VALUES has no effect. If the field you are describing is referenced by an input-capable field at display file creation time, VALUES is duplicated into the display file, where it tests the validity of data keyed into the input-capable field.

When specified at the select/omit level, this entry selects or omits records retrieved from the physical file(s) on which the logical file is based if they pass the specified test.

For VALUES, the test is that the value of the field specified in positions 19-28 must be equal to one of the values specified on the VALUES keyword.

```
VALUES(value-1 [value-2 ... [value-100]])
```

Level	Group
Field	Validity check
Select/omit	Select/omit

Example: `VALUES( 'A'  'B'  'C')`

VARLEN	**Variable-length field**
	Defines a character field as a variable-length field.
	VARLEN

Level	Group
Field	Miscellaneous

Example: VARLEN

ZONE	**Zone**
	Only the zone portion (high-order 4 bits) of each byte of the key field is used to build a key value.

Level	Group
Key field	Access path

Example: ZONE

Appendix B

CL Command Descriptions for Database Files

Full Command Descriptions
CRTPF (Create Physical File)
CRTLF (Create Logical File)

Abbreviated Command Descriptions
ADDLFM (Add Logical File Member)
ADDPFCST (Add Physical File Constraint)
ADDPFM (Add Physical File Member)
ADDPFTRG (Add Physical File Trigger)
CHGLF (Change Logical File)
CHGLFM (Change Logical File Member)
CHGPF (Change Physical File)
CHGPFCST (Change Physical File Constraint)
CHGPFM (Change Physical File Member)
CHGSRCPF (Change Source Physical File)
CLRPFM (Clear Physical File Member)
CPYF (Copy File)
CRTLIB (Create Library)
CRTSRCPF (Create Source Physical File)
DLTF (Delete File)
DSPCPCST (Display Check Pending Constraint)
DSPDBR (Display Database Relations)
DSPFD (Display File Description)
DSPFFD (Display File Field Description)
DSPPFM (Display Physical File Member)
EDTCPCST (Edit Check Pending Constraint)
INZPFM (Initialize Physical File Member)
MOVOBJ (Move Object)
OPNQRYF (Open Query File)
OVRDBF (Override with Database File)
RGZPFM (Reorganize Physical File Member)
RMVM (Remove Member)
RMVPFCST (Remove Physical File Constraint)
RMVPFTRG (Remove Physical File Trigger)
RNMM (Rename Member)
RNMOBJ (Rename Object)
WRKF (Work with Files)
WRKPFCST (Work with Physical File Constraint)

Using Command Descriptions

The following command descriptions for CRTPF (Create Physical File) and CRTLF (Create Logical File) provide a syntax diagram and a full description of all parameters. (The CRTLF parameters that have identical meanings as the respective CRTPF command parameters are described in full only for the CRTPF command.) The CRTPF and CRTLF commands are the most important for creating DB2/400 files. Other database-related commands have an abbreviated description that lists the parameters and allowable values, but no detailed explanation. You can get additional information on any command by prompting for it (using the F4 key) and pressing the Help (or F1) key. The *OS/400 CL Reference* provides complete command descriptions for all DB2/400-related commands.[1]

The "railroad track" syntax diagrams for CRTPF and CRTLF provide a quick guide to the commands. By following the tracks (left-to-right, top-to-bottom) you can see a command's keywords and allowable values. A correctly entered command will result from following a path through the diagram. A parameter whose keyword appears on the "base track" (the main line running through the diagram) is a required parameter. (For CRTPF and CRTLF, only the FILE parameter is required.) A parameter whose keyword appears on a "branch track" is optional. If a parameter has a default value, it appears as the choice *above* the track on which the parameter keyword appears (e.g., *FILE is the default value for the SRCMBR parameter on CRTPF and CRTLF).

Predefined parameter values start with * (e.g., *FILE) or Q (e.g., QDDSSRC). Other parameter values are user-defined (e.g., physical-file-name), and you supply an appropriate value. The parameter descriptions that follow the syntax diagrams list parameters in the same order as they appear on the diagram. Default parameter values are underlined in the descriptions.

---

[1] SQL/400-related commands (e.g., STRSQL, RUNSQLSTM, and CRTSQLxxx) are documented in *DB2 for OS/400 SQL Programming*.

CRTPF (Create Physical File) Command [2]

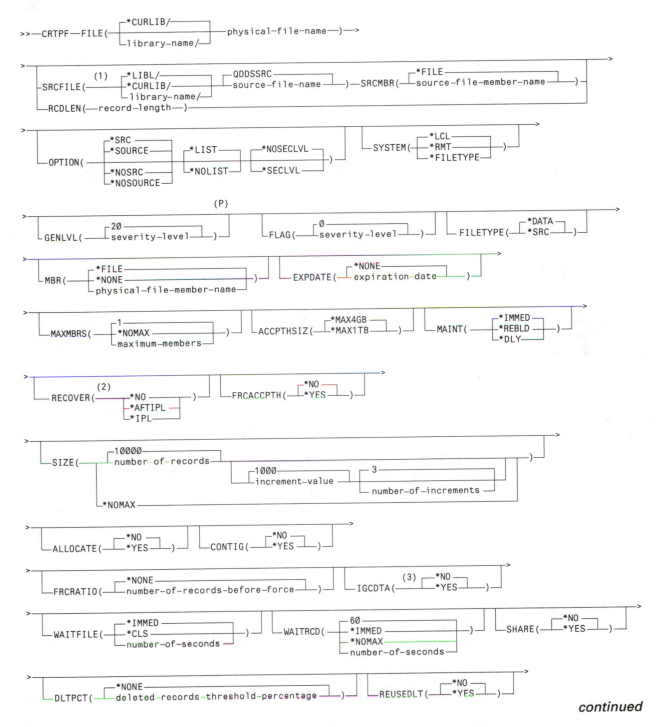

continued

[2] Reprinted with changes by permission from *AS/400 CL Reference Version 3* (IBM manual SC41-4723-00) copyright 1995 by International Business Machines Corporation.

CRTPF (Create Physical File) Command *continued*

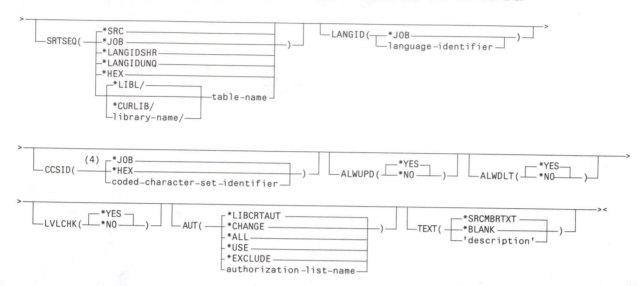

Notes:

(1) To code the following parameters positionally, the user must code them in this order, using *N for those not being specified: SRCFILE, SRCMBR, and RCDLEN.

(P) All parameters preceding this point can be specified in positional form.

(2) Refer to the parameter description for the default action for this parameter.

(3) DBCS systems only.

(4) If the CCSID parameter is specified, the RCDLEN parameter must also be specified.

Purpose

The Create Physical File (CRTPF) command creates a physical file in the database. A physical file is created from the file description parameters in the CRTPF command and (optionally) from a previously entered data description specification (DDS) source file member that contains the source description of the file. If the desired physical file has a record format with only one character field in arrival sequence or if the file is a source file, a DDS source file is not needed. To override attributes of the file after it has been created, use the Override Database File (OVRDBF) command before the file is opened. To change attributes of the file after it has been created, use the Change Physical File (CHGPF) command.

Restriction:

A saved keyed physical file can contain up to 3999 members. A saved nonkeyed physical file can contain up to 7999 members. A single save operation can save up to 8000 objects.

Required Parameter

FILE

Specifies the qualified name of the file being created. If the file is used by a high-level language (HLL) program, the file name must be consistent with the naming rules of that language; otherwise, the file must be renamed in the program.

physical-file-name: Specify the name of the physical file.

The name of the file can be qualified by one of the following library values:

*CURLIB: The file is created in the current library for the job. If no library is specified as the current library for the job, the QGPL library is used.

library-name: Specify the name of the library where the file is created.

Optional Parameters

SRCFILE

Specifies the qualified name of the source file used when the physical file is created. The source file contains the specifications that describe the record format and its fields, and the access path for the file and its members. The specifications that are made in DDS are described in Part I of this book and in *DB2 for OS/400 Database Programming* and *DDS Reference.*

If SRCFILE is specified, the RCDLEN parameter cannot be specified.

QDDSSRC: The source file, QDDSSRC, contains the DDS used to create the physical file.

source-file-name: Specify the name of the source file that contains the DDS used to create the physical file.

The name of the source file can be qualified by one of the following library values:

*LIBL: All libraries in the job's library list are searched until the first match is found.

*CURLIB: The current library for the job is searched. If no library is specified as the current library for the job, the QGPL library is used.

library-name: Specify the name of the library to be searched.

RCDLEN

Specifies the length (in bytes) of the records stored in the physical file. If RCDLEN and FILETYPE(*DATA) are specified, the physical file is created with a record format that has only one field. The file is then restricted to an arrival sequence access path. The record format and the field are both assigned the same name as that of the file, specified in the FILE parameter. A value ranging from 1 through 32766 bytes can be specified for the record length.

If RCDLEN and FILETYPE(*SRC) are specified, the record format has three fields: SRCSEQ (source sequence number), SRCDAT (source date), and SRCDTA (source data). The RCDLEN parameter must provide six positions for the source sequence number, six positions for the date field, and at least one position for source data, which are required in each record. These fields are defined with fixed attributes and names. If records are copied into the file by the CPYF command and the records are longer than the length specified, the records are truncated on the right.

If RCDLEN is specified, SRCFILE and SRCMBR cannot be specified; RCDLEN is used to specify a fixed record length for the record format when a source file is not needed (when only one field exists in each record or when the file being created is a source file). The high-level language program that processes the file must describe the fields in the record in the program.

Double-Byte Character Set Considerations:
If IGCDTA(*NO) is specified, the field is assigned the data type of character whose length is the same as the record length specified. A value ranging from 1 to 32766 bytes can be specified for the record length. If IGCDTA(*YES) is specified, the field is assigned the data type of DBCS-open and a value ranging from 4 to 32766 can be specified.

The RCDLEN parameter must provide six positions for the source sequence number, six positions for the date field, and at least four positions for source data when FILETYPE(*SRC) and IGCDTA(*YES) are specified.

SRCMBR

Specifies the name of the source file member that contains the DDS for the physical file being created; the member is in the source file specified in the SRCFILE parameter (or its default, QDDSSRC). If SRCMBR is specified, RCDLEN cannot be specified.

*FILE: The source file member name is the same as that of the physical file being created.

source-file-member-name: Specify the name of the member in the source file specified by SRCFILE used to create the physical file.

OPTION

Specifies the type of printout produced when the file is created. Up to three of the following values can be specified in any order on this parameter. If neither or both of the values in each group are specified, the underlined value will be used.

Note: The underlined values for this parameter are similar to, but not actually default values, and therefore, cannot be changed with the CHGCMDDFT (Change Command Default) command.

Source Listing Options

*SRC or ***SOURCE**: A printout is created of the source statements used to create the file, and of errors that occur.

*NOSRC or ***NOSOURCE**: No printout of the source statements is created unless errors are detected. If errors are detected, they are listed along with the keyword or record format that caused the error.

Program Listing Options

*LIST: An expanded source printout is created, showing a detailed list of the file specifications that result from the source statements and references to other file descriptions.

*NOLIST: An expanded source printout is not created.

*NOSECLVL: The messages section of the DDS printout does not contain the second-level message for the errors found during DDS processing.

*SECLVL: Second-level message text is included in the source listing.

SYSTEM

Specifies the system on which the physical file is created.

*LCL: The physical file is created on the local system.

*RMT: The physical file is created on a remote system using distributed data management (DDM). The physical file name specified on the FILE parameter must be the name of the DDM file (created using the CRTDDMF command). The DDM file contains the name of the physical file being created (RMTFILE parameter on the CRTDDMF command) and the name of the remote system (RMTLOCNAME parameter on the CRTDDMF command) on which the file is created.

*FILETYPE: If the name specified on the FILE parameter is a DDM file, the physical file is created on the remote system specified by the RMTLOCNAME parameter on the CRTDDMF command for the DDM file. Otherwise, the name on the FILE parameter cannot be the same as an existing file, since a physical file of that name is created on the local system.

GENLVL

Specifies the severity level at which the create operation fails. If errors occur that have a severity level greater than or equal to this value, the operation ends.

Note: This parameter applies only to messages created while processing the DDS source. Messages created elsewhere in the file creation process are not affected by this parameter.

20: If errors occur in the DDS source file with a severity level greater than or equal to 20, the file is not created.

severity-level: Specify a severity level ranging from 0 through 30. The file is not created if the severity level specified for this parameter equals 0 or is less than the severity level that occurs in the DDS source. This value must be greater than or equal to the value specified on the FLAG parameter.

FLAG

Specifies the minimum severity level of messages to be listed in the DDS source listing.

0: All messages are listed.

severity-level: Specify the minimum severity level of messages to be listed. Valid values range from 0 through 30. The severity level specified must be less than or equal to the severity level specified on the GENLVL parameter.

FILETYPE

Specifies whether each member of the physical file being created contains data records or contains source records (statements) for a program or another file. The file can contain, for example, RPG source statements for an RPG program or DDS source statements for another physical, logical, or device file.

Note: FILETYPE(*SRC) is specified only when including DDS field definitions in the source file. Otherwise, use the Create Source Physical File (CRTSRCPF) command to create a source file.

*DATA: The physical file contains data records.

*SRC: The physical file contains source records.

MBR

Specifies the name of the physical file member added when the physical file is created. Other members can be added to the file after it is created by using the ADDPFM (Add Physical File Member) command.

*FILE: The member being added has the same name (specified in the FILE parameter) as the physical file that contains the member.

*NONE: No member is added when the file is created.

physical-file-member-name: Specify the name of the member added when the physical file is created.

EXPDATE

Specifies the expiration date. The file cannot be overwritten until the expiration date. The expiration date must be later than or equal to the current date.

Note: An attempt to open a file member that has an expiration date that has been exceeded causes an error message to be sent to the user. The RMVM command is used to remove the member from the file.

*NONE: No expiration date is specified.

expiration-date: Specify the date after which the physical file member is not used. The date must be in the format specified by the QDATFMT and QDATSEP job attributes. The date must be enclosed in apostrophes if special characters are used in the format.

MAXMBRS

Specifies the maximum number of members that the physical file being created can have at any time.

1: Only one member can be contained in the file.

*NOMAX: The system maximum is used.

maximum-members: Specify the value for the maximum number of members that the physical file can have. Valid values range from 1 through 32767.

ACCPTHSIZ

Specifies the maximum size of auxiliary storage that can be occupied by the following kinds of access paths:

- The access paths that are associated with a physical file that has a keyed sequence access path.

- The access paths that are created for referential or unique constraints, and that can be added to this file with the ADDPFCST (Add Physical File Constraint) command.

This parameter does not apply to access paths that are created for logical files or for queries that refer to the data in a physical file.

*MAX4GB: The access paths associated with this file can occupy a maximum of four gigabytes (4,294,966,272 bytes) of auxiliary storage. This value provides compatibility with operating system release V3R1M0 and earlier.

*MAX1TB: The access paths associated with this file can occupy a maximum of one terabyte (1,099,511,627,776 bytes) of auxiliary storage.

Note: This value is not supported on releases of the system earlier than V3R6M0. Therefore, if an attempt is made to save a physical file that has this attribute, and the save operation specifies a target release earlier than V3R6M0, the save operation might be unsuccessful, or if successful, the access paths are not saved. If the save operation is successful and the saved version of the file is then used to restore the physical file, the system rebuilds all the access paths.

MAINT

Specifies, for files with keyed sequence access paths only, the type of access path maintenance used for members of the physical file.

*IMMED: The access path is maintained for each physical file member whether the source physical file is opened or closed. The access path is changed whenever a record is updated, added to, or deleted from a member of this file or a logical file member based on a member of this file.

*REBLD: The access path is completely rebuilt when a file member is opened during the running of the program. The access path is continuously maintained until the member is closed; the access path maintenance is then ended. *REBLD is not valid for access paths that require unique key values.

*DLY: The maintenance of the access path is delayed until the physical file member is opened for use. Then the access path is changed only for records that have been added, deleted, or changed since the file was last opened. While the file is open, changes made to its members are immediately reflected in the access paths of those members, no matter what is specified for MAINT. To prevent a lengthy rebuild time when the file is opened, *DLY should be specified only when the number of changes to the access path between successive opens are small; that is, when the file is opened frequently or when the key fields in records for this access path change infrequently. *DLY is not valid for access paths that require unique key values.

If the number of changes between a close and the next open reaches approximately 10 percent of the access path size, the system stops saving changes and the access path is completely rebuilt the next time the file is opened.

RECOVER

Specifies, for files having immediate or delayed maintenance on their access paths, when recovery processing of the file is performed after a system failure has occurred while the access path was being changed. This parameter is valid only for a file with a keyed access path.

If *IMMED is specified for the MAINT parameter, the access path can be rebuilt during initial program load (IPL) (before any user can run a job), or after IPL has ended (during jobs running at the same time), or when the file is next opened. While the access path is being rebuilt, the file cannot be used by any job.

During the IPL, an Override Access Path Recovery display lists those access paths that must be recovered and the RECOVER parameter value for each access path. The user can override the RECOVER parameter value on this display.

If *REBLD is specified for the MAINT parameter, the access path is rebuilt the next time its file is opened.

*NO: The access path of the file is not rebuilt during or after an IPL. The file's access path, if not valid, is rebuilt when the file is next opened.

Note: *NO is the default for all files that do not require unique keys.

*AFTIPL: The file's access path is rebuilt after the completion of the IPL. This option allows other jobs not using this file to start processing immediately after the completion of the IPL. If a job tries to allocate the file while its access path is being rebuilt, a file open exception occurs.

Note: *AFTIPL is the default for all files that require unique keys.

*IPL: The file's access path is rebuilt during the IPL. This ensures that the file's access path is rebuilt before the first user program tries to use it; however, no jobs can start running until after all files that specify RECOVER(*IPL) have their access paths rebuilt.

FRCACCPTH

Specifies, for files with keyed access paths only, whether access path changes are forced to auxiliary storage along with the associated records in the file whenever the access path is changed. FRCACCPTH(*YES) minimizes (but does not remove) the possibility that an abnormal job end may cause damage to the access path that requires it to be rebuilt.

*NO: The access path and changed records are not forced to auxiliary storage whenever the access path is changed.

*YES: The access path and changed records are forced to auxiliary storage whenever the access path is changed. If FRCACCPTH(*YES) is specified, MAINT(*REBLD) cannot be specified.

FRCACCPTH(*YES) slows the response time of the system if the access path is changed in an interactive job. If the access path is changed frequently, the overall performance of the system is decreased.

SIZE

Specifies the initial number of records in each member of the file, the number of records in each increment that can be automatically added to the member size, and the number of times the increment can be automatically applied. The number of records for each file member is specified as the number of records that can be placed in it (this number includes any deleted records).

When the maximum number of records has been reached, a message (stating that the member is full) is sent to the system operator, giving the choice of ending the request or extending the member size. The operator can extend the member by 10% or by the number of records specified as the increment value, whichever is greater, each time the message is received.

A list of three values is specified to indicate the initial size of each member and the automatic extensions that can be added when needed, or *NOMAX can be specified. If SIZE is not specified, SIZE(10000 1000 3) is assumed by the system.

Element 1 — Number of Records

Use one of the following to specify the initial number of records in the member before automatic extension of the member occurs. The ALLOCATE parameter determines when the required space for the initial number of records is allocated. If *YES is specified, the space is allocated when a new member is added. If *NO is specified, the initial space is allocated as determined internally by the system.

10000: Initially, up to 10,000 records can be inserted into each member of the file before any extension occurs.

number-of-records: Specify the number of records (ranging from 1 through 16777215) that can be inserted before an automatic extension occurs. If automatic extensions are not wanted, enter zeros for the second and third values in the list.

Element 2 — Increment Value

Use one of the following to specify the number of records that can be additionally inserted in the member when the initial member size is exceeded and an automatic extension occurs. The minimum size of an increment is 10% of the size of the member at the time the maximum number of records is reached.

1000: The member size is increased by 10% or 1000 records, whichever is greater.

increment-value: Specify the number of additional records (ranging from 0 through 32767) which, if greater than 10% of the size of the member when the maximum number of records is reached, are to be added to the member during an automatic extension.

If the number specified is not greater than 10% of the member size and not equal to zero, the member size is increased by 10%.

Specify 0 to prevent automatic extensions. This value must be 0 if the value for the number of increments is 0.

Element 3: Maximum Number of Increments

Use one of the following to specify the maximum number of increments that are automatically added to the member. If 0 is specified for the increment amount (element 2), and the number of increments is not specified; 0 is the default value instead of 3 (a message is sent to the user issuing the command).

3: Up to three increments are automatically added to the member size.

number-of-increments: Specify the maximum number of increments, ranging from 0 through 32767, that are automatically added to the member. To prevent automatic extensions, specify a value of 0.

Additional Single Value for the SIZE Parameter

*NOMAX: The system maximum is used.

ALLOCATE

Specifies whether storage space is allocated for the initial number of records (SIZE parameter) for each physical file member when it is added. The allocation provides enough space to hold the number of records specified by the SIZE parameter. Allocations that occur when a record cannot be added to a member without exceeding its capacity are determined by the system and by the SIZE parameter values.

*NO: When a new member is added, the system determines whether additional space is needed and allocates that amount.

*YES: The amount of storage space specified in the first value of the SIZE parameter is allocated each time a new member is added. If that amount of storage space is unavailable, the member is not added, and a message is sent to the user. If this parameter value is used, SIZE(*NOMAX) cannot be specified.

CONTIG

Specifies whether records in the initial allocation in each physical file member are stored contiguously (next to each other) on auxiliary storage. If so, and the necessary contiguous space is unavailable, the system sends a message to the job log and allocates the storage space noncontiguously. The file is still entirely usable. This parameter does not affect additional allocations that might be needed later, which would probably be noncontiguous.

*NO: The storage space for each member does not have to be contiguous.

*YES: The system allocates contiguous space for each member of the physical file being added. If it cannot, the user is notified and a message is put in the job log. The affected member is still added, even if the storage space is allocated noncontiguously. The member is just as usable in noncontiguous form. If *YES is specified for CONTIG, then ALLOCATE(*YES) must also be specified.

FRCRATIO

Specifies the number of inserted, updated, or deleted records that are processed before they are forced to auxiliary (permanent) storage.

If this physical file is being journaled, either a large number or *NONE should be used. *NONE may cause long synchronization of the journal and physical files.

*NONE: There is no force write ratio; the system determines when the records are written to auxiliary storage.

number-of-records-before-force: Specify the number of inserted, updated, or deleted records processed before being explicitly forced to auxiliary storage.

IGCDTA

Specifies whether the program-defined physical files can contain double-byte character set (DBCS) data.

Note: This parameter has no meaning with DDS files, because the use of DBCS data is specified in the DDS.

*NO: The file does not process DBCS data.

*YES: The file processes DBCS data.

Double-Byte Character Set Considerations:

If the user creates a physical file and specifies the RCDLEN parameter, the system creates a default record format.

If IGCDTA(*YES) is specified, the default record format can contain DBCS data (as if the record were specified with the DBCS-open (O in column 35 of DDS specification) data type).

If IGCDTA(*NO) is specified, the default record format cannot contain DBCS data (as if the record were specified with the character (A or blank in column 35 of DDS specification) data type).

The system ignores the IGCDTA parameter value if a value for the RCDLEN parameter is not specified.

The user cannot override the IGCDTA value for a physical file.

WAITFILE

Specifies the number of seconds that the program waits for the file resources and session resources to be allocated when the file is opened, or for the device or session resources to be allocated when an acquire operation is performed to the file. If those resources are not allocated within the specified wait time, an error message is sent to the program.

Note: An immediate allocation of the device by the device resource is required when an acquire operation is performed to the file.

*IMMED: The program does not wait; when the file is opened, an immediate allocation of the file resources is required.

*CLS: The job default wait time is used as the wait time for the file resources being allocated.

number-of-seconds: Specify the number of seconds a program waits for the file resources to be allocated to the job. Valid values range from 1 through 32767 seconds.

WAITRCD

Specifies the number of seconds that a program waits for a record to be updated or deleted, or for a record read in the commitment control environment with LCKLVL(*ALL) specified. More information on record locking is in Chapter 17 and the *DB2/400 Database Programming* manual. If the record is not allocated in the specified wait time, an error message is sent to the program.

60: The program waits for 60 seconds.

*IMMED: The program does not wait; when a record is locked, an immediate allocation of the record is required.

*NOMAX: The system maximum is used.

number-of-seconds: Specify the number of seconds a program waits for the record to be allocated. Valid values range from 1 through 32767 seconds.

SHARE

Specifies whether the open data path (ODP) for the physical file is shared with other programs in the routing step. When an ODP is shared, the programs accessing the file share facilities such as the file status and the buffer. More information on shared database files is in Chapter 17 and the *DB2/400 Database Programming* manual.

*NO: The ODP created by the program with this attribute is not shared with other programs in the routing step. Every time a program opens the file with this attribute, a new ODP to the file is created and activated.

*YES: The ODP created with this attribute is shared with each program in the routing step that also specifies SHARE(*YES) when it opens the file.

DLTPCT

Specifies the maximum percentage of deleted records allowed for any member in the physical file. The percentage is based on the number of deleted records compared with the total record count in a member. The percentage check is made when a member of the file is closed or a logical file member based on a member of the file is closed. If the number of deleted records exceeds the percentage, a message is sent to the system history log (QHST) to inform the user.

*NONE: No percentage is specified; the number of deleted records in the file members is not checked when a member is closed.

deleted-records-threshold-percentage: Specify the largest percentage of deleted records in any member in the file. Valid values range from 1 through 100. If this percentage is exceeded, a message is sent to the system history log (QHST) when the file is closed.

REUSEDLT

Specifies whether the space used by deleted data entries is reclaimed by future insert requests.

Note: If a *YES value is specified for this parameter, the key ordering attribute for the physical file must be allowed to default or must be FCFO instead of FIFO or LIFO. If *YES is specified for this parameter, the key ordering attributes of FIFO and LIFO are not allowed.

*NO: The file does not reclaim space used by deleted data entries.

*YES: The file reclaims space used by deleted data entries.

SRTSEQ

Specifies the sort sequence used for this file. The sort sequence is used with the LANGID and CCSID parameters to determine which sort sequence table is used.

*SRC: The table specified in the data description specification (DDS) on the ALTSEQ keyword is used. If ALTSEQ is not used in the DDS, use the value specified for *JOB on this parameter.

*JOB: The sort sequence value used is the value for the job issuing this command to create the physical file.

*LANGIDSHR: The sort sequence table uses the same weight for multiple characters, and is the shared-weight sort sequence table associated with the language specified on the LANGID parameter.

*LANGIDUNQ: The sort sequence table must contain a unique weight for each character in the code page.

*HEX: A sort sequence table is not used. The hexadecimal values of the characters are used to determine the sort sequence.

The name of the table can be qualified by one of the following library values:

*LIBL: All libraries in the job's library list are searched until the first match is found.

*CURLIB: The current library for the job is searched. If no library is specified as the current library for the job, the QGPL library is used.

library-name: Specify the name of the library to be searched.

table-name: Specify a table name.

LANGID

Specifies the language identifier used when *LANGIDSHR or *LANGIDUNQ is specified on the SRTSEQ parameter. The language identifier is used with the SRTSEQ and CCSID parameters to determine which sort sequence table the file will use.

*JOB: The language identifier specified for the job is used.

language-identifier: Specify a language identifier.

CCSID

Specifies the coded character set identifier (CCSID) used to describe character data in the fields of the file. If this parameter is specified, the RCDLEN parameter and FILETYPE(*SRC) must also be specified.

A CCSID is a 16-bit number identifying a specific set of encoding scheme identifiers, character set identifiers, code page identifiers, and additional coding-related information that uniquely identifies the coded graphic representation used.

*JOB: The current job's default CCSID is used.

*HEX: The CCSID 65535 is used, which indicates that the character data in the fields is treated as bit data and is not converted.

coded-character-set-identifier: Specify the CCSID to be used. More information on valid CCSIDs is in the *National Language Support* manual.

ALWUPD

Specifies whether records can be updated in the physical file. Records in a logical file can be updated only when the records in each physical file, on which the logical file is based, can be updated.

*YES: Records can be updated in the physical file.

*NO: Records cannot be updated in this physical file or in any logical file built over this physical file.

ALWDLT

Specifies whether records can be deleted from the physical file. Records in a logical file can be deleted only when the records in each physical file on which the logical file is based can be deleted.

*YES: Records can be deleted in this physical file.

*NO: Records cannot be deleted in this physical file or from any logical file built over this physical file.

LVLCHK

Specifies whether the record format level identifiers in the program are checked against those in the physical file when the file is opened. If so, the record format identifiers in the program must match those in the physical file. This value can be overridden by the Override with Database File (OVRDBF) command at run time.

*YES: The level identifiers of the record formats are checked when the file is opened. If the level identifiers do not match, an error message is sent to the program requesting the open, and the file is not opened.

*NO: The level identifiers are not checked when the file is opened.

AUT

Specifies the authority given to users who do not have specific authority to the physical file, who are not on an authorization list, and whose user group has no specific authority to the physical file.

*LIBCRTAUT: The public authority for the physical file is taken from the value on the CRTAUT parameter of the target library (the library that is to contain the physical file). The public authority is determined when the physical file is created. If the CRTAUT value for the library changes after the physical file is created, the new value does not affect any existing objects.

*CHANGE: The user can perform all operations on the physical file except those limited to the owner or controlled by object existence authority and object management authority. Change authority provides object operational authority and all data authority.

*ALL: The user can perform all operations except those limited to the owner or controlled by authorization list management authority. The user can control the object's existence, specify the security for the object, change the object, and perform basic functions on the object. The user can also change ownership of the physical file.

*USE: The user can perform basic operations on the physical file, such as reading the file. *USE authority provides object operational authority, read authority, and execute authority.

*EXCLUDE: The user cannot access the physical file.

authorization-list-name: Specify the name of the authorization list used.

TEXT

Specifies text that briefly describes the physical file.

*SRCMBRTXT: The text is taken from the source file member being used to create the physical file. If the source file is a database file, the text is taken from the source member. Text can be added or changed for a database source member by using the Source Entry Utility or by using either the Add Physical File Member (ADDPFM) command or the Change Physical File Member (CHGPFM) command. If the source file is an inline file or a device file, the text is blank.

*BLANK: Text is not specified.

'*description*': Specify no more than 50 characters of text, enclosed in apostrophes.

CRTLF (Create Logical File) Command [3]

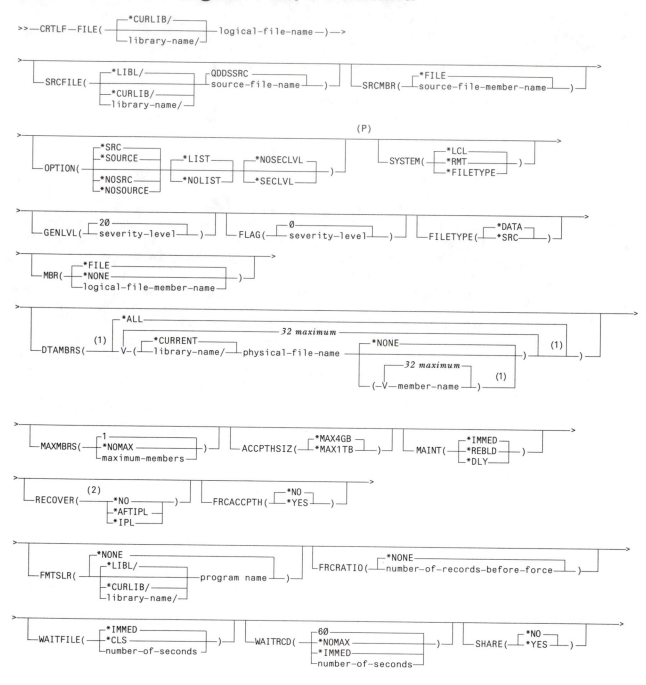

continued

[3] Reprinted with changes by permission from *AS/400 CL Reference Version 3* (IBM manual SC41-4723-00) copyright 1995 by International Business Machines.

CRTLF (Create Logical File) Command *continued*

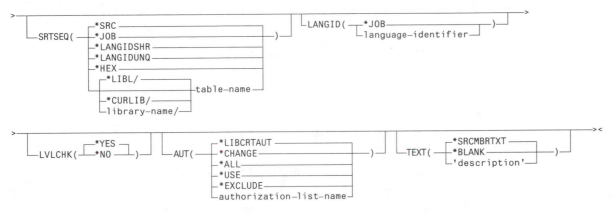

Notes:

(1)   The sum of all member names specified for all specified files cannot exceed 32.

(P)   All parameters preceding this point can be specified in positional form.

(2)   Refer to the parameter description for the default action taken for this parameter.

Purpose

The Create Logical File (CRTLF) command creates a logical file in the database. The logical file is created from the file description parameters in this CRTLF command and from the previously entered data description specifications (DDS) that contain the source description of the logical file. A logical file is a database file that describes how data records contained in one or more physical files are presented to a program. The logical file does not contain data records. The data records are contained in the physical files associated with the logical file. To override the attributes of the logical file after it has been created, use the Override Database File (OVRDBF) command before the file is opened. To change the attributes of the logical file after it has been created, use the Change Logical File (CHGLF) command.

Restriction:

To create a keyed logical file over one or more physical files, the user must have object operational and object management authorities or object alter authority for each of the files specified on the PFILE or JFILE keywords in DDS. To create a non-keyed logical file, only object operational authority is required.

Required Parameter

FILE

Specifies the qualified name of the logical file being created. If the file is used by a high-level language (HLL) program, the file name must be consistent with the naming rules of that language; otherwise, the file must be renamed in the program.

logical-file-name: Specify the name of the file that is to be created.

The name of the logical file can be qualified by one of the following library values:

> ***CURLIB**: The logical file is created in the current library for the job. If no library is specified as the current library for the job, the QGPL library is used.
>
> *library-name*: Specify the name of the library where the logical file is created.

Optional Parameters

SRCFILE

See description of this parameter under CRTPF Command, page 639.

SRCMBR

See description of this parameter under CRTPF Command, page 640.

OPTION

See description of this parameter under CRTPF Command, page 640.

SYSTEM

See description of this parameter under CRTPF Command, page 640.

GENLVL

See description of this parameter under CRTPF Command, page 641.

FLAG

See description of this parameter under CRTPF Command, page 641.

FILETYPE

See description of this parameter under CRTPF Command, page 641.

MBR

Specifies the name of the logical file member that is added when the logical file is created. Other members can be added to the file after it is created by using the Add Logical File Member (ADDLFM) command.

See description of this parameter under CRTPF Command, page 641.

DTAMBRS

Specifies the names of the physical files and members that contain the data associated with the logical file member being added by this command. A logical file member can be based on all of the physical files and members on which the logical file itself is based, specified by DTAMBRS(*ALL), or the member can be based on a subset of the total members and files, specified by DTAMBRS(qualified-file-names (member-names)).

When the FILE parameter specifies a join logical file or an arrival sequence logical file, only one data member must be specified on the DTAMBRS parameter for each physical file that was specified on the PFILE or JFILE keyword in the DDS. *ALL is valid only if each based-on physical file has only one member. If any of the physical files has more than one member, the specific physical file member must be specified on the DTAMBRS parameter.

The same physical file name can be specified more than once on the JFILE keyword. In this case, each occurrence of the file name is treated as a different based-on physical file, and must be specified on the DTAMBRS parameter.

*ALL: The logical file member being added is based on all the physical files and members (that exist at the time this CRTLF command is entered) used by the logical file. At least one member must exist in at least one of the physical files. The physical file names are specified on the PFILE or JFILE parameter in the DDS.

The physical file names must match a name on the PFILE or JFILE keywords in the DDS and cannot be specified more often on the DTAMBRS parameter than on the PFILE or JFILE keywords in the DDS. For join logical files, all physical files specified on the JFILE keyword must be specified on the DTAMBRS parameter and each physical file must contain only one member. If a physical file name is not specified for a physical file that is on a

PFILE or JFILE keyword in the DDS, the logical file member is not based on any member of that physical file.

Up to 32 qualified physical file names and physical file member names can be specified. Also, the total number of member names cannot exceed 32. For example, one file can specify 32 members, two files can each have 16 members, or 32 files can each have one member specified.

When a logical file is created, the physical files specified on the PFILE or JFILE DDS keyword are used to create the logical file. If no library name is specified for the physical files on the PFILE or JFILE keyword, the library list (*LIBL) at file creation time is used to find the physical files; the physical files from the library list are used to create the logical file. The qualified physical files from the PFILE or JFILE keyword (regardless of whether a library name was specified or if the library list was used to find the files) are the physical files associated with the logical file. The names of the physical files associated with the logical file are saved in the description of the logical file. When a member is added to the logical file, the DTAMBRS parameter is used to specify the physical file members associated with the logical file member. Each physical file name specified on the DTAMBRS parameter must be the name of a physical file that is associated with the logical file (saved in the description of the logical file).

If a library name is not specified, the current library name (*CURRENT) from the logical file description is used. If the library name is specified, the physical file must be a physical file associated with the logical file. If the logical file is associated with more than one physical file of the same name, the library name must be specified.

Element 1 — Names of Physical Files
physical-file-name: Specify the names of the physical files that contain the data being accessed by the logical file member being added.

Element 2 — Names of Members
NONE: A member name is not specified.

member-name: Specify the names of the members that contain the data being accessed by the logical file member being added.

MAXMBRS
Specifies the maximum number of members that the logical file being created can contain. See description of this parameter under CRTPF command, page 642.

ACCPTHSIZ
See description of this parameter under CRTPF Command, page 642.

MAINT
See description of this parameter under CRTPF Command, page 642.

Note: For a join logical file, this parameter value applies to all join secondary files even if the join file is not a keyed file.

RECOVER
See description of this parameter under CRTPF Command, page 643.

FRCACCPTH
See description of this parameter under CRTPF Command, page 643.

FMTSLR

Specifies the qualified name of a record format selector program that is called when the logical file member contains more than one record format. The user-written selector program is called when a record is inserted into the database file and a record format name is not included in the high-level language program. The selector program receives the record as input, determines the record format used, and returns it to the database. This program must perform this function for every member in the logical file that has more than one record format, unless the high-level language program itself specifies the record format name. More information about the use of format selector programs is in *DB2/400 Database Programming* manual.

This parameter is not valid if the logical file has only one record format.

*NONE: There is no selector program for this logical file. If the file has more than one logical record format, the high-level language program must specify the record format name.

program-name: Specify the name of the format selector program to be called when a record is inserted into a member having more than one format.

The name of the program can be qualified by one of the following library values:

> ***LIBL**: All libraries in the job's library list are searched until the first match is found.

> ***CURLIB**: The current library for the job is searched. If no library is specified as the current library for the job, the QGPL library is used.

> *library-name*: Specify the name of the library to be searched.

A program specified as the format selector program cannot be created with USRPRF(*OWNER) specified in its create program command.

FRCRATIO
See description of this parameter under CRTPF Command, page 645.

WAITFILE
See description of this parameter under CRTPF Command, page 646.

WAITRCD
See description of this parameter under CRTPF Command, page 646.

SHARE
See description of this parameter under CRTPF Command, page 647.

SRTSEQ
See description of this parameter under CRTPF Command, page 647.

LANGID
See description of this parameter under CRTPF Command, page 648.

LVLCHK
See description of this parameter under CRTPF Command, page 649.

AUT
See description of this parameter under CRTPF Command, page 649.

TEXT
See description of this parameter under CRTPF Command, page 649.

ADDLFM (Add Logical File Member) Command

Add a member to a logical file

Required Parameters

FILE   **File name**
   logical-file-name   Logical file to add member to. Name can be qualified with
                    *LIBL, *CURLIB, or library name.

MBR   **Member name**
   member-name   Name of logical file member to add.

Optional Parameters

DTAMBRS   **Files and members that contain data**
   *ALL   All physical files.

   physical-file-name member-name

                    Physical file(s) and member(s) that contain the data to be
                    accessed by the logical file member being added.

SHARE   **Share open data path**
   *NO   ODP is not shared
   *YES   ODP is shared

TEXT   **Descriptive text**
   *BLANK   Text is not specified.
   '*description*'   No more than 50 characters of text, enclosed in apostrophes.

ADDPFCST (Add Physical File Constraint) Command

Add a primary, unique, or foreign key constraint to a single-member physical file.

Required Parameters

FILE   **File name**
   physical-file-name   Physical file to add constraint to. Name can be qualified with
                    *LIBL, *CURLIB, or library name.

TYPE   **Type of constraint**
   *PRIKEY   A primary key constraint is being added.
   *UNQCST   A unique constraint is being added.
   *REFCST   A referential (foreign key) constraint is being added.

KEY   **Key field name(s)**
   field-name ...   One or more primary, unique, or foreign key field names.

Optional Parameters

CST   **Specifies the name of the constraint being added**
   *GEN   The system generates a constraint name.
   constraint-name   The name of the constraint.

PRNFILE   **Specifies the parent file and qualifying library of a referential constraint.** The file must be a physical file and it must allow a maximum of one member (MAXMBRS(1)).
   parent-file-name   Parent file for referential constraint. Name can be qualified with: *LIBL, *CURLIB, or library name.

PRNKEY	**Specifies the parent key, which is the definition of the access path on a parent file of a referential constraint**
*PRNFILE	The access path of the parent file is used when the access path is either a primary key constraint or a unique constraint.
field-name ...	Field name(s) for the referential constraint key you are defining. Each field name must exist in the file specified on the PRNFILE parameter.
DLTRULE	**The delete rule for a referential constraint between a parent file and dependent file**
*NOACTION	The no action delete rule is used. The delete rule is enforced at the end of the delete request.
*RESTRICT	The restrict delete rule is used. The delete rule is enforced at the beginning of the delete request.
*CASCADE	The cascade delete rule is used.
*SETNULL	The set null delete rule is used.
*SETDFT	The set default delete rule is used.
UPDRULE	**The update rule for a referential constraint between a parent file and dependent file**
*NOACTION	The no action update rule is used. The update rule is enforced at the end of the delete request.
*RESTRICT	The restrict update rule is used. The update rule is enforced at the beginning of the delete request.

ADDPFM (Add Physical File Member) Command

Add a member to a physical file.

Required Parameters

FILE	**File name**
physical-file-name	Physical file to add member to. Name can be qualified with *LIBL, *CURLIB, or library name.
MBR	**Member name**
member-name	Name of physical file member to add.

Optional Parameters

SRCTYPE	**Source type**
*NONE	No source type is specified.
source-type	Source type of the added member.
EXPDATE	**Expiration date**
*NONE	No expiration date is specified.
expiration-date	Date after which the member cannot be used.
SHARE	**Share Open Data Path**
*NO	ODP is not shared.
*YES	ODP is shared.

TEXT   **Descriptive text**

    *BLANK   Text is not specified.

    '*description*'   No more than 50 characters of text, enclosed in apostrophes.

ADDPFTRG (Add Physical File Trigger) Command

Add a trigger to a physical file.

Required Parameters

FILE   **File name**

    physical-file-name   Physical file to add trigger to. Name can be qualified with *LIBL, *CURLIB, or library name.

TRGTIME   **Trigger time**

    *BEFORE   Call trigger before the file operation occurs.

    *AFTER   Call trigger after the file operation occurs.

TRGEVENT   **Trigger event**

    *INSERT   Call trigger for insert operation.

    *DELETE   Call trigger for delete operation.

    *UPDATE   Call trigger for update operation.

PGM   **Trigger program name**

    program-name   Program to call for trigger. Name can be qualified with *LIBL, *CURLIB, or library name.

Optional Parameters

RPLTRG   **Replace trigger**

    *NO   Trigger doesn't replace any existing trigger for same event and time.

    *YES   Trigger replaces any existing trigger for same event and time.

TRGUPDCND   **Conditions under which update event calls trigger program associated with the update event**

    *ALWAYS   An update event always calls a trigger program.

    *CHANGE   An update event calls a trigger program only when a value is changed.

ALWREPCHG   **Allow repeated change**

    *NO   Do not allow changes to record being updated

    *YES   Allow changes to record being updated

CHGLF (Change Logical File) Command

Change the attributes of a logical file and its members. The changed attributes are used for all members subsequently added to the file. Where noted, the allowable parameter values are the keyword *SAME or the set of values described under the CRTLF command. To change the attributes of a specific member, use the CHGLFM command.

Required Parameter

FILE   **File name**
    logical-file-name   Logical file to change. Name can be qualified with *LIBL, *CURLIB, or library name.

Optional Parameters

SYSTEM   **Specifies local system or remote system**
    *LCL   Logical file is changed on the local system.
    *RMT   Logical file is changed on a remote system.
    *FILETYPE   If the name specified on the FILE parameter is a DDM file, the logical file is changed on the remote system specified by the RMTLOCNAME parameter of that DDM file.

MAXMBRS   **Maximum number of members**
    *SAME or one of the CRTLF command's allowable MAXMBRS parameter values.

MAINT   **Type of access path maintenance**
    *SAME or one of the CRTLF command's allowable MAINT parameter values.

RECOVER   **Recovery of the file is done if a system failure occurs**
    *SAME or one of the CRTLF command's allowable RECOVER parameter values.

FRCACCPTH   **Access path changes are forced to auxiliary storage**
    *SAME or one of the CRTLF command's allowable FRCACCPTH parameter values.

FMTSLR   **Record format selector**
    *SAME or one of the CRTLF command's allowable FMTSLR parameter values.

FRCRATIO   **Number of records processed before forced to storage**
    *SAME or one of the CRTLF command's allowable FRCRATIO parameter values.

WAITFILE   **Number of seconds that the program waits for the file resources and session resources to be allocated when the file is opened**
    *SAME or one of the CRTLF command's allowable WAITFILE parameter values.

WAITRCD   **Number of seconds that a program waits for a record to be updated or deleted**
    *SAME or one of the CRTLF command's allowable WAITRCD parameter values.

SHARE   **Share open data path**
    *SAME or one of the CRTLF command's allowable SHARE parameter values.

LVLCHK   **Record format level identifiers in the program are checked against those in the logical file**
    *SAME or one of the CRTLF command's allowable LVLCHK parameter values.

TEXT   **Descriptive text**
    *SAME or one of the CRTLF command's allowable TEXT parameter values.

CHGLFM (Change Logical File Member) Command
Change the attributes of a logical file member.

Required Parameter
FILE   **File name**
    logical-file-name   Logical file that contains the member that is changed. Name can be qualified with *LIBL, *CURLIB, or library name.

Optional Parameters
MBR   **Member name**
    *FIRST   First member in the database file is used.

    logical-file-member-name Logical file member that is changed.

SHARE   **Logical file member shared with other programs**
    *SAME   Value does not change.

    *NO   ODP created by the program with this attribute is not shared.

    *YES   ODP created with this attribute is shared.

TEXT   **Descriptive text**
    *SAME   Value does not change.

    *BLANK   Text is not specified.

    '*description*'   No more than 50 characters of text, enclosed in apostrophes.

CHGPF (Change Physical File) Command
Change the attributes of a physical file and all its members. The changed attributes are also used for all members subsequently added to the file. Where noted, the allowable parameter values are the keyword *SAME or the set of values described under the CRTPF command. To change the attributes of a specific member, use the CHGPFM command.

Required Parameter
FILE   **File name**
    physical-file-name   Name of the physical file to be changed. File name can be qualified with *LIBL, *CURLIB, or library name.

Optional Parameters
SYSTEM   **Specifies local system or a remote system**
    *LCL   Physical file is changed on the local system.

    *RMT   Physical file is changed on a remote system.

    *FILETYPE   If the name specified on the FILE parameter is a DDM file, the physical file is changed on the remote system specified by the RMTLOCNAME parameter of that DDM file.

SRCFILE   **DDS source file**
    *SAME or one of the CRTPF command's allowable SRCFILE parameter values.

SRCMBR   **DDS source member**
　　　*SAME or one of the CRTPF command's allowable SRCMBR parameter values.

OPTION   **Compile options**
　　　*SAME or one of the CRTPF command's allowable OPTION parameter values.

GENLVL   **Compile error level**
　　　*SAME or one of the CRTPF command's allowable GENLVL parameter values.

FLAG   **Compile error flag level**
　　　*SAME or one of the CRTPF command's allowable FLAG parameter values.

DLTDEPLF   **Delete logical files dependent on deleted field**
　　*NO   The logical files are not deleted. The command fails.

　　　*YES   The logical files that are dependent on a field that is
                                        removed from the file are deleted.

RMVCST   **Remove constraint relationships in the associated set of
                                        dependent files when you are deleting a parent file of a
                                        referential constraint.** This parameter is valid only when
                                        DLTDEPLF(*YES) is specified.
　　*RESTRICT   The constraint relationships are not removed. The com-
                                        mand fails.

　　*REMOVE   The constraints that are dependent on a field that is
                                        removed from the file are removed.

EXPDATE   **Expiration date**
　　　*SAME or one of the CRTPF command's allowable EXPDATE parameter values.

MAXMBRS   **Maximum number of members**
　　　*SAME or one of the CRTPF command's allowable MAXMBRS parameter values.

ACCPTHSIZ   **Maximum size of access paths**
　　　*SAME or one of the CRTPF command's allowable ACCPTHSIZ parameter values.

MAINT   **Type of access path maintenance**
　　　*SAME or one of the CRTPF command's allowable MAINT parameter values.

RECOVER   **Recovery of the file is done if a system failure occurs**
　　　*SAME or one of the CRTPF command's allowable RECOVER parameter values.

FRCACCPTH   **Access path changes are forced to auxiliary storage**
　　　*SAME or one of the CRTPF command's allowable FRCACCPTH parameter values.

SIZE   **Number of records in each member of the file**
　　　*SAME or one of the CRTPF command's allowable SIZE parameter values.

ALLOCATE   **Storage space is allocated for the initial number of records**
　　　*SAME or one of the CRTPF command's allowable ALLOCATE parameter values.

FRCRATIO   **Number of changed records processed before being
                                        forced to storage**
　　　*SAME or one of the CRTPF command's allowable FRCRATIO parameter values.

WAITFILE   **Number of seconds the program waits for the file resources**
*SAME or one of the CRTPF command's allowable WAITFILE parameter values.

WAITRCD   **Number of seconds that a program waits for record lock**
*SAME or one of the CRTPF command's allowable WAITRCD parameter values.

SHARE   **Share Open Data Path**
*SAME or one of the CRTPF command's allowable SHARE parameter values.

DLTPCT   **Maximum percentage of deleted records that any member in the physical file can have**
*SAME or one of the CRTPF command's allowable DLTPCT parameter values.

REUSEDLT   **Specifies whether the space made available by deleting data entries is reclaimed**
*SAME or one of the CRTPF command's allowable REUSEDLT parameter values.

CCSID   **The coded character set identifier used to describe character data**
*SAME or one of the CRTPF command's allowable CCSID parameter values.

LVLCHK   **Record format level identifiers in the program are checked against those in the physical file when the file is opened**
*SAME or one of the CRTPF command's allowable LVLCHK parameter values.

TEXT   **Descriptive text**
*SAME or one of the CRTPF command's allowable TEXT parameter values.

CHGPFCST (Change Physical File Constraint) Command
Change the state of one or more referential (foreign key) constraints for a physical file.

Required Parameters
FILE   **File name**
physical-file-name   Physical file which has constraint(s) to be changed. Name can be qualified with *LIBL, *CURLIB, or library name.

CST   **Specifies the constraint(s) to be changed**
  *ALL   All constraints for the specified file.
  *CHKPND   All constraints with a "check pending" status for the specified file.
  constraint-name   The name of the constraint to change.

Optional Parameter
STATE   **The state to which the constraint is being changed**
  *SAME   The value does not change.
  *ENABLED   The constraint that was disabled starts providing referential integrity again.
  *DISABLED   The constraint stops providing referential integrity.

CHGPFM (Change Physical File Member) Command

Change the attributes of a physical file member.

Required Parameters

FILE   **File name**

   physical-file-name   File that contains the member to be changed. Name can be qualified with <u>*LIBL</u>, *CURLIB, or library name.

MBR

   *FIRST   First member in the database file is used.

   member-name   Name of the physical file member to be changed.

Optional Parameters

SRCTYPE   **Source type**

   <u>*SAME</u>   Value does not change

   *NONE   No source type is specified.

   source-type   Source type of a member.

EXPDATE   **Expiration date**

   <u>*SAME</u>   Value does not change

   *NONE   No expiration date is specified.

   expiration-date   Date after which the member cannot be used.

SHARE   **Share Open Data Path**

   <u>*SAME</u>   Value does not change

   *NO   ODP is not shared.

   *YES   ODP is shared.

TEXT   **Descriptive text**

   <u>*SAME</u>   Value does not change

   *BLANK   Text is not specified.

   '*description*'   No more than 50 characters of text, enclosed in apostrophes.

CHGSRCPF (Change Source Physical File) Command

Change the attributes of a source physical file and its members. Where noted, the allowable parameter values are the keyword *SAME or the set of values described under the CRTPF command. The changed attributes are also used for all members subsequently added to the file.

Required Parameter

FILE   **File name**

   source-physical-file-name   File that is changed. File name can be qualified with <u>*LIBL</u>, *CURLIB, or library name.

Optional Parameters

SYSTEM   **Local or remote system**

   <u>*LCL</u>   Source physical file is changed on the local system.

   *RMT: Source physical file is changed on a remote system.

*FILETYPE   If the name specified on the FILE parameter is a DDM file, the physical file is changed on the remote system specified by the RMTLOCNAME parameter of that DDM file.

EXPDATE   **Expiration date**

*SAME or one of the CRTPF command's allowable EXPDATE parameter values.

MAXMBRS   **Maximum number of members**

*SAME or one of the CRTPF command's allowable MAXMBRS parameter values.

MAINT   **Type of access path maintenance**

*SAME or one of the CRTPF command's allowable MAINT parameter values.

RECOVER   **Recovery of the file is done if a system failure occurs**

*SAME or one of the CRTPF command's allowable RECOVER parameter values.

FRCACCPTH   **Access path changes are forced to auxiliary storage**

*SAME or one of the CRTPF command's allowable FRCACCPTH parameter values.

SIZE   **Number of records in each member of the file**

*SAME or one of the CRTPF command's allowable SIZE parameter values.

ALLOCATE   **Storage space is allocated for the initial number of records**

*SAME or one of the CRTPF command's allowable ALLOCATE parameter values.

FRCRATIO   **Number of changed records processed before being forced to storage**

*SAME or one of the CRTPF command's allowable FRCRATIO parameter values.

WAITFILE   **Number of seconds the program waits for the file resources**

*SAME or one of the CRTPF command's allowable WAITFILE parameter values.

WAITRCD   **Number of seconds that a program waits for a record lock**

*SAME or one of the CRTPF command's allowable WAITRCD parameter values.

SHARE   **Share Open Data Path**

*SAME or one of the CRTPF command's allowable SHARE parameter values.

DLTPCT   **Maximum percentage of deleted records that any member in the physical file can have**

*SAME or one of the CRTPF command's allowable DLTPCT parameter values.

CCSID   **The coded character set identifier used to describe character data**

*SAME or one of the CRTPF command's allowable CCSID parameter values.

TEXT   **Descriptive text**

*SAME or one of the CRTPF command's allowable TEXT parameter values.

CLRPFM (Clear Physical File Member) Command

Remove all the data (including deleted records) from the specified member of a physical file.

Required Parameter

FILE   **File name**

    physical-file-name   File that contains the member being cleared. Name can be qualified with *<u>LIBL</u>, *CURLIB, or library name.

Optional Parameter

MBR   **Member name**

    <u>*FIRST</u>   First member in the physical file is used.

    *LAST   Last member of the specified physical file is cleared.

    member-name   Physical file member that is cleared.

CPYF (Copy File) Command

Copy all or part of a database or external device file to a database or external device file. Copy operations can be done from physical, logical, diskette, tape, inline, or DDM files to physical, diskette, tape, printer, or DDM files.

Required Parameters

FROMFILE   **File that contains the records being copied**

    file-name   File from which data is copied. Name can be qualified with *<u>LIBL</u>, *CURLIB, or library name.

TOFILE   **File that receives the copied records**

    file-name   File to which data is copied. Name can be qualified with *<u>LIBL</u>, *CURLIB, or library name.

    *PRINT   Data is copied to the IBM-supplied printer device file QSYSPRT

Optional Parameters

FROMMBR   **The file member that is copied**

    <u>*FIRST</u>   First member in a database from-file is copied.

    *ALL   All members of a database from-file copied.

    member-name   The from-file member being copied.

    generic-member-name*   All database members that have names with the same prefix.

TOMBR   **File member that receives the copied records**

    <u>*FIRST</u>   First member in the database to-file receives the copied records.

    *FROMMBR   Corresponding from-file and to-file member names

    member-name   Physical to-file member to receive the copied records.

MBROPT   **New records replace or are added to the existing records**

    <u>*NONE</u>   Parameter does not apply to this copy operation.

    *ADD   System adds the new records to the end of the existing records.

	*REPLACE	System clears the existing member and adds the new records.
	*UPDADD	The system updates duplicate key records and adds new records to the end of the file.
CRTFILE		**Creates a physical file if the to-file does not exist**
	*NO	File is not created to receive the data.
	*YES	File is created with the name specified on the TOFILE parameter.
PRINT		**Copied records, excluded records, or both are printed**
	*NONE	Neither copied nor excluded records are printed.
	*EXCLD	Records excluded from the copy operation are printed.
	*COPIED	Copied records are printed.
	*ERROR	The number of recoverable output error records specified on the ERRLVL parameter are printed.
RCDFMT		**Name of the record format that is copied**
	*ONLY	The only record format in the from-file is copied.
	*ALL	All record formats in the logical from-file are used.
	record-format-name	Name of the record format copied.
FROMRCD		**The record number of the first record in the from-file copied**
	*START	Copy operation begins with the first record in the file.
	starting-record-number	First record copied from the from-file.
TORCD		**Record number of the last record in the from-file copied**
	*END	Records are copied until the end-of-file is reached.
	ending-record-number	Last record copied from the from-file.
FROMKEY		**Key value of the first record in the from-file is copied**
	*NONE	First record copied is not selected by key.
	nbr-of-key-fields '*key-value*'	Number of key fields and single character key value.
	*BLDKEY '*key-value*' ...	List of one or more key field values.
TOKEY		**Key value of the last record in the from-file copied**
	*NONE	Last record copied is not selected by key.
	nbr-of-key-fields '*key-value*'	Number of key fields and single character key value.
	*BLDKEY '*key-value*' ...	List of one or more key field values.
NBRRCDS		**Number of records in the from-file copied to the to-file**
	*END	Records are copied until the end-of-file.
	number-of-records	Number of records copied to the to-file.
INCCHAR		**Records are copied or excluded based on the result of a comparison with a character string value**
	*NONE	No character string comparison is used

*RCD *start-position relop* '*comparison-string*' ...
>> List of comparisons for positions in the record.

field-name start-position relop '*comparison-string*' ...
>> List of comparisons for positions in each record's fields.

>> The valid *relop* values are:

>> *EQ Equal

>> *GT Greater than

>> *LT Less than

>> *NE Not equal

>> *GE Greater than or equal

>> *NL Not less than

>> *LE Less than or equal

>> *NG Not greater than

>> *CT Contains

INCREL **Records are copied or excluded based on whether certain fields in the record contain data that satisfies specified relationships**

NONE: No field value relationships are used to select records.

logical-op field-name relop '*comparison-string*' ...
>> The valid *logical-op* values are

>> *IF Identifies the first field value relationship that must be satisfied before a record is copied.

>> *AND The tests on both sides of the *AND element must all be satisfied before a record is copied.

>> *OR A test on either side of the *OR value must all be satisfied before a record is copied.

>> The valid *relop* values are the same as listed for the INCCHAR parameter, above.

FMTOPT **Specifies field-level record format processing**

*NONE No field mapping or dropping is done during the copy operation.

*NOCHK Copy operation continues even if the record formats of the database files are different.

*CVTSRC Convert from a data file to a source file or vice-versa.

*MAP Fields with the same name in the from-file and to-file record formats are copied.

*DROP For field-level mapping, specify *DROP if any of the field names in the from-file record format do not exist in the to-file format.

*CVTFLOAT Processes each floating point field identified by the external description of the output database physical file and convert it from System/370 hexadecimal format to the IEEE format used by AS/400 systems.

*NULLFLAGS	Takes the byte following each field identified as being nullable by the external description of the output file, and use it as a flag to indicate if the corresponding input field is null.

SRCOPT   **Sequence numbers are inserted in the sequence number fields, and date fields are set to zero**

*SAME	Value does not change.
*SEQNBR	New source sequence numbers are inserted in the records copied.
*DATE	Source date field is set to zero in the records copied to the to-file.

SRCSEQ   **Sequence number given to the first record copied to the to-file**

starting-value	Sequence number of the first source record copied to the to-file; increment is 1.00.
starting-value increment-value	Sequence number of the first source record copied to the to-file, and increment for following records.

OUTFMT   **Copied records are printed as character or hexadecimal**

*CHAR	Records are printed in character format only.
*HEX	Records are printed in character format and hexadecimal format.

ERRLVL   **Number of recoverable errors during the copy operation**

0	Copy operation ends at the file member in which the error occurs.
*NOMAX	All recoverable errors are tolerated.
number-of-errors	Maximum number of recoverable errors that is allowed.

COMPRESS   **To-file contains a compressed form of the from-file**

*YES	Records copied to the to-file are compressed.
*NO	Both the deleted and nondeleted records are copied to the to-file.

CRTLIB (Create Library) Command

Create a new library.

Required Parameter

LIB   **Name of the library being created**

library-name	Library to be created.

Optional Parameters

TYPE   **Type of library being created**

*PROD	Production library.
*TEST	Test library.

AUT   **Authority given to users**

*LIBCRTAUT	Authority is the same as the create authority for QSYS.

	*USE	Provides object operational authority, read authority, and execute authority.
	*CHANGE	User can perform all operations on the object except those limited to the owner or controlled by object existence authority and object management authority.
	*ALL	User can perform all operations except those limited to the owner.
	*EXCLUDE	User cannot access the library.
	authorization-list-name	Name of the authorization list used.
CRTAUT		**Authority given to users when object is created in library**
	SYSVAL	The QCRTAUT system value is used.
	*USE	User can perform basic operations on the object.
	*CHANGE	User can perform all operations on the object except those limited to the owner or controlled by object existence authority and object management authority.
	*ALL	User can perform all operations on the object except those limited to the owner .
	*EXCLUDE	User cannot access the object.
	authorization-list-name	Authorization list whose authority is used for the object.
CRTOBJAUD		**Auditing value for objects created in this library**
	SYSVAL	Value specified in the system value QCRTOBJAUD is used.
	*NONE	No audit entry will be sent to the security journal.
	*USRPRF	User profile is used to determine if an audit record will be sent for this access.
	*CHANGE	All change accesses to this object by all users are logged.
	*ALL	All change or read accesses to this object by all users are logged.
ASP	**Auxiliary storage pool**	
	1	Storage space is allocated from the system auxiliary storage pool.
	asp-identifier	Specify a value for the ASP identifier.
TEXT		**Descriptive text**
	BLANK	Text is not specified.
	'*description*'	No more than 50 characters of text, enclosed in apostrophes.

CRTSRCPF (Create Source Physical File) Command

Create a source physical file. All parameters have the same set of allowable values as described under the CRTPF command.

Required Parameter

FILE   **File name to be created**

Optional Parameters

RCDLEN	Length (in bytes) of the records being stored in the source file
MBR	Member name
SYSTEM	Specifies local system or a remote system
EXPDATE	Expiration date
MAXMBRS	Maximum number of members
ACCPTH	Type of access path
ACCPTHSIZ	Maximum size of access paths
MAINT	Type of access path maintenance
RECOVER	Recovery of the file is done if a system failure occurs
FRCACCPTH	Access path changes are forced to auxiliary storage
SIZE	Number of records in each member of the file
ALLOCATE	Storage space is allocated for the initial number of records
CONTIG	Records in each source file member are stored contiguously
FRCRATIO	Number of changed records processed before being forced to storage
IGCDTA	File contains double-byte character set (DBCS) data
WAITFILE	Number of seconds the program waits for the file resources
WAITRCD	Number of seconds that a program waits for a record lock
CCSID	The coded character set identifier used to describe character data
SHARE	Share Open Data Path
DLTPCT	Maximum percentage of deleted records that any member in the physical file can have
ALWUPD	Records are updated in the physical file
ALWDLT	Records can be deleted from the physical file
AUT	Authority given to users who do not have specific authority to the source file
TEXT	Descriptive text

DLTF (Delete File) Command

Delete the specified database or device file(s) from the system. Deleting a file also frees the storage space allocated to the file. If a database file (physical or logical) is deleted, all members contained in the file are also deleted.

Required Parameter

FILE	File name
file-name	File to be deleted. File name can be qualified with *LIBL, *CURLIB, *USRLIBL, *ALL, *ALLUSR, or library name.
generic-file-name*	All files that have names with the same prefix.

Optional Parameters

SYSTEM	File is deleted from the local or a remote system
*LCL:	File is deleted from the local system.
*RMT:	File is deleted from a remote system.
*FILETYPE:	If a DDM file is specified on the FILE parameter, the remote file identifier in the DDM file is deleted from the remote system.

RMVCST	Whether to remove constraints when a parent file is deleted
*RESTRICT	Parent file is not deleted and the constraint relationship is not removed, if one exists.
*REMOVE	The constraint relationship between the parent file and a dependent file is removed.
*KEEP	The constraint relationship is no longer established, but the constraint definition is not removed.

DSPCPCST (Display Check Pending Constraint) Command

Display records that are potentially in violation of foreign key (referential) constraints for a physical file.

Required Parameters

FILE	File name
physical-file-name	Physical file which has constraint. Name can be qualified with *LIBL, *CURLIB, or library name.

CST	The constraint whose records are displayed
constraint-name	The name of the constraint to display.

OUTPUT	Whether the output from the command is shown at the requesting workstation or printed with the job's spooled output
*	The output requested by an interactive job is shown on the display. The output requested by a batch job is printed with the job's spooled output.
*PRINT	The output is printed with the job's spooled output.

DSPDBR (Display Database Relations) Command

Display, print, or place in a file information about database files. The information identifies the physical and logical files that are dependent on a specific file, files that use a specific record format, or file members that are dependent on a specific file member.

Required Parameter

FILE	File name
*ALL	Display all files in specified libraries.
generic*-file-name	All files that have names with the same prefix are displayed.
file-name	File to display.
	*ALL, generic file name, or specific file name can be qualified with *LIBL, *CURLIB, *USRLIBL, *ALLUSR, or library name.

Optional Parameters

MBR	Member name to provide relations information on
*NONE	No information about file members' relations is provided.
member-name	Name of the physical file member to display the relations for.

RCDFMT	Record format name to provide relations information on
*NONE	No information about file record format relations is provided.
*ALL	All record format relations information is provided.
format-name	Name of the physical file record format to display the relations for.
generic*-format-name	All record formats that have names with the same prefix are displayed.

OUTPUT	Output from the command is provided at the requesting work station, printed, or placed in a database output file
*	Output requested by an interactive job is shown on the display.
*PRINT	Output is printed with the job's spooled output.
*OUTFILE	Output is directed to the database file specified on the OUTFILE parameter.

OUTFILE	Database output file to which the output is directed
database-file-name	Database file that receives the output of the command. File name can be qualified with *LIBL, *CURLIB, or library name.

OUTMBR	Database file member to which the output is directed
Element 1 — Member to Receive Output	
*FIRST	First member in the file receives the output.
member-name	File member that receives the output.
Element 2 — Operation to Perform on Member	
*REPLACE	System clears the existing member and adds the new records.
*ADD	System adds the new records to the end of the existing records.

DSPFD (Display File Description) Command

Display one or more types of information retrieved from the file descriptions of one or more database and/or device files.

Required Parameter

FILE	File name
*ALL	All files
generic-file-name*	All files that have names with the same prefix.
file-name	File whose description are displayed. *ALL, generic file name, or file name can be qualified with <u>*LIBL</u>, *CURLIB, *USRLIBL, *ALL, *ALLUSR, or library name.

Optional Parameters

TYPE	Types of file information that are provided
Single Values	
<u>*ALL</u>	All types of information that apply to the specified file are provided.
*BASATR	Basic attribute information common to all files is provided.
Multiple Values	
*ATR	Attribute information for the specified file is provided.
*ACCPTH	Access paths of the specified file are provided.
*MBRLIST	All members in the file and a brief description of each member is provided.
*SELECT	Select/omit attribute information is provided.
*SEQ	Collating sequence information is provided.
*RCDFMT	Record format names and record format level information for the file are provided.
*MBR	Information about the file members in the specified file is provided.
*SPOOL	Spooling attributes of the diskette or printer file are provided.
*JOIN	Join from-file, the join to-file, and the fields that are involved in the join are provided.
*TRG	Trigger information for each file with a trigger are provided.
*CST	Constraint relationships associated with the file are provided.

OUTPUT	Output from the command is provided at the requesting work station, printed, or placed in a database output file
<u>*</u>	Output requested by an interactive job is shown on the display.
*PRINT	Output is printed with the job's spooled output.
*OUTFILE	Output is directed to the database file specified on the OUTFILE parameter.

FILEATR	Type of file whose attributes are shown
<u>*ALL</u>	Attributes of all files are shown.
*DSPF	Attributes of display files are provided.

*PRTF	Attributes of printer files are provided.
*DKTF	Attributes of diskette files are provided.
*TAPF	Attributes of tape files are provided.
*CMNF	Attributes of communications files are provided.
*BSCF	Attributes of BSC communications files are provided.
*MXDF	Attributes of mixed files are provided.
*PF	Attributes of physical files are provided.
*LF	Attributes of logical files are provided.
*SAVF	Attributes of save files are provided.
*DDMF	Attributes of the Distributed Data Management files are provided.
*ICFF	Attributes of ICF files are provided.

OUTFILE   **Database output file to which the output is directed**
 database-file-name   Database file that receives the output of the command. File name can be qualified with *LIBL, *CURLIB, or library name.

OUTMBR   **Database file member to which the output is directed**
Element 1 — Member to Receive Output
  *FIRST   First member in the file receives the output.
  member-name   File member that receives the output.
Element 2 — Operation to Perform on Member
  *REPLACE   System clears the existing member and adds the new records.
  *ADD   System adds the new records to the end of the existing records.

SYSTEM   **Location of information about files**
  *LCL   The information is about local files only.
  *RMT   Information is about remote files.
  *ALL   Information is about files on both the local and the remote systems.

DSPFFD (Display File Field Description) Command

Display, print, or place in a database file, field-level information for one or more files.

Required Parameter
FILE   **File name**
  Same as for DSPFD command's FILE parameter.

Optional Parameters
OUTPUT   **Output is shown at the work station, printed with the job's spooled output, or placed in a database outfile**
  Same as for DSPFD command's OUTPUT parameter.

OUTFILE   **Database file where the displayed information is stored**
  Same as for DSPFD command's OUTFILE parameter.

OUTMBR   **Database file member to which the output is directed**
    Same as for DSPFD command's OUTMBR parameter.

SYSTEM   **Location of information returned by the DSPFFD command**
    Same as for DSPFD command's SYSTEM parameter.

DSPPFM (Display Physical File Member) Command

Display a physical database file member. Records are shown in arrival sequence, even if the file has a keyed access path.

Required Parameter

FILE   **File name**
    file-name   File that contains member to display. File name can be qualified with <u>*LIBL</u>, *CURLIB, or library name.

Optional Parameters

MBR   **Member name**
    <u>*FIRST</u>   First member in the database file is used.
    *LAST   Last member of the specified physical file is shown.
    member-name   Name of the physical file member to display.

FROMRCD   **Record shown on the initial display**
    <u>*FIRST</u>   First record in the database file is shown.
    *END   Last non-deleted record in the physical file is shown.
    record-number   Number of the record shown on the top line of the initial display.

EDTCPCST (Edit Check Pending Constraint) Command

Display list of referential constraints with "check pending" status. This command has no parameters.

INZPFM (Initialize Physical File Member) Command

Initialize records in a member of a physical file to the specified type of record (either default or deleted records). This command is usually used for files that are processed in arrival sequence or by relative record numbers. If the initialized member is empty, records are added and initialized to the specified type; if the member is not empty, records of the specified type are added to the member. As many records are added as is necessary to make the total record count specified.

Required Parameter

FILE   **File name**
    file-name   File that contains the member to be intialized. File name can be qualified with <u>*LIBL</u>, *CURLIB, or library name.

Optional Parameters

MBR   **Member name**
    <u>*FIRST</u>   First member in the database file is used.
    *LAST   Last member of the specified physical file is initialized.
    member-name   Name of member that is intialized.

RECORDS	Type of records that are initialized
*DFT	Member is initialized with default records.
*DLT	Member is initialized with deleted records.
TOTRCDS	Total number of records in the member after it is initialized
*NXTINCR	Number of records in the member is increased to the next file size increment.
total-records	Total number of records.

MOVOBJ (Move Object) Command

Move an object from its currently assigned library and place it in a different library.

Required Parameters

OBJ	Object being moved to another library
object-name	Name of the object that is moved. Object name can be qualified with *LIBL, *CURLIB, or library name.
OBJTYPE	Type of the object moved to another library
object-type	Any valid OS/400 object type (e.g., *FILE or *PGM)
TOLIB	Library to which the object is moved
*CURLIB	Object is moved to the current library.
library-name	Library to which the object is moved.

OPNQRYF (Open Query File) Command

Open a file that contains a set of database records that satisfies a database query request.

Required Parameter

FILE	File(s), member(s), and format(s) used in the query file
file-name member record-format-name ...	List of one or more file, member, and record format specifications. File name can be qualified with *LIBL, *CURLIB, or library name.
	Member is optional and can be *FIRST, *LAST, or member name.
	Record format name is optional and can be *ONLY or format name.

Optional Parameters

OPTION	Open option used for the query file
*INP	Open the file for input.
*OUT	Open the file for output.
*UPD	Open the file for update operations.
*DLT	Open the file for delete operations.
*ALL	Opens the file for all operations.

FORMAT	**Record format used for records made available by using the OPNQRYF command**
*FILE	The record format of the first or only entry on the FILE parameter is used.
file-name record-format-name	Database file that has the record format to be used.
	Record format name is optional and can be *ONLY or format name.
QRYSLT	**Expression used to select records (before grouping) that are included in the query file**
*ALL	All records are selected.
'query-selection'	Expression that describes the values used to determine which records are selected.
KEYFLD	**Key field(s) used to arrange the query records**
*NONE	Key fields are not used to arrange the query records.
*FILE	The query records have the same arrangement as the first file, file member, and record format specified on the FILE parameter.
key-field-name order absval ...	List of one or more field names used to define a keyed access path to arrange the query records.
	order is optional and can be *ASCEND or *DESCEND
	absval is optional and can be *ABSVAL.
UNIQUEKEY	**Specifies whether the query is restricted to records with unique key values, and specifies how many of the key fields must be unique**
*NONE	None of the key fields specified on the KEYFLD parameter must be unique.
*ALL	All key fields specified on the KEYFLD parameter must be unique.
number-of-key-fields	Specify the number of key fields that must be unique.
JFLD	**Query join specification**
*NONE	No join operation is specified.
field-name1 field-name2 join-operator ...	List of one or more fields to join records on.
	Second field name is optional
	join-operator is optional and can be *EQ, *GT, *LT, *NE, *GE, *LE
JDFTVAL	**Whether the query file includes join records that use default values for any of the fields**
*NO	Default values are not used to construct join query records.
*YES	Creates all records for the join operation, including those produced both with and without default values.

*ONLYDFT	Creates only the records produced by using default values in constructing the join operation.
JORDER	**Whether the join order must match the order specified on the FILE parameter**
*ANY	Any join file order is allowed, and any such arrangement may be used by the system to create the result records.
*FILE	The order of the file, file member, and record format elements specified on the FILE parameter are preserved in the join operation.
GRPFLD	**Field(s) used to group query results**
*NONE	Fields are not used to form groups.
qualified-group-field ...	List of field names to group the query results.
GRPSLT	**Expression used to select records (after grouping) that are included in the query file**
*ALL	All records defined by the grouping function described in the GRPFLD parameter description are selected.
'*group-selection*'	Expression that describes the values used to determine which records are selected.
MAPFLD	**Definition of query fields that are either mapped to, or derived from, other fields**
*NONE	Mapped fields are not used.
mapped-field-name '*mapped-field-definition*' *field-type field-length field-decimals field-CCSID*	List of one or more field mapping definitions. The mapped field definition is an expression that defines the mapped field in terms of other fields that exist in one of the file, file member, and record format elements specified on the FILE parameter, or are defined by some other mapped field definition appearing earlier in the MAPFLD list. The other parameter values are optional and define the mapped field.
IGNDECERR	**Whether the system ignores decimal data errors during query file processing**
*NO	The system does not ignore decimal data errors.
*YES	The system ignores decimal data errors.
OPNID	**The identifier used to name the query file for subsequent reference by CLOF or POSDBF commands**
*FILE	The name of the first or only file specified on the FILE parameter is used for the open query file identifier.
open-identifier-name	Specify the name to associate with this open query file.
SEQONLY	**Whether sequential-only processing is used for the query file, and also specifies the number of records that can be processed as a group when read or write operations are performed**
*YES *number-of-records*	The query file uses sequential-only processing, with the number of records specified being processed as a group.
*NO	The file does not use sequential-only processing.

COMMIT		Whether the I/O operations are run under commitment control
	*NO	The open query file is not placed under commitment control.
	*YES	The open query file is placed under commitment control.
OPNSCOPE		**The extent of influence (scope) of the open operation**
	*ACTGRPDFN	The scope of the open operation is determined by the activation group of the program that called the OPNQRYF command processing program.
	*ACTGRP	The scope of the open data path (ODP) is the activation group.
	*JOB	The scope of the open operation is the job in which the open operation occurs.
DUPKEYCHK		Whether duplicate key feedback is returned on input/output (I/O) operations
	*NO	Duplicate key feedback is not returned on I/O operations.
	*YES	Duplicate key feedback is returned on I/O operations.
ALWCPYDTA		**Whether the system is allowed to copy data from the files specified on the FILE parameter**
	*YES	The system may use a copy of data from the files.
	*NO	The system does not use a copy of data from the files.
	*OPTIMIZE	The system can use a sort routine to order the output from the files.
OPTIMIZE		**Specifies the most efficient way the system can perform the selection and join processing necessary to satisfy the other parameter specifications on the OPNQRYF command**
	*ALLIO	The system attempts to reduce the total input/output time required to process the whole query, assuming that all query records are read from the file.
	*FIRSTIO *number-of-records*	The system attempts to reduce the input/output time required to open the query file and to retrieve the first buffer of records from the file.
	*MINWAIT *number-of-records*	The system attempts to reduce the time required to open the query file by minimizing delays when records are read from the file.
OPTALLAP		**Whether the query optimizer should consider all potential access paths**
	*NO	Allow the query optimizer to operate normally.
	*YES	Force the query optimizer to ignore the internal timeout value and consider all available access paths.
SRTSEQ		**Sort sequence for character variables**
	*JOB	The SRTSEQ value for the job is retrieved for the command.

*HEX	A sort sequence table is not used.
*LANGIDUNQ	A unique-weight sort table is used.
*LANGIDSHR	A shared-weight sort table is used.
table-name	Specify the name of the sort sequence table to be used with this query. Table name can be qualified with *LIBL, *CURLIB, or library name.

LANGID	**Language identifier used when *LANGIDUNQ or *LANGIDSHR is specified for SRTSEQ**
*JOB	The LANGID value for the job is retrieved for the command.
language-ID	Specify the language identifier to be used by the command.
TYPE	**Invocation level at which the RCLRSC (Reclaim Resources) command closes the file**
*NORMAL	When the program that ran the OPNQRYF command is ended without closing the file.
*PERM	The file remains open until the Close File (CLOF) command closes it, or until the routing step or default activation group ends.

OVRDBF (Override with Database File) Command

Override (replace) the file named in a program, or override certain attributes of a file that is used by a program. Where noted, the allowable parameter values are the same as described under the CRTPF command.

Required Parameter

FILE	**File name**
file-name	File used by the program to which the override command is applied. File name can be qualified with *LIBL, *CURLIB, or library name.

Optional Parameters

TOFILE	**File used instead of the file specified in the FILE parameter**
*FILE	Use file named in FILE parameter.
database-file-name	File used instead of the file specified in the FILE parameter. File name can be qualified with *LIBL, *CURLIB, or library name
MBR	**Member to open**
*FIRST	First member in the database file is used.
*LAST	Last member of the specified physical file is used.
*ALL	All members in the file are processed sequentially.
member-name	The member name to open.
POSITION	**Starting position for retrieving records from the database file**
*NONE	No special positioning is specified.
*START	Starting position is the first record in the file.
*END	Starting position is the last record in the file.

*RRN *relative-record-number*

> Relative record number of first record to retrieve.

key-relop nbr-of-fields rcdfmt 'key-value'

> The *key-relop* is one of the following:

*KEYB (key-before)	Record that precedes the record identified by the remaining search values.
*KEYBE (key-before or equal)	Record identified by the search values, or the record before the specified key value, is the first record retrieved.
*KEY (key-equal)	Record identified by the search values is the first record retrieved.
*KEYAE (key-after or equal)	Record identified by the search values, or the record after the specified key value, is the first record retrieved.
*KEYA (key-after)	Record that follows the record identified by the remaining search values.

> The *nbr-of-fields* is the number of key fields to use in the search.
>
> The *rcdfmt* is the name of the record format in the database file that contains the key value specified.
>
> The '*key-value*' is a quoted string or hexadecimal value.

RCDFMTLCK   **Lock state of the named record format while it is used by the program**

record-format-name lock-type

> The *lock-type* is one of the following:

*SHRRD	Shared read.
*SHRNUP	Shared read, no update.
*SHRUPD	Shared update.
*EXCLRD	Exclusive allow read.
*EXCL	Exclusive no read.

FRCRATIO   **Number of insert, delete, or update operations that can occur on records before they are forced into storage**

Same as the CRTPF command's allowable FRCRATIO parameter values.

FMTSLR   **Record format selector**

program-name   Name of the format selector program called when a record is inserted into a member having more than one format. Program name can be qualified by *<u>LIBL</u>, *CURLIBL or library name.

WAITFILE	**Seconds the program waits for file resources and session resources to be allocated when the file is opened**

Same as the CRTPF command's allowable WAITFILE parameter values.

WAITRCD	**Seconds that a program waits for a lock for a record to be updated or deleted, or for a record read in the commitment control environment**

Same as the CRTPF command's allowable WAITRCD parameter values.

NBRRCDS	**Number of records moved as a unit from auxiliary storage to main storage**
number-of-records	Number of records to move at a time.
EOFDLY	**Number of seconds to delay when the end-of-file is reached before trying to retrieve additional records**
*NONE	Normal end-of-file processing is done.
number-of-seconds	Number of seconds that the program waits between each attempt to get a record when an end-of-file condition occurs.
LVLCHK	**Record format level identifiers in the program are checked against those in the device file when the file is opened**
*NO	The level identifiers are not checked.
EXPCHK	**Expiration date of the named member is checked**
*YES	Expiration date of the physical file member is checked.
*NO	Expiration date is not checked.
INHWRT	**Specifies whether the processed records are written, deleted, or changed in the database file**
*YES	Records are prevented from being written into the database.
*NO	Processed records are written into the database.
SECURE	**File is safe from previously executed file override commands**
*NO	File is not protected from the effects of other file overrides.
*YES	File is protected from the effects of any file override commands.
OVRSCOPE	**Specifies the extent of influence (scope) of the override**
*ACTGRPDFN	Scope of the override is determined by the activation group of the program that called the OVRDBF command processing program.
*CALLLVL	Scope of the override is determined by the current call level.
*JOB	Scope of the override is the job in which the override occurs.
SHARE	**Share Open Data Path**

Same as the CRTPF command's allowable SHARE parameter values.

OPNSCOPE	**Specifies the extent of influence (scope) of the open operation**
*ACTGRPDFN	Scope of the open operation is determined by the activation group of the program that called the OVRDBF command processing program.

*JOB	Scope of the open operation is the job in which the open operation occurs.
SEQONLY	**Files whose records are processed in sequential order only**
*NO	Database file is not restricted to sequential-only processing.
*YES	Database file uses sequential-only processing. The system calculates the block size.
*YES *number-of-records*	Database file uses sequential-only processing. Each block contains the number of records specified.

RGZPFM (Reorganize Physical File Member) Command

The Reorganize Physical File Member (RGZPFM) command compresses (removes deleted records) in one member of a physical file in the database, and it optionally reorganizes that member.

Required Parameter

FILE	**File name**
file-name	File that contains the member to be reorganized. File name can be qualified with *LIBL, *CURLIB, or library name.

Optional Parameters

MBR	**Member name**
*FIRST	First member in the database file is used.
*LAST	Last member of the specified physical file is reorganized.
member-name	File member to be reorganized.
SRCOPT	**For source files, whether reorganization places new numbers in the sequence number field, places zeros in the date field, or changes both fields**
*SAME	Values do not change.
*SEQNBR	Records have a new sequence number placed into the SRCSEQ (source sequence number) field.
*DATE	Records have a zero date (000000) placed in the SRCDAT (source date) field.
SRCSEQ	**For source files, sequence number given to the first record in the source file member and the increment value that is used to renumber all other records in the member**

Element 1 — Starting Value

1.00	First source record has a sequence number of 0001.00.
starting-value	Sequence number of the first record in the member.

Element 2 — Increment Value

1.00	Source records are renumbered in the member with whole number increments of 1
increment-value	Increment value for renumbering all source records following the first record.

KEYFILE	**Arrival sequence changed to match keyed sequence**
*NONE	Member is not reorganized.
*FILE	Sequence of the records changed to match keyed sequence.
logical-file-name member-name	
	Name of the logical file and member whose sequence is used to reorganize the physical file member. Logical file name can be qualified by *LIBL, *CURLIB, or library name.
RCDFMT	**Record format name if the physical file member is reorganized in the sequence of a multiple-format logical file**
*ONLY	Logical file specified by the KEYFILE parameter has only one record format.
record-format-name	Record format in the multiple-format logical file that is used to reorganize the physical file member.

RMVM (Remove Member) Command

Remove one or more members from a physical or logical file. Removing a physical file member deletes all the data in the member and frees the storage space allocated to that member and its access path. Removing a logical file member deletes its access path to the associated data stored in a physical file member.

Required Parameters

FILE	**File name**
file-name	Database file that contains the member being removed File name can be qualified with *LIBL, *CURLIB, or library name.
MBR	**Member name**
*ALL	All members found in the specified file are removed.
member-name	Name of the member to be removed.
g*eneric*-member-name*	All members that have names with the same prefix are removed.

RMVPFCST (Remove Physical File Constraint) Command

Remove one or more primary, unique, or foreign key (referential) constraints for a physical file.

Required Parameters

FILE	**File name**
physical-file-name	Physical file which has constraint(s) to be removed. Name can be qualified with *LIBL, *CURLIB, or library name.
CST	**Specifies the constraint(s) to be removed**
*ALL	All constraints for the specified file.
*CHKPND	All referential constraints with a "check pending" status for the specified file.
constraint-name	The name of the constraint to remove.

Optional Parameters

TYPE   **The type of constraints to remove**

    *ALL   All types of constraints that satisfy the CST parameter specification are removed.

    *REFCST   The referential constraints that satisfy the CST parameter specification are removed.

    *UNQCST   The unique constraints are removed.

    *PRIKEY   The primary key constraint is removed

RMVCST   **How much of the constraint relationship on the dependent file is removed when a primary key or unique constraint that is also a parent key is removed from the parent file of a referential constraint**

    *RESTRICT   The constraint is not removed if the constraint is either defined or established between the parent file and the dependent file.

    *REMOVE   The constraint and the constraint definition between the parent file and the dependent file are removed.

    *KEEP   The constraint between the parent file and the dependent file is removed, but the constraint definition is not removed.

RMVPFTRG (Remove Physical File Trigger) Command

Remove one or more triggers from a physical file.

Required Parameter

FILE   **File name**

    physical-file-name   Physical file to remove trigger from. Name can be qualified with *LIBL, *CURLIB, or library name.

Optional Parameters

TRGTIME   **Trigger time**

    *ALL   Remove triggers for both before and after events.

    *BEFORE   Remove triggers for before file operation events.

    *AFTER   Remove triggers for after file operation events.

TRGEVENT   **Trigger event**

    *ALL   Remove triggers for insert, delete, and update events.

    *INSERT   Remove triggers for insert events.

    *DELETE   Remove triggers for delete events.

    *UPDATE   Remove triggers for update operation.

RNMM (Rename Member) Command

Change the name of a file member.

Required Parameters

FILE

File name

file-name

Database file that contains the member being renamed. File name can be qualified with *LIBL, *CURLIB, or library name.

MBR Member name

member-name

Name of member to be renamed.

NEWMBR

New name of the member being renamed

new-member-name

New name of member.

RNMOBJ (Rename Object) Command

Change the name of an object.

Required Parameters

OBJ

Object name

object-name

Object to be renamed. Object name can be qualified with: *LIBL, *CURLIB, or library name.

OBJTYPE

object-type

Any valid OS/400 object type (e.g., *FILE or *PGM).

NEWOBJ

New name of the object being renamed

new-object-name

New name of object.

Optional Parameters

SYSTEM

Specifies local system or remote system

*LCL

Object is changed on the local system.

*RMT

Object is changed on a remote system.

*FILETYPE

If the name specified on the OBJ parameter is a DDM file, the file is changed on the remote system specified by the RMTLOCNAME parameter of that DDM file.

WRKF (Work with Files) Command

Show the Work with Files display that lets you copy, delete, display descriptions, save, and restore files that you have authority to use.

Required Parameter

FILE

File name

*ALL

Display all files in specified libraries.

generic-file-name*

All files that have names with the same prefix are displayed.

file-name

File to display.

*ALL, generic file name, or specific file name can be qualified with *LIBL, *CURLIB, *USRLIBL, *ALLUSR, or library name.

Optional Parameter
FILEATR   **Type of file for displayed files**
    *ALL   All types of files are shown.
    file-type   Any valid OS/400 file type (e.g., LF or PF).

WRKPFCST (Work with Physical File Constraint) Command
Show the Work with Physical File Constraints display that lets you remove one or more primary, unique, or foreign key (referential) constraints for a physical file or display referential constraints in "check pending" status.

Optional Parameters
FILE   **File name**
    *ALL   Display constraints for all files in specified libraries.
    generic-file-name*   Constraints for all files that have names with the same prefix are displayed.
    physical-file-name   Physical file with constraints to display.

                                          *ALL, generic file name, or specific physical file name can be qualified with *LIBL, *CURLIB, *ALL, or library name.

TYPE   **The type of constraints to display**
    *ALL   All types of constraints are displayed.
    *REFCST   Referential constraints are displayed.
    *UNQCST   Unique constraints are displayed.
    *PRIKEY   The primary key constraint is displayed.
    *CHKPND   Referential constraints with "check pending" status are displayed.

Appendix C

Using Programming Development Manager (PDM)[1]

Introduction

PDM is an AS/400 programming environment that provides access to OS/400 and HLL compiler functions through a standard list interface. PDM is not a part of the OS/400 operating system. Rather, it's a component of IBM's Application Development ToolSet/400 (ADTS/400) product, which also includes Source Entry Utility (SEU), Screen Design Aid (SDA), Report Layout Utility (RLU), and Interactive Source Debugger (ISDB). Most AS/400s used for application development have ADTS/400 installed.

PDM is not an end-user tool. The functions that PDM provides are specifically designed for AS/400 programmers and system administrators. PDM includes functions to copy files, move objects from one library to another, edit (using SEU) and compile database files and HLL programs, display the contents of a library, and perform many other typical application development tasks. Most AS/400 programmers work from PDM as they develop and test application files and programs.[2]

As described in Chapter 1, OS/400 is an object-based architecture. Among the object types are libraries, programs, and files, which play an important role in PDM. OS/400 objects have other attributes, in addition to an object type, including a subtype. For example, recall that database files include data files (subtype PF-DTA and LF-DTA) and source files (subtype PF-SRC). Also recall that database files have members, and that source file members are where you store DDS, SQL, and HLL source code. Each source file member also has an attribute that identifies the type of source it contains. For example a PF source member type indicates the member contains DDS statements for a physical file, whereas RPGLE indicates a member contains RPG IV source code.

PDM as a Navigational Tool

PDM provides access to three levels of the OS/400 object-based architecture: the library level, the object level, and the member level. With PDM you can navigate the various levels of OS/400 and move from one level to the next. For example, you can start at the library level, then select a library and drop

---

[1] This appendix is based on "Appendix B: Programming Development Manager (PDM)" in *Control Language Programming for the AS/400*, by Bryan Meyers and Dan Riehl, copyright 1993 by Duke Press. The material is used with the authors' permission.

[2] As noted in Chapter 1, there are at least two PC-based alternatives to PDM and SEU: IBM's CODE/400 product and Aldon Computer Group's Flex/EDIT product.

down to the object level. From the object level, you can either go back up to the library level or select a database file and drop down to the member level.

You can start a PDM session from several AS/400 menus (e.g., use GO PROGRAM to display the Programming menu) or with one of the following commands:

- STRPDM (Start PDM)
- WRKLIBPDM (Work with Libraries Using PDM)
- WRKOBJPDM (Work with Objects Using PDM)
- WRKMBRPDM (Work with Members Using PDM)

The STRPDM command displays the PDM main menu shown in Figure C.1. Selecting option 1 (Work with libraries) is comparable to the WRKLIBPDM command. Option 2 (Work with objects) is comparable to the WRKOBJPDM command. And option 3 (Work with members) is comparable to the WRKMBRPDM command. Option 9 (Work with user-defined options) lets you set various PDM options that are described in the *ADTS/400: Programming Development Manager* manual.

Figure C.1
PDM Main Menu

```
                    AS/400 Programming Development Manager (PDM)

        Select one of the following:

              1. Work with libraries
              2. Work with objects
              3. Work with members

              9. Work with user-defined options




        Selection or command
        ===> _____
        _____
        F3=Exit         F4=Prompt        F9=Retrieve       F18=Command entry
        F12=Cancel      F18=Change defaults
                                        (C) COPYRIGHT IBM CORP. 1981, 1995.
```

Working with Libraries Using PDM

When you select option 1 from the PDM main menu, you're presented with the display shown in Figure C.2 on which you specify the libraries you want to work with. In this example, the entry app* specifies that all libraries whose names begin with APP should be included in the PDM list that's displayed next. You can enter a single library name, a generic name (as in this example), or one of the following special values:

- *ALL (all libraries)
- *LIBL (all libraries in the job's library list)
- *ALLUSR (all user, i.e., non-IBM, libraries on the system)
- *USRLIBL (all libraries in the user part of the job's library list)
- *CURLIB (the current library)

You can also use the * character as a wildcard in other parts of the library name. For example, *DTA specifies all libraries with names that end in DTA.

Figure C.2
Library Selection Display

```
                        Specify Libraries to Work With

 Type choice, press Enter.

     Library . . . . . . . . . .    app*          *LIBL, name, *generic*, *ALL,
                                                  *ALLUSR, *USRLIBL, *CURLIB











     F3=Exit      F5=Refresh      F12=Cancel
```

If you need more information about this or any other PDM prompt, you can position the cursor on an input field and press the Help or F1 key to display an explanation of the allowable choices.

After you specify the libraries you want to work with, PDM shows the Work with Libraries Using PDM display in Figure C.3 As an alternative to the PDM menu, you can get to the same display by entering the following command:

```
WRKLIBPDM LIB( app* )
```

The Work with Libraries using PDM display lists all the libraries you selected. For each selected library there's an option field, followed by the library name, type (production or test), and descriptive text. This display also has several input fields that control what's displayed and options for the listed

Figure C.3
Work with Libraries
Using PDM Display

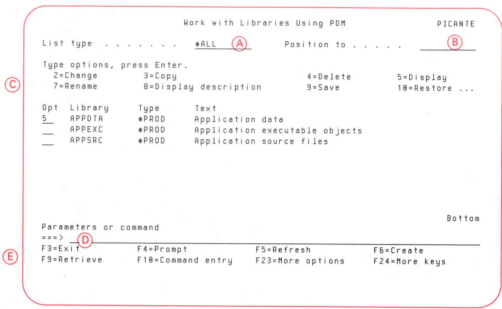

```
                              Work with Libraries Using PDM                    PICANTE
    List type  . . . . . . .   *ALL    Ⓐ      Position to  . . . . .              Ⓑ

    Type options, press Enter.
      2=Change          3=Copy                    4=Delete        5=Display
      7=Rename          8=Display description      9=Save          10=Restore ...

    Opt  Library    Type      Text
    5    APPDTA     *PROD     Application data
    __   APPEXC     *PROD     Application executable objects
    __   APPSRC     *PROD     Application source files




                                                                          Bottom
    Parameters or command
    ===>    Ⓓ
    F3=Exit            F4=Prompt         F5=Refresh          F6=Create
    F9=Retrieve        F10=Command entry F23=More options    F24=More keys
```

libraries. To change the list of displayed libraries, you can enter *ALL, *LIBL, *ALLUSR, or *USRLIBL in the List type field (A). The Position to input field (B) lets you position the list starting at a specified library. This is useful when the list contains many libraries.

The list of options (C) indicates values that can be entered in the Opt field to the left of each listed library. For example, to display the contents of the APPDTA library, you enter 5 in the Opt field next to that library and then press the Enter key.

There are more options available than PDM shows on a single display, so you can press the F23 (More options) key to toggle the display between sets of options. The valid options for the Work with Libraries Using PDM display are shown in Figure C.4. You can enter any valid option in the Opt field regardless of whether it's currently shown in the list of options.

As you can see from Figure C.4, there's a corresponding CL command for most PDM options. The PDM environment provides a list-oriented front-end for many CL commands. Options 20 through 23 let you reorder the job's library list, if the current display has selected *LIBL libraries. These four options don't perform any operations on the libraries themselves.

This display also includes a command line (D), which can be used to enter any AS/400 command. The F4 (Prompt) key is available for commands entered on this line. You can also retrieve previously entered commands by pressing the F9 (Retrieve) key.

The command line also serves another function within PDM. When an option is entered next to an entry in the list, the command line can be used to enter command parameters. When you enter command parameters on the command line, PDM uses them with the CL command associated with

Figure C.4
Work with Libraries
Using PDM Options

Option	Operation	CL Command Used
2	Change the type and text of a library	CHGLIB
3	Copy the contents of one library to another	CPYLIB
5	Display a list of objects in a library	DSPLIB
7	Rename a library	RNMOBJ
8	Display a library's description	DSPOBJD
9	Save a library and its contents	SAVLIB
10	Restore a library and its contents	RSTLIB
12	Show the Work with Objects Using PDM display	WRKOBJPDM
13	Change the descriptive text of a library	CHGOBJD
20	Move a library to a different location in the job's library list	(built-in PDM function, when *LIBL list is selected)
21	Move another library before this library in the job's library list	(built-in PDM function, when *LIBL list is selected)
22	Move another library after this library in the job's library list	(built-in PDM function, when *LIBL list is selected)
23	Remove a library from the job's library list	(built-in PDM function, when *LIBL list is selected)

the option, as listed in Figure C.4. For example, when you enter option 5 (Display), you can also enter OUTPUT(*PRINT) on the command line. PDM uses this parameter when it executes the DSPLIB command for the library entry. If you specify options for more than one list entry, any parameters you specify on the command line should be valid for all the options.

A partial list of valid function keys is shown at the bottom of the Work with Libraries Using PDM display (E). You can press F24 to toggle this list to show other keys. Figure C.5 lists all the function keys that are valid on PDM displays. You can use any valid function key regardless of whether it's currently shown in the list of keys.

Working with Objects Using PDM

When you select option 2 from the PDM main menu, PDM shows the display in Figure C.6, on which you specify which objects you want to include in the list. In this example, all objects in the APPDTA library are specified. You can restrict the objects by entering a specific, generic, or wildcard object

Figure C.5
PDM Function Keys

Function Key	Function	What the Function Does
F1	Help	Provides additional information. Place the cursor on a field and press F1.
F3	Exit	Exits from PDM
F4	Prompt	Prompts for a command associated with an option or entered on command line
F5	Refresh	Refreshes the list
F6	Create	Prompts for appropriate CRTxxx command.
F9	Retrieve	Retrieves previous command entered on command line
F10	Command Entry	Displays the Command Entry display.
F11	Toggle displayed list fields	Toggles between different formats for what's shown in the library, object, or member lists.
F12	Cancel	Cancels options or return to previous display
F13	Repeat	Repeats option at position of cursor for all entries following the entry where cursor is positioned
F14	Display object sizes, or display member last-change dates	For WRKOBJPDM, displays each object's size. For WRKMBRPDM, displays the date each member was last changed
F15	Order member list by last-change date	For WRKMBRPDM, orders the member list based on the date each member was last changed
F16	User options	Shows display for changing PDM options
F17	Subset	Shows display to select a subset of list entries
F18	Change defaults	Shows display to change PDM defaults
F21	Print the list	Prints entries of the current list
F23	More options	Toggles display to show additional option values
F24	More keys	Toggles display to show additional function keys

name; an object type; and a specific or generic object attribute (subtype). For example, if you want to work only with objects whose name starts with the letter L, you can enter L* in the Name field; or, if you want to work only with file objects, you can enter *FILE into the Type field.

Figure C.6
PDM Object
Selection Display

```
                              Specify Objects to Work With

      Type choices, press Enter.

          Library  . . . . . . . . .     appdta       *CURLIB, name

          Object:
            Name  . . . . . . . . . .    *ALL         *ALL, name, *generic*
            Type  . . . . . . . . . .    *ALL         *ALL, *type
            Attribute  . . . . . . . .   *ALL         *ALL, attribute, *generic*,
                                                      *BLANK








      F3=Exit      F5=Refresh      F12=Cancel
```

As an alternative to the PDM menu option 2, you can enter a WRKOBJPDM command with parameters that correspond to the fields shown in Figure C.6.

The Work with Objects Using PDM display (Figure C.7) shows a list of all selected objects. The display works much like the Work with Libraries Using PDM display, except that it lists objects within one or more libraries, and the options correspond to functions for objects rather than functions for libraries. This display also has fields to control what's displayed and various operations.

Figure C.7
Work with Objects Using
PDM Display

```
                              Work with Objects Using PDM                   PICANTE

      Library . . . . .   APPDTA (A)      Position to . . . . . . . .          (B)
                                          Position to type  . . . . .


      Type options, press Enter.
        2=Change         3=Copy          4=Delete       5=Display       7=Rename
        8=Display description             9=Save        10=Restore     11=Move ...

      Opt   Object     Type        Attribute    Text
            QSQJRN0001  *JRNRCV                  COLLECTION - created by SQL
       _    QSQJRN      *JRN                     COLLECTION - created by SQL
       _    AUTOLOAN    *FILE       PF-DTA       Auto loans
       _    BUILDING    *FILE       PF-DTA       Buildings
       _    CONTRACTOR  *FILE       PF-DTA       Contractors
       _    COURSE      *FILE       PF-DTA       Courses
       _    CUSTOMER    *FILE       PF-DTA       Customers
       _    EMPLOYEE    *FILE       PF-DTA       Employees
                                                                          More...
      Parameters or command
      ===> _____
      F3=Exit            F4=Prompt              F5=Refresh            F6=Create
      F9=Retrieve        F10=Command entry      F23=More options      F24=More keys
```

Figure C.8
Work with Objects Using
PDM Options

Option	Operation	CL Command Used
2	Change object attributes	CHGxxx (depending on object type)
3	Create duplicate object	CRTDUPOBJ
4	Delete object	DLTxxx (depending on object type)
5	Display information about an object	DSPxxx (depending on object type)
7	Rename an object	RNMOBJ
8	Display an object's description	DSPOBJD
9	Save an object	SAVOBJ or SAVSAVFDTA
10	Restore an object	RSTOBJ
11	Move an object from one library to another	MOVOBJ
12	For files, show the Work with Members Using PDM display. For other object types, show the appropriate "Work with ..." display	WRKMBRPDM or WRKxxx (depending on object type)
13	Change the descriptive text of an object	CHGOBJD
15	Copy data from one file to another	CPYF or CPYSRCF
16	Run an object	CALL (programs), CHGDTA (for DFU applications), or RUNQRY (for query definitions)
18	Change database file data	UPDDTA or STRDFU
25	Find a specified string in a physical file	(built-in PDM function)
26	Create program	CRTPGM
27	Create service program	CRTSRVPGM
34	Run debugger	STRISDB
54	Compare physical file members	CMPPFM

You can enter a library name (A) to work with the objects in a different library. You can also position the display to a specified object and object type (B).

The options available on the Work with Objects using PDM screen are listed in Figure C.8. Some options are valid only for specific object types. For example, Option 16 (Run) is valid for *PGM objects, but not for *FILE objects.

Working with Members Using PDM

The lowest level in the object hierarchy that PDM provides access to is file members. Programmers frequently use this level of PDM because it lets you edit source and submit DDS and HLL program compiles. PDM provides three ways to display the Work with Members Using PDM display:

- From the PDM main menu, select option 3 – Work with members
- From the Work with Objects Using PDM display, enter option 12 next to a file object
- Enter the WRKMBRPDM command

Figure C.9 shows the member selection display on which you specify a file name as well as the specific, generic, or wildcard member name and member type.

Figure C.9
Member Selection
Display

```
                        Specify Members to Work With

  Type choices, press Enter.

      File  . . . . . . . . . .     LFSRC          Name, F4 for list

        Library . . . . . . . .     APPSRC         *LIBL, *CURLIB, name

      Member:
        Name  . . . . . . . . .     *ALL           *ALL, name, *generic*
        Type  . . . . . . . . .     *ALL           *ALL, type, *generic*, *BLANK








    F3=Exit       F4=Prompt     F5=Refresh     F12=Cancel
```

The Work with Members Using PDM display (Figure C.10) shows a list of all specified members. You can change the file whose members are displayed (A) and position to a specified member (B).

The list of members lets you change the member type and descriptive text. The rest of the Work with Members Using PDM display is similar to the other PDM "work with" displays. The function keys are the same as with the other PDM displays, but the options are different.

Figure C.10

Work with Members
Using PDM Display

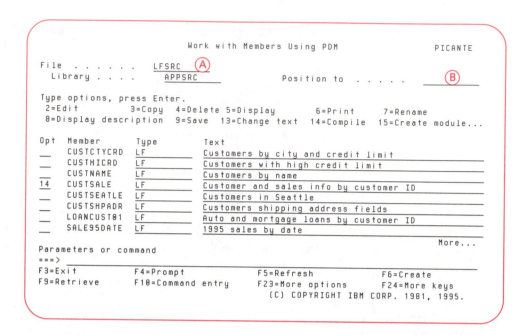

```
                    Work with Members Using PDM              PICANTE

File . . . . . .   LFSRC   Ⓐ
  Library . . . .  APPSRC              Position to . . . . .        Ⓑ

Type options, press Enter.
  2=Edit          3=Copy  4=Delete 5=Display     6=Print     7=Rename
  8=Display description  9=Save  13=Change text  14=Compile  15=Create module...

Opt  Member      Type    Text
__    CUSTCTYCRD  LF      Customers by city and credit limit
__    CUSTHICRD   LF      Customers with high credit limit
__    CUSTNAME    LF      Customers by name
14    CUSTSALE    LF      Customer and sales info by customer ID
__    CUSTSEATLE  LF      Customers in Seattle
__    CUSTSHPADR  LF      Customers shipping address fields
__    LOANCUST01  LF      Auto and mortgage loans by customer ID
__    SALE95DATE  LF      1995 sales by date
                                                            More...
Parameters or command
===> _____
F3=Exit         F4=Prompt          F5=Refresh          F6=Create
F9=Retrieve     F18=Command entry  F23=More options    F24=More keys
                               (C) COPYRIGHT IBM CORP. 1981, 1995.
```

The member options have slightly different meanings, depending on the member type. Some options (e.g., option 2 – edit with SEU) are valid only with source file members. Figure C.11 lists the valid options for members.

As mentioned earlier, you can press the F4 key to prompt for a command associated with a PDM option. Figure C.12 shows an example of the CRTLF command prompt displayed when you use option 14 for an LF type source file member (see Figure C.10). You can use the prompt to change command defaults or to supply additional parameter values. On a CL prompt display, you can press F11 to toggle between the prompt format shown in Figure C.12 and the keyword format shown in Figure C.13. The keyword format can be helpful if you're using CL examples in this book that list commands with the parameter keywords.

Changing PDM Defaults and Options

When you start PDM with a command (e.g., STRPDM or WRKMBRPDM), PDM uses various defaults that affect the way PDM performs certain functions. For example, one PDM default is the library into which file and program objects are created when you compile a source file member. By pressing the F18 function key, each PDM user can customize the PDM defaults for his or her sessions. On-line help and the *ADTS/400: Programming Development Manager* provide a complete description of the PDM defaults and the valid settings.

In addition to the IBM-supplied options available for each PDM "work with" display, you can create your own user-defined PDM options. These user-defined options allow you to specify a new option value and an associated command that PDM executes when you enter the option. PDM lets you

Figure C.11
Work with Members
Using PDM Options

Option	Operation	CL Command Used
2	Edit a source file member with SEU	STRSEU OPTION(2)
3	Copy a member	CPYF or CPYSRCF
4	Remove member	RMVM
5	Display data in physical file member	DSPPFM
6	Print a source file member	STRSEU OPTION(6)
7	Rename a member	RNMM
8	Display a member's description	(built-in PDM function)
9	Save the file containing a member	SAVOBJ
13	Change the descriptive text of a member	CHGPFM or CHGLFM
14	Compile a source file member to produce an object	CRTxxx (depending on member type)
15	Compile an HLL source file member to produce an ILE module object	CRTxxx (depending on member type)
16	Run the procedure contained in a source file member	STRREXPRC (for REXX procedures), or STRBASPRC (for Basic), or STRS36PRC (for S/36 OCL)
17	Change the DDS source for a display file using SDA	STRSDA
18	Change database file data	UPDDTA
19	Change the DDS source for a printer file using RLU	STRRLU
25	Find a specified string in a member	(built-in PDM function)
54	Compare physical file members	CMPPFM
55	Merge source file members	MRGSRC

Figure C.12
Prompted CRTLF
Command

```
                          Create Logical File (CRTLF)

  Type choices, press Enter.

  File  . . . . . . . . . . . . . . >  CUSTSALE      Name
    Library  . . . . . . . . . . . >   APPSRC       Name, *CURLIB
  Source file  . . . . . . . . . . >  LFSRC         Name
    Library  . . . . . . . . . . . >   APPSRC       Name, *LIBL, *CURLIB
  Source member  . . . . . . . . . >  CUSTSALE      Name, *FILE
  Generation severity level  . . .   20             0-30
  Flagging severity level  . . . .   0              0-30
  File type  . . . . . . . . . . .   *DATA          *DATA, *SRC
  Member, if desired . . . . . . .   *FILE          Name, *FILE, *NONE
  Physical file data members:                  _
    Physical file  . . . . . . . .   *ALL           Name, *ALL
      Library  . . . . . . . . . .                  Name, *CURRENT
      Members  . . . . . . . . . .                  Name, *NONE
                       + for more values
                       + for more values    _

                                                                    More...
  F3=Exit   F4=Prompt   F5=Refresh   F10=Additional parameters   F12=Cancel
  F13=How to use this display       F24=More keys
```

Figure C.13
Prompted CRTLF
Command with
Parameter Keywords

```
                          Create Logical File (CRTLF)

  Type choices, press Enter.

  File  . . . . . . . . . . . . . .  FILE      >  CUSTSALE
    Library  . . . . . . . . . . .             >   APPSRC
  Source file  . . . . . . . . . .   SRCFILE   >  LFSRC
    Library  . . . . . . . . . . .             >   APPSRC
  Source member  . . . . . . . . .   SRCMBR    >  CUSTSALE
  Generation severity level  . . .   GENLVL       20
  Flagging severity level  . . . .   FLAG         0
  File type  . . . . . . . . . . .   FILETYPE     *DATA
  Member, if desired . . . . . . .   MBR          *FILE
  Physical file data members:        DTAMBRS
    Physical file  . . . . . . . .            _
                                               *ALL
      Library  . . . . . . . . . .
      Members  . . . . . . . . . .
                       + for more values
                       + for more values    _

                                                                    More...
  F3=Exit   F4=Prompt   F5=Refresh   F10=Additional parameters   F12=Cancel
  F13=How to use this display       F24=More keys
```

code substitution values for each element of a list entry (e.g., the library, file, and member names for an entry on the Work with Members Using PDM display), so commands can take their parameter values from the entry. The *ADTS/400: Programming Development Manager* manual provides a complete description of PDM user-defined options.

Appendix D

Using Source Entry Utility (SEU)[1]

Introduction

SEU is a full-screen, source code editor for the AS/400. SEU is not a part of the OS/400 operating system. Rather, it's a component of IBM's Application Development ToolSet/400 (ADTS/400) product, which also includes Programming Development Manager (PDM), Screen Design Aid (SDA), Report Layout Utility (RLU), and Interactive Source Debugger (ISDB). Most AS/400s used for application development have ADTS/400 installed. SEU is not an end-user tool and it's specifically designed for AS/400 programmers to enter and modify DDS, HLL, SQL, and other source code.[2] Among SEU's features are built-in statement prompting and syntax checking for many languages, including DDS, RPG IV, COBOL/400, and embedded SQL statements.

Running SEU

You can run SEU in several ways:

- Enter STRSEU on any command line
- Enter option 2 (Edit) or 5 (Display) for a member on the Work with Members Using PDM display (described in Appendix C)
- From within SDA, edit DDS comment lines

The following command runs SEU and edits the CUSTSALE member of the APPSRC/LFSRC source file. Figure D.1 shows the SEU Edit display that's presented when you enter this command.

```
STRSEU SRCFILE( appsrc/lfsrc )
       SRCMBR( custsale )
```

Four main sections comprise the SEU Edit display. At the top (A) is the SEU command line where you can enter various editing commands (e.g., FIND). This command line is different from the standard AS/400 command line shown on other displays; it's provided solely as a means to enter SEU commands. On the left (B) SEU displays the source sequence numbers. This area is also where you enter SEU line commands (typing over the sequence

---

[1] This appendix is based on "Appendix C: Source Entry Utility (SEU)" in *Control Language Programming for the AS/400*, by Bryan Meyers and Dan Riehl, copyright 1993 by Duke Press. The material is used with the authors' permission.

[2] As noted in Chapter 1, there are at least two PC-based alternatives to PDM and SEU: IBM's CODE/400 product and Aldon Computer Group's Flex/EDIT product.

Figure D.1

SEU Edit Display

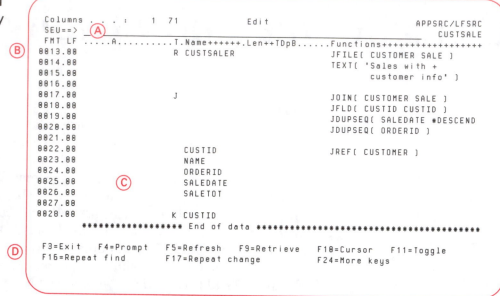

```
    Columns . . . :    1  71            Edit                      APPSRC/LFSRC
    SEU==>  Ⓐ                                                              CUSTSALE
    FMT LF .....A..........T.Name++++++.Len++TDpB.....Functions+++++++++++++++++++
Ⓑ  0013.00                  R CUSTSALER              JFILE( CUSTOMER SALE )
    0014.00                                          TEXT( 'Sales with +
    0015.00                                                 customer info' )
    0016.00
    0017.00                  J                        JOIN( CUSTOMER SALE )
    0018.00                                          JFLD( CUSTID CUSTID )
    0019.00                                          JDUPSEQ( SALEDATE *DESCEND
    0020.00                                          JDUPSEQ( ORDERID )
    0021.00
    0022.00                    CUSTID                JREF( CUSTOMER )
    0023.00                    NAME
    0024.00                    ORDERID
    0025.00   Ⓒ               SALEDATE
    0026.00                    SALETOT
    0027.00
    0028.00                  K CUSTID
    ****************** End of data *********************************************

Ⓓ  F3=Exit    F4=Prompt    F5=Refresh   F9=Retrieve   F10=Cursor    F11=Toggle
    F16=Repeat find          F17=Repeat change            F24=More keys
```

numbers), such as D to delete a line. The main area of the Edit display shows the source statements (C), which you can type over to change or insert new source. A partial list of valid function keys is shown at the bottom of the Edit display (D). You can press F24 to toggle this list to show other keys. Figure D.2 lists all the function keys that are valid on the Edit display. You can use any valid function key regardless whether it's currently shown in the list of keys. (Function keys are discussed in more detail later.)

The Source Sequence Number Area

In the source sequence number area, SEU displays each line's sequence number (stored as part of the records in a source file member) using the format of 9999.99. Although SEU doesn't allow you to directly change the sequence number of an existing line, you can type SEU line commands over the sequence number that's displayed. You use line commands for inserting, deleting, moving, and copying lines. You can also use line commands to position the display so a specified source line appears as the first line in the typing area.

Before getting into a full discussion of SEU line commands, let's look at a simple example of moving a source line within the member (Figure D.3).

Figure D.2
SEU Edit Display
Function Keys

Function Key	Function	What the Function Does
F1	Help	Provides additional information. Place the cursor on a field and press F1.
F3	Exit	Exits from SEU
F4	Prompt	Prompts for a statement based on the type of source
F5	Refresh	Refreshes the Edit display, undoing any changes since the Enter key was last pressed
F6	Move the split line	When working with split screen, repositions the split line to the line containing cursor
F9	Retrieve	Retrieves previous SEU command entered on command line
F10	Cursor	Moves the cursor from the editing area to the SEU command line and vice-versa
F11	Toggle, or Previous record	When not prompting, toggle display between leftmost and rightmost parts of source lines When prompting, prompts for previous source line
F13	Change session defaults	Shows display to change session defaults
F14	Find/Change options	Shows display to search for strings, and optionally replace matches with a new string
F15	Browse/Copy options	Shows display to browse other source members or spool files and optionally copy source to the member being edited
F16	Repeat find	Repeats the last FIND operation
F17	Repeat change	Repeats the last CHANGE operation
F18	DBCS conversion	Displays converted DBCS (double-byte character set) characters
F19	Left	Shifts the editing area so it displays information to the left of what's currently displayed
F20	Right	Shifts the editing area so it displays information to the right of what's currently displayed
F21	System command	Displays a command line for entering CL commands
F23	Select prompt	Shows the Select Prompt display from which you can select source language prompts
F24	More keys	Toggles display to show additional function keys

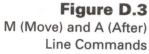

Figure D.3
M (Move) and A (After)
Line Commands

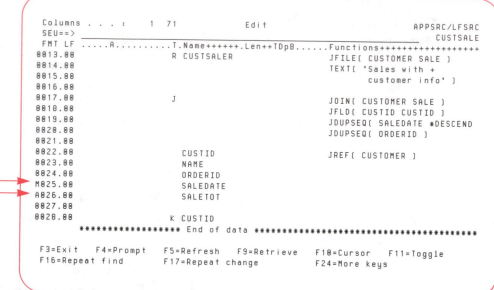

```
 Columns . . . :    1  71              Edit               APPSRC/LFSRC
 SEU==>  _____    CUSTSALE
 FMT LF .....A..........T.Name++++++.Len++TDpB.....Functions++++++++++++++++++
 0013.00                R CUSTSALER                JFILE( CUSTOMER SALE )
 0014.00                                           TEXT( 'Sales with +
 0015.00                                             customer info' )
 0016.00
 0017.00                J                          JOIN( CUSTOMER SALE )
 0018.00                                           JFLD( CUSTID CUSTID )
 0019.00                                           JDUPSEQ( SALEDATE *DESCEND
 0020.00                                           JDUPSEQ( ORDERID )
 0021.00
 0022.00                  CUSTID                   JREF( CUSTOMER )
 0023.00                  NAME
 0024.00                  ORDERID
 M025.00                  SALEDATE
 A026.00                  SALETOT
 0027.00
 0028.00                K CUSTID
      ***************** End of data ****************************************

 F3=Exit    F4=Prompt    F5=Refresh    F9=Retrieve    F10=Cursor    F11=Toggle
 F16=Repeat find         F17=Repeat change           F24=More keys
```

To move the source line that appears at line 0025.00 in Figure D.3 to the position immediately following line 0026.00, we enter the M (Move) line command on line 0025.00, and place the A (After) line command on line 0026.00, then press the Enter key. The combination of these two line commands tells SEU to move line 0025.00 after line 0026.00. After the move operation, there is no line 0025.00 and the moved line has the line number 0026.01 (see Figure D.4). You also can move lines to appear before a line, by specifying B instead of A for the target location.

Other commonly used line commands are C (Copy) to copy a line to another location while retaining it at the original location, and D (Delete) to delete a line from the source member. You can also use the X (eXclude) line command to "hide" lines from the editing area. Excluded lines remain in the file, but aren't displayed. This feature can be helpful if you need to work on sections of code that aren't adjacent and you want the sections' lines to appear together in the editing area.

In the previous example, we moved one source line to another position. You can also move several lines together in one operation; this is called a block operation. Consider the example shown in Figure D.5. Here we want to move the source lines 0023.00 through 0024.00 after line 0026.02. We place the MM block move command on the first and last lines to be moved, and place the A (After) command on line 0026.02. When you press the Enter key, SEU moves all the lines between (and including) the two lines containing MM.

As an alternative to the block operation using MM, you can use the SEU line command M*n*, where *n* is the number of lines you want to move. In this example, we could have specified M2 on line 0023.00 to move the two lines.

Figure D.4
Result of the
Move/After Operation

```
 Columns . . . :    1  71              Edit                    APPSRC/LFSRC
 SEU==> _____ CUSTSALE
 FMT LF .....A..........T.Name++++++.Len++TDpB......Functions++++++++++++++++++
 0013.00                  R CUSTSALER              JFILE( CUSTOMER SALE )
 0014.00                                           TEXT( 'Sales with +
 0015.00                                               customer info' )
 0016.00
 0017.00                  J                        JOIN( CUSTOMER SALE )
 0018.00                                           JFLD( CUSTID CUSTID )
 0019.00                                           JDUPSEQ( SALEDATE *DESCEND
 0020.00                                           JDUPSEQ( ORDERID )
 0021.00
 0022.00                    CUSTID                 JREF( CUSTOMER )
 0023.00                    NAME
 0024.00                    ORDERID
 0026.00                    SALETOT
 0026.01                    SALEDATE
 0027.00
 0028.00                  K CUSTID
 ******************* End of data ********************************************

   F3=Exit    F4=Prompt    F5=Refresh    F9=Retrieve   F10=Cursor   F11=Toggle
   F16=Repeat find         F17=Repeat change           F24=More keys
```

Figure D.5
Sample Block Operation

```
 Columns . . . :    1  71              Edit                    APPSRC/LFSRC
 SEU==> _____ CUSTSALE
 FMT LF .....A..........T.Name++++++.Len++TDpB......Functions++++++++++++++++++
 0013.00                  R CUSTSALER              JFILE( CUSTOMER SALE )
 0014.00                                           TEXT( 'Sales with +
 0015.00                                               customer info' )
 0016.00
 0017.00                  J                        JOIN( CUSTOMER SALE )
 0018.00                                           JFLD( CUSTID CUSTID )
 0019.00                                           JDUPSEQ( SALEDATE *DESCEND
 0020.00                                           JDUPSEQ( ORDERID )
 0021.00
 0022.00                    CUSTID                 JREF( CUSTOMER )
 MM23.00                    NAME
 MM24.00                    ORDERID
 0026.01                    SALEDATE
 A026.02                    SALETOT
 0027.00
 0028.00                  K CUSTID
 ******************* End of data ********************************************

   F3=Exit    F4=Prompt    F5=Refresh    F9=Retrieve   F10=Cursor   F11=Toggle
   F16=Repeat find         F17=Repeat change           F24=More keys
```

Other common block commands are CC (Copy) to copy a block of source lines to another location while retaining them at the original location, DD (Delete) to delete a block of lines, and XX (eXclude) to exclude a block of lines.

Line Commands for Positioning within a Source Member

When SEU first displays a member, the first record is shown at the top of the editing area. You can use the RollUp/RollDown (or PageUp/PageDown) keys to scroll forward and backward through the file. You can also use line commands to change positions in the member. SEU has commands for both absolute and relative positioning.

To use absolute positioning, type a sequence number over an existing sequence number, and press the Enter key. This brings the line that has the sequence number you entered to the top of the typing area.

To specify relative positioning, overtype a sequence number with a plus sign (+) or a minus sign (−) followed by the number of source lines to be scrolled forward (+) or backward (−). For example, if you want to move the sixth record that's displayed to the top of the display, you would enter +5. If you want to then move back to the original position, you would use the command −5.

Inserting New Lines

The I (Insert) line command is used to add new source statements to an existing member. To insert a line after an existing line, enter the I command on the existing line and press Enter. SEU inserts a new, empty line and you can enter the new source statement on this line. After you've entered the new source statement, you can press Enter and SEU inserts another empty line following the one you just added. You can continue adding new source in this fashion until you press Enter without typing anything on one of the new lines.

You can enter the I*n* command to have SEU insert *n* empty lines at once. For example, entering I5 inserts 5 new lines. After the empty lines are inserted, you can type new source into them.

Find/Change Options

As mentioned, SEU supports the function keys listed in Figure D.2. For several of these function keys, SEU shows additional displays.

The F14 key shows the Find/Change Options display (Figure D.6). On this display, you can specify a string for SEU to locate in the source member and, optionally, a replacement string for any matches. In the example in Figure D.6, SALETOT is the search string, and SALETOTAL is the replacement string.

When you're browsing a spool file that contains a compiler listing, you can use the *ERR special value in the Find field to match error messages in the listing.

The From column number and To column number option fields let you specify the range of columns to search. This option is useful with DDS, RPG/400, and RPG IV, which have fixed-columnar syntax.

Figure D.6
Find/Change
Options Display

```
                         Find/Change Options

    Type choices, press Enter.

        Find  . . . . . . . . . . . .  SALETOT_____
        Change  . . . . . . . . . . .  SALETOTAL_____
        From column number  . . . . .  1___     1-80
        To column number  . . . . . .  80       1-80 or blank
        Occurrences to process  . . .  1        1=Next, 2=All
                                                 3=Previous
        Records to search . . . . . .  1        1=All, 2=Excluded
                                                 3=Non-excluded
        Kind of match . . . . . . . .  2        1=Same case
                                                 2=Ignore case
        Allow data shift  . . . . . .  N        Y=Yes, N=No

        Search for date . . . . . . .  96/07/86 YY/MM/DD or YYMMDD
           Compare  . . . . . . . . .  _        1=Less than
                                                 2=Equal to
                                                 3=Greater than


    F3=Exit   F5=Refresh     F12=Cancel   F13=Change session defaults
    F15=Browse/Copy options  F16=Find     F17=Change
```

The Occurrences to process option lets you specify whether you want to process the next occurrence where the search string is found in the member, the previous occurrence, or all occurrences in the member.

The Records to search option lets you specify whether excluded records are to be included within the scope of the search. Excluded records are those that have been "hidden" from the display with the X line command.

The Kind of match option lets you specify whether the search is case sensitive. For example, if the search string is specified as SALETOT and you want to match SaleTot and saletot, you must specify 2 for this option to ignore case when matching strings.

When you specify a replacement string that's not the same length as the search string, the Allow data shift option determines if the data on a line is shifted when a match is found. For example, if you're searching for the string SALETOT, which is seven characters long, and you want to replace it with the string SALETOTAL, which is nine characters long, you'll shift source to the right of the match by two characters after the replacement is performed. When you specify N for this option, SEU blank-pads a replacement string that's shorter then the search string, and (if possible) overwrites adjacent blanks for a search string that's shorter then the replacement string.

The last options on this display are Search for date and Compare. These options let you find source member records that were modified before, on, or after a specified date. If you enter a value for the Compare option, SEU performs a search for records that meet the date search criteria. Date values should be specified in YY/MM/DD format.

Once you've entered values for the search string and other options, you press the F16 (Find) or F17 (Change) function key to start the search.

While the Find/Change Options display provides a helpful guide for new SEU users, many experienced AS/400 programmers perform searches directly from the SEU Edit display using the FIND and CHANGE commands on the SEU command line (covered later in this appendix).

Browse/Copy Options

The F15 key shows the Browse/Copy Options display (Figure D.7). On this display, you can select another source member or a spool file to view on the bottom of a split screen display, such as that shown in Figure D.8. In this example, the CUSTOMER member of the APPSRC/PFSRC source file is displayed for browsing below the CUSTSALE member that's being edited.

The Browse section of the display does not allow any editing; however, you can copy source lines from a source member in this part of the display. To copy lines, enter C, CC, or Cn line commands in the source sequence area of the browsed member and A or B line commands in the source sequence area of the member being edited.

The Browse/Copy Options display's Selection option (see Figure D.7) lets you select a source member, spooled output file, or output queue to browse. The value for this option determines which of the other options are applicable. You specify appropriate values for either the Browse/copy member, the Browse/copy spool file, or the Display output queue sets of options. For several of these options (e.g., Browse/copy member), you can place the cursor in the field and press the F4 key to display a selection list of available members, etc. This is handy when you don't know the exact name of a member or a spool file that you want to browse.

Figure D.7
Browse/Copy
Options Display

```
                         Browse/Copy Options
 Type choices, press Enter.


   Selection . . . . . . . . . .       1            1=Member
                                                    2=Spool file
                                                    3=Output queue
   Copy all records . . . . . .        N            Y=Yes, N=No
   Browse/copy member . . . . . .      CUSTOMER     Name, F4 for list
      File . . . . . . . . . . .       PFSRC        Name, F4 for list
         Library . . . . . . . .       APPSRC       Name, *CURLIB, *LIBL

   Browse/copy spool file . . . .      CUSTSALE     Name, F4 for list
      Job . . . . . . . . . . . .      CUSTSALE     Name
         User . . . . . . . . .        QPGMR        Name, F4 for list
         Job number . . . . . . .      *LAST        Number, *LAST
      Spool number . . . . . . .       *LAST        Number, *LAST, *ONLY

   Display output queue . . . . .      QPRINT       Name, *ALL
      Library . . . . . . . . . .      *LIBL        Name, *CURLIB, *LIBL

 F3=Exit       F4=Prompt       F5=Refresh      F12=Cancel
 F13=Change session defaults   F14=Find/Change options
```

Figure D.8
Browsing a Second File
with Split-Screen Display

```
Columns . . . :   1  71            Edit                    APPSRC/LFSRC
SEU==>                                                         CUSTSALE
FMT LF  .....A..........T.Name++++++.Len++TDpB.....Functions++++++++++++++++
0013.00                    R CUSTSALER               JFILE[ CUSTOMER SALE ]
0014.00                                              TEXT[ 'Sales with +
0015.00                                                    customer info' ]
0016.00
0017.00                    J                         JOIN[ CUSTOMER SALE ]
0018.00                                              JFLD[ CUSTID CUSTID ]
0019.00                                              JDUPSEQ[ SALEDATE *DESCEND

Columns . . . :   1  71            Browse                  APPSRC/PFSRC
SEU==>                                                         CUSTOMER
0014.00
0015.00                    R CUSTOMERR               TEXT[ 'Customers' ]
0016.00         *          ===============================================
0017.00                    CUSTID        7P 0        TEXT[ 'Customer ID' ]
0018.00
0019.00                                              COLHDG[ 'Cust.'
0020.00                                                      'ID' ]

  F3=Exit    F4=Prompt    F5=Refresh    F9=Retrieve   F11=Toggle   F12=Cancel
  F16=Repeat find         F17=Repeat change           F24=More keys
```

When you browse a source member or spool file, the result is a split-screen display, as in Figure D.8. When you display an output queue, no split screen is provided; you simply go to the DSPOUTQ (Display Output Queue) command display.

Also, if you enter 1 (Member) for the Selection option and Y for the Copy all records option, SEU places CC line commands on the first and last lines in the browsed member. You can then enter an A (after) or B (before) line command in the member being edited to tell SEU where to copy the records to.

Saving Your Work

When you've completed editing a source member, you can press the F3 (Exit) key to exit from the current editing session. SEU than shows the Exit display (Figure D.9). On this display, you specify how to end the editing session.

To save editing changes, you enter a Y (the default) in the Change/create member option. If you specify N, the work performed in your editing session is discarded. When you edit a source member with SEU, you're not working directly on the member itself; you're working on a temporary copy created by SEU when you begin editing a member. When you save your changes, (i.e., by specifying Y for the Change/create member option), SEU copies the temporary member to the member specified in the next three options (Member, File, Library). If you don't save your work, SEU discards the temporary copy.

For the Member, File, and Library options, you specify where SEU should store the member. By default, these show the member you specified when you started the editing session. You can change these to save the

Figure D.9
SEU Exit Display

```
                              Exit

Type choices, press Enter.

   Change/create member  . . . . . . .    Y           Y=Yes, N=No
     Member  . . . . . . . . . . . .      CUSTSALE    Name, F4 for list
     File  . . . . . . . . . . . . .      LFSRC       Name, F4 for list
       Library . . . . . . . . . . .      APPSRC      Name
     Text  . . . . . . . . . . . . .      Customer and sales info by customer ID

   Resequence member . . . . . . . .      Y           Y=Yes, N=No
     Start . . . . . . . . . . . . .      0001.00     0000.01-9999.99
     Increment . . . . . . . . . . .      01.00       00.01-99.99

Print member  . . . . . . . . . .         N           Y=Yes, N=No

Return to editing . . . . . . . . .       N           Y=Yes, N=No

Go to member list . . . . . . . . .       N           Y=Yes, N=No



F3=Exit    F4=Prompt    F5=Refresh    F12=Cancel
```

(revised) temporary copy to a different member — in which case, the original member is *not* changed.

The Text option lets you specify the descriptive text for the saved source member. If you're not saving the member, the Text option is ignored.

The Resequence member options let you specify that SEU should assign new sequence numbers to the source member's lines. If you're not saving the member, this option is ignored.

The Print member option lets you to print the contents of the member.

The Return to editing option lets you return to the editing session, with or without saving the previous changes. If syntax errors have been detected by SEU and not resolved in your editing session, SEU places Y in this option; otherwise, the option defaults to N.

The Go to member list option shows the Work with Members Using SEU list display from which you can select another source member to edit.

The SEU Command Line

Most functions that you can perform from the Find/Change Options, Browse/Copy Options, and Exit displays, can also be performed from the SEU command line.[3] As an example of an SEU command, Figure D.10 shows the FIND SALETOT command, which searches the source member for the first occurrence of the string SALETOT. If the string is found, the line containing

---

[3] Note that CL commands cannot be entered on the SEU command line. Use the F21 key to display a CL command line. Also, the commands you use on the SEU command line are not the same as SEU's line commands, discussed earlier.

Figure D.10

Using the SEU
Command Line

```
  Columns . . . :    1  71              Edit                    APPSRC/LFSRC
  SEU==> FIND SALETOT                                               CUSTSALE
  FMT LF .....A..........T.Name++++++.Len++TDpB......Functions+++++++++++++++++
  0013.00              R CUSTSALER              JFILE( CUSTOMER SALE )
  0014.00                                       TEXT( 'Sales with +
  0015.00                                             customer info' )
  0016.00
  0017.00              J                        JOIN( CUSTOMER SALE )
  0018.00                                       JFLD( CUSTID CUSTID )
  0019.00                                       JDUPSEQ( SALEDATE *DESCEND
  0020.00                                       JDUPSEQ( ORDERID )
  0021.00
  0022.00                CUSTID                 JREF( CUSTOMER )
  0023.00                NAME
  0024.00                ORDERID
  0025.00                SALEDATE
  0026.00                SALETOT
  0027.00
  0028.00              K CUSTID
  ****************** End of data ********************************************

  F3=Exit   F4=Prompt   F5=Refresh   F9=Retrieve   F10=Cursor   F11=Toggle
  F16=Repeat find        F17=Repeat change          F24=More keys
```

it is displayed in the editing area. The FIND command invokes the same SEU search that you can specify with on the Find/Change Options display.

The FIND command (or the abbreviation: F) has the basic form

FIND *search-string*

You can specify *ERR as the search string to find syntax errors in a compile listing spool file. If the search string includes blanks, you must enclose the search string in single quotes, as in the following example:

FIND 'Customer name'

Figure D.11 shows an example of entering the SEU CHANGE command on the SEU command line; Figure D.12 shows the result of the command. Notice how SEU marks line 0026.00 as CHANGED after the operation.

The CHANGE (or C) command has the basic form:

CHANGE *search-string replacement-string*

As with the FIND command, single quotes must be used to delimit search or replacement strings with embedded blanks. For both the FIND and CHANGE commands, you can specify various options following the string(s). In this example the ALL option specifies that all matches are to be replaced by this operation. To see an explanation of the options, type FIND or CHANGE on the command line and press the F1 key.

You can use the TOP (or T) command to position the source member to the first line. The BOTTOM (or BOT or B) command positions the source member so the last line is displayed at the bottom of the editing area.

Figure D.11
Using an SEU
CHANGE command

```
 Columns . . . :   1  71              Edit                        APPSRC/LFSRC
 SEU==> CHANGE SALETOT SALETOTAL ALL_____         CUSTSALE
 FMT LF .....A..........T.Name++++++.Len++TDpB.....Functions+++++++++++++++++
 0013.00                   R CUSTSALER              JFILE( CUSTOMER SALE )
 0014.00                                            TEXT( 'Sales with +
 0015.00                                                   customer info' )
 0016.00
 0017.00                   J                        JOIN( CUSTOMER SALE )
 0018.00                                            JFLD( CUSTID CUSTID )
 0019.00                                            JDUPSEQ( SALEDATE *DESCEND
 0020.00                                            JDUPSEQ( ORDERID )
 0021.00
 0022.00                     CUSTID                 JREF( CUSTOMER )
 0023.00                     NAME
 0024.00                     ORDERID
 0025.00                     SALEDATE
 0026.00                     SALETOT
 0027.00
 0028.00                   K CUSTID
       ****************** End of data ******************************************

 F3=Exit    F4=Prompt    F5=Refresh   F9=Retrieve   F10=Cursor   F11=Toggle
 F16=Repeat find         F17=Repeat change          F24=More keys
```

Figure D.12
Result of the SEU
CHANGE Command

```
 Columns . . . :   1  71              Edit                        APPSRC/LFSRC
 SEU==> _____         CUSTSALE
 FMT LF .....A..........T.Name++++++.Len++TDpB.....Functions+++++++++++++++++
 0013.00                   R CUSTSALER              JFILE( CUSTOMER SALE )
 0014.00                                            TEXT( 'Sales with +
 0015.00                                                   customer info' )
 0016.00
 0017.00                   J                        JOIN( CUSTOMER SALE )
 0018.00                                            JFLD( CUSTID CUSTID )
 0019.00                                            JDUPSEQ( SALEDATE *DESCEND
 0020.00                                            JDUPSEQ( ORDERID )
 0021.00
 0022.00                     CUSTID                 JREF( CUSTOMER )
 0023.00                     NAME
 0024.00                     ORDERID
 0025.00                     SALEDATE
 CHANGED                     SALETOTAL
 0027.00
 0028.00                   K CUSTID
       ****************** End of data ******************************************

 F3=Exit    F4=Prompt    F5=Refresh   F9=Retrieve   F10=Cursor   F11=Toggle
 F16=Repeat find         F17=Repeat change          F24=More keys
 String SALETOT changed 1 times.
```

You can use the SAVE command to save changes you've made to the current source member. The SAVE command performs the same function as saving your work from the SEU Exit display, but does not end the editing session. To save the member, simply type the command SAVE on the SEU command line. If you want to save the current source member to a different source member, specify the command as

SAVE *library-name/file-name member-name*

If you're saving the member to a different member of the same source file, you can simply use the command

SAVE *member-name*

The FILE command is similar to the SAVE command except the FILE command ends the current editing session.

You can use the CANCEL (or CAN) command to exit from SEU without saving your work. You also can use the CANCEL command on the bottom portion of a split-screen display to remove the split screen.

You can use the SET (or S) command to set SEU edit session defaults. The SET CAPS ON command converts all input to uppercase, the SET CAPS OFF command lets you enter uppercase and lowercase source.

The SET ROLL command sets the number of lines to scroll forward or backward for RollUp/RollDown (or PageUp/PageDown) keys. The alternatives are:

SET ROLL FULL — a full screen of lines
SET ROLL HALF — half the lines that fit on a screen
SET ROLL CSR — position the line with the cursor at the top or bottom of display
SET ROLL *nn* — *nn* lines

SEU Session Defaults

You can customize various SEU editing defaults (e.g., mixed-case/uppercase entry) by pressing F13 (Change session defaults) from the SEU Edit display. On-line help and the *ADTS/400: Source Entry Utility* manual provide complete information about changing your session defaults. Most session defaults can be saved and remain in effect for subsequent editing sessions.

Appendix E

Using Interactive SQL/400 (ISQL)

IBM's DB2 Query Manager and SQL Development Kit for OS/400 product includes a facility known as Interactive SQL (ISQL). ISQL lets you enter almost all SQL/400 statements interactively. Through ISQL, you can create collections, tables, views, and other SQL objects. You can also retrieve and display, print, or store data from the database. And with proper authority, you can add new rows and update or delete existing rows in database tables.

Entering SQL Statements

To run ISQL, you enter the STRSQL (Start SQL) command. You can use F4 to prompt for the STRSQL command parameters shown in Figure E.1. These parameters set the session attributes for the ISQL session that's started. For example, if you want to use change-level commitment control, you can enter *CHG for the COMMIT parameter. These session attributes can also be changed during a session, as we'll discuss later.

Figure E.1
STRSQL Command
Prompt

```
                    Start SQL Interactive Session (STRSQL)

 Type choices, press Enter.

 Commitment control . . . . . . .  COMMIT        *NONE
 Naming convention  . . . . . . .  NAMING        *SYS
 Statement processing . . . . . .  PROCESS       *RUN
 Library option . . . . . . . . .  LIBOPT        *LIBL
 List type  . . . . . . . . . . .  LISTTYPE      *ALL
 Data refresh . . . . . . . . . .  REFRESH       *ALWAYS
 Allow copy data  . . . . . . . .  ALWCPYDTA     *YES
 Date format  . . . . . . . . . .  DATFMT        *JOB
 Date separator character . . . .  DATSEP        *JOB
 Time format  . . . . . . . . . .  TIMFMT        *HMS
 Time separator character . . . .  TIMSEP        *JOB
 Decimal point  . . . . . . . . .  DECPNT        *SYSVAL
 Sort sequence  . . . . . . . . .  SRTSEQ        *JOB
    Library  . . . . . . . . . . .
 Language identifier  . . . . . .  LANGID        *JOB

                                                                      Bottom
 F3=Exit    F4=Prompt    F5=Refresh    F12=Cancel    F13=How to use this display
 F24=More keys
```

When you start an ISQL session, you see the statement entry display shown in figure E.2. This is a free-format display that lets you enter SQL/400 statements. The example shown in Figure E.2 was entered directly (without prompting) to provide an easily read sample. You don't have to align elements of SQL statements, as in this example.

Figure E.2
ISQL Statement
Entry Display

```
                          Enter SQL Statements
Type SQL statement, press Enter.
===> Create Table AppDta/Customer
     (CustID    Dec(    7, 0 ) Not Null,
     CustName              For Name     Char(  30  ) Not Null,
     CustShipLine1         For ShpLine1 Char( 100  ) Not Null,
     CustShipLine2         For ShpLine2 Char( 100  ) Not Null,
     CustShipCity          For ShpCity  Char(  30  ) Not Null,
     CustShipState         For ShpState Char(   2  ) Not Null,
     CustShipPostalCode1   For ShpPsCd1 Char(  10  ) Not Null,
     CustShipPostalCode2   For ShpPsCd2 Char(  10  ) Not Null,
     CustShipCountry       For ShpCntry Char(  30  ) Not Null,
     CustPhoneVoice        For PhnVoice Char(  15  ) Not Null,
     CustPhoneFax          For PhnFax   Char(  15  ) Not Null,
     CustStatus            For Status   Char(   1  ) Not Null
                                                    With Default ' ',
     CustCreditLimit       For CrdLimit Dec(   7, 0) With Default Null,
     CustEntryDate         For EntDate  Date          Not Null,
     Primary Key( CustID ) )
                                                                  Bottom
F3=Exit    F4=Prompt    F6=Insert line   F9=Retrieve   F10=Copy line
F12=Cancel                 F13=Services     F24=More keys
```

As you enter statements, ISQL retains them in a session log. You can page up to view previous statements. By placing the cursor on a statement and pressing F9, you can copy a previously entered statement to the statement input area of the display where you can edit it (if desired) and re-execute it. By default, when you exit a session, ISQL saves the log and restores it the next time you run ISQL. Thus, unless you take some action such as clearing the session log (discussed below), your previously entered statements are available across multiple sessions.

When you're working in the statement entry display, the following function keys are available:

F3   Exit ISQL

F4   Prompt statement

F6   Insert a blank line after the line with the editing cursor

F9   Retrieve the previous statement, or the statement on which the cursor is positioned

F10   Copy the line with the editing cursor to the next line

F12   Exit ISQL (same as F3)

F13   Display Session Services menu (discussed below)

F14   Delete line on which the cursor is positioned

F15   Split the line at the current cursor position; contents of line from the cursor position to the end of the line are moved to the next line

F16   Display a collection selection list

F17 Display a table and view selection list

F18 Display a column selection list

F24 Toggle the command-keys that are listed at the bottom of the display

The best way to familiarize yourself with ISQL statement editing is to create a test collection and then try out the various editing and other operations.

For many statements you'll find ISQL's prompting facility helpful, especially if you're just learning SQL. To prompt for a statement, enter the beginning of the statement (e.g., Create Table), and press F4. If you're not sure of the statement name, press F4 on a blank line to get a list of SQL statements from which you can select one to prompt.

When you prompt a statement, ISQL presents a display such as the one for the Create Table statement shown in Figure E.3. You enter the appropriate column names or other parts of the command into entry fields of the prompt. For most entries that require a table, view, or column name, you can put the editing cursor in the entry field and press F4 to display a list of available tables, views, or columns. You can then select one of these for the entry.

Figure E.3
ISQL Statement
Prompting

```
                        Specify CREATE TABLE Statement

Type information, press Enter.

    File . . . . . . . . . .   Customer              Name
       Library  . . . . . . .      AppDta            Name, F4 for list

Nulls:  1=NULL, 2=NOT NULL, 3=NOT NULL WITH DEFAULT

Field                   FOR Field      Type            Length  Scale  Nulls
CustID                                 Dec                  7     0      2
CustName                Name           Char                30            2
CustShipLine1           ShpLine1       Char               100     __     2
CustShipLine2           ShpLine2       Char               100     __     2
CustShipCity            ShpCity        Char                30     __     2
CustShipState           ShpState       Char                 2     __     2
CustShipPostalCode >    ShpPsCd1       Char                10     __     2
CustShipPostalCode >    ShpPsCd2       Char                10     __     2
                                                                     More...

    File CONSTRAINT  . . . . . . . . . . . . . .   Y      Y=Yes, N=No

F3=Exit    F4=Prompt            F5=Refresh   F6=Insert line     F10=Copy line
F11=Display more attributes     F12=Cancel   F14=Delete line    F24=More keys
```

To retrieve data, you enter a Select statement (as described in Chapter 14). ISQL presents the retrieved columns and rows in a rudimentary display as shown in Figure E.4, which is the result of entering the following Select statement:

```
Select      *
   From      AppDta/Employee
   Order By EmpID
```

You can page up and down in this display or use the Position to line entry field to display a particular row as the top row. The positioning options are T (top, or first row), B (bottom, or last row), or a number (e.g., 20). You can use the scalar functions listed in Figure 14.7 (e.g., SubStr) to improve the formatting of the displayed output somewhat, but ISQL displays are meant for ad hoc retrieval, not frequently-run queries where formatting is more important.

By changing the session's Select output attribute prior to executing a Select statement, you can redirect the retrieved rows to a printer file or to a new or existing database file. Changing the session's Select output attribute is discussed later.

Figure E.4
ISQL Output Display for Select Statement

```
                                        Display Data
                                                   Data width . . . . . . :        79
   Position to line  . . . . .  _____        Shift to column  . . . . . .      _____
   ....+....1....+....2....+....3....+....4....+....5....+....6....+....7....+....
   Employee   First              M  Last                                   Manager
   ID         Name               I  Name                                   Employee
                                                                           ID
     104,681  Barb               L  Gibbens                                898,613
     191,944  Hunter             F  Thompson                               707,504
     212,333  Heide              J  Smith                                  898,613
     227,504  Greg               J  Zimmerman                              668,466
     234,876  Rick               O  Millhollin                             709,453
     400,301  Raplh              S  Sport                                  898,613
     567,989  Ralph              H  Peck                                   707,504
     598,213  Sybil              M  Taylor                                 668,466
     668,466  Dave               R  Bernard                                709,453
     707,504  Bill               R  Dutcher                                668,466
     767,424  Alfred             W  Harris                                 608,466
     812,213  Joe                L  Cone                                   898,613
     898,613  Trish              S  Faubion                                668,466
     899,001  Rick               D  Castor                                 898,613
                                                                           More...
   F3=Exit      F12=Cancel      F19=Left      F20=Right      F21=Split
```

By default, when you start an ISQL session, the processing mode is *RUN, which means ISQL actually executes any statements you enter. You can specify the STRSQL command's PROCESS(*SYN) parameter (or change the session's process attribute, as described below) so that ISQL will only syntax check statements, and won't actually run them. This lets you use ISQL to construct SQL statements that you then put in a source file member, either for later execution with the RUNSQLSTM (Run SQL Statement) command or for use as embedded SQL statements in an HLL program. Another level of statement checking is available if you specify PROCESS(*VLD). With this session setting, ISQL syntax checks the statement and also verifies that all referenced tables and columns exist. The *VLD setting provides an appropriate level of checking for data manipulation language (DML) statements that use existing tables and views, while *SYN is appropriate when some of the referenced objects don't yet exist.

When you use ISQL to check statements that will be embedded in an HLL language, you should also specify an appropriate PGMLNG parameter value for the target programming language. For RPG IV and RPG/400, specify *RPG; for COBOL/400, specify *CBL.

Saving Statements to a Source Member

To save a statement to a source file member, enter the statement and, if necessary, revise it so it's syntactically correct and (optionally) validity checked. Then press the F13 key to display the Session Services menu, as shown in Figure E.5. Enter 4 to show the display in Figure E.6 where you can enter a source file and member name into which the current session log is saved. You can subsequently execute the saved statements in the source member using the RUNSQLSTM command, or use SEU (or other editor) to copy the saved statements to a source member for an HLL program.[1]

Figure E.5
ISQL Session
Services Menu

```
                      Interactive SQL Session Services

Select one of the following:

       1. Change session attributes
       2. Print current session
       3. Remove all entries from current session
       4. Save session in source file








Selection
    4

F3=Exit      F12=Cancel
```

[1] Although the ability to save SQL statements to a source member is quite handy, programmers who use a workstation-based editor have an easier solution. With an editor such as IBM's CODE/400 or Aldon Computer Group's Flex/EDIT for Windows, you can simply copy-and-paste from the 5250 emulation window in which you're running ISQL to a CODE/400 or Flex/EDIT editing window where you're working with HLL source code. With these editors, the reverse technique is also possible — you can use the editor to construct an SQL statement, then copy-and-paste to the ISQL window to syntax check or run it. All the examples in this book were checked that way, using Flex/EDIT to construct the statements and then checking them in ISQL.

Figure E.6
Save ISQL Session to
Source File Display

```
                            Change Source File
Type choices, press Enter.

    File . . . . . . . . .   sqlsrc        Name
      Library  . . . . . .   appsrc        Name
    Member . . . . . . . .   crtcust       Name, *FILE, *FIRST

    Option . . . . . . . .   1             1=Create new file
                                           2=Replace file
                                           3=Create new member
                                           4=Replace member
                                           5=Add to member

    For a new file:
      Authority  . . . . .   *LIBCRTAUT    *LIBCRTAUT, *CHANGE, *ALL
                                           *EXCLUDE, *USE
                                           authorization list name

      Text . . . . . . . .   Create Customer table

 F3=Exit      F5=Refresh      F12=Cancel
```

To clear statements you don't want to save, select option 3 from the Session Services menu. Be aware that this option clears *all* statements, so be sure you don't clear statements you'll want to retrieve or save later.

Changing Session Attributes

You can change session attributes, such as the commitment control level or the processing option for statements, by selecting option 1 from the Session Services menu. This will display a prompt to change session attributes, as shown in Figure E.7. After making your changes on this display, press Enter twice to return to the statement entry display with the new session attributes in effect.

The SELECT output entry field on the Change Session Attributes display is where you redirect rows retrieved by the Select statement to a printer or database file, instead of the display. If you enter a 3 (file) in this entry field and press Enter, you see a display such as the one in Figure E.8 where you specify the output file member and various options. Subsequent Select statement output is sent to the specified member and not displayed. A similar option is available to send the output to a printer file.

Figure E.7

Change ISQL Session
Attributes Display

```
                        Change Session Attributes

Type choices, press Enter.

    Statement processing . . . . .   *RUN          *RUN, *VLD, *SYN
    SELECT output  . . . . . . . .   1             1=Display, 2=Printer
                                                   3=File
    Commitment control . . . . . .   *NONE         *NONE, *CHG, *CS, *ALL, *RR
                                                   *NC, *UR, *RS
    Date format  . . . . . . . . .   *ISO          *JOB, *USA, *ISO, *EUR, *JIS
                                                   *MDY, *DMY, *YMD, *JUL
    Time format  . . . . . . . . .   *ISO          *HMS, *USA, *ISO
                                                   *EUR, *JIS
    Data refresh . . . . . . . . .   *ALWAYS       *ALWAYS, *FORWARD
    Allow copy data  . . . . . . .   *YES          *YES, *OPTIMIZE, *NO
    Naming convention  . . . . . .   *SYS          *SYS, *SQL
    List of libraries  . . . . . .   *LIBL         Name, *LIBL, *USRLIBL
                                                   *ALLUSR, *ALL, *CURLIB
    List type  . . . . . . . . . .   *ALL          *ALL, *SQL
    Decimal point  . . . . . . . .   *PERIOD       *SYSVAL, *PERIOD, *COMMA

                                                                   More...

F3=Exit    F4=Prompt    F5=Refresh    F12=Cancel
```

Figure E.8

Specifying the Output
Database File for
Select Statements

```
                        Change Session Attributes

Type choices, press Enter.

    Statement processing . . . . .   *RUN          *RUN, *VLD, *SYN
    SELECT output  . . . . . . . .   3             1=Display, 2=Printer
                                                   3=File
    Output file:
      File . . . . . . . . . . .     empltmp       Name
        Library  . . . . . . . .     appdta        Name
      Member . . . . . . . . . .     empltmp       Name, *FILE, *FIRST
      Option . . . . . . . . . .     1             1=Create file
                                                   2=Replace file
                                                   3=Create member
                                                   4=Replace member
                                                   5=Add to member
      Authority  . . . . . . . .     *LIBCRTAUT    *LIBCRTAUT, *CHANGE, *ALL
                                                   *EXCLUDE, *USE
                                                   authorization list name
      Text . . . . . . . . . . .     Temporary copy of Employee table

                                                                   More...

F3=Exit    F4=Prompt    F5=Refresh    F12=Cancel
```

Exiting ISQL

To exit an ISQL session, press F3 or F12 and you'll see the Exit display shown in Figure E.9. Normally, you can take the default option (1), which causes ISQL to save your session so it can be reloaded and resumed the next time you run ISQL under the same user profile.[2] The other Exit menu options let you exit without saving the session, resume (return to) the current session, or save the session to a source file member, as described above. Unfortunately, ISQL provides no way to read previously entered and saved SQL statements from a source member, so if you save a session to a source member instead of letting ISQL save the session to it's own internal area, you won't be able to reload the log for this session in a future ISQL session.

ISQL provides comprehensive online help, and is documented in the *DB2 for OS/400 SQL Programming* manual.

Figure E.9
Exit ISQL Display

```
                              Exit Interactive SQL

Type choice, press Enter.

    Option . . . . . . . . .     1        1=Save and exit session
                                          2=Exit without saving session
                                          3=Resume session
                                          4=Save session in source file












F12=Cancel
```

[2] If you run simultaneous ISQL sessions at different workstations, each workstation's sessions are saved independently. You can only resume the session saved for a workstation by running ISQL on the same workstation.

Annotated Bibliography

Recommended books are grouped by topics. Within each topic, they're listed alphabetically by title.

AS/400 Architecture, OS/400, and Related Topics

Application Developer's Handbook for the AS/400, Otey, Michael, ed., Duke Press 1993
A highly recommended collection of technical explanations and programming techniques for AS/400 application developers.

Control Language Programming for the AS/400, Meyers, Bryan and Riehl, Dan, Duke Press 1993
A comprehensive textbook, with exercises, for learning CL. (An Instructor's Guide is available also.)

Desktop Guide to AS/400 Programmers Tools, Riehl, Dan, Duke Press 1995
A handy, desk-sized reference for PDM, SEU, and other programming tools on the AS/400. This isn't a complete textbook, but provides adequate tutorial material for someone just learning to program on the AS/400.

Implementing AS/400 Security, 2nd Edition, Madden, Wayne, Duke Press 1995
An excellent practitioner's handbook for setting up AS/400 security.

Inside the AS/400, Soltis, Frank G., Duke Press 1996
Soltis was the chief architect of the AS/400, and his book is an interesting, clear, and authoritative explanation of the hardware and software architecture of the AS/400.

Power Tools for the AS/400, Volumes I and II, Dick, Frederick L. and Riehl, Dan, ed., Duke Press 1993
Another highly recommended collection of programming tips and techniques for AS/400 application developers. Comes with diskette.

RPG IV and RPG/400

Programming in RPG/400, 2nd Edition, Yaeger, Judy, Duke Press 1996
An excellent and widely used RPG/400 textbook. (An Instructor's Guide is available also.)

Programming in RPG IV, Yaeger, Judy, Duke Press 1996.
An excellent and widely used RPG IV textbook. (An Instructor's Guide is available also.)

RPG IV Jump Start, Meyers, Bryan, Duke Press 1995.
A concise guide to RPG IV for programmers who already know RPG/400.
This book provides a quick way to make the transition to RPG IV.

Database Books

Handbook of Relational Database Design, Fleming, Candace C., and Barbara
von Halle, Addison-Wesley Publishing Co. 1989.
These two "designing women" have written the best step-by-step guide to
practical database design. Much of Chapters 10 and 12 in *Database Design
and Programming for DB2/400* is based on the process described in the *Handbook*. The authors understand both the formal foundations of the relational
model and the practical aspects of business database design. This book is an
absolute must-have for anyone serious about database design.

An Introduction to Database Systems, Sixth Edition, Date, C.J., Addison-
Wesley Publishing Co. 1995
This book is another must-have for the professional database designer. Date
provides a highly readable, comprehensive, technically accurate explanation
of the relational database model, as well as other important database topics.
Chapters 9, 10, and 11 provide a very good explanation of normal forms.

Inside ODBC, Kyle Geiger, Microsoft Press 1995
This book provides an excellent explanation of ODBC programming.
An accompanying CD-ROM provides many Visual Basic and C++ sample
programs.

*CASE*Method Entity Relationship Modelling*, Barker, Richard, Addison-
Wesley Publishing Co. 1990
Barker provides an excellent book on business data modeling. The empha-
sis is on entity-relationship diagrams (ERDs), which can be useful for recording or presenting parts of the data model. Chapter 11 in *Database Design
and Programming for DB2/400* is based on the ERD notation described in
Barker's book.

Microsoft ODBC 2.0 Programmer's Reference and SDK Guide, Microsoft
Press 1994
This is an essential book for using the ODBC interface from a Windows
application. It's comprehensive and well-written, with lots of short examples.

Object Lifecycles, Modeling the World in States, Shlaer, Sally, and Stephen
J. Mellor, Prentice-Hall, Inc. 1992
This is a good book for anyone worried that "relational" is passé and who
wants to be "OO courant." It provides a good introduction to object-oriented
database design, which, by the way, is not completely antithetical to relational
design — the two approaches are compatible, and you can effectively use
techniques from both.

General Design and Programming Books

Code Complete, Steve McConnell, Microsoft Press 1993
This is my top recommendation for improving your programming skills. The author captures many essential principles and programming practices that separate the "amateur" from the "professional" programmer. The list of books and other references in Chapter 33 ("Where to Go for More Information") is excellent. This is a "must read" for any serious programmer.

Object-Oriented Design With Applications, Grady Booch, Benjamin/Cummings Publishing Company, Inc. 1991
This is a clear introduction to OO design. Although some people try to position "relational" and "OO" as competing methodologies, they're actually quite complimentary. In my own experience, many OO design concepts work well when interviewing end-users; however, relational (table-oriented) concepts work better for designing physical implementations, especially with most currently available DBMS.

Object-oriented Software Construction, Bertrand Meyer, Prentice-Hall International 1988
This is an excellent book that explains OO language and programming principles using the language Eiffel. Although there are commercial Eiffel compilers available, not many AS/400 programmers will use Eiffel; for most AS/400 programmers, the main value of the language is that it lets Meyers show real programming examples for each of the OO facilities he discusses, and it provides a basis for his discussions on various language design tradeoffs. Meyer has an excellent command of language principles, both in theory and practice.

The Practical Guide to Structured Systems Design, Meilir Page-Jones, Yourdon, Inc. 1980
Of several books produced by Ed Yourdon and his colleagues, I find this one the clearest on structured analysis and design. The data flow diagram (DFD) notation is quite handy for sketching the process part of a logical system model and dovetails nicely with relational data modeling techniques. Although structured analysis and design have given way to "OO" analysis and design, DFDs remain valuable and are an important diagramming component of many CASE (Computer Aided Software Engineering) tools.

IBM Manuals

The following are publications available from IBM, listed alphabetically. The publication number follows the title. Many of the annotations are drawn from IBM descriptions of the manuals. The *Publications Reference* manual for each release of OS/400 provides a comprehensive catalog of all IBM AS/400 manuals.

ADTS/400: Programming Development Manager, SC09-1771
(V3R2 and V3R6)
The PDM reference and user's guide.

ADTS/400: Source Entry Utility, SC09-1774 (V3R2 and V3R6)
The SEU reference and user's guide.

Backup and Recovery — Basic, SC41-3304 (V3R2) or SC41-4304 (V3R6)
This guide contains a subset of the information found in the *Backup and
Recovery — Advanced* manual. The manual contains information about
planning a backup and recovery strategy, the different types of media available to save and restore procedures, and disk recovery procedures. It also
describes how to install the system again from backup.

Backup and Recovery — Advanced, SC41-3305 (V3R2) or SC41-4305 (V3R6)
This manual provides information about the recovery tools available on the
system, such as save and restore operations, save while active, commitment
control, journal management, disk recovery operations and power loss recovery. It also provides guidelines for developing a backup and recovery strategy.
It contains procedures for save and restore operations, such as saving and
restoring the entire system, saving storage and restoring licensed internal
code, and it provides examples of using the save and restore commands. The
manual also contains procedures for data and disk recovery, such as using
journal management and disk recovering operations, instructions for planning and setting up mirrored protection, and information on uninterrupt-
ible power supply. The manual contains the appendices for SRC codes,
example Disaster Recovery Plan and the IPL process.

CL Programming, SC41-3721 (V3R2) or SC41-4721 (V3R6)
This guide provides a wide-ranging discussion of AS/400 programming topics, including a general discussion of objects and libraries, CL programming, controlling flow and communicating between programs, working with
objects in CL programs, and creating CL programs. Other topics include
predefined and impromptu messages and handling, defining and creating
user-defined commands and menus, application testing, including debug
mode, breakpoints, traces, and display functions.

CL Reference, SC41-3722 (V3R2) or SC41-4722 (V3R6)
This set of manuals provides detailed information about AS/400 control
language (CL) and the OS/400-related commands. All non-OS/400 CL
commands associated with other IBM AS/400 software products, including
all the various languages and utilities, are described in the manuals for
those products.

Client Access Windows 3.1 Client for OS/400 ODBC User's Guide,
SC41-3533 (V3R2 and V3R6)
This book describes how to set up and run ODBC applications using Client
Access for OS/400 ODBC. Included in this document are chapters on

performance, examples, and configuring specific applications to run with Client Access for OS/400 ODBC.

COBOL/400 Reference, SC09-1813 (V3R2 and V3R6)
This reference covers the older (non-ILE) version of COBOL on the AS/400. See *ILE COBOL/400 Reference* for the current version.

COBOL/400 User's Guide, SC09-1812 (V3R2 and V3R6)
This user's guide covers the older (non-ILE) version of COBOL on the AS/400. See *ILE COBOL/400 Programmer's Guide* for the current version.

Data Management, SC41-3710 (V3R2) or SC41-4710 (V3R6)
This guide provides information about using database and device files in application programs. The information is not as specific to database files as that contained in *DB2 for OS/400 Database Programming*.

DB2/400 Database — An Overview, SC41-3700 (V3R2 and V3R6)
This book provides a high-level discussion of the AS/400 integrated database, including information on related products. Introduces the database to programmers and end-users who are not currently using an AS/400.

DB2 for OS/400 Advanced Database Functions, GG24-4249 (V3R2 and V3R6)
This book provides suggestions, guidelines, and practical examples for using DB2/400 features such as triggers, referential integrity, DRDA, two-phase commit, and stored procedures. The book provides examples developed in several programming languages (RPG, COBOL, C), using native and SQL data access interfaces.

DB2 for OS/400 Database Programming, SC41-3701 (V3R2) or SC41-4701 (V3R6)
This guide provides a detailed description of the AS/400 database organization, including information on how to create, describe, and update database files on the system.

DB2 for OS/400 Query Manager Use, SC41-3212 (V3R2) or SC41-4212 (V3R6)
This guide describes the SQL/400 Query Manager and how to use its different options.

DB2 for OS/400 Query Management Programming, SC41-3703 (V3R2) or SC41-4703 (V3R6)
This book describes how to define an SQL query definition and define a report form definition using OS/400 query management. Also explains the relationship between the OS/400 query management and the Query/400 licensed program.

DB2 for OS/400 SQL Call Level Interface, SC41-3806 (V3R2) or SC41-4806 (V3R6)
This book describes how to use X/Open SQL Call Level Interface to access SQL functions directly through procedure calls to a service program provided by DB2/400.

DB2 for OS/400 SQL Programming, SC41-3611 (V3R2) or SC41-4611 (V3R6)
This manual provides an overview of how to design, write, run, and test
SQL/400 statements. The manual provides examples of how to write
SQL/400 statements in COBOL, RPG, and C programs on the AS/400.

DB2 for OS/400 SQL Reference, SC41-3612 (V3R2) or SC41-4612 (V3R6)
The reference for Structured Query Language (SQL) on the AS/400.

DDS Reference, SC41-3712 (V3R2 and V3R6)
The Data Description Specification reference. It covers DDS for physical and
logical database files; as well as display, printer, and intersystem communications function (ICF) device files.

Distributed Data Management, SC41-3307 (V3R2) or SC41-4307 (V3R6)
This guide provides information about remote file processing. It describes
how to define a remote file to OS/400 distributed data management (DDM),
how to create a DDM file, what file utilities are supported through DDM, and
the requirements of OS/400 DDM as related to other systems.

Distributed Database Programming, SC41-3702 (V3R2 and V3R6)
This guide provides information on preparing and managing an AS/400 system in a distributed relational database using the Distributed Relational Database Architecture (DRDA). Describes planning, setting up, programming,
administering, and operating a distributed relational database on more than
one AS/400 system.

Getting Started with AS/400, SC41-3204 (V3R2) or SC41-4204 (V3R6)
This book helps new or novice AS/400 users get started on the AS/400 system.
Shows how to perform simple tasks and introduces key AS/400 functions.

ILE C/400 Programmer's Guide, SC09-1820 (V3R2) or SC09-2069 (V3R6)
Provides information on how to develop applications using the ILE C/400
language. It includes information about creating, running and debugging
programs. It also includes programming considerations for interlanguage
program and procedure calls, locales, handling exceptions, database, externally described and device files. Some performance tips are also described.

ILE C/400 Programmer's Reference, SC09-1821 (V3R2) or SC09-2070 (V3R6)
The C reference for the AS/400.

ILE C/400 Reference Summary, SX09-1288 (V3R2) or SX09-1304 (V3R6)
Provides quick reference information about ILE C/400 command syntax,
elements of C, C library functions, and ILE C/400 Machine Interface (MI)
library extensions.

ILE COBOL/400 Programmer's Guide, SC09-1522 (V3R2) or SC09-2072
(V3R6)
Provides information about how to write, compile, bind, run, debug, and
maintain ILE COBOL/400 programs on the AS/400 system. It provides

programming information on how to call other ILE COBOL/400 and non-ILE COBOL/400 programs, share data with other programs, use pointers, and handle exceptions. It also describes how to perform input/output operations on externally attached devices, database files, display files, and ICF files.

ILE COBOL/400 Reference, SC09-1523 (V3R2) or SC09-2073 (V3R6)
The COBOL reference for the AS/400. This reference covers the ILE version of COBOL.

ILE COBOL/400 Reference Summary, SX09-1260 (V3R2) or SX09-1305 (V3R6)
Provides quick reference information on the structure of the ILE COBOL/400 programming language and the structure of an ILE COBOL/400 source program. It also provides syntax diagrams of all Identification Division paragraphs, Environment Division clauses, Data Division clauses, Procedure Division statements, and Compiler-Directing statements.

ILE Concepts, SC41-3606 (V3R2) or SC41-4606 (V3R6)
This guide explains concepts and terminology pertaining to the Integrated Language Environment (ILE) architecture of the OS/400 licensed program. Topics covered include creating modules, binding, running programs, debugging programs, and handling exceptions.

ILE RPG/400 Programmer's Guide, SC09-1525 (V3R2) or SC09-2074 (V3R6)
This guide provides information about the ILE RPG/400 (RPG IV) programming language. It includes information on creating and running programs, with considerations for procedure calls and interlanguage programming. The guide also covers debugging and exception handling and explains how to use AS/400 files and devices in RPG IV programs. Appendixes include information on migration to RPG IV from (non-ILE) RPG/400 and sample compiler listings. It is intended for people with a basic understanding of data processing concepts and of the RPG language.

ILE RPG/400 Reference, SC09-1526 (V3R2) or SC09-2077 (V3R6)
The RPG IV reference. This manual describes, position by position and keyword by keyword, the valid entries for all RPG IV specifications, and provides a detailed description of all the operation codes and built-in functions. This manual also contains information on the RPG IV logic cycle, arrays and tables, editing functions, and indicators.

ILE RPG Reference Summary, SX09-1261 (V3R2) or SX09-1306 (V3R6)
Provides information about the (non-ILE) RPG/400 and (ILE) RPG IV versions of RPG. This manual contains tables and lists for all specifications and operations in both versions. A key is provided to map RPG/400 specifications and operations to RPG IV specifications and operations.

International Application Development, SC41-3603 (V3R2 and V3R6)
This guide provides information required to understand and use the national language support function on the AS/400 system. This book prepares the AS/400 user for planning, installing, configuring, and using AS/400 national language support (NLS) and multilingual support of the AS/400 system. It also provides an explanation of the database management of multilingual data and application considerations for a multilingual system.

Master Glossary, SC41-3006 (V3R2) or SC41-4006 (V3R6)
This manual provides definitions for many technical terms used on the AS/400 system, including for OS/400 and some IBM licensed programs.

National Language Support, SC41-3101 (V3R2 and V3R6)
This guide describes national language support concepts, using national language support functions in a multilingual environment, and how IBM licensed programs are affected by national language support functions in a multilingual environment.

Programming Reference Summary, SX41-3720 (V3R2) or SX41-4720 (V3R6)
This manual is a quick-reference of programming information relating to OS/400 and programming tools, including SEU. Included are summaries of OS/400 object types, IBM-supplied objects, CL command list, CL command matrix, DDS keywords and monitorable error messages.

Publications Reference, SC41-3003 (V3R2) or SC41-4003 (V3R6)
This manual describes the printed and online information in the AS/400 library, and also lists other publications about the AS/400 system. Includes cross-reference information between the current library and the previous version library.

Query/400 Use, SC41-3210 (V3R2) or SC41-4210 (V3R6)
This guide provides the end-user or programmer with information about using AS/400 Query to get data from any database file. It describes how to start Query, and how to define and run queries to create reports containing the selected data.

RPG/400 Reference, SC09-1817 (V3R2 and V3R6)
This reference covers RPG/400, the older (non-ILE) version of RPG on the AS/400. See *ILE RPG/400 Reference* for the current version (RPG IV).

RPG/400 User's Guide, SC09-1816 (V3R2 and V3R6)
This user's guide covers RPG/400, the older (non-ILE) version of RPG on the AS/400. See *ILE RPG/400 Programmer's Guide* for the current version (RPG IV).

Security — Basic, SC41-3301 (V3R2 and V3R6)
This guide explains why security is necessary, defines major concepts, and provides information on planning, implementing, and monitoring basic security on the AS/400 system.

Security — Reference, SC41-3302 (V3R2) or SC41-4302 (V3R6)
This manual provides information about system security concepts, planning for security, and setting up security on the system. It also gives information about protecting the system and data from being used by people who do not have the proper authorization, protecting the data from intentional or unintentional damage or destruction, keeping security up-to-date, and setting up security on the system.

Sort User's Guide and Reference, SC09-1826 (V3R2 and V3R6)
This manual provides information about the OS/400 sort utility, including how to identify input and output files and how to specify sort options

Tips and Tools for Securing AS/400, SC41-3300 (V3R2) or GC41-0615 (V3R6)
This guide explains how to use the AS/400 security functions and several new tools supplied by IBM to improve your AS/400 security.

Work Management, SC41-3306 (V3R2) or SC41-4306 (V3R6)
This guide provides information about how to create and change an AS/400 work management environment. It also includes a description of tuning the system, collecting performance data including information on record formats and contents of the data being collected, working with system values to control or change the overall operation of the system, and a description of how to gather data to determine who is using the system and what resources are being used.

Glossary

For additional definitions, see IBM's *AS/400 Master Glossary* publication.

access method — The method used to read records in a file: sequential, direct, or a combination of sequential and direct.

access path — The order in which records are organized for processing by a program: either arrival sequence or keyed sequence.

algebraic closure — In the relational database model, the property of relational algebra such that the result of any operation is a relation.

alias — In DDS, the alternative field name up to 30 characters long.

arrival sequence — The ordering of records by their relative record numbers.

AS/400 — IBM's midrange business computer system.

ASP — See **auxiliary storage pool**.

assertion — In a data model, a rule that must be satisfied by the data and/or operations on the data.

atomic — Indivisible. This term may apply to attributes in the relational database model, to SQL/400 functions, or to transactions running under commitment control.

attribute — In the relational database model, a named property of the entity represented by a relation.

attribute integrity — In the relational database model, the rule that values for attributes come only from their respective domains.

authority — The right or capability to do something. On the AS/400 there are system-defined public and private authorities that govern a user profile's access to an object.

authorization list — An OS/400 object (type *AUTL) that controls access to one or more other objects.

auxiliary storage pool (ASP) — An AS/400 configuration feature that identifies one or more disk units as a specific location for storing objects.

backup — A copy of saved system objects, usually on magnetic tape. The process of making a backup.

base relation — A relation that represents an entity. Contrast with **view relation**.

base table — In SQL, a table that contains data. In SQL/400, a base table is a physical file. Contrast with **view**.

basic predicate — An SQL predicate that tests a simple condition, such as equality.

Between predicate — An SQL predicate that tests for a range of values.

binary — In DB2/400, a numeric data type that stores numbers using a representation of the number in base 2.

blocked Insert — In SQL/400, an Insert statement that inserts multiple rows in a single operation.

C-spec — See **calculation specification**.

calculation specification (C-spec) — In RPG IV and RPG/400, a statement that generally contains an executable operation such as assignment or I/O.

candidate key — In the relational database model, a minimal set of attributes that are non-null and always contain a unique value for each tuple in the relation. If there are multiple candidate keys, one is selected to serve as the relation's primary key.

cardinality — The number of tuples in a relation. Also, in entity relationship diagrams, the number of instances of one entity that can be associated with an instance of another entity.

catalog — In general, the system information that describes database objects. In SQL, the tables that contain descriptions of the database objects (e.g., tables, views, indexes, and packages).

character field — In DB2/400, a database field that contains character data.

CODASYL data model — See **network data model**.

code reuse — An implementation technique in which previously created code is reused in a subsequent application.

collection — In SQL, a container for database objects, such as tables and views. In SQL/400, a collection is an OS/400 library object.

column — In SQL, the element of a table or view that represents some property of an entity. In SQL/400, a column is a field in a database file.

column function — In SQL, a function that calculates a value from a set of rows. Contrast with **scalar function**.

command — A statement used to request a system function. On the AS/400, these are known as CL (Command Language) commands.

commitment boundary — In OS/400, the point at which there are no uncommitted operations. This point is the end of the previous transaction (if any) and the beginning of the next transaction.

commitment control — An OS/400 facility that allows all-or-none execution of a transaction.

commutative — The mathematical property that the order of operands is insignificant (e.g., A+B = B+A).

composite key — A database file key, or relation key, that's composed of more than one field or attribute.

composite primary key — A primary key that's composed of more than one field or attribute.

concatenate — To join together two character strings.

conceptual schema — See **schema**.

constraint — A restriction or limitation specified in a data model or specified for an SQL table or database file.

continuation symbol — In DDS, the + or − character that indicates a statement is continued on the following source record.

correlated subquery — In SQL, a subquery that references a table or view named in an outer subselect.

correlation name — In SQL, an identifier that designates a table, a view, or an individual row of a table or view within a single SQL statement.

cursor — On a display, a movable symbol that indicates the location of input or some other operation. In SQL, a named structure that's used to access rows individually within an HLL program.

data authority — In OS/400, one of the following specific authorities: *READ, *ADD, *UPD, *DLT, *EXECUTE.

data definition language (DDL) — In SQL, the set of statements that are used to create new database objects (e.g., Create Table).

Data Description Specifications (DDS) — An AS/400 language for defining database and device files.

data dictionary — In a logical data model or physical database design, the containers used to hold everything recorded during the modeling process. These may include word-processing documents, database files, CASE design tool project folders, or other types of containers.

data manipulation language (DML) — In SQL, the set of statements that are used to manipulate the contents of database objects (e.g., Update).

data model — An abstract representation of the content and structure of the information of interest to an organization.

data modeling — See **logical data modeling**.

data type — In general terms, a definition of a set of allowable values and operations. In DDS and SQL, the attribute of a field or column that determines how values are stored (e.g., character or packed decimal) and the allowable operations.

database — A set of computer files for storing information that's used by a business or other organization. With respect to SQL/400, all the database objects on one AS/400 constitute a single database.

database design — See **physical database design**.

database file — In OS/400, a physical or logical file object (type *FILE).

database management system (DBMS) — The software to create files and retrieve and update file contents.

date — A DB2/400 field and column data type that stores values for calendar dates.

date duration — In SQL, a value for an interval of time (e.g., a number of days).

DB2 Query Manager and SQL Development Kit for OS/400 — The IBM product that contains SQL/400 and Query Management/400.

DB2/400 — The name of the AS/400's integrated, relational DBMS.

DBMS — See **database management system**.

DDL — See **data definition language**.

DDM — See **Distributed Data Management**.

degree — In the relational database model, the number of attributes of a relation. In entity relationship diagramming, the number of relations participating in a relationship.

delayed access path maintenance — A DB2/400 feature that logs changes to a nonunique, keyed access path and updates the access path when the file is next opened. Contrast with **immediate** and **rebuild access path maintenance**.

Delete statement — An SQL statement to remove one or more rows from a table.

delete-update-insert rules — For foreign key integrity or referential constraint specifications, the actions to take when a delete, update, or insert operation would leave an orphan row in the dependent file.

dependent file — The file in a referential constraint that contains the foreign key.

derived attribute — See **virtual attribute**.

device parity protection — An AS/400 feature that protects data on disk from being lost due to a single disk unit failure.

difference — A relational algebra operation that returns a relation with all tuples in the first relation but not in the second.

direct access — A file access method that allows reading records in an arbitrary order by key value or relative record number. Contrast with **sequential access**.

direct attribute — In the relational database model, an attribute that's not derived; i.e., one that represents an intrinsic property of an entity.

Distributed Data Management (DDM) — An IBM standard and DB2/400 facility that lets an application program on one system use database files stored on remote systems, as if the remote files were local.

Distributed Relational Database Architecture (DRDA) — An IBM standard and DB2/400 facility that lets an application on one system use SQL to perform operations on database files stored on remote systems, as if the remote files were local.

division — A relational algebra operation that takes two relations and returns a relation consisting of all values of one set of attributes in the first relation, for those tuples that match on the remaining attributes (in the first relation) all tuples in the second relation.

DML — See **data manipulation language**.

DRDA — See **Distributed Relational Database Architecture**.

dynamic record selection — A DDS access path option and DB2/400 facility to evaluate record selection criteria when records are read, rather than when records are added to a file.

EBCDIC — See **Extended Binary Coded Decimal Interchange Code**.

embedded dynamic statement — In SQL, one of the DML statements (e.g., Execute) to prepare and execute an SQL statement stored as a character string in a program variable.

embedded SQL statement — An SQL statement coded in an HLL program.

embedded statement — See **embedded SQL statement**.

entity — In data modeling, one instance of an entity type.

entity integrity — In the relational database model, the rule that each tuple in a relation must be unique.

entity relationship diagram (ERD) — A graphical diagram using a notation that represents entity types as boxes and relationships between entity types as lines.

entity subtype — An entity type that has all the properties — and possibly more — of another entity type. All entities that are instances of the entity subtype are also instances of the other entity type (the entity supertype).

entity type — A representation of a set of objects, events, or associations of interest in a data model. The entity type defines properties of all instances of the type.

entity type hierarchy — A set of entity types arranged in a subtype/supertype hierarchy.

equijoin — A join that selects rows based on equal values in specified columns of the joined tables.

ERD — See **entity relationship diagram**.

exclusive relationship — In entity relationship diagramming, a set of relationships for which each instance can participate in exactly one of the possible relationships.

Exists predicate — An SQL predicate that tests for a nonempty result set for a subquery.

Extended Binary Coded Decimal Interchange Code (EBCDIC) — The 8-bit per character encoding used for most DB2/400 character data.

external schema — See **subschema**.

externally described file — An OS/400 file that's created from DDS or SQL and that has field-level definitions for the file's records. Contrast with **program-described file**.

F-spec — See **file description specification**.

Fetch statement — An SQL statement to change position in a cursor and/or to read a row from the cursor's result set.

field — The smallest named unit of data in a database. A named group of bytes used to store a value in a record.

field dictionary — A set of definitions for database fields used in one or more applications.

field mapping — The specification of how fields in a logical file or OPNQRYF command's record format are derived from an underlying file.

field reference file — A physical file used solely to contain field definitions that can be referenced by the DDS for other file definitions.

field usage — In DDS, whether a field can be used for input, output, or both input and output.

field-level — In DDS, the group of keywords that can be specified on individual field definitions.

fifth normal form (5NF) — In the relational database model, the normal form of relations such that no further decomposition is possible without loss of information.

file access routine — A programming technique in which a program or procedure is implemented to provide all file access for higher-level application programs.

file description — The description of a file's layout, access path, and other information that OS/400 stores in the file object's header.

file description (FD) entry — A COBOL statement that declares a file's record layout in a program.

file description specification (F-spec) — In RPG IV and RPG/400, a statement that declares a file.

file information data structure — In RPG IV and RPG/400, a language-defined data structure that's filled with status information after each I/O operation.

file pointer — An internal pointer that keeps track of a location in a database file.

first normal form (1NF) — In the relational database model, the normal form of relations such that each attribute value is atomic (i.e., not a set).

floating point — In DB2/400, a numeric data type that stores real numbers using a representation of the number as a mantissa and exponent.

foreign key — A set of columns that reference the primary key of a table. Used to associate rows in a dependent table with rows in a (not necessarily distinct) parent table.

foreign key constraint — In SQL/400 and DB2/400, a **referential constraint**.

fourth normal form (4NF) — In the relational database model, the normal form of relations such that no more than one multivalued fact exists in a relation.

full outer join — A join in which unmatched rows in both joined tables are included in the result and are paired with null or default values.

fullselect — A form of SQL Select that is a subselect, or the union of multiple subselects.

group profile — An AS/400 user profile that's referenced as a group profile by some (nongroup) user profile.

grouping column — A column used in an SQL subselect to group rows into subsets for the purpose of selection and aggregation.

hexadecimal (hex) field — In DB2/400, a field data type that stores data as unencoded bits.

hierarchic data model — A data model that represents the structure of information in a hierarchy, with parent/child relationships among nodes in the hierarchy.

high-level language (HLL) — A general-purpose programming language, such as RPG IV or COBOL/400.

HLL — See **high-level language**.

host structure array — In SQL/400, a program variable declared as an array of structures. This type of variable can be used in multiple-row Fetch or blocked Insert operations.

host structure variable — In SQL/400, a program variable declared as a structure (e.g., an RPG data structure or a COBOL/400 group item).

host variable — In SQL/400, an HLL program variable used in an embedded SQL statement.

I-spec — See **input specification**.

IFS — See **Integrated File System**.

impact analysis — The analysis of what other changes will be required when a file definition or program change is made.

implementation — The actual coding and other tasks required to create a working application.

In predicate — An SQL predicate that tests for membership in a set of values.

index — In DB2/400, an internal structure that contains key values for records and their corresponding relative record numbers. In SQL, an object used to enforce unique keys and to provide an internal index to aid performance.

indicator variable — In SQL, a host variable that contains a Boolean value indicating whether a column or expression is null.

inner join — A join in which unmatched rows in both joined tables are not included in the result.

input specification (I-spec) — In RPG IV and RPG/400, a statement that declares an input record or field.

Insert statement — An SQL statement to add one or more new rows to a table.

instance — In the relational database model, one occurrence of an entity type. Represented by a tuple in a relation or a row in a table.

Integrated File System (IFS) — A Unix-like directory structure and set of interfaces that's part of OS/400. The /QSYS.LIB subdirectory under the root directory of IFS contains DB2/400 files.

integrity constraint — See **constraint**.

Interactive SQL (ISQL) — An IBM interactive tool for entering SQL statements. A component of the DB2 Query Manager and SQL Development Kit for OS/400 product.

intersection — A relational algebra operation that returns a relation with all tuples that occur in both the first relation and the second.

intersection entity — In entity relationship diagramming, an entity that represents an association among two or more entities.

inverted list data model — A data model that resembles a conventional file system with enhanced file index facilities to aid in record retrieval

ISQL — See **Interactive SQL**.

join — A relational algebra operation that returns a relation that is the subset of the product of two relations, such that each row of the result satisfies a specified condition. The term "join" is frequently used to mean **equijoin**.

join field — In DDS, a comparison field that identifies records from two files to be combined into one record.

join logical file (join file) — A logical file that combines (in one record format) fields from two or more physical files.

join specification — In DDS, the statements that describe how to join pair(s) of files.

journal — An OS/400 object (type *JRN) that identifies the objects being journaled and the attached and detached journal receivers.

journal entry — A record in a journal receiver that contains information about changes to a journaled file or other activity.

journal receiver — An OS/400 object (type *JRNRCV) that contains entries for changes to files and other journaled activities.

key field — In DB2/400, a field used to identify or arrange the records in a file member.

key list — In RPG IV and RPG/400, an identifier defined on a KLIST statement for a set of fields specified on KFLD statements.

keyed access path — An access path that provides keyed sequence access to a file's records.

keyed sequence — The ordering of records by values in their key fields.

keyword — In DDS, a name that identifies a function. In CL, HLLs, and SQL, a language-defined identifier that specifies a statement parameter.

keyword entry — In DDS, one of the specification entries (e.g., TEXT) that must be coded in the Function column (positions 45–80) of the statement.

labeled duration — In SQL, a number and keyword (e.g., 2 Days) that represents a duration of years, months, days, hours, minutes, seconds, or microseconds.

left outer join — A join in which unmatched rows in the primary (left hand) joined table are included in the result and are paired with null or default values.

level checking — An OS/400 function that compares the record-level identifiers of a file to be opened with the file description that's part of a compiled program to determine if the record format for the file has changed since the program was compiled.

library — An OS/400 object (type *LIB) that contains other OS/400 objects.

Like predicate — An SQL predicate that tests for a match with a string pattern.

lock level — The specification of when record locks should be obtained under commitment control and the type and duration of record locks.

logical data modeling — The process of analyzing and specifying the information required by an organization.

logical file — A DB2/400 file that provides an alternative means of accessing data in one or more underlying physical files. Contrast with **physical file**.

major key — The most significant field or column in a composite key.

member — The component of a physical or logical file that contains records.

minor key — The least significant field or column in a composite key.

mirrored disk protection — An AS/400 function that protects data by duplicating all disk data in an auxiliary storage pool (ASP) to another disk unit in the same ASP.

multi-format logical file — A logical file with two or more record format definitions.

multiple-row Fetch statement — An SQL/400 Fetch statement that retrieves multiple rows on each execution.

multirow predicate — A predicate that requires values from multiple rows in a table to evaluate.

multitable predicate — A predicate that requires values from rows in multiple tables to evaluate.

multivalued fact — In the relational database model, a dependency in which a value for one attribute may determine several values for another attribute (e.g., an employee ID may determine multiple courses taken by the employee).

natural join — An equijoin in which one of the two matching columns (or sets of columns) are not included in the result.

network (CODASYL) data model — A form of data model that uses nodes and explicit links to represent information. Unlike in the hierarchical data model, a node may have more than one "parent."

normal form — A form of relations that satisfies certain criteria related to the elimination of redundant representation of facts.

normalization — A process to make sure the relations or tables in a data model conform to a particular normal form.

null — In the relational database model, a placeholder that signifies a missing or unknown value.

Null predicate — An SQL predicate that tests for a column or expression being null.

null-capable — A field or column that can be set null. In DDS, a field defined with the ALWNULL keyword. In SQL, a column defined without the Not Null clause.

numeric field — In DB2/400, a database field that contains numeric data.

O-spec — See **output specification**.

object — On the AS/400, a named storage space that consists of a set of characteristics that describe the object and, in some cases, data.

object authority — A specific authority (e.g., *OBJMGT) that controls how a user profile can operate on an entire object.

object lock — An AS/400 resource allocation mechanism that guarantees certain types of access by the process placing the lock and prevents certain types of access by other processes.

ODBC — See **Open Database Connectivity**.

ODP — See **open data path**.

ODP scope — For an open operation, the scope within which the ODP can be shared and the boundary at which the system will automatically delete the ODP.

open data path (ODP) — An OS/400 control block created when a file is opened and used to provide access to the file's data.

Open Database Connectivity (ODBC) — A Microsoft-developed standard for database access. Primarily used for access from Windows-based applications.

open scope — See **ODP scope**.

OS/400 — The AS/400 operating system.

outer join — A join in which unmatched rows in the one or both of the joined tables are included in the result and are paired with null or default values. See **full outer join**, **left outer join**, and **right outer join**.

output specification (O-spec) — In RPG IV and RPG/400, a statement that declares an output record or field.

override scope — For an OVRDBF command, the scope within which file opens and other overrides are affected by this command.

packed decimal — In DB2/400, a numeric data type that stores numbers using a representation of the number with one digit per half byte.

parameter marker — In SQL, a ? character used to mark the location of a parameter in a string that's dynamically prepared for subsequent execution.

parent file — The file containing a primary or unique key referenced by a foreign key in the dependent file.

parent key — The primary or unique key in a file referenced by a foreign key.

partial key — In RPG IV and RPG/400, a list of key fields that doesn't include all the fields in a composite key.

PDM — See **Programming Development Manager**.

physical data independence — The DBMS architecture concept that users are not affected when the *physical* structure of stored data is changed, as long as the *logical* structure remains the same.

physical database design — The process designing the files and other application objects needed to implement a particular logical data model.

physical file — A DB2/400 file that contains data. Contrast with **logical file**.

positional entry — In DDS, one of the specification entries (e.g., field name) that must be coded in specific positions of the statement.

positioned Delete statement — In SQL, a Delete statement with a Where Current Of clause. Used to delete a row that has been Fetch'd through a cursor. Contrast with **searched Delete statement**.

positioned Update statement — In SQL, an Update statement with a Where Current Of clause. Used to update a row that has been Fetch'd through a cursor. Contrast with **searched Update statement**.

precompilation — A source translation process that occurs before the compilation step.

precompiler directive — A source language statement that causes some action during precompilation.

predicate — A logical expression that has a true or false value. In SQL, an expression that has a value of true, false, or unknown.

primary file — In a join logical file, the first file listed on the JFILE statement. Contrast with **secondary file**.

primary key — In the relational database model, the candidate key used to identify rows in the table. In DB2/400, the key identified on a physical file's primary key constraint.

primary key constraint — In SQL/400 and DB2/400, a physical file constraint that requires a set of fields to have unique, nonnull values.

privilege — In SQL, a capability given to a user by a Grant statement. In SQL/400, privileges correspond to OS/400 specific authorities.

product — A relational algebra operation that returns a relation consisting of all possible combinations of two tuples, one from each of two specified relations..

program adopted authority — The authority of the owner of a program, service program, or SQL package given to a user who is executing the object.

program-described file — A file created without DDS or SQL and for which the fields in the records are described only in programs that process the file. Contrast with **externally described file**.

Programming Development Manager (PDM) — An IBM programming utility that provides a list-oriented interface for working with libraries, objects, and file members. A component of the ADTS/400 product.

projection — A relational algebra operation that returns a relation with all remaining (sub)tuples in a relation after specified attributes have been dropped.

property — In a data model, some characteristic of an entity.

public authority — The authority governing access by a user profile that has no private authority to an object.

qualified name — In OS/400, the combination of a library name and an object name.

quantified predicate — An SQL predicate that tests a basic predicate against all rows in a subquery's result table.

query definition — An OS/400 object (type *QRYDFN) produced when the Query/400 specification of a query is saved.

Query Manager/400 — An IBM data retrieval utility for use with DB2/400 files. A component of the DB2 Query Manager and SQL Development Kit for OS/400 product.

Query/400 — An IBM data retrieval product for use with DB2/400 files.

rebuild access path maintenance — A DB2/400 feature that rebuilds a nonunique, keyed access path when the file is next opened. Contrast with **delayed and immediate access path maintenance**.

record — A named collection of fields stored or accessed together.

record format — A named part of an OS/400 file that identifies records with a specific layout.

record lock — A DB2/400 allocation mechanism that prevents certain types of conflicting record access.

record-oriented file — A file organized as sequence of records. Contrast with **stream-oriented file**.

recovery — The process of re-creating damaged files and other objects from a backup.

referential constraint — In SQL/400 and DB2/400, a physical file constraint that requires a set of nonnull fields in a dependent file to have a matching value in the primary or unique key of a record in the parent file.

referential integrity — In the relational database model, the requirement that tuples that exist in separate relations, but that are interrelated, be unambiguously interrelated by corresponding attribute values.

regular entity — In entity relationship diagramming, an entity type that is not a weak entity. Contrast with **weak entity**.

relation — In the relational database model, a relation heading and body. Informally, a relation can be thought of as a table.

relation body — In the relational database model, a relation's set of tuples.

relation heading — In the relational database model, the set of attribute-and-domain pairs.

relational database model — A general model for representing information as a set of relations.

relational model — See **relational database model**.

relationship — Some form of association or interdependence between two or more entity types.

relative file number — In DDS, the number representing a file's position on the JFILE statement.

relative record number (RRN) — The number representing a record's physical location in a file member, relative to the first location.

result table — In SQL, the conceptual table defined by a fullselect.

right outer join — A join in which unmatched rows in the secondary (right hand) joined table are included in the result and are paired with null or default values.

row — In SQL, a row consists of a sequence of column values. In SQL/400, a row corresponds to a database record.

RRN — See **relative record number.**

save-while-active — An AS/400 save operation performed while application programs that change objects are running.

save/restore facilities — AS/400 facilities to create backups and use those backups in subsequent recovery operations.

scalar function — In SQL, a function that calculates a value from an expression that involves no more than one row. Contrast with **column function.**

schema — In a logical data model, the part of the model that represents the overall, integrated description of the data.

scrollable cursor — An SQL cursor declared with the Scroll keyword to allow nonsequential Fetch operations.

search condition — In SQL, one or more predicates that specify the criteria for selecting rows from a table.

searched Delete — In SQL, a Delete statement with an optional Where clause that specifies a search condition. Contrast with **positioned Delete statement.**

searched Update — In SQL, an Update statement with an optional Where clause that specifies a search condition. Contrast with **positioned Update statement.**

second normal form (2NF) — In the relational database model, the normal form of relations such that each non-key attribute is dependent on the entire primary key.

secondary file — In a join logical file, the second or later file listed on the JFILE statement. Contrast with **primary file.**

Select clause — In COBOL, the clause of a File-Control paragraph that declares a file.

Select statement — An interactive SQL statement to retrieve rows from one or more tables or views. Also, a fullselect and an optional Order By, For Update Of, For Read Only, or Optimize For clause.

select/omit — In DDS, statements that specify the record selection criteria for a logical file.

selection — A relational algebra operation that returns a relation with all tuples in a relation that satisfy a specified condition.

sequential access — A file access method that allows reading records in their physical order in a file member or by the order of their key field values. Contrast with **direct access**.

set-at-a-time operation — In SQL, the capability of a Select, Insert, Update, or Delete statement to operate on a set of rows in one operation.

SEU — See **Source Entry Utility**.

shared access path — An internal DB2/400 index used by two or more database file's keyed access paths.

shared ODP — An ODP that's used by more than one open file in CL and HLL programs.

sort — A physical re-ordering of the records in a file, based on the values in one or more fields.

source code editor — A programming tool for entering and modifying source code.

Source Entry Utility (SEU) — An IBM full-screen source code editor for the AS/400. A component of the ADTS/400 product.

source file — A physical file that contains source records.

source file member — A member in a source file.

source type attribute — An attribute of a source file member that indicates the type of source code contained in the member.

special authority — An OS/400 authority (e.g., *SAVSYS) associated with a user profile and providing various access and system management capabilities.

specific authority — An OS/400 authority (e.g., *READ) granted to a user profile to allow a specific type of access to an object.

SQL — See **Structured Query Language**.

SQLCA — See **SQL communication area**.

SQL communication area (SQLCA) — A program record structure that's updated after every SQL operation.

SQL special register — One of the system-defined storage areas (e.g., Current Date) that contain information that can be used in SQL statements.

static execution — In SQL, the execution of a static statement. Contrast with **dynamic execution**.

static statement — An embedded SQL statement that's prepared during program creation and executed when the program is run.

stored procedure — In SQL, a procedure that can be called with a Call statement. In SQL/400, a stored procedure is an HLL program object.

stream-oriented file — A file organized as sequence of bytes. Contrast with **record-oriented file**.

Structured Query Language (SQL) — An industry-standard language for defining and manipulating relational database objects.

subquery — A subselect that's part of a predicate.

subschema — In a logical data model, the part of the model that represents specific end-user views.

subselect — An SQL expression that begins with the Select keyword and that defines a result table. A subselect is a component of a fullselect.

substring — A portion of a character string.

surrogate key — A column used as a primary key and that contains a meaningless, system-assigned number.

system catalog — See **catalog**.

system column name — In SQL/400, the 10-character (or shorter) physical file field name used for a column.

system dictionary — See **catalog**.

table — A database object with rows and columns. A table may be a base table or a view table; however, "table" by itself is frequently used to mean base table.

table lock — In SQL, a lock placed on a base table. In SQL/400 a table lock is an object lock on a physical file.

theta-join — A general term for any join that uses any operator (represented by the Greek symbol θ) to compare values in joined rows.

third normal form (3NF) — In the relational database model, the normal form of relations such that each non-key attribute is dependent on nothing but the primary key.

three-valued logic — In SQL, computational logic that uses the three values true, false, and unknown.

time — A DB2/400 field and column data type that stores values for time.

time-dependent property — In a data model, a property (e.g., a product's price) whose values must be stored for different date or time intervals.

timestamp — A DB2/400 field and column data type that stores values for system timestamps (e.g., a combination of data and time).

transaction — A group of individual changes to objects on the system that should appear as a single atomic change to the user.

transition constraint — In a data model, a rule governing changes to values.

translate table — An OS/400 table object (type *TBL) that provides entries for translating characters from one set of encodings to another (e.g., from lowercase to uppercase). Do not confuse with SQL/400 tables, which are *FILE objects.

trigger — In general database terms, a condition that causes some procedure to be executed.

trigger program — An HLL program associated with a trigger condition for a physical file.

triggered procedure — In general database terms, a procedure executed for some trigger.

tuple — In the relational database model, a set of attribute-and-value pairs. A tuple corresponds to a row in a table representation of a relation.

union — A relational algebra operation that returns a relation with all tuples that occur in either the first relation or the second.

union-compatible — In the relational database model, the property of two relations that have the same attributes. In SQL, two tables that have the same number of columns and for which corresponding columns have compatible data types.

unique constraint — See **unique key constraint**.

unique key — A database file key that doesn't allow duplicate values.

unique key constraint — In SQL/400 and DB2/400, a physical file constraint that requires a set of fields to have unique values. Null values are allowed.

unit of work — See **transaction**.

Update statement — An SQL statement to update one or more rows in a table.

user profile — An OS/400 object (type *USRPRF) that represents a system user, and that is the basis for controlling access to system objects and functions.

user-defined data type — A data type defined by the user (programmer) rather than one that's part of the programming language.

view — In SQL, a table-like object that provides an alternative means of accessing data in one or more underlying base tables. In SQL/400, a view is a logical file. Contrast with **base table**.

view relation — In the relational database model, a named, derived relation that represents an alternative way to view the contents of one or more base relations. Contrast with **base relation**.

virtual attribute — In the relational database model, a view relation's attribute that's derived by some expression from one or more attributes in a base relation.

weak entity — In entity relationship diagrams, an entity for which an instance cannot exist unless a corresponding entity on the other end of a relationship exists. Contrast with **regular entity**.

zoned decimal — In DB2/400, a numeric data type that stores numbers using a representation of the number with one byte per digit.

Index

THE A TO Z OF EDI

By Nahid M. Jilovec

Electronic Data Interchange (EDI) can help reduce administrative costs, accelerate information processing, ensure data accuracy, and streamline business procedures. Here's a comprehensive guide to EDI to help in planning, startup, and implementation. The author reveals all the benefits, challenges, standards, and implementation secrets gained through extensive experience. She shows how to evaluate your business procedures, select special hardware and software, establish communications requirements and standards, address audit issues, and employ the legal support necessary for EDI activities. 263 pages.

APPLICATION DEVELOPER'S HANDBOOK FOR THE AS/400

Edited by Mike Otey, a **NEWS/400** *technical editor*

Explains how to effectively use the AS/400 to build reliable, flexible, and efficient business applications. Contains RPG/400 and CL coding examples and tips, and provides both step-by-step instructions and handy reference material. Includes diskette. 768 pages, 48 chapters.

AS/400 DISK SAVING TIPS & TECHNIQUES

By James R. Plunkett

Want specific help for cleaning up and maintaining your disk? Here are more than 50 tips, plus design techniques for minimizing your disk usage. Each tip is completely explained with the "symptom," the problem, and the technique or code you need to correct it. 72 pages.

AS/400 SUBFILES IN RPG

On the AS/400, subfiles are powerful and easy to use, and with this book you can start working with subfiles in just a few hours — no need to wade through page after page of technical jargon. You'll start with the concept behind subfiles, then discover how easy they are to program. The book contains all of the DDS subfile keywords announced in V2R3 of OS/400. Five complete RPG subfile programs are included, and the book comes complete with a 3.5" PC diskette containing all those programs plus DDS. The book is an updated version of the popular *Programming Subfiles in RPG/400*. 200 pages, 4 chapters.

C FOR RPG PROGRAMMERS

By Jennifer Hamilton, a **NEWS/400** *author*

Written from the perspective of an RPG programmer, this book includes side-by-side coding examples written in both C and RPG to aid comprehension and understanding, clear identification of unique C constructs, and a comparison of RPG op-codes to equivalent C concepts. Includes many tips and examples covering the use of C/400. 292 pages, 23 chapters.

CL BY EXAMPLE

By Virgil Green

CL by Example gives programmers and operators more than 850 pages of practical information you can use in your day-to-day job. It's full of application examples, tips, and techniques, along with a sprinkling of humor. The examples will speed you through the learning curve to help you become a more proficient, more productive CL programmer. 864 pages, 12 chapters.

CLIENT ACCESS TOKEN-RING CONNECTIVITY

By Chris Patterson

Attaching PCs to AS/400s via a Token-Ring can become a complicated subject — when things go wrong, an understanding of PCs, the Token-Ring, and OS/400 is often required. *Client Access Token-Ring Connectivity* details all that is required in these areas to successfully maintain and trouble-shoot a Token-Ring network. The first half of the book introduces the Token-Ring and describes the Client Access communications architecture, the Token-Ring connection from both the PC side and the AS/400 side, and the Client Access applications. The second half provides a useful guide to Token-Ring management, strategies for Token-Ring error identification and recovery, and tactics for resolving Client Access error messages. 125 pages, 10 chapters.

COMMON-SENSE C
Advice and warnings for C and C++ programmers

By Paul Conte, a **NEWS/400** *technical editor*

C programming language has its risks; this book shows how C programmers get themselves into trouble, includes tips to help you avoid C's pitfalls, and suggests how to manage C and C++ application development. 100 pages, 9 chapters.

CONTROL LANGUAGE PROGRAMMING FOR THE AS/400

By Bryan Meyers and Dan Riehl, **NEWS/400** *technical editors*

This comprehensive CL programming textbook offers students up-to-the-minute knowledge of the skills they will need in today's MIS environment. Progresses methodically from CL basics to more complex processes and concepts, guiding readers toward a professional grasp of CL programming techniques and style. 512 pages, 25 chapters.

DDS BY EXAMPLE

By R S Tipton

DDS by Example provides detailed coverage on the creation of physical files, field reference files, logical files, display files, and printer files. It includes more than 300 real-life examples, including examples of physical files, simple logical files, multi-format logical files, dynamic selection options, coding subfiles, handling overrides, creating online help, creating reports, and coding windows. 360 pages, 4 chapters.

DDS PROGRAMMING FOR DISPLAY & PRINTER FILES

By James Coolbaugh

Offers a thorough, straightforward explanation of how to use Data Description Specifications (DDS) to program display files and printer files. Covers basic to complex tasks using DDS functions. The author uses DDS programming examples for CL and RPG extensively throughout the book, and you can put these examples to use immediately. Focuses on topics such as general screen presentations, the A specification, defining data on the screen, record-format and field definitions, defining data fields, using indicators, data and text attributes, cursor and keyboard control, editing data, validity checking, response keywords, and function keys. A complimentary diskette includes all the source code presented in the book. 446 pages, 13 chapters.

DESKTOP GUIDE TO THE S/36

By Mel Beckman, Gary Kratzer, and Roger Pence, **NEWS/400** *technical editors*

This definitive S/36 survival manual includes practical techniques to supercharge your S/36, including ready-to-use information for maximum system performance tuning, effective application development, and smart Disk Data Management. Includes a review of two popular Unix-based S/36 work-alike migration alternatives. Diskette contains ready-to-run utilities to help you save machine time and implement power programming techniques such as External Program Calls. 387 pages, 21 chapters.

THE ESSENTIAL GUIDE TO CLIENT ACCESS FOR DOS EXTENDED

By John Enck, Robert E. Anderson, and Michael Otey

The Essential Guide to Client Access for DOS Extended contains key insights and need-to-know technical information about Client Access for DOS Extended, IBM's strategic AS/400 product for DOS and Windows client/server connectivity. This book provides background information about the history and architecture of Client Access for DOS Extended; fundamental information about how to install and configure Client Access; and advanced information about integrating Client Access with other types of networks, managing how Client Access for DOS Extended operates under Windows, and developing client/server applications with Client Access. Written by industry experts based on their personal and professional experiences with Client Access, this book can help you avoid time-consuming pitfalls that litter the path of AS/400 client/server computing. 430 pages, 12 chapters.

ILE: A FIRST LOOK

By George Farr and Shailan Topiwala

This book begins by showing the differences between ILE and its predecessors, then goes on to explain the essentials of an ILE program — using concepts such as modules, binding, service programs, and binding directories. You'll discover how ILE program activation works and how ILE works with its predecessor environments. The book covers the new APIs and new debugging facilities and explains the benefits of ILE's new exception-handling model. You also get answers to the most commonly asked questions about ILE. 183 pages, 9 chapters.

IMPLEMENTING AS/400 SECURITY, SECOND EDITION
A practical guide to implementing, evaluating, and auditing your AS/400 security strategy

By Wayne Madden, a **NEWS/400** *technical editor*

Concise and practical, this second edition brings together in one place the fundamental AS/400 security tools and experience-based recommendations that you need and also includes specifics on the latest security enhancements available in OS/400 Version 3 Release 1. Completely updated from the first edition, this is the only source for the latest information about how to protect your system against attack from its increasing exposure to hackers. 389 pages, 16 chapters.

INSIDE THE AS/400
An in-depth look at the AS/400's design, architecture, and history

By Frank G. Soltis

The inside story every AS/400 developer has been waiting for, told by Dr. Frank G. Soltis, IBM's AS/400 chief architect. Never before has IBM provided an in-depth look at the AS/400's design, architecture, and history. This authoritative book does just that — and also looks at some of the people behind the scenes who created this revolutionary system for you. Whether you are an executive looking for a high-level overview or a "bit-twiddling techie" who wants all the details, *Inside the AS/400* demystifies this system, shedding light on how it came to be, how it can do the things it does, and what its future may hold — especially in light of its new PowerPC RISC processors. 475 pages, 12 chapters.

INTRODUCTION TO AS/400 SYSTEM OPERATIONS

by Patrice Gapen and Heidi Rothenbuehler

Here's the textbook that covers what you need to know to become a successful AS/400 system operator. System operators typically help users resolve problems, manage printed reports, and perform regularly scheduled procedures. *Introduction to AS/400 System Operations* introduces a broad range of topics, including system architecture; DB2/400 and Query; user interface and Operational Assistant; managing jobs and printed reports; backup and restore; system configuration and networks; performance; security; and Client Access (PC Support).

The information presented here covers typical daily, weekly, and monthly AS/400 operations using V3R1M0 of the OS/400 operating system. You can benefit from this book even if you have only a very basic knowledge of the AS/400. If you know how to sign on to the AS/400, and how to use the function keys, you're ready for the material in this book. 234 pages, 10 chapters.

AN INTRODUCTION TO COMMUNICATIONS FOR THE AS/400, SECOND EDITION

By John Enck and Ruggero Adinolfi

This second edition has been revised to address the sweeping communications changes introduced with V3R1 of OS/400. As a result, this book now covers the broad range of AS/400 communications technology topics, ranging from Ethernet to X.25, and from APPN to AnyNet. The book presents an introduction to data communications and then covers communications fundamentals, types of networks, OSI, SNA, APPN, networking roles, the AS/400 as host and server, TCP/IP, and the AS/400-DEC connection. 210 pages, 13 chapters.

JIM SLOAN'S CL TIPS & TECHNIQUES

By Jim Sloan, developer of QUSRTOOL's TAA Tools

Written for those who understand CL, this book draws from Jim Sloan's knowledge and experience as a developer for the S/38 and the AS/400, and his creation of QUSRTOOL's TAA tools, to give you tips that can help you write better CL programs and become more productive. Includes more than 200 field-tested techniques, plus exercises to help you understand and apply many of the techniques presented. 564 pages, 30 chapters.

MASTERING THE AS/400
A practical, hands-on guide

By Jerry Fottral

This introductory textbook to AS/400 concepts and facilities has a utilitarian approach that stresses student participation. A natural prerequisite to programming and database management courses, it emphasizes mastery of system/user interface, member-object-library relationship, utilization of CL commands, and basic database and program development utilities. Also includes labs focusing on essential topics such as printer spooling; library lists; creating and maintaining physical files; using logical files; using CL and DDS; working in the PDM environment; and using SEU, DFU, Query, and SDA. 484 pages, 12 chapters.

OBJECT-ORIENTED PROGRAMMING FOR AS/400 PROGRAMMERS

*By Jennifer Hamilton, a **NEWS/400** author*

Explains basic OOP concepts such as classes and inheritance in simple, easy-to-understand terminology. The OS/400 object-oriented architecture serves as the basis for the discussion throughout, and concepts presented are reinforced through an introduction to the C++ object-oriented programming language, using examples based on the OS/400 object model. 114 pages, 14 chapters.

PERFORMANCE PROGRAMMING — MAKING RPG SIZZLE

By Mike Dawson, CDP

Mike Dawson spent more than two years preparing this book — evaluating programming options, comparing techniques, and establishing benchmarks on thousands of programs. "Using the techniques in this book," he says, "I have made program after program run 30%, 40%, even 50% faster." To help you do the same, Mike gives you code and benchmark results for initializing and clearing arrays, performing string manipulation, using validation arrays with look-up techniques, using arrays in arithmetic routines, and a lot more. 257 pages, 8 chapters.

POWER TOOLS FOR THE AS/400, VOLUMES I AND II

Edited by Frederick L. Dick and Dan Riehl

NEWS 3X/400's Power Tools for the AS/400 is a two-volume reference series for people who work with the AS/400. Volume I (originally titled *AS/400 Power Tools*) is a collection of the best tools, tips, and techniques published in *NEWS/34-38* (pre-August 1988) and *NEWS 3X/400* (August 1988 through October 1991) that are applicable to the AS/400. *Volume II* extends this original collection by including material that appeared through 1994. Each book includes a diskette that provides load-and-go code for easy-to-use solutions to many everyday problems. *Volume I:* 709 pages, 24 chapters; *Volume II:* 702 pages, 14 chapters.

PROGRAMMING IN RPG IV

*By Judy Yaeger, Ph.D., a **NEWS/400** technical editor*

This textbook provides a strong foundation in the essentials of business programming, featuring the newest version of the RPG language: RPG IV. Focuses on real-world problems and down-to-earth solutions using the latest techniques and features of RPG. Provides everything you need to know to write a well-designed RPG IV program. Each chapter includes informative, easy-to-read explanations and examples as well as a section of thought-provoking questions, exercises, and programming assignments. Four appendices and a handy, comprehensive glossary support the topics presented throughout the book. An instructor's kit is available. 450 pages, 13 chapters.

PROGRAMMING IN RPG/400, SECOND EDITION

*By Judy Yaeger, Ph.D., a **NEWS/400** technical editor*

This second edition refines and extends the comprehensive instructional material contained in the original textbook and features a new section that introduces externally described printer files, a new chapter that highlights the fundamentals of RPG IV, and a new appendix that correlates the key concepts from each chapter with their RPG IV counterparts. Includes everything you need to learn how to write a well-designed RPG program, from the most basic to the more complex, and each chapter includes a section of questions, exercises, and programming assignments that reinforce the knowledge you have gained from the chapter and strengthen the groundwork for succeeding chapters. An instructor's kit is available. 440 pages, 14 chapters.

PROGRAMMING SUBFILES IN COBOL/400

By Jerry Goldson

Learn how to program subfiles in COBOL/400 in a matter of hours! This powerful and flexible programming technique no longer needs to elude you. You can begin programming with subfiles the same day you get the book. You don't have to wade through page after page, chapter after chapter of rules and parameters and keywords. Instead, you get solid, helpful information and working examples that you can apply to your application programs right away. 204 pages, 5 chapters.

THE QUINTESSENTIAL GUIDE TO PC SUPPORT

By John Enck, Robert E. Anderson, Michael Otey, and Michael Ryan

This comprehensive book about IBM's AS/400 PC Support connectivity product defines the architecture of PC Support and its role in midrange networks, describes PC Support's installation and configuration procedures, and shows you how you can configure and use PC Support to solve real-life problems. 345 pages, 11 chapters.

RPG ERROR HANDLING TECHNIQUE
Bulletproofing Your Applications

By Russell Popeil

RPG Error Handling Technique teaches you the skills you need to use the powerful tools provided by OS/400 and RPG to handle almost any error from within your programs. The book explains the INFSR, INFDS, PSSR, and SDS in programming terms, with examples that show you how all these tools work together and which tools are most appropriate for which kind of error or exception situation. It continues by presenting a robust suite of error/exception handling techniques within RPG programs. Each technique is explained in an application setting, using both RPG III and RPG IV code. 164 pages, 5 chapters.

RPG IV BY EXAMPLE

By George Farr and Shailan Topiwala

RPG IV by Example addresses the needs and concerns of RPG programmers at any level of experience. The focus is on RPG IV in a practical context that lets AS/400 professionals quickly grasp what's new without dwelling on the old. Beginning with an overview of RPG IV specifications, the authors prepare the way for examining all the features of the new version of the language. The chapters that follow explore RPG IV further with practical, easy-to-use applications. 500 pages, 15 chapters.

RPG IV JUMP START
Moving ahead with the new RPG

By Bryan Meyers, a **NEWS/400** *technical editor*

Introducing the "new" RPG, in which the columnar syntax has been challenged (all the specifications have changed, some vestigial specifications from an earlier era have been eliminated, and new specifications and data types have been added), this book shows you RPG IV from the perspective of a programmer who already knows the old RPG. Points out the differences between the two and demonstrates how to take advantage of the new syntax and function. 193 pages, 12 chapters.

RPG/400 INTERACTIVE TEMPLATE TECHNIQUE

By Carson Soule, CDP, CCP, CSP

Here's an updated version of Carson Soule's *Interactive RPG/400 Programming.* The book shows you time-saving, program-sharpening concepts behind the template approach, and includes all the code you need to build one perfect program after another. These templates include code for cursor-sensitive prompting in DDS, for handling messages in resident RPG programs, for using the CLEAR opcode to eliminate hard-coded field initialization, and much more. There's even a new select template with a pop-up window. 258 pages, 10 chapters.

S/36 POWER TOOLS

Edited by Chuck Lundgren, a **NEWS/400** *technical editor*

Winner of an STC Award of Achievement in 1992, this book contains five years' worth of articles, tips, and programs published in *NEWS 3X/400* from 1986 to October 1990, including more than 290 programs and procedures. Extensively cross-referenced for fast and easy problem solving, and complete with diskette containing all the programming code. 737 pages, 20 chapters.

STARTER KIT FOR THE AS/400, SECOND EDITION
An indispensable guide for novice to intermediate AS/400 programmers and system operators

By Wayne Madden, a **NEWS/400** *technical editor*
with contributions by Bryan Meyers, Andrew Smith, and Peter Rowley

This second edition contains updates of the material in the first edition and incorporates new material to enhance it's value as a resource to help you learn important basic concepts and nuances of the AS/400 system. New material focuses on installing a new release, working with PTFs, AS/400 message handling, working with and securing printed output, using operational assistant to manage disk space, job scheduling, save and restore basics, and more basic CL programming concepts. Optional diskette available. 429 pages, 33 chapters.

SUBFILE TECHNIQUE FOR RPG/400 PROGRAMMERS

By Jonathan Yergin, CDP, and Wayne Madden

Here's the code you need for a complete library of shell subfile programs: RPG/400 code, DDS, CL, and sample data files. There's even an example for programming windows. You even get some "whiz bang" techniques that add punch to your applications. This book explains the code in simple, straightforward style and tells you when each technique should be used for best results. 326 pages, 11 chapters, 3.5" PC diskette included.

TECHNICAL REFERENCE SERIES

Edited by Bryan Meyers, a **NEWS/400** *technical editor*

Written by experts — such as John Enck, Bryan Meyers, Julian Monypenny, Roger Pence, Dan Riehl — these unique desktop guides put the latest AS/400 applications and techniques at your fingertips. These "just-do-it" books (featuring wire-o binding to open flat at every page) are priced so you can keep your personal set handy. Optional online Windows help diskette available for each book.

Desktop Guide to CL Programming

By Bryan Meyers, a **NEWS/400** *technical editor*

This first book of the **NEWS/400** *Technical Reference Series* is packed with easy-to-find notes, short explanations, practical tips, answers to most of your everyday questions about CL, and CL code segments you can use in your own CL programming. Complete "short reference" lists every command and explains the most-often-used ones, along with names of the files they use and the MONMSG messages to use with them. 205 pages, 36 chapters.

Desktop Guide to AS/400 Programmers' Tools

By Dan Riehl, a **NEWS/400** *technical editor*

This second book of the **NEWS/400** *Technical Reference Series* gives you the "how-to" behind all the tools included in *Application Development ToolSet/400* (ADTS/400), IBM's Licensed Program Product for Version 3 of OS/400; includes Source Entry Utility (SEU), Programming Development Manager (PDM), Screen Design Aid (SDA), Report Layout Utility (RLU), File Compare/Merge Utility (FCMU) — *new in V3R1,* and Interactive Source Debugger — *new in V3R1.* Highlights topics and functions specific to Version 3 of OS/400. 266 pages, 30 chapters.

Desktop Guide to DDS

By James Coolbaugh

This third book of the **NEWS/400** *Technical Reference Series* provides a complete reference to all DDS keywords for physical, logical, display, printer, and ICF files. Each keyword is briefly explained, with syntax rules and examples showing how to code the keyword. All basic and pertinent information is provided for quick and easy access. While this guide explains every parameter for a keyword, it doesn't explain every possible exception that might exist. Rather, the guide includes the basics about what each keyword is designed to accomplish. The *Desktop Guide to DDS* is designed to give quick, "at your fingertips" information about every keyword — with this in hand, you won't need to refer to IBM's bulky *DDS Reference* manual. 132 pages, 5 major sections.

Desktop Guide to RPG/400

By Roger Pence and Julian Monypenny, **NEWS/400** *technical editors*

This fourth book in the *Technical Reference Series* provides a variety of RPG templates, subroutines, and copy modules, sprinkled with evangelical advice, that will help you write robust and effective RPG/400 programs. Highlights of the information provided include string-handling routines, numeric editing routines, date routines, error-handling modules, tips for using OS/400 APIs with RPG/400, and interactive programming techniques. For all types of RPG projects, this book's tested and ready-to-run building blocks will easily snap into your RPG. The programming solutions provided here would otherwise take you days or even weeks to write and test. 211 pages, 28 chapters.

Desktop Guide to Creating CL Commands

By Lynn Nelson

In this most recent book in the *Technical Reference Series*, author Lynn Nelson shows you how to create your own CL commands with the same functionality and power as the IBM commands you use every day, including automatic parameter editing, all the function keys, F4 prompt for values, expanding lists of values, and conditional prompting. After you have read this book, you can write macros for the operations you do over and over every day or write application commands that prompt users for essential information. Whether you're in operations or programming, don't miss this opportunity to enhance your career-building skills. 164 pages, 14 chapters.

UNDERSTANDING BAR CODES

By James R. Plunkett

One of the most important waves of technology sweeping American industry is the use of bar coding to capture and track data. The wave is powered by two needs: the need to gather information in a more accurate and timely manner and the need to track that information once it is gathered. Bar coding meets these needs and provides creative and cost-effective solutions for many applications. With so many leading-edge technologies, it can be difficult for IS professionals to keep up with the concepts and applications they need to make solid decisions. This book gives you an overview of bar code technology including a discussion of the bar codes themselves, the hardware that supports bar coding, how and when to justify and then implement a bar code application, plus examples of many different applications and how bar coding can be used to solve problems. 70 pages.

USING QUERY/400

By Patrice Gapen and Catherine Stoughton

This textbook, designed for any AS/400 user from student to professional with or without prior programming knowledge, presents Query as an easy and fast tool for creating reports and files from AS/400 databases. Topics are ordered from simple to complex and emphasize hands-on AS/400 use; they include defining database files to Query, selecting and sequencing fields, generating new numeric and character fields, sorting within Query, joining database files, defining custom headings, creating new database files, and more. Instructor's kit available. 92 pages, 10 chapters.

USING VISUAL BASIC WITH CLIENT ACCESS APIs

By Ron Jones

This book is for programmers who want to develop client/server solutions on the AS/400 and the personal computer. Whether you are a VB novice or a VB expert, you will gain by reading this book because it provides a thorough overview of the principles and requirements for programming in Windows using VB. Companion diskettes contain source code for all the programming projects referenced in the book, as well as for numerous other utilities and programs. All the projects are compatible with Windows 95 and VB 4.0. 680 pages, 13 chapters.

FOR A COMPLETE CATALOG OR TO PLACE AN ORDER, CONTACT

NEWS/400
Duke Communications International
221 E. 29th Street • Loveland, CO 80538-2727
(800) 621-1544 • (970) 663-4700 • Fax: (970) 669-3016